Side-by-Side Survey
Comparative Regional Studies
in the Mediterranean World

Side-by-Side Survey

Comparative Regional Studies in the Mediterranean World

Edited by

Susan E. Alcock and John F. Cherry

Oxbow Books

Published by
Oxbow Books, Park End Place, Oxford OX1 1HN

ISBN 1 84217 096 1

A CIP record for this book is available from the British Library

Cover image: The Balkans.
http://visibleearth.nasa.gov/cgi-bin/viewrecord?25304
Jacques Descloitres, MODIS Rapid Response Team, NASA/GSFC

This book is available direct from
Oxbow Books, Park End Place, Oxford, OX1 1HN
(Phone: 01865-241249; Fax: 01865-794449)

and

The David Brown Book Company
PO Box 511, Oakville, CT 06779, USA
(Phone: 860-945-9329; Fax: 860-945-9468)

and

via our website
www.oxbowbooks.com

Printed in Great Britain by
Antony Rowe, Chippenham

Contents

List of Figures

List of Tables

List of Contributors

Alcock, Susan E., Department of Classical Studies, University of Michigan, 2160 Angell Hall, 435 S. State Street, Ann Arbor, MI 48109-1003, USA.

Attema, Peter, Groningen Institute of Archaeology, Poststraat 6, 9712 ER Groningen, The Netherlands.

Blanton, Richard E., Department of Sociology and Anthropology, Purdue University, West Lafayette, IN 47907, USA.

Casana, Jesse, The Oriental Institute, University of Chicago, 1155 East 58th Street, Chicago, IL 60637, USA.

Cherry, John F., Department of Classical Studies, University of Michigan, 2160 Angell Hall, 435 S. State Street, Ann Arbor, MI 48109-1003, USA.

Cunningham, Tim, Département d'Archéologie, Université Catholique de Louvain, Place B. Pascal 1, 1348-Louvain-la-Neuve, Belgium.

Davis, Jack L., Department of Classics, University of Cincinnati, Cincinnati, OH 45221-0226, USA.

Driessen, Jan, Département d'Archéologie, Université Catholique de Louvain, Place B. Pascal 1, 1348-Louvain-la-Neuve, Belgium.

Fentress, Elizabeth, Arco degli Acetari 31, Rome 00186, Italy.

Fontana, Sergio, Via Clementina 11, Rome 00186, Italy.

Gates, Jennifer, Interdepartmental Program in Classical Art and Archaeology, University of Michigan, Kelsey Museum of Archaeology, 434 S. State Street, Ann Arbor, MI 48109-1390, USA.

Given, Michael, Department of Archaeology, University of Glasgow, Gregory Building, Lilybank Gardens, Glasgow G12 8QQ, United Kingdom.

Hitchner, Robert Bruce, Department of Classics, Tufts University, Eaton Hall, Medford, MA 02155, USA.

Mattingly, David J., School of Archaeology and Ancient History, University of Leicester, Leicester LE1 7RH, United Kingdom.

Osborne, Robin, Faculty of Classics, University of Cambridge, Sidgwick Avenue, Cambridge CB3 9DA , United Kingdom.

Perkins, Philip, Department of Classical Studies, The Open University, Walton Hall, Milton Keynes MK7 6AA, United Kingdom.

Stone, David L., Deptartment of Classics, The Florida State University, Tallahassee, FL 32306-1510, USA.

Terrenato, Nicola, Department of Classics, University of North Carolina at Chapel Hill, Chapel Hill, NC 27599-3145, USA.

Thompson, Stephen, 142 Westwood Circle, Charlottesville, VA 22903, USA.

Ur, Jason, The Oriental Institute, University of Chicago, 1155 East 58th Street, Chicago, IL 60637, USA.

van Leusen, Martijn, Groningen Institute of Archaeology, Poststraat 6, 9712 ER Groningen, The Netherlands.

Wandsnider, LuAnn, Department of Anthropology and Geography, University of Nebraska-Lincoln, 126 Bessey Hall, Lincoln, NE 68588-0368, USA. *and* Statistical Reasearch, Inc., 6099 E. Speedway Blvd., Tucson, AZ 85751-1865, USA.

Wilkinson, T. J., Department of Archaeology, University of Edinburgh, The Old High School, Infirmary Street, Edinburgh EH1 1LT, United Kingdom.

Witcher, Rob, British School at Rome, Via A. Gramsci 61, 00197 Rome, Italy.

Wright, James C., Department of Classical and Near Eastern Archaeology, Bryn Mawr College, 101 North Merion Avenue, Bryn Mawr, PA 19010-2899, USA.

Preface

This volume is the outcome of an advanced Workshop, entitled "Side-by-Side Survey: Comparative Regional Studies in the Mediterranean World", which we organized at the University of Michigan, April 5–7, 2002. Its primary goal was to facilitate intensive discussion among a representative range of experienced practitioners of archaeological survey in a number of circum-Mediterranean countries. Our intention was not to provide a showcase for individual recent projects, nor a general update on the state of the survey art in the Mediterranean area, let alone to lay down guidelines or standards for how surveys could or should be conducted. The purpose, rather, was to discuss some of the potential scholarly benefits of working in a comparative format with the evidence that has accumulated over the past 30 years or more from many different survey projects, and to consider solutions to some of the practical obstacles that currently present roadblocks to achieving that objective. Landscape archaeology and the analysis of regional survey data having been for us subjects of sustained interest over many years, we had come to feel that insufficient attention had yet been given to such matters of comparison. How, for example, can we evaluate the intriguing contrasts or similarities between many individual projects' datasets, given the marked differences that often exist in their environmental and cultural contexts, in their intensity and spatial coverage, and in the protocols adopted for data collection and reporting? Or how can we build towards interesting pictures at the macro-regional scale (the only one appropriate for certain sorts of questions) from the disparate – sometimes even wholly non-comparable – bits of evidence provided by a myriad of local-level surveys, generally of non-contiguous blocks of landscape, conducted with a very wide range of research objectives in mind?

We provide further discussion of these important issues and questions in our Introduction (Chapter 1). But it seemed obvious to us, as we thought about them ourselves and pondered the idea of convening a group of colleagues to discuss them, that the University of Michigan would offer a particularly suitable venue for hosting such a Workshop, in view of this University's long-standing and distinguished involvement in regional archaeological survey in many parts of the world, including the Mediterranean. Accordingly, once we had taken the decision to organize the meeting, we drew up a 'dream team' of archaeological colleagues to invite: those who had organized at least one (in most cases, several) survey projects, whose published work indicated a real interest in issues relating to comparative regional studies, and who between them could provide geographical coverage of both the northern and southern shores of the Mediterranean, and from Iberia to the Near East. It was a matter of considerable gratification that virtually all those whom we contacted accepted our invitation, and those who could not take part were prevented from doing so only by prior fieldwork commitments or by personal circumstances. Our first thanks, then, go to these participants and, now, contributors to the present volume: we are grateful for their enthusiastic involvement in the Workshop and for their co-operation throughout the editorial process.

Others who took part, but who are not represented in the pages that follow, also deserve mention here for contributing to the liveliness of the occasion. They include our colleagues from the University of Michigan's Museum of Anthropology, Henry Wright, Jeff Parsons and Carla Sinopoli, who served both as session moderators and as engaging discussants on the final day. More by chance than design, both Jeff Parsons and we were teaching relevant graduate seminars during the winter term of 2002 when the Workshop took place (Classical Archaeology 820, 'Approaches to Archaeological Survey' and Anthropology 691, 'Settlement Pattern Archaeology'); this provided welcome opportunities for some meaningful bridging of the so-called 'Great Divide', for helpful advance discussion of the papers, and for significant student involvement in the Workshop itself. Among these students were: Shilpi Bhadra, Hendrik Dey, Elissa Faro, Matthew Harrington, Cat Lyon Crawford, Ben Rubin, Dan Shoup, and Drew Wilburn. Other participants who were able to contribute from their first-hand experience of Mediterranean survey fieldwork included Vince Gaffney, Jennifer Gates, Rob Schon, Shari Stocker and Laurie Talalay.

An important element in the Workshop's organization was the pre-circulation of papers, since we conceived of the occasion as involving mainly well-informed discussion, of the sleeves-rolled-up variety. In the age of the Internet, it has become possible to use electronic means of dissemination – all the more desirable for papers of this sort, with abundant use of color images, GIS output, links to websites, and so on. Thus we arranged for the establishment of a closed-corral website, for the use of the participants, to which were posted abstracts and full texts of all the papers, with embedded images. We are very grateful to Drew Wilburn (of the University of Michigan's Interdepartmental Program in Classical Art and Archaeology [IPCAA]) for his hard work in creating and maintaining this website. Another way in which we attempted to inform the discussion was through the creation of a Filemaker Pro™ database of websites containing useful information about regional archaeological projects in the Mediterranean region; this was done in collaboration with Jennifer Gates (IPCAA), and a revised and somewhat simplified version of it has been included as an Appendix to this volume.

The Workshop took place in a fine state-of-the-art conference room on the 8th floor of the University's Harlan Hatcher Graduate Library – affording fine views, during session breaks, of the elegant Law School, of the largest college football stadium in the country, and of the crowds assembled on April 6th for the annual celebration of Hash Bash (a demonstration in support of the legalization of marijuana)! We are most grateful to Traianos Gagos (Papyrology Collection) and Karl Longstreth (Map Library) for their assistance in securing the use of these excellent facilities. Thanks are also due to Matthew Harrington for his knowledgeable technical support to all the participants in negotiating the complexities of the audio-visual system. The Department of Classical Studies kindly allowed our use of its library for our concluding round-table discussion on Sunday morning, while the Kelsey Museum of Archaeology provided one of its memorably lavish receptions amongst its galleries, following a public lecture by David Mattingly, entitled 'From Mystery to History: The Garamantes of Southern Libya'.

None of the foregoing could have taken place without financial support from a number of units within the University of Michigan. We take special pleasure, therefore, in offering our thanks to those who helped sponsor this Workshop and, by extension, who helped make possible this volume: the Horace H. Rackham School of Graduate Studies, the Office of the Vice President for Research, the International Institute, the Interdepartmental Program in Classical Art & Archaeology, the Department of Classical Studies, and the Kelsey Museum of Archaeology. In addition to the grants received from all these units, the Workshop was supported with personal research funds made available to Sue Alcock via her Arthur F. Thurnau Professorship, and to John Cherry as Director of IPCAA. These funds, and various other logistical arrangements, were ably administered by Pat Berwald and Anne Shore (Department of Classical Studies), Helen Baker (Kelsey Museum of Archaeology) and Debbie Fitch (IPCAA). We are pleased to be associated with a university that takes advanced research seriously, and that is prepared to make tangible contributions in its support.

Finally, we thank our friends at Oxbow Books, David Brown and Charles Watkinson, who offered their support for this venture as soon as they heard of it, and long before they actually saw any of its final product.

Sue Alcock & John Cherry
Ann Arbor, Michigan
February 2003

INTRODUCTION

1. Introduction

Susan E. Alcock and John F. Cherry

GROWTH AND CHANGE IN MEDITERRANEAN SURVEY

As is well known, one of the most striking changes in the practice of archaeology throughout much of the Mediterranean area during the past quarter-century has been the extraordinary growth of interest in field survey projects and regional analysis. For a number of reasons, the relative rate of growth in survey work and its local impact has been quite variable from one region to another. Yet there

can be no doubt at all about the overall increase in the numbers of regional projects that have been undertaken, or that are currently in progress.

One of us has recently made some preliminary attempts to quantify this growth, both in the Mediterranean region as a whole (Figure 1.1), and in specific parts of it (Cherry 2003: 138–40; in press: fig. 1; cf. Cherry and Parkinson 2003: fig. 4.1). In Greece, for example, where only a handful of surveys took place in the three decades after

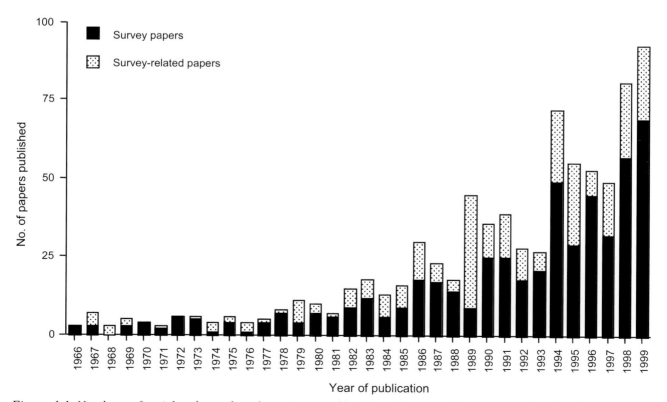

Figure 1.1 Numbers of articles devoted to the primary publication of survey data, or to studies drawing on survey evidence, as published during the period 1967–1999 in 15 archaeological journals providing coverage of archaeological research in the majority of circum-Mediterranean countries. (For the journals consulted in this study, see Cherry and Parkinson 2003: fig. 4.1.)

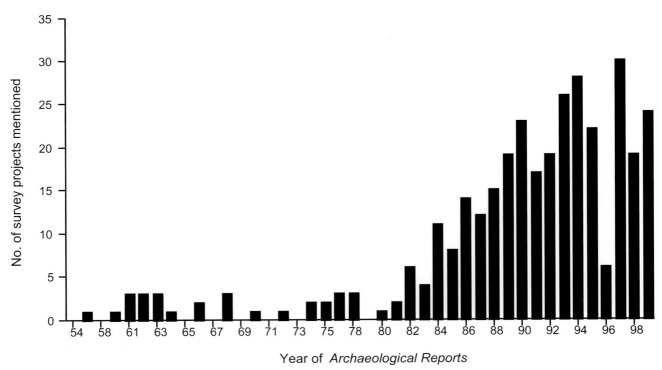

Figure 1.2 Numbers of archaeological survey projects in Greece reported annually in the journal Archaeological Reports, *1954–1999.*

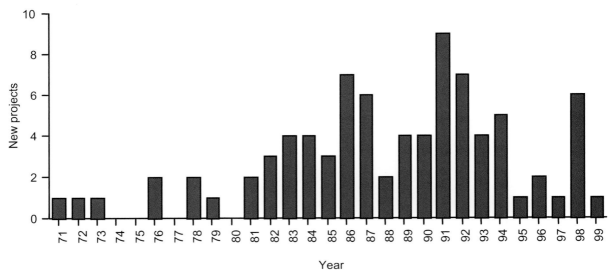

Figure 1.3 Annual start-ups of new survey projects in Greece, 1971–1999.

World War II, there has been an explosion of activity since *c.* 1975, with almost 100 formal projects initiated subsequently (Figures 1.2 and 1.3). Likewise, Kletter and De-Groot (2001), in their recent study of the licenses and permits issued for archaeological fieldwork in Israel during the period 1989–98, tabulate no less than 394 "surveys", which – even if many of them were short-lived and very small-scale – nonetheless reveal a significant stepping-up in the pace of activity. This, incidentally, is not a purely Mediterranean phenomenon, for similar growth is apparent in certain other parts of the world too: Fish (1999: table 14.1), for instance, documents a ten-fold increase over the past four decades in the percentage of lead articles in *American Antiquity* that deal with settlement pattern

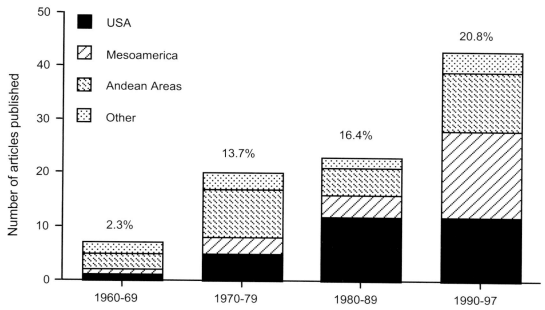

Figure 1.4 Lead articles with settlement pattern themes published in American Antiquity, *1960–1997, showing a tenfold increase between the 1960s and the 1990s. (Data from Fish 1999: table 14.1.)*

themes (Figure 1.4). Our point, however, is a simple one (even if its accurate quantification is impossible): millions of hectares of the Mediterranean landscape have now been subjected to inspection via pedestrian reconnaissance of one sort or another. What is being done with all the newly available data resulting from this fieldwork?

Equally apparent over this same time-span are the vast improvements in the sophistication of many of these surveys. In earlier years, regional fieldwork was often regarded primarily as a means of producing a 'sites-and-monuments record' (in the form of a gazetteer or a set of map sheets), or even merely as a preliminary step in the process of locating a site suitable for excavation. Experience revealed a number of critical weaknesses in the reliability of data collected in this way (Barker 1996), prompting methodological experimentation and reflexive self-criticism of a kind not often encountered in relation to excavation data. Many newer-style Mediterranean projects of the past couple of decades thus share some features which set them apart from the surveys of earlier generations. Among them are the following:

(a) A clearly demarcated territory as the target of fieldwork.
(b) The region itself as the focus of research design.
(c) The use of labour-intensive pedestrian survey by teams of surveyors.
(d) A more systematic approach to the coverage of terrain, often involving explicit sampling designs.
(e) Carefully thought-out procedures for standardizing the collection and recording of data.
(f) An interest in recovering information about the full range of archaeological phenomena surviving on the surface, including very small-scale sites and (often, but by no means always) 'non-site' or 'off-site' artifact distributions as well.

(g) The full integration within project design of studies of erosion, alluviation, soil formation, coastal change, vegetation history, etc., since landscape settings are not static and are themselves impacted by human occupation.

(h) The expansion of regional projects to become progressively more multi- or inter-disciplinary (*e.g.* through the incorporation of parallel studies in such fields as cultural anthropology, ethnohistory, ethnoarchaeology, historical geography, archival research, analysis of travel literature, geophysical prospection, etc.).

(i) A growing interest in the material culture and regional archaeology of the Mediterranean in periods (*e.g.* Arab, Frankish, Crusader, Venetian, Ottoman, early modern) hitherto undervalued or poorly studied by earlier surveys.

(j) Greatly increased use of relational databases, Geographical Information Systems, and the Internet for storing, analyzing and serving data.

Needless to say, the extent to which these characteristics apply varies greatly from country to country, from one project to another, and especially in relation to the date of inception of fieldwork, the local and national organizational frameworks within which archaeological research must be conducted, and divergent regional traditions of archaeological history and thought (*cf.* Hodder 1991); but, in general, they surely represent dominant trends in many areas. One good measure of just how far Mediterranean survey work has progressed in the past couple of decades is a comparison of the papers of the 1981 Athens conference on "Archaeological Survey in the Mediterranean Area" (Keller and Rupp 1983) with those in the five volumes of the POPULUS project, a decade and a half later, on "The Archaeology of Mediterranean Landscapes" (Barker and Mattingly 1999–2000).

COMBINING AND COMPARING SURVEY DATA

Thus, at the outset of the 21st century, we are faced with an influx of regionally based archaeological data of unprecedented quantity, quality, and diversity from hundreds of individual survey projects – but no widely agreed procedures for juxtaposing, combining, or synthesizing individual survey datasets. This is disappointing. As long as 20 years ago, reflecting on the state of Mediterranean survey at that time, Cherry (1983: 406) wrote:

> A vast data bank has been built up, willy-nilly, containing information of very variable quality, patchily distributed, and generally published in ways that impede the direct comparison of one survey with another. Nonetheless, information is pouring in at an unprecedented rate. What are we to do with it all? I am enough of an optimist to believe that we are at, or fast approaching, the stage when synthesis and comparison at a geographical scale considerably larger than that of the individual survey would be worthwhile.

The primary basis for such optimism, as a matter of fact, lay not in the Mediterranean itself, but in the civilizational heartlands of Mesoamerica and Mesopotamia. For example, the fruits of numerous separate, but adjacent and interlocking regional surveys, undertaken in and around the Basin of Mexico in the 1950s and 1960s (*e.g.* Parsons 1972; Blanton 1972), had allowed – for the first time – truly macro-regional, diachronic synthesis based on staggering quantities of surface data (*e.g.* Sanders *et al.* 1979). Juxtaposed with comparable data from similarly extensive research efforts in the Valley of Oaxaca and in the Maya lowlands, these results opened the way for pan-regional comparison of the sort perhaps best represented by the book *Ancient Mesoamerica: A Comparison of Change in Three Regions* (Blanton *et al.* 1982). Likewise, survey reconnaissance in numerous parts of lowland Mesopotamia over many years (*cf.* Adams 1965; Adams and Nissen 1972) culminated, eventually, in R. McC. Adams' pioneering work *Heartland of Cities: Surveys of Ancient Settlement and Land Use on the Central Floodplain of the Euphrates* (1981). Writing in 1981, then, it seemed reasonable to suppose that the surge of interest in survey in many parts of the Mediterranean would shortly bring us to the point where big questions of inter-regional scope could be tackled in illuminating ways with very large quantities of fresh data – just as the synthetic and comparative analysis of multiple sets of survey results had helped rewrite and reorient the archaeology of important parts of Mesopotamia

and Mesoamerica. But a dozen years later it had to be conceded that "it has taken rather longer than... expected to reach this stage" (Cherry 1994: 95).

The factors underlying this relative sluggishness in the development of *comparative* regional studies in the Mediterranean area are multiple, and would repay closer examination. (So too, parenthetically, would the reasons for the wide variations in the extent to which systematic regional surveys have penetrated standard archaeological practice around the Mediterranean.) Delays in the full publication of data from some of the more ambitious, intensive surveys begun in the late 1970s and continuing throughout the 1980s are certainly one part of the explanation. Another may be that the healthy experimentation with field methods and the general move toward more intensive and inclusive data collection over the past couple of decades have resulted in datasets that provide information in quite strikingly different forms. This appears to have led to some understandable hesitancy about direct, side-by-side comparison of results from different projects: one does not want to be accused of making invalid comparisons between apples and oranges. In our estimation, nonetheless, there does now seem to be a growing interest and willingness to attempt intra- and inter-regional studies encompassing multiple sets of survey data.

For purposes of illustrating this point, let us focus briefly on Greece (only because this is the area with whose archaeology we are most familiar). Many would point to Alcock's *Graecia capta: The Landscapes of Roman Greece* (1993) as the first sustained attempt to deploy survey data, as they existed in the late 1980s, to investigate regional variation in the rural, civic, provincial, and sacred landscapes that emerged with Greece's incorporation into the Roman imperial sphere. This study drew on 21 principal survey projects, which (in theory) provided examination of some 20,824 sq. km; but less than half the projects fell into her top category in terms of intensity of coverage and general reliability, and these had actually surveyed less than 400 sq. km in total. *Graecia capta* may have served as a catalyst; or it may simply be that, as more surveys are now reaching full publication, it has become more feasible to begin to set side-by-side the data from projects in closely adjacent areas. In the past several years, at any rate, survey data from Greece have been used comparatively, for example, to investigate such diverse topics as:

- the apparent north-south divide in Greek prehistory (Halstead 1994);
- the development of states on the southern Greek mainland in the later Bronze Age (Cavanagh 1995);
- the seeming northwestward shift in the centre of gravity of political power in mainland Greece throughout the first millennium B.C. (Bintliff 1997);
- long-term patterns in the prehistory of the Peloponnese (Mee 1999);
- the role of pastoralism in the Greek Neolithic (Cavanagh 1999);
- the regional context for the emergence of the palatial

centre of Mycenae and the polity it controlled (Cherry and Davis 2001);

- divergent political hierarchies in different areas of Crete in the Old and New Palace periods (Driessen 2001; Cunningham 2001).

On a substantially larger canvas (and now moving well beyond Greece), some recent work in a similar vein includes:

- an attempt to provide a comparative context for Hellenistic through Byzantine settlement patterns of the coastal area of western Rough Cilicia in Turkey, via structured comparison with 18 other surveys in areas ranging from Spain to Cyprus (Blanton 2000; *cf.* Ch. 15);
- a study of the rural settlement patterns of the Hellenistic kingdoms, all the way from Greece to Afghanistan, using evidence from some 50 surveys in a dozen countries (Alcock 1994);
- comparative use of survey data from all parts of Tunisia to evaluate the transformative impact of Roman rule on local rural landscapes (Stone 1997; *cf.* Ch. 10);
- a review of long-term patterns in environment, urbanism, and demography, based on data from 42 surveys in southeastern Turkey, Syria and Iraq (Wilkinson 2000; *cf.* Wilkinson *et al.*, Ch. 14).

It is not irrelevant also to mention here comparative studies that are not so much geographically based, as longitudinal – that is, the comparison of renewed (and usually far more intensive and interdisciplinary) survey in areas in which considerable surface reconnaissance had already taken place some years earlier. Notable examples of research in this vein are the fieldwork of the Pylos Regional Archaeological Project during the early 1990s (Davis *et al.* 1997; Davis 1998) within the territory in southwestern Greece explored in the 1960s by the University of Minnesota Messenia Expedition (McDonald and Rapp 1972); or the Tiber Valley Project's return to landscapes and artifacts first examined by the British School at Rome's surveys of Southern Etruria (Patterson *et al.* 2000; *cf.* Potter 1979). Stephen Thompson's contribution to the present volume (Ch. 6), in his case set in the countryside around Metaponto in southern Italy (Carter 2003), offers a further variation on this style of analysis, since it concerns a single project that has been in progress sufficiently long to require careful evaluation of data collected at different stages of fieldwork.

These are encouraging and exciting developments – and there are, we know, other examples from elsewhere in the Mediterranean that we have no space to mention here. Indeed, as one reads through the hundred or more papers published in the volumes of the POPULUS project (Barker and Mattingly 1999–2000), there is the sense of a new interest in building constructively and comparatively on others' data. This is hardly surprising, in light of the stated objective of this research network, which was "to in-vestigate the feasibility of establishing a common series of research goals and standards in Mediterranean landscape archaeology so as to advance the study of the ancient demography of the region on a broad comparative front" (Barker and Mattingly 1999: iv).

It is notable, nonetheless, that most of these efforts to utilize survey data in a comparative mode have barely scratched the surface of the richness and complexity of the available information. For instance, the comparison is often decidedly primitive, structured merely in terms of asking whether there is an increase or a decrease in the number of known sites (or a higher or lower site density) from period A to period B in a number of surveyed areas within a region, or between regions. This, of course, begs a number of critical and central questions – how sites have been defined; the relationship between on- and off-site data; the intensity of search procedures; the representativeness of the sample; the relative confidence with which material can be dated in different regions; the differing lengths of chronological phases, which may affect the likelihood that sites were in use contemporaneously; the degree of comparability between chronological schemes employed by different projects; the extent to which environmental changes may have differentially affected site visibility and obtrusiveness in different regions at different times; and so on.

Anyone who has been involved in the collection, analysis, or publication of survey data knows all too well the importance of factors such as these, but the project-specific solutions adopted to deal with them vary enormously and these may seriously impede direct comparison. One very recent example of this is the use by Given and Knapp (2003), in their final publication of the Sydney Cyprus Survey Project (SCSP), of an elaborately computed "pottery index", mapped in GIS for every surveyed unit, and intended to assess the relative presence of a period within a given survey unit, based on counts and weights of observed material, classified by "chronotypes" and corrected for unit size, visibility, and "background confusion". Their system is sophisticated and logically coherent; but, inevitably, it does not allow direct comparison of SCSP data with that from earlier projects. Similarly, because of operational and definitional matters (such as the means used to estimate the size of a multi-period site in each of its periods of occupation, or the spatial configuration of the sampled units of the landscape), it may be that comparative indexes of site nucleation or dispersion in different areas at different times reflect methodological differences as much as any underlying archaeological reality (for additional discussion, *cf.* Cherry *et al.* 1991: 457–79).

To use any individual set of survey data requires a degree of "archaeological source criticism" (Alcock 1993: 49–53), in order to understand the constraints, limitations and uncertainties inherent in the data. To compare *multiple* datasets – especially the use of results from recent, intensive surveys alongside older, extensive and relatively unsystematic investigations – makes such source criticism imperative. (Similar concerns, it may be noted, also have to be faced in other areas of archaeological endeavour, such as provenience studies, where some very tricky problems arise when trying to build a cumulative picture based on analytical data from numerous laboratories, using disparate techniques in studies conducted at various times and to differing standards: see Knapp and Cherry 1994.) This issue of comparability is one which we feel has not yet been squarely tackled by Mediterranean survey as a whole, and yet it is one of real and growing importance, as the corpus of survey results across the entire region continues to expand.

THEMES AND ISSUES

This, then, was the general context for the Workshop convened at the University of Michigan in April 2002. The resulting papers, collected in the present volume, constitute the contributions and responses of a range of archaeologists to our two primary objectives: to discuss some of the potential scholarly benefits of working in a comparative format with evidence from many different survey projects, and to consider solutions to some of the practical obstacles that currently present roadblocks in achieving that objective. Rather than rehearsing at this point the specific arguments of the various papers, which can speak for themselves, we offer a few comments which might be useful in providing some orientation for the reader.

One initial caveat, for example, may help prevent later disappointment. Although some of the papers do touch on the question of whether there is any realistic hope of promoting standards of comparability that have a chance of wide acceptance, it was never the intention of this Workshop to develop agreed guidelines or standards for how surveys could or should be conducted. It is natural, of course, to want to think in these terms, when faced with seeming deficiencies in other people's data ("If only Project X had thought to collect data on… "). Textbooks on archaeological methods have generally been written as though there do indeed exist standard, widely agreed procedures for the conduct of regional survey; but closer inspection shows them to be reflections of the author's own experience, often very firmly rooted in nationally specific traditions of fieldwork (e.g. Greene 2002: Ch. 2; Banning 2002). There have been calls, from time to time, for the development of common standards in Mediterranean landscape archaeology, most recently by the organizers of the POPULUS project, who had hoped to produce a "Manual of Best Practice" (Barker and Mattingly 1999: ix). But, as Martin Millett wrote, in his commentary on some of the POPULUS papers (Francovich *et al.* 2000: 93):

> …we do not need to insist that methods are the same. Indeed, given the geographical and historical variability of our discipline and its data, I would argue that methodological uniformity would be entirely

inappropriate… I shudder at the thought of a European working party trying to produce a thesaurus of standardized terms. Careful and explicit explanation by each project is what we need to facilitate worthwhile comparisons.

We agree with this view. As Millett also points out, the comparison of datasets is not rendered unproblematic simply because they were generated by the self-same methods, and "in order to use the results of another piece of work we need first to understand it and second to know the limits of its validity" (*ibid.*).

In order to use others' results, needless to say, one must have some means of gaining access to them: it is only the availability of basic survey data, in sufficient detail to allow "source criticism" and non-trivial comparisons, that makes it possible to put regional surveys side-by-side. This too has become a pressing issue on which we hoped participants in the Workshop might express their views. As surveys have become more sophisticated and ambitious, the data they produce have inevitably become more voluminous and – especially with the advent of relational databases and GIS – more difficult and costly to publish in the traditional formats of the printed article or monograph. Obviously, the expansion of the Internet and new technologies now make possible, in principle, the rapid and wide sharing (whether with fellow scholars, students, or the general public) of large textual, numerical, or graphical datafiles. But to what extent is "Internet publication" taking place, and does it meet the need for access to primary data?

We have looked into the first part of that question, as part of our preparation for the Workshop, by compiling a fairly systematic database of survey projects available via the Internet (see Gates *et al.*, Appendix, this volume). Our main conclusions from this exercise are these: that there currently exist only a modest number of websites serving information about Mediterranean survey projects, that few of them provide much more than brief illustrated accounts, and that virtually none aims at full "publication" (i.e., in as much detail as would be expected in a final report). One can imagine a number of factors that might be in play here: the time and effort required to establish a website serving data on a large scale (especially with interactive search and query functions), the real difficulties of maintaining such a site in good working order over the long term, an unwillingness to make proprietary databases widely accessible (particularly prior to their dissemination in traditional printed formats), and so on. Mattingly and Witcher (Ch. 13, p.177, this volume), while admiring the potential of "user-driven" interrogation of integrated, multi-scale GIS (online or as down-loadable data), nonetheless rightly do not see this as

> … an argument for simply putting all survey data on the Internet and letting the user get on with it. It is still vital for surveyors to take responsibility for the explanation and interpretation of their results – no

amount of metadata can be a substitute for first-hand experience of a survey.

In short, if the Internet ought not to be used as a dumping-ground for undigested, raw survey data, yet if few archaeologist at present seem willing or able to make full on-line disclosures of their project results, is there nonetheless a case to be made for serving digital information about Mediterranean surveys via some centralized archive or databank? This might be something akin to the Archaeology Data Service (1986–2003) in the United Kingdom, for example, whose chief mission is "to collect, describe, catalogue, preserve, and provide user support for digital resources that are created as a product of archaeological research". (In the USA, the Archaeological Data Archive Project [2002], under way for almost a decade, ceased operation in August 2002, having archived only a very few files of unproven utility.) The more recently established Collaboratory for GIS and Mediterranean Archaeology (Foss 2001; CGMA 2002) perhaps offers another model for the future. But how might such an archive work, without necessitating an unlikely level of agreement about standards for data format, imposing undesirable uniformity of hardware and software systems, or expecting unrealistic levels of familiarity with advanced GIS? Somewhat similar issues, incidentally, were being confronted 30 years ago by the Southwestern Archaeological Research Group (1974), in its attempts to share survey data for purposes of macro-regional comparison (albeit in a technologically simpler age). The present volume by no means resolves all these matters, but it does at least highlight them as important issues requiring thought and effort, if we are to make further progress.

Another area engaged, especially by the authors of the first group of papers that follow (Chapters 2–5), is discussion of the practical, methodological problems already enumerated above (such as incompatibilities in density estimates, site definition, sample sizes, etc.) encountered by those who have attempted to work with results from multiple survey datasets, set side-by-side. Just how truly limiting are these problems? To what extent can they be circumvented, without compromising research objectives – and how? Do these problems relate primarily to the inherent nature of survey data, to the way in which individual projects have been conducted, or to the form in which their results have been published? Are there certain types of information whose more routine incorporation in survey publications would facilitate and enhance comparison? Above all, if we wish to compare, what hope is there that we can agree about the standards for comparison to be employed? This plays out both at the relatively mundane level of sherd densities (Given, Ch. 2) or discovery rates of prehistoric pottery (Davis, Ch. 3), and at the more abstract level of definitional terms such as "site", "off-site", "intensity", "chronotype", and so on (Terrenato, Ch. 4; Wandsnider, Ch. 5). While none of these authors would venture to suggest that these issues are easily resolved, and disagreements (even among the Workshop

participants themselves) clearly remain, their systematic discussion here at least offers a point of departure for future, more clear-headed analysis.

Moving beyond our methodological tangles, it is entirely appropriate to ask what, exactly, it is that we seek to compare, and to what end. Of course, one can envisage both purely local, intra-regional comparisons (perhaps devoted to a specific research problem, such as the rise of an individual Mycenaean kingdom), as well as studies of much broader geographical scope, crossing a number of modern-day national borders. Yet other sorts of case-studies might involve comparison within broadly similar types of environments and landscapes (*e.g.*, upland or montane settings, islands, alluvial plains), or between them (*e.g.*, the regional highland/lowland contrasts explored, for some Roman landscapes of the Mediterranean, in Barker and Lloyd [1991]). In compiling this volume, we asked for empirically based studies of any sort, utilizing survey data from the Mediterranean area – provided they were strongly comparative in nature. Chapters 6–10 play out that challenge in various ways: from the longitudinal study of Thompson at Metaponto (Ch. 6), to two papers exploring the variable impact of Roman incorporation upon particular local landscapes in Italy and Tunisia (Attema and van Leusen, Ch. 7; Stone, Ch. 10), to observations relating to Bronze Age sociopolitical development on Crete and on the Greek Mainland (Cunningham and Driessen, Ch. 8; Wright, Ch. 9). Each addresses different questions, with often quite different approaches; together, they offer a range of perspectives on how to put surveys "side-by-side".

That range is extended by papers which – while taking their starting-place with comparative regional data – move in other directions: the distribution of a particular form of highly identifiable pottery types (Fentress *et al.*, Ch. 11); the fraught difficulties of deriving reliable demographic estimates from survey data (Osborne, Ch. 12); and the additional challenges posed by regional research to the mapping and representation of the ancient world (Mattingly and Witcher, Ch. 13).

The volume concludes with two contributions that adopt even more ambitious ambits, taking us well beyond the bounds of the Mediterranean world: Wilkinson *et al.* (Ch. 14) write on settlement pattern trends across the Fertile Crescent, while Blanton (Ch. 15) compares settlement and population change in Mesoamerican and Mediterranean civilizations. These last two wide-ranging papers, especially, bring into sharp focus an issue to which the conjoint, comparative use of multiple survey data sets might be seen as one response – namely, the "myopia" with which Blanton (2001) has charged Mediterranean archaeologists. Noting that data collection in the Mediterranean (because of decisions prioritizing ever increasing spatial resolution) is often from very small areas or "micro-regions" of at most 100 sq. km (and sometimes much smaller still), Blanton wonders whether such methodology "will actually inhibit meaningful comparison" and if it is in fact ill-suited to regional research aimed at large-scale social and demographic processes. He points out, with much justice, that

> ... the hinterlands of single Roman period administrative centres are often in the 50–200 sq. km range, but can extend over 600 sq. km, and a regional system may be made up of multiple interacting territories of this scale... Mediterranean nodal regions integrated by upland-lowland symbiosis typically occupy hundreds or thousands of sq. km... Mediterranean survey archaeology as a whole... now prioritizes high-resolution method over theory and problem orientation (Blanton 2001: 628–29).

Mediterranean archaeologists, in short, might do well to reflect, with Blanton, on whether their emphasis on high-quality data at the micro scale has resulted in a myopic lack of attention to wider vistas of interest. But to the extent that this is so, the case for building back up to larger synthetic structures, by utilizing the results of multiple projects comparatively, is surely given even greater justification.

One obvious conclusion to be drawn from this collection of papers is that comparative regional analysis can manifestly take many forms, and at various temporal and geographical scales. Another is that – notwithstanding the concerns raised by nearly every author (sometimes in quite strong terms) about methodological difficulties and the dangers of facile comparison of data which are to some extent non-comparable – the benefits of comparative analysis and the validity of what can actually be achieved by adopting such an approach nonetheless emerge largely intact. This volume does not try to gloss over real procedural obstacles that stand in our way, but it is also intended, unashamedly, to proselytize intelligently: that is, to encourage further critical exploration of forms of "side-by-side" analysis which we believe have a vital contribution to make to our understanding of the ancient Mediterranean world.

REFERENCES

Adams, R. McC. (1965) *Land Behind Baghdad: A History of Settlement on the Diyala Plain.* Chicago, Chicago University Press.

Adams, R. McC. (1981) *Heartland of Cities: Surveys of Ancient Settlement and Land Use on the Central Floodplain of the Euphrates.* Chicago, Chicago University Press.

Adams, R. McC. and Nissen, H J. (1972) *The Uruk Countryside: The Natural Setting of Urban Societies.* Chicago, Chicago University Press.

Alcock, S. E. (1993) *Graecia capta: The Landscapes of Roman Greece.* Cambridge, Cambridge University Press.

Alcock, S. E. (1994) Breaking up the Hellenistic world: survey and society. In I. Morris (ed.), *Classical Greece: Ancient Histories and Modern Archaeologies*: 171–90. Cambridge, Cambridge University Press.

Archaeological Data Archive Project (2002) http://csanet.org/archive/adap/adaplond.html

Archaeology Data Service (1986–2003) http://ads.ahds.ac.uk/

Banning, E. B. (2002) *Archaeological Survey.* (Manuals in Archaeological Method, Theory, and Technique.) New York, Kluwer Academic/Plenum Publishers.

Barker, G. (1996) Regional archaeological projects: trends and traditions in Mediterranean Europe. *Archaeological Dialogues* 3.2: 160–75.

Barker, G. and Lloyd, J. (eds.) (1991) *Roman Landscapes: Archaeological Survey in the Mediterranean Region.* (Archaeological Monographs of the British School at Rome 2). London, British School at Rome.

Barker, G. and Mattingly, D. (1999) General Editors' introduction: the POPULUS Project. In J. Bintliff and K. Sbonias (eds.), *The Archaeology of Mediterranean Landscapes 1: Reconstructing Past Population Trends in Mediterranean Europe*: iii–ix. Oxford, Oxbow Books.

Barker, G. and Mattingly, D. (series eds.) (1999–2000) *The Archaeology of Mediterranean Landscapes* (5 vols.). Oxford, Oxbow Books.

Billman, B. R. and Feinman, G. M. (eds.) (1999) *Settlement Pattern Studies in the America: Fifty Years Since Virú.* Washington D. C., Smithsonian Institution Press.

Bintliff, J. L. (1997) Regional survey, demography, and the rise of complex societies in the ancient Aegean: core-periphery, neo-Malthusian, and other interpretive models. *Journal of Field Archaeology* 24: 1–38.

Blanton, R. E. (1972) *Prehispanic Settlement Patterns of the Ixtapalapa Peninsula Region, Mexico* (Occasional Papers in Anthropology, Department of Anthropology, The Pennsylvania State University 6). University Park, Pennsylvania, The Pennsylvania State University.

Blanton, R. E. (2000) *Hellenistic, Roman and Byzantine Settlement Patterns of the Coast Lands of Western Rough Cilicia* (BAR International Series 879). Oxford, Archaeopress.

Blanton, R. E. (2001) Mediterranean myopia. *Antiquity* 75: 627–29.

Blanton, R. E., Kowalewski, S. A., Feinman, G. M. and Finsten, L. M. (1993) *Ancient Mesoamerica: A Comparison of Change in Three Regions.* Cambridge, Cambridge University Press.

Carter, J. C. (2003) *Discovering the Greek Countrside at Metaponto* (The Thomas Spencer Jerome Lectures). Ann Arbor, University of Michigan Press.

Cavanagh, W. G. (1995) Development of the Mycenaean state in Laconia: evidence from the Laconia survey. In R. Laffineur and W.-D. Niemeier (eds.), *POLITEIA: Society and State in the Aegean Bronze Age* (*Aegaeum* 12): 81–87. Liège, Université de Liège, Histoire de l'art et archéologie de la Grèce antique.

Cavanagh, W. G. (1999) Revenons à nos moutons: surface survey and the Peloponnese in the Late and Final Neolithic. In J. Renard (ed.), *Le Peloponnèse: archéologie et histoire*: 31–65. Rennes, Les Presses Universitaires.

CGMA (2002) http://www.depauw.edu/acad/geology/website/cgma/index.html

Cherry, J. F. (1983) Frogs round the pond: perspectives on current archaeological survey projects in the Mediterranean region. In D. R. Keller and D. W. Rupp (eds.) *Archaeological Survey in the Mediterranean Region* (BAR International Series 155): 375–416. Oxford, British Archaeological Reports.

Cherry, J. F. (1994) Regional survey in the Aegean: the 'New Wave' (and after). In P. N. Kardulias (ed.), *Beyond the Site: Regional Studies in the Aegean Area*: 91–112. Lanham, Rowman and Littlefield.

Cherry, J. F. (2003) Archaeology beyond the site: regional survey and its future. In J. Papadopoulos and R. Leventhal (eds.) *Theory and Practice in Mediterranean Archaeology: Old World and New World Perspectives*: 137–60. Los Angeles, Cotsen Institute of Archaeology, University of California at Los Angeles.

Cherry, J. F. (in press) Cyprus, the Mediterranean, and survey:

current issues and future trends. In M. Iacovou (ed.) *Archaeological Field Survey in Cyprus: Past History, Future Potentials. Proceedings of a Conference Held at the University of Cyprus, 1–2 December 2000* (BSA Studies). London, British School at Athens.

Cherry, J. F. and Davis, J. L. (2001) 'Under the sceptre of Agamemnon': the view from the hinterlands of Mycenae. In K. Branigan (ed.), *Urbanism in the Aegean Bronze Age* (Sheffield Studies in Aegean Archaeology 4): 141–59. Sheffield: Sheffield Centre for Aegean Archaeology, University of Sheffield.

Cherry, J. F., Davis, J. L. and Mantzourani, E. (1991) *Landscape Archaeology as Long-Term History: Northern Keos in the Cycladic Islands.* (Monument Archaeologica 16.) Los Angeles, Institute of Archaeology, University of California at Los Angeles.

Cherry, J. F. and Parkinson, W. A. (2003) Lithic artifacts from surveys: a comparative evaluation of recent evidence from the southern Aegean. In P. N. Kardulias and R. W. Yerkes (eds.) *Written in Stone: The Multiple Dimensions of Lithic Analysis*: 35–57. Lanham, Lexington Books.

Cunningham, T. (2001) Variations on a theme: divergence in settlement patterns and spatial organization in the far east of Crete during the Proto- and Neopalatial periods. In K. Branigan (ed.), *Urbanism in the Aegean Bronze Age* (Sheffield Studies in Aegean Archaeology 4): 72–86. Sheffield: Sheffield Centre for Aegean Archaeology, University of Sheffield.

Davis, J. L. (ed.) (1998) *Sandy Pylos: An Archaeological History from Nestor to Navarino.* Austin, University of Texas Press.

Davis, J. L., Alcock, S. E., Bennet, J., Lolos, Y. G. and Shelmerdine, C. W. (1997) The Pylos Regional Archaeological Project. Part I: Overview and the archaeological survey. *Hesperia* 66: 391–494

Driessen, J. (2001) History and hierarchy: preliminary observations on the settlement pattern in Minoan Crete. In K. Branigan (ed.), *Urbanism in the Aegean Bronze Age* (Sheffield Studies in Aegean Archaeology 4): 51–71. Sheffield: Sheffield Centre for Aegean Archaeology, University of Sheffield.

Fish, S. K. (1999) Conclusions: the settlement pattern concept from an Americanist perspective. In B. R. Billman and G. M. Feinman (eds.) *Settlement Pattern Studies in the Americas: Fifty Years since Virú*: 203–208. Washington, D.C., Smithsonian Institution Press.

Foss, P. (2001) GPS, GIS, and WWW in archaeological survey comparability. Paper presented at the electronic symposium "Crossroads in Mediterranean Landscape Archaeology" at the April 2001 meeting of the Society for American Archaeology.

Francovich, R., Patterson, H. and Barker, G. (eds.) (2000) *The Archaeology of Mediterranean Landscapes 5: Extracting Meaning from Ploughsoil Assemblages.* Oxford, Oxbow Books.

Given, M. and Knapp, A. B. (2003) *The Sydney Cyprus Survey Project: Social Approaches to Regional Archaeological Survey.*

(Monumenta Archaeologica 21.) Los Angeles, Cotsen Institute of Archaeology, University of California at Los Angeles.

Greene, K. (2002) *Archaeology: An Introduction* (4th edition). London, Routledge.

Halstead, P. (1994) The north-south divide: regional paths to complexity in prehistoric Greece. In C. Mathers and S. Stoddart (eds.), *Development and Decline in the Mediterranean Bronze Age*: 195–219. Sheffield, J.R. Collis Publications

Hodder, I. (ed.) (1991) *Archaeological Theory in Europe: The Last Three Decades.* London, Routledge.

Keller, D. R. and Rupp, D. W. (eds.) (1983) *Archaeological Survey in the Mediterranean Region* (BAR International Series 155). Oxford, British Archaeological Reports.

Kletter, R. and De-Groot, A. (2001) Excavating to excess? Implications of the last decade of archaeology in Israel. *Journal of Mediterranean Archaeology* 14: 76–85.

Knapp, A. B. and Cherry, J. F. (1994) *Provenience Studies and Bronze Age Cyprus: Production, Exchange and Politico-economic Change.* (Monographs in World Archaeology 21.) Madison, Prehistory Press.

McDonald, W. A. and Rapp, G. R., Jr (eds.) (1972) *The Minnesota Messenia Expedition: Reconstructing a Bronze Age Regional Environment.* Minneapolis, University of Minnesota Press.

Mee, C. B. (1999) Regional survey projects and the prehistory of the Peloponnese. In J. Renard (ed.), *Le Peloponnèse: archéologie et histoire*: 67–79. Rennes, Les Presses Universitaires.

Patterson, H., di Gennaro, F., di Giuseppe, H., Fontana, S., Gaffney, V., Harrison, A., Keay, S. J., Millett, M., Rendeli, M., Roberts, P., Stoddart, S. and Witcher, R. (2000) The Tiber Valley Project: the Tiber and Rome throughout two millennia. *Antiquity* 74: 395–403.

Parsons, J. R. (1972) *Prehistoric Settlement Patterns in the Texcoco Region* (Memoirs of the Museum of Anthropology, University of Michigan, Vol. 3). Ann Arbor, Museum of Anthropology, University of Michigan.

Potter, T. W. (1979) *The Changing Landscape of Southern Etruria.* London, Paul Elek.

Sanders, W. T., Parsons, J. R. and Santley, R. S. (1979) *The Basin of Mexico: Ecological Processes in the Evolution of a Civilization.* New York, Academic Press.

Southwestern Archaeological Research Group (1974) SARG: a co-operative approach towards understanding the locations of human settlement. *World Archaeology* 6: 107–116.

Stone, D. L. (1997) *The Development of an Imperial Territory: Romans, Africans and the Transformation of the Rural Landscape of Tunisia.* PhD dissertation, Interdepartmental Program in Classical Art and Archaeology, The University of Michigan.

Wilkinson, T. J. (2000) Regional approaches to Mesopotamian archaeology: the contribution of archaeological surveys. *Journal of Archaeological Research* 8: 219–67.

METHODOLOGICAL ISSUES

2. Mapping and Manuring: Can We Compare Sherd Density Figures?

Michael Given

INTRODUCTION

In the literature on intensive survey in the Mediterranean, there are several comparisons of the results and interpretations of different survey projects (*e.g.* Alcock 1993), and numerous comparisons of their methods (*e.g.* Mattingly 2000). Is it also possible to carry out a direct, quantitative comparison of the primary data from such survey projects – namely, their artefact density figures? Is 20 sherds per 100 sq. m in one project, for example, in any way equivalent to 20 sherds per 100 sq. m in another? More fundamentally, what does '20 sherds per 100 sq. m' actually *mean*?

This has ramifications for our whole understanding of survey. Is intensive survey a science, which uses statistics and GIS to produce absolute figures that can be tested by means of repeatability experiments and then directly compared? Or is it an art, an adjunct to ancient history, with its results and interpretations determined by the knowledge, experience and creativity of its project directors and specialists?

It is hardly surprising that different survey projects have developed different methods. Across the Mediterranean there are great variations in local physical conditions, land use and landscape history, while the variations between the research aims and contexts of different projects are if anything even greater. Such variations are for the most part entirely legitimate and appropriate. If we are going to try and compare intensive survey data, however, we need to know our limitations. Are these differences too fundamental to allow direct comparison, or can they somehow be taken into account and compensated for?

There are clearly several levels on which survey projects can be compared, and several different objects of comparison (Attema and van Leusen, Ch. 7, this volume). The present paper is concerned mainly with the artefact density data at the lower end of the analytical scale, rather than higher-level questions and processes such as rural colonisation and the control of agricultural production. Yet primary data of this kind are fundamental to most issues examined by survey projects. Many projects, for example, make 'sites' or 'settlements' their main objects of analysis and comparison. If the pottery density figures used to define such 'sites' cannot be compared, this invalidates any comparison of 'site densities' or 'settlement patterns' – quite apart from ignoring the complex, continuous and multi-period nature of human activity in the landscape and its material traces (Wandsnider, Ch. 5, this volume). Higher-level questions such as population figures also depend on the definition of site size, which in turn generally depends on artefact density: choosing different thresholds and definitions can alter the proposed population figures to an almost absurd degree (Osborne, Ch. 12, this volume).

The object of comparison on which I wish to focus in this paper consists of the broad but low-density 'field scatters' of artefacts which are often attributed to ancient manuring. These have been reported from England to Iraq and beyond, and certainly all across the Mediterranean. Assuming physical conditions, chronology and methodology are all roughly equivalent, can we identify general 'manuring levels', or clear regional patterns of variation? Or are conditions and methods so variable that we can only examine field scatters on a case-by-case basis? After reviewing the density figures for such field scatters from a variety of survey projects, I discuss some of the obstacles that severely limit any attempt to compare such data.

COMPARING FIELD SCATTERS

The mapping of ancient cultivation by means of detecting residual artefacts spread on the fields along with manure and night soil has the potential for being one of the great success stories of intensive survey. It recognises that human activity is continuous across the landscape, rather than restricted to the black dots of 'sites' and 'settlements' on the map. It completely transcends the false dichotomy between on-site and off-site material, which is frequently tantamount to 'site' and 'junk' (Van de Velde 2001: 28–30). It also greatly increases the sophistication of our analysis of past rural economies and societies. This, to give one answer to Elizabeth Fentress' question (2000), is what we are counting for.

Clearly, many of these scatters can be attributed to the effects of long-term manuring, with domestic pottery being scattered on the fields along with the manure (Bintliff and Howard 1999). Equally clearly, there are many other potential explanations, both cultural and natural, and each candidate for manuring status needs to be scrutinised closely on an individual basis (Alcock *et al.* 1994). Particularly helpful here is the use of soil science techniques. Examination of buried agricultural horizons in Cypriot check dams dating back to the 8th century AD and later has produced organic material and pottery (Noller and Wells in press). Similar buried soil strata from the Minoan period on Pseira contain identifiable faecal bio-markers as well as pottery (Bull, Betancourt and Evershed 1999; 2001; Bull *et al.* 1999). Stable manure more generally can be identified by an 'indicator package' of dung, litter, and characteristic insects and parasites (Kenward and Hall 1997; Hall and Kenward 1998). Particularly suitable to intensive survey is the use of phosphate analysis across agricultural areas, not just on potential farmstead sites (Cavanagh *et al.* 1988; Wilkinson 1988).

Wilkinson's analysis of Early and Middle Bronze Age dry-farming states in Upper Mesopotamia is an excellent demonstration of the analytical potential of examining field scatters (Wilkinson 1994; Wilkinson and Tucker 1995). Field scatters surrounding tells show a clear pattern of intensive cultivation and manuring up to a radius of 5–6 km from the tell, while outlying satellite settlements have smaller scatters of about 1 km. These scatters are neatly matched by radial 'hollow ways', traces of the ancient roadways which provided access from the city to the fields. On the basis of this highly informative material, it is possible to establish rates of agricultural production, the populations that these catchments could have supported, and the economic relationships between major centres, satellites, and adjoining catchment areas. Thanks to the ability to date such field scatters, it is possible to see the changes and developments in such systems, in contrast to static and acontextual 'catchment analyses'.

The Sydney Cyprus Survey Project (SCSP) discovered equivalent patterns, particularly in a broad alluvial plain near the Archaic-Byzantine city of Tamassos (Given and Knapp 2003; 309–311) (see Figure 2.1). Rather than giving the raw counts per unit of square area, these density figures are expressed in terms of a 'Pottery Index'. This takes into account not just square area, but the ground visibility and background confusion recorded by the survey team (see below), and also projects from the approximately 30% representative collection to the entire assemblage in the survey unit. Rough calibration from across the survey area shows that levels substantially above a Pottery Index of 5,000 represent major dense settlement – such as here at Tamassos during the Roman period, just clipped by the survey transect in the southeast corner of the map (Figure

2.1). The map's two smaller density peaks of 4,000–5,000 represent smaller-scale and lower-intensity activity, most probably estates. This interpretation is supported by a similar density peak 1.5 km to the southwest of the map, which survives much better and is certainly a Late Roman agricultural estate.

The most interesting pattern on the map, however, consists of the even but low-density spread of material in between these points. A Pottery Index of 1,000 (roughly equivalent to 50 sherds per 100 sq. m on clear ground) is common for the Roman period on broad alluvial terraces across the survey area. Most of this alluvium dates to the early Holocene, so the Roman surface is essentially intact. These low-density field scatters clearly represent intensive agriculture during the Roman period, especially the Late Roman period, when it was based on estates and supported a substantial elite in the city of Tamassos. The contrast with earlier and later periods is marked; only in the Medieval-Ottoman periods do we see similar carpets, and then they are restricted to 'haloes' of about 1 km diameter round the villages.

There are broad comparisons that we can draw here between two different social systems: Early to Middle Bronze Age dry-farming states in Upper Mesopotamia; and Late Roman cities in Cyprus. Both are based on urban centres surrounded by zones of intensive agriculture. These zones extend as far as it is possible for farmers to commute each day and transport manure from urban latrines and animal pens, with extensions round outlying settlements or estates. Clearly this comparison is only in the broadest of terms, and the object of comparison consists of 'exploitation patterns' or 'zones of intensive agriculture', rather than actual sherd densities. If ancient manuring was indeed a widespread phenomenon which intensive survey can identify and record relatively easily, we would expect there to be broadly similar levels of density, given equivalent methods and environmental conditions. This would allow us to analyse phenomena such as state-controlled intensive agriculture on a comparative and regional footing, rather than merely looking at a handful of isolated case studies.

Earlier attempts to tabulate average densities of field scatters from different projects across the Mediterranean suggested a very general correspondence (Cherry *et al.* 1991: 47), or else a clear decrease from Mesopotamia in the east to England in the west (Bintliff and Snodgrass 1988: 510–12). More data have now been published, and there are clearly some very wide disparities (Table 2.1).

What is supposedly the same phenomenon is represented by 625 sherds per 100 sq. m in Oman and 0.01 sherds per 100 sq. m in Spain. How can this be? Perhaps such startling disparities actually show that 'ancient manuring' is a construct of local geomorphological conditions, or of projects' very different methodologies. Before it is possible to compare the density data of these field scatters, we need to examine the main factors which cause this variation, and which are therefore obstacles to the direct comparison of survey data. Based on my own

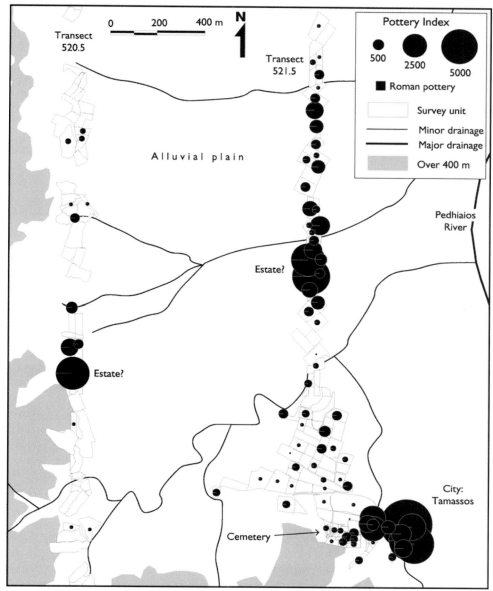

Figure 2.1 Sydney Cyprus Survey Project: Roman pottery distribution in the Tamassos plain. (See also colour version in Given and Knapp 2003: pl. LIII.)

active attempt to acquire, analyse and compare several data sets, I will discuss the following factors: dissemination; visibility; chronology; intensity; and geomorphology.

OBSTACLES TO COMPARING SHERD DENSITY FIGURES

Dissemination

A major problem in analysing and comparing raw survey data is that currently very little is available, in spite of the increasing numbers of projects that have been published. Sherd density maps such as those of the Pylos Regional Archaeological Project (Davis *et al.* 1996–2001) or the

Segermes Valley Survey (Sørensen *et al.* 1995) give the analysis, but not the primary data. This means that it is impossible to perform new calculations, analyses and tests. If site gazeteers and pottery catalogues are considered worthy of publication in some form, should not the same apply to pottery density data? Currently the best home for such data consists of public agencies that undertake to archive and disseminate digital data from archaeological projects, most notably the UK's Archaeology Data Service (2002).

Visual presentation is critical to the analysis and dissemination of survey data and results. Edward Tufte's criticisms of data-poor, acontextual, ambiguous diagrams cluttered with unnecessary 'chart-junk' are all too appropriate here (Tufte 1983; 1990). This is not a matter of

Project	Area	Period	Method	Source	Density (sherds per 100 sq. m)
Sohar	Main 'carpets'	Abbasid	100 sq. m squares	Wilkinson 1982: 328	625
Sweyhat	10 minutes from tell	Bronze Age; Hellenistic	100 sq. m squares	Wilkinson 1982: 330	58
Sweyhat	20 minutes from tell	Bronze Age; Hellenistic	100 sq. m squares	Wilkinson 1982: 330	30
Sweyhat	30 minutes from tell	Bronze Age; Hellenistic	100 sq. m squares	Wilkinson 1982: 330	20
SCSP	Transect 521.5	Roman	Survey units	Given & Knapp 2003: 309	0.3
SCSP	SCY110	Medieval-Modern	3.1 sq. m circles	Given & Knapp 2003: 186–87	30
SCSP	SCY209	Archaic-Classical	3.1 sq. m circles	Given & Knapp 2003: 197–99	16
SCSP	SCY215	Medieval-Modern	3.1 sq. m circles	Given & Knapp 2003: 200–201	27
Halieis	Calculation from *kopron*	Classical	–	Snodgrass 1994: 200	15.3
NVAP	Off-site overall mean	All	Survey units	Cherry *et al.* 1991: 47	2.0
Boeotia	Thespiae off-site (vis. adjusted)	Mostly Archaic-Classical	Survey units	Bintliff & Howard 1999: 53	26.4
Keos	Overall off-site average	All	Survey units	Cherry *et al.* 1991: 46	0.5
Methana	Average off-site density	All	Survey units	Mee & Forbes 1997: 36	0.1
Segermes	Typical off-site density	All	Survey units	Sørensen *et al.* 1995: 134–73	5
Riu Mannu	Transect 00, 50 m from farm	Roman	2 sq. m circles	Van de Velde 2001: 43–44	400
Riu Mannu	Transect 00, 100 m from farm	Roman	2 sq. m circles	Van de Velde 2001: 43–44	200
Tarragona	1/A halo round Site 1.6	Alto imperial	Survey units	Carreté *et al.* 1995: 169	0.02
Tarragona	2/C	Iberica	Survey units	Carreté *et al.* 1995: 185	0.02
Tarragona	2/D halo round Site 2.9	Republicana	Survey units	Carreté *et al.* 1995: 189	0.01

Table 2.1 Average pottery densities for field scatters from a selection of survey projects.

cosmetics: the inability to read published diagrams is a major obstacle to comparing survey projects. Examples encountered during research for this article include: scale labels (e.g. '1:5000') which were correct *before* reduction for publication; maps with no scales at all; multiple shades of grey which after printing become indistinguishable; graphs with unlabelled axes; sherd densities with no units expressed; and extreme information overload. My object here is not to cast blame (I have been guilty of several of these!), but to bring an important and neglected issue into public debate (*cf.* Sollars 2001).

A lesser problem is technical terminology. Intensive survey is now a highly complex and technical procedure, and different projects inevitably develop specific terms, such as ADABS, POSI, Pottery Index, and C-transforms. With proper definition and explanation, this should be no problem, though it could be asked how much statistical knowledge it is fair to ask of readers. When projects use different terms, the comparative worker has to impose some sort of system. For the unit of analysis variously called survey unit, field, tract, swath and transect, for example, I shall use the term 'survey unit' in this paper, as it is the basic spatial unit of analysis of most intensive survey projects. Similarly, I shall express densities in sherds per 100 sq. m, rather than per sq. m or per ha, to give relatively manageable numbers.

Visibility

If there is one universal in Mediterranean survey, it is that ground visibility is always a problem. Stubble, maquis, tomatoes, grass and pine needles all come between the fieldwalker and the artefacts with tedious and frustrating regularity. If we surveyed only those areas with over 90% visibility, then our sample of many rich and important areas would be minimal. Another option is to use very small sample units which can be entirely cleared of vegetation, such as the 2 sq. m circles of the Riu Mannu Survey Project (Van de Velde 2001: 34–35). More commonly, projects surveying much larger units have their fieldwalkers or team leaders estimate and record ground visibility, usually expressed as a percentage of the ground that can be seen. This can then be used to calculate a putative total number of sherds in the field, as is done, for example, on the Boeotia Project (Bintliff and Howard 1999: 53).

The problem with such a procedure is that there can be systematic biases in estimating visibility, as Bintliff and Howard point out (1999: 63, map 16), and that there are many factors other than ground cover which affect the percentage of sherds spotted by fieldwalkers (Thompson, Ch. 6, this volume). If we compare such visibility-corrected figures from different projects, we are dealing with numbers that are not 'real' (number of sherds seen), but are subjective and potentially inconsistent even within projects, let alone between them (Mattingly 2000: 12). SCSP carried out seeding experiments to test precisely this point, and discovered that in fields of poor visibility, sherd recovery rates were much better than the teams' visibility estimates would suggest (Schon 2000: 109; Meyer and Schon, in Given and Knapp 2003: 52–57). This means that simply increasing the sherd count in proportion to the ground visibility would produce a grossly inflated figure (as early analyses on SCSP did indeed do). Schon's more detailed experiments on the Eastern Korinthia Archaeological Survey demonstrated that even in very low visibility conditions, fieldwalkers recovered more sherds than expected. Conversely, sherd recovery was not total even in conditions of 100% visibility (Schon 2002: 153–54).

Several projects test the degree to which visibility

problems have affected their results (Cherry *et al.* 1991: 39–45), or adjust their figures based on careful experiment-ation and statistical analysis of their data (Terrenato 2000; Ch. 4, this volume). In SCSP's case, we flattened the visibility adjustment considerably: for a field of 50% visibility, for example, the sherd count was multiplied not by 2, but by only 1.14. When applied to our experimental data, these reduced multipliers gave us figures close to the known total of sherds sown in each field (Meyer and Schon, in Given and Knapp 2003: 52–57). Visibility is not the only factor which requires sherd density figures to be manipulated. Another particularly important one is background confusion, when weary fieldwalkers give up bending down to examine flat, red sherd-like stones, and so miss the actual sherds. SCSP's experiments showed this to have a greater impact than that of visibility, and we dealt with it using the same procedures as for visibility.

Different projects will clearly encounter different conditions and biases in their figures, and by doing this type of testing will establish different correction formulae. Should we therefore compare density counts after these formulae have been applied? Or should we compare raw densities without trying to compensate for the distortions produced by visibility and background confusion? The first alternative compares incompatible data, while the second compares deficient data.

Chronology

Dating surface pottery is another frequent challenge in analysing survey data, particularly in areas where there is no stratified sequence nearby which has been excavated and published. One very fruitful way forward is careful and wide-ranging fabric analysis of all coarse wares (*e.g.* Annis *et al.* 1995: 143, 147–48). Even so, a considerable proportion of material collected during intensive survey is datable only to very broad periods, or else overlaps two or more periods. A typical 'Roman' survey unit, for example, might have two sherds from the 4th century AD; five Hellenistic-Early Roman; three Late Roman; 15 Roman; 14 pre-Medieval; and 5 whose dates are unknown. How do we group these meaningfully, so we can compare the distributions of 'Roman' pottery from different pro-jects? One possibility is to distribute each sherd's chron-ological value across all years of its assigned period (Millett 2000: 54–57). This is a neat solution to a common problem, but requires the primary data to be available, and still faces the problem of regional biases in our knowledge of particular wares and periods.

Another requirement for comparing field scatters is that such scatters are not just clicker-counted, but a sufficient sample is collected for them to be dated with some degree of confidence. Some projects carried out their fieldwork before this need had become evident (Cherry *et al.* 1991: 52–53). Others have decided that such a procedure is too labour-intensive to be worth the gain in information (Fentress 2000). There is clearly no

point in trying to compare a clicker-counted pottery scatter (all periods), with one that has been dated as Roman. Just as importantly, we cannot compare a continuous scatter dated by means of a 30% representative sample with one dated by means of a grab of 'diagnostics'. This issue is particularly important when analysing field scatters. When such scatters are caused by *sebakh* (sherd-rich earth from tells which has been spread across fields as fertiliser in relatively recent periods), we can expect to find sherds of all periods. Pottery from a field scatter derived from ancient manuring will be limited to the periods when that manuring was carried out.

Clearly, every region has its own problems: local fabrics which stay the same for centuries; gaps in our knowledge because of lack of excavated material; possible 'aceramic' periods. This means that each project will have to make its own chronological groupings based on its own local conditions. Even when such groupings coincide in chron-ological terms, they will have very different assumptions built into them. Any direct comparison of 'Roman' pottery densities looks decidedly precarious.

Intensity

The term 'intensity' refers to the percentage of ground that field teams have actually examined for artefacts, the length of time they have spent on it, and the care with which they have examined it. If a project's survey units cover 12% of the survey area, this is only a 12% sample if the fieldwalkers have examined all of each survey unit. When fieldwalkers are 10 m or more apart, they can only examine a relatively narrow strip, typically 2 m wide. On the Tarragona survey fieldwalkers were 5 m apart: it was estimated 'that the field of vision of any individual walker is 2 to 2.5 m wide, with the result that the spacing produced a coverage of 40–50% of field surfaces' (Carreté *et al.* 1995: 52).

Another approach is for the fieldwalkers to be close together, no more than 5 m, and aiming to cover the entire area of the survey unit. This was SCSP's procedure, with fieldwalkers 5 m apart and covering 2.5 m on each side of them. By staying level and communicating with each other, they ensured that two walkers did not count the same sherd. The seeding experiments, however, showed that this hardly constituted total coverage (Meyer and Schon, in Given and Knapp 2003: 52–57). Even in a field with 90% visibility, zero background confusion and only 20 seeded sherds, recovery rates for the five teams ranged from 50% to 70%. This by no means makes the figures invalid. The team records a reasonable sample of what is on the ground, and does so in a sufficiently consistent fashion that general comparison across the survey area is possible. What this procedure does not produce, however, is an accurate and absolute record of sherd density which can be directly compared alongside other projects.

A further problem with the intensity of sherd recording is the drastic difference between a survey unit up to 100 m long, with a team walking and clicking across it, and a sample circle 2 m in diameter, with a fieldwalker on hands and knees scrutinising each clump of soil. The Riu Mannu Survey Project used circles 80 cm in diameter (*i.e.* with an area of 2 sq. m), usually on a 30 m grid (Van de Velde 2001: 30–34). Will these give significantly different pottery densities to 25 × 100 m survey units traversed in 20 minutes by five fieldwalkers?

This question can be answered by the simple method of resurvey using a different method. In 1995 a SCSP team surveyed two particularly dense units, using the standard procedure of walking 5 m apart and aiming to cover the whole field (Given *et al.* 1999: 27–29; Given and Knapp 2003: 159–60). Using this method, units 1268 and 1281 had overall densities of 91 and 25 sherds per 100 sq. m respectively (including tile fragments). The following year, after the field had been ploughed, we returned and set out a grid of sample circles 2 m in diameter and 10 m apart across each survey unit. Each circle was counted and collected by a single fieldwalker on hands and knees. They were examined with considerable care, particularly after the discovery of a Chalcolithic picrolite pendant in one of them. By this method, the averages for units 1268 and 1281 when extrapolated out from the circles to the entire units were 773 and 358 sherds per 100 sq. m respectively. Even allowing for possible fluctuations due to ploughing, it is clear that a small circle is examined with far greater intensity than a large survey unit, and the results cannot be directly compared.

Some of the differences in density figures in Table 2.1 are clearly due to the varying intensity of the scrutiny of the ground. This is clearest in the SCSP examples, where sample circles produced densities up to ten times greater than that of standard survey units. The very high densities on the Riu Mannu Survey Project may well be in part due to the small size of their survey units and consequent higher intensity of examination, as well as their guaranteed 100% visibility. Even when more or less the same level of intensity has been used, however, the differences are still too great to be attributed to minor variations of method.

Geomorphology

A whole range of geomorphological and other post-depositional factors can have a dramatic effect on the sherd densities that are recorded. This is by now well known (*e.g.* Taylor 2000; Wells 2001; Davis, Ch. 3, this volume; Thompson, Ch. 6, this volume; Wandsnider, Ch. 5, this volume). Before we can even begin to question the meaning of surface artefact densities, we have to ask if they have been brought in, covered or carried away by soil movements such as erosion and deposition, or disturbed in any way by anthropogenic processes such as ploughing, dumping, and bulldozing.

One post-depositional process with a particularly dramatic effect on artefact densities is deflation. In arid conditions, the light sand and soil particles are blown away,

while the heavier sherds remain in place, gradually piling up on each other as their matrix is removed from round them. In deflationary areas round Sohar in Oman, Wilkinson found field scatters with densities of up to 3,750 sherds per 100 sq. m (1982: 328).

In an even more extreme example, the Amheida Project in the Dakhleh Oasis (Egypt) carried out a series of exploratory test squares in a typically dense area on the Roman urban site of Amheida (Last 2001). Three such test squares demonstrated an on-site 'surface horizon' consisting almost entirely of pottery, with very little matrix. This horizon overlay sand and debris with much less pottery, and was clearly created mainly by deflation. These squares produced surface horizon densities of up to 400 sherds per sq. m, weighing 4.2 kg, or 40,000 sherds per 100 sq. m! The smallest degree of deflation, therefore, will grossly exaggerate pottery densities, whether on- or off-site.

This is only one cautionary example out of hundreds; clearly it is vital to investigate and analyse all such geomorphological processes. A further problem is how this geomorphological information should be integrated into the analysis of the pottery data. Should areas of erosion or deposition be simply excluded, and survey restricted to the 'windows' between them? Or is it possible to establish a formula to compensate for the effects of different soil movement processes, as with visibility or background confusion?

As with pottery chronology, so with geomorphological descriptors such as 'stable', 'slightly eroding', and 'depositional': clearly they have to be suited to local environmental conditions. So how can one project's 'slightly eroding' be compared to another's 'Stability Class B'? Besides, such terms by necessity have a coarse resolution. Even a small area of deposition in one part of a survey unit can drastically affect artefact densities, even though it is not large enough to be mapped at the scale at which transect survey operates.

Many intensive survey projects now have geomorphologists who map areas of erosion, instability, and deposition. The Eastern Korinthia Archaeological Survey and the Troodos Archaeological and Environmental Survey Project both have a geomorphology student on every field team, whose observations ensure that no survey unit straddles two different geomorphological zones (Given *et al.* 2002: 27). This means that artefact densities within each survey unit are reasonably coherent in terms of the extent to which they have been affected by geomorphological processes. Fieldwalking and geomorphological mapping can also be supplemented by more detailed geomorphological and micromorphological studies of erosion, soil management and site formation processes (*e.g.* French and Whitelaw 1999).

As our understanding of the complex relationship between surface process and artefact history increases, it may prove to be more helpful to measure sherd density in sherds per unit volume (Wilkinson 1988: 100–103), or

Cultural

1. Rate of artefact production
2. Rate of artefact disposal
3. Duration of artefact production
4. Duration of artefact deposition (*e.g.* continuous manuring for 300 years)
5. Manner of deposition: abandoned settlement, burial, dumping, manuring

Post-depositional

6. Build-up of incoming sediment over artefacts, covering and hiding them
7. Build-up of incoming sediment containing new artefacts from elsewhere
8. Erosion of existing sediment, removing artefacts with it
9. Stripping of existing sediment, exposing buried artefacts
10. Deflation of sediment leaving artefacts in place, causing greater surface densities
11. Movement because of recent anthropogenic disturbance (ploughing, dumping, bulldozing, etc.)
12. Differential sherd survival
13. *Sebakh*: the spreading of soil and sherds from ancient sites as agricultural fertiliser

Methodological

14. Ground visibility, and varying ways of estimating and compensating for it
15. Background confusion, and varying ways of estimating and compensating for it
16. Effects of sunlight, weather and soil moisture
17. Intensity of recording (how much of their strip do the fieldwalkers actually examine?)
18. Varying abilities of fieldwalkers to identify artefacts; fieldwalkers' state of mind and health
19. Definition of artefact (*e.g.* minimum sherd size)
20. Collection policy: relationship between sherds counted and sherds collected
21. Identification and grouping of fixed chronological periods
22. Data entry, processing and analytical methods (typos; formulae for calculating densities, etc.)
23. Presentation: choice of symbols, data ranges, and scales

Table 2.2 Factors that create surface artefact density figures.

else sherd mass per unit volume. The fourth relevant dimension is time, and we may even be able to factor rates of erosion, deposition or deflation into our measurement of human activity in the landscape (Jay Noller, personal communication; Wandsnider, Ch. 5, this volume).

CONCLUSION

The central question of this paper is whether we can carry out direct, quantitative comparison of artefact density figures from intensive survey projects. After several practical attempts to do so, my answer – in the current state of research – is 'no'. Table 2.2 suggests some of the factors which intervene between the past human activities under investigation, such as cooking or farming, and the tables and maps with which survey projects publish their results. To investigate any one of these (the deposition of artefacts with manure, for example), requires isolating it from the other 22, and making sure it is just that one which causes variation in the figures. Different survey

projects have different combinations of factors, and those factors have varying effects and are dealt with in different ways. This makes it logically impossible to isolate any one of them across two separate projects.

Given the dramatic effect that these factors can have, it is perhaps a challenge to ensure direct comparability *within* survey projects, let alone *between* them. This particularly applies when projects deliberately choose different topographical zones to give an environmental and cultural cross-section of their region. Can we really compare density figures from steep, pine-clad ridges with those from cultivated fields on alluvial terraces?

Each project needs to develop its own solution to its unique set of problems. Complex procedures to compensate for factors such as ground visibility, varying rates of pottery production, and fieldwalker biases can indeed have a local validity, when they are carefully tested against collected and experimental data. In a way, this is a form of calibration: individual projects suggest interpretations of various 'density' levels based on their own analyses and experience. Such procedures, for example SCSP's 'Pottery

Index', need to be published and explained in a transparent way, preferably with the original, raw data made available for that purpose.

This is clearly the way forward. Interpreting and comparing raw data without taking into account the many factors that affect sherd counts will only produce a regional map of fieldwalking conditions and methods. However interesting this might be, it is hardly the ultimate goal of regional survey. There are many possibilities for increasing the sophistication of our analyses and comparisons of surface material. Particularly important are seeding experiments, improved techniques of mapping pottery, and a fuller integration of geomorphological analyses of surface processes. We will probably never be able to set a Mediterranean standard for 'manuring' levels of sherd density; surface survey is too blunt a tool for that degree of precision and consistency. What we can do is to compare manuring scatters that have been identified by different projects on the basis of carefully tested and contextualised analysis.

ACKNOWLEDGMENTS

I am grateful to John Bintliff, Emeri Farinetti, Martin Millett and Peter van Dommelen for their generosity in providing me with unpublished survey data, and to the members of the Sydney Cyprus Survey Project, particularly Timothy E. Gregory, A. Bernard Knapp, Nathan Meyer, Jay Noller and Robert Schon. I would also like to thank Jay Noller, Peter van Dommelen and participants in the 'Side-by-Side' workshop in Ann Arbor in April 2002 for their comments on an earlier draft of this paper.

REFERENCES

Archaeology Data Service (2002) Website, available at http://ads.ahds.ac.uk/

Alcock, S. E. (1993) *Graecia Capta: The Landscapes of Roman Greece*. Cambridge, Cambridge University Press.

Alcock, S. E., Cherry, J. F. and Davis, J. L. (1994) Intensive survey, agricultural practice and the Classical landscape of Greece. In I. Morris (ed.) *Classical Greece: Ancient Histories and Modern Archaeologies*: 137–70. Cambridge, Cambridge University Press.

Annis, M. B., van Dommelen, P. and van de Velde, P. (1995) Rural settlement and socio-political organization: the Riu Mannu Survey Project in Sardinia. *Bulletin Antieke Beschaving* 70: 133–52.

Bintliff, J. L. and Howard, P. (1999) Studying needles in haystacks: surface survey and the rural landscape of Central Greece in Roman times. *Pharos* 7: 51–91.

Bintliff, J. L. and Snodgrass, A. (1988) Off-site pottery distributions: a regional and interregional perspective. *Current Anthropology* 29: 506–513.

Bull, I. D., Betancourt, P. P. and Evershed, R. P. (1999) Chemical evidence for a structured agricultural manuring regime on the island of Pseira, Crete, during the Minoan period. In P. P. Betancourt, V. Karageorghis, R. Laffineur and W.-D. Niemeier,

(eds.) *Meletemata: Studies in Aegean Archaeology Presented to Malcolm H. Wiener as He Enters His 65th Year*, Vol. I: 69–73. Liège, Université de Liège.

Bull, I. D., Betancourt, P. P. and Evershed, R. P. (2001) An organic geochemical investigation of the practice of manuring at a Minoan site on Pseira Island, Crete. *Geoarchaeology* 16: 223–42.

Bull, I. D., Simpson, I. A., van Bergen, P. F. and Evershed, R. P. (1999) Muck 'n' molecules: organic geochemical methods for detecting ancient manuring. *Antiquity* 73: 86–96.

Carreté, J.-M., Keay, S. and Millett, M. (1995) *A Roman Provincial Capital and its Hinterland: The Survey of the Territory of Tarragona, Spain, 1985–1990* (*JRA* Supplementary Series 15). Ann Arbor, Journal of Roman Archaeology.

Cavanagh, W. G., Hirst, S. and Litton, C. D. (1988) Soil phosphate, site boundaries, and change point analysis. *Journal of Field Archaeology* 15: 67–83.

Cherry, J. F., Davis, J. L. and Mantzourani, E. (1991) *Landscape Archaeology as Long-Term History: Northern Keos in the Cycladic Islands from Earliest Settlement until Modern Times* (*Monumenta Archaeologica* 16). Los Angeles, UCLA Institute of Archaeology.

Davis, J. L., Alcock, S. E., Bennet, J., Lolos, Y., Shelmerdine, C. W., and Zangger, E. (1996–2001) The Pylos Regional Archaeological Project: internet edition. Available at http://river.blg.uc.edu/prap/PRAP.html.

Fentress, E. (2000) What are we counting for? In R. Francovich and H. Patterson (eds.) *The Archaeology of Mediterranean Landscapes 5: Extracting Meaning from Ploughsoil Assemblages*: 44–52. Oxford, Oxbow.

French, C. and Whitelaw, T. (1999) Soil erosion, agricultural terracing and site formation processes at Markiani, Amorgos, Greece: the micromorphological perspective. *Geoarchaeology* 14: 151–89.

Given, M., Kassianidou, V., Knapp, A. B. and Noller, J. (2002) Troodos Archaeological and Environmental Survey Project, Cyprus: report on the 2001 season. *Levant* 34: 25–38.

Given, M. and Knapp, A. B. (2003) *The Sydney Cyprus Survey Project: Social Approaches to Regional Archaeological Survey* (*Monumenta Archaeologica* 21). Los Angeles, Cotsen Institute of Archaeology.

Given, M., Knapp, A. B., Meyer, N., Gregory, T. E., Kassianidou, V., Noller, J., Wells, L. E., Urwin, N. and Haddon, W. (1999) The Sydney Cyprus Survey Project: an interdisciplinary investigation of long-term change in the North Central Troodos, Cyprus. *Journal of Field Archaeology* 26: 19–39.

Hall, A. R. and Kenward, H. K. (1998) Disentangling dung: pathways to stable manure. *Environmental Archaeology* 1: 123–26.

Kenward, H. K. and Hall, A. R. (1997) Enhancing bioarchaeological interpretation using indicator groups: stable manure as a paradigm. *Journal of Archaeological Science* 24: 663–73.

Last, J. (2001) Columbia University Excavations at Amheida, Egypt: Exploratory Test Pits. Available at http://www.mcah.columbia.edu/amheida/html/2001_field_reports/testpits2001.html.

Mattingly, D. J. (2000) Methods of collection, recording and quantification. In R. Francovich and H. Patterson (eds.) *The Archaeology of Mediterranean Landscapes 5: Extracting Meaning from Ploughsoil Assemblages*: 5–15. Oxford, Oxbow.

Mee, C. and Forbes, H. (1997) (eds.) *A Rough and Rocky Place: The Landscape and Settlement History of the Methana Peninsula, Greece* (*Liverpool Monographs in Archaeology and Oriental Studies*). Liverpool, Liverpool University Press.

Millett, M. (2000) Dating, quantifying and utilizing pottery assemblages from surface survey. In R. Francovich and H. Patterson (eds.) *The Archaeology of Mediterranean Landscapes 5: Ex-*

tracting Meaning from Ploughsoil Assemblages: 53–59. Oxford, Oxbow.

Noller, J. and Wells, L. (in press) Bimillenary persistence of traditional systems of hill slope soil conservation in the Mediterranean. *Geoarchaeology*, (in press).

Schon, R. (2000) On a site and out of sight: where have our data gone? *Journal of Mediterranean Archaeology* 13: 107–11.

Schon, R. (2002) *Seeding the Landscape: Experimental Contributions to Regional Survey Methodology*. Unpublished Ph.D. dissertation, Bryn Mawr College.

Snodgrass, A. (1994) Response: the archaeological aspect. In I. Morris (ed.) *Classical Greece: Ancient Histories and Modern Archaeologies*: 197–200. Cambridge, Cambridge University Press.

Sollars, L. H. (2001) *Regional Survey in the Mediterranean: Presentations, Re-Presentations and Archaeological Landscapes*. Unpublished M. Phil. thesis, University of Glasgow.

Sørensen, L. W., Lund, J. and Carlsen, J. (1995) The survey. In S. Dietz, L. L. Sebaï and H. Ben Hassen (eds.) *Africa Proconsularis: Regional Studies in the Segermes Valley of Northern Tunesia*, Vol. I: 113–75. Copenhagen, Carlsberg Foundation and the Danish Research Council for the Humanities.

Taylor, J. (2000) Cultural depositional processes and post-depositional problems. In R. Francovich and H. Patterson (eds.) *The Archaeology of Mediterranean Landscapes 5: Extracting Meaning from Ploughsoil Assemblages*: 16–26. Oxford, Oxbow.

Terrenato, N. (2000) The visibility of sites and the interpretation of field survey results: towards an analysis of incomplete distributions. In R. Francovich and H. Patterson (eds.) *The Archaeo-*

logy of Mediterranean Landscapes 5: Extracting Meaning from Ploughsoil Assemblages: 60–71. Oxford, Oxbow.

Tufte, E. R. (1983) *The Visual Display of Quantitative Information*. Cheshire, CT, Graphics Press.

Tufte, E. R. (1990) *Envisioning Information*. Cheshire, CT, Graphics Press.

Van de Velde, P. (2001) An extensive alternative to intensive survey: point sampling in the Riu Mannu Survey Project, Sardinia. *Journal of Mediterranean Archaeology* 14: 24–52.

Wells, L. E. (2001) A geomorphological approach to reconstructing archaeological settlement patterns based on surficial artifact distribution. In P. Goldberg, V. Holliday and C. R. Ferring (eds.) *Earth Sciences and Archaeology*: 107–41. New York, Kluwer Academic/Plenum.

Wilkinson, T. J. (1982) The definition of ancient manured zones by means of extensive sherd-sampling techniques. *Journal of Field Archaeology* 9: 323–33.

Wilkinson, T. J. (1988) The archaeological component of agricultural soils in the Middle East: the effects of manuring in antiquity. In W. Groenman-van Waateringe and M. Robinson (eds.) *Man-Made Soils* (*BAR-IS* 410): 93–114. Oxford, British Archeological Reports.

Wilkinson, T. J. (1994) The structure and dynamics of dry-farming states in Upper Mesopotamia. *Current Anthropology* 35: 483–520.

Wilkinson, T. J. and Tucker, D. J. (1995) *Settlement Development in the North Jazira, Iraq: A Study of the Archaeological Landscape* (*Iraq Archaeological Reports* 3). London, British School of Archaeology in Iraq.

3. Are the Landscapes of Greek Prehistory Hidden? A Comparative Approach

Jack L. Davis

In collaboration with his colleagues, John Bintliff, co-director of the Boiotia Project, has argued in a series of publications and lectures over the past 15 years that the surface archaeological record of Greece for prehistoric periods is only an impoverished pale reflection of what was once present (Bintliff 1999; 2000; Bintliff and Snodgrass 1985; Bintliff *et al.* 1999; 2000; 2002). The conviction that survey teams in Boiotia did not find sufficient quantities of prehistoric artifacts is now deep-seated. Consequently, and logically, Bintliff and his colleagues have found it necessary not only to seek to explain this situation, but also to propose methods for constructing a more realistic picture of the prehistoric landscapes of Greece as they may have appeared before being ravaged by time and human interventions. These methods consist of multiplying observed data by specified constants, in order to adjust the figures to account for prehistoric remains that have supposedly been overlooked (see Schon 2000; 2002:138–77 for a critique of the use of such multipliers and an examination of the effects of differences in visibility on our perceptions of surface archaeological distributions).

Although these ideas were originally formulated to address specific concerns that arose in the course of fieldwork in Boiotia, they have recently been amalgamated into a general model that, it is argued, may be relevant for the interpretation of surface remains elsewhere in Greece – indeed in other parts of the Mediterranean and Europe too (see Bintliff *et al.* 1999). Bintliff and his colleagues (Bintliff *et al.* 2000) have not, however, asserted the universal validity of their model and invite others to test it by bringing to bear different sets of data.

This is a welcome invitation since not all projects operating in the Aegean area have encountered such difficulties in recognizing prehistoric artifacts, raising the possibility that problems in Boiotia arise from circumstances peculiar to the Boiotia Project and that the model proposed by Bintliff *et al.* is much more restricted in its applicability than imagined. My own experiences do not warrant any blanket generalization that surface densities of prehistoric finds are necessarily lower than those of

historical periods. Indeed, artifacts characteristic of certain post-prehistoric periods have been noticeably uncommon in some parts of Greece: not only, obviously, those of the Dark Ages, but also of the later Hellenistic and Early Roman periods and of the Archaic-Classical periods (*e.g.* see Davis and Cherry 1998, on the Dark Ages and Archaic periods in Keos, Attica, and Euboia; Alcock 1993, on the Late Hellenistic and Early Roman periods).

The purpose of this paper is to address several of the earlier arguments of Bintliff, Howard and Snodgrass by drawing comparatively on largely unpublished information in the archives of four regional studies projects in Greece and Albania. Members of the Boiotia Project have themselves taken the lead in testing their model, suggesting that fieldwork in other parts of Greece, such as that of the Pylos Regional Archaeological Project (hereafter, PRAP), provides support for their ideas. Most recently, Bintliff (2001) has argued that the results of the Keos survey (Cherry *et al.* 1991) and of Alcock's researches at Phlius (1991) support his arguments that Dark Age landscapes of Greece are also largely hidden. But the results of PRAP are not yet published in a sufficiently detailed manner so as to allow detailed comparison with those of the Boiotia Project.

Indeed the absence of fully available data sets is likely to plague attempts at comparing the results of surveys in Greece for some time to come. Possible remedies for this problem are addressed below. But comparison is also hindered by an equally serious difficulty – the continuing lack of standardization in field methods. This situation reflects the lack of any real system for training practitioners of survey. There has yet to emerge any formal means for apprenticing future directors of field projects, partly because of the relatively low status that regional studies have held within traditional structures of institutional power.

Survey developed without significant support from most of the foreign schools of archaeology in Greece, and at the fringes of the archaeological community. Although its reception by professional organizations such as the Archaeological Institute of America was somewhat better, William A. McDonald, co-director of the University of Minnesota Messenia Expedition (hereafter, UMME), could nonetheless wonder in 1981 about the criteria according to which its Gold Medal had been awarded to him: 'It is surely safe to eliminate practically every standard that is routinely used to measure achievement in classical archaeology' (Wilkie and Coulsen 1985: xiv). Regional studies projects continued to operate largely without close scrutiny until 1988, when official action was taken by the Greek Ministry of Culture to regulate and to control them. The decision was made that each foreign nation conducting archaeological research in Greece could only operate three surveys per year and that these projects needed to be selected and nominated by the appropriate national school in Greece, a pronouncement that was clearly modeled on an earlier statute that had restricted each foreign school to three excavations.

Those who organized surveys were usually younger than excavation directors and most had been influenced by anthropological archaeology. Survey was virtually the only arena in which a graduate student or recent Ph.D. could realistically expect to be able to organize a program of field research. Many directors were based in institutions that lay outside the traditional powerhouses of Classical archaeology. Although Greek governmental regulations have long required a prospective excavation director to serve an internship under the supervision of a previously approved excavator, there were no such requirements for surveyors. It is hardly surprising that such an environment encouraged experimentation and diversity in procedures.

The official changes in 1988 may eventually lead to greater procedural uniformity, but this has not yet happened. Even in the case of the American archaeological community, for example, the American School of Classical Studies at Athens responded to the new regulations simply by renaming its committee charged with vetting proposals for fieldwork (as the 'Excavation and Survey Committee') without taking further steps to ensure that the abilities of principal investigators or the soundness of research proposals would be adequately reviewed. Indeed, in the majority of years since 1988 there has been no member of the committee who has ever directed or has even participated in a survey. An opportunity to encourage the development of more standardized field procedures through critical review has thus been missed. At the same time, a tightening of Greek governmental control over surveys in the past decade has compelled further innovation and modification of research strategies and methods – but now for non-scientific reasons.

The preceding excursus on the development of survey in Greece is needed, it seems to me, in order to appreciate the enormous barriers that stand in the way of the development of comparative survey, at least in one part of the Mediterranean. In this paper, my own way out of the quandary created by lack of procedural uniformity and unavailability of sufficiently detailed information has been

to present, side-by-side, case studies from projects in which I have participated and that have employed broadly similar methods.

THE 'HIDDEN LANDSCAPE' OF PREHISTORIC GREECE

Bintliff and his colleagues were among the first to introduce a critical perspective to the analysis of data from survey in Greece. Most projects are now quite aware that factors, such as Shennan's (1985: 35) 'field effects' and 'walker effects,' may distort our perception of surface patterns, and most are sensitive to the possibility that the archaeological record of particular periods can be camouflaged by the deposition of soil units at a later date. Such *Quellenkritik* of data from surveys has increasingly come to be expected in the publication of the results of surveys (see Cherry *et al.* 1991 for an early example of such analyses; *cf.* Alcock 1993: 49–53). Still, Bintliff and his various co-authors are extremely skeptical about reliability of data when their conclusions are compared to those of other projects in Greece.

The fullest presentation of these ideas lies in the paper 'The hidden landscapes of prehistoric Greece,' published by John Bintliff, Phil Howard, and Anthony Snodgrass in the *Journal of Mediterranean Archaeology* (Bintliff *et al.* 1999). Arguments are developed there as follows. Surveys in Greece have supposedly found fewer prehistoric than historical sites, and the overall density of prehistoric artifacts is lower than that of historical remains. The Boiotia Project found that prehistoric components were few in number, their distribution 'patchy', and that most were from multi-component sites (the Boiotia Project's ratio of prehistoric components to area intensively surveyed [1.6 components per sq. km] is, however, higher than most other surveys in Greece). They then note that intensive survey was supposed to improve on UMME's picture of prehistoric periods which, as both Bintliff (1977: 6) and Cherry (1983: 392–93) had argued, probably missed smaller sites and favored larger, more obtrusive ones set in certain specific locations (*e.g.*, on hilltops). The authors of the "hidden landscape" model, however, claim that the results of UMME and PRAP were largely the same with regards to the overall distribution of prehistoric settlements, and that PRAP failed to improve on UMME by finding 'genuinely' small prehistoric sites (< 0.1 ha).

Such a comparison of the results of PRAP and UMME seems not only premature, but also inappropriate for historical reasons of which Bintliff and his colleagues may in part be understandably unaware. There is no room here for detailed discussion of this subject (which will be more fully elucidated in the final publication of the prehistoric material from PRAP), but it is worth making two points. In the first place, it is important to realize that the area around the Palace of Nestor that was reinvestigated by PRAP was studied by members of UMME with much greater intensity than other parts of Messenia, since McDonald was a member of Blegen's excavation team from 1939, long before UMME was formally constituted as a regional studies project. McDonald and Hope Simpson did not locate the vast majority of sites in the vicinity of the Palace of Nestor by applying their much-maligned predictive model of settlement location. In fact, many of the sites that UMME lists had already by 1929 been discovered by a local antiquary who conveyed information about them to Blegen, while McDonald found others in intensive explorations in 1953 and 1955 (McDonald and Hope Simpson 1961: 221, n. 1 and 222, n. 2). In the second place, it is incorrect to assert that PRAP did not detect the remains of very small prehistoric sites. For example, tiny components of the EBA were discovered by tract-walking at several locations on the Englianos Ridge within the area of the town that later surrounded the Palace of Nestor (Stocker 2004).

Bintliff, Howard and Snodgrass next suggest explanations for what they consider to be the astonishingly small quantities of prehistoric artifacts generally found by surveys in Greece. They are perplexed that no greater a density than 1–2 prehistoric sites per sq. km has been recorded by the Boiotia Project, and other surveys, and they maintain that such a density is not sufficiently great. This assertion is supported by reference to publications of the German *Landeskunde* school of geography, which predicts that any fertile catchment will always contain agricultural settlements, although their location and nature will shift through time.

Having constructed this problem, Bintliff *et al.* then set out to explain why it is that surveys have located what they regard as insufficient numbers of prehistoric sites. They ground their explanations in anecdotal observations from the Boiotia Project, suggesting that increases in search intensity unrelated to any attempt to locate prehistoric finds, or simply chance itself, resulted in the discovery of otherwise unsuspected prehistoric components. They thus conclude that the Boiotia Project failed to find certain prehistoric sites. It is, in fact, difficult to argue against this logic since it is largely circular: sites were not discovered because search intensity was not sufficiently high, and we can conclude that search intensity was not sufficiently high because sites were not discovered.

Bintliff and his colleagues discount soil erosion as the reason why their project did not find more prehistoric sites, since in their view erosion should have resulted in lag deposits containing artifacts. (In response to this claim, see Barker 2000; it is also worth noting that, despite rampant recent erosion, virtually all sites known to UMME in the 1950s were relocated by PRAP. There appears to be a slight inconsistency in their argument, since elsewhere they assert that exposed prehistoric artifacts will have entirely worn away.) Instead they believe that prehistoric sites are there to be found, but that we are failing to recognize them because so little survives. They outline several reasons why they believe this to be the case:

1) Coarse pottery is in the majority in household assemblages on prehistoric sites, but is of low durability (i.e., it tends entirely to be eroded away when brought to the surface) and it is difficult for fieldwalkers to recognize.

2) Fine pottery is in the minority and long-term erosion on the surface has greatly reduced its diagnosticity.

3) Finds of post-prehistoric periods are so much greater in density that they in effect 'swamp' those of prehistoric periods, making the prehistoric all the more difficult to locate.

4) Stone tools are more durable than pottery, but are difficult for any but specialist fieldwalkers to recover, particularly where bedrock consists of chert cobbles and where a majority of stone tools is manufactured of chert.

Bintliff *et al.* believe that prehistoric artifacts existed virtually everywhere in a given landscape, because in prehistory agriculture was based on a system of long fallow which encouraged a constant shifting of small-scale agricultural settlements. Such small single-period sites will be unobtrusive and their remains are likely to be very poorly preserved. They further suggest that the prehistoric pottery that today survives on the surface must be exclusively derived from recently exposed deposits and has not resulted from prehistoric manuring or casual activities. From this assumption it follows that in places where only prehistoric pottery has been found there must be buried deposits. In contrast, on multi-component sites, prehistoric artifacts are better protected, but – because they are drastically outnumbered by finds of later periods – only detailed gridded collection can open up windows through which one might catch a glimpse of the 'hidden' prehistoric landscape.

The preceding argumentation is complicated and warrants a much fuller examination than is possible in this chapter. An important component of Bintliff *et al.*'s 1999 paper, for example, is its consideration of the meaning of small quantities of prehistoric artifacts. The authors conclude that even the presence of a few prehistoric sherds is evidence for 'a sustained and intense level of prehistoric activity' (1999: 154; *cf.* the reactions to this proposition by Schon [2000] and Thompson [2000]). They also suggest that changes in field methods might result in the location of more satisfactory samples of prehistoric artifacts. I do not directly address either of these points here. Instead, I concern myself with evaluating the more basic assumptions from which the remainder of their arguments follow – namely, that patterns in the distribution of prehistoric artifacts that have been detected by intensive surveys are fundamentally flawed and provide an unreliable picture of prehistoric settlement and land use.

These are issues that are of obvious importance if the results of a variety of regional studies projects are to be compared. If the authors of the "hidden landscape" model are correct, there can be little point in contrasting published data, at least insofar as they pertain to prehistory (for purposes such as population estimation, Bintliff 1999 makes this same point). I will argue, however, that in many instances there is little reason to doubt the effectiveness of intensive survey in revealing general patterning in the distribution of prehistoric artifacts. I first consider the distribution of lithic finds, as they have been documented by three intensive surveys: the Pylos Regional Archaeological Project (PRAP), the Mallakastra Regional Archaeological Project (MRAP), and the Durrës Regional Archaeological Project (DRAP). There follows a discussion of the distribution of prehistoric pottery as observed by the Nemea Valley Archaeological Project (NVAP). One advantage of drawing on data from several projects, obviously, is that it is easier to evaluate the reliability of negative evidence.

THE EVALUATION OF LITHIC DISTRIBUTIONS

The Durrës Regional Archaeological Project

I first discuss the results of DRAP, the Durrës Regional Archaeological Project in central Albania. In antiquity Durrës was the location of a Greek colony known as Epidamnus, and later, to the Romans, as Dyrrachium. The ancient city covered hills overlooking the modern port and in antiquity it is clear that settlement also extended eastwards into lowlands by the sea. These lowlands had become marshes by modern times and were only drained for agricultural purposes in the 1960s. Any systematic survey of the lowlands is today difficult, since they have become the focus of illegal settlement by tens of thousands of new immigrants from northern Albania.

Our own work in Durrës focussed on a more accessible hilly area lying between the outskirts of the modern city and the village of Porto Romano to the north-northwest (Davis *et al.* 2003). These uplands may in antiquity have been largely surrounded by water, but the environmental researches needed to reconstruct the paleoenvironment of the area have yet to be undertaken. Six sq. km were intensively surveyed in a month-long field season in March and April 2001.

An almost continuous litter of artifacts was detected and documented by members of the two survey teams that investigated this area. But only a handful of lithics (15 in number) were observed and collected. We recognized no Paleolithic or Mesolithic artifacts. Several pieces could be of Neolithic or later prehistoric date, but it is not impossible that others are still more recent (*e.g.*, from relatively modern threshing sledges).

It would be tempting to imagine that such a low density of lithics was the result of 'walker effects' or 'field effects.' Did our fieldwalkers lack the aptitude to recognize chipped stone, or did particular conditions of the fields impede their abilities to do so? The fact that they also found almost no prehistoric pottery might be another indication that survey procedures were deficient. I strongly doubt, how-

ever, that methodology is the problem, since the lack of prehistoric lithics and pottery mirrors the results of 50 years of excavation in the city of Durrës and of extensive exploration in its vicinity (bibliography summarized in Davis *et al.*, 2003: 67–68) Only a few prehistoric artifacts have previously been noted in and around Durrës (*e.g.*, sherds and a hammerstone from the new port of Durrës are said to be of Late Bronze Age date [see Toçi 1976: 301]).

The Mallakastra Regional Archaeological Project

The contrast between the results of DRAP and those of MRAP, the Mallakastra Regional Archaeological Project (see Korkuti *et al.* 1998; Davis *et al.* n.d.b), is remarkable. Since 1998 members of MRAP have been investigating the hinterland of Apollonia, a Greek colony 60 km south of Durrës, through a combined program of survey and excavation. In campaigns in the summers of 1998, 1999, and 2000, a total of *c.* 22 sq. km have been examined (Figure 3.1). More than 1,500 individual lithic finds were observed and collected in tracts, and in the summer of 2001 the entire collection was studied in detail by Curtis Runnels and my co-director, Muzafer Korkuti. I quote from Runnels' report (available in full at http://river.blg.uc.edu/mrap/lithics01.html").

> The collection procedures employed by the survey teams ensured that lithics of all sizes and descriptions were collected... The wide range seen in the sizes of the artifacts, which range from large cobbles used as tested pieces down to worked flakes no more than one or two millimeters in maximum dimension, is testimony that few if any significant lithics were overlooked by the survey teams. Only a small number of pieces, fewer than five, turned out on closer inspection to be natural, i.e. unmodified stones... The majority of the artifacts are made from local raw materials, chiefly reddish-brown flint (chert). Only one small piece of obsidian (of unknown origin) was noted in the collection. Raw materials other than flint include quartzite, quartz, and cherty limestone... Only two major periods are represented: Palaeolithic and Mesolithic. Lower/Middle Palaeolithic artifacts are common, with smaller numbers of early Upper Palaeolithic artifacts. The other period represented in the assemblage can be described as Mesolithic (Epipalaeolithic). Other than for these two periods, evidence for human presence in the form of the lithics is very patchy and only a handful of artifacts were assigned to the Neolithic, Bronze, and Iron ages.

A third of the fieldwalkers who participated in the Durrës survey had previously worked in Mallakastra, and on both projects all fieldwalkers were routinely trained to recognize lithics and were instructed to collect all lithic artifacts (and, in doubtful instances, to error on the side of safety). In my view the obvious conclusion to be drawn from a

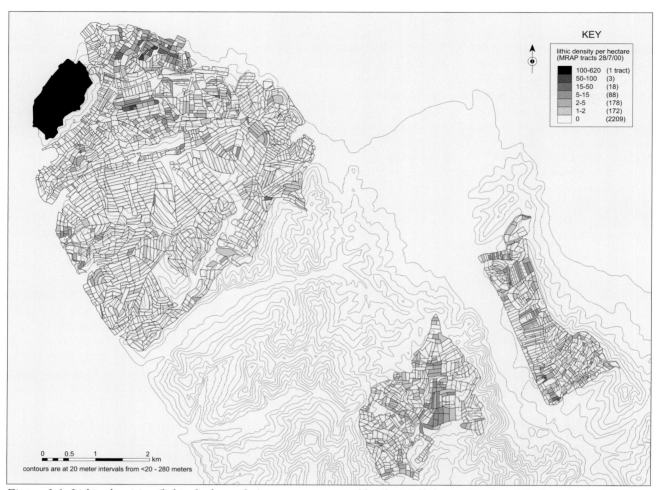

Figure 3.1 Lithic densities (lithic finds per ha) in areas surveyed by the Mallakastra Regional Archaeological Project.

comparison of the results of DRAP and MRAP is that the landscape around Apollonia was more intensively used in the Paleolithic and Mesolithic than was that around Durrës. Patterns detected by fieldwalking appear to reflect genuine differences in the prehistories of these two areas.

Nor does it seem likely that variation between the two projects can be explained as the result of 'field effects.' In 4,192 tracts defined by MRAP, mean visibility was 43% with a standard deviation of 23%, and mean visibility in tracts where lithics were collected was only slightly better (48%; s.d. 22%). Visibility at Durrës was significantly worse than at Mallakastra (Figure 3.2). Average visibility was 33% in the survey area as a whole (s.d. 21%), and was 30% or less in 72% (683) of all defined tracts (938). Nonetheless, it is difficult to see how bad visibility can be responsible for the fact that only a handful of lithics were found in the Durrës project. A substantial number of DRAP tracts fall well within the visibility range in which lithics were found at Apollonia, and the mean for visibility in DRAP tracts in which lithics were recognized is not much greater than the average for all tracts – 40%, with a standard deviation of 20% (Figure 3.3). Finally, the fact that lithics have commonly been found by MRAP and not

by DRAP runs contrary to expectations that the presence in the local bedrock of raw lithic material will seriously hamper the recognition of lithic artifacts. Chert cobbles are extremely common throughout the entire area investigated by MRAP, the same chert that was employed for the manufacture of chipped stone tools.

The Pylos Regional Archaeological Project

The results from these two pieces of fieldwork in Albania can usefully be compared to those from the Pylos Regional Archaeological Project (for prehistoric remains from PRAP, see Davis *et al.* 1997; Zangger *et al.* 1997; Davis 1998). PRAP has investigated the archaeology of a region in southwestern Greece that is about 100 sq. km in extent and is centered on the so-called Palace of Nestor, a Late Bronze Age Mycenaean administrative center. Within this broader region 10 distinct zones (totalling 40 sq. km) were chosen to reflect the geographical and geological variability representative of the larger region and were targeted for intensive survey (Figure 3.4). Chert artifacts (449) recovered in tract-walking were four times as common as obsidian (109), a lithic density many times that of Durrës,

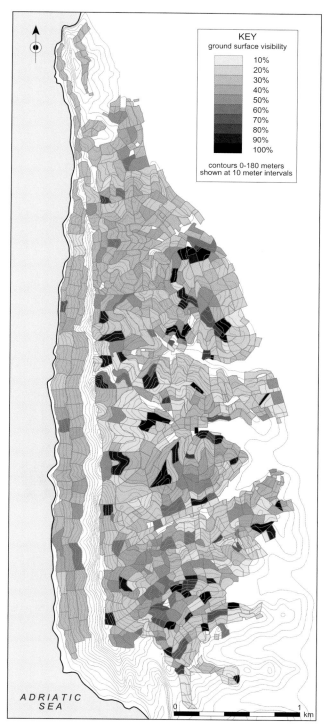

Figure 3.2 Durrës Regional Archaeological Project: map of tracts showing variability in visibility.

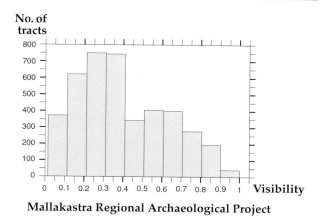

Mallakastra Regional Archaeological Project

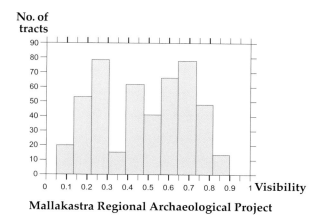

Mallakastra Regional Archaeological Project

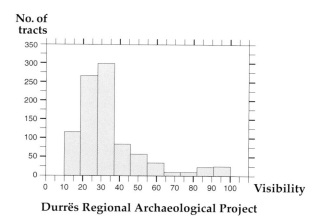

Durrës Regional Archaeological Project

Figure 3.3 Graphs comparing visibility in DRAP and MRAP tracts (the middle graph shows MRAP tracts with lithics).

but only one-third that of Mallakastra (Figure 3.5). For the most part, the finds are of Neolithic and Bronze Age types, but Middle and Late Paleolithic artifacts are also present (the first, in fact, to be documented in this part of Greece).

At first glance, the PRAP data appear to support concerns of Bintliff *et al.* about difficulties in the recog-

nition of lithics. Zones A and L are characterized by Oligocene conglomerate and Mesozoic limestone, and finds from them were significantly fewer in number than in places where base geology consisted of Pliocene marls and Eocene limestones. One of the main units of the conglomerate and limestone is 'thinly bedded black, red, and white chert of a Jurassic to Cenomanian radiolarite

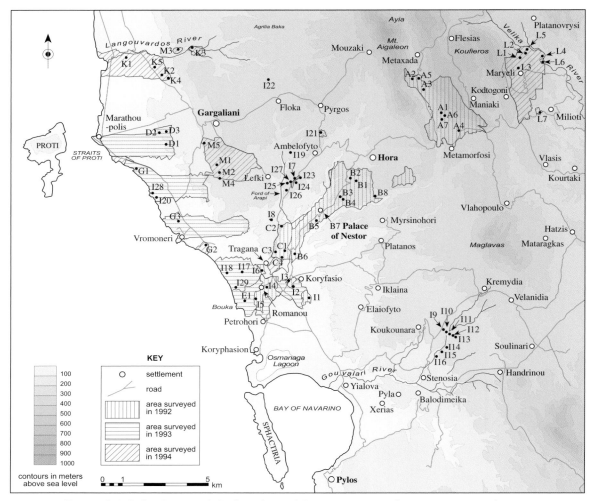

Figure 3.4 Pylos Regional Archaeological Project: surveyed areas, zones, and sites.

series' (Zangger *et al.* 1997: 555). But, on closer in-spection, it is difficult to see how 'field effects' alone can account for the patterning in the data. In the first place, Zones B, C, D, E, G, I, K, and M share similar geology among themselves, yet there are striking differences between them in the numbers of lithics recovered, both obsidian and chert. These contrasts are particularly accen-tuated when inland zones around the Palace of Nestor (B and C) are compared to those near the coast (D, E, G, I, and K) and south of the modern town of Gargaliani (M). Some of this patterning in the data surely has a cultural explanation. Cherry and Parkinson (1997) have already suggested that this is the case, referring to the striking concentration of obsidian around the village of Romanou. In the second place, a closer look at the results of fieldwork in Zone L, where chert cobbles in the conglomerate bedrock are most common, suggests that the low density of artifacts observed may reflect a real scarcity of lithics in the archaeological record as a whole. Subsequent to field-walking, systematic collection of three sites with prehistoric components (L1, L4, and L5) did not produce any lithics, despite the greatly elevated search intensity.

The data from PRAP also presents a good opportunity to evaluate the applicability of a second assertion made by Bintliff *et al.*: namely, that because certain fieldwalkers are exceptionally poor or good in their abilities to find lithics, any patterning in the archaeological record will be artificial, resulting from these 'walker effects.' The PRAP data suggest that certain individuals do have a greater propensity for recognizing lithics. Of a total of 42 field-walkers a handful (see Table 3.1) stand out as reporting higher lithic counts than the rest (i.e., average densities greater than 0.6 artifacts per linear km walked). It does not seem, however, that this fact has greatly interfered with the recognition of intra-regional variation in lithic distribution.

Since PRAP enjoyed a remarkable continuity in staff, it is possible to study the performance of most fieldwalkers over more than a single season, and thus in more than one zone. Their results can also be compared to those of others in their team so as to determine the extent to which their observations deviate from the average in any particular zone (Table 3.2; Figure 3.6). Fieldwalkers 14 and 23, for example, recorded the highest overall densities. In part,

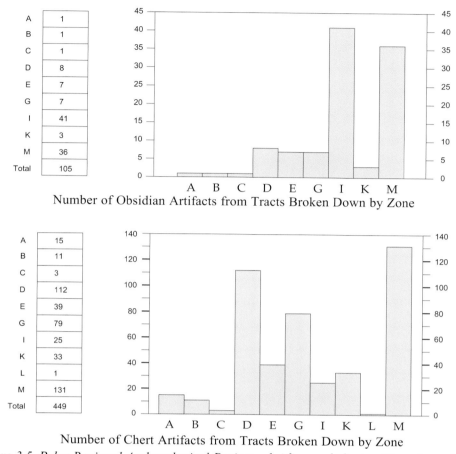

A	1
B	1
C	1
D	8
E	7
G	7
I	41
K	3
M	36
Total	105

Number of Obsidian Artifacts from Tracts Broken Down by Zone

A	15
B	11
C	3
D	112
E	39
G	79
I	25
K	33
L	1
M	131
Total	449

Number of Chert Artifacts from Tracts Broken Down by Zone

Figure 3.5 Pylos Regional Archaeological Project: obsidian and chert artifacts in each zone.

Fieldwalker	Average/1000 m.	Averages by Zones
23	1.62	I (1.99/.74), C (0.00/0.08)
14	1.57	M (3.37/1.01), D (2.49/0.82), A (0.02/0.01)
67	0.99	G (1.82/0.44), E (0.47/0.21)
68	0.89	G (0.78/0.44)
49	0.77	G (0.89/0.44), L (0.00/0.01)
62	0.73	D (0.73/0.82)

Table 3.1 PRAP: average number of lithics reported per km of field-walking (column 2); average numbers reported per zone compared to average for all field-walkers in that zone (column 3). Included in these statistics are only those individuals who traversed more than 14,000 m as regular field-walkers.

the averages for these two fieldwalkers are higher than those of their colleagues because each made a single large find. Fieldwalker 14 found 70 lithics in one place while working in Zone D. Fieldwalker 23 found 21 in one place in Area I. However, even if these finds are discounted, their averages would remain among the highest. Most importantly, moreover, their observations are correlated with those of their fellows. In zones where the entire team recorded higher densities, Fieldwalkers 14 and 23 did also. In zones where few lithics were found, Fieldwalkers 14 and 23 also observed little. One of these fieldwalkers (49) with a special aptitude for finding lithics was, in fact, a member of the team that investigated Area L where few

were found. It seems clear that the presence of a person with a special aptitude for lithics does not in itself ensure their discovery.

THE EVALUATION OF CERAMIC DISTRIBUTIONS: THE NEMEA VALLEY ARCHAEOLOGICAL PROJECT

Next is addressed the argument of Bintliff *et al.* that intensive surveys have failed to recognize unobtrusive prehistoric concentrations of pottery, because field procedures are not sufficiently sensitive to be able to detect

Zone	M	D	I	G	K	E	C	B	L	A
Density	1.01	0.82	0.74	0.44	0.27	0.21	0.08	0.02	0.01	0.01

Table 3.2 Average number of lithics per km of fieldwalking in all PRAP zones, ranked in descending order (from left to right).

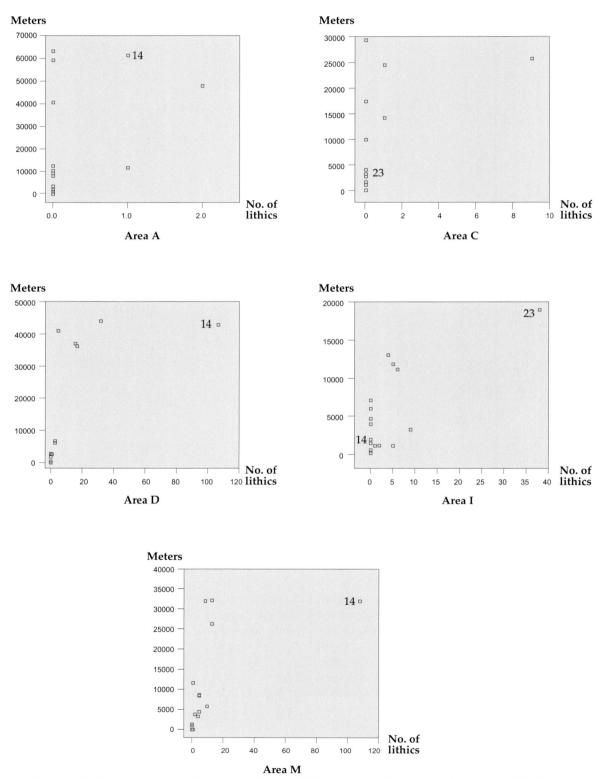

Figure 3.6 Linear meters walked vs. numbers of lithics observed by walkers in various PRAP zones.

Period	Total	Found in Site Collection
Neolithic	16	9
Early Helladic	28	12
Late Helladic	27	17

Table 3.3 Total numbers of prehistoric components on NVAP sites and the numbers of components discovered only in the course of site collection. No sherds were collected in initial tract-walking in the case of one Neolithic site (Site 922); four Early Helladic sites (Sites 910, 922, 923, and 931); and six Late Helladic sites (Sites 910, 922, 923, 925, 926, and 931).

extremely deflated small sites. I will be particularly concerned with their contention that, when previously surveyed areas are re-examined at a higher level of search intensity, prehistoric finds are discovered that previously escaped detection. In support of this contention, they note that the Boiotia Project first identified prehistoric components on historical sites when they were targets of systematic surface collection.

The data of the Nemea Valley Archaeological Project offer an appropriate base from which to test the preceding assertions. In four field seasons (1984–86, 1989), NVAP intensively surveyed an area of nearly 50 sq. km in the southern Corinthia, adjacent to the Argive Plain and within view of the citadel of Mycenae (for prehistoric remains from NVAP, see Cherry *et al.* 1988; Wright *et al.* 1990; Alram-Stern 1996: 234–35; Cherry and Davis 2001). Although the Corinthia and the Argolid had long been the focus of excavations and extensive surveys, NVAP was remarkably successful in discovering a large number of previously unknown prehistoric sites. Field procedures were broadly similar to those used later by PRAP, MRAP, and DRAP, and to those of the Boiotia Project. (In 1989, parts of the Nemea valley were systematically investigated, but without recording data for individual fieldwalkers.) Grids were used for surface collection of *c.* 10% of the 95 sites identified by the project. More typically, however, transects and various types of systematic grab samples were employed (see Wright *et al.* 1990; Alcock 1991). NVAP was the first project in Greece systematically to collect artifacts 'off-site', a practice that was soon afterwards adopted in Boiotia.

Excluding the large and very obtrusive sites of Tsoungiza and the Sanctuary of Zeus, where extensive prehistoric remains were well known prior to the start of our fieldwork, NVAP found prehistoric artifacts (Neolithic, Early Bronze, or Late Bronze Age) at 35 out of a total of *c.* 95 sites defined (*c.* 35%), an astonishing number considering that definite Classical remains were found only at *c.* 40 of these sites, and Hellenistic at only *c.* 25. Nor are the numbers of 'off-site' prehistoric finds appreciably lower than those of some historical periods. Approximately 7,500 individual sherds were collected from tracts. More than 400 of these can be dated to prehistoric periods: 78 to the Neolithic period, 110 to the Early Helladic period, and 173 to the Late Helladic period. Approximately 160 sherds can be dated to the Classical period, 179 to the Hellenistic period. Although 1,085 other sherds may date to the

Classical period and 876 to the Hellenistic period, it is not obvious from these data that NVAP field strategies were biased against the discovery of prehistoric finds or that our teams were unsuccessful in finding them.

How are we to interpret these figures? Because prehistoric phases are much longer than historical periods, should we have found still larger quantities of prehistoric artifacts? Bintliff, Howard, and Snodgrass would no doubt suggest that our finds are but the tip of an iceberg, and that we left many other potential prehistoric findspots unnoticed. Moreover, as in the Boiotia Project some prehistoric components were only recognized when sites were more intensively investigated (Table 3.3). However, finds from on-site tracts were not the only prehistoric finds. Indeed, for the Bronze Age more prehistoric sherds were discovered 'off-site' than 'on-site': 77 of the 110 Early Helladic sherds and 112 of the 173 Late Helladic sherds were collected in tracts that were *not* later defined as sites. Only for the Neolithic were more sherds collected from tracts that were defined as sites than from those that were not (66 of the total of 78).

In light of these figures from Nemea, John Cherry and I recently suggested that 'blankets', rather than 'windows', might be a more appropriate metaphor for the high-density concentrations of artifacts that we call 'sites' (Cherry and Davis 2001: 152–53). At sites it may be difficult to recognize prehistoric remains because they are covered by a thick mantle of later debris. This is the process that we imagined at work on Keos (Cherry *et al.* 1991), but which Bintliff has taken as evidence for his own notion of sites as windows. The fact that we have been able to recognize so many 'off-site' prehistoric finds makes us wonder if tract-walking would have been perfectly effective in locating prehistoric artifacts on sites, had a mantle of historical components not been present. For that reason, I would argue that the combination of intensive 'off-site' procedures and intensive 'on-site' collections gave us a good sample of the prehistoric artifacts that remained to be found. In short, the landscape of prehistoric Greece was not hidden at Nemea.

It is worthwhile comparing the results of NVAP more concretely with those of the Boiotia Project. NVAP and the Boiotia Project would appear to be remarkably similar in numbers of sites, leaving aside any possible differences in the way that sites were defined. Each project recognized a total of *c.* 35 prehistoric components in a total surveyed area of *c.* 50 sq. km (48.96 sq. km is the precise figure for

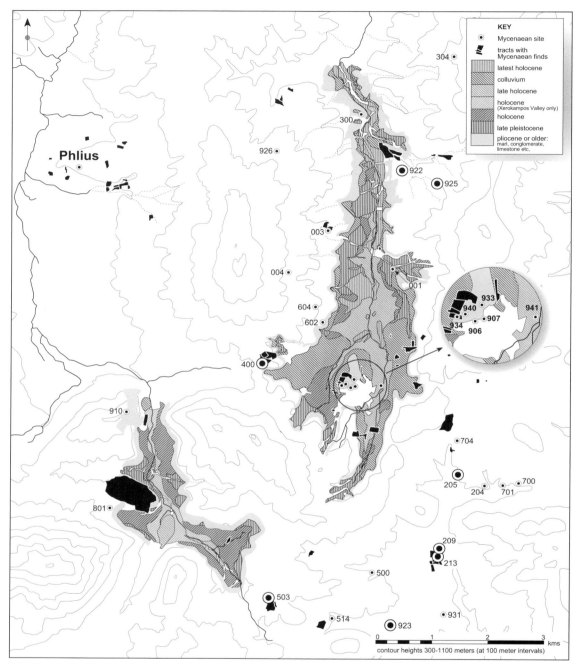

Figure 3.7 Nemea Valley Archaeological Project: Mycenaean sites and soil units (= Cherry and Davis 2001, fig. 10.6). Map of soil units courtesy of A. Demitrack.

the combined area of all tracts defined by NVAP in 1984–86 and 1989, a density of one prehistoric component per 1.4 sq. km. Approximately 2.0 sites of all periods were defined per sq. km.). NVAP differs from the Boiotia Project, however, in that the total number of sites with prehistoric components represents a much higher percentage of all sites. Moreover, NVAP teams in the course of regular tract-walking located prehistoric finds in a remarkably large number of locations: Neolithic in 18 tracts; Early Helladic in 64 tracts; and Late Helladic in 72 tracts. Almost two-thirds of these tracts were not associated

with sites. If these low density findspots were included, the actual number of prehistoric components would be more than doubled.

There are very significant differences between the Boiotia Project and NVAP that must have cultural explanations. Middle Bronze Age material is well-represented in Boiotia, but absent in Nemea. At NVAP the negative evidence from survey is supported by the results of long-term programs of excavation at Tsoungiza and the Sanctuary of Zeus at Nemea. Patterns in the distribution of prehistoric finds are strikingly different from those previously known. The differences are particularly clear in the Mycenaean period where NVAP has been successful in identifying four levels in a site hierarchy (Figure 3.7). Eight sites of 2 ha or less appear to be small settlements. But several dozen other locations that have produced prehistoric finds would seem to represent the remains of the 'genuinely small sites, of around 0.1 ha. or less,' whose absence are a concern to Bintliff and his colleagues (Cherry and Davis 2001). It seems doubtful that any component of the Mycenaean settlement system has entirely missed detection.

THE MORAL OF THE STORY

In the case studies that have been considered in this paper it seems that field methods adequately recognized meaningful patterning in the prehistoric archaeological records of the areas investigated. No doubt, had fieldwalkers dedicated to finding lithics been employed in the manner recommended by Bintliff *et al.*, more lithic artifacts would have been found by DRAP, MRAP, and PRAP. An increase in search intensity will almost always result in the discovery of greater quantities of any category of artifact. But there is little doubt in my mind that *overall* distributional patterns would remain the same.

The purpose of my paper is not to suggest that the observations of the authors of the "hidden landscape" model concerning the relative invisibility of certain parts of the prehistoric surface archaeological record are irrelevant or that their cautionary tales should be ignored. I would argue only that they are not of universal applicability. And lest I be accused of beating a dead horse – since several discussants in the *Journal of Mediterranean Archaeology* have already noted that results of their own fieldwork point to real spatial and temporal variation in the patterning of surface distributions (see Mee and Cavanagh 2000; Barker 2000) – I note that Bintliff has continued to apply the model of the 'hidden landscape' to the results of other projects (Bintliff *et al.* 2002).

Other aspects of the arguments of the 'hidden landscape' model need attention, in particular the observations regarding the durability of prehistoric pottery. Descriptions of friable fabrics that revert to mud when wet have struck a resonant chord in the experiences of some archaeologists who work elsewhere in Europe (*e.g.*, Barker 2000). But it seems to me highly unlikely that the presence of such wares has seriously skewed our perception of prehistoric patterns of settlement in parts of Greece other than Boiotia. In most parts of the Peloponnese, as Mee and Cavanagh (2000) have already noted for Laconia and Methana, coarse wares are hard-fired and in the later prehistoric periods are wheelmade. We need to transform the study of this problem into an objective examination of the durability of ceramic fabrics for each principal area where survey is being conducted. Anecdotal tales of 'soggy biscuits' serendipitously recognized in the field are not

the way forward. Even in Boiotia it would be useful systematically to evaluate and test alternative explanations for the observed data. Is it possible, for example, that rates of production, use, and deposition of ceramics were simply lower in the prehistoric periods, a point raised by Bintliff and his colleagues, but dropped without further discussion?

Was settlement and landuse more periodic and less continuous in prehistoric than in historical times? Bintliff *et al.* (1999: 159) tentatively suggest that 'small-site, shifting agriculture is especially important in the Final Neolithic-EBA. In the MBA and LBA, there is far more emphasis on larger settlement sites of hamlet-village size... alongside a less widespread small farm-site network in the countryside intervening between such minor foci.' It is not immediately clear, however, that such a model is completely transferable to Nemea. Re-use of sites seems to characterize the transition between the Neolithic and Early Helladic periods (Early Helladic pottery is present on five of seven Neolithic sites). Might this evidence suggest a stability in the location of agricultural installations quite unlike the scenario postulated for Boiotia?

It is both a strength and a weakness of the interpretative framework of Bintliff, Howard, and Snodgrass that the "hidden landscape" model was initially derived to explain observations in a particular part of Greece. While the formation of the archaeological record of Boiotia (or at least those parts of it investigated by the Boiotia Project) may be so explained, extreme caution should be exercised in applying the model deductively to other sets of data. Even in Boiotia there is a risk that real differences in empirical results may be 'massaged away' in order to make them conform to prior expectations derived from a non-archaeological theory. Bintliff *et al.* have been greatly influenced by adherence to ideas drawn from German geographical scholarship of the early 20th century. This so-called *Landeskunde* tradition subscribes to the tenet that certain 'chambers' of preferred land will be occupied in every period of the past, although the locus and nature of settlement in each chamber may change from period to period. Bintliff's thinking may be overly dependent on assumptions about the continuity of the regime of mixed farming that this model assumes and does not leave open the possibility that there have occurred in the past significant shifts in the nature of subsistence practices.

Comparative survey can help to determine if a particular interpretive model is genuinely of universal significance, by evaluating it inductively against the results of other projects in different geographical and geological settings. It is, of course, important to dodge accusations that our own perspectives are also parochial. I hope to have avoided this trap by using, side-by-side, case studies from four different surveys and by emphasizing differences between and within the areas that have been investigated. Ideally, one would like also to exploit for this purpose data from projects other than one's own, a goal that remains largely unattainable, not only because of variability in methods, but also because it is virtual impossible to include in printed reports the types of data that would have been needed for this paper. The 'Could you please send me?' approach to finding comparanda is an inadequate temporary fix that depends overly much on the kindness of friends and strangers. Full disclosure via the Internet is likely to be the long-term solution (*cf.* Davis *et al.* n.d.a, for one example).

ACKNOWLEDGMENTS

Comparative studies necessarily require a long list of acknowledgments. I am grateful to all of my colleagues in DRAP, MRAP, PRAP, and NVAP for making this paper possible by ensuring that data were collected systematically and processed effectively. Sharon R. Stocker (co-director at DRAP and museum co-director at MRAP), Debi Bennet (data manager for PRAP), Cynthia Shelmerdine (museum director for PRAP), Bob Sutton and Mary Dabney (museum directors for NVAP), John Wallrodt (information technology manager for MRAP and DRAP), Mike Galaty (field director for MRAP), and John Bennet (field director for PRAP), deserve much credit for the ease with which I was able to use databases for this comparative study. I thank my wife Sharon R. Stocker for her close reading and perceptive comments on several drafts of this paper. John Bennet, John Cherry, and Mike Galaty also helped me to improve it greatly. Bill Parkinson and John Cherry kindly shared their extensive knowledge of the PRAP lithic collection with me, as did Curtis Runnels and Muzafer Korkuti for MRAP. Jerry Rutter and Dan Pullen lent their considerable authority to the study of NVAP prehistoric ceramics. Finally, I gladly express my appreciation to Muzafer Korkuti, Skënder Muçaj, and Lorenc Bejko, my Albanian co-directors at MRAP, to Afrim Hoti and Iris Pojani, my Albanian co-directors at DRAP, and to John Cherry and Jim Wright, my co-directors at NVAP, for their continuing collegiality and friendship. All figures were produced by Rosemary J. Robertson, Figures 3.1 and 3.2 with John Wallrodt.

REFERENCES

Alcock, S. E. (1991) Urban survey and the polis of Phlius. *Hesperia* 60: 421–63.
Alcock, S. E. (1993) *Graecia Capta: the Landscapes of Roman Greece.* Cambridge, Cambridge University Press.
Alram-Stern, E. (1996) *Die Ägäische Frühzeit. 2. Serie. Forschungsbericht 1975–1993. 1. Band. Das Neolithikum in Griechenland.* Vienna, Österreichischen Akademie der Wissenschaften.
Barker, G. (2000) Hidden prehistoric landscapes: an Italian perspective. *Journal of Mediterranean Archaeology* 13: 100–102.
Bintliff, J. L. (1977) The history of archaeo-geographic studies of prehistoric Greece, and recent fieldwork. In J. L. Bintliff (ed.) *Mycenaean Geography: Proceedings of the Cambridge Colloquium September 1976*: 3–18.
Bintliff, J. L. (1999) Regional field surveys and population cycles. In J. L. Bintliff and K. Sbonias (eds.) *Reconstructing Past Population Trends in Europe* (*The Archaeology of Mediterranean Landscapes* 1): 21–43. Oxford, Oxbow Books.
Bintliff, J. L. (2000) Beyond dots on the map: the future of surface artefact survey in Greece. In J. L. Bintliff, M. Kuna, and N. Venclová (eds.) *The Future of Surface Artefact Survey in Europe*: 3–20. Sheffield, Sheffield Academic Press.
Bintliff, J. L. (2001) The contribution of archaeological survey to our understanding of Archaic Greece. Paper delivered to the Oxford Ancient History Seminar, Fall 2001.
Bintliff, J. L., Farinetti, E., Howard, P., Sarri, K. and Sbonias, K. (2002) Classical farms, hidden prehistoric landscapes and Greek rural survey: a response and an update, *Journal of Mediterranean Archaeology* 15: 260–66.
Bintliff, J. L., Howard, P. and Snodgrass, A. M. (1999) The hidden landscapes of prehistoric Greece. *Journal of Mediterranean Archaeology* 12: 139–68.
Bintliff, J. L., Howard, P. and Snodgrass, A. M. (2000) A rejoinder. *Journal of Mediterranean Archaeology* 13: 116–23.
Bintliff, J. L. and Snodgrass, A. M. (1985) The Boiotia Survey: a preliminary report: the first four years. *Journal of Field Archaeology* 12: 123–61.
Cherry, J. F. (1983) Frogs round the pond: perspectives on current archaeological survey projects in the Mediterranean region. In D. R. Keller and D. W. Rupp (eds.) *Archaeological Survey in the Mediterranean Area* (*BAR International Series* 155): 375–416. Oxford, British Archaeological Reports.
Cherry, J. F. and Davis, J. L. (2001) 'Under the sceptre of Agamemnon': the view from the hinterlands of Mycenae. In K. Branigan (ed.) *Urbanism in the Aegean Bronze Age* (*Sheffield Studies in Aegean Prehistory* 4): 143–61. Sheffield, Sheffield Academic Press.
Cherry, J. F., Davis, J. L., Demitrack, A., Mantzourani, E., Strasser, T. and Talalay, L. (1988) Archaeological survey in an artifact-rich landscape: a Middle Neolithic example from Nemea, Greece. *American Journal of Archaeology* 92: 159–76.
Cherry, J. F., Davis, J. L. and Mantzourani,. E. (1991) *Landscape Archaeology as Long-Term History: Northern Keos in the Cycladic Islands* (Monumenta Archaeologica 16). Los Angeles, Institute of Archaeology, UCLA.
Cherry, J. F. and Parkinson, W. A. (1997) Lithic studies and Pleistocene sites. In J. L. Davis, S. E. Alcock, J. Bennet, Y. G. Lolos, and C. W. Shelmerdine, The Pylos Regional Archaeological Project: Part I, overview and the archaeological survey. *Hesperia* 68: 414–17.
Davis, J. L. (ed.) (1998) *Sandy Pylos: An Archaeological History from Nestor to Navarino.* Austin, University of Texas Press.
Davis, J. L., Alcock, S. E., Bennet, J., Lolos, Y. G. and Shelmerdine, C. W. (1997) The Pylos Regional Archaeological Project: Part I, overview and the archaeological survey. *Hesperia* 68: 391–494.
Davis, J. L., Alcock, S. E., Bennet, J., Lolos, Y. G., Shelmerdine, C. W. and Zangger, E. (n.d.a) The Pylos Regional Archaeological Project: internet edition. Available at http://river.blg.uc.edu/prap/PRAP.html.
Davis, J. L. and Cherry, J. F. (1998) Northern Keos in context. In L. G. Mendoni and A. Mazarakis Ainian (eds.), *Kea-Kythnos: History and Archaeology*: 217–26. Paris, Diffusion de Boccard.
Davis, J. L., Hoti, A., Pojani, I., Stocker, S. R., Wolpert, A. D. and Acheson, P. E. (2003) Archaeological survey in the territory of Epidamnus/Dyrrachium (Albania). *Hesperia* 72: 41–119.
Davis, J. L., Korkuti, M., Bejko, L., Galaty, M. L., Muçaj, S. and Stocker, S. R. (n.d.b) The Mallakastra Regional Archaeological Project. Available at http://river.blg.uc.edu/mrap/MRAP.html.
Korkuti, M. M., Davis, J. L., Bejko, L., Galaty, M. L., Muçaj, S. and Stocker, S. R. (1998) The Mallakastra Regional Archaeological Project: first season, 1998. *Iliria* 1998: 253–73.

McDonald, W. A. and R. Hope Simpson, R. (1961) Prehistoric habitation in Southwestern Peloponnese. *American Journal of Archaeology* 65: 221–60.

Mee, C. and Cavanagh, W. (2000) The hidden landscape in Greece: a view from Laconia and Methana. *Journal of Mediterranean Archaeology* 13: 102–107.

Schon, R. (2000) On a site and out of sight: where have our data gone? *Journal of Mediterranean Archaeology* 13: 107–111.

Schon, R. (2002) *Seeding the Landscape: Experimental Contributions to Regional Survey Methodology*. Ph.D., Bryn Mawr College.

Shennan, S. J. (1985) *Experiments in the Collection and Analysis of Archaeological Survey Data: The East Hampshire Survey*. Sheffield, University of Sheffield.

Stocker, S. R. (in press) The Pylos Regional Archaeological Project: Part V, Deriziotis Aloni, a small Bronze Age site in Messenia. *Hesperia*.

Thompson, S. A. (2000) The still hidden landscape. *Journal of Mediterranean Archaeology* 13: 111–15.

Toçi, V. (1976) Popullsia ilire e Dyrrahut në dritën e të dhënave historiko-arkeologjike. *Iliria* 4: 301–306.

Wilkie, N. and Coulsen, W. D. E. (eds.) (1985) *Contributions to Aegean Archaeology: Studies in Honor of William A. McDonald*. Minneapolis, Center for Ancient Studies.

Wright, J. C., Cherry, J. F., Davis, J. L., Mantzourani, E. and Sutton, S. B. (1990) The Nemea Valley Archaeological Project: a preliminary report. *Hesperia* 59: 579–659.

Zangger, E., Timpson, M. E., Yazvenko, S. B., Kuhnke, F. and Knauss, J. (1997) The Pylos Regional Archaeological Project: Part II, landscape evolution and site preservation. *Hesperia* 68: 548–641.

4. Sample Size Matters!
The Paradox of Global Trends and Local Surveys

Nicola Terrenato

Survey archaeologists have always had to deal with a tantalizing mismatch, in terms of orders of magnitude, between their ambitions to reconstruct large-scale trends and processes and the material constraints inherent in the practice of field survey. Paradoxically, with the evolution of the discipline in the twentieth century, the contradiction has only become more acute and distressing. On the one hand, recent theorizing has brought survey archaeologists in contact with global concepts, such as world systems or core-periphery models (*e.g.*, Stein 1999; Champion 1989), but on the other, improved field methodologies have inevitably contracted the size of survey areas. Just as we are moving down from the hundreds into the tens of square kilometers surveyed, we contradictorily yearn to transcend local issues and take part in the debate with other specialists, and especially historians, who may not even conceive anything smaller than the territory of a city-state or an administrative region as a unit of study. More and more, survey people need a critical mass of data of considerable absolute size even to sit at the table where the big issues are under discussion. Spatial sampling seemed to offer some measure of relief for the problem; but it ended up producing a whole autonomous diatribe of its own, which is giving no sign yet of dying down and has done little to improve the wider credibility of field survey archaeologists. (It is enough to recall how the final discussion on sampling in Fish and Kowalewski [1990] still sounds very much like Flannery's [1976: 131–36] classic spoof of 15 years earlier.)

It is natural, thus, to see as the only hope the combination of results from different surveys, as well as the improvement and standardization of the quality of their results. Only by pooling the resources of different teams, operating over a long period of time, can one hope to gather data in sufficient quantity to address the global issues that have been raised. And this, precisely, was the dream of those new archaeologists who, from the 1960s onwards, strove to codify an optimal approach to regional studies (most famously, Binford 1964; Flannery 1976). This was obviously part and parcel of the revolution in

methods and theory that was being advocated at the time, but it is important to remark that field survey had a specific and prominent role in all this. Much more than excavation, survey was seen as the truly scientific approach to settlement archaeology, at least potentially. Its practice, in fact, could be seen as a repeatable experiment that would allow the objective testing of different strategies and approaches. Through systematic, controlled coverage of regions (or samples thereof), archaeologists would finally be able to obtain data in a standard format, thus susceptible of being analyzed statistically. Survey would provide, as it were, a 'clinical epidemiology' approach, which would allow the identification of global trends and would escape the inherent case-by-case variability and *ad hoc* decision-making of archaeological 'surgery' (that is, excavation).

The large-scale work carried out in Mexico and in the American Southwest seemed to confirm the validity of this approach, as valley after valley was surveyed and the data consolidated in grand syntheses (Blanton 1981 *et al.*; Euler and Gummerman 1978). Another exciting development was the use of spatial analysis, which would finally bring archaeologists on a par with the other envied social scientists (*e.g.*, Johnson 1977). Thus came into being a great chimera that proved as difficult to pursue as to abandon. Even future anti-positivist guru Ian Hodder was guilty of sowing a spatial wild oat in his youth (Hodder and Orton 1976). At the time Hodder and Orton's book *Spatial Analysis in Archaeology* was published, however, another young British archaeologist (also destined for a remarkable career) found himself in a position to evaluate and assess many of the strongest claims and hopes that were being built on survey at the time, especially in Europe.

Stephen Shennan, later to become Professor of Theoretical Archaeology at University College London, was wading through East Hampshire with a 'Job Creation' team (presumably composed of victims of early Thatcherite cuts). His idea was to take this opportunity to assess quantitatively the validity of field survey as a scientific data collection procedure. The results were not particularly encouraging: significant biases were being introduced by a host of factors linked to the conditions in which the survey was carried out. Shennan reported these finds only in 1985, and he appears to tread fairly cautiously in the conclusions about the far-reaching implications of his discovery. He conceded that the data show that a number of statistically significant distortions affect the recorded distributions and, revealingly, he mentioned his own 'flagging enthusiasm' in the effectiveness of 'regional fieldwalking' (Shennan 1985: 1). However, after having processed the numbers with a multi-stage regression analysis, based on several very strong assumptions, he was eager to assure us, as others were to do after him, that 'the distorting variables... are not overwhelming in their effects' (Shennan 1985: 44; cf. Cherry *et al.* 1991: 45, for a verbatim concordance). Such a conclusion is not so clearly supported by the data presented, especially since the limited experiments of replicated collections yield devastating results which are dismissed as statistically insignificant (Shennan 1985: 44).

If an ambivalent attitude was detectable here and elsewhere in the British discourse, such was not the case for another scholar who had also been doing field surveys in the 1970s. Prodded by Stanford experimentalists of the caliber of L. L. Cavalli-Sforza, Albert Ammerman was repeating coverages in Calabria on a much larger scale than Shennan's, in hopes of demonstrating to his colleagues in the hard sciences that field surveys were indeed replicable and reliable. Again the results failed to point in that direction at all (Ammerman and Feldman 1978) and the same thing happened when simulations were carried out on fields seeded with mock artifact scatters (Ammerman 1985). As a result, in a review article published as early as 1981, Ammerman was offering the admonition that the dynamism of the landscape had been up to then a grossly underestimated element in the game.

It has to be said that these cautionary tales and sobering voices failed to have any real impact on the discipline. The 1980s were spent, at least in Europe and the Mediterranean, focusing almost entirely upon the issue of intensity of coverage. In part this reaction was understandable, since intensity had been shown to be likely to be the most important factor affecting data recovery in surveys (Cherry 1983). But enthusiasm for the developments that were possible in this direction completely overshadowed the serious problems that were also emerging: by and large, surveys simply 'floored the intensity pedal' and hoped that this would make everything else all right. As a result, the number of person/days it took to cover one sq. km sky-rocketed in some cases to one hundred times what it had typically been in the 1960s.

The intensification of surveys thus became the dominant trend and the key issue in field survey practice and theory over the last 25 years. Behind all this, several different orders of reasoning can be gleaned. At a very basic level, among the many factors that are known to affect the outcome of surveys, intensity appears to be the one that could be the most easily controlled. In contrast with

vegetation or geopedological effects, intensity is purely a function of survey design: thus, going 'all out' on this aspect may have seemed a way to compensate for all the other variables about which, apparently, one could not do much.

At a deeper intellectual level, the intensification of survey in the Mediterranean may also have to do with a reaction to the sustained skepticism with which ancient historians have greeted survey results. It must not be forgotten that, of all the archaeological field methods, survey is the one that operates at the largest territorial scale, and this necessarily brings it into much closer debate with historians. By improving the quality of their data recovery, perhaps unconsciously, survey archaeologists have tried to strengthen their case as potential reconstructors of large-scale processes (the point is argued in full in Terrenato and Ammerman 1996). While busy doing this, they have largely swept under the carpet all the other recovery problems that have been well known at least since Shennan's work, hushing up the issue in fear that this would dramatically undermine the broader credibility of survey results. Yet the great irony here is that it can be argued (see below) that the higher the intensity of the survey, the larger the effects of the various biases at work.

The value and impact of this last methodological wave have still to be properly assessed. Certainly, artifact-level surveys are now considered the required standard by British and British-influenced (*e.g.*, Dutch) archaeologists in the Mediterranean (*cf.* the papers in Francovich *et al.* 2000), yet studies that effectively demonstrate and measure their benefits are still awaited. Above all, it remains to be proved that, once data are collected at that level, they can be then corrected for all the possible biases that affect those counts. The impact of the biases, on the other hand, has been conclusively established. It may be worth noting, in passing, that not only have other European archaeological schools not yet followed the British lead on this, but even Americanist archaeology has so far shown remarkably little interest in it. As a matter of fact, one of the founding fathers of survey, Robert McC. Adams, clearly warned, as early as 1981, about the dangers of artifact-level survey only achieving a spurious accuracy (Adams 1981: 43–47). His verdict seems to be still influencing practitioners based in the United States, in contrast with the prevalent mood in western Europe (the split is clearly illustrated by the papers in the special section that the journal *Antiquity* dedicated to the issue). It may also be significant that, in general, survey seems to become more intensive when it has to deal with cultural contexts characterized by a vast body of sceptical historiography based on literary sources (and hardly anyone is more sceptical than British ancient historians...).

An interesting, although perhaps predictable, development in recent years has been the emergence of a radical critique to quantitative approaches in field surveys. Building on by-now classic postmodern frameworks (as well as on parallel developments in human geography), an approach emphasizing individual perception has been steadily gaining ground in many scholarly circles. Underlining the inherent subjectivity of human observations of reality, scholars such as Tilley (1994) have argued that idiosyncratic, impressionistic narratives of one's experiences in the field are all that one can meaningfully share with others. It is easy to imagine how such a purely relativistic stance did not particularly impress those that for a generation had tried to standardize field survey as an objective procedure. As in many other areas of contemporary culture, an irreconcilable epistemological rift was created, with neither side showing much inclination to build bridges any time soon.

Both approaches, in their extreme forms, are equally unappealing. The philosophical weakness of assuming that one's observations are objective has been often remarked: indeed, virtually everybody now agrees, for instance, that there is no such thing as an impartial excavation record (Carver 1990) – so why hope that this might somehow be the case for survey? At the same time, the heuristic paralysis that results from a relativist credo has been even more frequently disparaged. So is there an alternative to an ongoing philosophical stand-off? This paper aims at exploring some options, as far as field surveys are concerned. While on the whole subscribing to the critiques of processualism, it will try to come up with something other than the simple 'cop-out' of pure relativism. What we should be seeking are ways to evaluate narratives based on field surveys, combined with a moderate use of heuristic quantitative and graphic tools that do not require exceedingly strong assumptions about the quality of the data. First, the problems inherent in most current approaches will be reviewed, and then some alternative views about the integration of different surveys will be suggested.

DARE TO COMPARE?

So why is it so hard to compare and integrate surveys? In a way, the key issue is what we want to compare, and for what purpose. Originally, the issue was a fairly straightforward one: field surveys were meant to produce a gazetteer of archaeological sites, and putting survey maps side-by-side would simply generate a larger and perfectly homogeneous map. Such was, and still is, the format of projects that aim to produce a catalog (often for Cultural Resource Management purposes) and that implicitly assume complete recovery, such as the *Forma Italiae* in Italy and others elsewhere (for Italy, Terrenato 1996; for Poland, Barford *et al.* 2000). Once a first measure of innocence was lost, however, the direct association between intensity of survey and density of sites found was fully realized and spelled out. It became clear at that point (as early as the 1970s in the United States) that only surveys of similar intensity could meaningfully be compared. Even if the dependence of survey results on the procedure adopted came as a shock for some, the news was not altogether seen

as too bad. After all, intensity could easily be standardized, and this was precisely what multi-team projects such as the Southwest Archaeological Research Group (SARG) set out to do efficiently (Plog *et al.* 1978).

But once the flea of critical doubt had entered the surveyor's ear, inquisitive minds could not rest until other possible biases were investigated. The obvious next step was to question the consistency of the very unit of analysis – *i.e.*, the site (Plog *et al.* 1978: 365). Site definition criteria had to be formalized and standardized if data were really to be comparable. This was easy to say in theory, but it proved to be a much harder nut to crack in terms of implementation (for a good survey of the problem, see Gallant 1986). In fact, the best practitioners in the discipline have been jousting with the problem for over 20 years now, and there is still very little consensus on a universal site-defining algorithm (Cherry *et al.* 1991: 45–47). As a by-product of this intellectual endeavor, however, the practice of field survey ended up being completely revolutionized. The quest for objective criteria of site definition necessarily involved dealing with the distribution of individual artifacts: indeed, the only way of approaching the problem was through accurate measures of their density on the ground and surveys began painstakingly to collect this kind of data.

Although these methodological developments are taken for granted today, at least in some quarters, not much effort has yet gone into evaluating their success. On the one hand, there can be no doubt that a permanent and extremely positive acquisition is the realization of the importance of off-site scatters for the reconstruction of landscape use (Bintliff and Snodgrass 1988; Wilkinson 1989; Stoddart and Whitehead 1991). On the other, as we will discuss shortly, it is still debatable whether these measures have made good on all their original promises. What is absolutely sure, however, is that this step-up in intensity has resulted in a dramatic decrease of the total covered area. In these smaller surveys the number of sites found, even if very high in terms of density per sq. km, dropped in the dozens in absolute terms. The thousands of sites discovered in surveys in Mesopotamia, Oaxaca or South Etruria were simply impossible to achieve at this level of detail. The trade-off was in favor of data quality (and thus objectivity and comparability across surveys), at the expense of sheer data quantity. Was it a good move? I want to advance the contentious view that this remains entirely to be proven: we are still awaiting studies that convincingly demonstrate the greater objectivity of artifact-level counts for purposes of defining sites. Worse than that, a body of literature has been accruing in recent years conclusively showing the presence of massive biases that affect the distribution of surface artifacts to the point where it becomes doubtful that density measures have any significance at all.

It might be useful at this point to briefly review some of the main documented processes at work in the formation and transformation of artifact scatters. For the sake of clarity, they can be divided into macroscopic, site-level

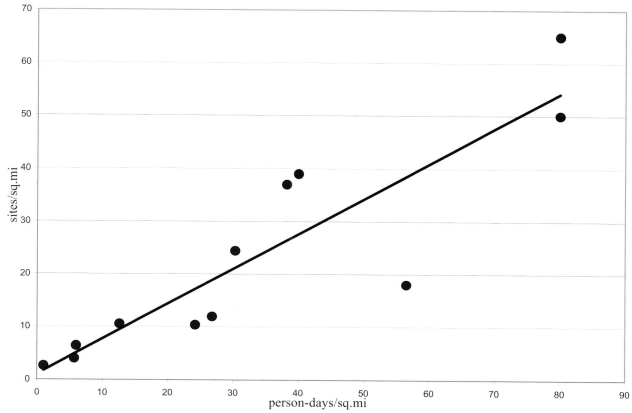

Figure 4.1 Association between intensity and site density (after Plog et al. 1978)

biases and microscopic, artifact-level ones (cf. Given's Table 2.2, this volume). The former group is composed of a few really major effects, which are, however, not impossible to assess and compensate for. Intensity we have already touched upon: like spatial sampling, it is an artifact of the research strategy itself, and thus, at least in theory, easier to control. The linear association that seems to exist between intensity and site density indeed suggests that calibration can be expected to work reasonably well (Figure 4.1). Another major problem is represented by recent geopedological processes. Erosion and alluviation, to name only the main ones, routinely destroy and conceal ancient surfaces, introducing remarkable gaps in the record obtained (Figure 4.2). The impact of these phenomena, known since Vita-Finzi's study of the Mediterranean valleys (Vita-Finzi 1969), was first assessed by Ammerman and his colleagues in the late 1970s (Ammerman and Bonardi 1981). It is somewhat harder to control than any human-made effect, but – provided the relevant geomorphological and pedological knowledge is accessible– it can be effectively tackled (the problem being that existing maps hardly ever have the topographic and chronological resolution that is required to calibrate for the bias). The landscape can be conceptualized, in this respect, as a palimpsest of windows dating to different periods. Sites will only be found if they happen to be in a window that is contemporaneous or earlier than them.

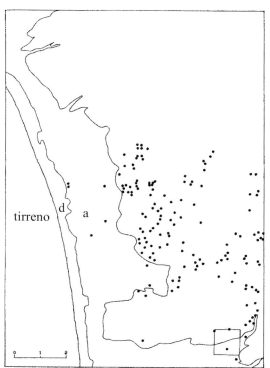

Figure 4.2 Distribution of sites in the Cecina Valley coastal area. Only a small minority of sites were found in the geopedologically unfavorable areas (indicated by the letters d=recent dunes, a=recent alluvium).

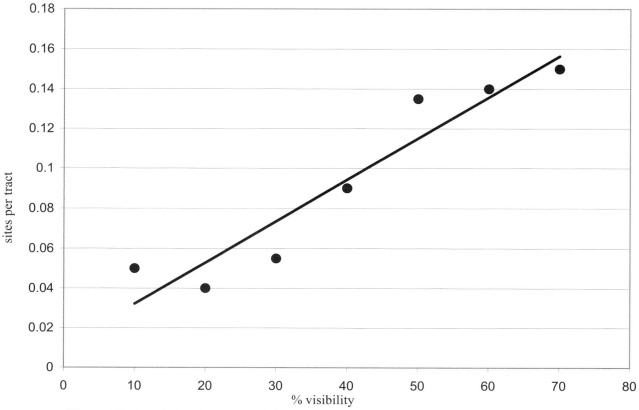

Figure 4.3 Association between visibility and site recovery at Keos (after Cherry et al. _1991)._

A similar situation obtains when it comes to vegetation and to other agents that may be obscuring the visibility of the actual soil surface. Woodland, tree groves, pasture, but also houses, gardens, quarries, terraces and landfills, military bases and artillery firing ranges are just some examples of the countless possible impediments to visibility. In contrast with geopedology, however, surface visibility is not binary, but rather can be characterized by an almost continuous scale, from vegetation-free plowed fields where heavy rains have made artifacts stand out on little towers of sediment, to woodland covered by a blanket of dead leaves a foot thick. In association with geopedology, they create extremely complex overlaying and intersecting patterns that massively constrain the possibility of recovering archaeological sites in most Mediterranean landscapes (Terrenato and Ammerman 1996). This is, of course, nothing new, and surface visibility measures have been incorporated in surveys ever since the 1970s. As with intensity, the existing data seem to show a linear association with site recovery, which again makes correcting for these effects not impossible (Figure 4.3). Taking on board the full range of implications of a formalization of this kind, however, involves a somewhat different approach to data analysis about which not everybody appears to be enthusiastic.

At the microscopic level of individual artifacts, things are, if possible, even more complicated. Not only has one to contend with the main biases discussed above (which, as they affect sites, do so even more with artifacts), but also with a host of others. The list is long and somewhat depressing, since all have been shown to have a significant impact on the density of artifacts on the surface. Plowzone effects should probably take pride of place. Repeated collections, experiments and simulations substantially agree in showing remarkable lateral displacement of artifacts at each plowing event (Figure 4.4; Ammerman and Feldman 1978; Ammerman 1985; Yorston _et al._ 1990; Taylor 2000), even with differential behavior for different objects (Figure 4.5). Moreover, artifacts cycle within the plowzone in a stochastic way, producing remarkably different sherd counts after each plowing. In fact, entire sites have famously been described as coming on and off in different years 'like traffic lights' (Lloyd and Barker 1981: 291). Sheet erosion in sloping fields can only add to the distortion of the original scatters (Allen 1991). These small-scale biases are extremely difficult, if not impossible, to compensate for, if one considers how the amount and nature of agricultural work, carried out over the centuries at each field, are completely unknown quantities, which cannot be estimated, even roughly.

A related issue is that of fragmentation. In frequently plowed fields, artifact counts will go up purely as a result of increased breakage rates. Worse, different artifact classes will be affected in different ways (Figure 4.6;

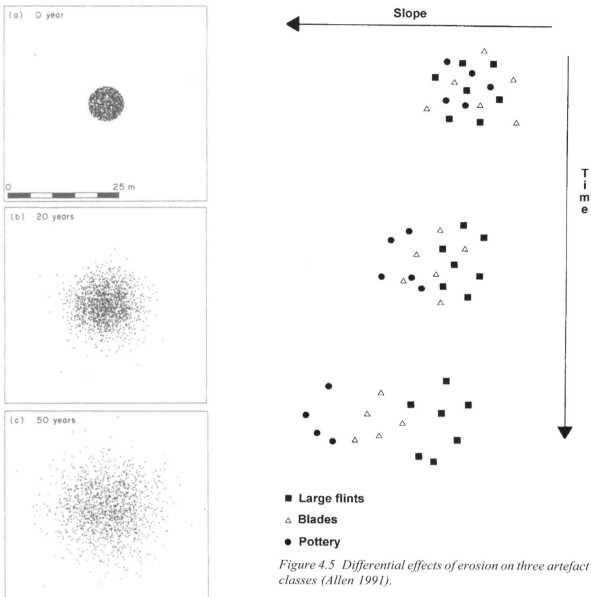

Figure 4.4 Simulated effects of repeated plowings on an artefact distribution over time (Yorston et al. 1990).

Figure 4.5 Differential effects of erosion on three artefact classes (Allen 1991).

Schiffer and Skibo 1989; Taylor 2000). In theory, sophisticated quantification techniques, such as EVEs (Estimated Vessel Equivalents), can address the problem, but they are hardly viable in field surveys. In any case, if different surveys define different lower size thresholds for their collections, or even ignore the problem altogether, major problems will arise for inter-survey comparisons.

Even regional artifact supply patterns can be an issue, since it has been shown how sites in different periods and/ or areas can use radically different quantities of objects. Thus a late Roman farm in Spain can on average have as little as one hundredth of the pottery that an Augustan one of the same size has in Italy (Millett 1991; Figure 4.7).

This will, of course, generate different surface densities for essentially comparable sites. The problem can be made yet worse by different chronological diagnosticity of artifacts of different periods and regions (Cherry *et al.* 1991: 327–33). Cultural contexts with nondescript, easily corroded or simply poorly studied materials may be grossly underrepresented if quantitative thresholds are used to define period occupation. Moreover, the nature of the underlying stratification itself can have a distorting role: sites characterized by deep features will produce lighter scatters than those with shallower ones (Taylor 2000). It has even been claimed that the geographical latitude of the research area can influence the average surface densities of different regions (Bintliff and Snodgrass 1988, although a wider study would be needed to prove this curious effect conclusively).

Another whole slew of problems derives from the

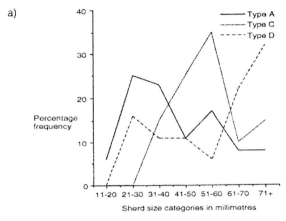

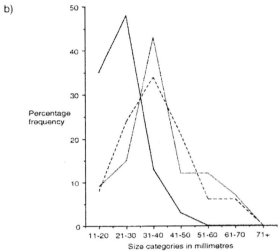

Figure 4.6 The percentage frequency distribution of three pottery assemblages of fabrics A (organic temper), C (sand temper) and D (no temper), a) before trampling and b) after trampling (Taylor 2000).

claiming that density measures allow a standardization of site definition across different survey projects. As a matter of fact, in most cases, they can hardly be claimed to produce the desired effect even within the boundaries of one and the same large-scale survey.

Noticing that the emperor had little in the way of clothes, Lisa Fentress (2000) finally dared to ask bluntly: 'What are we counting for?' I am afraid that the question still has not received a satisfactory answer. We should all, to be sure, record off-site scatters, but this does not necessarily involve density measures; we may certainly go on counting, in the hope that future studies will be able to come up with satisfactory answers to all of the potential biases. Yet we should also be clearly aware that our counting has had some undesirable effects. An approach to site definition based only on density counts, without adequate corrections for possible biases, paradoxically runs the risk of producing the opposite of the desired goal – *i.e.*, a higher variability (compared to the traditional empirical approach) in what counts as a site in different surveys. Given the significant but diverse impact of the microscopic biases on sherd counts, there is a definite danger that stochastic phenomena may account for most of the variability in artifact densities, especially when site status ends up being granted on the basis of a handful of diagnostic pieces (and several examples of this could be provided). While this potential problem can at least be circumvented using a pinch of common sense at the data-processing stage, there is another one that has even deeper and unavoidable consequences.

The intensity step-up has necessarily dramatically reduced the amount of land that we cover, all resources being equal. This, in turn, means that we now have to rely on a much smaller statistical basis for our inferences at the regional and interregional level, and this enormously weakens any kind of quantitative analysis of settlement patterns. One has to wonder if things were not better when we had many more sites, even though empirically defined, since the large numbers would have tended to compensate for any bias introduced by the absence of quantitative thresholds. And in any case it remains to be proved that the new system works much better than the old one for purposes of reliable site definition. (This would have to be verified through a double-blind test involving repeated non-pickup coverages of the same area by different teams using empirical and quantitative approaches to site definition, and then ground-truthing the different site attributions with shovel tests and boreholes.) At the same time, it has to be said that if we stopped gathering these data altogether, we will never have even the remotest chance of learning how to deal with the aforementioned biases.

Having said all that, it seems that a key issue in the future of artifact density measures is an operational one. Only if the collection process can be streamlined to the point where large regions can be covered and hundreds of sites can be found again, while still obtaining reliable density measures, will we find ourselves in a win-win

material conditions and the individual subjectivity of the survey itself. Conditions of light, rainfall, and time of the day may all play a role – even more so for differential abilities in picking up and dating sherds (see Shennan 1985, for a statistical treatment of all these factors). Keeping separate counts for each walker has shown how in some cases the differences can be significant. And again, it is not even a simple bias due to different recovery rates, but rather a complex one that varies by artifact class. Typically, for instance, certain walkers are much better than others at finding flints, and the same is very often true for metal objects. Especially if any materials are identified and left in the field (as often happens for surface scatters), significant chronological variation can be introduced by different individual abilities and backgrounds within the fieldwalking team. It is a common observation that, almost always, more material tends to be found and identified that dates to the broad era in which the researchers specialize (Ammerman 1981). All this – and more could be added – should invite extreme caution when

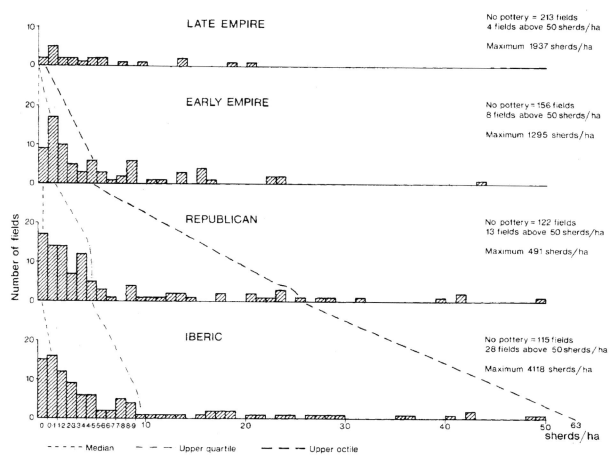

Figure 4.7 Histograms showing the distribution of numbers of fields in the Ager Tarraconensis *survey with different quantities of pottery per hectare (Millett 1991).*

situation, with no doubts raised about the justification of what we do. Some preliminary tests I have run seem to suggest that this elusive goal could be achieved through a massive use of GPS equipment, but this would take us into a different paper altogether. The provisional conclusion cannot but be that we had better confine ourselves to site-level data integration across different surveys. Actually, we cannot even rest on the assumption that site definition criteria are at all comparable. In plain words, what is interpreted as a dense off-site scatter in one project may well be treated as a site in another one. Or, perhaps even more easily, two concentrations separated by a lighter scatter may well show up as one site or two sites, depending on the approach.

In terms of strict experimental positivism (the one that guided the early advocates of field survey integration), we should simply give up hopes of any reliable quantitative analysis and go back to the drawing board (and to studying plowzone effects for the next 50 years). I suspect it is because of this unsettling implication that there has been a certain reticence in openly facing the problems posed by such biases, both macroscopic and microscopic. But perhaps some recent developments offer a theoretical

loophole, allowing us to escape the Newtonian strait-jacket. We can accept that individual judgment might have been exerted in defining sites, and we do not need to go to the extremes of pure relativism to do that; we simply have to come to terms with qualitative criteria of site definition, instead of quantitative ones. Not all will be perfectly consistent with each other, but, through explicit discussion, it should be possible for larger groups of practitioners to agree on acceptable ranges. Let us not forget that this was how clinical epidemiology was done when diagnoses were exclusively based on the five senses of each individual physician. And, to come back to archaeology, I have always wondered why hardly anybody questions the qualitative distinction of layers in excavations, whereas everybody is so desperately concerned with objective site definitions. Sites and layers are simply conventional units that come in handy to break down the continuum of reality into manageable chunks. They are by definition etic categories – which does not, however, make them fictional or non-existent.

Indeed, the conclusion of this paper will be that the integration of different sets of survey data is an exercise in global interpretation which can only be based on a variety of local interpretations, rather than objective observations. The prospect of combining ideas, readings and narratives (possibly containing numbers, graphs and GIS plots), rather than the numbers themselves, should not necessarily be a shocking one. I will argue that it can be seen as a sort of Bayesian approach; and let us not forget that in the days before telemetry and satellite images, Bayesian estimates for artillery ranges resulted in guns hitting their targets (Cowgill 1989).

LITTLE (FIELD) MAN, WHAT NOW?

This long digression makes it possible for the rest of this paper to focus on site-level issues, without having to worry about those at the artifact level. So what can we do with our empirically-defined sites? What kind of global trends can we reconstruct from local surveys, even without a guarantee of perfect comparability? More than 20 years ago, Cherry and Shennan (1978), in an extremely influential paper, defined four basic areas of research into site distributions; these still offer a convenient systematization of the range of questions that can be asked of survey results.

The first is the most basic and, ironically, also the toughest: how many sites? The task of coming up with even a very rough estimate of the total number of sites that existed within an area in the past is fraught with difficult problems. All three of the macroscopic biases (intensity, geopedology, visibility) are at work, and there may also have been imposed an artificial sampling design. We have seen earlier that (at least in theory) it is not impossible to deal with such macro-effects and compensate for them; but this only means that their impact can be somewhat equalized across the surveyed regions. Roughly speaking, if the average density of sites in tracts surveyed at low intensity is 2 per sq. km, and 5 per sq. km in those surveyed at a high intensity, then a density of sites 2.5 times higher can be estimated in the low-intensity tracts, everything else being equal. While partially correcting an internal bias of the recovered distribution, however, this gets us no closer to estimating the total number of sites. It has been known for a generation at least that by increasing the intensity or repeating the coverage (which are actually one and the same thing) more sites will always be found, 'with no signs of diminishing returns' (Plog *et al.* 1978). The disturbing implication, which has very far-reaching consequences, is that our site distributions cannot ever be complete, and – what is much worse – we have no idea whatsoever of what proportion of the total they represent. This will remain a major problem, simply because we are not likely to have test cases in which the total number of sites existing in antiquity is a given. Until then, we will not be able to assess the impact of any survey bias in absolute terms, but at the most in relative ones.

In the extremely intensive and full-coverage Boeotia survey (Bintliff and Snodgrass 1985), a recovery rate of

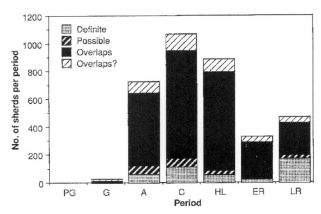

Figure 4.8 Differential diagnosticity of pottery for different periods at Keos (Cherry et al. *1991).*

57% was estimated on the basis (itself questionable) of literary sources. If such a detailed surface collection really only recovered about half of the sites, this suggests that there is a wide range of variability that this rate can have in different areas. For all of these considerations, the exercise of putting together survey data to reconstruct absolute numbers of sites appears for the moment pretty hopeless. This, of course, is particularly bad news for ancient demographers (Osborne [Chapter 12, this volume] comes to the same conclusion after a detailed critique of the Boeotian case; contrast the papers in Bintliff and Sbonias 1999): the best they can hope for is to detect relative increases and decreases over time, and even that appears extremely problematic.

But this already touches upon Cherry and Shennan's second area – *i.e.*, the investigation of site numbers in different chronological periods. This is a somewhat more promising approach (provided again we stick to relative rather than absolute comparisons) and probably also a more important one in heuristic terms. Two of the three biases thankfully cease to be a major problem: intensity will have little or no differential effect on different periods in the same region (except for periods particularly characterized by very small sites), and more or less the same can be said for vegetation. Geopedology on the other hand needs to be kept under tight control: if different periods have different amounts of exposed surface, this needs to be taken into account. Typically, Neolithic and earlier periods will have considerably smaller surface areas in which sites can be found. But, once the recent geopedological history has been reconstructed in sufficient detail, it should not be impossible to arrive at a figure of sites per sq. km of exposed surface, which can be considered a meaningful indicator of settlement changes over time. Some microscopic biases might be at work here, mainly those connected with different diagnosticity of artifacts of different periods, variations over time in artifact usage and supply, and differential detection and identification abilities among the surveyors; the possibility of lower survival rates for older sites has also recently been advanced (Bintliff 2000).

Even within the same survey all these biases need to be somehow equalized across the various periods, if significant comparisons between periods are to be made. Help can come from excavation data, as Martin Millett (1991) has shown, in the form of estimates of artifact supply per period, as well as of diagnosticity rates per period. With sufficiently large samples, thus at site level, these values might be used to correct for biases of this kind.

When it comes to individual surveyors' abilities, however, it is much harder even to assess the bias, especially across different surveys, unless one goes back to the material itself. Here is one of the junctures where it becomes absolutely necessary to switch to qualitative evaluations. Intellectual history and individual backgrounds need to be brought to bear on the issue. For instance, everything we know about the South Etruria Survey (Potter 1979) suggests that Ward-Perkins and his co-workers had only a very basic understanding of Hellenistic pottery, something that makes their distribution maps for this period very hard to compare with those of projects that had the benefit of the pottery studies conducted in the 1970s and 1980s. There is no easy way of making some quantitative correction. This is true also for a number of other problems connected with comparing surveys: it is an unavoidable consequence of the very nature of surveys (and, some would add, of human knowledge itself). Rather than throwing up our hands in despair, denying our problems, or wishing them away, we simply need to make the best of what we have. In the case of the South Etruria Survey, we must admit that while other parts of the project may still be considered reliable, extreme skepticism should be exercised concerning their reconstruction of the Hellenistic phase. This does not mean embracing relativism, but simply trying to come up with consistent narratives that can be accepted by the largest possible group of people.

Let us now consider relationships between sites and their environment. Locational studies can be in remarkably good shape in terms of their robustness in the face of possible sources of bias. Certainly, those that deal with individual sites (such as site catchment analysis: *e.g.*, Vita-Finzi 1978) are fairly safe, except of course if there are undetected contemporary sites within the catchment radius. Even summary statistics of locational preference (Figure 4.9, now enormously facilitated by GIS) are not at major risk from macroscopic biases, since they do not require a complete sample, but simply a representative one. Even if only an unknown proportion of Hellenistic farms has been recovered, their locations are nonetheless informative of the productive and perceptive choices of the farmers. The only serious problem can arise if the sample is skewed by some environmental factor that affects both modern visibility and ancient locational choices: in more formal terms, a spatial autocorrelation between visibility and environmental factors must be excluded. Let us consider a typical Mediterranean example. In a coastal plain, only paleodunes may be sticking out of recent, deep alluvium. They are the only tracts in which ancient sites can be found, and thus a

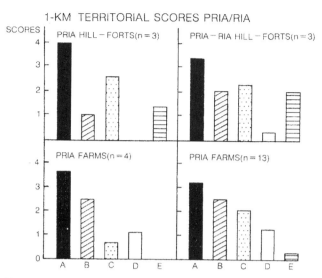

Figure 4.9 Locational choices for Pre-Roman Iron Age (PRIA) and Roman Iron Age (RIA) hill-forts and farms in the Neothermal Dalmatia Project. Land classes: A, stony; B, arable; C, terrace; D, bottom land; E, karst (Chapman 1991).

locational analysis would show a massive preference of sites for that kind of habitat. But of course the survey cannot recover anything that is under the deep alluvium, completely biasing the analysis precisely because the environmental pattern can affect both visibility and human settlement. To spell out the problem, it is possible that the dunes are the only soils light enough to be arable in the original landscape, or it might be the case that other acceptable habitats existed under the alluvium. Survey alone will not, by definition, allow us to opt for one or the other of these two radically different alternatives, nor will it even bring out the problem. Only a detailed environmental knowledge of the region (especially based on boreholes and observation of exposed sections) might be informative, and it will be at the level of interpretation, rather than of positive, quantitative determinations.

Aside from this issue, comparisons of interaction between sites and environments are comparatively reliable and very desirable. This is especially so because almost always the only possible integration will be at the qualitative level, given the high degree of environmental variability across Mediterranean regions. In other words, we are comparing interpretative accounts about locational preferences, instead of trying to obtain averages of sites per sq. km within each environmental unit.

Where things again become extremely complicated is with relationships *between* sites. This heading covers a very wide range of techniques and approaches to the study of site distribution (Hodder and Orton 1976; Johnson 1977). Most conclusions drawn from field surveys and dealing with political, social, and economic issues ultimately rest on analysis of relationships between sites.

Hierarchies, networks and configurations of sites are perceived as key indicators of past social systems. Besides basic impressionistic observations, which just about any dataset will support, a host of quantitative tools have commonly been employed, deriving mostly from human geography and particularly from the so-called 'New Geography' (Haggett 1965). Central place theory, nearest-neighbor analysis, and the rank-size rule, to mention some familiar concepts, all come to us from geography, and indeed they were conceived specifically for the analysis of modern, mapped, human landscapes. Precisely because of that fact, however, these analytical tools can safely rest only upon an assumption of completeness of those distributions. But as we have said several times, that is precisely an assumption that it is most unwise to make, as far as field survey results are concerned. All of the macroscopic biases tend to prevent total recovery, and it is virtually impossible to imagine a context in which none of them would have a significant effect, at least in the Mediterranean. This is why the simple transfer of geographical tools to archaeological analysis cannot safely happen unless we have first dealt properly with the issue of the completeness of the record.

THE REMAINS OF THE (FIELD) DAY

Both when interpreting a single survey, and much more so when integrating different ones, we need to be acutely aware that we are dealing with distributions that are all in various degrees of incompleteness. This is a major problem for many current approaches, and it is surprising how little willingness exists to admit it and to try and find ways to tackle it. Perhaps it is felt to be a crippling realization, or an involuntary gift to those historians that still refuse to take field surveys seriously into account; but the reticence, in any case, is nonetheless strong and tangible. I am certainly not claiming that those yawning gaps in the survey record are good news, but I believe that we need to confront the problem directly, by starting to develop a body of theory specifically designed to deal with incomplete distributions – *i.e.*, custom-made for archaeological field survey results. This involves coming up with our own tools, ones that are sufficiently robust to work for the kind of data with which we are stuck. At the same time, we need to change our expectations about the type and level of the quantitative analyses that we can perform. Both are serious challenges, but they can be easier to approach if taken with a pinch of post-modernism.

An example of an approach of this kind is represented by the application of trend-surfaces to express the likelihood of a site presence (Figure 4.10; for a fuller description, see Terrenato 2000: 66–69). This is an interpolation based on known site data, as well as on known active biases; it involves transforming distributions of dots into matrices of values that can be represented in 3-D or through contour lines, a process known as generalization. The map algebra

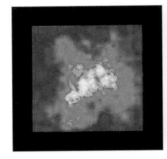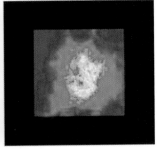

Figure 4.10 Trend surface plottings showing the likelihood of site presence corrected for visibility factors (Terrenato 2000).

involves a circular box of definable radius that moves across the landscape. At each location, the likelihood of site presence is estimated on the known distribution, corrected for intensity, surface visibility and geopedological factors. It is important to stress that this is not a site prediction approach based on reconstructed locational choices, but rather a form of visualization that combines survey results with a correction of macroscopic biases. It transforms an incomplete distribution of sites into visual patterns that should reflect more closely the actual settlement concentrations that existed in antiquity. The replacement of site locations with abstract surfaces may seem an unacceptable loss of detail, but it probably is a more realistic representation, in epistemological terms, of our effective knowledge of the ancient landscape. The sites that we happen to recover are not an ancient distribution, but at most a pale and partial reflection that reaches us through several distorting mirrors, the original image being entirely beyond our grasp. If we are lucky, we can produce visualizations that share some of its spatial properties. Their shape, however, will also be a function of how we conceive, model and approximate the biasing processes and are thus inevitably linked with our prejudices and assumptions (and the wide variety of methodological approaches to these problems is the best demonstration of this).

The relativity of any visualization that we can produce should not make us think that we have necessarily abandoned any hope of quantitative analysis. The trend surfaces themselves, for instance, are susceptible of being spatially analyzed. Clustering can be detected by means of a comparison with randomly generated surfaces, paralleling the approach of nearest-neighbor analysis. It is important to remember, however, that we can make these representations realistic and convincing, but not objective and independent of our assumptions. They are best seen as rhetorical devices that allow us to communicate better what we think we have found, and ultimately to enhance the internal consistency of our narratives, at least in our hopes. They work like metaphors do in our language: we can shape them freely, but only some of them will be recognizable and meaningful for the recipients of our communication.

CONCLUSION

My conclusion here derives from these reflections. If we want to integrate field survey results, it might be convenient to take a leaf out of the postmodern book. We have to accept that different people will produce different accounts of the same landscape, especially because of the many layers of potential recovery biases that make incontrovertible observations impossible. We will necessarily have to simplify and approximate such complexity in some way, and this will result in a variety of formats, representations and reconstructions. This does not mean that some of them will not be more persuasive and widely acceptable than others. It is better to see survey results as narratives, travelogues if you want, but they can still contain maps, graphs and tables that help convey our understanding of the evolution of human landscapes. These quantitative and spatial forms of communication can be of great help in our evaluation of the appropriateness and internal consistency of each of these rich survey texts, but they cannot turn them into objective descriptions.

The key thought, throughout this chapter, is that giving up on objectivity does not render all interpretations epistemologically equal, nor equally worthless. Such a general philosophical stance is nowhere more relevant than in the reconstruction of global narratives on the basis of survey results. While in fact there will always be different ways of combining data, some approaches and some datasets will make our end-product more convincing and useful than others.

We have discussed at some length above how certain ways of collating information better suit our understanding of survey data quality. To sum up, any analytical tool that works without assuming complete or near-complete recovery is definitely going to serve us better. The same can be said for data collected with a watchful eye for macroscopic sources of bias. But above all, perhaps, no refinement in field collection technique is worth a drastic reduction of sample size. That size matters (at least in this context) is a slogan on which both positivist and post-modern views can converge. It makes good statistical sense, as we all know, and it makes good narratological sense too. It is much safer to decode a few large-scale surveys than lots of small ones: for one thing, it requires less work, but it also involves fewer interpretative steps, allowing us to stay closer to the original data and facilitating the game of inference. It is easier to handle a few hopefully self-consistent research universes than dozens of microworlds that do not even have the critical mass, individually, to produce a structured account within their own boundaries.

We should deal with each survey as a detective does with an eyewitness, rather than as a literary critic does with a text. This involves considering its background, recalling the intellectual climate which influenced it, badgering it for contradiction and inconsistency, and in the end assessing its reliability and its use for our investigative purposes. Before any other consideration, however, witnesses count only inasmuch as they have seen some-thing significant: any jury would rather have a couple of middle-aged witnesses that each saw an hour of the crime, rather than 30 youngsters each relating a different four-minute segment of it. All the accounts will have their biases, but it is easier and epistemologically sounder to work with a few long stories than with a lot of soundbites. This is why we should pause and think about Mediterranean survey's move from a few 'old-fashioned' projects with hundred of sites each, to a lot of sophisticated ones with only a couple of dozen sites apiece. Life becomes much harder for people interested in the 'big picture', as the pieces of the puzzle get smaller and smaller.

There are reconstructions of past events – be they farming activities or felonies – that satisfy the courts and the public better than others, even if they cannot ever be the pure truth. Sample size, recovery biases and incompleteness of distributions are what archaeologists need to keep their eyes on, if they want to reconstruct global trends from local survey results.

REFERENCES

Adams, R. McC. (1981) *Heartland of Cities: Surveys of Ancient Settlement and Land Use on the Central Floodplain of the Euphrates.* Chicago, University of Chicago Press.

Allen, M. J. (1991) Analysing the landscape: a geographical approach to archaeological problems. In A. J. Schofield (ed.) *Interpreting Artefact Scatters: Contributions to Ploughzone Archaeology*: 39–58. Oxford, Oxbow Books.

Ammerman, A. J. (1981) Surveys and archaeological research. *Annual Review of Anthropology* 10: 63–88.

Ammerman, A. J. (1985) Plow-zone experiments in Calabria, Italy. *Journal of Field Archaeology* 12: 33–40.

Ammerman, A. J. and Bonardi, S. (1981) Recent developments in the study of Neolithic settlements in Calabria. In G. W. W. Barker and R. Hodges (eds.) *Archaeology and Italian Society*: 335–42. Oxford, British Archaeological Reports .

Ammerman, A. J. and Feldman, M. (1978) Replicated collection of site surfaces. *American Antiquity* 43: 734–40.

Barford, P., Brzezinski, W. and Kobylinski, Z. (2000) The past, present and future of the Polish Archaeological Record Project. In J. Bintliff, M. Kuna and N. Venclova (eds.) *The Future of Surface Artefact Survey in Europe*: 73–92. Sheffield, Sheffield Academic Press.

Binford, L. R. (1964) A consideration of archaeological research design. *American Antiquity* 29: 425–45.

Bintliff, J. (2000) Beyond dots on the map: future directions for surface artefact survey in Greece. In J. Bintliff, M. Kuna and N. Venclova (eds.) *The Future of Surface Artefact Survey in Europe*: 3–20. Sheffield, Sheffield Academic Press.

Bintliff, J. and Sbonias, K. (eds.) (1999) *Reconstructing Past Population Trends in Mediterranean Europe (3000 BC – AD 1800)*. Oxford, Oxbow Books.

Bintliff, J. and Snodgrass, A. (1985) The Cambridge/Bradford Boeotia Expedition: the first four years. *Journal of Field Archaeology* 12: 123–61.

Bintliff, J. and Snodgrass, A. (1988) Off-site distributions: a regional and interregional perspective. *Current Anthropology* 29: 506–513.

Blanton, R. E., Kowalewski, S. A., Feinman, G. M. and Appel, J. (1981) *Ancient Mesoamerica: A Comparison of Change in Three Regions*. New York, Cambridge University Press.

Carver, M. O. H. (1990) Digging for data: archaeological approaches to data definition, acquisition and analysis. In R. Francovich and D. Manacorda (eds.) *Lo scavo archeologico: dalla diagnosi all'edizione*: 45–120. Florence, Insegna del Giglio.

Champion, T. C. (ed.) (1989) *Centre and Periphery: Comparative Studies in Archaeology*. London, Unwin Hyman.

Cherry, J. F. (1983) Frogs around the pond: perspectives on current archaeological survey in the Mediterranean region. In D. R. Keller and D. W. Rupp (eds.) *Archaeological Survey in the Mediterranean Area*: 375–416. Oxford, British Archaeological Reports.

Cherry, J. F., Davis, J. L. and Mantzourani, E. (1991) *Landscape Archaeology as Long-term History: Northern Keos in the Cycladic Islands from Earliest Settlement until Modern Times* (*Monumenta Archaeologica* 16). Los Angeles, UCLA Institute of Archaeology.

Cherry, J. F. and Shennan, S. J. (1978) Sampling cultural systems: some perspectives on the application of probabilistic regional survey in Britain. In J. F. Cherry, C. S. Gamble and S. J. Shennan (eds.) *Sampling in Contemporary British Archaeology*: 17–48. Oxford, British Archaeological Reports.

Cowgill, G. (1989) Formal approaches in archaeology. In C. C. Lamberg-Karlovsky (ed.) *Archaeological Thought in America*: 74–88. Cambridge, Cambridge University Press.

Euler, R. C. and Gumerman, G. J. (eds.) (1978) *Investigations of the Southwestern Anthropological Research Group: An Experiment in Archaeological Cooperation. The Proceedings of the 1976 Conference*. Flagstaff, Museum of Northern Arizona.

Fentress, E. (2000) What are we counting for? In R. Francovich, H. Patterson and G. Barker (eds.) *Extracting Meaning from Ploughsoil Assemblages*: 44–52. Oxford, Oxbow Books.

Fish, S. K. and Kowalewski, S. A. (eds.) (1990) *The Archaeology of Regions: A Case for Full-coverage Survey*. Washington, Smithsonian Institution Press.

Flannery, K. V. (ed.) (1976) *The Early Mesoamerican Village*. New York, Academic Press.

Francovich, R., Patterson, H. and Barker, G. (eds.) (2000) *Extracting Meaning from Ploughsoil Assemblages*. Oxford, Oxbow Books.

Gallant, T. W. (1986) Background noise and site definition: a contribution to site methodology. *Journal of Field Archaeology* 13: 403–418.

Haggett, P. (1965) *Locational Analysis in Human Geography*. London, Edward Arnold.

Hodder, I. and Orton, C. (1976) *Spatial Analysis in Archaeology*. Cambridge, Cambridge University Press.

Johnson, G. A. (1977) Aspects of regional analysis in archaeology. *Annual Review of Anthropology* 6: 479–508.

Lloyd, J. and Barker, G. W. W. (1981) Roman settlement in rural Molise: problems of archaeological survey. In G. W. W. Barker and R. Hodges (eds.) *Archaeology and Italian Society*: 375–416. Oxford, British Archaeological Reports.

Millett, M. (1991) Pottery: population or supply patterns? The Ager Tarraconensis approach. In G. W. W. Barker and J. Lloyd (eds.) *Roman Landscapes*: 18–26. London, British School at Rome.

Plog, S., Plog, F. and Wait, W. (1978) Decision making in modern surveys. In M. Schiffer (ed.) *Advances in Archaeological Method and Theory* 1: 383–421. New York, Academic Press.

Potter, T. W. (1979) *The Changing Landscape of South Etruria*. London, Paul Elek.

Schiffer, M. B. and Skibo, J. B. (1989) A provisional theory of ceramic abrasion. *American Anthropologist* 91: 101–115.

Shennan, S.J. (1985) *Experiments in the Collection and Analysis of Archaeological Survey Data: The East Hampshire Survey*. Sheffield, University of Sheffield Department of Prehistory and Archaeology.

Stein, G.J. (1999) *Rethinking World-systems: Diasporas, Colonies, and Interaction in Uruk Mesopotamia*. Tucson, University of Arizona Press.

Stoddart, S. K. F. and Whitehead, N. (1991) Cleaning the Iguvine stables: site and off-site analysis from a central Mediterranean perspective. In A. J. Schofield (ed.) *Interpreting Artefact Scatters: Contributions to Ploughzone Archaeology*: 141–48. Oxford, Oxbow Books.

Taylor, J. (2000) Cultural depositional processes and post-depositional problems. In R. Francovich, H. Patterson and G. Barker (eds.) *Extracting Meaning from Ploughsoil Assemblages*: 16–28. Oxford, Oxbow Books.

Terrenato, N. (1996) Field survey methods in Central Italy (Etruria and Umbria). *Archaeological Dialogues* 3: 216–30.

Terrenato, N. (2000) The visibility of sites and the interpretation of field survey results: towards an analysis of incomplete distributions. In R. Francovich, H. Patterson and G. Barker (eds.) *Extracting Meaning from Ploughsoil Assemblages*: 60–71. Oxford, Oxbow Books.

Terrenato, N. and Ammerman, A. J. (1996) Visibility and site recovery in the Cecina Valley Survey, Italy. *Journal of Field Archaeology* 23: 91–109.

Tilley, C. (1994) *A Phenomenology of Landscape: Places, Paths, and Monuments*. Oxford, Berg.

Vita-Finzi, C. (1969) *The Mediterranean Valleys: Geological Changes in Historical Times*. Cambridge, Cambridge University Press.

Vita-Finzi, C. (1978) *Archaeological Sites in their Setting*. London, Thames and Hudson.

Wilkinson, T. W. (1989) Extensive sherd scatters and land-use intensity: some recent results. *Journal of Field Archaeology* 16: 31–46.

Yorston, R., Gaffney, V. L. and Reynolds, P. R. (1990) Simulation of artefact movement due to cultivation. *Journal of Archaeological Science* 17: 67–83.

5. Solving the Puzzle of the Archaeological Labyrinth: Time Perspectivism in Mediterranean Surface Archaeology

LuAnn Wandsnider

PROLOGUE

Everyone knows the story of Icarus. His father Daedalus was the clever fellow who helped Pasiphae, wife of King Minos of Crete, in her assignations with the bull. She gave birth to the Minotaur and, for his part in this indelicate act, Daedalus was put to work by King Minos to fashion the Labyrinth on Crete in which the Minotaur (and his mother) might be confined. King Minos also imprisoned Daedalus, who did not suffer confinement lightly: he crafted wings, like those of a bird, so that he and his children could make their escape. Icarus was warned, and warned again, by his father about the dangers of flying too near the sun. Nevertheless, Icarus swooped into the heavens, shouting back his joy in flying and the wonders he beheld from his perch on high. Of course, soon the wax binding the feathers to the frame began to melt, the feathers came free, and Icarus himself plunged into the sea, much to his father's anguish. Daedalus was successful in escaping King Minos' Labyrinth.

Little known, however, is the story of Icarus' sister. Although her father also fashioned a pair of wings for her, Icarus' sister refused to wear them and pleaded with her father and brother to stay longer and try another means. She feared for both their lives. Alas, they left her, and we know what became of them. As for her, she studied hard other avenues of escape: how olive leaves floated on the sea breezes, how spiders rode silk filaments, how hawks with fixed wings soared on thermal currents. From these initial studies, Icarus' sister began a methodical study of aerodynamics, first inventing calculus and using it to explore aspects of lift and drag. By this time, she had determined that her intuition about bird-like wings and a flapping propulsion was correct; wings would not support her and again she mourned her lost father and brother. She eventually settled that a kite would be her vehicle, but what kind of envelope would support her weight? How would she control it? She considered in turn diverse fabrics and their properties. But, to understand the stresses and strains they would have to bear, she found she needed vector algebra and it took her a couple of years to master

this. She experimented with parchment and flax and also the webbing produced by spiders. This latter seemed to serve best, but it took some time to establish spider ranches (those early days of spider study were challenging indeed) throughout Crete to grow enough silk with which to weave her kite. Weeks of trial flights now followed. Of course, by this time, Icarus' sister was rather advanced in years. Consulting a local oracle, finally, a departure day was set. One fine June dawn, with a silver kite arching above her and invoking the fortitude of Artemis, Icarus' sister launched herself over the sea, dipping low and then catching an updraft. Her fate? Did she successfully escape the Labyrinth? Unknown. King Minos' archers last saw her sailing low over Crete before heading towards the mainland.

I use the strained metaphor of Icarus and his sister to characterize the state of archaeological landscape studies in the Mediterranean (and elsewhere). The Labyrinth of the archaeological record, fashioned not by Daedalus but by human activities and that of other species and geological processes over the millennia, is our puzzle, perhaps not to be escaped, but to be solved. With ever greater technical sophistication, Mediterranean (and other) archaeologists have crafted finer wings with which to document and interpret past landscapes in terms of sites and settlements, settlement patterns and settlement systems. A better binding agent has been sought, reinforced feathers developed, and Icarus has been put on steroids so that he might beat his wings with greater strength. Yet, the vehicle of 'settlements' – the propulsion system, as it were, predominating in Mediterranean (indeed, worldwide) landscape archaeology – is flawed, fatally so. Such studies may from time to time correctly represent the past (Daedalus, after all, was able to make shore even with analog bird-wings), but this may be more the result of chance than design. Icarus' fate is more typical of settlement pattern studies in general: both their authors and their audience think they are flying, for they report credible results which seem to satisfy how we think the past should be understood. But the sun is beginning to melt the wax,

Icarus can't beat his arms fast enough, and he is losing altitude: the full potential of archaeological landscapes will not be realized through settlement studies, no matter how well executed.

As for his unnamed sister, who fashioned a propulsion system based on knowledge gained from a hard-won understanding of available materials and how they might work, her fate is at present unknown. The value of these other means by which to negotiate the Labyrinth – to approach the archaeological landscape, that is – emanating from a growing understanding of archeological deposits, how they form and how they can be interpreted in a way that does not abuse or deny their formation history, remains to be seen.

INTRODUCTION

This volume is devoted to furthering the exchange of information among and between the many high-quality, pedestrian archaeological surveys being conducted in the Mediterranean Basin. Comparing and contrasting these rich records of human endeavor promises to yield critical regional-scale insights, building on and complementing those from earlier syntheses in the Mediterranean (Alcock 1994) and the Near East (Wilkinson 2000), and correcting 'Mediterranean myopia' (Blanton 2001).

To a greater or lesser extent, such an enterprise requires that insight-sharing researchers also share a common paradigm (Kuhn 1970), including an understanding of how archaeological surface deposits form, what information they may yield, relevant *chronotypes, i.e.*, models of causation, agent, and temporality (following Bender and Wellbery 1991; *contra* Gregory, forthcoming), methods, and empirical and conceptual units (*sensu* Ramenofsky and Steffen 1998). While agreement on all aspects of the interpretative enterprise that is archaeology is not expected, some common ground is necessary. In what follows, I will point to a condition of multiple paradigm disorder, with elements of at least two paradigms guiding research: a regional studies paradigm seated in a functional, processual metaphysic, and a multi-temporal paradigm seated in a formational metaphysic. Such a condition suggests we are still somewhat far from that common ground. Nevertheless, confusion of this sort is to be expected during a paradigm shift and can be interpreted as a sign of disciplinary vitality.

I begin by reviewing the several paradigms within which the archaeological landscape has been approached in the Mediterranean. Beginning in the 1950s, the text-inspired historicist approach, emphasizing monuments, was supplanted by a regional studies or settlement archaeology approach. Other recent approaches I characterize as employing a multi-temporal chronotype, such as that from archaeological *Annaliste* adaptations (Barker 1995; Bintliff 1991a; Knapp 1992), Bailey's (1981; 1983; 1987) time perspectivism, or McGlade's (1995; 1999a; 1999b) eco-dynamics. Recently, such approaches have been ex-

plicitly tied to a formationally nuanced understanding of archaeological deposits (Knapp 1992; Murray 1999; Smith 1992). Mediterranean practice has long reflected a keen appreciation for the formationally complex surface record. Moreover, to a limited extent, researchers often rely on chronotypes or models of causation, agent, and temporality that are also complex. Curiously (and evidencing multiple paradigm disorder), however, the parlance of Mediterranean survey is based, superficially at least, in the regional studies paradigm – *i.e.*, in discussion of sites and settlements and other functional entities.

In part, this situation is due to conceptual and methodological impoverishment. Conceptual tools for interpreting the taphonomically or formationally complex landscape in terms of a variety of short-, medium-, and long-term processes are still under construction. I attempt to address this impoverishment, specifically referring to current work in southern Turkey and concluding with a more general discussion of methodological issues.

MEDITERRANEAN ARCHAEOLOGICAL LANDSCAPE PARADIGMS

Kardulias (1994) and others (Bennet and Galaty 1997; Dyson 1982; Morris 1994) nicely review the paradigm shift that occurred in Mediterranean prehistory and Classical archaeology, as text-inspired archaeological research gave way to anthropologically-oriented work in the 1950s to 1970s. Earlier archaeological work focused on specific sites mentioned in historical texts, seeing such monuments as material testimony of Hellenism, the spirit of which infuses Western thought. Past change, when it occurred, did so because of invading armies, migrating populations, and diffusing ideas (Jacobsen 2000; Snodgrass 1985). That is, the chronotype of culture history or historicism, seen also in European Paleolithic (Clark 1994) and Iron Age (Olivier 1999) analyses, also organized Mediterranean studies. The methods employed came from art history, emphasizing detailed description of the unique (Kardulias 1994; Renfrew 1980). Empirical and conceptual units were of the classically informed common-sense world.

Regional Studies and Settlement Archaeology

The shift to a regional studies paradigm in the Mediterranean, grounded by a functional metaphysic, seems to have been shaped by developments both internal and external to the discipline (Athanassopoulos and Wandsnider, forthcoming). Fotiadis (1995: 99–100) notes the general move of the social sciences towards scientific humanism, wherein 'universal man,' endowed with 'adaptive flexibility,' was taken as the natural-technical object of research. This functional metaphysic is evident in various British geographical approaches to archaeology and the environment, to be seen in the work of O. G. S. Crawford, Grahame Clark, and their heirs (Daniel 1975;

Jacobsen 2000; Trigger 1989). It is also evident in the cultural ecology of Americanist archaeology, which guided Gordon Willey's (1953) initial efforts in settlement pattern archaeology in the Virú Valley of Peru and Robert Braidwood's (1937) work at Antioch; and it reached an apogee of sorts in the processual archaeology of David Clarke and Lewis Binford (Trigger 1989). In the Mediterranean, the Minnesota Messenia Expedition (McDonald and Rapp 1972) set the standard for regional, multi-disciplinary work focused on 'man and his environment.' Reflecting internal developments, Renfrew's (1972) study of the emergence of complex society in the Cyclades marks the first explicitly anthropological treatment of a subject in the classical world. These two benchmark studies inspired three decades of high-quality survey in the Mediterranean basin, culminating, for instance, in the sort of studies presented in the series *The Archaeology of Mediterranean Landscapes* (Barker and Mattingly 1999; 2000).

The orienting chronotype (or model of causation, agent, and temporality) of the regional studies paradigm was explicitly anti-historicist and processual (Kardulias 1994); causation was seen as complex and as due to demographic, internal social, economic, and political dynamics. Each of these different forces operated to create the organization seen at each spatial scale in a hierarchy of settlement (household, community, region) (Ammerman 1981; Gowlett 1997; Parsons 1972; Trigger 1967). For a given time period, settlement patterns, thus, represent a snapshot of demographic trends and the social, economic, political, and religious institutions that govern daily life. As such, regional settlement pattern studies epitomize a structural-functional approach closely approximating that in Durkheimian social anthropology (Trigger 1989: 284–85).

Within this paradigm, empirical units include ceramic types (carriers of chronological information) and regions. Sites are recognized as problematic empirical entities that require interpretation to be distinguished (Cherry *et al.* 1991). They are conventionally defined as 'anomalously dense concentrations of artifacts [and features; (Kardulias *et al.* 1995: 9)] with definable spatial limits' (Cherry and colleagues, in Wright *et al.* 1990: 606), 'which provide an opportunity to discuss functional interrelationships between data elements' (Given *et al.* 1999: 24). That is, they are empirical entities owed to ethnographically referable human endeavors, but seriously affected by other (less interesting) processes through time.

Conceptual units, on the other hand, include settlements and settlement patterns. Settlements, occupied by communities and perhaps materially represented by sites, are also problematic in their definition. Gordon Willey (1968: 216) clearly conceived of this definition as an important issue with two parts: (1) creating sites as analytic units derived from observed structures and features; and (2) demonstrating that a site was indeed the material reflection of a community, *i.e.*, a settlement. In the end, he could specify no objective criteria for doing either and so recognized settlements as preliminary designations. Given

et al. (1999: 24), concerned more with recognizing domestic space as opposed to community space, stipulate:

> We define a settlement as any site that has material culture remains in close association with architectural features spread over a hectare or more, including several distinct structures. Wherever a dense scatter of sherds is accompanied by an equally dense spread of roofing tiles and rubble that could indicate architectural remains of the same date as the sherds, we tentatively regard this combination of features as a settlement...

That they recognize the same interpretive problem as had Willey is suggested by their use of the word 'tentatively.'

Settlement patterns are 'a set of culturally significant locations, each of which occupies a specified position within an array that makes up a coherent distribution' (Fish 1999: 203). Importantly, settlement patterns are the essential conceptual device that 'enables archaeologists to efficiently relate large bodies of data to complicated assumptions in a widely comprehensible manner' (*ibid.*). Using versions of settlement pattern analyses, demographic and structural issues have been addressed throughout the Mediterranean (*e.g.* Bintliff and Sbonias 1999), although at a more local scale than that reported for other parts of the world (Blanton 2001).

Methodologically, Mediterranean regional studies of the 1970s and 1980s were coherently interdisciplinary and focused on the region as a fundamental unit of interaction. Systematic survey, complemented by geoarchaeological and geophysical studies, was and is the primary means for locating temporally sensitive artifacts and sites (Kardulias 1994). It was recognized early on as particularly effective in the Mediterranean, with its excellent surface exposure promoted by a long history of grazing and plowing and also by erosion (Dyson 1982).

Settlement pattern studies, undergirded by functional, processual principles, have come to be one of the dominant interpretative vehicles employed in archaeology today (Fish 1999: 207, table 14.1; *cf.* also Alcock and Cherry, Ch. 1, this volume, Figure 1.4): 20% of the recent articles appearing in *American Antiquity* and *Latin American Antiquity* rely upon settlements and settlement patterns to interpret past cultural dynamics, as do most of the contributors to the series *The Archaeology of Mediterranean Landscapes* (Barker and Mattingly 1999; 2000). As Fish (1999: 203) notes, most archaeologists 'have internalized the concept [of settlement patterns] to the point that there are few reflections on its impact...' and that the concept of settlement patterns is 'so fundamental to reconstructing past lifeways... that after its influential articulation by Willey, and exemplary implementation in the Virú Valley, it became a basic tenet of subsequent method and theory....' But challenges to the efficacy of the regional studies paradigm and to the interpretative convention of settlement patterns were voiced even as early as the 1970s and continue to be voiced today.

The chronotype (model of causation, agent, and temporality) of the regional studies paradigm has been challenged as non-comprehensive and unsound. Echoing a general critique of processual studies, Bintliff (1991b) notes that the structural-functional chronotype appears to work well for describing and generalizing about regional communities and societies, but not about individuals; it emphasizes major trends, de-emphasizing short-term events; and, finally, the associated positivistic approach is recognized as flawed. Specifically focusing on approaches to the archaeological landscape, Tilley (1994: 11) argues for the abandonment of a false objective consideration of 'geometrical universal space,' reflected in a concern for site catchments and regional economic models and the embrace of an approach that considers the construction of human places in space through on-going human experience and action in the world. The contributors to Ashmore and Knapp (1999) explore these constitutive acts further, considering landscapes as memory, identity, social order and transformation (see also Anschuetz *et al.* 2001).

In the methodological realm, other disjunctures have been recognized. In a seminal paper, Cherry acknowledged various 'truths' about the surface archaeological record and recognized operational problems at both the site and regional spatial scales:

(a) The necessarily coarse chronological framework, seldom more precise than a century and often much vaguer than that, which results from the use of aggregate collections of poorly preserved surface material, so that

(b) Maps of site distributions based on survey data to some degree (often unknown) must be take to represent 'palimpsests' of sites, not all of which were necessarily in use simultaneously (cf. Hamond 1978).

(c) The smearing and blending of surface finds, by natural or human agencies, means that small sites may often go unrecognized and sites of all sizes and types may be difficult to define accurately in spatial terms.

(d) Information about the internal organization and function of sites is usually very difficult to obtain. (Cherry 1983: 379).

Moreover, the surface archaeological record 'is likely to consist of *a virtually continuous spatial distribution of material over the landscape*, but a distribution extremely variable in density' (Cherry 1983: 395, emphasis in original; see also Dunnell and Dancey 1983: 272). The character of this distribution is owed to a number of factors, including human activities, by which artifacts and features are created and deposited; these include organized long-term behavior that results in some places on the landscape accumulating more artifacts more than others (Binford 1981a; Foley 1981; Cherry *et al.* 1991: 48); and subsequent human or natural activities which move or concentrate artifacts (Alcock *et al.* 1994; Cherry *et al.* 1991; Given *et*

al. 1999). Furthermore, the surface record is dynamic, even on an annual time scale: archaeological materials may appear and disappear as a result of surface geomorphological processes (Ammerman 1981; Dunnell 1988; 1992; Taylor 2000).

Related temporal issues have also surfaced. Plog (1974) labeled Cherry's (1983: 379) point b (above) the 'synchronic assumption.' (See also the 'contemporaneity problem' [Dewar 1991; Schacht 1984; and Wright, Ch. 9, this volume].) In addition, he noted that because of 'periodization' (Cherry's point a, above), change, when detected by archaeologists, would appear to be sudden and transformative, rather than gradual and evolutionary. Chapman (1999: 66, 69) adds two other distinctions. Noting our dependence on surface ceramics for dating, the 'tyranny of pot typology' assumes that when – archaeologically – we see a change in ceramics, then this indeed registers a change in behavior, and that moreover ceramics are a good indicator of change in general. This tyranny generates a concern for temporal boundaries, wherein archaeologists feel compelled to impose an order on what may be chaos. Second, when we find a larger-than-average number of sherds in a surface scatter, is this concentration the result of more intensive deposition, of higher site population (which has implications for interpretations of nucleation and dispersion in the Mediterranean), or of longer occupation (see also Sbonias 1999)?

At the site level, operational or measurement problems included the consistent and reliable definition of sites in the field, and their functional and temporal attribution. In an extended discussion, participants in a colloquium on archaeological survey in the Mediterranean area, held in the early 1980s, could not agree on an operational definition for site (Keller and Rupp 1983). Various non-site methods and *post hoc* assessments (Cherry *et al.* 1991; Gallant 1986) have brought internal consistency to the definition of sites. But revisiting this issue in 1994, Cherry (1994) called attention to the persistent problem of functional assignment. Finally, regarding settlement patterns, Hope Simpson (1983; 1984), echoing Taylor (1972), noted the difficulty of recovering an entire settlement pattern, because of differential burial and erosion and the obfuscation of the surface by building and vegetation (though see Terrenato, Ch. 4, this volume).

Bintliff (1999a: 21) has recognized much of the above as 'methodological hindrances' to which one must attend before demographic inferences can be sustained. But might not these 'methodological hindrances' in fact signal that something is amiss with the regional studies paradigm, which we dismiss at our peril? Other empirical indicators suggest this to be true. Firstly, Sutton (1994), in her analysis of contemporary Greek settlement systems, highlights two dynamics: that of the community as a coalition of a patrilines that is constantly being negotiated, and that of the geographic reference of these communities. Communities are 'of the moment,' as are the spatial loci of settlements occupied by communities. One could dismiss this settlement instability as a product of modernity, but we appreciate that some of the circumstances of modernity that affect settlement stability long have been felt in the Mediterranean (Cherry 1983: 376–77); indeed, this is one of its unique features as an arena for research on humans through time.

Secondly, when archaeological temporal indicators of finer resolution are available, they reveal much more settlement instability. For instance, radiocarbon dates from excavations on the Hungarian Plain indicate multiple, shifting occupations responsible for creating a surface expression that to the eye indicates continuous occupation by a large population (Chapman 1999). Similarly, comparing the record from Cycladic mortuary contexts with that from site survey, Whitelaw (2001) again finds evidence for settlement instability operating at a level not currently resolvable using survey ceramic data.

These many paradigmatic dissonances point toward a set of formational principles (*i.e.* a metaphysic) that underlie the conduct of surface archaeology, very different from the functional principles underpinning regional studies (Wandsnider and Holdaway 2003). Rather than surface variation being solely or even mostly attributable to functional settlement behaviors, the archaeological landscape is recognized fundamentally as a formational and taphonomic entity (Cherry 1983; Cherry *et al.* 1991; Dunnell 1992). Importantly, archaeological materials, being durable and substantive, are not of any 'one functional moment,' but potentially and actually of 'many functional moments.' To treat formational entities as functional units, whether empirical or conceptual, is to make them temporally flat (Bailey 1983) – *i.e.* as attributable to narrow spans of time, and thus, to deny their formational heritage (Rossignol and Wandsnider 1992; Murray, forthcoming). As Dunnell notes more generally:

> No one would contest that settlements, camps, villages, activity loci, and the like can produce what we see today as more or less dense clusters of artifacts, but there is no necessary relation between such ethnographic concepts, many of which are themselves suspicious as units of ethnographic observation, and high-density clusters of artifacts. Not all such clusters are the product of behaviors implied by the ethnographic categories, nor do all such ethnographic units leave high-density artifact clusters. Settlement, occupation, and activities are not agents of deposition; at best they are highly interpretive summaries of relations among such agents. Sites are not units of deposition; they are accretionary phenomena. The historical relatedness of their pieces is highly variable and not directly correlated with spatial proximity (Dunnell 1992: 27).

In that settlement pattern studies depend on flawed units of sites and settlements, they, too, must be suspected as equally flawed. Dewar and McBride (1992) add time to the equation and argue that we should conceptualize our surface deposits not in terms of settlement patterns, but as remnant settlement patterns (*i.e.* patterns due to the operation of settlement over the short-, medium-, and long-term). In this case, pattern reflects not function, but a history that includes both rare and common events. The distinction may seem semantic rather than substantive, but it betrays a fundamentally different metaphysical commitment.

That the settlement pattern vehicle is so entrenched in current archaeological practice is perhaps the consequence of two things. One is the 'tyranny of familiar materials' (after Plog 1974). We see things in the field that are interpretable using our well-tested common-sense (*sensu* Dunnell 1982). It takes little effort to extend experientially-informed ideas about pots and structures into the past. Likewise, Alcock (1993: 24–32) refers to a 'tyranny of historical documents,' similar to Wobst's (1978) 'tyranny of the ethnographic record.' These records appear so much richer than archaeological materials that they are also regarded as necessarily more accurate; and indeed they can be, but only for very narrow temporalities. Nevertheless, we feel compelled to hold archaeological materials to a 'quick-time' ethnographic standard, when in reality they inform on temporalities of different orders (Binford 1981a).

The second reason why settlement pattern studies are so attractive is that they sometimes seem to work. That is, when the historic period is considered, there appears to be some agreement between the two records, historical and settlement pattern (*e.g.* Athanassopoulos 1997; Bintliff 1991b). The question to be asked, then, is why this agreement exists, rather than to extend apparent agreement into the past.

In short, the regional studies/settlement pattern paradigm, like Icarus' wings, is simply not working. Its underpinning metaphysic and chronotype (or model of causation, agent, and temporality) have been queried and it has failed various methodological challenges. But, as discussed below, there is more than one way to solve the puzzle of the Labyrinth, and more than one way to fly.

Time Perspectivism

Since the mid-1980s, several changes have occurred in how Mediterranean landscapes are approached. For one, an orienting concept of 'landscape' has appeared, incorporating and reconfiguring that of the earlier 'regional studies' orientation (Anschuetz *et al.* 2001; Kardulias 1994; Knapp and Ashmore 1999). Concordant with the shift to a landscape perspective, another chronotype – this one multi-temporal, wherein causation is complex and not proximally attributable – has appeared in Mediterranean landscape archaeology. It takes several forms, from an antecedent in the *Annales* School (Barker 1995; Bintliff 1991b; 1999b; Cherry 1983; Knapp 1992), from Mc-Glade's (1995; 1999a, b) eco-dynamics, and from Bailey's (1981; 1983; 1987) time perspectivism.

Bintliff's (1991b; 1999b) adaptation of the *Annales*

construct is multi-temporal and distinguishes between structures (arising from almost imperceptible medium- and long-term processes) and the events of daily life constrained by those structures. In practice, archaeologists emphasize that archaeology is well-suited to seeing the material results of the operation of medium-term processes – Bintliff points to agrarian and political cycles – which may be further animated or elaborated upon by short-term data coming from texts when available. Furthermore, the longer-term structures that operate as contingent factors influencing shorter-term historical trajectories are exposed through comparative historical analysis. For example, he compares the emergence of the Greek city-states (in the context of no constraining political power) to the western European Medieval landscape (wherein powerful states and feudal lords did not allow the development of Greek-like city-states; Bintliff 1999b). Each historical trajectory is a contingent response to a biological structural constraint of how effective communication occurs as population size increases. In the case of Greek city-states, while population sizes were large, the development of a hierarchy meant that rather fewer members of that population were in fact effective communicators. In the case of western Medieval Europe, communication stress precipitated fissioning and the landscape became populated by small villages, with all villagers participating as effective communicators.

Bintliff's structural-contingent approach considers causation as hierarchical; processes operating over the longer-term frame those operating over the shorter-term. His approach is evolutionary, in the sense that different historical trajectories follow from different contingencies. For him, while proximate causation is complex, ultimate causation is attributed to demographic change and, in the example here, to the biological constraint of information processing. Perhaps because of the commitment to demographic change driving critical aspects of culture change, Bintliff feels compelled to discuss demographic entities, like settlements and villas. But his analysis depends not on settlements and villas *per se*, but on indicators of structural organization: the presence of a powerful hierarchy in the case of western Medieval Europe and its lack in the Greek case; the size and degree of integration of populations in each case; the degree to which all individuals or only some individuals are counted as effective communicators. In other words, he does not require fully developed functional entities, but indications that particular conditions hold (powerful hierarchy; integrated communities that are smaller or larger than communication threshold; many *vs.* few effective communicators).

In McGlade's (1995; 1999a; 1999b) eco-dynamics, a multi-temporal construct comes from an understanding of complex, nonlinear systems as applied in the New Ecology. For him, time is inherent in biological, economic, political and ideological processes. Space is socially constructed and time-dependent (as discussed by Sutton [1994] for ethnographically documented Greek villages). Nonlinear interactions have their own complex dynamic and these

may lead to the reorganization of the social-natural system; thus, small-scale events are important because they can be a source of major change. Landscape structure emerges as a result of the operation of social and natural processes with different temporalities. McGlade suggests we eschew concepts of adaptation and system stability for those of self-organization and system resilience, and proposes to map system resiliency in terms of bifurcation history. Yet, despite his example (McGlade 1999a), it remains unclear (to me, at least) how this is effected in the field or laboratory.

Time perspectivism refers to Bailey's (1981; 1983; 1987) biologically-based hierarchical scheme of time – *i.e.* of multiple, systemic-realm processes operating at a variety of rates. In a seminal paper, Bailey (1983) argued that 'past behaviour represents an amalgamation and intersection of many different processes operating over different time spans and defined by different time boundaries.' He elaborated:

> (a) that there are essentially only two scales of behavior – long-term and short-term; (b) that long-term processes are dominated by environmental and biological interactions, by relationships between genetics, demography, and economic exploitation of the natural environment, whereas short-term processes are dominated by social and psychological processes, by social rules and relationships and individual goals and motivations; [and] (c) that behavior at these different scales requires different sorts of explanations expressing varying degrees of proximate or ultimate causation and varying emphasis on historical (in terms of the past), functional (in terms of the present), or teleological (in terms of the future) causes (Bailey 1983: 180).

It can be noted that Murray (1999) amends Bailey's hierarchical construct, saying that it is likely that many processes, operating at many temporal scales, are at work.

Bailey (1983) thus explicitly addressed the role of causation and the nature of explanation. For those processes operating at different time-scales, they may be viewed as hierarchical and independent of each other, as for Bintliff (1999b). For those processes operating at similar or overlapping time scales, then interactions become important. Fletcher (1992; 1995), for example, focuses on various interacting medium-scale processes related to communication stress and architecture in communities.

Importantly, Bailey (1981:110) explicitly acknowledged the ontological nature of archaeological deposits, seeing them as being due to temporal and social aggregates of human behavior occurring over archaeological time (hundreds to thousands of years) rather than ethnographic time (one to ten years). Only in the last decade has this aspect of time perspectivism, also alluded to in Binford's (1981a) discussion of the 'Pompeii Premise,' been widely appreciated and actively pursued. That is, Knapp (1992), Murray (1997; 1999) and Smith (1992) have explicitly linked the time-averaged, formational nature of archaeological deposits to multi-temporal chronotypes, like time perspectivism and the *Annaliste* schemes.

The units necessary to undertake interpretation within a multi-temporal chronotype that acknowledges the formational nature of the archaeological landscape have not been well discussed. Sullivan (1978: 195) points to *traces*, alterations in the physical properties of an object (or relations between objects and a surface or the relations between surfaces) and their accumulation by artifacts and surfaces as their formational history unfolds. Dunnell (1992: 34) has specifically commented on this topic, emphasizing that artifacts and artifact attributes represent fundamental formational units, which may thus serve as empirical units. By extension, feature elements, the atoms of which features are made and remade, may also serve in this fundamental formational capacity.

Conceptual units, constructed from formational empirical units, are also under-discussed and under-developed. Barton *et al.* (1999; 2002) offer one treatment, giving substance to the conceptual unit of settlement intensity. This analysis relies on functional entities (tools), rather than formational entities. Settlement intensity is determined on the basis of the spatial and temporal distribution of tool densities across the landscape, prorated for length of time period.

Other conceptual tools are offered by Stern, who focuses on deposits at Olduvai Gorge and their potential information content (Stern 1993; 1994; 1995; Stern *et al.* 2002). Specifically, she notes that at Olduvai, the fluvial nature of those deposits constrains their minimum temporal resolution. In fluvial systems, deposits of cultural and faunal remains may represent primary accumulations, but also secondary or tertiary reworked accumulations flushed from a variety of older temporal planes from throughout the basin. In the case of the Okote member at Koobi Fora, Stern argues that these remains accumulated over a span of 60,000 to 70,000 years, with the temporal boundaries of the sedimentary envelope defined by a dateable ash lens (on the bottom) and a calcareous sandstone lens (on the top). Cultural and faunal remains, thus, are time-averaged over this span; finer temporal slices cannot be securely identified and patterning in them is attributable to multiple agents, including hominids, the ecological organization of communities in which hominids participated, taphonomic processes, fluvial events, and so on. Attempts to interpret cultural and faunal remains from the Okote member in terms of behavioral or even ecological processes, thus, are sadly misdirected. Since the minimum temporal resolution of this deposit is 60,000–70,000 years, only processes with frequency on the order of 150,000 years or longer can be addressed. Stern – echoing Binford (1981a) and Bailey (1981), and anticipating Murray and Chapman – is emphatic that archaeologists recognize archaeological deposits for what they are: time-averaged entities:

> The potential of the... archaeological record for enhancing our understanding of human behavioural

evolution derives not only from the long time span it offers but also from the time resolution of the archaeological materials being studied. However, this unique potential cannot be exploited unless researchers are willing to first acknowledge the singular character of the archaeological record and second to explore uncharted theoretical ground that provides a more appropriate understanding of these data as a record of human action (Stern 1993: 202).

A final aspect of time perspectivism pertains to measurement decisions. Three strategies for using archeological materials to learn about temporalized conditions appear to be available (Wandsnider, forthcoming). For one, we can elect to look at our landscape assemblages in terms of *point indicators* – functionally specific artifacts, features, assemblages or surfaces that originated at a particular (narrow) point in time, presumably reflecting and informing on prevailing conditions. Archaeologists routinely consider the temporal and spatial distribution of such point indicators to infer prevailing conditions. For example, Alcock (1993: 172–214) looks at the contextual development of the sacred landscape, as indicated in the spatial and temporal distribution of cult sites and sanctuaries. Crumley and Marquardt (1987) consider the find population of artifacts from different time periods with respect to different geostructural features, to make arguments for the role those features played in people's lives. Wells (1999) focuses on the population of graves and their contents with respect to the changing Roman frontier to infer the nature of tribal-Roman interaction.

Secondly, Chapman (1999) suggests focusing on changes in monuments, Plog (1979) considered changes in surface use, and Alcock (1993) looks at displaced cults and the 'symbolic violence' they may indicate. (See also contributions to *World Archaeology* [1998] on the theme 'The Past in the Past.') That is, these researchers rely on *material histories* that relate to and inform on changing conditions. People construct monuments that serve as lightning rods for further human activity, be it augmentive or destructive. For example, Chapman (1994) reports on the deliberate damage and destruction of more than 50% of the mosques in Bosnia and Hercegovina during the recent conflict there. Assuming that damaged buildings and building foundations persist, these will serve as material testimony both to their construction and to their damage and destruction. Of course, based on archaeological evidence alone, it may be difficult to establish that such massive destruction occurred during a very short interval of time; and the conditions about which these material histories inform us remain to be established through middle-range research and an elaboration of their contexts of discovery.

Finally, we can elect to look at the distinctive character of assemblages that accumulate over a span of time and, based on that character, infer prevailing conditions. For example, the relative ratio of thick-walled, long-lived storage vessels compared with fragile, short-lived, fine table vessels at a location informs possibly on function (that storage and dining activities occurred here), but also potentially on the length of occupation (*i.e.* occupation stability). Similarly, Foxhall (2000) discusses long-lived sanctuaries and the short-lived votive offerings they attracted. Qualitative, comparative analysis of an aggregate assemblage that includes short-lived and long-lived artifacts or features, or artifacts and features that are introduced into the archaeological record at very different rates, may inform as *span indicators* of prevailing conditions.

Time perspectivism encompasses the view that archaeological deposits are created by many different processes operating at many different tempos, similar to that discussed by Bintliff and McGlade. Some of those contributing processes and temporalities are knowable, as set by the temporal resolution of the assemblage. But time perspectivism also focuses analytic attention on the material implications of those processes, considering artifacts, features, and surfaces, or landscapes and their material histories. As such, time perspectivism embraces a formational metaphysic.

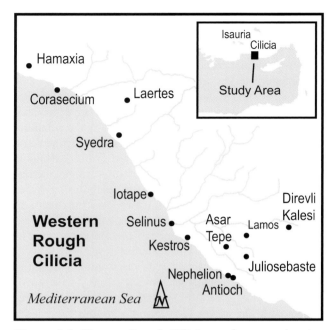

Figure 5.1 Western Rough Cilicia study area, showing cities known through historic and epigraphic texts.

WESTERN ROUGH CILICIA

Since 1998, the Rough Cilicia Project, based in southern Turkey (Figure 5.1), has been experimenting with the collection and integration of a variety of different historical and material data sources. Ultimately, we want to say something about how the 'local' Cilician population, likely derived from indigenous and Mediterranean-wide sources, interacted with various expanding cores through the Hellenistic and Roman periods. We have some Classical references to the area, but these are very geographically and temporally coarse; historical texts in the form of inscriptions are also available. Moreover, using pollen and macrobotanical data, we are presently building a paleoenvironmental sequence for the area. Here, I detail an approach that has evolved over the last four years of fieldwork for developing information on past processes and their temporalities as evidenced materially. Of course, the very interesting exercise upon which we are just now embarking is the integration of these various strands of evidence. The following brief discussion is organized in terms of *surfaces*, *features*, and *artifacts and artifact assemblages*.

Surfaces

Landscape surfaces are the dynamic and evolving stage on which people, past and present, organize themselves, plants and animals, and technology (McGlade 1995). But just as artifacts and features on the contemporary archaeological landscape can be considered palimpsests (*i.e.* lingering from remote points of introduction), the modern landscape is a mosaic of surfaces of different ages and subject to different geomorphological processes (Barton

et al. 2002; Bettis and Mandel 2002). This has several important implications. For one, surfaces of the time period of interest to us may be buried (van Andel and Runnels 1987), or they may be present but contain transported assemblages. Thus, much geoarchaeology over the last 20 years has focused on establishing chronostratigraphy and on understanding the formation of deposits (Mandel 2000; Stein 2000). Wells (2001) nicely describes laboratory and field techniques useful in defining morphostratigraphic (similarly appearing) and chronostratigraphic (chronologically sequenced) units for archaeological survey.

But a corollary observation deserves mention: the ages of contemporary surfaces in a study area will not all be the same. Furthermore, different surfaces represent different samples of time and taphonomy (Bettis and Mandel 2002). In other words, morpho-chronostratigraphic units can be further discriminated as *taphostratigraphic* units, *i.e.* surfaces exposed for about the same length of time and being affected by the same suite of surface processes. (Paleontologists argue that paleontological assemblages be compared among and between *isotaphonomic* units [Behrensmeyer 1991].) Moreover, as discussed above for time-averaged assemblages, different processes are accessible with different taphostratigraphic units with assemblages that are differentially time-averaged.

The distinction I am making is subtle but important. Wells (2001) and others (Barker 1995; Bintliff *et al.* 1999; van Andel and Runnels 1987) are interested in learning what fraction of the landscape might be eroded or buried, because of the commitment to a sited, synchronic, essentialist metaphysic. But if the landscape is approached as a formational phenomenon, then it is important to identify quasi-taphostratigraphic units, because they define the temporality of the processes and process temporalities that can be addressed archaeologically (Bettis and Mandel 2002). The completeness of a settlement pattern is not an issue.

In the Rough Cilicia study area, Sancar Ozaner (see Rauh and Wandsnider 2002) has developed a morpho-stratigraphic map that serves as the base from which to develop a taphostratigraphic map. The latter takes into account not only surface ages and geomorphological processes, but also where modern fields provide good surface exposure and the degree to which looting makes available subsurface remains in and around architecture.

Coarse-grained Phase 1 of the field survey was designed to locate all massive architecture. With this information, we are now looking to sample taphostratigraphic units of different ages, time spans, and surface process suites.

Features

Features can be considered both as point indicators and in terms of their material histories. For example, several Roman baths are preserved in the study area. Their presence advertises a commitment of some members of the local populace to participation in the pan-Mediterranean ethos of what it means to be a good Roman. But exactly when and for how long this sentiment held is something we are presently trying to establish.

Similarly, the fact that large architectural aggregates are found on hilltops which, through independent analysis, appear to be selected for their defensibility suggests that security issues were prominent at times in the Hellenistic past. That either the need for, or the mode of, defense was not constant is implied by the lack of fortification walls at the site of Asar Tepe (with much early Roman pottery; see Figure 5.1); but the fortification walls at the massive site of Lamos, with later Roman and Byzantine ceramics, suggest that security issues again became important. It is vital to note, however, that the siting of a settlement or the construction of a fortification wall has long-term material consequences that persist in time beyond the presence of initial condition, such as a threat. The walls at Lamos are intact today, yet defend against no one.

Other work on architecture attempts to address the construction history at specific locations. Consistency in building styles, ceramic sherds in the mortar, and the degree to which construction appears agglutinated (or not) assist in this respect. (With limited success, we have also experimented with lichenometric dating and limestone weathering as ways independently to date architectural elements.) Subsurface testing will prove critical in developing construction histories for particular places.

Artifacts and Artifact Assemblages

Our 2002 field methods involved sampling survey units in different taphostratigraphic strata. Units are the size of fields, or smaller areas (*c.* 50 x 50 m) are established as our analytic units. Within the unit, we walk transects about 5 m apart and flag artifacts along a 1-m wide transect. All temporally diagnostic sherds, as well as all rim, base, and handle sherds, are described (data entered in the field in hand-held computers) and mapped using hand-held GPS devices (yielding a spatial resolution of 20 m). An un-systematic walk through the unit is also carried out to locate other temporally interesting sherds. Description includes information on chronotype (*sensu* Gregory, forthcoming), form, size, temper, interior and exterior markings, and rim and base radius estimates. Sherds designated as interesting are photographed and sherds identified as potentially temporally diagnostic are returned to the field laboratory.

Needless to say, these field documentation procedures are very time-consuming. This investment is warranted by the information they yield beyond standard temporal information. For example, sherd size distributions inform on the formation history of the deposit. Small, battered sherds were found on the Haçimusa floodplain and represent a sample from throughout the Haçimusa catchment; large sherds, exposed by looters, occur amidst architecture; and intermediate-to-large sherds occur in cultivated fields, telling us about how the plowzone is being sampled.

More importantly, artifacts, by their presence, also communicate information about local conditions. The presence of an African Red Slip sherd indicates that some sort of interaction with North Africa occurred at some point in time contemporaneous with or after the production of such wares. We look to the population of sherds from exotic vessels to help establish the nature and timing of that interaction (Millett 2000). The presence of press- and grinding-stones likewise indicates something about mode of production.

The issue of how to report sherd finds is likewise being addressed (Orton 1993). Should one large storage vessel sherd be counted the same as one small fineware sherd? Should they instead be counted in terms of portions of vessels represented? Should they be inventoried in terms of vessel use-life or relative vessel cost or vessel adaptability? Because of the measurements made in the field, we can begin to pose questions of this kind. Ultimately, we plan to develop a series of ratio measures to use in characterizing the history of arbitrarily defined assemblages sampled from taphostratigraphic strata.

From his analysis of the Iron Age Princely grave at Hochdorf, Olivier (1999) offers a model for how to incorporate material histories into multi-temporal narratives about the past. These approaches – along with analyses of Cilician myths in the Luwian language of Anatolia, and textual and inscriptional evidence – will be used to approach a developmental history of the dynamic, socio-natural landscape of western Rough Cilicia.

METHODOLOGICAL ISSUES

While time perspectivism seated in a formational paradigm may seem another form of empiricism, that is only because our inferential tools are still under development. Nevertheless, their development is essential. The scientific positivism explicitly embraced by the early New Archaeology during the 1960s and 1970s has been supplanted by a mitigated objectivism (Wylie 1982; 1989a; 1989b; 1995), in which knowledge about the past is constituted in terms of independent and (to greater or lesser degrees) secure inferential tools – *i.e.* Binford's (1981b) middle-range theory. That this solution to the fundamental interpretive dilemma of archaeology has been widely recognized (*contra* Cunningham and Driessen, Ch. 8, this volume) is evident in work of a diverse group of researchers (*e.g.* Hodder 1999; Tilley 1994; Trigger 1995). Nevertheless, interpretation of processes with different tempos using material histories is hardly a simple matter. The same issues that concern archaeological inference in general apply here as well.

Middle-range theories and bodies of reference knowledge used to undergird inferences have typically been built using observations made during short-term actualistic studies. Bailey (1983) suggests that, of and by themselves, such studies cannot be extended to interpret the long-term, although what he appears to be critiquing is analogical reasoning supported by a substantive uniformitarianism (Gould 1965). Some instrumental knowledge (*i.e.* knowledge used for making inferences) is of this sort – *e.g.* portraits of the supposedly timeless Greek farmers used as analogs for earlier agriculturalists, as critiqued by Fotiadis (1995). But all instrumental knowledge need not be analogical or conventional. For example, understanding the placement of threshing floors on ridge crests, where strong breezes winnow away the chaff, is a type of knowledge that is timeless and spaceless (*i.e.* Gould's [1965] methodological uniformitarianism), but that must be used in contextually informed ways. In other words, understanding that chaff is lighter than wheat helps us understand that threshing floors occur on ridgetops, but not necessarily *which* ridgetops.

Murray (1997), however, is not convinced that observations made in the short-term can be used to understand medium-term processes. He, especially, seeks the Holy Grail of social theory of the medium- to long-term that has archaeological referents, suggesting four strategies for developing this theory:

1. Search for anomalous events or situations that challenge our understanding of the past (similar to a learning strategy offered by Richard Gould [1978]; and see Stephen Jay Gould [1986] for a discussion of the 'panda principle').
2. Establish performance limits for theory with regard to the empirical archaeological record.
3. Search for a body of theory that more directly speaks to the problem of palimpsest and scale than current

social theory does. In fact, many possible theoretical constructs are available in anthropology. But, Murray would emphasize that they must be refashioned to make them archaeologically accessible in a way that does not make ontologically unsupportable demands of the archaeological record. Fletcher (1992; 1995), for example, depends on communication theory to look at the flow of information in communities of various sizes and uses it to predict when settlements may approach a communicative crisis as population size increases. When these communication thresholds are approached, settlements may be reconfigured and Fletcher details expectations for what remodeling should look like.

4. Engage in fiction writing at different temporal scales.

Curiously, Murray does not suggest the strategy that has been offered up several times (Clarke 1973; Sabloff 1986; Smith 1992; Snodgrass 1985): to use the historical record to build inferential tools. It may be that such middle-range information exists, but has not been organized in a way that is presently useable. For example, when Roman baths are constructed, what set of social, economic, and political conditions do they imply? When they are destroyed by earthquakes and not rebuilt, what conditions might this indicate? What is the temporality of those conditions? Under what conditions are tombs remodeled into temples and temples into baths? Again, what are the social, political and temporal entailments of this material history? Textual records may allow the establishment of such conditions.

Another strategy was pioneered by Darwin (Gould 1986) – that is, the development of an historical hypothesis that specifies various material stages in the operation of a long-term process. Darwin proposed a hypothesis that linked fringeing, barrier and atoll coral reefs, using the historical thread of island subsidence: fringeing reefs first develop and, as the island subsides, grow into barrier reefs, and then atolls. Independent verification (drilling and dating) has since confirmed Darwin's hypothesis. Archaeologists engage in building historical hypotheses all the time – Flannery's (1972) argument about the development of hierarchies being a classic example. The part of the enterprise involving independent verification, however, is often lacking.

Middle-range theory for material histories is also required. It is relatively easy to recognize sequences in assemblage and feature development and modification (Sullivan 1992), but more difficult to draw substantive inferences about those sequences. Sequential modeling (Bleed 2001) embedded in a matrix of knowledge about temporal and spatial distributions of material culture may be useful here.

Finally, middle-range theory for span indicators is also required. Several authors (Binford 1977; Shiner *et al.* forthcoming) consider hunter-gatherer assemblage character as a result of the accumulation of artifacts with different use-lives and discard rates. For example, Binford

(1977) postulates that conditions of tool curation *vs.* those of expedient material use can be inferred on the basis of various ratios, such as broken to complete tools, cores to tools, and so forth. For these inferences to be supported, however, ethnographic or historical studies on artifact and feature use-lives are critical. Behavioral archaeologists have been investing in such information for decades.

CONCLUDING THOUGHTS

The currently embraced paradigm in Mediterranean surface archaeology of regional/settlement pattern studies – seated in flat-time functional metaphysic – is imperiled. As shown by Mediterranean archaeologists, that chronotype does not deal well with either complexity or history. And, attending methods, also as demonstrated by Mediterranean archaeologists, do not consistently accommodate or satisfactorily assign meaning to the varied archaeological landscape. But another formational metaphysic exists and seems better to comprehend the complex, historical world and to acknowledge landscape variation.

Rather than continuing the 'multiple paradigm disorder' practice of using intensive non-site methods, best suited to documenting taphonomic variation, in order to pursue flawed functional goals (settlement pattern reconstruction), it seems clear that a full acceptance of the formational metaphysic is in order. Time perspectivism, while still cohering, offers both an understanding of agent, causation, and temporality fundamentally wedded to an understanding of archaeological materials and how they may inform on human and natural processes operating at various temporal scales. Other concepts of time and causation, such as McGlade's eco-dynamics or Bintliff's structural-contingency approach, have the potential to speak to the historical complexity of the archaeological landscape, but must be refashioned to engage that landscape in archaeological terms.

Icarus, on steroids and with bird wings of titanium, will be bested by Poseidon or will meet some other lamentable fate. His sister, however, having studied the properties of flight and materials (and if she lives long enough) has the chance to make it out of the Labyrinth. But time is drawing short. In the Mediterranean Basin, agro-business and development have already remodeled extensive portions of the land surface. For this reason, it is essential that the issues of unit definition and of measurement be given top priority. By failing to give such issues the attention they require, survey (especially non-collection survey) not only risks squandering scarce resources, but also perpetuates a complacent charade of formational facts masquerading as functional knowledge.

ACKNOWLEDGMENTS

I extend my deep gratitude to Susan Alcock and John Cherry for making possible the very rich 'Side-by-Side Survey' conference and this resulting volume. I am also thankful to my Rough Cilician team-mates – Nicholas Rauh, Michael Hoff, Rhys Townsend, and Matthew Dillon – for their invitation to join the team and thereby think about these matters, which have consumed me for quite some time. Thanks to Simon Holdaway, who has helped in hatching many of the ideas presented here. I thank Peter Bleed, Christopher Dore, and Nicholas Rauh for their comments. I alone am responsible for errors of fact and reason. This material is based upon work supported by the National Science Foundation under Grant No. 0079951. Any opinions, findings, and conclusions or recommendations expressed in this material are those of the author and do not necessarily reflect the views of the National Science Foundation.

REFERENCES

Alcock, S. E. (1993) *Graecia Capta: The Landscapes of Roman Greece*. Cambridge, Cambridge University Press.

Alcock, S. E. (1994) Breaking up the Hellenistic world: survey and society. In I. Morris (ed.) *Classical Greece: Ancient Histories and Modern Archaeologies*: 171–90. Cambridge, Cambridge University Press.

Alcock, S. E., Cherry, J. F. and Davis, J. L. (1994) Intensive survey, agricultural practice and the Classical landscape of Greece. In I. Morris (ed.) *Classical Greece: Ancient Histories and Modern Archaeologies*: 137–70. Cambridge, Cambridge University Press.

Ammerman, A. J. (1981) Surveys and archaeological research. *Annual Review of Anthropology* 10: 63–88.

Anschuetz, K. F., Wilhusen, R. H. and Scheick, C. L. (2001) An archaeology of landscapes: perspectives and directions. *Journal of Archaeological Research* 9: 157–211.

Ashmore, W. and Knapp, A. B. (eds.) (1999) *Archaeologies of Landscape*. Walden, MA, Blackwell.

Athanassopoulos, E. (1997) Landscape archaeology of Medieval and pre-Modern Greece: the case of Nemea. In P. N. Kardulias and M. T. Shutes (eds.) *Aegean Strategies: Studies of Culture and Environment on the European Fringe*: 79–105. Lanham, Rowman and Littlefield.

Athanassopoulos, E. and Wandsnider, L. (forthcoming) Introduction: Mediterranean landscape archaeology past and present. In E. Athanassopoulos and L. Wandsnider (eds.) *Mediterranean Archaeological Landscapes: Current Issues. (*Under review.)

Bailey, G. (1981) Concepts, timescales and explanations in economic prehistory. In A. Sheridan and G. Bailey (eds.) *Economic Archaeology: Towards an Integration of Ecological and Social Approaches*. British Archaeological Report 96: 97–117. Oxford, British Archaeological Reports.

Bailey, G. N. (1983) Concepts of time in Quaternary prehistory. *Annual Review of Anthropology* 12: 165–92.

Bailey, G. (1987) Breaking the time barrier. *Archaeological Review from Cambridge* 6: 5–20.

Barker, G. (1995) *A Mediterranean Valley: Landscape Archaeology and Annales History in the Biferno Valley*. London, Leicester University Press.

Barker, G. and Mattingly, D. (series eds.) (1999; 2000) *The Archaeology of Mediterranean Landscapes*. Oxford, Oxbow Books.

Barton, C. M., Bernabeu, J., Aura, J. E. and Garcia, O. (1999)

Land-use dynamics and socioeconomic change: an example from the Polop Alto Valley. *American Antiquity* 64: 609–634.

Barton, C. M., Bernabeu, J., Aura, J. E., Garcia, O. and La Roca, N. (2002) Dynamic landscapes, artifact taphonomy, and landuse modeling in the Western Mediterranean. *Geoarchaeology* 17: 155–90.

Behrensmeyer, A. K. (1991) Terrestrial vertebrate accumulations. In P. A. Allison and D. E. G. Briggs (eds.) *Taphonomy: Releasing the Data Locked in the Fossil Record* (Vol. 9): 291–335. New York, Plenum Press.

Bender, J. and Wellbery, D. E. (1991) Introduction. In J. Bender and D. E. Wellbery (eds.) *Chronotypes: The Construction of Time*: 1–15. Stanford, Stanford University Press.

Bennet, J. and Galaty, M. (1997) Ancient Greece: recent developments in Aegean archaeology and regional studies. *Journal of Archaeological Research* 5: 75–120.

Bettis, E. A., III and Mandel R. E. (2002) The effects of temporal and spatial patterns of Holocene erosion and alluviation on the archaeological record of the Central and Eastern Great Plains, U.S.A. *Geoarchaeology* 17: 141–54.

Binford, L. R. (1977) Forty-seven trips: a case study in the character of archaeological formation process. In R. V. S. Wright (ed.) *Stone Tools as Cultural Markers*: 24–36. Canberra, Australian Institute of Aboriginal Studies.

Binford, L. R. (1981a) Behavioral archaeology and the 'Pompeii Premise'. *Journal of Anthropological Research* 37: 195–208.

Binford, L. R. (1981b) *Bones: Ancient Men and Modern Myths.* New York, Academic Press.

Bintliff, J. L. (ed.) (1991a) *The* Annales *School and Archaeology.* Leicester, Leicester University Press.

Bintliff, J. L. (1991b) The contribution of an *Annaliste*/structural history approach to archaeology. In J. L. Bintliff (ed.) *The* Annales *School and Archaeology*: 1–33. Leicester, Leicester University Press.

Bintliff, J. L. (1999a) Regional field surveys and population cycles. In J. L. Bintliff and K. Sbonias (eds.) *Reconstructing Past Population Trends in Mediterranean Europe (3000 BC – AD 1800)*: 21–33. Oxford, Oxbow Books.

Bintliff, J. L. (1999b) Structure, contingency, narrative, and timelessness. In J. L. Bintliff (ed.) *Structure and Contingency in the Evolution of Life, Human Evolution, as Human History*: 132–148. London, Leicester University Press.

Bintliff, J. L., Howard, P. and Snodgrass, A. (1999) The hidden landscapes of prehistoric Greece. *Journal of Mediterranean Archaeology* 12: 116–23.

Blanton, R. E. (2001) Mediterranean myopia (Review of G. Barker and D. Mattingly (series eds.) *The Archaeology of Mediterranean Landscapes*, Oxford, Oxbow Books 1999–2000). *Antiquity* 75 (289): 627–29.

Bleed, P. (2001) Trees or chains, links or branches: conceptual alternatives for consideration of stone tool production and other sequential activities. *Journal of Archaeological Method and Theory* 8: 101–127.

Braidwood, R. (1937) *Mounds in the Plain of Antioch: An Archaeological Survey.* Chicago, University of Chicago Oriental Institute Publication.

Chapman, J. (1994) Destruction of a common heritage: the archaeology of war in Croatia, Bosnia, and Hercegovina. *Antiquity* 68: 120–26.

Chapman, J. (1999) Archaeological proxy-data for demographic reconstructions: facts, factoids, or fiction? In J. L. Bintliff and K. Sbonias (eds.) *Reconstructing Past Population Trends in Mediterranean Europe (3000 BC – AD 1800)*: 65–76. Oxford, Oxbow Books.

Cherry, J. F. (1983) Frogs around the pond: perspectives on current archaeological survey projects in the Mediterranean region. In D. R. Keller and D. W. Rupp (eds.) *Archaeological Survey in*

the Mediterranean Area. BAR International Series 155: 375–416. Oxford, British Archaeological Reports.

Cherry, J. F. (1994) Regional survey in the Aegean: the 'New Wave' (and after). In P. N. Kardulias (ed.) *Beyond the Site: Regional Studies in the Aegean Area*: 91–112. Lanham, University Press of America.

Cherry, J. F., Davis, J. L. and Mantzourani, E. (1991) *Landscape Archaeology as Long-Term History: Northern Keos in the Cycladic Islands.* Monumenta Archaeologica 16. Los Angeles, Institute of Archaeology, University of California.

Clark, G. A. (1994) Migration as an explanatory concept in Paleolithic archaeology. *Journal of Archaeological Method and Theory* 1: 305–344.

Clarke, D. L. (1973) Archaeology and the loss of innocence. *Antiquity* 46: 6–18.

Crumley, C. L. and Marquardt, W. H. (eds.) (1987) *Regional Dynamics: Burgundian Landscapes in Historical Perspective.* San Diego, Academic Press.

Daniel, G. (1975) *A Hundred and Fifty Years of Archaeology.* London, Duckworth.

Dewar, R. E. (1991) Incorporating variation in occupation span in settlement-pattern analysis. *American Antiquity* 56: 604–620.

Dewar, R. E. and McBride, K. A. (1992) Remnant settlement patterns. In J. Rossignol and L. Wandsnider (eds.) *Space, Time, and Archaeological Landscapes*: 227–55. New York, Plenum Press.

Dunnell, R. C. (1982) Science, social science, and common sense: the agonizing dilemma of modern archaeology. *Journal of Anthropological Research* 38: 1–25.

Dunnell, R. C. (1988) Low-density archaeological records from plowed surfaces: some preliminary considerations. In L. Wandsnider and J. Ebert (eds.) *Issues in Archaeological Surface Survey: Meshing Method and Theory. American Archaeology* 7(1): 29–37. Ridgefield, CT, Atechiston Press.

Dunnell, R. C. (1992) The notion site. In J. Rossignol and L. Wandsnider (eds.) *Space, Time, and Archaeological Landscapes*: 21–41. New York, Plenum Press.

Dunnell, R. C. and Dancey, W. S. (1983) The siteless survey: a regional-scale data collection strategy. In M. B. Schiffer (ed.) *Advances in Archaeological Method and Theory*, Vol. 5: 267–87. New York, Academic Press.

Dyson, S. L. (1982) Archaeological survey in the Mediterranean basin: a review of recent research. *American Antiquity* 47: 87–98.

Fish, S. (1999) Conclusions: the settlement pattern concept from an Americanist perspective. In B. R. Billman and G. Feinman (eds.) *Settlement Pattern Studies in the Americas: Fifty Years since Virú*: 203–208. Washington, D.C., Smithsonian Institution Press.

Flannery, K. V. (1972) The cultural evolution of civilizations. *Annual Review of Ecology and Systematics* 3: 399–426.

Fletcher, R. (1992) Time perspectivism, *Annales*, and the potential of archaeology. In A. B. Knapp (ed.) *Archaeology,* Annales*, and Ethnohistory*: 35–50. Cambridge, Cambridge University Press.

Fletcher, R. (1995) *The Limits of Settlement Growth.* Cambridge, Cambridge University Press.

Foley, R. A. (1981) A model of regional archaeological structure. *Proceedings of the Prehistoric Society* 47: 1–17.

Fotiadis, M. (1995) Modernity and the past-still-present: politics of time in the birth of regional archaeological projects in Greece. *American Journal of Archaeology* 99: 59–78.

Foxhall, L. (2000) The running sands of time: archaeology and the short-term. *World Archaeology* 31: 484–98.

Gallant, T. W. (1986) 'Background noise' and site definition: a contribution to survey archaeology. *Journal of Field Archaeology* 13: 403–418.

Given, M., Knapp, A. B., Meyer, N., Gregory, T. E., Kassianidou, V., Noller, J., Wells, L., Urwin, N. and Wright, H. (1999) The Sydney Cyprus Survey Project: an interdisciplinary investigation of long-term change in North Central Troodos, Cyprus. *Journal of Field Archaeology* 26: 19–39.

Gould, R. A. (1978) Beyond analogy in ethnoarchaeology. In R. A. Gould (ed.) *Explorations in Ethnoarchaeology*: 249–93. Albuquerque, School of American Research, University of New Mexico Press.

Gould, S. J. (1965) Is uniformitarianism necessary? *American Journal of Science* 263: 223–228.

Gould, S. J. (1986) Evolution and the triumph of homology, or Why history matters. *American Scientist* 74: 60–69.

Gowlett, J. A. J. (1997) High definition archaeology: ideas and evaluation. *World Archaeology* 29: 152–71.

Gregory, T. E. (forthcoming) Less is better: the quality of ceramic evidence from archaeological survey and practical proposals for low-impact survey in a Mediterranean context. In E. Athanassopoulos and L. Wandsnider (eds.) *Mediterranean Archaeological Landscapes: Current Issues* (Under review.)

Hamond, F. W. (1978) The contribution of simulation to the study of archaeological processes. In I. Hodder (ed.) *Simulation Studies in Archaeology*: 1–9. Cambridge, Cambridge University Press.

Hodder, I. (1999) *The Archaeological Process: An Introduction*. Oxford, Blackwell.

Hope Simpson, R. (1983) The limitations of surface surveys. In D. R. Keller and D. W. Rupp (eds.) *Archaeological Survey in the Mediterranean Area*. BAR International Series 155: 45–49. Oxford, British Archaeological Reports.

Hope Simpson, R. (1984) The analysis of data from surface surveys. *Journal of Field Archaeology* 11: 115–17.

Jacobsen, T. W. (2000) Background of the Franchthi Project. In W. R. Farrand (ed.) *Depositional History of Franchthi Cave: Sediments, Stratigraphy, and Chronology*, Vol. 12: 1–10. Bloomington, Indiana University Press.

Kardulias, P. N. (1994) Paradigms of the past in Greek archaeology. In P. N. Kardulias (ed.) *Beyond the Site: Regional Studies in the Aegean Area*: 1–23. Lanham, University Press of America.

Kardulias, P. N., Gregory, T. E. and Sawmiller, J. (1995) Bronze Age and Late Antique exploitation of an islet in the Saronic Gulf, Greece. *Journal of Field Archaeology* 22: 3–21.

Keller, D. R. and Rupp, D. W. (eds.) (1983) *Archaeological Survey in the Mediterranean Area*. BAR International Series 155. Oxford, British Archaeological Reports.

Knapp, A. B. (1992) Archaeology and *Annales*: time, space, and change. In A. B. Knapp (ed.) *Archaeology,* Annales*, and Ethnohistory*: 1–21. Cambridge, Cambridge University Press.

Knapp, A. B. and Ashmore, W. (1999) Archaeological landscapes: constructed, conceptualized, ideational. In W. Ashmore and A. B. Knapp (eds.) *Archaeologies of Landscape*: 1–30. Walden, MA, Blackwell.

Kuhn, T. S. (1970) *The Structure of Scientific Revolutions*. Chicago, University of Chicago Press.

Mandel, R. E. (2000) Introduction. In R. E. Mandel (ed.) *Geoarchaeology in the Great Plains*: 3–9. Norman, University of Oklahoma Press.

McDonald, W. M. and Rapp, G. R., Jr (eds.) (1972) *The Minnesota Messenia Expedition: Reconstructing a Bronze Age Regional Enviornment*. Minneapolis, University of Minnesota Press.

McGlade, J. (1995) Archaeology and the eco-dynamics of human-modified landscapes. *Antiquity* 69: 113–32.

McGlade, J. (1999a) Archaeology and the evolution of cultural landscapes: towards an interdisciplinary research agenda. In P. J. Ucko and R. Layton (eds.) *The Archaeology and Anthropology of Landscape*: 458–82. London, Routledge.

McGlade, J. (1999b) The times of history: archaeology, narrative and non-linear causality. In T. Murray (ed.) *Time and Archaeology*: 141–63. London, Routledge.

Millett, M. (2000) Dating, quantifying and utilizing pottery assemblages from surface survey. In R. Francovich, H. Patterson and G. Barker (eds.) *Extracting Meaning from Ploughsoil Assemblages*: 53–59. Oxford, Oxbow Books.

Morris, I. (1994) Archaeologies of Greece. In I. Morris (ed.) *Classical Greece: Ancient Histories and Modern Archaeologies*: 8–48. Cambridge, Cambridge University Press.

Murray, T. (1997) Dynamic modelling and new social theory of the mid- to long-term. In S. E. van der Leeuw and J. McGlade (eds.) *Time, Process and Structured Transformation in Archaeology*: 449–63. London, Routledge.

Murray, T. (1999) A return to the 'Pompeii Premise'. In T. Murray (ed.) *Time and Archaeology*: 8–27. London, Routledge.

Murray, T. (forthcoming) Archbishop Ussher and archaeological time. In L. Vishnyatsky (ed.) *The Archaeologist as Detective: The Leo Klejn Festschrift*. St. Petersburg, Folio Press.

Olivier, L. (1999) The Hochdorf 'Princely' Grave and the question of the nature of archaeological funerary assemblages. In T. Murray (ed.) *Time and Archaeology*: 109–138. London, Routledge.

Orton, C. (1993) How many pots make five? An historical review of pottery quantification. *Archaeometry* 35: 169–84.

Parsons, J. R. (1972) Archaeological settlement patterns. *Annual Review of Anthropology* 1: 127–50.

Plog, F. (1974) *The Study of Prehistoric Change*. New York, Academic Press.

Plog, F. T. (1979) Alternative models of prehistoric change. In C. Renfrew and K. L. Cooke (eds.) *Transformations: Mathematical Approaches to Culture Change*: 221–36. New York, Academic Press.

Ramenofsky, A. F. and Steffen, A. (1998) Units as tools of measurement. In A. F. Ramenofsky and A. Steffen (eds.) *Unit Issues in Archaeology*: 3–17. Salt Lake City, University of Utah Press.

Rauh, N. K. and Wandsnider, L. (2002) Dağlik Kılıkıa Yüzey Araştirma Projesı: 2001 Sezonu Raporu. In *24th International Symposium of Excavations, Surveys and Archaeometry. 25–29 May 2002*, T.C. Kültür Bakanliği Antilar ve Müzeler Genel Müdürlüglü.

Renfrew, C. (1972) *The Emergence of Civilization: The Cyclades and the Aegean in the Third Millennium B.C.* London, Methuen.

Renfrew, C. (1980) The Great Tradition versus the Great Divide: archaeology as anthropology? *American Journal of Archaeology* 84: 287–98.

Rossignol, J. and Wandsnider, L. (eds.) (1992) *Space, Time, and Archaeological Landscapes*. New York, Plenum Press.

Sabloff, J. A. (1986) Interaction among Classic Maya polities: a preliminary examination. In C. Renfrew and J. F. Cherry (eds.) *Peer Polity Interaction and Socio-Political Change*: 109–116. New York, Cambridge University Press.

Sbonias, K. (1999) Investigating the interface between regional survey, historical demography, and paleodemography. In J. Bintliff and K. Sbonias (eds.) *Reconstructing Past Population Trends in Mediterranean Europe (3000 BC – AD 1800)*: 219–34. Oxford, Oxbow Books.

Schacht, R. M. (1984) The contemporaneity problem. *American Antiquity* 49: 678–95.

Shiner, J., Holdaway, S., Allen, H. and Fanning, P. (forthcoming) Understanding stone artifact assemblage variability in late Holocene contexts in Western New South Wales, Australia: Burkes Cave, Stud Creek and Fowlers Gap. In C. Clarkson and L. Lamb (eds.) *Rocking the Boat: New Approaches to Stone Artefact Reduction, Use and Classification in Australia*. BAR International Series. Oxford, Archaeopress.

Smith, M. E. (1992) Braudel's temporal rhythms and chronology theory in archaeology. In A. B. Knapp (ed.) *Archaeology,*

Annales, *and Ethnohistory*: 23–33. Cambridge, Cambridge University Press.

Snodgrass, A. M. (1985) The New Archaeology and the Classical archaeologist. *American Journal of Archaeology* 89: 31–37.

Stein, J. K. (2000) Stratigraphy and archaeological dating. In S. E. Nash (ed.) *It's About Time: A History of Archaeological Dating in North America*: 14–40. Salt Lake City, University of Utah Press.

Stern, N. (1993) The structure of the Lower Pleistocene archaeological record. *Current Anthropology* 34: 201–225.

Stern, N. (1994) The implications of time-averaging for reconstructing the land-use patterns of early tool-using hominids. *Journal of Human Evolution* 27: 89–105.

Stern, N. (1995) The 'Blue' Tuff locality at Koobi Fora in Northern Kenya: archaeological time and the record of past human behaviour. *The Artefact* 18: 49–59.

Stern, N., Porch, N. and McDougall, I. (2002) FxJj43: a window into a 1.5-million-year-old palaeolandscape in the Okote Member of the Koobi Fora Formation, Northern Kenya. *Geoarchaeology* 17(4): 349–92.

Sullivan, A. P. (1978) Inference and evidence in archaeology: a discussion of the conceptual problems. *Advances in Archaeological Method and Theory* 1: 183–222.

Sullivan, A. P. (1992) The role of theory in solving enduring archaeological problems. In L. Wandsnider (ed.) *Quandaries and Quests: Visions of Archaeology's Future* (Center for Archaeological Investigations, Occasional Paper 20): 239–53. Carbondale, IL, Center for Archaeological Investigations, Southern Illinois University at Carbondale.

Sutton, S. B. (1994) Settlement patterns, settlement perceptions: rethinking the Greek village. In P. N. Kardulias (ed.) *Beyond the Site: Regional Studies in the Aegean Area*: 313–37. Lanham, University Press of America.

Taylor, C. C. (1972) The study of settlement pattern in pre-Saxon Britain. In P. J. Ucko, R. Tringham and G. W. Dimbleby (eds.) *Man, Settlement and Urbanism*: 109–114. London, Duckworth.

Taylor, J. (2000) Cultural depositonal processes and post-depositional problems. In R. Francovich, H. Patterson and G. Barker (eds.) *Extracting Meaning from Ploughsoil Assemblages*: 16–26. Oxford, Oxbow Books.

Tilley, C. (1994) *A Phenomenology of Landscape: Places, Paths, and Monuments*. Oxford, Berg.

Trigger, B. G. (1967) Settlement archaeology – its goals and promise. *American Antiquity* 32: 149–160.

Trigger, B. G. (1989) *A History of Archaeological Thought*. Cambridge, Cambridge University Press.

Trigger, B. G. (1995) Expanding middle-range theory. *Antiquity* 69: 449–58.

van Andel, Tj. H. and Runnels, C. N. (1987) *Beyond the Acropolis: A Rural Greek Past*. Stanford, Stanford University Press.

Wandsnider, L. and Holdaway, S. (2003) The problem with palimpsests. Paper submitted to *American Antiquity*.

Wandsnider, L. (forthcoming) Artifact, landscape and temporality in eastern Mediterranean archaeological landscape studies. In E. Athanassopoulos and L. Wandsnider (eds.) *Mediterranean Archaeological Landscapes: Current Issues*. (Under review.)

Wells, L. E. (2001) A geomorphological approach to reconstructing settlement patterns based on surficial artifact distribution: replacing humans on the landscape. In P. Goldberg, V. T. Holliday and C. R. Ferring (eds.) *Earth Sciences and Archaeology*: 107–141. New York, Kluwer Academic/Plenum.

Wells, P. S. (1999) *The Barbarians Speak: How the Conquered Peoples Shaped the Roman Empire*. Princeton, Princeton University Press.

Whitelaw, T. (2001) Settlement instability and landscape degradation in the southern Aegean in the third millenium BC. In P. Halstead and C. Frederick (eds.) *Landscape and Land Use in Postglacial Greece*: 135–61. Sheffield, Sheffield Academic Press.

Wilkinson, T. J. (2000) Regional approaches to Mesopotamian archaeology: the contribution of archaeological surveys. *Journal of Archaeological Research* 8: 219–67.

Willey, G. R. (1953) *Prehistoric Settlement Patterns in the Virú Valley, Peru*. Washington D.C., Bureau of American Ethnology.

Willey, G. R. (1968) Settlement archaeology: an appraisal. In K. C. Chang (ed.) *Settlement Archaeology*: 208–226. Palo Alto, CA, National Press.

Wobst, H. M. (1978) The archaeo-ethnology of hunter-gatherers, or the tyranny of the ethnographic record in archaeology. *American Antiquity* 43: 303–309.

Wright, J. C., Cherry, J. F., Davis, J. L., Mantzourani, E., Sutton, S. B. and Sutton, R. F., Jr. (1990) The Nemea Valley Archaeological Project: a preliminary report. *Hesperia* 59: 579–659.

Wylie, A. (1982) An analogy by any other name is just as analogical: a commentary on the Gould-Watson dialogue. *Journal of Anthropological Archaeology* 1: 382–401.

Wylie, A. (1989a) Archaeological cables and tacking: the implications of practice for Bernstein's 'Options beyond objectivism and relativism'. *Philosophy of the Social Sciences* 19: 1–18.

Wylie, A. (1989b) The interpretive dilemma. In V. Pinsky and A. Wylie (eds.) *Critical Traditions in Contemporary Archaeology*: 18–27. Cambridge, Cambridge University Press.

Wylie, A. (1995) An expanded Behavioral Archaeology. In J. M. Skibo, W. H. Walker and A. E. Nielsen (eds.) *Expanding Archaeology*: 198–209. Salt Lake City, University of Utah Press.

COMPARATIVE STUDIES
IN THE MEDITERRANEAN

6. Side-by-Side and Back-to-Front: Exploring Intra-Regional Latitudinal and Longitudinal Comparability in Survey Data. Three Case Studies from Metaponto, Southern Italy

Stephen Thompson

INTRODUCTION

This paper presents three case studies that grew out of an effort to evaluate the accuracy of, and interpretive limits inherent to, a body of regional surface survey data collected by University of Texas field crews in the territory of colonial Greek Metaponto in southern Italy between 1981 and 1984. Like the field methods of many other Mediterranean surveys of two decades ago, those employed at Metaponto in the early 1980s (D'Annibale 1983a; 1983b) may appear rather naïve and uncomplicated by modern standards. The basic assumption underlying the project was that discoverable, empirical phenomena called archaeological sites are 'out there' in the landscape and that the goal of survey is to identify them and to collect information from their surfaces pertaining to their dates of occupation and to the types of human behavior that produced them. Despite its relatively lower levels of methodological sophistication compared to what since has come to characterize survey archaeology in the Mediterranean, the 1980s Metaponto survey was very successful – in fact, incredibly so – in realizing its basic goal of site identification. Between 1981 and 1984 the project recorded a total of 528 archaeological sites, the vast majority of which date broadly to the Greek colonial period (600 BC – 200 BC), in an area of just over 23 sq. km. Overall site densities of this magnitude are unknown elsewhere in the Mediterranean and, in fact, it was precisely this incomparable – indeed, ultimately nonreplicable – character of the 1980s Metaponto survey results that stimulated much of the work reported in this paper.

The three studies reported here were conceived within a broader effort to consolidate and publish the findings of the 1980s survey at Metaponto, and to incorporate the results of more recent survey (and resurvey) in the region carried out between 1999 and 2001. Of fundamental interest to each of these case studies are the ways in which the structure of the surface archaeological record is perceived, measured, and portrayed by survey archaeologists, both across space and through time. Following a brief overview of the local historical and geographical context of Meta-

ponto and a summary of the survey methods employed there twenty years ago and today, this paper moves through the set of three case studies, each of which explores a different aspect of what might generally be termed 'archaeological visibility'. The three 'visibility factors' considered below include vegetation, routine survey and artifact collection methods, and diachronic structural transformation of the archaeological record itself. Although the data used are specific to Metaponto, the analyses and conclusions reached should have implications for the broader discussion surrounding the reliability and comparability of survey data that continues to influence methodological and interpretive developments in Mediterranean archaeology.

HISTORICAL AND GEOGRAPHICAL SETTING

Colonial Greek Metaponto is located on the Ionian coast of southern Italy in the province of Basilicata (Figure 6.1). Achaean Greeks from the northeastern Peloponnese founded the colony in the later 7th century BC. Metaponto's colonial Greek neighbors were Taras (modern Taranto), located some 40 km to the northeast, and Siris/Heraclea (modern Policoro) approximately 20 km to the southwest. According to ancient sources, Metaponto's agricultural territory (*chora*) was bounded to the north and south by the Bradano and Cavone Rivers, respectively. The territory, encompassing an area of approximately 225 sq. km, is believed to have reached inland for a distance of some 15 km, with its interior limit being marked in the northwest by the settlement/*phrourion* at Cozzo Presepe.

Geologically, the Metapontino is located along the coastal facies of a broad northwest-trending fore-arc basin known as the *Fossa Bradanica* or Bradano Trough. To the north the Fossa Bradanica is bounded by the limestone plateau of the Apulian Murge that extends from the 'heel' of the Italian peninsula northwest along the Adriatic coast. To the south, the Calabrian foothills of the Apennine mountain chain form the margin of the Fossa Bradanica. The primary soils of the Metapontino consist of deep late

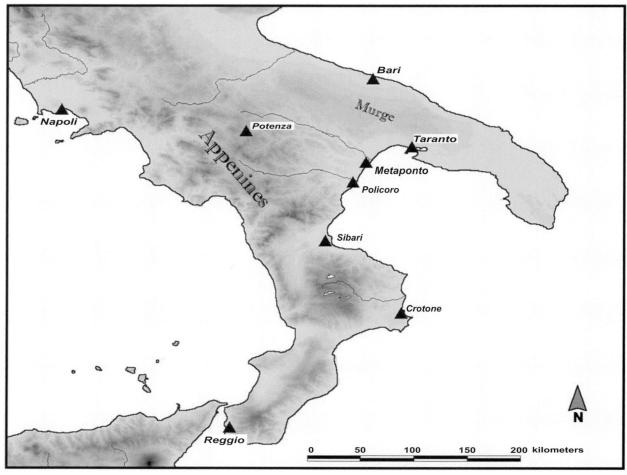

Figure 6.1 Map of southern Italy.

Pliocene-early Pleistocene marine sediments that were shed from the surrounding landforms when the basin was inundated by the sea. The sea gradually withdrew during the middle-late Pleistocene, leaving in its retreat a number of relic beach lines that parallel the modern coastline and that gently model this low-relief landscape into a series of step-like marine terraces that gradually rise from the modern coastline towards the interior. Relatively coarse sands and gravels, up to 30 m in depth, mantle these marine terraces. These coarser surface deposits in turn rest on extremely thick beds of dense Plio-Pleistocene clays. Although the Metapontino is extremely flat, its soils – particularly the deep clay 'bedrock' – are extremely susceptible to erosion, and the marine terraces have been deeply incised by both the major and minor streams that drain the region. Because of poor natural drainage due to the region's low relief and massive sedimentation towards the mouths of the major rivers, the Metapontino was very swampy and malarial, and little inhabited until extensive land reclamation efforts were implemented following World War II. This overview of regional geography and the geomorphological map of the Metapontino presented in Figure 6.2 draw heavily on the doctoral research of Jim Abbott (Abbott 1997).

TWENTY YEARS OF SURVEY IN THE METAPONTINO

In the summer of 2001, the Institute of Classical Archaeology (ICA) of the University of Texas at Austin carried out its eleventh season of intensive archaeological survey in the territory of colonial Greek Metaponto. Earlier campaigns included four years of survey in the early 1980s – focused on a 10 x 4 km transect between the Bradano and Basento Rivers and a ca. 2 sq. km zone at Pantanello, both in the northern half of the chora – followed by a season of selective site revisiting in 1990, all under the direction of Cesare D'Annibale (D'Annibale 1983a; 1983b). Between 1992 and 1994, the late Jon Morter directed three additional seasons of survey, this time between the Basento and Cavone Rivers to the south in an extension of the original study transect. In 1999, at the request of the Archaeological Superintendency of Basilicata, ICA surveyed a narrow swath of land between the Cavone and Bradano Rivers in advance of a major oil pipeline (Thompson 1999b). The 2000 and 2001 field seasons have included new survey coverage, in both the Bradano-Basento and Basento-Cavone transects, as well as a program of resurvey across

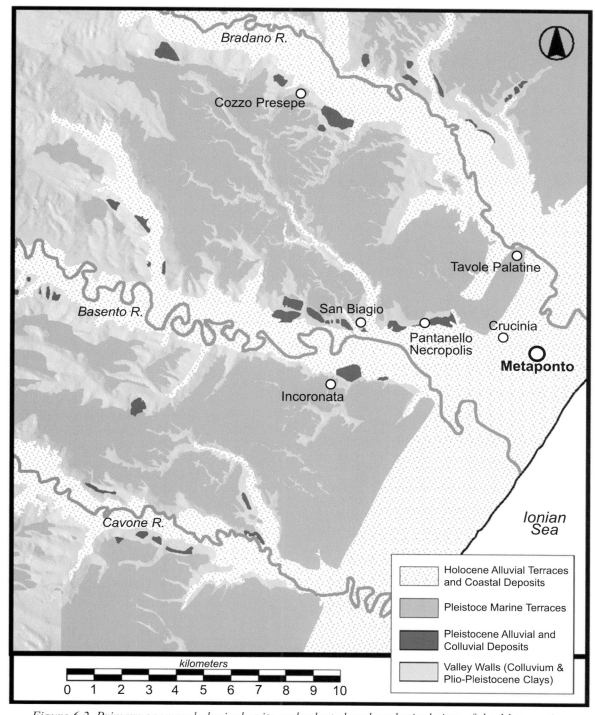

Figure 6.2 Primary geomorphological units and selected archaeological sites of the Metapontino.

selected portions of the area between the Bradano and Basento first covered during the early 1980s (Prieto 2000; 2001; Thompson 2002) (Figure 6.3).

The total area intensively surveyed by ICA crews now stands at 37 sq. km, with more than 800 sites documented. Approximately 63% (23.34 sq. km) of this total area was covered and 67% (n = 528) of all sites were discovered during the four seasons of the early 1980s survey campaign. The overall density of sites in the Metapontino – around 22 per sq. km – is truly staggering. Even more remarkable is the fact that roughly 80% of these sites are characterized by significant ancient Greek components. In fact, the density of ancient Greek sites alone (*c*. 17/sq. km) is typically five to ten times greater than the *total* site densities encountered by survey projects elsewhere in the Mediterranean basin (Figure 6.4). Furthermore, the sizes

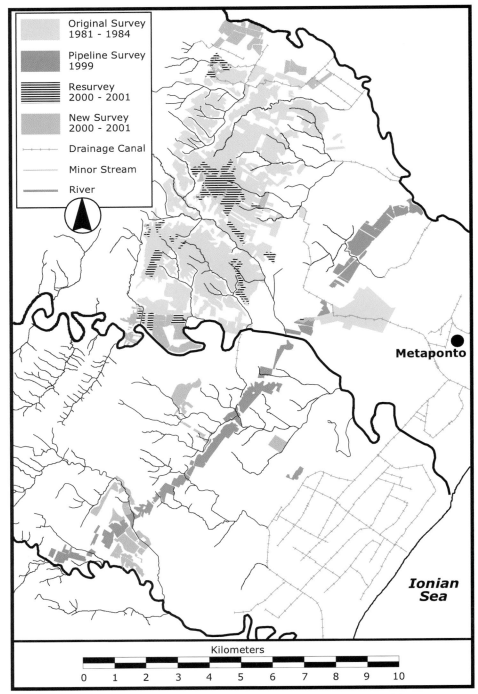

Figure 6.3 Survey zones in the Metapontino, 1981 – 2001.

of surface sites recorded in the Metapontino, at least during the early 1980s, are comparatively small, averaging just over 1200 sq. m. Only 15 (3%) of the more than 500 sites recorded during the early 1980s exceeded half a hectare in size, while only three sites have areas greater than one hectare.

Why the archaeological landscape of the Metapontino should appear to be so atypical in comparison to other Mediterranean regions known through intensive survey remains an open question with several possible answers.

The density of sites, particularly for the Greek colonial period, may be a function of the relatively large size of Metaponto's chora and the distance from the urban center (*c.* 5–15 km) of the ICA survey zones. Preservational factors, too, may play a role, as the Metapontino clearly appears to have been relatively little inhabited and exploited from the post-Greek period down to the middle of the 20th century, when land reclamation efforts reopened the region to an increasingly intensive agriculture. Finally, it might be argued that the high site counts recorded here,

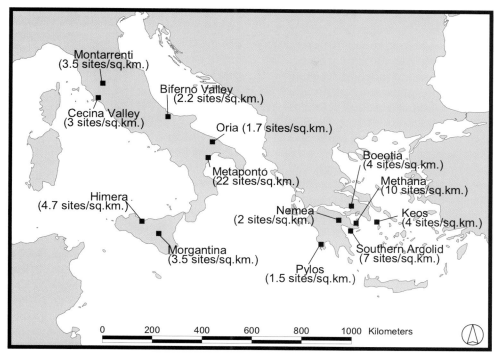

Figure 6.4 Overall site densities in Greece and Italy as recorded by a selection of survey projects (Oria: Yntema 1993; Biferno Valley: Barker 1995a; 1995b; Cecina Valley: Terrenato and Ammerman 1996; Montarrenti: Barker et al. 1986; Himera: Belvedere 1988; Morgantina: Thompson 1999a; Methana: Mee and Forbes 1997; Southern Argolid: Jameson et al. 1994; Keos: Cherry et al. 1991; Boeotia: Bintliff and Snodgrass 1985; Nemea Valley: Wright et al. 1990; Pylos: Davis et al. 1997).

particularly during the early 1980s, may in part derive from the survey methods used – that is, that the project was either extremely adept at recognizing surface sites or was simply much more liberal than most other surveys in assigning site status. Much in this paper, in fact, was first prompted by the realization that the results of the 1999 pipeline survey were quite different from those of the early 1980s. Albeit in an area of the Metapontine chora typically much closer to the coast than the 1980s study zone, the 1999 survey, while identifying sites of different periods in roughly the same proportions as the earlier survey, recorded an overall site density of only (!) 13 sites/sq. km and an average site size (5540 sq. m) nearly five times that recorded during the early 1980s. In order to evaluate the possibility that methodological factors may have contributed to this disparity of results, a more detailed examination of the survey methods employed (both then and now) and of the conditions of survey was begun, a process that in 2000 and 2001 led to a program of systematic resurvey of portions of the original study area.

SURVEY METHODS AT METAPONTO

... Then

The University of Texas survey during the early 1980s within the Bradano-Basento transect and the smaller study zone around ICA's long-standing excavation site at Pantanello can be described as both systematic and intensive. Although deliberately focused upon the 'heart' of the colonial Greek chora, the project aimed to collect material of all periods of human occupation (D'Annibale 1983a: 6) and to systematically cover all terrain within the designated study areas. The project relied on 10 m intervals between field walkers during routine survey. An explicit effort was made to survey land only under conditions of 'good' surface visibility, a requirement that necessitated long autumn field seasons in 1982 and 1983 to accommodate the local agricultural calendar. Occasionally, whenever low visibility fields could not be avoided, walker intervals may have been collapsed in an effort to compensate for the effects of reduced visibility (see Yntema 1993: 20 for a comparable practice within the contemporaneous Oria survey). Over the course of its four seasons the typically 5-person field crew attained an average rate of coverage of approximately 1 sq. km/week.

Despite systematic walking of all accessible land within the study zone, survey during the early 1980s focused exclusively upon site identification and collection. A map outlining the areas covered by the field crew was maintained daily during the course of the project. However, apart from this record of surveyed and unsurveyed fields, no additional field-by-field 'off-site' information was recorded. Thus, the primary documents of the project contain no records concerning variations in surface visibility, walker interval, artifact density, or contemporary land use across the study area. Furthermore, artifacts were never collected from non-site areas, nor was their presence (or absence) ever noted. The lack of these sorts of continuous 'background' data for the surveyed zone imposes certain interpretive limits upon the site data collected in the 1980s and, as is discussed in more detail below, helped to motivate the resurvey program.

Sites recorded during the 1980s survey campaign were typically defined on the basis of bounded concentrations of surface artifacts or, much less frequently, by the presence of rare single artifacts (such as fragments of tomb architecture) or landscape modifications (*in situ* architectural remains, soil discolorations, or quarrying cuts, for example). On-site collection of artifacts entailed total inspection of the surface of each site and focused upon chronologically and functionally diagnostic ceramic vessel fragments and feature sherds (rims, bases, handles). Small samples of roof tile as well as of common undecorated ceramic wares were also routinely collected. A standardized notebook entry was completed in the field for each site identified. On-site land use (though not surface visibility) was usually recorded for each site, as were relative measurements of both roof tile and sherd densities. The site records also contain brief descriptions of local topography and frequently mention materials present on the surface of sites that were not collected.

Each site located during the 1980s survey was indicated (by a point and site number) on a series of 1:10,000 topographic maps provided to the project by the Archaeological Superintendency of Basilicata. In the early 1990s, Jon Morter initiated computerization of many of the survey's primary documents and encouraged the development of a GIS database devoted to the project. Towards this end, a computerized data base of sites was compiled that included an x,y coordinate pair, site number, topographical setting and land use information, distances to nearest water and to urban Metaponto, and provisional occupation date(s) and functional class (*e.g.* 'domestic', 'funerary', 'manufacturing', 'unknown') for each of the 528 sites recorded.

... And now

Survey at Metaponto now uses a system of continuous, field-by-field recording of a range of information, including contemporary land use, type and density of vegetation, type of plowing or surface treatment, relative surface artifact density, walker interval, and crew composition. Chronologically and functionally diagnostic artifacts (all recognized and potentially datable artifacts and all feature sherds), as well as all lithics and fragments of prehistoric pottery, are collected for each surveyed field or 'plot'. As in earlier campaigns, routine survey uses a 10 m walker interval, although this occasionally is modified slightly to accommodate the planting intervals of orchards and other row crops. For the past two seasons, the survey has used a

portable differential Global Positioning System (GPS) receiver and data recorder to map all surveyed plot boundaries (to sub-meter accuracy). Spatial data collected with the GPS are downloaded daily and imported into the project's (ArcView 3.2) GIS database. Descriptive plot data and artifact information, recorded on standardized paper forms in the field, are entered daily into a series of spreadsheets and databases that can be imported or related to the GIS spatial database.

Although incorporating continuous, 'non-site' (Dunnell and Dancey 1983) or 'distributional' (Ebert 1992) recording methods, survey at Metaponto continues to recognize the existence of sites and to treat these areas more intensively than non-site areas. Assignment of site status follows closely the criteria forwarded by Plog *et al.* (1978: 389): 'A site is a discrete and potentially interpretable locus of cultural materials', in which 'discrete' means that the boundaries of the concentration are marked by at least relative changes in artifact density. Adherence to this definition does not imply that all sites so defined are *easily* interpretable, nor that all 'sited' human behavior results in clearly recognizable and enduring material signatures (Pettegrew 2001), nor that 'sites' are solely the consequences of past human agency (Dunnell 1992: 27), nor that sites constitute the totality of the archaeological record (Dunnell and Dancey 1983: 272; Ebert 1992), nor that artifacts or landscape features occurring between sites are fundamentally not interpretable.

Site identification continues to be based upon the recognition *during routine survey* of bounded concentrations of surface artifacts. All concentrations and potential concentrations of surface artifacts, however, are now routinely 'density mapped' both to confirm their existence and to document more completely and accurately their shape, size, structure, and location (Figure 6.5). Using 100 m tapes, hand-held compasses, and wire flags, a grid is quickly established across the site area and drawn on a scaled paper map. Armed with hand-held clickers and using the brightly colored flags to mark their lines, field crew systematically walk the site's surface, calling out artifact counts (for both roof tile and sherds) at measured intervals (typically every 5 or 10 m) which the crew leader records on the scaled site map. Density mapping typically extends in all directions until the concentration is fully defined, and in certain ambiguous cases may be extended to cover entire fields or groups of fields. Following completion of the density map, the field crew again uses the grid flags to orient themselves for close-interval walking (2 to 5 m) focused upon artifact collection. On-site collection criteria are the same as are used in off-site contexts (all potentially diagnostic pottery, all feature sherds, all lithics, and all prehistoric pottery). Before removing the flagged grid, real-world coordinates are collected using the GPS unit for a series of flagged points around the perimeter of the grid.

Computerization of site data entails entering the arbitrary coordinates and artifact counts of the field density

Figure 6.5 Site density mapping, Metaponto Survey 2001.

maps into spreadsheets. These tabular data files are imported into the project's GIS as point coverages, and the real-world GPS coordinates collected in the field at flagged points on the mapping grid are used to register each coverage to a standard coordinate system and map projection. Site boundaries and areas are determined from the digitized density maps, and other computerized descriptive information and artifact inventories compiled for each location are integrated with the GIS database.

WHY RESURVEY?

At least half of both of the 2000 and 2001 field seasons has been dedicated to resurveying, using the methods just described, areas first covered during the early 1980s. To date, ICA field crews have resurveyed approximately 2.5 sq. km, or roughly 10%, of the total 23.34 sq. km area originally covered in the early 1980s between the Bradano and Basento Rivers. The resurvey program has made a

concerted effort to revisit areas across the full range of geomorphological and topographical settings in the original survey transect and to reinvestigate areas of both high and low site densities as documented in the early 1980s. The primary goals motivating the resurvey project are summarized below. Following this brief synopsis, the three case studies are presented, two of which draw heavily on the resurvey data of the past two years.

To evaluate the regional distribution patterns of rare artifact classes

As discussed above, survey in the early 1980s relied on an exclusively site-centered strategy, and neither recorded nor collected information concerning surface artifacts (or land use or visibility conditions) in non-site areas. Consequently, the regional sample of collected surface artifacts, particularly as regards classes of relatively rare though widely dispersed materials, is potentially biased towards areas characterized by high densities of sites, which were typically identified on the basis of visually obtrusive concentrations of historic (Greek and post-Greek) ceramic and architectural remains. For example (and as is developed in more detail in the second case study below), although prehistoric remains were collected at 11% (n = 59) of all sites documented during the survey campaign of the early 1980s, more than three-quarters (n = 47) of these locations yielded fewer than 10 prehistoric artifacts, suggesting that the regional distribution of prehistoric remains in the Metapontino is characterized by relatively low density and spatially extensive scatters, rather than by clearly bounded, high density 'sites'. The possibility exists, then, that much of what we can see of the prehistoric landscape in the 1980s survey data reflects the locations of 'windows' opened only where higher density historic sites were recognized and surface artifacts were subsequently collected. Selective resurvey using off-site collection strategies helps to evaluate and to correct this potential bias in the data set from the 1980s.

To evaluate site location and site size data

In 1999, the Metaponto survey began to experiment with the use of portable differential GPS receivers during fieldwork and in 2000 procedures for their use were standardized and incorporated into routine field practices. GPS units are now used for the mapping of all survey unit boundaries, including off-site 'plots' as well as sites. Since 1999, the project has also routinely carried out artifact density mapping of all site surfaces to provide both a detailed record of each site surface as well as to ensure a consistent basis for the calculation of site size. Employing these methods during the resurvey program allows us to assess the reliability of the locations and sizes of sites recorded during earlier survey campaigns, in addition to providing an extremely detailed and spatially accurate 'document' (Wandsnider and Camilli 1992: 170, see also Shott 1995) against which future work can be compared (see also the section on 'longitudinal transformations', below).

To make additional artifact collections from identified sites

Occupation dates and interpretation of site function are based typically upon the analysis of collected artifact assemblages, sometimes in consideration with various aspects of site structure (*e.g.* size, artifact density) and location. Approximately 13% (n = 67) of the 528 sites identified between 1981 and 1984 were revisited in 1990, providing an important 'second look' at our sample of their artifact assemblages. Unfortunately, the 1990 revisiting program focused exclusively upon artifact collection, and made no records of field conditions (land use, visibility, etc.) or site structure (size, artifact density) at the time of re-collection. The 2000–2001 resurvey program has sought to increase the total number of sites revisited

and, for specific sites, to increase the number of revisits. Artifact collections made during revisits allow us more fully to evaluate the representativeness or *reliability* (following Wandsnider and Camilli 1992: 170–71) of the original site collections and to assess the extent to which interpretations of occupation date(s) and function(s) may be altered by repeated visits and collections.

To study longitudinal transformations of the surface record

Given the fairly rapid and continuous refinement of methods that has characterized Mediterranean survey archaeology over the past several decades, and given a still marked level of methodological idiosyncrasy even between contemporaneous surveys, data collected by different projects are not always directly or easily made comparable. The problem of data comparability between projects separated by both space and time, however, is not strictly a methodological one. Over the past 20 years, survey archaeologists increasingly have come to realize that the archaeological record, particularly as it is manifested or seen on the surface, is highly dynamic and in a constant state of transformation (see, for example, Ammerman and Feldman 1978; Ammerman 1985; 1995; Davis and Sutton 1995; Van der Velde 1987; Yorston *et al.* 1990; Boismier 1997). In addition to our methodological lenses, natural processes of decay and decomposition – as well as the effects of regionally and temporally variable geomorphological processes, natural vegetation regimes, and human land use practices – influence not only what we *can* see of the surface archaeological record, but also what *is* *there* to see. In light of the ever-intensifying character of agriculture in the Metapontino, a final objective of the resurvey project has been to document and describe potential diachronic changes to the structure and composition of the region's archaeological record over the past 20 years and to establish a more comprehensive regional data set or 'document' that can be used by future longitudinal studies.

CASE STUDY 1. VEGETATION, SURFACE VISIBILITY, AND VISIBILITY OF THE ARCHAEOLOGICAL RECORD

Among the assorted visibility variables that influence our ability to see the surface archaeological record, vegetation certainly must rank as one of the most widely acknowledged and recorded (see, for example, Schiffer *et al.* 1978: 6–7; Ammerman 1993: 369–71). In fact, there likely exists not a single contemporary survey project, at least in the Mediterranean basin, that does not diligently record the amount of vegetation present in each field. Indeed, the masking effects of vegetation are so obvious that, for many, vegetation and visibility would appear to be virtually synonymous quantities (*e.g.* Mee and Forbes 1997: 34).

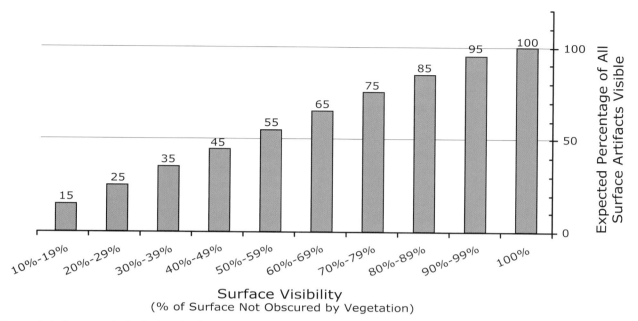

Figure 6.6 Bar graph depicting the linear relationship between vegetation and surface artifact visibility assumed by standard 'visibility correction equations' in which a 'corrected' count of surface artifacts in any given survey unit is equal to OA/V, where OA is the number of observed artifacts and V is that portion of the surface not obscured by vegetation at the time of survey.

While some projects have been content to simply overlay vegetation/surface visibility maps on those of artifact distributions and site locations and point towards general potential biases in the archaeological data due to visibility problems caused by dense vegetation (*e.g.* Cherry *et al.* 1991: 40–45), others go the further step of mathematically 'up-grading', 'correcting', or 'normalizing' survey data by applying a simple and intuitive multiplication formula that treats vegetation and visibility of the archaeological record as standing in a direct, inverse relationship to one another (*e.g.* Gaffney *et al.* 1991: 64; Whitelaw 1991: 202; Gillings and Sbonias 1999: 36; Bintliff *et al.* 1999: 153). This latter approach, typically tied to efforts to study surface artifact density as a continuously varying quantity across space, makes the perfectly commonsensical assumption (graphically depicted in Figure 6.6) that if vegetation obscures, for example, 50% of the ground surface in a given survey unit, then 50% fewer artifacts will be seen than would be the case were there no vegetation growing. Although some (*e.g.* Lock *et al.* 1999: 59–60; Schon 2000: 109; Given, Ch. 2, this volume) have cautioned against the appropriateness or accuracy of this 'correction formula', the general paucity of empirical evidence refuting the suitability of this highly instinctual approach seems to guarantee its continued use.

At Metaponto, one of the most glaring omissions among the records of the 1980s survey, at least to the modern eye, is the complete absence of any indication of visibility conditions during fieldwork. Although, as mentioned, a concerted effort was made by the project to survey fields only under 'good' visibility conditions, a quick browse through the photographic record of sites identified reveals considerable variation in both the types and amounts of vegetation present from site to site. Presumably, a similarly broad range of 'good' visibility conditions characterized the non-site areas surveyed in the early 1980s as well. Not only, then, is it impossible to explore the possible effects that variable surface visibility may have had upon site identification in the 1980s data, but direct comparisons of site artifact assemblages (presence/absence, density) would also appear to be compromised if we assume that variable visibility conditions during survey had a pronounced effect upon what was seen and collected from site to site.

Ideally, study of the relationship between vegetation and visibility of the archaeological record would rely on a highly controlled experiment, such as repeated survey of a series of fields with known, or at least constant, artifact content under a range of vegetation covers. At Metaponto such a study has begun; however, given the slight influence archaeologists have upon the plowing and planting practices of local farmers (as well as upon the growing habits of crops and weeds), development of an adequate data set remains a long way off. In the meantime, data collected at Metaponto between 1999 and 2001 can be used to explore the relationship between vegetation and visibility of the archaeological record. Indeed, if the assumed relationship between vegetation and visibility depicted in Figure 6.6 is an accurate one, it should be more or less apparent in our raw, uncorrected survey results.

Between 1999 and 2001 a total of 681 discrete units covering a representative range of geomorphological and topographical settings, and comprising a combined area

Visibility	Number of Survey Units	Area (sq. km)	Percentage of Total Area	Mean Artifact Density (per ha.)	Number of Sites Discovered	Mean Site Density (per sq. km)
100%	193	4.09	34%	110	53	13
90-99%	145	2.31	19%	126	33	14
80-89%	69	1.08	9%	67	11	10
70-79%	61	1.07	9%	97	17	16
60-69%	44	0.61	5%	94	14	23
50-59%	67	1.21	10%	83	20	16
40-49%	43	0.85	7%	83	12	14
30-39%	20	0.41	3%	21	2	5
20-29%	24	0.39	3%	57	3	8
10-19%	15	0.19	2%	42	4	21

Table 6.1 Total area surveyed and surface visibility conditions in the Metapontino, 1999–2001.

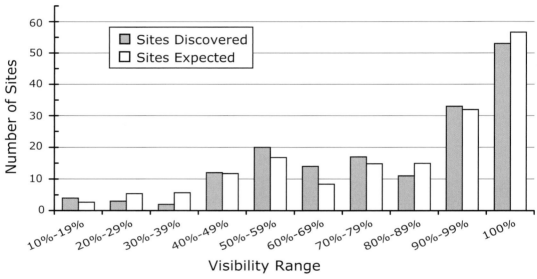

Figure 6.7 Numbers of sites discovered and expected according to the percentage of the total area surveyed (1999–2001) across the full range of surface visibility conditions.

of 12.21 sq. km, have been surveyed at Metaponto. As detailed in Table 6.1, visibility conditions (measured as that percentage of the ground surface not obscured by vegetation) are, on the whole, extremely good. Across more than half of the terrain surveyed vegetation covered 10% or less of the ground, while in only 15% of the surveyed area did vegetation obscure 50% or more of the surface. It is also the case that vegetation appears to have had little if any effect upon site discovery. In fact, mean site densities actually are higher towards the middle of the visibility range than at the top. Examination of the numbers of sites discovered, as compared to the numbers expected given the total area surveyed in each visibility range (Figure 6.7), further indicates that no relationship exists between vegetation density and site discovery, an impression further supported by a chi-square goodness-of-fit test. Indeed, Figure 6.7 indicates that site discovery was slightly less than expected under optimal (100%) visibility conditions and consistently higher than expected under more middling visibility conditions. The lower than

expected number of sites discovered towards the low end of the visibility range, particularly between 20% and 39% visibility, suggests that at this lowest level of visibility site identification may be compromised. This impression, however, cannot be supported statistically. The high mean site density value for the lowest visibility range (10% – 19%) is surprising but may be a product of the small sample size at this visibility level. At least in the extensively plowed lands of the Metapontino, then, there exists in these data little indication that site discovery has been adversely affected by vegetation. In general, the relationship between vegetation and site discovery apparent in the Metapontine data is quite similar to results reported for the Nemea Valley (Davis and Sutton 1995: 116, table 2) and Keos (Cherry *et al.* 1991: 45, figure 3.6) surveys, where site discovery also seems to have been compromised only when visibility conditions, as measured by vegetation, fell below 30%–40%.

Although the typically sparse vegetation of the Metapontino appears to have little effect upon the recognition

Visibility Range	Maximum Artifact Density (per ha.)	Minimum Artifact Density (per ha.)	Mean Artifact Density (per ha.)	Artifact Density Expressed as Percentage of Mean Density at 100% Visibility
100%	2057	0	110	100%
90-99%	3998	0	126	115%
80-89%	1034	0	67	61%
70-79%	1389	0	97	88%
60-69%	930	0	94	85%
50-59%	1755	0	83	75%
40-49%	738	0	83	75%
30-39%	133	0	21	19%
20-29%	931	0	57	52%
10-19%	353	0	42	38%

Table 6.2 Maximum, minimum, and mean artifact densities by surface visibility class for all areas surveyed (sites and off-site 'plots') in the Metapontino, 1999–2001.

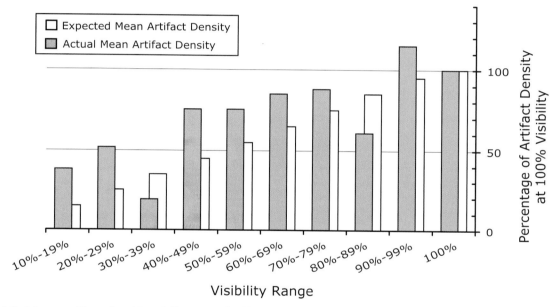

Figure 6.8 Mean artifact densities (all on- and off-site locations) for different visibility ranges, expressed as the percentage of mean artifact density at 100% visibility.

of discrete concentrations of surface artifacts, such identifications are, of course, made relative to the surrounding 'background'. Thus, these results indicate primarily that variations in vegetation alone are not sufficiently great so as to obscure relative increases and decreases in the density of surface artifacts. The question remains as to what extent vegetation affects surface artifact density in an *absolute* way and whether or not the one-to-one relationship between vegetation and artifact density depicted in Figure 6.6 is an accurate one.

Table 6.2 presents absolute maximum, minimum, and mean surface artifact densities across the full range of visibility classes for all on-site and off-site areas surveyed between 1999 and 2001. These density values, it should be stressed, are based upon the assemblage of *collected* artifacts rather than on the full complement of artifacts seen during survey, as survey at Metaponto does not

routinely count all artifacts seen in off-site areas. Calculation of the artifact density figures in Table 6.2 begins with the assumption that each field walker visually monitors a two-meter-wide swath during survey. Thus, the sample fraction (or that percentage of the ground surface subjected to visual inspection) is equal to 2/WI, in which WI represents the interval (in meters) between walkers. Multiplying the sample fraction by the total area of each survey unit (a value calculated by the project's GIS software) provides a measure of sample size, or the absolute area of terrain subjected to direct visual inspection, for each unit. Dividing the number of artifacts collected in each unit by the unit's sample size, in turn, provides an absolute surface artifact density. This density value, of course, represents an average value for the entire unit. To construct Table 6.2, all of the units (both sites and off-site 'plots') have been grouped according to visibility range and the artifact

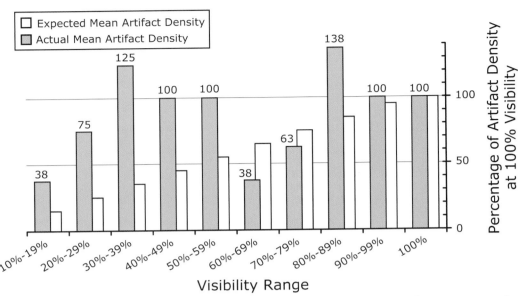

Figure 6.9 Mean off-site artifact densities for different visibility ranges, expressed as the percentage of mean artifact density at 100%.

densities of all the units within a given visibility range have been used to calculate a mean density value for that range.

As is apparent in Table 6.2, both maximum and mean artifact densities exhibit the general trend of increasing from low to high visibility conditions. Plotting the mean values for each visibility class as the percentage of mean artifact density at 100% visibility (Figure 6.8) allows for a direct comparison with the idealized vegetation/artifact density relationship depicted in Figure 6.6. Although once again these data show a general tendency for surface artifact densities to increase as vegetative cover decreases, there is nonetheless a significant, consistent divergence from the idealized one-to-one relationship. A chi-square goodness-of-fit test confirms the disparity between the real and idealized density data sets and provides the further insight that, in general, deviation from the 'expected' idealized mean increases as surface visibility decreases. In addition to recorded artifact densities being consistently higher than expected, also evident in Figure 6.8 is the surprising detail that the mean surface artifact density of survey units in the 90%–99% visibility range actually exceeds that of the 'optimal' 100% visibility class.

Breaking the surface artifact density data down into off-site (Figure 6.9) and on-site groups (Figure 6.10) is a useful next step given that on-site artifact densities can be expected, virtually by definition, to be higher than those in off-site areas. In fact, the similarity between Figures 6.8 (all units) and 6.10 (on-site) and their disparity with Figure 6.9 (off-site) clearly indicates that much of the structure observed in the combined dataset derives from the high values of on-site artifact densities. Both the on- and off-site density datasets show, however, mean artifact densities in the 80%–99% visibility ranges as high as or

higher than the mean at 100% visibility. Furthermore, with very few exceptions, recorded artifact densities from both on-site and off-site contexts are consistently higher than the one-to-one intuitive model would predict. On face value, these data could be used to argue that the general increase in measured artifact density as visibility decreases is a consequence of only sites with progressively higher artifact densities being recognizable as vegetation increases. Yet the earlier analysis, demonstrating no relationship between site identification and vegetation, argues strongly against such an interpretation.

Although relatively few comparative data are available, a very similar pattern of higher than expected artifact densities at lower visibility ranges also appears to exist in the raw artifact density data presented by the Keos project (Cherry *et al.* 1991: 45, figures 5a, 5b), while in the Nemea Valley (Cherry *et al.* 1988; Wright *et al.* 1990) there is some indication, at least for Neolithic artifacts, that recovery rates are greater under conditions of more dense vegetation (Davis and Sutton 1995: 114, table 1). In Gallant's Lefkas-Pronnoi survey (1986: 410–11, figure 7, table 1) it also appears that the highest artifact densities were consistently recorded between 40% and 80% surface visibility. The need to substantiate these data with those from more controlled experiments notwithstanding, the pattern that emerges from the above analysis is, upon reflection, perhaps not so surprising. Despite the tendency among many survey projects to conflate vegetation and visibility, the potential of numerous other 'field' factors to obscure the surface archaeological record has long been recognized. Lighting conditions provide a widely acknowledged example, as does the time since the last cleansing rains and the relative contrast between the visual patterning of 'background' surface soils and those of the common

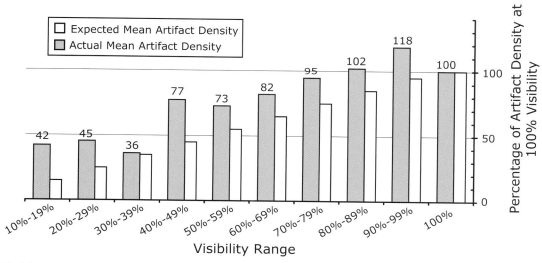

Figure 6.10 Mean on-site artifact densities for different visibility ranges, expressed as the percentage of mean artifact density at 100%.

sorts of surface artifacts that survey aims to 'foreground'. Variables such as these, however, are invariably more difficult to treat quantitatively than is the case with vegetation. Furthermore, none of these particular variables can be reasonably expected to have exerted the sort of *systematic* influence apparent in the raw artifact density data *vis-à-vis* vegetation presented above. Indeed, given the consistently higher artifact densities than are predicted by the current intuitive understanding of vegetation's masking effects, it would appear that our data have been systematically structured, at least in part, by the effects of some other visibility (enhancing) factor. That is, concomitant with the increase in vegetation, some other (perhaps related) variable operates to partially ameliorate the obvious masking effects of plants.

The interpretation proposed here is that in recording the amount of vegetation present on a given agricultural surface, we are also providing a proxy measure for the amount of weathering to which that surface has been exposed. In the heavily farmed and plowed lands of the Metapontino, 100% visibility (or 0% vegetation) is virtually synonymous with freshly plowed fields. Following plowing, both sown crops and/or weeds gradually establish themselves, while at the same time the plowed surface weathers, settles, and deflates. One of the consequences of this weathering process is that, in addition to being cleaned by rain and irrigation water, artifacts previously lying at least partially *within* the surface gradually come to rest *on* the surface and typically with their broadest (and most visible) dimension being the most fully exposed. Although weeds and crops may grow up through this surface, partially obscuring it in the process, weathering of the surface soils actually acts to make the archaeological component of these soils more visible. Of course, as

vegetation becomes increasingly dense, the advantages in terms of artifact recognition are progressively diminished. In addition, it is probably the case that the maximum potential of weathering to expose artifacts at or in the surface is probably reached relatively rapidly. This interpretation is perfectly consistent with the above finding that surface artifact densities in the 80%–99% visibility class are higher on average than at 100% surface visibility, strongly suggesting that this slightly weathered but relatively unvegetated state provides more optimal conditions for surface survey than does the complete absence of vegetation. In fact, equating 'optimal' visibility (of the archaeological record) with approximately 90% surface visibility, as measured by the amount of vegetation present, goes some way towards minimizing the disparity observed above between actual and expected artifact densities.

In the absence of additional supporting data, both from Metaponto and from other comparable regions, proposing a revamped formula for the 'up-grading' of survey data is obviously premature. To the extent that the same general pattern concerning vegetation and visibility can be extended backwards in time – and there is really no sound reason for assuming that it cannot – these findings do help to clarify the interpretive potential and limits of the 1980s Metaponto survey data. Thus, especially given the efforts made twenty years ago to survey only under 'good' visibility conditions, there exist few grounds for assuming that the survey failed to recognize sites because of relatively poor surface visibility conditions – a fact further borne out by the resurvey results presented below. Additionally, in terms of the uncertainties outlined at the beginning of this section regarding the analytic comparison of site assemblages from the 1980s Metaponto survey, this study also suggests that the contribution made by variable on-site visibility conditions to inter-site variations in collected artifact assemblages is probably less severe than might have previously been assumed. Finally, this second conclusion may prove relevant to other efforts elsewhere in Mediterranean to incorporate the results of additional earlier, less rigorous surveys into broader, pan-regional syntheses.

CASE STUDY 2. THE INFLUENCE OF METHODOLOGICAL FACTORS UPON THE VISIBILITY AND APPEARANCE OF THE PREHISTORIC RECORD IN THE METAPONTINO

As detailed above, archaeological survey in the Metapontino during the early 1980s employed an exclusively site-centered approach. Although non-site areas were routinely walked at 10m intervals, surface artifacts were only collected from within the confines of areas of relatively high artifact concentration defined as sites. The preceding discussion concluded that surface vegetation probably had little effect upon site recognition and that vegetation probably did little to distort or obscure patterning in the surface archaeological record. This case study, in contrast, considers the effects of survey and collection methods upon the visibility of, and structure seen in, the surface record, at least in terms of one relatively rare artifact class.

In the vast majority of cases, the more than 500 archaeological surface sites recorded during the 1980s survey are characterized by assemblages dominated by historic (Greek and later) roof tile and ceramic vessel fragments. Only in extremely few cases is it clear that sites were defined solely, or even in part, on the basis of recognized concentrations of prehistoric artifacts; in only 15 cases do prehistoric artifacts constitute 25% or more of the total assemblage collected at a site, while in only eight cases do they account for more that half of the total collected assemblage. Furthermore, the 'on-site' density of prehistoric artifacts is typically extremely low; in only four cases does it rise to more than 1 artifact/10 sq. m, while the highest prehistoric artifact density among the sites defined during the 1980s reaches only 5 artifacts/10 sq. m. These low density values for prehistoric materials are made more significant by the fact that while historical era artifacts were sampled (for diagnostics and feature sherds), all pieces of prehistoric pottery and flaked stone seen (on-site) were collected. Thus, even though prehistoric materials were recognized and collected at more than 10% of all sites documented during the early 1980s, very few of these locations can be accurately described as prehistoric 'sites', at least in the traditional sense of this term. Rather, the evidence available strongly suggests that the distribution of prehistoric materials in the region is characterized by a diffuse, very low density 'carpet' of material remains. Whether or not this distributional pattern is but a highly degraded remnant of a once far more obvious or obtrusive mosaic of artifact-rich prehistoric sites (*e.g.* Bintliff *et al.* 1999) is not really

the issue here. Although such may well be the case, of more fundamental concern is the extent to which the recording and recovery methods used during the 1980s were sufficient to accurately capture patterning among those prehistoric remains that have survived and were recognized and collected during survey in the region. In point of fact, very strong patterning exists among the prehistoric find spots recorded during the early 1980s survey. The question considered in this case study is the extent to which this patterning can be considered an accurate, albeit partial, reflection of prehistoric discard patterns, as opposed to an artifact or unintended consequence of the site-centered survey methodology employed and of the distributional patterning characteristic of the large corpus of historical era sites documented by the project.

As illustrated in Figure 6.11, find spots of prehistoric artifacts recovered during the early 1980s show a very strong tendency to cluster on and near the margins of the relatively steep valley walls that separate the higher Pleistocene marine terraces and the incised stream valleys in the study area. Although nearly half (11.33 sq. km) of the total area surveyed during the 1980s lies more than 100 m from a valley wall and roughly 20% of the surveyed area lies more than 300 m from a valley wall, only 13 (22%) of the 59 prehistoric find spots were made more than 100 m and only two find spots are more than 300 m from a valley wall. At face value, this evidence suggests that prehistoric settlement in, and exploitation of, the region was heavily focused upon this rather specific topographical setting. This distributional pattern of prehistoric find spots, however, closely mirrors that of historical era sites, which also are most heavily concentrated on and near valley walls, a pattern that has been explained by the fact that natural springs and seeps are heavily concentrated at such (exposed) contact points between the coarser surface soils and the underlying, dense and relatively impermeable Plio-Pleistocene clays (Carter 1980: 6; see also Abbott 1997: 29–30). Furthermore, find spots of prehistoric artifacts are even more strongly weighted towards those more restricted areas in which above average densities of historical era sites were encountered (Figure 6.12). While it may well be that prehistoric and historical era settlement in the region were conditioned by much the same factors, the possibility cannot be ruled out that the distributional patterns seen among the prehistoric remains collected by the site-centered survey of the early 1980s may be a product of the methods employed. The resurvey campaign of 2000–2001, using off-site collection methods, was intended, in part, to evaluate this possibility.

Resurvey over the past two seasons of approximately 2.5 sq. km of land originally covered in the early 1980s routinely collected all recognizable prehistoric artifacts both from on-site and off-site contexts. During the course of these two resurvey seasons 167 items of prehistoric pottery and flaked stone were collected from 39 discrete survey units comprised of 25 off-site 'plots' and 14 sites. As was the case during the original 1980s survey, most of

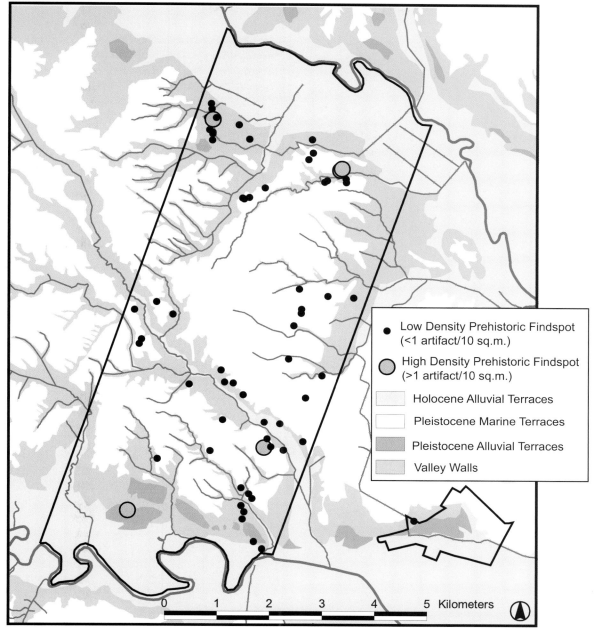

Figure 6.11 All prehistoric findspots (ceramic and flaked stone) of the early 1980s survey.

these find spots produced very few prehistoric artifacts and always at very low overall densities. Among the 14 sites at which prehistoric artifacts were found, only four lie more than 100 m and two more than 200 m from a valley wall. Of the 25 off-site contexts that produced at least one prehistoric artifact, more than 70% (n = 18) lie wholly or primarily within 100 m of a valley wall. Furthermore, of the 87 off-site units located more than 100 m of a valley wall (which together comprise 60% [1.5 sq. km] of the 2.5 sq. km resurveyed area), only seven units (8%) yielded prehistoric remains.

These results strongly suggest that, although the locations of prehistoric find spots recorded during the 1980s

may be skewed towards localized areas characterized by above average (historical era) site densities, the more general pattern of prehistoric artifacts clustering along the valley margins is a true characteristic of the archaeological record and not an artifact of the site-centered recovery methods employed during this earlier work. That the site-based collection strategy of the 1980s should have been so successful in picking up this patterning among diffusely distributed prehistoric remains is likely a consequence both of the strength of the patterning and of the very large number of sites identified, and hence of 'samples' or 'windows' opened to the surviving prehistoric landscape, across a wide range of topographical settings.

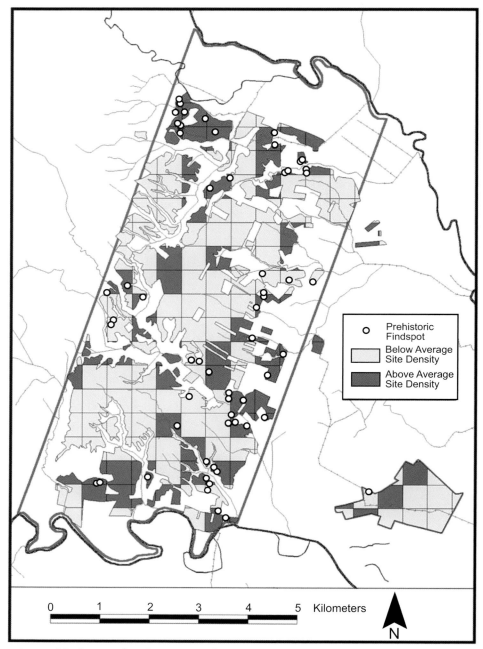

Figure 6.12 Locations of findspots of prehistoric artifacts (1981–1984) in relationship to areas of above- and below-average overall site densities.

CASE STUDY 3. BACK-TO-FRONT COMPARABILITY: DOCUMENTING DIACHRONIC TRANSFORMATIONS OF THE SURFACE ARCHAE-OLOGICAL RECORD IN THE METAPONTINO

As mentioned, over the course of the 2000 and 2001 field seasons, ICA field crews have resurveyed approximately 10% (2.5 sq. km) of the area originally covered in the early 1980s between the Bradano and Basento Rivers (Figure 6.3). A concerted effort has been made to revisit areas across the full range of geomorphological and topographical settings in the original survey transect and to

reinvestigate areas of both high and low site densities as documented in the early 1980s. In addition to gathering new types of information deemed necessary for the interpretation of existing data, as exemplified by the preceding case study, another basic objective of the resurvey program was to confirm the extremely high overall site densities (and small site sizes) documented by this earlier work.

In terms of site numbers, the results of the resurvey program are extremely surprising. According to the original survey records, there should have been 81 sites located within the 2.5 sq. km thus far resurveyed. Resurvey, however, has located only 45 (55%) of these sites. Despite

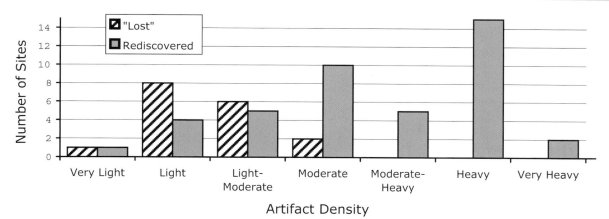

Artifact Density

Figure 6.13 Relationship between on-site surface artifact density (early 1980s) and site rediscovery (2000–2001).

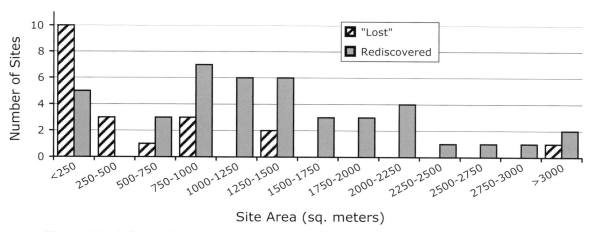

Site Area (sq. meters)

Figure 6.14 Relationship between site size (early 1980s) and site rediscovery (2000–2001).

the evidence presented in the first case study indicating little, if any, relationship between vegetation and site discovery, it nevertheless seemed prudent to exclude from this analysis (for the time being) unrediscovered sites in cases of extremely low (< 40%) surface visibility. Thus, of the 36 unrelocated or 'lost' sites, 15 have been discounted from the following analysis as resurvey in these locations was under relatively poor surface visibility conditions. Nonetheless, we are left with 21, or roughly one-quarter, of the original 81 sites that we were unable to relocate – even though surface visibility during resurvey was good and very intensive techniques, including density mapping of entire fields, were often employed. So what has happened to the 'lost' sites?

Almost without exception, the 'lost' sites are characterized in the original records as having relatively small overall areas and relatively low artifact densities (Figures 6.13–14). It is unlikely that the original survey simply imagined or invented these relatively more ephemeral 'sites of low obtrusiveness' (Schiffer *et al.* 1978), particularly at such a high rate, given that other sites of comparable structure were rediscovered and others continue to be discovered by new survey elsewhere in the Metapontino.

On the other hand, it is widely acknowledged that plow zone sites with artifact densities below a certain minimum threshold can appear to 'turn off and on' with each new plowing due solely to the operation of stochastic mixing and movement of artifacts in an actively plowed soil (Ammerman and Feldman 1978: 734–40; Ammerman 1985; 1993: 370–71; Barker 1991: 5; Shott 1995: 476, 481; Terrenato and Ammerman 1996: 93–95). So, were these sites 'lost' or, more accurately, unrecognized because of such uncontrollable plow zone processes? While this explanation may account for some of the loss, it cannot account for all because – by the same logic – resurvey should have discovered an additional 20 or so new sites not recognized during the early 1980s for precisely the same reasons. Thus far, however, the resurvey program has recorded only three sites not identified 20 years ago.

Currently, the most parsimonious explanation for the loss of roughly one-quarter of the sites recorded in the Metapontino 20 years ago is that they have truly disappeared, or have been so transformed as to no longer be recognizable as bounded concentrations of surface artifacts. Following widespread drainage and land reclamation in the Metapontino in the post-World War II years, the

LANDUSE CHANGE (early 1980s – 2000/2001)	Rediscovered Sites		"Lost" Sites		% of all "Lost" Sites
	#	%	#	%	
Vineyard ---- Fruit Trees	7	47%	8	53%	
Vineyard ---- Plowed	0	0%	2	100%	
Vineyard ---- Market Vegetables	1	50%	1	50%	
Vineyard ---- Citrus	1	100%	0	0%	
Vineyard ---- Grain	1	100%	0	0%	
total **Vineyards** ---- Other Crops	**10**	**48%**	**11**	**52%**	**52%**
Plowed ---- **Vineyard**	4	57%	3	43%	
Tomato ---- **Vineyard**	0	0%	1	100%	
Grain ---- **Vineyard**	2	100%	0	0%	
Nut Trees ---- **Vineyard**	1	100%	0	0%	
total Other Crops ---- **Vineyards**	**7**	**64%**	**4**	**36%**	**19%**
Vineyard ---- **Vineyard**	**0**	**0%**	**2**	**100%**	**10%**
Market Vegetables ---- Citrus	1	33%	2	67%	
Olive ---- Olive	3	75%	1	25%	
Plowed ---- Uncultivated	2	67%	1	33%	
Olive ---- Fruit Trees	6	100%	0	0%	
Plowed ---- Olive	4	100%	0	0%	
Grain --- Fruit Trees	3	100%	0	0%	
Grain ---- Citrus	2	100%	0	0%	
Fallow ---- Grain	1	100%	0	0%	
Grain --- Market Vegetables	1	100%	0	0%	
Olive ---- Olive, Citrus, Fruit Trees	1	100%	0	0%	
Plowed ---- Fruit Trees	1	100%	0	0%	
Plowed ---- Market Vegetables	1	100%	0	0%	
Plowed ---- Olive, Fruit Trees	1	100%	0	0%	
Plowed ---- Plowed	1	100%	0	0%	
total Other Crops ---- Other Crops	**28**	**88%**	**4**	**12%**	**19%**
Totals	45		21		

Table 6.3 Relationship between land use change and surface site loss in the Metapontino, 1981–2001.

region has been characterized by an increasingly intensive agriculture tied closely to national and international markets. Furthermore, agricultural practices are highly dynamic, such that what crops are being grown and, more importantly, what is being grown where, changes quite rapidly. Examination of the relationship between local land use changes over the past 20 years and the locations of the 'lost' sites (Table 6.3) indicates, first, that with 84% of all sites, whether rediscovered or not, the specific crops in these locations are different from what they were 20 years ago. A second and more specific observation is that roughly 80% of all 'lost' sites are associated with areas where grapes either were or now are being grown. The proportion of lost sites in lands associated with vineyards, in fact, is more than twice as high as would be expected were there no relationship between these two variables.

Over the past two seasons, the Metaponto survey project has also been collecting information on the various techniques of soil preparation and routine maintenance practiced in the Metapontino, and has discovered a remarkable variation according to crop and to the cropping strategies of individual farmers. Significantly, preparation of land for grape growing throughout the Metapontino is very intensive and intrusive, and routinely entails working the surface (either through deep plowing or mechanical turning) to depths ranging between 80 and 120 cm to break up and aerate the subsoil for the deeply rooted vines. Once planted, however, maintenance of vineyard soils entails only intermittent shallow harrowing of the surface to inhibit weeds. For various reasons – including the long-term viability of vines, changing preferences for different grape stocks, and the desire to install new and more efficient irrigation and arbor systems – local farmers report that the average vineyard has a roughly 20 year lifespan before the land will be completely reworked, even if grapes are to be replanted. Fruit-bearing tree crops, which to a lesser degree also are associated with site loss in the Metapontino, are both longer lived than vineyards and typically do not entail such pronounced surface preparations.

As Shott (1995: 477) and others have noted, arable agriculture represents a 'decidedly mixed blessing' for survey archaeology. On the one hand, through the removal of vegetation and the disturbance of buried strata, plowing does much to expose the archaeological record across often vast expanses of the landscape. On the other hand, it is important to recognize that in exposing the record, 'Cultivation practices [also] fundamentally alter and, in some ways, degrade the structure of the archaeological record' (Shott 1995: 477). Existing studies of the effects of contemporary land use practices upon the surface record report that crops requiring more pronounced surface preparation can actually *increase* the visibility of the record by bringing fresh artifacts to the surface, often for the first time since their deposition (Ammerman 1993: 370; 1995; Davis and Sutton 1995). In a related vein, it was clearly recognized during the original ICA survey of the early 1980s that the recent introduction of deep plowing to the Metapontino was an extremely important agent in exposing the region's archaeological record (J. C. Carter and C. D'Annibale, pers. comm.). Indeed, the proximity in time of the original survey to these changes to routine plowing practices, combined with a remarkably high level of preservation of the rural archaeological record due ultimately to long-standing natural drainage problems and malaria in the region, undoubtedly contributed to the pronounced richness of the record documented in the early 1980s. The results of the resurvey project, however, suggest that such gains in visibility due to the introduction of more intensive and intrusive agricultural practices may be relatively short-lived. The tide, in fact, appears to have turned for the Metapontino's rural record and at least one aspect of its overall structure has been transformed significantly from that evident 20 years ago. Although our results indicate that thus far the relatively more ephemeral rural sites have been most severely affected, some indications are also emerging that these processes are beginning to impact more substantial sites in the region. For example, although a relatively dense 'background' was recorded in 2001 throughout much of the (new) vineyard where Site 401 was identified in 1982, extensive density mapping in 2001 was unable to detect a discrete, bounded concentration of surface remains associated with this site, which is among the largest (and richest) of the sites identified in the early 1980s and the one large-site 'outlier' in Figure 6.14. Elsewhere, in areas that have been mechanically leveled we have encountered a number of oddly shaped linear and curvilinear 'sites' that clearly are the result of the bulldozing of artifact-rich surface soils.

Should a resurvey project continue at Metaponto, it will likely document other systematic transformations – beyond simple loss – to the more substantial and enduring elements of the regional record. The pronounced disparity in site sizes recorded in the 1980s and in recent work remains a specific point of interest. Although the increase in the areal extent of surface sites over time is very likely another consequence of ongoing plowing (Van der Velde 1987; Yorston *et al.* 1990; Boismier 1997: 234–37; Orton 2000: 63), uncertainties about how (and how accurately) site sizes were measured during the 1980s campaign currently inhibit a more detailed understanding of this process.

CONCLUSION

Throughout these three case studies, I have tried to stress that what we see of the archaeological record is conditioned strongly by a variety of visibility factors. Although I make no claim that the case studies presented here exhaust the full range of these factors, they do perhaps illustrate the several broad classes into which such variables can be grouped. In addition, the case studies suggest the differing scales, both spatial and temporal, at which visibility factors can exert their influences. The first two visibility factors considered above, vegetation and survey/collection methodology, fit neatly into what Shennan (1985) has termed 'field' and 'walker' effects, respectively. The above analysis of the relationship between vegetation and surface artifact density strongly suggests that the effects of this ubiquitous field effect upon visibility (*of the surface archaeological record*) are considerably less pronounced than many have assumed and, furthermore, that the application of intuitive 'correction formulae' to compensate for the presumed masking effects of vegetation obscure rather than clarify perception of the archaeological record. Although the relationship between vegetation, surface weathering, and archaeological visibility presented here may not be wholly accurate nor universally applicable, it is only through such explorations of actual data that we can reliably probe the veracity of our existing, largely subjective assumptions about visibility (Shennan 1985: 44). Similarly, it is only through direct comparison of the results produced by differing survey methods across the same landscape, as in the second case study, that a full understanding of the limitations and potentials of differing methods will be achieved. Again, at least in terms of the specific issue addressed above, the masking or distorting effects of method appear to have been less pronounced than initially assumed.

Although the first two studies presented here fit more or less comfortably within existing understandings of visibility – that is, that visibility factors are largely independent filters or lenses that we must see through (and with) to see the archaeological record – the third study makes the point that even though what we see of the record is, at least in part, a reflection of the physical properties of the record, the physical structure and composition of the archaeological record are in a constant state of change. As Ammerman (1981: 82) has noted, survey takes place in space *and* time, and 'time itself introduces relativity into the relationship between the observer and that which is observed ... [such that] ... on any given day in the field, time's arrow conditions in part what we will happen to see'. Over the short-term, plow zone dynamics, in conjunction with other surface effects such as vegetation and weathering, appear to have a somewhat cyclical – or 'on again, off again' – effect upon the visibility of the record. Consequently any given synchronic 'snapshot' provided by survey must be regarded as necessarily partial, as well as potentially biased or systematically distorted in this partiality. In addition to reminding us that the archaeological record is both a finite and highly vulnerable element of the Earth's surface, the Metaponto resurvey project foregrounds this fundamental historicity of the archaeological record, while also clearly revealing that over the longer-term directional changes to the structure and composition of the record are likely. As the interest in synthesizing the results of geographically and temporally disparate survey projects gains momentum in Mediterranean archaeology, we are reminded that, in addition to past human behavior and contemporary discovery and recording methods, our data may also be structured by locally and temporally variable transformational histories.

ACKNOWLEDGEMENTS

The fieldwork and analysis presented here were carried out during my employment at the Institute of Classical Archaeology, University of Texas at Austin and were supported by a generous grant from the Packard Humanities Institute. I thank ICA's director, Professor Joseph Carter, for permission to publish this work, and the Packard Humanities Institute for its strong support of archaeology at Metaponto.

REFERENCES

Abbott, J. T. (1997) *Late Quaternary Alluviation and Soil Erosion in Southern Italy.* Unpublished Ph.D. Dissertation, Department of Geography, University of Texas at Austin.

Ammerman, A. J. (1981) Survey and archaeological research. *Annual Review of Anthropology* 10: 63–88.

Ammerman, A. J. (1985) Plow-zone experiments in Calabria, Italy. *Journal of Field Archaeology* 12: 33–40.

Ammerman, A. J. (1993) Review of J. F. Cherry *et al., Landscape Archaeology as Long-Term History: Northern Keos in the Cycladic Islands* (Los Angeles: UCLA Institute of Archaeology, 1991). *Journal of Field Archaeology* 20: 367–72.

Ammerman, A. J. (1995) The dynamics of modern land use and the Acconia survey. *Journal of Mediterranean Archaeology* 8: 77–92.

Ammerman, A. J. and Feldman, M. W. (1978) Replicated collection of site surfaces. *American Antiquity* 43: 734–40.

Barker, G. (1991) Approaches to survey. In G. Barker and J. A. Lloyd (eds.) *Roman Landscapes: Archaeological Survey in the Mediterranean Region.* BSR Archaeological Monographs 2: 1–9. London, British School at Rome.

Barker, G. (1995a) *A Mediterranean Valley: Landscape Archaeology and Annales History in the Biferno Valley.* London, Leicester University Press.

Barker, G. (1995b) *The Biferno Valley Survey: The Archaeological and Geomorphological Record.* London, Leicester University Press.

Barker, G., Coccia, C., Jones, D. A. and Sitzia. J. (1986) Integrating archaeological, environmental, and historical data. *Archeologia Medievale* 13: 291–320.

Belvedere, O. (1988) Metodologia e finalità della ricerca. In V. Alliata, O. Belvedere, A. Cantoni, G. Cusimano, P. Marescalchi and S. Vassallo (eds.) *Himera III. Prospezione Archeologica nel Territorio:* 3–16. Rome, Bretschneider.

Bintliff, J. L. and Snodgrass, A. M. (1985) The Cambridge/Bradford Boeotian Expedition: the first four years. *Journal of Field Archaeology* 12: 123–61.

Bintliff, J., Howard, P. and Snodgrass, A. (1999) The hidden landscape of prehistoric Greece. *Journal of Mediterranean Archaeology* 12: 139–68.

Boismier, W. A. (1997) *Modeling the Effects of Tillage Processes on Artefact Distributions in the Ploughzone: A Simulation Study of Tillage-Induced Pattern Formation.* British Archaeological Reports, British Series 259. Oxford, Archaeopress.

Carter, J. C. (1980) *Excavations in the Territory, Metaponto, 1980.* Annual Report of the Institute of Classical Archaeology, University of Texas at Austin.

Cherry, J. F., Davis, J. L., Demitrack, A., Mantzourani, E., Strasser, T. F. and Talalay, L. E. (1988) Archaeological survey in an artifact-rich landscape: a Middle Neolithic example from Nemea, Greece. *American Journal of Archaeology* 92: 159–76.

Cherry, J. F, Davis, J. L. and Mantzourani, E. (1991) Data evaluation and off-site distributions. In J. F. Cherry, J. L. Davis, and E. Manzourani, *Landscape Archaeology as Long-Term History: Northern Keos in the Cycladic Islands.* Monumenta Archaeologica 16: 37–54. Los Angeles, UCLA Institute of Archaeology.

D'Annibale, C. (1983a) Field survey of the Chora of Metaponto, 1981–82. In J. C. Carter (ed.) *The Territory of Metaponto 1981–1982.* Annual Report of the Institute of Classical Archaeology, University of Texas at Austin: 5–9. Austin, Institute of Classical Archaeology.

D'Annibale, C. (1983b) Field survey of the chora of Metaponto. In D. R. Keller and D. W. Rupp (ed.) *Archaeological Survey in the Mediterranean Area.* BAR International Series 155: 191–93. Oxford, British Archaeological Reports

Davis, J. L., Alcock, S. E., Bennet, J., Lolos, Y. and Shelmerdine, C. W. (1997) The Pylos Regional Archaeological Project. Part I: Overview and the archaeological survey. *Hesperia* 66: 391–494.

Davis, J. L. and Sutton, S. B. (1995) Response to A. J. Ammerman, 'The dynamics of modern land use and the Acconia survey'. *Journal of Mediterranean Archaeology* 8: 113–23.

Dunnell, R. C. (1992) The notion site. In J. Rossignol and L. Wandsnider (ed.) *Space, Time, and Archaeological Landscapes:* 21–41. New York, Plenum Press.

Dunnell, R. C. and Dancey, W. S. (1983) The siteless survey: a regional scale data collection strategy. In M. B. Schiffer (ed.) *Advances in Archaeological Method and Theory* 6: 267–87. New York, Academic Press.

Ebert, J. I. (1992) *Distributional Archaeology.* Albuquerque, University of New Mexico Press.

Gaffney, V., Bintliff, J. and Slapšak, B. (1991) Site formation processes and the Hvar survey project, Yugoslavia. In A. Schofield (ed.) *Interpreting Artifact Scatters: Contributions to Ploughzone Archaeology*: 59–77. Oxford, Oxbow Books.

Gallant, T. W. (1986) 'Background noise' and site definition: a contribution to survey methodology. *Journal of Field Archaeology* 13:403–418.

Gillings, M. and Sbonias, K. (1999) Regional survey and GIS: the Boeotia Project. In M. Gillings, D. Mattingly, and J. van Dalen (ed.) *Geographical Information Systems and Landscape Archaeology*: 35–54. Oxford, Oxbow Books.

Jameson, M. H., Runnels, C. N. and van Andel, T. H. (1994) *A Greek Countryside: The Southern Argolid From Prehistory to the Present Day*. Stanford, Stanford University Press.

Lock, G., Bell, T. and Lloyd, J. (1999) Towards a methodology for modeling surface survey data: the Sangro Valley Project. In M. Gillings, D. Mattingly, and J. van Dalen (ed.) *Geographical Information Systems and Landscape Archaeology*: 55–63. Oxford, Oxbow Books.

Mee, C. and Forbes, H. (1997) *A Rough and Rocky Place. The Landscape and Settlement History of the Methana Peninsula, Greece: Results of the Methana Survey Project*. Liverpool, Liverpool University Press.

Orton, C. (2000) *Sampling in Archaeology*. Cambridge, Cambridge University Press.

Pettegrew, D. K. (2001) Chasing the classical farmstead: assessing the formation and signature of rural settlement in Greek landscape archaeology. *Journal of Mediterranean Archaeology* 14: 189–209.

Plog, S., Plog, F. and Wait, W. (1978) Decision-making in modern surveys. In M. B. Schiffer (ed.) *Advances in Archaeological Method and Theory* 1: 383–421. New York, Academic Press.

Prieto, A. (2000) Field survey 2000, Metaponto. In J. C. Carter (ed.) *The Study of Ancient Territories, Chersonesos and Metaponto*. Annual Report of the Institute of Classical Archaeology, University of Texas at Austin: 15–22. Austin, Institute of Classical Archaeology.

Prieto, A. (2001) Metaponto: the 2000 field season. Paper presented at the 102nd Annual Meeting of the Institute of Classical Archaeology, San Diego, CA, January 3–6, 2001.

Shennan, S. (1985) *Experiments in the Collection and Analysis of Archaeological Survey Data: The East Hampshire Survey*. Sheffield, University of Sheffield Department of Prehistory and Archaeology.

Schiffer, M. B., Sullivan, A. P. and Klinger, T. C. (1978) The design of archaeological surveys. *World Archaeology* 6: 107–116.

Schon, R. (2000) On a site and out of sight: where have our data gone? *Journal of Mediterranean Archaeology* 13: 107–111.

Shott, M. J. (1995) Reliability of archaeological records on cultivated surfaces: a Michigan case study. *Journal of Field Archaeology* 27: 475–90.

Terrenato, N. and Ammerman, A. J. (1996) Visibility and site recovery in the Cecina Valley Survey, Italy. *Journal of Field Archaeology* 23: 91–108.

Thompson, S. M. (1999a) *A Central Sicilian Landscape: Settlement and Society in the Territory of Ancient Morgantina (5000 BC – AD 50)*. Unpublished Ph.D. dissertation, Department of Anthropology, University of Virginia.

Thompson, S. M. (1999b) Survey campaigns: Metaponto, summer and fall. In J. C. Carter (ed) *Ancient Territories, Metaponto and Chersonesos*. Annual Report of the Institute of Classical Archaeology, University of Texas at Austin: 12–17. Austin, Institute of Classical Archaeology.

Thompson, S. M. (2002) Archaeological survey in the chora of Metaponto, 2001: resurvey and longitudinal study of the surface archaeological record. Poster presented at the 103rd Annual Meeting of the Archaeological Institute of America, Philadelphia, PA, January 3–6, 2002.

Van der Velde, P. (1987) Post-depositional decay: a simulation. *Analecta Praehistorica Leidensia* 20: 168–73.

Wandsnider, L. and Camilli, E. L. (1992) The character of surface archaeological deposits and its influence on survey accuracy. *Journal of Field Archaeology* 19: 169–88.

Whitelaw, T. (1991) Investigations at the Neolithic sites of Kephala and Paoura. In J. F. Cherry, J. L. Davis, and E. Manzourani, *Landscape Archaeology as Long-Term History: Northern Keos in the Cycladic Islands*. Monumenta Archaeologica 16: 199–216. Los Angeles, UCLA Institute of Archaeology.

Wright, J. C., Cherry, J. F., Davis, J. L., Mantzourani, E., Sutton, S. B. and Sutton, R. F. Jr. (1990) The Nemea Valley Archaeological Project: an interim report. *Hesperia* 59: 579–659.

Yntema, D. (1993) *In Search of An Ancient Countryside: The Amsterdam Free University Field Survey at Oria, Province of Brindisi, South Italy (1981–1983)*. Amsterdam, Thesis Publishers.

Yorston, R. M., Gaffney, V. and Reynolds, P. J. (1990) Simulation of artifact movement due to cultivation. *Journal of Archaeological Science* 17: 67–83.

7. Intra-regional and Inter-regional Comparison of Occupation Histories in Three Italian Regions: The RPC Project

Peter Attema and Martijn van Leusen

BACKGROUND: THE RPC PROJECT

Trajectories towards social complexity in protohistoric Italian regions are best expressed in the landscape through the centralization of settlements and through forms of early urbanization. Excavations and surveys have shown that in this process Greek and Roman colonization were potent forces of change. But social complexity was not solely brought about by colonists – some regions already had complex societies at the time that they were colonized (8th – 4th centuries BC), others less so. In addition, the nature and intensity of indigenous contacts with the colonial presence differed, with some regions less directly involved than others.

The *Regional Pathways to Complexity* (RPC) project studies and compares three areas that show such diverging trajectories. These are the Pontine region in central Italy, the Salento Isthmus in Puglia and the Sibaritide in Calabria, all of which have a tradition in Dutch archaeological fieldwork (Figure 7.1). In these areas the research team of the RPC project compares the modes of interaction between the Italic peoples and Greek and Roman colonialism (cf. Attema *et al.* 1998; Attema 2001). The project uses a comparative format, with evidence collected from a range of sources for each region (Attema *et al.* 1999).

The project, which began in September 1997, is now nearing its end. The project is managed by Professor Peter

Attema at the Groningen Institute of Archaeology and Dr. Gert-Jan Burgers at the Archaeological Institute of the Free University of Amsterdam. Related doctoral research is being carried out by Froukje Veenman (the study of pastoral land use; Veenman 2002), Benoît Mater (the study of ceramic production technology; Mater in prep.), Ester van Joolen (the study of land evaluation techniques; van Joolen forthcoming), and Martijn van Leusen (the study of regional settlement pattern analysis; van Leusen 2002). With two of the four theses completed and two more nearing completion, the project team has already begun work on a synthetic volume. A volume of conference proceedings has already appeared (Attema *et al.* 2002). Here we present, in the form of a discussion paper, issues that are relevant to comparative survey archaeology and illustrate these with case studies drawn from the project (see separate text boxes).

SOME INSIGHTS RESULTING FROM THE WORK SO FAR

Although the project team is still comparing and synthesizing the data and regional interpretations, some significant insights into the potential and problems of comparative research have already emerged from the work:

- Our surveys have allowed us to begin to differentiate settlement histories according to land system, liberating us from describing these histories on a simplified regional scale. A land system is an area or group of areas with a recurring pattern of land forms, soils and vegetation. The impact of proto-urbanization and Roman colonization on the various land systems in the Pontine region, for instance, was far from equal and appears to have had a complex spatial, functional and chronological patterning. For a more detailed discussion and examples, see Box 1.
- Our intensive surveys in both centrally located and 'marginal' areas (we use the latter term to refer to both geographical and socio-economic marginality,

Figure 7.1 Location map: Italy and the three RPC study regions.

especially in relation to the 'core') have added large numbers of less obtrusive sites, both 'Classical' and (especially significant) protohistoric sites. For example, our Doganella di Ninfa survey in the Pontine region, covering 3 sq. km of the colluvial footslopes of the Monti Lepini, demonstrates the incompleteness of earlier 'topographic' and 'extensive' surveys in the same area (van Leusen 1998; van Leusen 2002, chapter 9). This has important consequences for the settlement histories of these areas, and of the wider region of which they are a part, especially in the area of interaction between indigenous settlement patterns and Greek/Roman colonization (see Box 2).

- Our greater awareness of the role of biases and of problems in survey methodology in creating potentially misleading patterns in the data set has led to a (re-) interpretation of existing data sets created over the past 30 years, and to a more critical assessment of data acquired through our own field walking surveys (see Box 3).
- Our emphasis on *rural* histories of settlement and land use, as in other recent survey projects, complements the traditional urban focus of classical studies, and thus provides a broader base to the interpretation of 'core' processes such as centralization, urbanization and colonization (see Box 4).

BOX 1. LAND SYSTEMS, SOCIAL STRATEGIES AND VARIABLE RATES OF SETTLEMENT DEVELOPMENT IN THE PONTINE REGION DURING PROTOHISTORY AND THE ROMAN PERIOD (Figure 7.2)

Archaeological evidence that adjacent land systems were used in a complementary fashion to support a regional economy may be read as signs of a complex society. Field walking surveys can be used to study long-term changes in the exploitation of those land systems. This provides the basis for the intra-regional comparative approach used by the RPC project. Here we present two examples of this approach, one dating from the protohistoric period, the other from the Roman colonial period.

On the strength of the present data we may, in the case of the Pontine region, hypothesize complex and

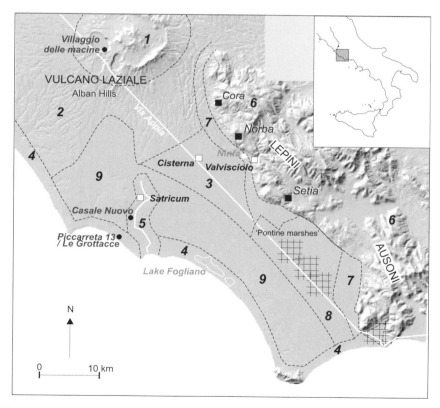

Figure 7.2 Land systems of the Pontine region. 1: Alban caldera; 2: steeply dissected volcanic landscape; 3: flat alluvial area; 4: coastal strip; 5: Astura valley; 6: limestone mountains; 7: calcareous alluvial/colluvial system; 8: Pontine marsh; 9: sandy/clayey terraces. Hachures indicate (presumed) mid-Republican centuriations.

long-term functional inter-relationships between the various land systems. To understand these relationships we have found it useful to subdivide the main physiographical units of the Pontine Region (volcanic area of the Alban hills, calcareous pre-Apennine mountains, coastal plain; see Figure 7.2) into their various land systems, each with their own specific combination of environmental characteristics and potential for human exploitation. A land system can be defined as an area or group of areas with a recurring pattern of land forms, soils, and vegetation. The Alban hills, for example, can be subdivided into the caldera with its lakes, the fertile hilly and dissected volcanic landscape that slopes towards the Tyrrhenian sea, and the Astura river valley. The Lepine and Ausonic mountains can be subdivided into uplands and footslopes, and the Pontine plain into the marshes, the sandy/clayey terraces, and the coastal strip with its lagoons.

Recent research indicates that socio-economic relationships above the level of a largely pastoral economy developed already in the Bronze Age between these units (see Angle *et al.* 1987). In the Alban lake, for instance, a substantial submerged settlement of the later Middle Bronze Age excavated by Italian archaeologists provided evidence for a developed agricultural economy (the so-called Villaggio delle Macine; Chiarucci 1985; 1994). In the Astura valley environment a site from the Recent and Final Bronze Age was excavated with evidence for metallurgy and contacts with the Mycenaean world (Casale Nuovo, Angle *et al.* 1987). A recent excavation by the Groningen Institute of Archaeology in the coastal strip has furnished strong evidence for a salt or fish producing site of late Bronze Age date (Piccarreta 13; Attema *et al.* in prep.). Several sites of the latter type must have existed along the coast, as demonstrated by earlier topographical work (Piccarreta 1977) and confirmed by recent surveys by the Groningen Institute of Archaeology. This and other (old and new) evidence from the Lepine mountains and the dissected volcanic landscape, in combination with data from pollen studies of the various land systems (van Joolen forthcoming), points to a differentiated Bronze Age economy in the Pontine region, in which the various land systems may have served specific roles within a developing settlement hierarchy. To construct a long-term comparative settlement history we must monitor these roles through time. In the agricultural economy of the later Iron Age in the Pontine region, it appears that the dissected volcanic landscape provided the best conditions for the development of an urban society. It is here that we find the first towns with substantial rural infill in their catchments (for example, Lanuvium, Ardea, and Satricum). Other land systems either did not undergo such developments (such as the southern coastal strip and the Monti Lepini uplands) or experienced them to a much lesser extent (for example, the slopes and foothills of the Lepine mountains).

For our second example we discuss the differential development of land units in the Pontine plain in the period of Roman colonization from the 5th century BC onwards. Here we want to discuss briefly the rate of Roman colonization in the Lepine mountains in comparison to similar developments in the coastal strip. Our surveys have shown that the Lepine footslopes were already busily farmed in the Archaic period, prior to the Roman colonization of that area. Historically, the change-over from a society consisting of relatively autonomous Latin tribes to one increasingly controlled by the Romans is dated in the 5th/4th century BC (a period which we call the post-Archaic), when Roman and Latin colonists are said to have founded fortified colonies on the Lepine scarp. Norba is an example of such a colony; according to Livy, it was founded in 492 BC. Such foundation dates are hard to verify archaeologically, but from our surveys it appears that the nearby protohistorical settlement of Valvisciolo contracts or even disappears in the 5th century BC (Attema 1993: 157–80), while Norba appears as a heavily fortified site in the course of the 4th century BC. Tied to these urban developments taking place at Norba itself, at Cora and at Setia, is a rapid development of so-called 'platform villas' that are founded on the Lepine scarp and footslopes – a development that may be linked to intensive oleoculture as suggested by pollen evidence for this period (Haagsma 1993). These rural farmsteads were built on platforms of heavy polygonal masonry, a technique also used in the fortifications around the Roman colonies. Our most recent (as yet unpublished) survey indicates a starting date for these platform villas around 300 BC on account of specific black glaze ware. The archaeological evidence therefore indicates a rapid and successful romanization of the Lepine scarp and footslopes, probably already in the late 4th century BC. This extended into the adjacent colluvial areas, such as we found, for instance, in the *ager* of Setia in earlier surveys. To this may be added the historical, archaeological, and air photographic evidence for infrastructural works such as the Via Appia (312 BC) and for large scale land divisions that are dated even before that (according to Cancellieri 1990: 61–71; see also Attema 1993: 233–36).

It has now become possible to compare and contrast this early Roman activity in the Lepine foothills and adjacent colluvial areas, with the situation in a different land system along the coast. Our recent surveys in the coastal strip suggest that Roman interest in exploiting this land system came much later and was of a different nature. An intensive survey carried out by us at the Fogliano lagoon in 1998 and 1999 indicates that this area was not developed on a substantial scale until the later Republic and early Imperial period (Attema *et al.* 2001). This relatively late development may have been triggered by Roman economic interest in marine resources and pottery production along the coast. A mapping of Roman remains exposed by marine erosion along the coast at a site called Le Grottace near Nettuno (carried out by us in 2001 and 2002) has indicated that, prior to the appearance of the luxurious Imperial maritime villas of the Roman upper class, commercial activities had taken place during the Republican period. These activities left vast quantities of Roman amphorae of Graeco-Italic and other Republican types, recorded in strata below the Imperial villa and in several pockets nearby. The preparation of fish and/or fish sauce may have been part of these activities, while there may also have been production of amphorae on the spot. The case presented here shows how, within the relatively small area of the Pontine region, we may begin to differentiate the nature of Roman interest in, and the rate of Roman development of, the various land systems.

We intend to extend our use of the land systems approach to a study of the transformation and modification patterns of settlement and land use in the area of the Alban hills and the adjacent territory to the coast from the 5th century BC onwards. In this area the Archaic (6th century BC) Latial city state system was romanized during the 5th and 4th centuries, but a systematic regional study has been lacking. Of the larger excavated urban lowland settlements, we know that at Satricum, for instance, the settlement structure was completely transformed in the 5th and 4th centuries BC, and that this ultimately resulted in a small rural Republican settlement. Other Archaic centers such as Ardea, however, have shown more of an urban continuity in recent excavations. The situation in the dissected landscape of the Alban hills also suggests a strong urban continuity similar to that of Ardea. Of equal interest are the land use, infrastructure, and settlement patterns of the late Antique and early Medieval period. These are the subject of study at this moment, and may provide parallels with the protohistorical situation in some of the land systems mentioned above. Comparison of developments in adjacent land systems may thus also reveal comparable patterns within the same region over very long stretches of time.

BOX 2. COMPARING INTENSIVE AND EXTENSIVE PROSPECTION: THE DOGANELLA DI NINFA SURVEY (Figure 7.3)

In April 1998 we conducted a survey of the lower Lepine slopes in the Doganello di Ninfa area. This survey area, of about 5 km by 750 m and dominated by the Monte Arrestino massif (862 masl), is bounded by the Canale delle Acque Alte (Canale Mussolini) and Fosso del Cavone on the west and north sides, by the steep uncultivated slopes and cliffs of the Lepine hills, and by the Cora gap in the north. Nowadays it consists mostly of large and small fields with olive trees, with smaller areas devoted to fruit trees, viticulture, and grazing. The slopes are cut in two or three places by (nearly) dry gullies, and drainage at the foot of the slope is directed NW-SE because of the elongated tuff hill geomorphology there. The area is dotted with small farming cabins and, increasingly, with modern houses. The two main rubble-metalled tracks running through the area perpendicular to the slopes, and many minor paths too, are in heavy use and there is much evidence of fields being worked with machinery in order to remove stones. This included the removal of terrace walls and remains of Roman architecture. Increasingly, the steeper slopes are also cleared, ploughed and enclosed. Most of this area was included in the earlier topographic survey conducted by Paola Brandizzi Vittucci (Brandizzi Vittucci 1968), which centered on Cora.

Our team systematically surveyed a total of 27 fields, and discovered or reconfirmed the presence of 20 sites reported by Brandizzi Vittucci (Figure 7.3; van Leusen 1998). Figure 7.3 shows the locations of these fields and sites on a topographical background. Although the stated purpose of the survey was to map sections of a system of 'platform villas' associated with the early historic (5th – 4th century BC) Roman colonies of Setia and Norba on the Lepine scarp and connected by the *pedemontana* road, most of the survey area proved to be rich in 6th century Archaic finds, with Roman Republican sites (often without any platform walls) generally overlying Archaic predecessors. This confirmed that the Romans should not be seen as colonisers in the sense that they brought a previously marginally used landscape under cultivation. Instead, a fairly dense and possibly differentiated Archaic settlement pattern seems to be present, which will force a partial readjustment of current views regarding the settlement history of the area. Beginning already in the later Iron Age, Latial tribes had apparently fully colonized these footslopes during the Archaic period; their population was not simply concentrated in the few larger settlements known just outside the surveyed area (such as Valvisciolo, Satricum, Cisterna di Latina).

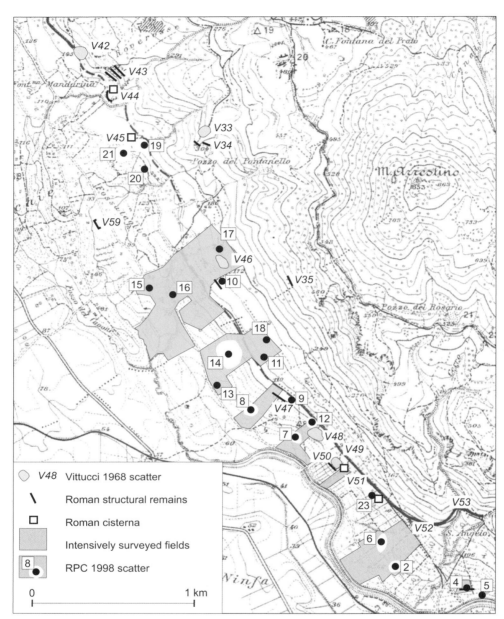

Figure 7.3 1:25,000 scale topographic map of the Doganella di Ninfa survey area. See Figure 7.2 for general location. Fields surveyed by the RPC in gray; new Archaic and/or Roman Republican sites are represented by small black dots with site identifications in roman type. Italic numbers prefixed by a 'V' are sites identified by Brandizzi Vittucci (1968). Just left of center is a larger site (14) that hints at the potential complexity of the Archaic settlement system.

BOX 3. INTENSIVE SURVEY IN THE SIBARITIDE: INVESTIGATING BIASES IN THE SURFACE RECORD (Figure 7.4)

The Sibaritide is an alluvial plain on the Gulf of Taranto (part of the Ionian Sea), bounded on the landward side by the Pollino massif (to the north) and the Sila mountain range (to the south). It is named after the ancient Greek colony of Sybaris, which lies in the approximate centre of its coastline. Following the discovery of Sybaris and its Hellenistic and Roman successor towns through the combined efforts of the

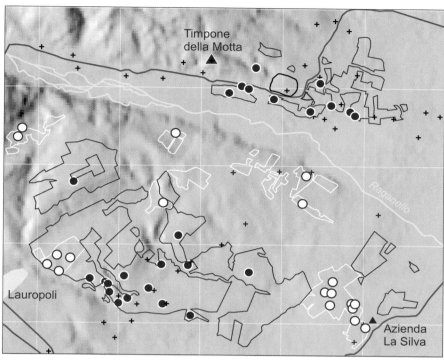

Figure 7.4 The SIBA 2000 fieldwork transect (excluding Monte S Nicola), with extensive (black outline) and intensive (white outline) survey areas shown. Plus signs: Quilici sites; circles: RPC project sites and scatters 1995–2001. Grid spacing: 1 km.

University of Pennsylvania Museum and the Lerici foundation (Lerici 1960: 303–37; Rainey and Lerici 1967; Rainey 1969: 261–73), an approximately 21 by 24 km (500 sq. km) area in the centre of the region was surveyed by a team under the direction of Lorenzo Quilici. Quilici aimed both to provide a context for the excavations starting at Sybaris in 1969 and to record surface archaeology in advance of land development schemes funded by the Italian Cassa per il Mezzogiorno (De Rossi *et al.* 1969:147).

In addition to revisiting and evaluating the known sites, many new sites and monuments were discovered as well. The results were recorded on a total of 858 forms and 23 sheets of the 1:10,000 topographic map series, but were considerably condensed for publication. The whereabouts of the original survey archive are currently unknown. The nearly 800 sites of archaeological interest collected from documented evidence, or recorded in the field by this team, still provide the bulk of the archaeological record for the region. Our systematic field walking survey for the year 2000 in the Sibaritide (SIBA 2000 survey) targeted an approximately six km long and 1.5 km wide transect through the transitional zone, consisting of marine and fluvial terraces, between the coastal plain and its mountainous hinterland between the valley of the Raganello river

and the modern town of Lauropoli (see Figs. 7.4 and 7.6). This survey aimed to see how the recorded sizes, locations, interpretations and dating of the sites mapped in De Rossi *et al.* 1969 compare with the current archaeological surface record (van Leusen and Attema, in press).

As can be seen in Figure 7.4, both intensive and extensive surveying methods recovered about twice the number of sites mapped by De Rossi *et al.* 1969 in the study area, despite the deterioration of the soil archive in the intervening decades. The resultant site distribution suggests, but does not prove, that the 'villages' in the 1969 publication are artefacts of research and visibility biases. A definite answer to this question will require targeting a wider area for extensive survey in the future, and obtaining access to the original research records. Although routes may well have existed where they are posited in De Rossi *et al.* 1969, sites also occur well away from these along all 'minor' terrace edges. With respect to dating, the materials collected in the SIBA 2000 survey also suggest consistently earlier dates (Archaic to late Republican) than those proposed in De Rossi *et al.* 1969 (late Hellenistic to early Imperial); and these results may tentatively be extrapolated across all of the Sibaritide.

The adverse conditions for retrieval of protohistoric ceramics on the intensively worked terraces must be taken into account when interpreting the archaeological record of relatively well preserved upland protohistoric sites (van Leusen 2001). There is currently no evidence that protohistoric (Bronze Age – early Iron Age) settlement occurred anywhere in the survey transect but at the very highest elevations (the Monte San Nicola at 500 masl stands some 150 m above the highest terrace). This can be interpreted as confirmation of existing thought about protohistoric settlement patterns being geared to the needs of pastoralism – winter grazing in the plain. For the later Iron Age and Archaic periods, the evidence from the survey is equivocal. Despite the historical evidence for the establishment of Sybaris around 720 BC and the archaeological evidence for continued use of the sanctuary and necropolis at neighbouring Timpone Motta into the late 6th century BC (Attema *et al.* 2000), no securely datable materials from this period have been found in our survey. Given our experience with the very low visibility of coarse impasto wares in the stony soils of the survey area, we must conclude that neither our own surveyors nor the team led by Lorenzo Quilici were able to identify low density scatters of such material with any degree of reliability. We cannot, therefore, infer anything from its absence. For the Archaic period,

much will depend on a closer dating of the coarse wares, which make up more than half of the finds by weight, through association with datable fine wares or through typological comparison with excavated material within the region.

No such visibility problem occurred with the classical Hellenistic and Roman ceramic types. It appears from the results of our field work that the large-scale spatial patterns mapped in De Rossi *et al.* 1969 are, at least for the transitional zone between the plain and the hinterland, realistic. Large and small sites of the Hellenistic/Roman period do occur in elongated clusters along 'major' terrace edges. However, such sites also appear to cluster locally along the edges of small secondary valleys cut into the terraces; this is at least the case along the eastern edge of the Vallone Organata /di Franceschiello which runs just to the east of Lauropoli. The possibility that the site clusters in De Rossi *et al.* 1969 are caused by, rather than merely correlated to, modern accessibility and land use must remain a hypothesis at this stage; it may eventually be confirmed or rejected when working with the original survey archive. Among the 'new' small classical sites identified by our intensive survey, several are located within the clusters initially identified in De Rossi *et al.* 1969, while others are scattered all over.

BOX 4. RURAL LANDUSE AND 'CORE' PROCESSES IN THE SALENTO PENINSULA (Figure 7.5)

Intensive surveys in the Salento peninsula, where the Archaeological Institute of the Free University of Amsterdam has a long tradition of fieldwork, have focussed above all on the Brindisi plain (see, for example, Yntema 1993a; 1993b; Burgers 1998). Early urbanization is attested here, notably during the late Archaic and early Hellenistic periods (550–250 BC), while romanization of that early urban landscape proceeded after the Roman conquest of Salento in the first half of the third century BC. Little was known, however, of the Murge limestone plateau and the adjacent coastal plain to the east of the Brindisino. The rolling landscape of the Murge itself is an agriculturally marginal area with thin soils, while the alluvial coastal plain is largely devoted to olive cultivation. A major question regarding these land systems was, therefore, to what degree the lack of data in this area reflected a lack of intensive, problem oriented research, or marginal human exploitation in the past (Burgers *et al.* in

press). The decision to carry out an intensive survey in these areas was motivated by the wish to complement the excellent data set from the Brindisi plain with data from adjacent physiographical units with quite different land systems, so as to understand the impact that the core processes taking place in the Brindisi plain might have on the adjacent Murge.

The fieldwork was undertaken within the framework of the RPC project in a survey that was carried out in 1999, and which shows that these territories only attracted substantial rural settlement in the early Hellenistic period (325 – 200 BC; Figure 7.5). In the coastal survey area 100, following a pattern observed earlier at Oria (Yntema 1993a), these sites appear to be located along a line running just beneath and parallel to the Murge cliff edge, suggesting the existence of a *pedemontana* road. Unlike similar farms in the Oria and Valesio survey areas, some of these sites lack identifiable tile, which suggests that a much simpler construction method was used for farm buildings. The Salento Murge was thought to be an archaeologically marginal landscape, even in the Hellenistic period, until the sites and off-site material detected by our survey in

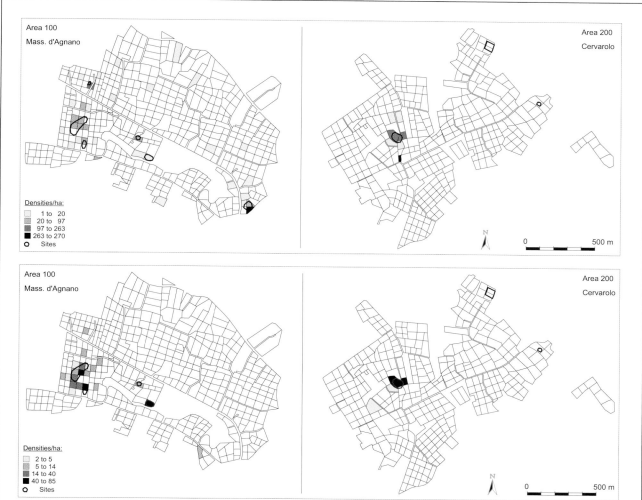

Figure 7.5 Density distribution maps of early Hellenistic (top) and Roman Imperial finds (bottom), corrected for surface visibility factors, in Areas 100 and 200 of the Ostuni survey 1999.

the upland area 200 showed that this landscape in fact also participated in the early Hellenistic regional trend of agricultural expansion and intensification, established on the basis of a study of farmsteads in urban catchment survey areas on the Salento Isthmus (Burgers 1998: 226–63). At seven to eight km from the nearest contemporaneous urban centers in the Murge (at Ceglie Messapico and Ostuni), the presence of these farmsteads suggests that a regional trend extended to the cultivation of even the most outlying, previously untilled, lands outside the urban catchment areas.

The agricultural transformation indicated by these results can be linked to other major contemporaneous early Hellenistic developments, such as demographic growth and urban rearrangement of the larger settlements, which also reached their maximum expansion in this period. These urban transformations can be shown to have occurred simultaneously at sites throughout the Salento peninsula. Relating them to the rural infill of

the landscape surrounding these major sites, one observes the parallel emergence of pronounced local settlement hierarchies throughout the region (as discussed in more detail in Burgers 1998: 226–63). On the basis of our survey, events in the Murge area can now be linked to events in the wider peninsula, with isolated farmsteads even appearing on the rolling land of the high plateau. It can be concluded that, with the rearrangement of the wider landscape, the Murge towns became central places serving extensive rural hinterlands in the early Hellenistic period. The variability in the ceramic repertoires of the rural sites detected in both survey areas is indicative of this development, and suggests articulation with a market system – besides tiles and local coarse kitchen and plain wares, these repertoires include fine wares such as Apulian Black Gloss, Gnathia ware and Apulian Red Figure.

As is clear from Figure 7.5, neither of the two survey areas shows significant changes in the number or location of sites of the late Republican and Imperial periods, as compared to the early Hellenistic period. A basic continuity seems to exist for these phases, suggesting that the Murge landscape was not much affected when the centre of power in the region shifted towards the direct hinterland of the Latin colony of Brundisium (Brindisi). Brundisium was founded around the middle of the 3rd century BC as Rome's satellite in the newly conquered Salento peninsula. In the late Republican period it grew into one of the major Italian harbours for communication with the eastern Mediterranean, as well as into a regional centre for the overseas export of agricultural products, notably wine and olive oil. With the emergence of an export-oriented market economy, there is evidence to suggest the formation of a regional landscape which was differentiated in various zones of profitability (Burgers 1998: 265–92). Market-oriented wine and olive oil production can be argued to have concentrated in the immediate hinterland of Brindisi, as well as along the major new transport axis of the Via Appia. As a consequence, the role of the former Hellenistic towns as central places in these areas was lost, which may be one of the major reasons for their decline. Areas further removed from Brindisi and the Via Appia (including the Ostuni survey areas) must also have become economically peripheral, with subsistence farming likely to have prevailed in the late Republican period. The lack of systematic archaeo-

logical research conducted at the Murge towns warns against drawing definite conclusions regarding their development in the Roman period. However, judging from the scarcity of Roman finds so far, they do seem to have contracted considerably.

In relative contrast, the rural landscape of the Murge upland and the coastal plain seems not to have suffered similarly, as demonstrated by the Roman sites in these survey areas. The presence of considerable amounts of fine wares on these sites also suggests that the area as a whole still had access to a wider market system. This rural continuity also holds good for the Roman Imperial period, at least for the lowland survey area 100, for which African Red Slip wares are amply attested. In this regard, one may also point to the existence of the nearby Via Traiana, running along the coast from the Bari district to Brindisi. Its course has been studied by Uggeri (1983: 228–64) who relates the ancient written sources mentioning the road to actual field observations. The Via Traiana is likely to have considerably improved the accessibility of this part of the Murge, not least for the transport of agricultural products. In contrast, Imperial fine wares are less conspicuous in the upland zone 200. Other contemporary diagnostic wares are lacking as well, suggesting that the area was abandoned in the 2nd century AD and that the Murge upland now became peripheral to the wider region.

We will first illustrate the effect these insights have already had on our conception of regional settlement histories with examples taken from all three areas, and then discuss the more general effect they have had on our view of the 'core' processes in all three regions.

INTRA-REGIONAL DIFFERENCES IN SETTLE-MENT HISTORY WITHIN THE PONTINE REGION

We find that intra-regional differences in settlement and land use of the Classical landscape tend to have deep roots, often already becoming apparent in protohistory (later Bronze Age and Iron Age), and that these can be linked to the physical geography. For example, proto-urbanization of the Iron Age/Archaic Latial society took place principally in the volcanic landscape of the Alban hills, and appears to be related to earlier late Bronze Age centralized settlements in and around the Alban caldera (see Bietti Sestieri 1992: 45–62).

In the settlement history of the Pontine region it is, moreover, evident that intra-regional differences, besides being conditioned and constrained by a pre-existing physical and social landscape, can also arise from historical contingencies and supra-regional factors. As an

example of the former we may mention the strategic placement of Roman colonies on the Lepine scarp in answer to specific perceived threats emanating from inland tribes, as reported in ancient sources. The latter is illustrated in Box 1 by the chronological gap between mid-Republican economic development along the axis of the Via Appia and late Republican exploitation of the lagoonal landscape, which we link to Rome's military and economic needs. In terms of formal models, the Pontine region appears to have been the scene of core-periphery interactions in the Roman period as well as in protohistory.

OUR ALTERED VIEW OF THE CORE PROCESSES

In common with other recent students of Italian proto-history, we now no longer feel that the alteration of the landscape through the process of proto-urbanization is either well-understood or archaeologically well demonstrated. It is generally assumed that the increasing complexity of Late Bronze and Iron Age societies was physically translated into settlement nucleation in all three regions, a process often referred to as 'proto-urbanization'. However, the sizes of many of these central sites, and their density of habitation, are still a matter of conjecture and knowledge of the rural component of these societies is only gradually beginning to be collected (*cf.* Vanzetti 2002).

In contrast, Late Iron Age and Archaic urbanization can now more clearly be observed to be a supra-regional phenomenon, albeit regionally differentiated and locally truncated in the south by Greek colonization (7th century BC) and in central Italy by early Roman colonization (around 500 BC). Outside these areas directly influenced by colonizers we observe continuity in urban development (*e.g.* Salento outside the sphere of influence of Taras). A discussion of these issues can be found in Attema (forthcoming).

Comparing survey results for our three study regions has also highlighted what appears to be an intensive and widespread 4th century BC development of the rural landscape, with Hellenistic and Roman farms occurring in even the most marginal and distant parts of the landscape. For example, in the Sibaritide highlands we recently found Hellenistic farmstead scatters at the maximum elevation at which emmer wheat can still be grown; in the Salento such scatters have been found in the marginal uplands of the Murge as well (Burgers *et al.*, in press). This indicates a (to us) surprising degree of penetration of Hellenistic and Roman material culture outside the traditional colonial core areas. Likewise, a general drop in the number of sites of the early Imperial period, observed in all three regions, is consistent with the idea that intensive rural exploitation in the Hellenistic/Republican period was replaced by more extensive exploitation in the form of *latifundiae*, although this model certainly is far too generic and specific field studies need to be performed in future work.

Generally, *non-urban* aspects of the regional histories of settlement and land use in our study areas are now slowly coming into focus, allowing us to abandon the monolithic use of concepts such as centralization and colonization. One example is formed by the hilltop sites, apparently linked to transhumance, which we found in the Sibaritide highland survey and which add another component to a system known otherwise only by its large central settlements. This example is elaborated in Box 5. A second example comes from the Pontine region, where we have evidence for the existence of special activity sites both on the coast and along the Astura river; these sites probably functioned in conjunction with the known central settlements of the Alban core area as is argued in Box 1. Both examples indicate the complexity of Late Bronze and Iron Age centralization. There are also examples pertaining to colonization processes. As shown in Box 1, the growth of a dispersed rural settlement, and an economy tied to a small number of Roman villas exploiting local resources in the coastal landscape near Fogliano, can be seen as a late expression of Roman colonization in the Pontine region (Attema *et al.* 2001).

BOX 5. SURVEY IN THE HIGHLANDS OF THE SIBARITIDE (Figure 7.6)

As in most other Mediterranean landscapes, archaeological surveys in Italy have mostly been carried out in the coastal plains and adjacent foothills. The accessibility of these cultivated terrains generally presents no problem, while visibility conditions are favourable due to intensive ploughing. On the whole, much less attention has been paid to the less accessible uplands and highlands of Italy. Projects like Barker's Biferno valley survey (Barker 1995) or, more recently, Vermeulens' Potenza valley survey (Vermeulen 2002) show, however, the importance of linking the archaeology of the plains to that of the mountainous hinterlands in a single survey programme. In this way the relationships between the Mediterranean uplands and coastal plains will become comparable across various Italian regions. One goal of our work in the Sibaritide is to illustrate the long-term socio-economic relationships between the settlement and exploitation patterns of the uplands of the Pollino massif and those in the plain of Sybaris.

In our study area (see Figure 7.6) the protohistoric settlement patterns mapped through survey in the plain and foothills are difficult to understand without knowledge of the contemporaneous settlement and exploit-ation patterns in the highland. The larger Middle and Late Bronze Age settements, such as Torre Mordillo, Francavilla Marittima and Broglio di Trebisacce, are located on the foothills bordering the alluvial plain and in strategic positions with regard to the main rivers. These sites are generally assumed to have controlled transit routes between the coast and the hinterland; moreover, some – if not all – may have derived much of their importance from the historically known practice of short distance transhumance. This took place along routes linking the summer pastures in the highland of the Pollino massif to winter pastures in the plain of Sybaris.

The surveys carried out by the Groningen Institute of Archaeology in the plain and foothills (Figure 7.6; see also Box 3) are therefore being complemented by a mapping of archaeological sites in the mountainous hinterland of the Pollino massif. This highland survey programme is being carried out in close collaboration with the local speleological society 'Sparviere' based at Alessandria del Carretto (located at the top of the map). At present, the focus of this programme is on the mapping of hilltop sites, rock shelters and caves of protohistorical date that are already known to the Sparviere society. These sites are located along, or in

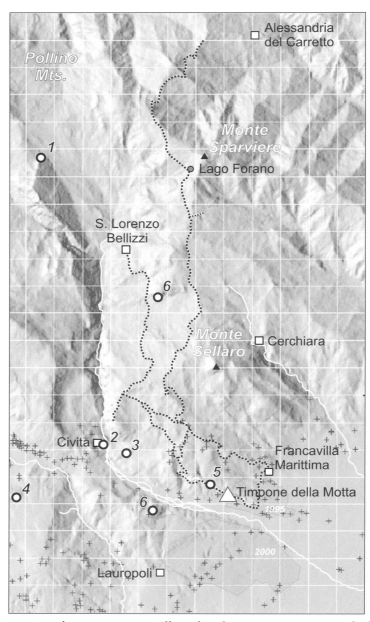

Figure 7.6 Short-distance transhumance routes still used in the recent past connect the highland of the Pollino mountains to the plain of the Sibaritide. Our survey along some of these routes (indicated by dotted lines) has identified several small protohistoric highland sites (circles) which may provide evidence for the existence of similar transhumant practices during protohistory. 1: Trizzòne della Scala; 2: Madre Chiesa; 3: Timpa del Demanio; 4: Timpone delle Fave; 5: Grotta del Caprio; 6: Banco del Ferro. This use of highland and lowland land systems may be complementary to the contemporary agricultural exploitation, characterised by larger centralised settlements such as at the Timpone della Motta (triangle). Sites mapped by De Rossi et al. 1969 are indicated by plus signs (the boundary of this survey lies just north of Civita), with Groningen Institute of Archaeology survey transects (1995–2000) added for reference. Grid spacing: 1 km.

close proximity to, the main historical transhumance routes, and our strategy consists of the digital mapping of these routes and their associated archaeology using a small handheld computer (PDA) containing mapping and database software linked to a handheld satellite-navigation system (GPS; the technology for this aspect of the survey is being developed by Nick Ryan from the University of Kent at Canterbury). One such route, of *c*. 13.5 km in length, is indicated in Figure 7.6 and runs from the Timpone della Motta at Francavilla Marittima to San Lorenzo Bellizzi at the sources of the river Raganello.

The sites surveyed up to the year 2000 campaign are located on limestone outcrops of modest size in positions with a good view over the surrounding landscape. One good example is provided by a number of sites located on either side of the canyon of the Raganello near present-day Civitá (such as Madre Chiesa and Timpa del Demanio). These were in a position to control the routes that went up into the Pollino on either side of the river, while the site of Timpone delle Fave could have controlled the passage into the adjacent upper Coscile watershed. Recent research has proved that small protohistorical sites appear as high up as 1420 m in the Pollino (for example, at Trizzòne della Scala), where they dominate the saddles leading into different valleys. There is reason to believe that we deal here with a regionally structured system of sites indicative of the relative complexity of late Bronze Age society in the Sibaritide. Studies of the surface pottery collections carried out by us so far suggest a general date for most of these sites in the later Bronze Age/early Iron Age. An interesting phenomenon is constituted by the existence of rock shelters and caves along these same routes, some of which (such as the Grotta del Caprio near Timpone della Motta) have been in use for a very long time, from protohistory to at least the late antique period; in some cases these can be assigned a cultic function (such as the cave of Banco del Ferro near S. Lorenzo Bellizzi).

Provided that the small upland sites can be dated to within reasonable timespans of one or two centuries, our site database for the protohistorical period in both the foothills and the uplands of the Sibaritide will furnish a good basis for the analysis of the socio-economic relationships between the uplands and lowlands, especially in combination with the results of survey work by the team of Renato Peroni (Peroni and Trucco 1994). To this end, small excavations of upland sites are foreseen in the near future. Regarding the later periods, we have not yet found firm evidence for the presence of later Iron Age and Archaic sites in the uplands. Whether this indicates a substantial change in the regional settlement pattern and the socio-economical relationships between highlands and lowlands will have to be clarified by further and more intensive survey work and pottery studies. It is clear, however, that in the Hellenistic period small rural sites again appear in the uplands as high up as 1000 m: a sign of agricultural land use expanding into the uplands.

PROBLEM AREAS

In accordance with the aims of this publication and the original Workshop, we will now discuss some of the more significant problem areas identified by our project. These concern the definition of the object of comparison, the methodology of comparison, the significance of biases, the limits to chronological resolution, and the logic of interpretative processes.

1. First of all, the *object* of comparison must be defined. Do we want to compare the archaeological finds, sites, and monuments, *patterns* in those objects, or our *interpretations* of those patterns (which interpretations are mainly based on historical sources and anthropological concepts)? Current high level interpretations concerning our own study regions only have a loose relation to the underlying archaeological data and patterns, the study of which still requires much work on methodological issues.

2. Regarding the methodology of intra- and inter-regional comparison, we can distinguish problems relating to the mechanics of comparison, and problems relating to differences in research tradition. The former relates to questions such as how to store different types and qualities of digital (site) data for comparison in a single database; how to handle incompatible site type classifications; and how to arrive at sound quantitative comparisons. In short, comparison of archaeological *data sets* is only possible if these are classified (described) in an identical, or at least compatible, manner. The latter has resulted in regional differences in interpretative frameworks, terminology and periodization, thus obstructing direct comparison of archaeological data. Nor is comparison of *processes* such as colonization and urbanization possible unless a single and unambiguous definition is adhered to (see van Leusen 2002, ch. 13).

3. When comparing regional data sets, the role of bias factors such as physical landscape dynamics and land use histories becomes especially important, as these selectively tend to obscure some settlement phases rather than others. Sedimentation in the coastal plain of the Sibaritide, for example, obscures all but the most recent settlement phases, making unfeasible any comparison with settlement development in other coastal plains (Cherubini *et al.* 1994; Cotecchia and Pagliarulo 1996; Hofman 2002); our coring program in sections of the Pontine colluvium has shown that sedimentation has covered protohistoric settlement phases, leaving a predominantly Roman landscape to

be discovered (Attema and Delvigne 2000; van Joolen forthcoming). Regarding the influence of recent land use histories, we merely note that unobtrusive remains have been, and are still likely to be, unnoticed by the archaeologist unless circumstances are especially favorable (*eg.* intensive survey in tilled landscapes). Hence, more effort will be needed to study the geological processes occurring in conjunction with human presence, and the degree to which our data collection is biased by factors such as the recent (post-War) history of land use (for example, through the study of historic maps; Feiken and van Leusen 2000). The retrospective study of older archaeological data sets is an important area of application here.

4. The ultimate goal of comparative chronology must be to tie local (regional) cultural periodizations to absolute chronology in centuries. Comparative chronology, on which inter-regional demographic and settlement histories should be based, is predicated on the compatibility of relevant ceramic typochronologies; however, we find that these chronologies are not sufficiently comparable and precise with regard to the material retrieved in surface collections. Moreover, surface collections consist of 99% coarse and plain wares, but dating is still largely dependent on fine wares. For these reasons, a team from the Groningen Institute of Archaeology has been working on the establishment of local fabric-based chronologies that are embedded in excavation contexts (Attema 2000; Attema *et al.* in press). These have facilitated the identification of, for example, the 6th century BC red ceramics of the Pontine region from survey contexts because these coarse fabrics are well-known from stratigraphic contexts at the Satricum excavations (Maaskant-Kleibrink 1987; 1992). No such precision has yet been achieved for local ceramics of the same period in the Sibaritide. Our inability to recognize Archaic rural settlement in the Sibaritide (van Leusen 2002, chapter 12) is a direct consequence of this, and of the almost complete lack of diagnostic fine wares. Pottery studies of the Sibaritide wares are currently taking place to address this problem.

5. The strength of archaeological interpretations depends on being able to specify the relation between archaeologically observable patterns and high-level processes. Some processes, such as the early phases of colonial contact between Greek traders and indigenous peoples of southern Italy, are not visible at all in surface survey and can only be studied at the scale of individual sites (see, for example, the recent discussions in Kleibrink [in press] and Yntema [2000]). Others remain problematic; we provide a few examples here:

    • Few, if any, models exist to link rural settlement trends unambiguously to processes such as proto-urbanization and colonization. In other words, the question – 'What, if any, patterns of rural evidence *should* we consistently find if such processes occurred?' – has not been answered. Whilst Iron Age rural infill complementing the central proto-urban settlements has been found in the Alban hills, no such phenomenon has yet been found in the foothills of the Sibaritide. Should we regard the Alban pattern as standard, implying that the lack of infill in the Sibaritide is due to visibility problems? This same problem is also expressed in the relation between archaeology and historical evidence. For example, the 'platform' villas of the Lepine margins are characterized by their uniform appearance and spacing of architectural remains (Attema 1993: 233–35). In what way are they (chronologically and functionally) related to the historically attested 4th century establishment of Roman colonies at Norba, Signium, and Setia, given that current opinion dates the villas to the 3rd and 2nd centuries BC (see, for example, Quilici 1995)?

    • The nature of settlement and population dynamics is dependent on the highly problematic functional interpretation of survey scatters. For example, Archaic ceramic scatters in the Pontine region can be interpreted as evidence for subsistence farms or for temporary work-related shelters (Osborne 1987); choosing between the two will deeply affect our interpretation in terms of the nature of Archaic rural infill and of continuity or discontinuity into the Roman period.

    • We have become increasingly aware that the surface record may contain information on spatially distinct functional components ('subsystems') within each broad period. For example, the Bronze Age special activity sites mentioned in Box 1 should be interpreted in conjunction with habitation sites of the same period, rather than as isolated phenomena. But can we reliably recognize special activity sites from a surface scatter alone? This calls for a more thorough study of survey assemblages in the context of local land systems.

FUTURE RESEARCH

Although we have begun to make inroads on each of the problem areas identified in the previous section within the framework of the RPC project, that project is now nearing its end. The synthetic volume being prepared at the moment will represent our first formal attempt at inter-regional comparison of the settlement histories of the three regions in southern Lazio, the Salento, and northern Calabria. On the basis of this work, we feel that future research should be aimed at improving the regional data sets before a higher quality inter-regional comparison can be attempted. In practical terms this means that:

1. We will continue to study, and experiment with, ways

of improving the comparibility of surface collections, ultimately aiming to arrive at more objective and comparable data retrieval in surface surveys;

2. We plan to extend the field study of 'marginal' areas into the uplands and highlands of all three regions, developing appropriate methods including the use of portable digital location and mapping equipment as we go along (Ryan and van Leusen 2002);

3. In order to establish criteria for the functional interpretation of survey scatters, we plan to excavate examples of all the more frequently occurring site types encountered in surface surveys in the Pontino and Sibaritide (besides the coastal sites mentioned above, obvious targets include Iron Age hilltop sites without Archaic or Roman successors, rural Archaic scatters, and Republican 'platform villas');

4. We will continue our reconstruction of ancient land systems by extending our geoarchaeological and bioarchaeological work (sedimentation history, pollen cores) in the Pontino and Sibaritide, aiming to provide a more detailed environmental context to the archaeological data collected in surveys;

5. We intend to do further fabric research in order to increase the resolution of local ceramic chronologies.

REFERENCES

Angle, M., Caneva, C., Conti, A. M., Dottarelli, R., Gianni, A., Giardino C. and Persiani, C. (1987) Casale Nuovo (LT) e la tarda età del Bronzo nel Lazio Meridionale. *Atti del 3° Convegno di studi "Un millenio di relazioni fra la Sardegna e i Paesi del; Mediterraneo"*: 265–303. Selargius-Cagliari, Edizioni Della Torre.

Attema, P. A. J. (1993) An archaeological survey in the Pontine Region, Vols. 1–2. PhD dissertation, University of Groningen.

Attema, P. A. J. (2000) Ceramics of the first millennium BC from a survey at Lanuvium in the Alban Hills, Central Italy: method, aims, and first results of regional fabric classification. *Palaeohistoria* 39/40 (1997/1998): 413–39.

Attema, P. A. J. (2001) Early urban and colonized regions of Central and South Italy: a case study in comparative landscape archaeology. In T. Darvill and M. Gojda (eds.) *One Land, Many Landscapes*. BAR International Series 987:147–56. Oxford, Archaeopress.

Attema, P. A. J. (forthcoming) Early urbanization between 800 and 600 BC in Lazio, Apulia and the Sybaris. In B. Cunliffe and R. Osborne (eds.) *Mediterranean Urbanization 800–600 BC*. Oxford, University Press.

Attema, P. A. J., Burgers G.-J., Kleibrink, M. and Yntema, D. G. (1998) Case studies in indigenous developments in Early Italian centralization and urbanization: a Dutch perspective. *European Journal of Archaeology* 1 (3): 326–81.

Attema, P. A. J., Joolen, E. van, Leusen, P. M. van, Burgers, G.-J., Mater, B. and Veenman, F. (1999) Regional Pathways to Complexity: landscape and settlement dynamics in early Italy. In C. Fabech and J. Ringtved (eds.) *Settlement and Landscape, Proceedings of a Conference in Århus, Denmark, May 4–7 1998*: 475–77. Moesgard, Jutland Archaeological Society.

Attema, P. A. J., Burgers, G.-J., Joolen, E. van, Leusen, P. M. van and Mater, B. (eds.) (2002) *New Developments in Italian Landscape Archaeology. Proceedings of a Three-day International Conference held at Groningen, April 13–15, 2000.* BAR International Series 1091. Oxford, Archaeopress.

Attema, P. A. J. and Delvigne, J. J. (2000) Settlement dynamics and alluvial sedimentation in the Pontine Region, Central Italy: a complex relationship. In F. Vermeulen and M. de Dapper (eds.) *Geoarchaeology of the Landscapes of Classical Antiquity*: 35–47. Leiden, Stichting Babesch.

Attema, P. A. J., Delvigne J. J., Drost, E. and Kleibrink, M. (2000) Habitation on plateau I of the hill Timpone della Motta (Francavilla Marittima, Italy): a preliminary report based on surveys, test pits and test trenches. *Palaeohistoria* 39/40 (1997/1998): 375–411.

Attema, P. A. J., Joolen, E. van and Leusen, P. M. van (2001) A marginal landscape: field work on the beach ridge complex near Fogliano (South Lazio). *Palaeohistoria* 40/41 (1998/1999): 149–62.

Attema, P. A. J., Beijer, A., Kleibrink, M., Nijboer, A. and Oortmerssen, G. van (in press) Pottery classifications: ceramics from Satricum and Lazio, Italy 900–300 BC. *Palaeohistoria* 42/43 (2001/2002).

Attema, P. A. J., De Haas, T. and Nijboer, A. J. (in prep.) Preliminary report on the protohistorical and Roman remains investigated in the campaigns 2000–2002 by the Groningen Institute of Archaeology along the coast between Nettuno and Astura (South Lazio). *Bulletin Antieke Beschaving*.

Barker, G. (1995) *A Mediterranean Valley: Landscape Archaeology and Annales History in the Biferno Valley*. London, Leicester University Press.

Bietti Sestieri, A. M. (1992) *The Iron Age Community of Osteria dell'Osa: A Study of Socio-political Development in Central Tyrrhenian Italy*. Cambridge, Cambridge University Press.

Brandizzi Vittucci, P. (1968) *Cora*. Forma Italiae, I, 5. Roma, Istituto di topografia antica dll'Università di Roma, De Luca editore.

Burgers, G.-J. (1998) *Constructing Messapian Landscapes*. Amsterdam, Gieben.

Burgers, G.-J., Leusen, P. M. van and Attema, P. A. J. (in press) Walking the Murge: interim report of the Ostuni Field Survey (Apulia, Southern Italy). *Studi di Antichità*.

Cancellieri, M. (1990) Il territorio pontino e la via Appia. *Archeologia Laziale* X, 1. Quaderni del Centro di studio per l'archeologia Etrusco-Italica 18: 61–72. Rome, Consiglio nazionale delle ricerche.

Cherubini, C., Cotecchia, V. and Pagliarulo, R. (1994) Geological and geotechnical problems connected with the disappearance of the ancient city of Sybaris. *Science and Technology for Cultural Heritage* 3: 95–112.

Chiarucci, G. (1985) Materiali dell'età del bronzo nelle acque del lago Albano. *Archeologia Laziale* VII. Quaderni del Centro di studio per l'archeologia Etrusco-Italica 11: 34–39. Rome, Consiglio nazionale delle ricerche.

Chiarucci, G. (1994) *Il villaggio delle Macine sommerso nelle Acque del Lago Albano*. Bolletttino di Archeologia subacquea 1. Rome, Istituto Poligrafico dello Stato.

Cotecchia, V. and Pagliarulo, R. (1996) State of the art in geological, hydrogeological and geotechnical researches carried out on the archaeological site of Sybaris. *Geologia applicata e idrogeologia* 31: 43–54.

De Rossi, G. M., Pala, M., Quilici, L. and Quilici Gigli, S. (1969) *Carta archeologica della Piana di Sibari*. Atti e memorie della Società Magna Grecia, nuova Serie IX–X (1968–1969): 91–155. Roma, Società Magna Grecia.

Haagsma, B. J. (1993) A pollen core from Monticchio in the Agro Pontino (South Lazio): a study of human impact in the Agro Pontino during the first millennium BC. In P. A. J. Attema, An archaeological survey in the Pontine Region, Vol. 1: 249–55. PhD dissertation, University of Groningen.

Hofman, B. (2002) The sedimentation history of the Sybaris plain, new radio carbon dates. Unpublished report, Groningen Institute of Archaeology.

Feiken, H. and van Leusen, P. M. (2001) Interpreting field survey results in the light of historic relief change: the Fogliano beach ridges (south Lazio, Italy). In Z. Stančič and T. Veljanovski (eds.) *Computing Archaeology for Understanding the Past. CAA 2000: Computer Applications and Quantitative Methods in Archaeology, Proceedings of the 28th Conference, Ljubljana, April 2000.* BAR International Series 931: 205–11. Oxford, Archaeopress.

Joolen, E. van (forthcoming) Potential land evaluation in archaeology. A reconstruction of ancient landscapes for land utilization types in Italy during the 1st millennium BC. PhD dissertation, University of Groningen.

Kleibrink, M. (in press) The search for Sybaris: an evaluation of historical and archaeological evidence. *Bulletin Antieke Beschaving.*

Lerici, C. M. (1960) *I nuovi metodi di prospezione archeologica alla scoperta della civiltà sepolte.* Milano, Lerici.

Leusen, P. M. van (1998) Archaic settlement and Early Roman colonisation of the Lepine foothills. *Assemblage* 4; http://www.shef.ac.uk/~assem/4/.

Leusen, P. M. van (2001) Marginal landscapes: survey and interpretation biases in low finds density regions in Italy. In T. Darvill and M. Gojda (eds.) *One Land, Many Landscapes.* BAR International Series 987: 71–73. Oxford, Archaeopress.

Leusen, P. M. van (2002) Pattern to Process: Methodological Investigations into the Formation and Interpretation of Spatial Patterns in Archaeological Landscapes. PhD dissertation, University of Groningen (http://www.ub.rug.nl/eldoc/dis/arts/p.m.van.leusen)

Leusen, P. M. van and Attema, P. A. J. (in press) Regional archaeological patterns in the Sibaritide: preliminary results of the RPC field survey campaign 2000. *Palaeohistoria* 42/43 (2000/2001).

Maaskant-Kleibrink, M. (1987) *Settlement Excavations at Borgo Le Ferriere "Satricum", Vol. I.* Groningen, Egbert Forsten.

Maaskant-Kleibrink, M. (1992) *Settlement Excavations at Borgo Le Ferriere "Satricum", Vol. II.* Groningen, Egbert Forsten.

Mater, B. (in prep.) Pre- and protohistoric pottery production in the course of urbanization and colonization in three Italian regions. PhD dissertation, Free University of Amsterdam.

Osborne, R. (1987) *Classical Landscape with Figures: The Ancient Greek City and its Countryside.* London, George Philip.

Peroni, R. and Trucco, F. (eds.) (1994) *Enotri e Micenei nella Sibaritide.* Taranto, Istituto per la storia e l'archeologia della Magna Grecia.

Piccarreta, F. (1977) *Astura.* Forma Italiae I, XIII. Firenze, L. S. Olschki.

Quilici, L. (1995) Interventi di incentivazione agraria in un fundus visto da Varrone lungo la via Salaria. In L. Quilici and S. Quilici-Gigli (eds.) *Interventi di bonifica agraria nell'Italia romana.* Atlante tematico di topografia antica 4: 157–81. Roma, "L'Erma" di Bretschneider.

Rainey, F. G. (1969) The location of Archaic Greek Sybaris. *American Journal of Archaeology* 73: 261–73.

Rainey, F. G. and Lerici, C. M. (1967) *The Search for Sybaris: 1960–1965.* Roma, Lerici.

Ryan, N. and van Leusen, P. M. (2002) Educating the digital fieldwork assistant. In G. Burenhult and J. Arvidsson (eds.) *Archaeological Informatics: Pushing the Envelope. CAA 2001: Computer Applications and Quantitative Methods in Archaeology, Proceedings of the 29th Conference, Gotland 2001.* BAR International Series 1016: 401–12. Oxford, Archaeopress.

Uggeri, G. (1983) *La viabilità romana nel Salento.* Mesagne, Museo civico archeologico "Ugo Granafei".

Vanzetti, A. (2002) Some current approaches to protohistoric centralization and urbanization in Italy. In P. A. J. Attema, G.-J. Burgers, E. van Joolen, P. M. van Leusen and B. Mater (eds.) *New Developments in Italian Landscape Archaeology. Proceedings of a Three-day International Conference held at Groningen, April 13–15, 2000.* BAR International Series 1091: 36–51. Oxford, Archaeopress.

Veenman, F. A. (2002) Reconstructing the pasture: a reconstruction of pastoral landuse in Italy in the 1st millennium BC. PhD dissertation, Free University of Amsterdam.

Vermeulen, F. (2002) Uit de lucht gegrepen: de bijdrage van archeologische luchtfotografie in het 'Potenza Valley Survey project'. *Tijdschrift voor Mediterrane Archeologie* 26: 33–42.

Yntema, D. G. (1993a) *In Search of An Ancient Countryside: The Amsterdam Free University Field Survey at Oria, Province of Brindisi, South Italy (1981–1983).* Amsterdam, Thesis Publishers.

Yntema, D. G. (1993b) The settlement of Valesio, Southern Italy: final report on the field survey. *Bulletin Antieke Beschaving* 68: 49–70.

Yntema, D. G. (2000) Mental landscapes of colonization: the ancient written sources and the archaeology of early colonial-Greek southeastern Italy. *Bulletin Antieke Beschaving* 75: 1–49.

8. Site by Site:
Combining Survey and Excavation Data to Chart Patterns of Socio-political Change in Bronze Age Crete

Tim Cunningham and Jan Driessen

INTRODUCTION

In this paper we concentrate on Bronze Age Crete. While this is a narrow focus for a volume aimed at broad comparisons, there is an argument to be made for Crete as its own microcosm, at least insofar as the history of archaeological exploration is concerned (Bennet 2002: 215). Indeed, all considerations of archaeological data must be limited geographically, temporally and method-ologically; our own constraints are set out below.

Geographically, the mere island nature of Crete compli-cates issues of comparability across any broader spectrum. Although the picture of islands as isolated laboratories for study has been challenged (Cherry 1999: 19; Broodbank 2000: 1; Hamilakis 2002: 17), there is still ample evidence to suggest that prehistoric Crete may have evolved fairly idiosyncratic social forms and furthermore that its size prevents direct comparisons with the many smaller islands in the Aegean.

Temporally, most survey projects on the island have been carried out by and for prehistorians. Though no-one nowadays spurns the later periods and careful recording of all remains is standard practice, this is still a very different beast from a survey planned and executed by a scholar of Byzantine, Roman or even Hellenistic Crete. It may well be that surveys with an explicitly historical bias would have already produced 'better' results in terms of generating useful and coherent reconstructions of human interaction with and within landscapes, with broader relevance to events and trends elsewhere. This said, we ourselves are both prehistorians and unfortunately will not be helping matters much from that point of view.

Methodologically, one must select what *sort* of data to consider, both in terms of how it has been produced and how it has been made available (*i.e.* final publication, preliminary report, personal communication, etc.). One also naturally employs the data that most suits one's own interpretive methodology. In the present paper, as implied by its title, we do not consider survey data alone, but rather all archaeological data, whether derived from excavation, casual reconnaissance, or modern, systematic

and intensive survey methods. In fact, the inter-relationship of survey datasets and results from excavations, their integration and the development of a more holistic ap-proach form a major theme of this paper. We do not try to account for all available evidence, but have sifted the data according to the questions we seek to answer (for a broader summary of Cretan survey projects, see Driessen 2001a). While in no way disputing the usefulness of collecting data as broadly as possible, on the interpretive side we belong to what Bennet (2002: 218) identifies as an anti-'generalising' trend in Minoan studies.

We will begin by considering the state of survey data from the island on two levels: first, how it has been produced and used; and second, what has actually been produced (*i.e.* the dataset itself). We propose a method-ology for the comparative use of survey data as well as for future fieldwork research design that emphasizes the generation of clear, *testable* hypotheses. Comparisons must take place at a post-interpretive stage and must not be limited to what is felt to be certain, immediately provable, or safe. Work aimed at and limited to systematizing the transition from raw statistical data (such as sherd counts) to the identification of specific human action is important, but only as a means to an end – an end which must be ever in mind. Modern intensive survey techniques have pro-duced data on a level that is far more precise than is necessary in many cases, while at the same time often restricting interpretation to a general, coarse-grained summary of results. Although the more intensive and systematic data retrieval methods sacrifice area covered and can inhibit the use of judgment sampling, in most cases the results have vindicated the research design. Still, the trade-off should never be left unexamined, and no single methodology should ever be accepted as appropriate to all cases.

It is clear now that sherd density maps cannot and should not be compared across projects save in exceptional circumstances (see many of the papers in this volume, particularly Ch. 2 by Michael Given). Indeed, most middle-range issues must be worked out in a more site-specific manner: broad rules or formulae applicable to projects separated by time and space are not possible, not needed, and unworthy even as a goal. A simple method, starting with the generation of hypotheses that can then be tested, is a more suitable (though perhaps less mathematically sexy) way to make the transition from raw data to understandable conclusions about past human behavior. Hypotheses at the generation stage should be elaborate and must go beyond the current data or evidence. This last point (that in order to be testable, a hypothesis must predict future results), though an obvious one, is often ignored by scholars who have confused generation with confirmation and therefore limit their interpretations to what they feel could be safely confirmed using only the evidence available to them. More far-ranging interpretations stimulate discourse, can be easily tested and modified, and will hopefully inspire a more readable and appealing literature (Whittlesey 2000). A palpable fear of being wrong often infuses much archaeological writing, and this hesitancy profoundly handicaps the discipline.

We propose in this paper to test survey data by applying it to more finely-grained questions than has perhaps been the norm. We will present a hypothesis about the development of 'palatial' culture on Crete – a hypothesis that does not seek to account for all evidence, but is based on or derived from observation of certain key pieces of evidence (or what we think are key pieces, at least) which should prove testable. We will be concerned with working through the predictive aspects of our hypothesis and proposing a means for future tests.

Finally, we will briefly address two major hurdles that stand in the way of improving the scope and resolution of archaeological discourse. These are, first, the rate of publication, not only for survey, but for all archaeological fieldwork; and second, the present permit structure which prohibits proper implementation of many modern advances in fieldwork methodology and would certainly inhibit our proposed model for future work.

ARCHAEOLOGICAL SURVEY ON CRETE: SOME THOUGHTS ON WHERE WE ARE, AND HOW WE GOT THERE

The island of Crete covers 8,305 sq. km and is dominated by mountain chains that make up 52% of the surface. Overall, roughly 1,100 sq. km of the island has been subjected to survey, with an obvious bias towards coastal and upland plains (Figure 8.1) (Driessen 2001a: 52–53). Unfortunately, only a little less than half of this area has been published. It is not our purpose to focus on the limitations of the data, but it is worth pointing out that this article could not even begin to be written without extensive reliance on preliminary reports, personal communication, our own experience and even hearsay.

Modern systematic survey techniques have been enthusiastically accepted, by and large, although certain features, often in extremely remote and difficult terrain, such as 'refuge' sites and peak sanctuaries have more often been located and explored by more traditional, one-person methods (for refuge and defensible sites, see Nowicki 2000; for roads and 'watchtowers', Tzedakis *et al.* 1989; 1990). Probably the most useful aspect of modern systematic and intensive surveys, utilizing teams of fieldwalkers and employing carefully chosen sampling strategies, has been the degree of confidence attributable to negative results. Finding and recording sites is not particularly difficult and requires little more than a single person equipped with a compass, a pencil and a notebook (Whitley *et al.* 1999: 257–58). All surveys, whether one-man or team-based, miss sites, sometimes because sites can appear and disappear, and sometimes because they just miss them. However, a large-scale team survey, walking measured and evenly-spaced transects will tend to produce a dataset far more *convincingly* complete. Considering that all surveys and indeed all archaeological explorations are in the end only samples, it is likewise reassuring to have the sampling strategy itself a topic of some consideration.

Of course, this only concerns prospection. A parallel development, still in its infancy, but sure to improve the quality of the dataset by at least an order of magnitude, has been the development and incorporation of geo-archaeological and paleo-environmental research into the survey process. We say these are in their infancy not as a slight to what they have produced so far, but rather in recognition of their potential. Geoarchaeology, in particular, as a combined discipline, holds great promise. Projects in which the research design is driven by geo-archaeological concerns, rather than merely incorporating them, will no doubt become the rule.

There is, of course, an enormous amount of uncertainty in survey archaeology, including the very definition of a site, dating of coarse wares, and understanding depositional and post-depositional processes without recourse to excavation. Frequently, and especially with small sites, the relation of the surface scatter to past behavior is anything but clear; and, in some areas, surface survey is better described as a charting of various post-depositional processes than of past settlement patterns or human activity.

However, this is a well-worn subject and we will not rehash it here, except to make two points. First, even in the worst-case scenario of unreliability, from human error, unrecognized post-depositional processes, and mistakes in sampling and research design, surface survey on Crete has produced enough data of enough quality to begin moving on – moving on from what has been at times an exhausting and even detrimental self-referential focus on field methodology. It will improve, no doubt, but it works, it produces important and usable data, and it is time to make something of it. Second, due to the lack of textual evidence and sources for almost all of the Bronze Age, a 'first stage' of survey was required simply to produce

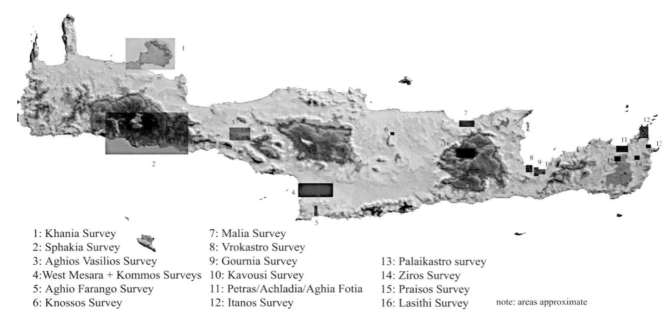

1: Khania Survey
2: Sphakia Survey
3: Aghios Vasilios Survey
4: West Mesara + Kommos Surveys
5: Aghio Farango Survey
6: Knossos Survey

7: Malia Survey
8: Vrokastro Survey
9: Gournia Survey
10: Kavousi Survey
11: Petras/Achladia/Aghia Fotia
12: Itanos Survey

13: Palaikastro survey
14: Ziros Survey
15: Praisos Survey
16: Lasithi Survey

note: areas approximate

Figure 8.1 Map of Crete showing locations of survey areas considered in the text.

enough background data to begin the process of hypothesis generation and testing. This was not necessary, for example, in the Near East or for historical periods, where literary sources supplied such material for hypotheses, so that survey projects could begin at the level of testing and confirmation/refutation – or at least with a good head start.

The impetus behind recent survey projects on Crete and their aims has been the generation of broadly diachronic data applicable to reconstructions of past settlement (and, more generally, human activity) and environment. The push has been for objective or raw data, acquired through standardized methods, as if trying to produce a dataset comparable at a pre-interpretive stage, though this has rarely been done.

Not surprisingly, the questions asked by survey projects on Crete tend to be as broad as possible. What was the environment/landscape like during particular time periods and what did humans do there? Such coarse-grained questions are combined with a focus on methods of data recovery, the unspoken methodological assumption being that more systematized field-walking will produce better results – an assumption tautologically confirmed by heralding whatever does result as better by virtue of the recovery methodology employed. Unfortunately, broad questions, painstaking recovery methods that limit the amount of area covered, and a fear of over-interpretation tend not to produce very interesting reconstructions of the past. In response, projects sometimes expand their time scales – *i.e.* lower their resolution to a point where at least some kind of picture, however fuzzy, emerges, using broad periods such as 'prehistoric', 'Greco-Roman' and 'modern'. Subsequent work often seeks to formalize the relationship of surface remains to past activity rather than simply

accepting that this relationship can only be interpreted, never known or mathematically demonstrated.

The downside of all this is a lack of 'exciting' results given the mass of data. The upside is that the data themselves, having been gathered without strong predispositions and agendas, are more trustworthy. But can data generated in this way from different projects simply be juxtaposed, combined or even synthesized, and thereby produce answers? And even if so, in practice, is this the only or even the best way forward? It is our contention that increasing the resolution of the data retrieval, though obviously beneficial, is not the answer; nor is simply assembling raw datasets from larger areas. We must increase the resolution of the questions we ask of the data and increase the resolution of the interpretations we give, with the understanding that these are hypotheses, which must be formulated and proposed before they can even be tested – let alone confirmed.

On a more practical level, the current state of data dispersal or dissemination, though improving all the time, is still lagging far behind its potential. A serious clean-slate reconsideration of the process of fieldwork publication is in order, for excavation as well as survey. This topic will be taken up in the conclusions, along with the related need for a reconsideration of the way such field projects are conceived and implemented: it will be argued that a new paradigm is needed for initial fieldwork as well as subsequent publication of results, not so much as a replacement of existing strategies, but as a necessary next step.

Moving on to consider the actual results of survey work on Crete, we should mention some of the background of archaeological work on the island, most of which has focused on the Bronze Age culture dubbed 'Minoan' by Sir Arthur Evans. Minoan civilization is an excellent example of a modern archaeological construct imposed on a past unable to defend itself (MacGillivray 2000), not having produced any history of its own (that has been found). Partly discovered and partly created by Evans in the early twentieth century, Minoan culture has long fascinated specialists and laymen alike, enticing them, like Evans, to a mixture of discovery and invention. Although scrutiny, skepticism and deconstructivist analysis have been liberally applied, and reconstructions questioned, oddly enough it turns out that – however unsound his methods, or influential his preconceptions – Evans was often right. For example, Minoan artistic styles and decorative schemes really were strikingly similar to the Art Nouveau/Arts and Crafts movements of Evans' own time (Farnoux 1996: 107–109); and, more importantly, Bronze Age Cretan culture really does form a perceptible unity, worthy of a special name.

In point of fact, that which we call 'Minoan civilization', and around which we have built our modern construct, was every bit as much a construct in its own time. In other words the archaeological record itself suggests the application of a synthetic construct to reconstitute the society that produced it. This cultural self-awareness, coupled with the fact that this was an island civilization and hence strongly filtered by geographic constraints, increases the chances of building a comparatively complete picture of a certain human condition at a certain place and time in remote antiquity and hence speaks directly to what is certainly one of the most prevailing and deeply-rooted of human fascinations – that of the 'lost civilization'. Consequently, most of the energy put into archaeology in Crete, whether survey or excavation, has gone towards building such a picture; even revisionist notions – and, incidentally, ones applauded by the present authors (*e.g.* Hamilakis 2002) – are little more than a way of 're-mystifying' Cretan prehistory to allow a new generation of researchers the thrill of discovering the newly lost. Broader issues, such as why people moved to islands throughout the whole East Mediterranean in the Neolithic period, receive less attention. Likewise, the study of later periods has often been separated from that of the Bronze Age. Despite these admittedly limiting biases, what has survey been able to contribute?

One of us has already attempted a summary comparison of survey data for Crete (Driessen 2001a). This approach was felt to be valid as a first step, but ultimately failed to provide the kind of information that was sought. What it did provide was a basis for further questions and for the construction of hypotheses. Simple diachronic changes in settlement patterns were about as far as the data went, and these are outlined briefly below:

- An increase in settlement, perhaps reflecting an influx of new people in the Final Neolithic.
- A rapid increase and dispersal of settlement in the Middle Minoan I–II periods.
- A leveling-off and often a contraction, possibly nucleation, in Late Minoan I.

- The phenomenon of defensible/refuge sites in Late Minoan IIIB and IIIC.
- Considerable diversity from region to region on Crete, perhaps reflecting local trajectories and development.

These changes all come from the realm of basic site prospection. A few other phenomena are particularly well suited to recovery by survey techniques: peak sanctuaries, roads, and the occurrence of isolated structures, whether they be 'farmhouses', 'road stations', or 'watchtowers'; the so-called 'villas' can be included here as well. As for some of the other disciplines implicated in the 'multi-disciplinary' approach favored by modern surveys, some of the most interesting work on paleoclimatic and environmental reconstruction has been done by Jennifer Moody, who in a recent paper (Moody, forthcoming) proposed a 'little ice age' period coincident with palatial civilization on Crete, running from roughly 1900 BC to 1200 BC, with a possible climatic maximum at *c.* 1630 BC. These data are interesting not so much from a causal point of view (since the development, growth and decline of a civilization is always a complex issue and best understood as an emergent phenomenon, with many interacting influences), but contextually: that is, when this civilization was being formed, it was within a landscape considerably wetter than previously thought and consequently more productive – which may be a significant factor in the *nature* of the society that developed and what it was like to live in it.

Though not a comprehensive overview, these comments hopefully are enough to provide a sense of the kind of data being produced. It is not our intention to summarize or attempt to account for all the various information available, but rather to select what we feel are potentially interesting features of the dataset so far gathered and to use these as 'test cases' to frame questions and propose hypotheses. We begin by considering the apparent drop in settlement numbers in Late Minoan I and move on to a discussion of the development and nature of political organization for the Bronze Age generally.

TEST CASE 1: WHAT HAPPENED IN LATE MINOAN I?

The conventional tripartite chronological divisions of Early, Middle and Late Minoan (EM, MM, LM), based on ceramic styles, were later merged by Platon into a scheme based on architectural phases thought to apply to the major ('palatial') sites: Prepalatial (EMI-MMI), Protopalatial (MMIB-MMII), Neopalatial (MMIII-LMIB), and Post- (now sometimes 'Final') palatial (LMIII).

In the traditional view, population and social complexity grew steadily from the end of the Neolithic to EMII, culminating in a kin-based society with village-level rather than regional organization. EMIII represented for some a period of smooth transition, for others decline and fragmentation, for yet others a period improperly defined ceramically, after which in MMI population and social complexity grew more rapidly than before, culminating in the construction of the palaces and the establishment of palatial civilization by MMII (for a fuller discussion and bibliography see Watrous 1994: 712–20, though his position on EMIII is perhaps more idiosyncratic than one might expect in a general review article).

The transition to palatial society has been seen by some as sudden and dramatic (Cherry 1983; Watrous 1994), by others as fairly gradual (Renfrew 1972; Warren 1987: 50; and more recently Sbonias 1999). Once established, palaces and palatial civilization were thought to have grown smoothly and uninterruptedly until LMIB, when a wave of destructions occurred throughout the island and only Knossos, of the palaces, survived.

Cherry's peer-polity model, with larger regional entities organized around each of the larger palaces, has been widely accepted for the Protopalatial period (Cherry 1986). Most scholars accept a Knossian domination of the island starting by the beginning of the Neopalatial period (MMIII) and lasting until its end (LMIB). This scheme has led to a blurring of the Neopalatial phases – *contra* Evans, who noted major architectural revisions and differences between MMIII and LMIA. Recent developments have supported Evans' original distinctions and demonstrated that the major palaces did not have coincident architectural phasing (Macdonald 2002; La Rosa 2002). It has already been suggested, on the basis of architectural and ceramic changes, that a new political force incorporating a much larger territory emerged at Knossos only in LMIA (Driessen 2001a: 63). Likewise, survey data have suggested some significant changes in socio-political organisation and possibly in demography for these periods.

A drop in settlement numbers for LMIA was found in surveys at Malia, Kavousi, Gournia, Praisos, Lasithi, Kommos, and the Western Mesara. The most extreme case is at Malia, where the number of sites drops from over 75 for the Protopalatial to just 9 for the Neopalatial period (Driessen 2001a: 51, table 4.1). This cannot be described as nucleation, as the town of Malia is also known to have shrunk in this period, as did the palace. In the Western Mesara, the slight decline in settlements in LMIA is accompanied by a simplification (or even the establishment) of hierarchy. The wide variation in settlement size noted for the Protopalatial period is replaced by a three-tiered hierarchy with a couple of large sites (Kommos, Phaistos/Aghia Triada), many medium-size sites (small hamlet or village), and somewhat fewer small sites (one or two houses) (Watrous *et al.* 1993: 225–26).

When the surveys at Kommos and in the Western Mesara were conducted, little was made of this phenomenon, as certain major buildings at the centers (especially the palace at Phaistos and the massive Building T at Kommos) were thought to belong to this period. Now, new information has radically altered the context of the data collected by these projects. While surveys are often carried out with the stated intent of contextualizing ex-

cavated sites, the inverse is often more true – that the surveys are carried out *within* the context of the excavated sites, even when territorially removed.

If we consider the Kommos and Western Mesara surveys this is abundantly clear. Strong evidence was found for a major shift in population and settlement patterns from the Protopalatial to the Neopalatial periods, particularly in the Western Mesara where the overall number of sites not only dropped, but the hierarchy simplified. In the *context* of presumed continuity and growth from the Proto- to Neo-palatial periods, this was dismissed as a curiosity, or simply nucleation (though Watrous *et al.* [1993: 226] do speculate about a population drop).

Starting with Kommos, Building T has now been shown to have been built early in MMIII (Shaw *et al.* 2001: 8) and to have had only limited use in early LMIA, after which it underwent a radical change in function (demonstrated by a pottery kiln built atop what had been a stoa at one end of the court). Kalamaki, which may have been the second largest site in the immediate vicinity of Kommos, shows signs of a burned destruction in LMIA (Hope Simpson *et al.* 1995: 396).

At Phaistos, re-examination of deposits has conclusively dated the 'new palace' to LMIB (La Rosa 2002). After the destruction of the first palace at the end of MMII there is some re-use of the ruined structure throughout the subsequent periods – but major reconstruction does not happen until LMIB and it has been suggested that, while administrative control passed to Kommos in MMIII and Aghia Triada in LMIA, there was *no palatial center* in the Mesara for the period in question.

Already, the drop in settlement numbers and the simplification in size hierarchy are looking more interesting, and the case for emerging Knossian dominance more convincing. A recently discovered palace at Galatas, only some 20 km from Knossos, was built in MMIII and destroyed early in LMIA, with only squatter occupation thereafter (Rethemiotakis 1999: 721).

The decline at Malia has already been mentioned. Meanwhile, the Pediada, an area of rich agricultural potential just southeast of Knossos, saw site numbers jump from 125 in the Protopalatial to 230 in the Neopalatial period (Driessen 2001a: 65, n. 3; these numbers are to be used with extreme caution, pending publication), and the urban site of Knossos likewise grew considerably. The palace at Knossos was rebuilt with a new, heavily restricted and fortified northern entrance passage, flanked by a bastion decorated with a monumental relief fresco of a bull. This is what Colin Macdonald calls the 'Frescoed Palace' (Macdonald 2002); and a new decorative and iconographic scheme is incorporated at this time, along with the re-introduction of figurative art, rare or unknown during MMIII.

Likewise, while MMIII is a period of conservatism and regionalism in ceramic terms, in LMIA island-wide styles in both fine and plain wares emerge, including a standardization of size for the conical cup (Van de Moortel 1997:

266–67 and n. 157, citing work of K. Petruso; also, for this trend at Palaikastro, Knappett and Cunningham 2003). We believe all of this signals a major political shift on the island. The fact that it seems to affect even rural settlement patterns, which, if anything, should be *longue durée* or at least '*longue*-ish', emphasizes the point that this was not a gradual, organic growth, nor a smooth transition, but the comparatively sudden and deliberate imposition of a new system, quite possibly applied forcibly over a large region and at all levels of society. For example, in the Kavousi region on the Gulf of Mirabello in East Crete, Haggis (1996: 403) finds in LMIA a 'significant restructuring of the spatial patterns of habitation and land use, suggesting changes in political and economic conditions', and he has recently suggested (2002: 138) an 'imposed hierarchy' in the Neopalatial period.

One could argue that the survey results were significant enough to warrant more notice, but they were lost against the background of evidence from excavated centers. Given that palatial society was held to be a continuous development, the survey data were left as a bit of a puzzle – that is, under-interpreted, perhaps with the off-hand suggestion that they might simply indicate nucleation. This does not seem to be so, and, particularly in the case of Malia, one has to wonder if there was not even some kind of coerced relocation of inhabitants – a forced depopulation of the largest and closest rival.

Furthermore, in compiling the survey data referred to above, archaeologists were expecting and looking for a general growth in population and increase in settlements in the Neopalatial period, and assuming continuity or gradual evolution of cultural and political systems from the Protopalatial onwards. Also, MMIII and LMIA ceramics are often not distinguished, and have even been lumped together into a single 'transitional' period. Yet despite these obstacles, evidence *still* surfaced to suggest a more radical hypothesis.

What might the picture be if a project, asking fine-grained questions, were set up explicitly to test this hypothesis – a project that set out rigorously to distinguish LMI from MMIII, and to isolate LMI components in multi-period sites; a project that was able to check all possible candidates for 'nucleation' to see if the LMI scatter showed expansion, and to use predictive modeling to suggest under-explored areas where people might have moved or been moved to? Such resolution is not possible in broad, regional, diachronic, multi-disciplinary surveys that explicitly seek to avoid preconceptions or interpretive axe-grinding, but it is still possible. Is it not worthwhile?

If, as we believe, there was at the beginning of LMIA a comparatively sudden change in the political structure on the island, not simply a smooth continuous trend, nor even a sudden spurt towards centralization, but a real change, however short-lived (and we doubt it lasted beyond the eruption of Thera), then what was the nature of social and political organization before? If the nature of Protopalatial society was flowing towards an emerging Knossian 'state',

we do not think we would see such fundamental changes as outlined above; but what kind of organizational principles are required that could allow for such a contrast, and what happens to them afterwards? We must expand our hypothesis to account for the nature and development of palatial society in the Cretan Bronze Age.

TEST CASE 2: A CORPORATE POLITY IN MINOAN CRETE?

Before we consider the implications of survey data for our hypothetical reconstruction of Minoan socio-political development and structure, we should consider the issue from a more general standpoint. Minoan civilization presents us with a paradox. There is a striking unity to its material culture, especially reflected in architecture, ceramics, prestige goods and iconography. This is particularly notable in, but not restricted to, the elite sphere and this coherence spans the island and even spills out across the Aegean. Yet there is never any sign of a lasting island-wide administrative system; no ruler iconography; few elite burials; and no explicit indications of territorial boundaries or allegiances – in fact, no evidence outside similarities in material culture for the kind of state such similarity implies.

Indeed, locating a state on Bronze Age Crete has always had more to do with redefining the term 'state' than anything else. Can a centralized state be found in survey data? Considerations of settlement distribution, patterns in resource exploitation, rank-size distributions, and specialized sites dependent on larger centers have so far failed to produce such evidence. In short, the answer is no.

Should there have been such a state? Do we need Minos after all? Complexity theory and emergent order are by now sufficiently well-established concepts (Schoep and Knappett, forthcoming) that we no longer have to assume that something like palatial civilization must be forced onto or coerced out of a basically unwilling or at least indifferent populace. A 'bottom-up' paradigm for the emergence and subsequent formulation of Minoan society is at the very least possible. Schoep and Knappett (forthcoming) argue for an interweaving of top-down and bottom-up organizing principles in the development of Minoan palatial society; while we do not exclude the former, we emphasize the latter. Certainly, the ubiquity and similarity of forms of social reproduction on the island (Cunningham 2001: 84), and the iconographic focus on crowd scenes and public ritual, suggest that Minoans were self-aware as a civilization (or culture group) and quite intentionally sought to maintain links with island-wide ideological unities – without in any way requiring or even implying any larger political or even economic system.

Such a formulation presupposes a lack of intensive competition for basic resources, a kind of self-sufficiency for regional groups. Was this possible? We have mentioned indications that the climate during the time in

DEM created by S. Soetens, A. Sarris

Figure 8.2 Relief map of East Crete.

question (1900–1200 BC) was, in fact, wetter than at any time since. Estimation of ancient agricultural yields, like population estimates, is notoriously difficult and combining the two can only provide a ball-park figure of primarily illustrative value (see Nowicki 1999 for a good recent example) – essential in fleshing out our understanding of daily life, perhaps, but unsuitable as proof. Still, the question being posed here is simply answered. To take East Crete as an example (Figure 8.2), could Petras, Palaikastro and Zakros, the three central places in the far eastern end of the island, have coexisted without needing to encroach on each other's 'territories' for agricultural subsistence?

Hamlets and farmhouses near possible 'borders' in the region tend to show a relatively even mix of ceramics from the two putative centers (for Azokeramos, between Zakros and Palaikastro, see Day 1997: 225), and no sign of defensibility as a high priority. Where we do see signs of defensive concerns (most notably in the Petras area, see Tsipopoulou 1999: 848), these seem to be in response to extremely local conditions, and not a result of competition *between* centers. Indeed, in the Minoan period no

indication of borders or territorial markers have been found and such borders are only reconstructable based on topographic features or on hypothetical comparison with much later historical times (Bennet 1990).

Furthermore, as Chaniotis (1999: 182–85) points out for the Hellenistic period, a basic social order of economic autarchy was able to persist through the occasional drought-inspired raid on a neighboring territory and survived integration into the larger Hellenistic world. How deep-rooted was this kind of autarchy?

The only known instances in the region of inter-village conflict have either been opportunistic and ideological (Christian/Muslim conflict at the turn of the century), or concerned with revenue derived from extra-regional sources (the argument over the income from the Sanctuary of Diktaean Zeus). And of course Minoan settlements generally were unwalled and undefensible. Basic self-sufficiency, or economic autarchy, was not only possible, it seems, but is suggested by the data.

Other survey-based analyses have shown that divergent trajectories in settlement patterns demonstrate local autonomy (Driessen 2001a; Cunningham 2001). The Siteia basin, for example, is dominated by Petras, a small (2.5 ha) palatial center, ringed by three smaller (*c.* 1 ha) sites with a scatter of farmhouses or isolated dwellings occupying the lowest tier. Palaikastro, one of the largest towns of Bronze Age Crete (*c.* 30 ha) is surrounded only by isolated dwellings or very small hamlets (*c.* 0.25 – 0.5 ha). The evidence suggests local autonomy in growth and distribution of habitation, and possibly resource exploitation as well. For example, an extensive road network linking coastal and upland sites and particularly well documented in the Zakros region, though seen as a defensive system by Tzedakis *et al.* (1989; 1990), may also have facilitated the movement of agricultural produce or even the export of timber.

The lack of clear patterns in rank-size distribution may likewise suggest local agency in the development of economic and political systems. If no clear centers (or conversely too many) can be found to link second-order settlements, then the system can be considered non-radiating (or non-dendritic). Likewise, lower-order sites might cluster in the general vicinity of a larger settlement, but without any clear pattern to their distribution. Such is the case for Minoan Crete, so far at least. When radiation does occur (around Petras, for example, but not Palaikastro or Zakros), it seems locally determined. Site locations correlate with a wide variety of possible determinatives, such as environmental factors (elevation, geology, water), proximity to neighboring sites, and routes, again in such a way as to seem locally (*i.e.* opportunistically) determined (see Moody 1987 for the best examples). Such a non-radiating, opportunistic settlement pattern suggests to us local agency in the development and structure of local area relations.

We also see local agency demonstrated in response to extra-regional stimuli. The Gulf of Mirabello region, like most of the island, shows signs of significant developments in LMIA (for Kavousi, see Haggis 1996; for Gournia, see Watrous and Blitzer 1995). At Kavousi, 24 of 53 sites are abandoned; these are all single houses or small clusters. Two coastal sites grow: one, Tholos (3.5 ha), was most likely a port, and the other (2.5 ha) is located close by. This is the first sign of site-size ranking since the Early Bronze Age in the survey area. It is accompanied by an increase in local production of coarse-ware pottery. Similarly, at Gournia, there is at this time a drop in site numbers and an increase of activity at the port. These areas are contiguous and the new port at Tholos is only 9 km from Gournia, though it is that much closer to the offshore island communities at Pseira (1.5 ha) and Mochlos (2.5 ha). Gournia, at 5 ha and sporting a palace, is the only candidate for a regional center. Even at such a small scale (the combined area of the two surveys is less than 100 sq. km), it seems that local sites reacted directly to the extra-regional stimulus (whatever it was) and that that stimulus was not filtered through or distributed by Gournia. Again, local agency would seem to be the dominant force in structuring regional relations.

In such a system, allegiance to local centers would be largely a matter of mutual self-interest. This can be contrasted with clear patterns of site spacing according to 'production zones' (such as Wilkinson [2000: 58] has suggested for the Early Bronze Age North Jazira) which indicate a level of hierarchical organization scaled to match the extent of the observable pattern in traditional rank-size analysis. In such cases, even if still restricted to localized units, the pattern suggests a stronger degree of control radiating from the central place.

Such patterns cannot be found with any regularity at any scale for Minoan Crete. Archanes, for example, is too rich, too large and too close to Knossos to function as a second-tier center distributing power from and sourcing goods to Knossos; likewise harbor towns, such as Kommos, Poros, Amnisos, Palaikastro, and Zakros, show signs of benefiting directly from their own trading ventures (for Kommos, see Cline 1999), despite in some cases (Kommos, Amnisos and Poros) a level of proximity to other centers that could be perceived as competitive or even threatening. Blanton (1996: esp. 79–80), discussing dendritic vs. non-dendritic market systems (for which see also Smith 1976) in the Basin of Mexico, finds some irregularities in the distribution of market centers, route placement, and connectivity as indicative of a less than fully developed dendritic system; but the situation on Crete has been very difficult to fit into any existing models for market systems at all. Knappett (1999) demonstrated the lack of correlation between the growth of political and economic systems, showing that the wide distribution of Mirabello pottery could not be linked to the growth of Malia as a palatial center, and indeed it seems that the spread of Isthmus wares and fabrics throughout the Bronze Age must be first understood as a locally emerging phenomenon.

Curiously, in LMIII, the time of the Linear B archives at Knossos (known as the 'Final Palatial' period), settlement patterns change drastically. This has long been considered a time of Mycenaean domination, whether political or cultural, and though many scholars now reject a simplistic conquest model, most agree on the essential 'un-Minoanness' of the end of the Bronze Age. The political entity represented by the Knossos archives, which probably start as early as LMII and last through LMIIIA2 (*c.* 1450–1300 BC), has been characterized as having a specialized extraction economy (Driessen 2001b), and Halstead (1999: 161) has pointed out that, while the palace sought to ensure a steady flow of certain products, actual ownership of such things as flocks was left to the people. Even this system is only centralized in certain aspects and falls short of a fully organized bureaucratic 'state'; but for most of the island, the patterns of habitation and land use (new settlements, usually small and dispersed, and a much lower density of occupation in towns) suggest a reorganization on grounds or criteria determined by the needs of, or importance to, the center – that is, Knossos (Bennet 1985; 1987; 1990).

After the final destruction of the palace at Knossos,

Cretan society reverted to a simple village-based system with little sign of integration on an island-wide scale. Much of the work on settlements at the end of the Bronze Age and beginning of the Iron Age has been done in the Isthmus of Ierapetra, where they are described by Haggis (1996: 414) as 'lineage based... miniature communities'. There are continuing similarities in aspects of material culture, particularly cultic aspects, that suggest a lingering thread of cultural consciousness. We propose a similar lingering thread in social, economic and political organizational patterns – a thread that lingers, in our view, because it was a foundational aspect of Bronze Age Cretan (or Minoan) society.

Local elements did not need any larger centralized authority to order their society or compose their cultural identity. LMIA Knossian hegemony was in this view an aberration, a warping of the basic structure of that society; the LMIII Knossian 'state', a parasitic growth. Both may have co-opted or made use of an integrated island-wide cultural 'system', but neither was responsible for, and indeed both were ultimately damaging to, the basic principles of integration and order of what was an essentially corporate polity.

We borrow the phrase 'corporate polity' from Blanton *et al.* (1996: 7) to indicate, in an admittedly vague way, a polity where a significant proportion of the strategies used to create and maintain economic and political structures were essentially corporate. Most of the work on corporate strategies in early societies has been focused on Mesoamerica (Berdan *et al.* 1996; Blanton *et al.* 1996; Blanton 1998; Feinman *et al.* 2000; Saitta 1997; for Crete, see Vansteenhuyse 2002). While outside our present scope, we would point especially to the discussion in Feinman *et al.* (2000: 453) of 'corporate organizations' characterized by 'dispersed economic resources', a 'less personalized' leadership with fewer ostentatious displays and a lack of 'individual aggrandizement' replaced by 'communal ritual... public construction... large co-operative labor tasks... shared power...' and whose 'social segments [are] woven together through broad integrative ritual and ideological means'. Likewise, Blanton's five 'main elements constituting corporate political economy in archaic states' (1998: 154–55), especially the 'ritual sanctification of the corporate cognitive code and ritualization of political communication' seem especially relative to Minoan Crete. And Saitta (1997: 7) makes a very important caution against the assumption that power correlates with and implies coercive control of labor, and points out that 'power, property and labor relations can vary independently of each other'.

For the Minoan period, at least until LMIA, the profusion and wide distribution of centers for social reproduction, whether 'court compounds', peak sanctuaries, feasting centers or 'villas' already suggested a lack of centralized authority. If our hypothesis is correct, there should be still more of these, especially in rural or remote areas. Almost any small agglomeration of dwellings should have a local

space, most probably a court of some kind, for feasting and communal rituals, and until the encroachment of a centralized power in LMIA there should be no restrictions on the number and distribution of peak sanctuaries and indeed a looser typology of such sites. Can such information be recovered from surface survey? Assemblages dominated by drinking vessels and particularly conical cups might indicate a rural feasting center. Conical cup distributions are by no means consistent in excavated sites, and are not all that common in surface scatters. (For a discussion of conical cup deposits concentrated near entrances, see Rupp and Tsipopoulou 1999; for a similar pattern noted at Palaikastro, see Knappett and Cunningham, in press; see also Vlasaki 1996: 42 and pl. 8, for a pit at Nopigeia filled [according to Vlasaki, pers. comm.] with *c.* 3,000 conical cups.)

Work on peak sanctuaries being done now by our colleague Steven Soetens will, we think, greatly enhance our understanding of the role these may have played in organizing the Minoan countryside (Soetens *et al.* 2002). In the Khania Survey (Moody 1987), for the MMI-II period, 11 ritual sites and two 'hilltop shrines' were found. The latter were not considered peak sanctuaries because they did not exactly conform to the established (and since unestablished) topographical criteria; however, such variation is exactly what we would expect for a locally emerging cultic phenomenon.

Our hypothesis also holds certain implications for the *development* of palatial civilization. It predicts a stepping-stone or link between the individually complex, but regionally independent, villages known from Early Minoan II sites and the emergence of island-wide palatial culture – a transitional phase where the EMII 'nodes' began interacting and establishing order at a higher scale. If such transitional linkages are not present, we would be forced to concede that the palaces, along with a new social order, had been imposed from above, as it were. Happily, we do not have to do this, at least not yet. Recent work by Haggis (1999: 53–84) and by Wilson and Day (1999: 43–44; and especially 2002: 160–61) has shown the emergence and importance of both peak sanctuaries and communal feasting activities well prior to the establishment of the palaces. Indeed, such communal ritual foci (which should also include the Mesara tholoi) are the first sign of what has been seen as the emerging 'palatial' order.

It is worth noting that peak sanctuaries are a particularly communicative phenomenon (Haggis 1999). Contrary to popular belief, peak sanctuaries do not tend to share intervisibility with habitation sites, but rather with each other, providing a sphere of communication and interaction between otherwise autonomous communities, already in the process of evolving similar ritualized constructions of group identity. As these communities grow to a size where communication between local communities becomes relatively instantaneous, much larger regions can function adaptively and institutions – 'palaces' – emerge. Monumental building then commemorates the 'awakening' of an island-wide consciousness of a shared cultural sphere with the elaboration of the traditional communal feasting centers.

Oral tradition and subsequent mythologized history likewise suggest an island with a profusion of hierarchically equal cities. Even the fabled and now often discounted thalassocracy and 'pax Minoica' (Cherry 1999: 19) might be better understood as a kind of 'neighborhood watch' program (*i.e.* the impact of local agents acting in common self-interest) than the decree of a Minos.

We therefore posit a society with a cellular or corporate political and economic structure, bound together through a shared cultural identity, ideologically defined and ritually composed. The predominance of iconographic depictions of communal ritual support this idea, as does the nature of most burial sites, now including Poros, which show a mix of elite and common burials (Dimopoulou and Rethemiotakis 1999).

 Once established, such a system would, of course, be ripe for co-option. Human nature being what it is, we should expect that at some time the system would have shifted and a dynast or dynasty emerge that at least tried to 'take over' and impose a top-down centralized power structure. As outlined above, we believe that this is exactly what happened in LMIA at Knossos. Such a 'dynasty' was short-lived and must not have survived the eruption of Thera (indeed, the evidence that the LMIA Knossian state had particular interest in trade and colony routes to Anatolia via Thera would only have increased the devastating effect of the eruption) – a time span of possibly only 20 or 30 years. The basic social structure that pre-existed the more unified state would have survived and should be seen as one of the causal ingredients in the development of the city-state, a legacy not unlike Cretan-born Zeus.

This is, as noted, simply a proposal; evidence has been sifted and interpreted to demonstrate our reasons for proposing it. Proof may never come, but testing can be done even with the data already gathered, and, perhaps more effectively, with the implementation of new research projects specifically geared toward selected aspects of it.

CRITIQUE: A PROPOSAL FOR FUTURE WORK

We suggest that one way forward is to frame projects around such specific questions. Material must be re-examined and sites revisited. Projects must be initiated with specific investigative aims. A simple compilation of data, no matter how sophisticated the number-crunching gets, will never be able to provide confirmation or refutation of such questions – and yet survey itself could provide such answers. What we propose, then, is the construction of clear, developed and testable hypotheses. Much of what is written nowadays about survey is highly specialized and inwardly focused (see, for example, many papers in the POPULUS volumes: Barker and Mattingly

1999–2000). While useful for the further refinement of methodology or as a venue for shoptalk among specialists, such work is of little interest outside the discipline. Correlatives and multipliers are all well and good, but what are obviously needed are more people in the field who not only understand what they are looking at, but also have a good idea of what they are looking for.

Hypothesis confirmation must not be confused with hypothesis generation, and a hypothesis need not be proved to be welcomed, as long as it can be tested. Too often projects try to combine the steps, to summarize all the evidence and confirm what should only be proposed; or they shy away from proposing anything that they do not feel can be proved, lowering the bar of reconstructing the past to a point where it ceases to be of interest to anyone (see Whittlesey 2000, for a similar argument regarding archaeology in the American Southwest). Synthesis, explanation, and interpretation in archaeology are primarily ways of translating evidence about the past into a language that can be understood and has relevance to a given audience – an audience which cannot be limited to specialists schooled to speak the jargon of much scientific archaeological practice.

What does all this have to do with surface survey? As noted above, we have been able to find some evidence for our hypothesis from survey results. Perhaps more importantly in the context of this volume, we are proposing what might be an inversion of the standard approach. Instead of asking what we as archaeologists can do for survey data, we suggest asking what surveys can do for us. One answer is that survey projects be formulated with specific research goals aimed at answering carefully chosen questions, or testing a particular hypothesis.

Just as we favor an approach that makes use of *all* forms of data in generating hypotheses, so too we advocate a holistic approach to fieldwork, making use of whatever techniques or methodologies best suit the questions being asked and the region being examined. This is admittedly not possible under the current permit system, which if anything seems to grow more restrictive, but is nonetheless worth framing. Wide-bore coring, 'shovel-testing' and limited test-excavation would radically alter the degree of resolution of survey results and especially aid in establishing the impact of geomorphological factors within a given area. Likewise excavation projects should generally include a survey component, not as an adjunct, but as an integral part of the investigative strategy.

Finally, it has become very clear, in our part of the world at least, that something is wrong at a systemic level with the current conventions for all fieldwork publication. We need to get rid of the concept of 'final publication' and consider exactly what is needed, who needs it, and how to get it to them. For example, basic, raw data should be processed (finds conserved, drawn, inventoried, photographed if need be; sections, plans, maps etc. scanned) and made available as soon as possible, whether or not it has been 'understood'. Basic summary interpretations can be (and usually are, anyway) presented in preliminary reports. Actual materials should be available for study, limited only by practical concerns (*i.e.* it is not fair to hold on to material out of purely territorial impulses). Many, if not all projects nowadays are at least headed in the right direction (internet publication like PRAP, for example: Davis *et al.* 1996–2001), and at least starting to make use of advances in digital storage and dispersal. What is needed is a concerted restructuring of typical fieldwork/study protocol and especially the reorientation of funding and permit-granting/sponsoring institutions. Typically, a project in the data recovery phase will carry out a kind of triage of archival recording and recording, and then, through the course of a series of study seasons, gradually prepare material for publication. A system aimed at making material directly ready for publication prior to mastication (in other words, publishing sherds and pots before they have been dated, or rather finished being dated) could move much faster. Raw material, notebooks, etc. should not be hoarded, but made available to those with the time, energy, and ability to study them. It would mean much more of a flux; there would be no 'final' word on what was found – but is there ever anyway? We think it will be healthier for the discipline, and more fun anyway, to be moving forward, even though mistakes will be made, corrected, and corrected again.

ACKNOWLEDGMENTS

This paper was prepared as part of the 'Topography of Power' project carried out at the Université Catholique de Louvain (Fonds Spécial de Recherche 2000, 2001). We would like to thank Philip Betancourt, Cyprian Broodbank, Charles Frederick, Florence Gaignerot, Donald Haggis, Sandy MacGillivray, Jenny Moody, Sylvie Müller, Lucia Nixon, Kristof Nowicki, Nikos Panagiotakis, Alan Peat-field, Mieke Prent, Norbert Schlager, Annie Schnapp, Stuart Thorne, Didier Viviers, Vance Watrous and James Whitley, who have generously shared information, but who should by no means be held accountable for any of our hypotheses. Likewise, the other members of our project, Steven Soetens, Peter Tomkins, and Klaas Van-steenhuyse, and especially colleagues Carl Knappett and Ilse Schoep, have provided invaluable help, but bear no responsibility for the outcome.

REFERENCES

Barker, G. and Mattingly, D. (series eds.) (1999–2000) *The Archaeology of Mediterranean Landscapes*. 5 volumes. Oxford, Oxbow Books.

Bennet, J. (1985) The structure of the Linear B administration at Knossos. *American Journal of Archaeology* 89: 231–49.

Bennet, J. (1987) The Wild Country east of Dikte: the problem of East Crete in the LM III period. In J. T. Killen, J. L. Melena and J.-P. Olivier (eds.) *Studies in Mycenaean and Classical Greek Presented to John Chadwick* (*Minos* 20–22): 77–88. Salamanca, Ediciones Universidad de Salamanca.

Bennet, J. (1990) Knossos in context: comparative perspectives on the Linear B administration of LM II-III Crete. *American Journal of Archaeology* 94: 193–211.

Bennet, J. (2002) Millennial ambiguities. In Y. Hamilakis (ed.) *Labyrinth Revisited: Rethinking 'Minoan' Archaeology*: 214–25. Oxford, Oxbow Books.

Berdan, F. F., Blanton, R. E., Boone, E., Hodge, M., Smith, M. E., and Umberger, E. (eds.) (1996) *Aztec Imperial Strategies*. Washington D.C., Dumbarton Oaks.

Blanton, R. E. (1996) The Basin of Mexico market system and the growth of empire. In F. F. Berdan, R. E. Blanton, E. Boone, M. Hodge, M. E. Smith, and E. Umberger (eds.) *Aztec Imperial Strategies*: 47–84. Washington, D.C., Dumbarton Oaks.

Blanton, R. E. (1998) Beyond centralization: steps toward a theory of egalitarian behavior in Archaic states. In G. M. Feinman and J. Marcus (eds.) *Archaic States*: 135–72. Sante Fe, School of American Research Press.

Blanton, R.E., Feinman, G. M., Kowalewski, S. A. and Peregrine, P. N. (1996) A dual-processual theory for the evolution of Mesoamerican civilization. *Current Anthropology* 37: 1–14.

Broodbank, C. (2000) *An Island Archaeology of the Early Cyclades*. Cambridge, Cambridge University Press.

Chaniotis, A. (1999) Milking the mountains: economic activities on the Cretan uplands in the Classical and Hellenistic period. In A. Chaniotis (ed.) *From Minoan Farmers to Roman Traders: Sidelights on the Economy of Ancient Crete*: 53–85. Stuttgart, Franz Steiner Verlag.

Cherry, J. F. (1983) Evolution, revolution, and the origins of complex society in Minoan Crete. In O. Krzyszkowska and L. Nixon (eds.) *Minoan Society: Proceedings of the Cambridge Colloquium 1981*: 33–45. Bristol, Bristol Classical Press.

Cherry, J. F. (1986) Polities and palaces: some problems in Minoan state formation. In C. Renfrew and J. F. Cherry (eds.) *Peer Polity Interaction and Socio-political Change*: 91–112. Cambridge, Cambridge University Press.

Cherry, J. F. (1999) Introductory reflections on economies and scale in prehistoric Crete. In A. Chaniotis (ed.) *From Minoan Farmers to Roman Traders: Sidelights on the Economy of Ancient Crete*: 17–23. Stuttgart, Franz Steiner Verlag.

Cline, E. (1999) The nature of the economic relations of Crete with Egypt and the Near East during the Late Bronze Age. In A. Chaniotis (ed.), *From Minoan Farmers to Roman Traders: Sidelights on the Economy of Ancient Crete*: 115–44. Stuttgart, Franz Steiner Verlag.

Cunningham, T. F. (2001) Variations on a theme: divergence in settlement patterns and spatial organization in the far east of Crete during the Proto- and Neopalatial periods. In K. Branigan (ed.) *Urbanism in the Aegean Bronze Age*: 72–87. Sheffield, Sheffield Academic Press.

Davis, J. L., Alcock, S. E., Bennet, J., Lolos, Y., Shelmerdine, C. W., and Zangger, E. (1996–2001) The Pylos Regional Archaeological Project: internet edition. Available at http://river.blg.uc.edu/prap/PRAP.html

Day, P. M. (1997) Ceramic exchange between towns and outlying settlements in Neopalatial East Crete. In R. Hägg (ed.) *The Function of the 'Minoan Villa'*: 219–27. Stockholm, Skrifter utgivna av Svenska Institutet i Athen.

Day, P. M. and Wilson, D. E. (2002) Landscapes of memory, craft, and power. In Y. Hamilakis (ed.) *Labyrinth Revisited: Rethinking 'Minoan' Archaeology*: 143–66. Oxford, Oxbow Books.

Dimopoulou, N. and Rethemiotakis, G. (1999) The Sacred Conversation Ring from Poros. In I. Pini and W. Muller (eds.) *Minoisch-Mykenisch Glyptik: Stil, Ikonographie, Funktion. 5th Internationales Siegel-Symposium, Marburg. CMS Beiheft 6*: 39–56. Mainz, Mann Verlag.

Driessen, J. (2001a) History and hierarchy: preliminary observations on the settlement pattern of Minoan Crete. In K. Branigan (ed.) *Urbanism in the Aegean Bronze Age*: 51–71. Sheffield, Sheffield Academic Press.

Driessen, J. (2001b) Centre and periphery: some observations on the administration of the Kingdom of Knossos. In S. Voutsaki and J. T. Killen (eds.) *Economy and Politics in the Mycenaean Palace States*. Cambridge Philological Society Supplementary Vol. 27: 96–112. Cambridge, Cambridge Philological Society

Driessen, J. (2002) 'Kretes and Ijawones': some observations on the identity of Late Bronze Age Knossians. In J. Bennet and J. Driessen (eds.) *A-NA-QO-TA: Studies in Mycenaean Society and Economy offered to J.T. Killen. Minos* Supplement 33–34 [1998–99]: 83–105. Salamanca, Ediciones Universidad de Salamanca.

Farnoux, A. (1996) *Knossos: Unearthing a Legend*. London, Thames and Hudson.

Feinman, G. M., Lightfoot, K. G. and Upham, S. (2000) Political hierarchies and organizational strategies in the Puebloan Southwest. *American Antiquity* 65(3):449–70.

Haggis, D. (1996) Archaeological survey at Kavousi, East Crete: preliminary report. *Hesperia* 65(4): 373–432.

Haggis, D. (1999) Staple finance, peak sanctuaries, and economic complexity in Late Prepalatial Crete. In A. Chaniotis (ed.), *From Minoan Farmers to Roman Traders: Sidelights on the Economy of Ancient Crete*: 53–85. Stuttgart, Franz Steiner Verlag.

Haggis, D. (2002) Integration and complexity in the Late Prepalatial Period. In Y. Hamilakis (ed.) *Labyrinth Revisited: Rethinking 'Minoan' Archaeology*: 120–42. Oxford, Oxbow Books.

Halstead, P. (1999) The meaning and wider significance of *o* in Knossos sheep records. *Annual of the British School at Athens* 94: 145–66.

Hamilakis, Y. (2002) What future for the Minoan past? In Y. Hamilakis (ed.) *Labyrinth Revisited: Rethinking 'Minoan' Archaeology*: 2–29. Oxford, Oxbow Books.

Hope Simpson, R., Betancourt, P. P., Callaghan, P. J., Harlan, D. K., Hayes, J. W., Shaw, J. W., Shaw, M. C., and Watrous, L. V. (1995) The archaeological survey of the Kommos area. In J. W. Shaw and M. C. Shaw (eds.) *Kommos I. The Kommos Region and Houses of the Minoan Town. Part 1: The Kommos Region, Ecology, and Minoan Industries*: 325–402. Princeton, Princeton University Press.

Knappett, C. (1999) Assessing a polity in Protopalatial Crete: the Malia-Lassithi state. *American Journal of Archaeology* 103: 615–39.

Knappett, C. and Schoep, I. M. Y. (2000) Continuity and change in Minoan palatial power. *Antiquity* 74: 365–71.

Knappett, C. and Cunningham, T. F. (2003) Three Neopalatial deposits from Palaikastro, East Crete. *Annual of the British School at Athens* 98 (in press).

La Rosa, V. (2002) Pour une révision préliminaire du second palais de Phaistos. In J. Driessen, I. Schoep and R. Laffineur (eds.) *Monuments of Minos: Rethinking the Minoan Palaces. Proceedings of the International Workshop 'Crete of the 100 Palaces?' held at the Université Catholique de Louvain, Louvain-la-Neuve, 14–15 December 2001 (Aegaeum 23)*: 71–97. Liège, University of Liège; Austin, University of Texas at Austin.

Macdonald, C. F. (2002). The Neopalatial Palaces of Knossos. In J. Driessen, I. Schoep and R. Laffineur (eds.) *Monuments of Minos: Rethinking the Minoan Palaces. Proceedings of the International Workshop 'Crete of the 100 Palaces?' held at the Université Catholique de Louvain, Louvain-la-Neuve, 14–15 December 2001 (Aegaeum 23)*: 35–54. Liège, University of Liège; Austin, University of Texas at Austin.

MacGillivray, J. A. (2000) *Minotaur: Sir Arthur Evans and the Archaeology of the Minoan Myth*. New York: Hill and Wang.

Moody, J. (1987) *The Environmental and Cultural Prehistory of the Khania Region of West Crete: Neolithic through Late Minoan III*. Unpublished PhD dissertation, University of Minnesota.

Moody, J. (forthcoming) The impact of Little Ice Age events on the cultural history of Crete in the Medieval, Bronze and Neolithic Periods. Paper presented at the 9th International Congress for Cretological Studies, Elounda, Crete, October 2001.

Nowicki, K. (1999) Economy of refugees: life in the Cretan mountains at the turn of the Bronze Age and Iron Ages. In A. Chaniotis (ed.) *From Minoan Farmers to Roman Traders: Sidelights on the Economy of Ancient Crete*: 53–85. Stuttgart, Franz Steiner Verlag.

Nowicki, K. (2000) *Defensible Sites in Crete (Aegaeum 21)*. Liège, University of Liège; Austin, University of Texas at Austin.

Renfrew, C. (1972) *The Emergence of Civilisation: The Cyclades and the Aegean in the Third Millennium B.C.* London, Methuen.

Rethemiotakis, G. (1999) The hearths of the Minoan palace at Galatas. In P. P. Betancourt, V. Karageorghis, R. Laffineur and W.-D. Niemeier (eds.) *MELETEMATA: Studies in Aegean Archaeology presented to Malcolm H. Wiener as He Enters His 65th Year (Aegaeum 20)*, III: 721–28. Liège, University of Liège; Austin, University of Texas at Austin.

Rupp, D. and Tsipopoulou, M. (1999) Conical cup concentrations at Neopalatial Petras : a case for a ritualized reception ceremony with token hospitality. In P. P. Betancourt, V. Karageorghis, R. Laffineur and W.-D. Niemeier (eds.) *MELETEMATA: Studies in Aegean Archaeology presented to Malcolm H. Wiener as He Enters His 65th Year (Aegaeum 20)*, III: 729–40. Liège, University of Liège; Austin, University of Texas at Austin.

Saitta, D. J. (1997) Power, labor, and the dynamics of change in Chacoan political conomy. *American Antiquity* 62(1): 7–26.

Sbonias, K. (1999) Social development, management of production, and symbolic representation in Prepalatial Crete. In A. Chaniotis (ed.) *From Minoan Farmers to Roman Traders: Sidelights on the Economy of Ancient Crete*: 53–85. Stuttgart, Franz Steiner Verlag.

Schoep, I. and Knappett, C. (forthcoming) Dual emergence: evolving heterarchy, exploding hierarchy. Paper presented at the Sixth Round Table on Aegean Archaeology, Sheffield, January 2002.

Shaw, J. W. and Shaw, M.C. (1995) *Kommos I. The Kommos Region and Houses of the Minoan Town, Part 1: The Kommos Region, Ecology, and Minoan Industries*. Princeton, Princeton University Press.

Shaw, J. W. *et al.* (2001) *A LMIA Ceramic Kiln in South-Central Crete: Function and Pottery Production (Hesperia* Supplement 30). Athens, American School of Classical Studies.

Smith, C. (ed.) (1976) *Regional Analysis*, Volume I. New York, Academic Press.

Soetens, S., Driessen, J., Sarris, A. and Toupazi, S. (2002) The Minoan peak sanctuary landscape through a GIS approach. *Archeologia e calcolatori* 13: 161–70.

Tsipopoulou, M. (1999) Before, during, after: the architectural phases of the palatial building at Petras, Siteia. In P. P. Betancourt, V. Karageorghis, R. Laffineur and W.-D. Niemeier (eds.) *MELETEMATA: Studies in Aegean Archaeology presented to Malcolm H. Wiener as He Enters His 65th Year (Aegaeum 20)*, III: 847–54. Liège, University of Liège; Austin, University of Texas at Austin.

Tsipopoulou, M. and Papacostopoulou, A. (1997) 'Villas' and villages in the hinterland of Petras, Siteia. In R. Hägg (ed.), *The Function of the 'Minoan Villa'*: 203–214. Stockholm, Skrifter utgivna av Svenska Institutet i Athen.

Tzedakis, Y., Chrysoulaki, S., Voutsaki, S. and Venieri, Y. (1989) Les routes minoennes. Rapport préliminaire: défense de la circulation ou circulation de la défense ? *Bulletin de correspondance hellénique* 113: 43–76.

Tzedakis, Y., Chrysoulaki, S., Venieri, Y. and Argouli, M. (1990)

Les routes minoennes: le poste de Choiromandres et le contrôle des communications. *Bulletin de correspondance hellénique* 114: 43–65.

Van der Moortel, A. M. P. A. (1997) *The Transition from the Protopalatial to the Neopalatial Society in South-Central Crete: A Ceramic Perspective*. Ph.D. Dissertation, Bryan Mawr College.

Vansteenhuyse, K. (2002) A study of the political institution in Neopalatial Minoan Crete. In G. Muskett, A. Koltsida and M. Georgiadis (eds.) *SOMA 2001: Symposium on Mediterranean Archaeology. Proceedings of the Fifth Annual Meeting of Postgraduate Researchers, The University of Liverpool, 23–25 February 2001*. British Archaeological Reports International Series1040: 157–60. Oxford, Archaeopress.

Vlasaki, M. (1996) Nopigeia, Kissamos. *Kritiki Estia* Periodos D, Tomos 5: 11–45.

Warren, P. M. (1987) The genesis of the Minoan palace. In R. Hägg and N. Marinatos (eds.) *The Function of the Minoan Palaces*: 47–56. Stockholm, Skrifter utgivna av Svenska Institutet i Athen.

Watrous, L. V. (1994) Review of Aegean Prehistory III: Crete from the earliest prehistory through the Protopalatial period. *American Journal of Archaeology* 98: 695–753.

Watrous, L. V. and Blitzer, H. (1995) The Gournia Survey Project: a preliminary report on the 1992–1994 field seasons. *American Journal of Archaeology* 99: 313 [abstract].

Watrous, L. V., Khatzi-Vallianou, D., Pope, K., Shay, J., Shay, C.T., Bennet, J., Tsoungarakis, D., Angelomati-Tsoungaraki, E., Vallianos, C. and Blitzer, H. (1993) A survey of the Western Mesara plain in Crete: preliminary report of the 1984, 1986 and 1987 field seasons. *Hesperia* 29: 90–108.

Whittlesey, S. M. (2000) Review of S. H. Lekson, *The Chaco Meridian: Centers of Political Power in the Ancient Southwest* (Walnut Creek, CA, AltaMira Press, 1999). *Journal of Field Archaeology* 27: 359–64.

Whitley, J., Prent, M. and Thorne, S. (1999) Praisos IV: a preliminary report on the 1993 and 1994 survey seasons. *Annual of the British School at Athens* 94: 215–64.

Wilkinson, T. (2000) Case studies from the Levant and the Near East. In J. Bintliff and K. Sbonias (eds.) *Reconstructing Past Population Trends in Mediterranean Europe (The Archaeology of Mediterranean Landscapes* 1): 45–64. Oxford, Oxbow Books.

Wilson, D. E. and Day, P. M. (1999) EMIIB Ware groups at Knossos: the 1907–8 South Front tests. *Annual of the British School at Athens* 94: 1–62.

9. Comparative Settlement Patterns during the Bronze Age in the Northeastern Peloponnesos, Greece

James C. Wright

INTRODUCTION

Despite a long interest in collecting data on prehistoric site location on the mainland of Greece, there has been a dearth of analytical and synoptic research on the distribution of these remains. Since Blegen's overview in 1928 there has been very little comparative study of changes in settlement among regions (Haley and Blegen 1928). Bintliff's doctoral dissertation (1977) *Natural Environment and Human Settlement in Prehistoric Greece* is a notable exception. Although the primary source for such study – the *Gazetteer and Atlas of Mycenaean Sites* by Hope Simpson and Dickinson (1979) – has been around since its inception nearly four decades ago (Hope Simpson 1965), there is little more on the subject for the entire Bronze Age than Dickinson's article of two decades ago, revisiting the core problems of settlement distribution in the Peloponnesos (Dickinson 1982; see McDonald and Hope Simpson 1972; Rutter 1993b; Shelmerdine 1997; Bennet and Galaty 1997).

Bintliff (1977) had noted an apparent disparity in distribution between the evidence from excavation and from survey (*i.e.* many more sites collected through survey), and this spurred Dickinson's re-evaluation. Although Dickinson (1982: 129) allowed that these distributions – and presumably the disparities among them – would almost certainly be revised as a result of increased survey field-work and better reckoning of site size, he did not believe that the numbers produced by extensive surveying were so inaccurate as to be in danger of being overturned by intensive survey. Thus, he argued forcefully that the variation in the density and even in the size of settlements observable from the evidence assembled in the *Gazetteer* reflected a true pattern (1982: 131).

The problem with this point of view is that the comparisons were primarily being made according to a coarse temporal scale, punctuated only by the distinctions of Early, Middle and Late Bronze Ages (Fig.9.1), and, except in a few instances, involved very broad geographical units, largely reflecting modern political (prefecture) boundaries. Dickinson continued the tradition, begun by Blegen, of

Figure 9.1 Overall site distribution in the northeastern Peloponnesos (n=104).

thinking about prehistoric settlement in the Peloponnesos in imprecise, static, and stage-defined terms. This is illustrated by his assessment of the mainland during the Middle Bronze Age as 'poor and backward in comparison with the Cycladic and Cretan civilisations,' with the conditions of settlement being nothing more than 'farming villages' (1982: 134). Only with the late phase of this period did he see emerging the 'origins of Mycenaean civilisation'.

In the intervening 20 years the new information available from excavation and survey has made the problem of analysis much more complicated (*e.g.* Morgan 1999: 347–67). We are now more critical of interpretations comparing the major subdivisions of the Bronze Age across broadly defined geographic boundaries. Curiously, however, although there has been much more work on this problem for the Early Bronze Age (Forsén 1992; Maran 1998), there is a continuing reluctance to do the same for the Middle and Late Bronze Ages. Thus, despite an increasingly sophisticated and detailed understanding of the relative stratigraphic correlations during the Middle Helladic and early Mycenaean periods, and a richly documented picture of sites of activity and settlement on the mainland and among the Aegean islands, there has been no detailed accounting of settlement distribution for the Middle and Late Bronze Ages that explores the dynamic processes of settlement, landuse, and interaction of regions and sub-regions of the geographically fragmented Peloponnesos. Instead only generalized discussions, such as those of Kilian (1987; 1988a; 1988b; 1994), Cavanagh and Mee (1998), Barber (1992), Shelmerdine (1997), Dabney and Wright (1990), Wright (1995), and Dickinson (1999) have been published.

In a 21st-century collection of essays such as this, where scholars working in such broad traditions as that of American, Roman, British, Greek, Cypriot, and Near Eastern archaeology are conferring, it is readily apparent that it is long past the time that those of us working in the Aegean adjust our focus from one of 'Mediterranean myopia' as Blanton (2001) has termed it, to one of *evriopa* (s.v. ευρύοπα, the term used by Homer) – a term that Strabo, Braudel, and the European Union would approve for its multiple connotations of the vision of far-seeing Zeus and of supra-national perspective. Surely the purpose of comparing data from surveys is to understand better the dynamic pathways of different civilizations, cultures, and communities. And, despite a post-modern recognition of the difficulty of comparing them to each other, or comparing them against an abstracted background of generalizing theories and models like state formation, a broad framework for the prehistory of the Aegean is long past due (with appropriate nods of respect to Renfrew's seminal *The Emergence of Civilisation* [1972] and Broodbank's recent *An Island Archaeology of the Cyclades* [2000]). After all, the models for fieldwork and interpretation have been around since *The Basin of Mexico: Ecological Processes in the Evolution of a Civilization* (Sanders *et al.* 1979) and *Ancient Mesoamerica: A Comparison of Change in Three Regions* (Blanton *et al.* 1981).

Fundamental to any such examination is an inspection of the overall trends in human activity within any given region. I use the term 'human activity' for two reasons: it comprehends everything from hunting and foraging to highly nucleated urban formations; and it suggests that, at a general and initial level of investigation, it is not necessary to qualify the data, for there is room and time for that after rough models have been constructed for further, closer, even myopic investigation. Thus, the purpose of this paper is to see what kind of picture we can construct with the information gathered unsystematically over the course of the last century and a half, and then to compare it to the more systematically and intensively gathered data from surveys in order to see if and how the picture is different. Ultimately, I hope to propose ways for further examination, and to point to specific research strategies that might fill lacunae, as well as to wonder if the patterns observed in our setting are similar at other times within our own study region, as well as beyond it to other places in the world. Specifically, I will show in my conclusions that patterns emerge which support three different models, which I will term *Central Place*, *Dependency*, and *Periphery*.

With this scope in mind, several considerations must be taken into account. Paramount are the scales of examination in terms of space and time; then considerations of size (both absolute and rank size) and function should come into play. Also, it will be necessary to keep in mind the nature of the evidence – disparities in the quality and quantity of information available, limitations due to the incomparability of methods of collection, the inadequacy

of evidence for certain kinds of questions. But none of these should limit the scope for, if nothing else, the questions that can be asked on the basis of our knowledge of basic human needs and of fundamental ways of acting in the landscape will, in and of themselves, point in directions of value.

SPACE

The problem of defining regions for study and determining meaningful boundaries of human activities and habitation is, of course, one of the central difficulties of regional studies (Steward 1950; Adams 1981; Bintliff 1977; Plog *et al.* 1978; Sanders *et al.* 1979; Sutton 1994). Even though the boundaries of communities change according to different economic and political conditions and the flux of social relations (Sutton 1988; 1994; 1999; 2000a; 2000b), it is well worth the risk of looking at data through a grid of smaller units that have some potential for catching local-scale activities (see Lukerman 1972).

In the Aegean, now that we have finely-grained information from intensive surveys, we must use those results to provide a more subtly graded and richly textured picture of settlement than we have traditionally done. In this manner, we can better take account of distinctions among different land-forms and better compare similar ones from one area to another, while also being sensitive to local responses to contact and exchange with external agencies. For example, while it is obvious that there are substantive geographical differences between the Corinthia and Argolis, and therefore that it is not especially meaningful to talk about the northeast Peloponnesos as a whole (Figure 9.2), it is not immediately apparent what the division between these two areas means. What is more apparent is that, in the Corinthia, the zone along the Gulf of Corinth is different from the interior, because the settlement patterns throughout the Bronze Age are not only different in these two areas, but sites also cluster together spatially (Morgan 1999: 347–67). Such an observation spurs other questions, so that an examination of this localization of sites is paired with geomorphological observations. More specifically, the sites on the Gulf's coast and on the Isthmus are situated on ancient marine terraces of soft limestone with abundant aquifers that discharge as springs and which provide much arable land – in marked contrast to the upland valleys, which are some 300+ m higher, are characterized by colluvial deposits, and are part of the ecology of the mountainous interior (Freytag 1973; Higgins and Higgins 1996).

The Argolid also is not meaningfully viewed as a whole (Figure 9.2). Instead, it breaks down into several regions (Jameson *et al.* 1994: 13–56). These are: (1) the great alluvial plan around the Gulf of Argos and the mountainous periphery which drains into it (further subdivided by catchments: Lehmann 1937; Zangger 1993); (2) the valleys to the southeast that include the settlements of Asine and

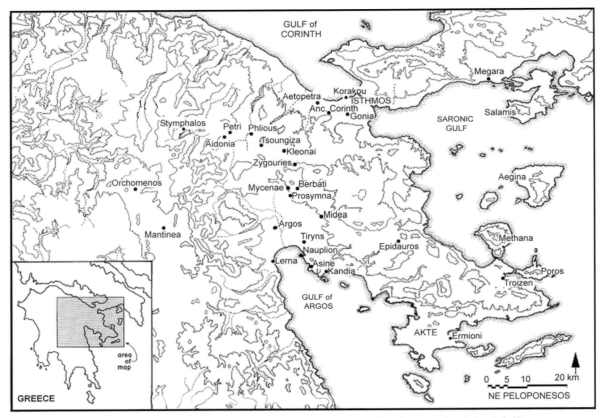

Figure 9.2 Map of the northeastern Peloponnesos (after drawing by Julia Pfaff).

Kandia; (3) the region further east known as the Epidauria, which has harborage on the Saronic Gulf; (4) the peninsular island-scape of Methana-Troizen-Poros; and (5) the Akte, or southern Argolid, separated from the rest by the massif of Didyma and extending as a peninsula out into the Aegean Sea.

All of these subdivisions (and others not discussed here) are amenable to analysis in terms of their potential for supporting communities. Fortunately, a number of them have been subjected to systematic intensive surveys, and there is much information available with which to begin this analysis.

TIME

If it is useful to argue that the lens used for analyzing spatial distributions needs to be focused more on localities, it is equally pertinent to suggest that we coordinate the evidence from our highly refined ceramic typologies with absolute chronological reckonings. The need for this is apparent merely by observing that our customary tripartite system of division is very much a relict of the culture-historical approach to Aegean prehistory which has accustomed us to think in terms of the largely meaningless stages 'Early', 'Middle', and 'Late' – even though we know that a more dynamic and process-oriented framework is available. Thus we need to work within temporal units

that capture shorter segments of time, in order to visualize better the variable tempos and modes of sociopolitical and political economic change. For example, the question today is not one of defining the culture of the 'Middle Helladics' (as Caskey [1960] referred to them), or in arguing that they were poor (as Dickinson [1982] would have it), but instead of assessing the differential local and regional dynamics that transpired throughout the second millennium B.C. – a period that witnessed multiple and differential episodes of cultural formation, consolidation and collapse.

From the perspective of method it is clearly misleading to construct maps or charts of site distribution merely on the basis of our nomenclature, since it is heavily biased towards the recognition of the most diagnostic ceramics (Rutter 1983). This is evident by looking at a table that coordinates absolute dates with ceramically defined subdivisions and shows how the recognition of ceramic styles creates classificatory phases of highly varying lengths of time in absolute terms (Table 9.1). Any presentation of these data in visual form is highly distorted, since the phases are incommensurate; thus, counts of sites for EH II representing a span of about 450 years are represented as being of the same scale as the count for MH III measured at 75 years.

This is a problem the Aegean shares with other archaeologically investigated areas of the world, and it is a necessary artifact of the culture-historical approach which

Phase	EH I–EH II	EH II–EH III	EH III–MH I	MH I–MH II	MH II–MH III	MH III–LH I	LH I–LH II	LH II–LH IIIA	LH III A–LH IIIB	LH IIIB–LH IIIC	LH IIIC–SubMyc/PG
HI Dates B.C. (Manning 1995)	3100–2650	2650–2200	2200–2000	2000–1900	1900–1750?	1750?–1675	1675–1600	1600–1435	1435–1360	1360–1200	1200–1065
Range	450	450	200	100?	150?	75	75	165	75	160	135
LO Dates B.C. (Warren and Hankey 1989)	3100–2650	2650–2200	2200–2000	2000–1850?	1850?–1700?	1700?–1600?	1600?–1500?	1500?–1390?	1390–1300	1300–1200	1200–1065
Range	450	450	200	150?	150?	100?	100?	110?	90	100	135

Table 9.1 Aegean Bronze Age phase designations and absolute dates, after Manning (1995) (high ^{14}C chronology) and, with adjustments, after Warren and Hankey (1989). I follow Wiener (1998) in dating the end of LH IIIA to c. 1300 B.C.

defined phases by assemblages of traits. By continuing such a nominalist approach to the study of the Bronze Age, however, we mask the problems inherent in studying the general and specific trajectories of cultural development in our region. Notwithstanding the difficulties of identifying surface material, researchers conducting intensive surveys are often reluctant to make chronological assessments more refined than Early, Middle and Late Bronze, as in the Methana survey (Mee and Forbes 1997). The problem is not confined to this instance, but creeps into the assessments of many modern researchers, in large part because there are two conflicting purposes at work: a traditional system of classification and one more functionally oriented and interpretative. Thus Rutter comments:

> In general, absolute dates for the Aegean Stone and Bronze Ages are not yet very reliable and many different sets of dates are often in use for one and the same phase or period. A major debate has been raging since 1987 over the absolute date of the great volcanic explosion of the island of Thera… early in the Late Bronze Age. As a result, absolute dates within the first two-thirds of the second millennium B.C. (ca. 2000–1350 B.C.) are presently in an unusually active state of flux. *It is therefore always best to describe an archaeological assemblage in terms of a relative chronological label… rather than in terms of its supposed duration in calendar years B.C.* (Rutter 2002; emphasis added).

Why should it be thought preferable to speak in relative terms? In my view, such a language of archaeology denies the volatility of human activity, collapsing long-term processes into a few words, distending rapid developments into arcane terminology. Archaeology studies the historically contingent phenomenon of culture; it is not an abstract and scientifically observable process like biological evolution, where notions of situated time are irrelevant (although not notions of process; Dunnell 1980).

Associated with this issue of developing meaningful instruments of temporal measurement is the problem of contemporaneity. This term was coined by Fred Plog in the 1970s and has been the subject of discussion since (Plog 1973; Schacht 1984; Dewar 1991; 1994; Kintigh 1994; Pollock 1999: 63). The counting of numbers of

sites by period is complicated by the observation that, while some sites are occupied for different intervals of time, simply counting the totals for each subjectively defined period creates a completely false and inflated number of occupations, since for any given period some sites will (a) originate or (b) be abandoned during the period, or (c) they will originate and be abandoned entirely within it. This will be especially true for periods of long duration, and simple counts of numbers for such phases compared to others that are temporally very short will woefully distort the picture. For example, a site occupied for only a part of the 450 years of EH II is weighed equally with one that was occupied throughout the entire phase and into the next phase of EH III.

Dewar (1991) has dealt with this problem by constructing a program based on formulae for the average number of sites that originate per year and the average number that are abandoned per year. In order to do this, however, it is necessary to count the number of sites according to the following four types:

a) sites occupied in the previous and the current phase;
b) sites occupied in the previous, the current and the next phase;
c) sites occupied in the current and the next phase;
d) sites occupied only during the current phase.

It is also necessary to know the number of years for the phase in question. In this study, Dewar's formula is applied using both the high and low absolute chronological reckonings for the Aegean (Warren and Hankey 1989; Manning 1995; Wiener 1998), in part to test the importance of the difference between them. In the graphs in this paper, the 'corrected' numbers of sites per period ('LO' representing the calculations based on Warren and Hankey's absolute chronology [and adjusted by Wiener 1998] and 'HI' based on those of Manning) are plotted against the raw numbers of sites counted per period.

Kintigh (1994) offered an alternative for calculating site numbers, and I did test some of the data according to his formulae, but I am not employing the results, which seem unsuitable in many cases (negative values, highly depressed numbers in some instances and wildly high numbers in others). One of the problems Kintigh correctly examines is that of extremely long periods and the assum-

	Corinthia	*Argolis*	*Lakonia*	*Messenia*
Total Sites	48	50	90	190*
Excavated	15	19	8+	48
Major Excavated Sites	14	13	4	9–11

*Table 9.2 Known sites in regions of the Peloponnesos. (*McDonald and Hope Simpson recognize 332 prehistoric sites in the broadly defined area of the Minnesota Messenia Survey and I have adjusted this number by comparing it to the later record of the Gazetteer (Hope Simpson and Dickinson 1979) and the more recent work of PRAP (2002), which is available online at http://river.blg.uc.edu/prap/PRAP.html).*

ptions that Dewar makes about occupations within them. There seems no suitable mathematical resolution for this problem, since it is primarily one stemming from the fieldworkers' inability to distinguish shorter intervals. As noted below, however, in the case of intensive surveying, where careful attention is paid (*e.g.* the Argolid Exploration Project), a much more refined analysis is attempted.

Additionally, it is possible to simulate the total settled area per period using Dewar's program (Pollock 1999: 64–65, fig. 3.12). For each period being investigated the sum of the area of the sites that fit into the four above-listed categories is substituted for the actual number of sites. The algorithm then simulates the total area occupied per period, which, when compared to the total area of all the sites for the phase, invariably is smaller. I will not attempt this analysis here because it is beyond the scope of this paper. In fact it is at this point unlikely that a study of the areas of settlements can be confidently conducted in the Aegean because of the many intractable problems with estimating site size (see below).

SIZE

Documentation of sites in the Aegean is plagued by the problem of measuring the size of sites. This seems to me a fourfold problem. It is an historical by-product of the simplistic assumption that virtually any artifact scatter represented a settlement or a tomb, the details of which would only be known through excavation. Traditionally, it is a problem of a lack of interest in calculating site size that accompanied the extensive documentation of sites. But above all are the problems of visibility and of multiple periods of occupation. Many sites are overgrown by garrigue, maquis and other vegetation, and thus extremely hard to document. Others have been occupied off and on for as much as 8,000 years, and it is usually unclear what the actual size was for any given period (*e.g.* Jameson *et al.* 1994: 417; Cherry and Davis 2001). I mention this issue here, because rank-size estimates are one of the critical initial steps of analysis necessary before more sophisticated levels of distributional analyses can be conducted (Hodder and Orton 1976: 69–73).

PROBLEMS WITH THE RECORD

Before proceeding I want to return to Dickinson's (1982) point about the disparity between excavated sites and those known through surface observation. Table 9.2 illustrates that there has been extensive excavation and surface collection throughout the Peloponnesos over the past 150 years. Clearly, the general distributions do not accurately reflect the record of prehistoric settlement and utilization of the different landscapes. These profiles may be misleading, for the simple reason that the core areas have received more attention through excavation and recording of surface finds than others. But, as Rutter (1983) cautioned, it may be exacerbated by variability in the recognition of diagnostic artifacts (such as MH pottery), and recent analysis by Bintliff *et al.* (1999) has claimed the problem is even more deleterious because of an imputed large-scale loss of the surface record. Cherry and Davis (2001) doubt that this problem exists; at least their work in the Nemea Valley indicates otherwise (see also Davis, Chapter 3, this volume). But that the issue must be taken seriously is evident when we recognize the relative dearth of intensive survey around core areas of habitation and our general ignorance of the hinterlands of these areas (see discussion below, pp. 127–28).

There is, then, a very real likelihood that the extensively gathered information is heavily biased. Lurking behind this doubt is the possibility that major sites have gone unnoticed or are not sufficiently appreciated. Thus in the Phliasian Valley, the discovery of major sites at Aidonia, Petri and Agia Irini are transforming our appreciation of that hitherto isolated rural setting. At Dimini Dr. V. Sismani-Adrimi has been uncovering over the last five years an entire Mycenaean palace complex. Therefore the data obtained from the intensive surveys in the Peloponnesos may be critical for assessing how much error the biased information from the 'core' areas creates and how much it distorts the record. Some work on this has already taken place. Bintliff and Snodgrass (1985: 135–36) claimed that the intensive survey of their region in Boeotia returned on the order of 50 times the number of sites than had been discovered in the extensive survey of Messenia by McDonald and Hope Simpson (1972). Of course, this comparison is specious if it turns out that the regions of Boeotia and Messenia are non-comparable, because of differences in climate, pedology, and hydrology, not to mention differing demographic and historic contingencies. These objections notwithstanding, subsequent research by the Pylos Regional Archaeological Project [PRAP] has confirmed the earlier Messenian pattern (Davis *et al.* 1997; 2002). Rutter (1993b) published a comparative chart that showed the differences in site density (sites/sq. km) between extensive and intensive surveys in Greece to vary from 10 to 100 times (see also Bintliff 1985; Cavanagh 1995; Cherry and Davis 2001); but this needs to be appreciated in terms of the relative number of sites by size, since the conclusions we might draw will be fundamentally different if the increase occurs among sites of the lower, middle or upper orders of magnitude. Therefore, for a reasonable comparative assessment of the growth and changing degree of socio-political integration among different areas, it is critically important to determine the difference in magnitude. It is no surprise that a primary result of intensive survey is an increase in the number of small sites, but of more importance will be determining the relative importance of such sites in periods prior to the emergence of centralized polities (see Jameson *et al.* 1994) and the nature of their relationship as such polities appear.

In the analysis which follows two different sets of data are examined. I begin with the extensively gathered record, which is drawn from the *Gazetteer* (Hope Simpson and Dickinson 1979); this I have updated from the annual reports in the *Chronique des fouilles* of the *Bulletin de correspondance hellénique* and the *Archaeological Reports* in the *Journal of Hellenic Studies*, together with Morgan's (1999) study of the Isthmia. In tabulating the data for insertion into Dewar's simulation, I have admitted all reported sites, whether mortuary or settlement or simple scatters, but I have not double-counted known settlements and their cemeteries.

I then consider the evidence from the intensive surveys, where again I recorded all sites published in the inventories. Here, however, I also introduce a second set of calculations, since efforts were rather systematically made to measure the size of sites, and the numbers of sherds and other artifacts were counted. Thus I include in these calculations only those sites whose area was measured and which have at least 50 sherds; the remainder is treated as scatters. In this regard, I do not vary much with the original analysts of the material. It is also necessary to say a word about the temporal divisions I employ. Aegeanists may wonder how I can count sites according to the division of the Middle Bronze Age into the phases MH I, II, III, and may likewise query why LH I and LH II are lumped together. I am able to distinguish these because recent study by Lambropoulou (1991), Nordquist (1987), Dietz (1991), and Zerner (1978; 1986; 1988; 1993) has re-evaluated the pottery from most of the primary excavated sites throughout this region. LH I and LH II are combined, because many sites are recorded as having pottery of MH-LH I or of LH II and LH I-II; I have assumed that in the first case the designation MH could only refer to MH III, since otherwise the range would not be given into LH I. Confirmation of this procedure is found in that in almost

every instance where I found pottery recorded as being of the range MH-LH I, so too was pottery recorded as LH I-II.

THE EXTENSIVELY GATHERED DATA FROM THE NORTHEASTERN PELOPONNESOS

The charts of Figures 9.3–9 show the raw and simulated values of site distributions throughout the sub-phases for the Early, Middle and Late Bronze Ages in the Corinthia and the Argolid. Figures 9.3 and 9.4 graph the distributions according to the borders of the modern prefectures. Although the raw total numbers of sites vary only slightly and the curves are similar, the simulated results are significantly different. But the results are probably skewed, since both represent current political boundaries that combine widely different landforms that traditionally have had different economic, political and social orientations (as noted above, pp. 115–16). It is worthwhile, then, to reconfigure this comparison to represent notional core areas of each region. For the Corinthia, I do this by subtracting the sites found in the upland valleys, leaving only the coastal margins and the Isthmus (Figure 9.5). For the Argolid, I subtract the sites from the Methana-Troizen-Poros area and those from the Southern Argolid (Figure 9.6) – counting the area from Asine to Epidauros as a part of the core.

The differences are dramatic. The Corinthia was actively settled during the EH II period and then dramatically depopulated, with only a few sites enduring through the early stages of the Middle Bronze Age. In the Argolid, by contrast, the drop-off in settlement after EH II was apparently more gradual and it left a larger base of sites that increased in the middle phase of the Middle Helladic; site numbers then took off sharply at its end and during the early phases of the Late Helladic, steadily increasing to a peak at the end of LH IIIA and beginning of LH IIIB, until finally dropping off during LH IIIB and IIIC. In the Corinthia, the Middle Helladic may be characterized as a low plateau of sites that – depending on whether one follows the high or low chronology – either steps up or dips during LH I-II and then steps up dramatically during LHIIIA and IIIB. Both graphs show significantly different curves between those of the raw number of sites and of the simulated calculations. Of course, we do not know even if these reconfigured distributions relate to the state of affairs during the Bronze Age, but an obvious notion to be pursued is that these differences may point to the apparent absence of a central palace settlement during the Late Bronze Age in the Corinthia, in contrast to the presence of several palatial centers in the Argive plain – a matter that has received much attention in scholarship (Blegen 1928: 221; Bintliff 1977: 346–47; Vermeule 1987; Wright 1990; Davis 1988; Morgan 1999: 352–53). I think it also important to explore if the stepwise progression in the Corinthian slope may reflect the extent to which settlement

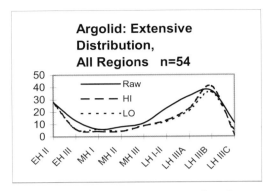

Figure 9.3 Argolid, extensive site distribution.

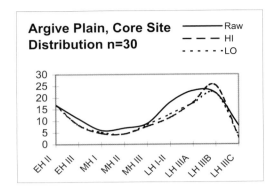

Figure 9.6 Argive Plain, extensive site distribution.

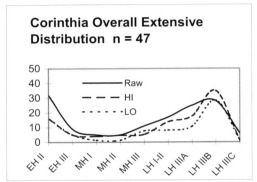

Figure 9.4 Corinthia, extensive site distribution.

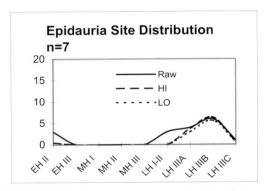

Figure 9.7 Epidauria, extensive site distribution.

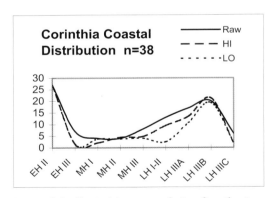

Figure 9.5 Corinthia, coastal site distribution.

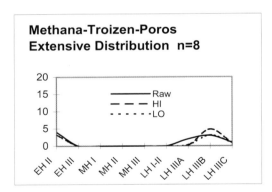

Figure 9.8 Methana-Troizen-Poros, extensive site distribution.

in the Corinthia is guided by other factors than that in the Argolid (see Morgan 1999: 349–58).

Continuing examination of the extensively gathered data, I show a further breakdown of the Argolid by separating the core area of the plain (Figure 9.6) from three regions: the Epidauria, the Methana-Troizen-Poros area and the southernmost region of the Argolid (Figures 9.7, 9.8 and 9.9). Although we know that the numbers of sites are much greater in the core area of the Argolid plain, the patterns of distributions in the outlying areas are significantly different. The Methana-Troizen-Poros region

was depopulated throughout the Middle Bronze Age; only slowly did settlement reappear, lagging behind the core area with its central places. In the Epidauria and the southern Argolid, however, the extensive record suggests some activity by the middle period of the Middle Helladic before taking off during the Mycenaean era. This pattern needs to be explored to try to understand why settlement refoundation occurred in the Middle Bronze Age and to what extent the distribution of sites was affected during LH III, when presumably the palaces in the central Argive plain were consolidating territory and economic control.

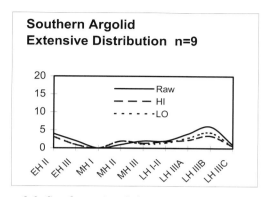

Figure 9.9 Southern Argolid, extensive site distribution.

In general, I query whether these fluctuations reflect relatively autonomous settlements or whether they record varying degrees of integration into, and dependence on, the palatial economy. All the areas that show variable and stepwise profiles of site distribution may be understood better if these patterns are examined in terms of evidence for local development and external influence.

INTENSIVE SURVEY

We are fortunate to have data from intensive survey available for these regions. As mentioned, those from the Methana survey cannot be usefully employed in this analysis, but the information from the Argolid Exploration Project, the Berbati-Limnes Survey, and the Nemea Valley Archaeological Project [NVAP] provides a detailed basis of comparison between intensive and extensive distributions. Perhaps more importantly, it offers insights into the variable trajectories of many localities in differing relationships to the core areas. Furthermore, Morgan's (1999) thorough reexamination of the extensive evidence from the Isthmia and the Corinthia in general provides an excellent basis for detailed comparison of these differently collected data.

The Southern Argolid Survey

I will begin by comparing the graph of the extensively collected data from the southern Argolid with that from the intensive regional survey by the Argolid Exploration Project (Figures 9.9 and 9.10). The survey was very successful in recognizing Early Bronze Age material (including EH I) and the pottery analysts boldly dated ceramics according to a fine division of phases (Nordquist 1995; Mountjoy 1995). The resulting graph (Figure 9.10) is the most detailed of any of the survey projects so far conducted, although it must be recognized that these data are not from a contiguous region, but rather from a variety of areas surveyed throughout the area (Jameson *et al.* 1994: 216–19, fig. 4.1). The results are strongly different in the record of Early Bronze Age sites, with many more sites

recognized by the intensive survey (50 total compared to 4), and these differences reflect many different levels of activity in the landscape rather than merely being a record of settlement (Jameson *et al.* 1994: 348–66). After that, however, both distributions show a stepwise progression of sites as the Late Bronze Age succeeds the Middle. Sites increase from MH II through LH I-II, and then rise higher during LH III. For the intensive survey, this distribution can also be plotted in terms of those sites which were assessed as probable habitation sites (Figure 9.11; Jameson *et al.* 1994: 366–72; compare to the EBA list in their table 6.5, p. 360). For this analysis I have added 10 sites to the tally of those whose size was measured or coarsely estimated; these were sites which had 50 or more sherds (Jameson *et al.* 1994: 417 and list in table B2, p. 544; Runnels *et al.* 1995: appendix 2). This is an arbitrary cut-off determined by looking at the data and deciding that those sites with fewer than 50 sherds consistently showed almost no concentrations for any particular period. Figure 9.11 shows the distribution of measured ('primary') sites. It confirms the overall impression of strong settlement during EH II, but for the late Middle Bronze Age and early Mycenaean period shows a much more pronounced increase than the other graphs. This is followed by a dramatic increase in sites during LH IIIB before the collapse in LH IIIC.

In general, the intensive survey recorded two to three times the number of Middle and Late Bronze Age sites than had previously been known, and the total (22 LH IIIA, 19 LH IIIB) is close to that of the Argive plain (27 LH IIIA and 28 LH IIIB). The major difference, however, is in site size, since this core area comprises the citadels and towns of Mycenae, Argos, Tiryns, Midea, Asine, Nauplion, Lerna and a number of substantial villages – settlements in size no less than 1.5 ha (*e.g.* Asine during MH, Nordquist 1987: 24) and as much as 35–50 ha (Mycenae, Tiryns). The distribution of sites by size from the intensive survey in the southern Argolid is as shown in Table 9.3 (after Jameson *et al.* 1994: 544–45, table B.2), and it demonstrates the magnitude of difference that separates settlement in the southern Argolid from that in the region of the plain of Argos. Notably, the 12 sites with specific estimates all have EH material, while the remaining 25 of the EH sites are recognized only from artifact distributions. For the MH and LH sites, only eight of the MH and LH I-II distributions and 11 of the LH III correspond with measured sites, leaving between two and five of the former and eight and 11 of the latter as artifact distributions over unmeasured sites. This analysis suggests simply that accompanying the rise in settlement activity during these periods is a natural rise in other activities in the landscape. This is a matter discussed by Jameson *et al.* (1994: 348–68; see also Runnels and Van Andel 1987: 314–16, 325–26) in their consideration of the complex hierarchy and functional differences of settlement during the Early, Middle and Late Bronze Ages.

The results of the intensive survey of the peninsula of

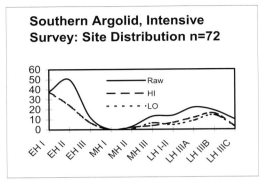

Figure 9.10 *Southern Argolid, intensive survey, all sites.*

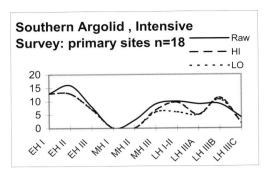

Figure 9.11 *Southern Argolid, primary site distribution from the intensive survey.*

Size in ha.	Total measured sites	EH I	EH II	EH III	MH I	MH II	MH III	LH I	LH II	LH IIIA	LH IIIB	LH IIIC
TOTAL all Sites	12	38	50	12	2	4	13	11	14	23	20	12
0.00–0.5	4	4	4	1	0	0	1	1	1	2	2	1
0.51–1.0	1	0	0	0	0	0	0	1	1	1	1	0
1.01–2.0	4	1	3	2	0	0	0	1	2	2	2	1
2.01–3.0	3	2–3	2–3	1	0	0	0	0	0	1	1	0
3.01–	1	1	1	0	0	0	0	0	0	1	1	0
LARGE	3	1	1	0	0	0	0	0	0	1	1	0

Table 9.3 *Site size distribution of measured sites from the Argolid Exploration Project.*

Methana also confirm the discovery of more sites during the EH and LH periods than the extensive record indicated (Mee and Forbes 1997). Figures 9.8 and 9.9 show the extensive record for Methana (8 sites) and the southern Argolid (9 sites) to be about the same, whereas the gross plot of sites from the survey projects (Figure 9.12) shows they are quite different, with Methana having many more EH sites than previously thought, but few MH and LH (50, 4, 8, respectively, of a total of 53 sites), and the southern Akte region having more of all (59, 18, 44, respectively, of a total of 72). The preponderance of evidence from Methana is of sites with five sherds or fewer, which leaves us with little basis for assessing the functional meaning of the increased distribution.

The question of the relationship between settlement and activity in the landscape can be analyzed in more detail. The investigators of the Argolid Exploration Project argue that settlement during EH I-II formed a three-tier hierarchy (Jameson *et al.* 1994: 253–54, 348–66). Settlement in the area was undoubtedly affected by the disturbances at the major centers throughout the Aegean at the end of EH II, since there is a dramatic decrease of sites during EH III (1994: 366–67), after which the area was largely but not completely abandoned. Beginning in MH II, occupation reappeared at three sites (F5, E13, and A6), but then rose during MH III to as many as four (F5, E9, E13, A6). (Jameson *et al.* [1994: 367–68] list only three

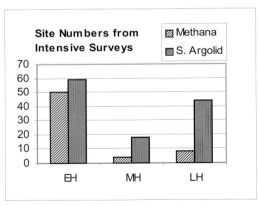

Figure 9.12 *Methana and Southern Argolid: gross comparison of sites by period.*

MH sites – F5, E13, A6 – but I have added E9, Sambariza Magoula, which has consistent and substantial evidence for EH, MH and LH occupation [Jameson *et al.* 1994: 484–85; Runnels *et al.* 1995: 275–79].) An additional 11 had small scatters of MH III pottery and another four disclosed pottery only identifiable as MH. This wide distribution I believe indicates that by the end of the Middle Bronze Age the inhabitants of the few occupied settlements had began to utilize the landscape more extensively, as a prelude to the consolidation of settlement during the early Mycenaean period. The publication of the pottery by Nordquist (1995) enables a more subtle analysis that permits relating the location of sherd scatters to major sites. Thus the distribution of those locations with few sherds shows that most of them are scattered outwards (between 0.55 and 2.3 km) from the major sites of F5, E13, E9, and A6. The evidence to determine what kind of activity created such distributions, however, despite careful analysis of the remains, does not exist (Jameson *et al.* 1994: 368–72), but may be governed by a variety of activities, including cultivation, burial, and routes of communication.

LH I-II witnesses a consolidation marked especially by a dispersed pattern of settlement that continues throughout the LH III period. (Jameson *et al.* 1994: 368). However one reads the different plots in Figures 9.11 and 9.12, LH IIIA and B show variability rather than a steady increase in sites. In their analysis of the sites in terms of size and function, the investigators suggest that the predominant settlement was the small village, though in the later Mycenaean period a higher order may again have been achieved (Jameson *et al.* 1994: 253–54, 366–72). This, however, is not easily confirmed by architectural or mortuary remains.

It is yet unclear how and to what extent occupation and use of the southern Argolid during the Middle and Late Bronze Age was affected by the distant core area of the Argive plain, but no doubt it was (Runnels and Van Andel 1987: 326–30). As Forbes observes, the region's long-term history is one that alternates between 'a largely inward looking, agrarian-based economy' and engagement with central polities in the core region of the Argolid, as well as with maritime economies of the Saronic Gulf (Forbes 2000: 41, 68–70; Van Andel and Runnels 1987: 164–76). Ethnographic and historical studies (Sutton 2000a; 2000b; Forbes 2000; Petronoti 2000; Topping 2000) show that the region's economy and demography, though agrarian and rural in character, are closely and opportunistically linked to the chances for political and economic relationships with polities in both the Argive plain and throughout the maritime Attic-Saronic region.

The Nemea and Berbati-Limnes Valleys Surveys

I now turn to the surveys in the Nemea and the Berbati-Limnes Valleys (Figure 9.2). They mediate between the more densely settled areas of coastal Corinthia to the north and the Argive Plain to the south. Figures 9.13 and 9.14 show very different patterns of site distribution, in part because the Nemea chart only shows the 10 sites with significant quantities of material and not the remaining 17 tracts with finds (Cherry and Davis 2001). If the Berbati survey results are similarly reckoned, a total of 11 sites might be identified as significant (Figure 9.15) – 3 with 50 or more sherds, 8 with more than 100. By sub-phase, the Berbati-Limnes data show relatively high numbers of EH II sites compared to virtually none of EH III through

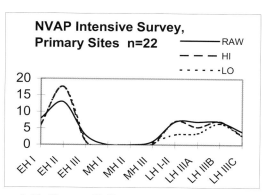

Figure 9.13 Nemea Valley intensive survey, site distribution.

MH II. The remarkable similarity of both the graph of overall and of primary site distribution in the Berbati-Limnes area in large part reflects the consistency of occupation or activity at the primary site of Mastos and its impact on activities in the area. This changes with the dramatic rise in the number of sites in LH IIIA and B; again both distributions display a similar curve, which suggests the extent to which occupation and activities are significantly correlated. Compared to the graph of the core region of the Argolis (Figure 9.6), the near abandonment of the area throughout the Middle Bronze Age is clear. The extent to which its exploitation was tied in with Mycenae during the Late Bronze Age is equally apparent and confirms the similar observations of Wells (1996). The profile of this valley system looks much more like that of the marginal areas of Methana, Troizen and Poros (Figure 9.8) and displays none of the activity recorded in the Akte region (Figures 9.9–11).

In the Berbati-Limnes system (Table 9.4), other than the main and excavated site of Mastos, only one other site of significant size was discovered, FS 14, which measures 6.5 ha. Schallin (1996: 133–34, 173) suggests this unusual site, with traces of walls and many fine-ware sherds and some figurine fragments, but neither coarse wares nor stone implements, was a special facility for the Mycenaean road which runs by it. Of the remaining 10 sites for which size estimates were made, six were between 0.05 and 0.1 ha and four were less than 0.05 ha (Table 9.4). Three of these are tombs (of a total of seven tomb sites found in the survey region), six are thought to have been farmsteads (FS 428, 301, 306, 414, 443, 444; Schallin 1996: 167), and one is suggested to have been a sheep/goat shelter (FS 416, Schallin 1996: 167). In other words, the principal activity in the region seems to have been food production, which primarily took place during the late 14th and 13th centuries, when Mycenae was at its peak of power and population (Schallin 1996: 171–72). The role of the main settlement at Mastos is unclear, but it must have been the controlling agency of the region from early on, as both the MH III/LH I tombs and LH II built tholos tomb demonstrate. Since Mastos was later the site of a pottery kiln

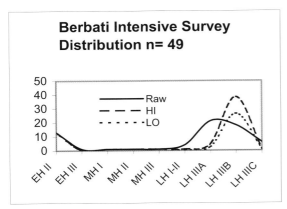

Figure 9.14 *Berbati-Limnes, intensive survey, site distribution.*

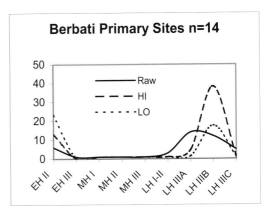

Figure 9.15 *Berbati-Limnes, intensive survey, primary site distribution.*

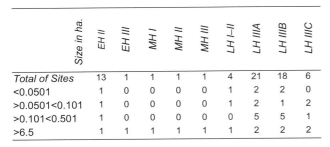

Size in ha.	EH II	EH III	MH I	MH II	MH III	LH I-II	LH IIIA	LH IIIB	LH IIIC
Total of Sites	13	1	1	1	1	4	21	18	6
<0.0501	1	0	0	0	0	1	2	2	0
>0.0501<0.101	1	0	0	0	0	1	2	1	2
>0.101<0.501	1	0	0	0	0	0	5	5	1
>6.5	1	1	1	1	1	1	2	2	2

Table 9.4 *Measured sites, Berbati-Limnes survey.*

(Åkerström 1940; 1968), it may have performed a variety of important roles for its own population as well as for Mycenae. Finally, the intensive survey shows that agricultural sites are centered in the plain between Mastos and the village of Prosymna, while tombs lie more in the western end, in proximity to the settlement on Mastos. The importance of agriculture is further emphasized by the presence of many agricultural terraces and check dams, which illustrate the intensification of food production for the growing population of the palace center (Wells *et al.* 1990: 223–28, 237; 1993).

In the Nemea Valley there are also relatively many sites of EH II date (18 maximum) and a sharp decrease in EH III (5 maximum) (Kalogerou n.d.). After that there is no MH at all until MH III, when the hill of Tsoungiza was reoccupied. At this time activity in the valley also begins, with four primary sites in LH I, six in LH II and nine in LH III – and an additional 17 when all levels of site magnitude are included (Cherry *et al.* 2002; Cherry and Davis 2001). The graph in Figure 9.13 only shows data for the primary sites, since a breakdown of the ceramic dates of small scatters is presently not available. The strength of the reoccupation of the valley during MH III and the early phases of the Late Bronze Age is apparent. There are interesting similarities between the neighboring Berbati-Limnes and Nemea valleys. Both had a central site during the Early and Late Bronze Ages. But whereas Mastos continued to be inhabited throughout the Middle

Bronze Age, Tsoungiza and the entire Nemea Valley were abandoned. This difference is probably the reason that near Mastos lies a MH III/LH I cemetery and then a LH II tholos, but the habitation and exploitation of the Berbati-Limnes system is ultimately more an artifact of the proximity of this valley to Mycenae. Certainly, the distributional curves for the Berbati-Limnes region emphasize the dramatic increase in exploitation of the area during the height of the Mycenaean palatial era, and this stands in contrast to the more plateau-like profile of the Nemea Valley, which seems to demonstrate a maintenance of sites throughout the Mycenaean period (*cf.* Cherry and Davis 2001: 147–52). Perhaps also the greater distance of the Nemea Valley from Mycenae sheltered settlement from the immediate control of the palace; certainly the lower profile of sites during LH III implies a less intense exploitation than in the Berbati-Limnes valleys.

In this regard the data may be usefully compared to those from the intensive survey of the southern Argolid. The correspondence of the pattern in the Nemea Valley to that of the Akte is of interest (Figures 9.10–11, 9.13), since both show a climax of sites during the early Mycenaean period and a further increase during the palatial period. If the explanation for this phenomenon in the southern Argolid is to be found in its ability to exist somewhat independently of central agencies (*i.e.* capable of interacting with different markets), is there a similar explanation for the Nemea Valley? This is a very important question because it asks how we compare regions to one another.

The NVAP survey demonstrated that the valley was inextricably tied to the Argolid, but indirectly through the major route of communication, the Kelossa Pass (Wright *et al.* 1990: 585), which begins at the southeastern end of the Phliasian Plain. Furthermore, the detailed investigation of the settlement on Tsoungiza has provided a wealth of information about settlement and consumption patterns during all phases of the Mycenaean period (Rutter 1990; 1993a; Dabney 1997). On the basis of analysis of the pottery, among which are none of the Minoanizing and

Site No.	Name	Min Size in ha.	Max Size in ha.	FN/EHI	EH I	EHI/II	EH II	EH III	EH III/MH	MH I	MH II	MH III	LH I	LH II	LH IIIA	LH IIIB	LH IIIB/C
003	Schinochoritika		0.84		×	×	×						×			×	×
204	Hani Anesti	0.37		×	×	×	×										
205	Hani Anesti		0.60					×					×	×	×		
209/213	Dervenakia	0.50	1.00		×	×	×						×				
400	A. Sotira	0.32	1.96												×		
500	Zaharias	0.26		×	×		×										
503	Diaselo Tourkovrisi	0.23					×			×	×	×	×	×	×	×	×
512	Tourkovrisi		3.84							×	×						
514	Palaiochoro		1.21							×	×						
922	Bekiri Rahi	0.28	1.50		×		×								LH	LH	
923	Ano Vounaki	0.88	1.70		×		×	×					×	×	×	×	×
925			4.24?												×	×	
906, 907, 933, 934, 940	Tsoungiza	1.45	7.5	×	×	×	×						×	×	×	×	×
941	Sanctuary Zeus								×					×	×	×	
TOTAL = 14																	

Table 9.5 Sites in the Nemea Valley (from Cherry and Davis 2001, table 10.1 and Kalogerou n.d.).

fine lustrous-decorated wares known in the Argolid, Rutter has argued (1990) that the original settlement may have been founded from the Corinthia. This situation shifts during LH II and IIIA when the inhabitants on Tsoungiza increased contact with the markets in the Argolid, presumably with Mycenae (Rutter 1993a; Dabney 1997; *cf.* Morgan 1999: 232, 358–61). Yet the connection was not necessarily direct, for, as Susan Sutton's research informs us, 'in modern times the Phliasian Plain emerges as an almost constant demographic and economic center' (in Wright *et al.* 1990: 601–602). This should give us cause for reflection, since during the Late Bronze Age settlement to the west was also well established and potentially dominant. The settlement at Aidonia commanding the western side of the Phliasian Plain was flourishing (Demakopoulou 1996), and, although we do not know the extent of others, at Ayia Irini and Phlius there were likely substantial settlements (Alcock 1991: 458; Cherry and Davis 2001: 150). Thus the graphed form of the distribution of sites in the valley may be a consequence of a more complex and indirect set of political-economic and social relationships, rather than a reflection of a mere linear relationship with Mycenae (compare Morgan's analysis of the Isthmia region; 1999: 353, 388). In this way we have a basis for comparison with the region of southern Argolis, where, as we have seen, a complex geography and economy of settlement also existed. But this realization uncovers yet another, namely our continuing ignorance of the potentially rich areas of settlement and agricultural production that define the hinterlands of the major centers. In part, this is a consequence of the bias inherent in archaeology in Greece, where Classical sites and the visibility of major monuments (e.g. Venetian and Ottoman fortifications) prejudice our view towards and orientation of the landscape. Thus, prior to the discovery of the Mycenaean cemetery at Aidonia, the Phliasian Valley was viewed from its eastern side, in terms of the perspective from the acropolis of ancient Phlius over its region, the Phliasia (Alcock 1991: 425–33, 460–

63). This example must lead us to comparison of the situation in the Plain of Argos (sic), where, for example, the vast, rich and largely unstudied northwestern reaches of the Inachos drainage behind Argos are largely unstudied, just as the fertile area surrounding Midea (Figure 9.2). In other words, it is insufficient to attempt comparison between extensive distributions and intensively surveyed areas without taking into account the wider contexts of integration in the landscape.

If we turn to consider the internal development of settlement in the Nemea Valley, the picture during LH III seems to be one of consolidation and centralization. According to information published by Cherry *et al.* (2002; Cherry and Davis 2001: 148), during LH III there develops a substantial spread of sites around the study area, especially larger sites (approx > 1.0 ha). They have suggested the emergence of a four-tier hierarchy of settlement and activity in the valley during the Mycenaean period (2001: 150), and although I am skeptical that we should include activities in the landscape (as opposed to settlement) as a part of this hierarchy, they are surely correct in pointing to the emergence of settlement at a lower order than Tsoungiza. In the intensive field investigation of the Nemea Valley survey area, no site was found as large as that on Tsoungiza, which covered at least 7.5 ha. Cherry and Davis (2001: 148) estimate the size of eight (Sites 003, 205, 213, 400, 503, 922, 923, 925) of the most significant of the 25 sites discovered, in addition to those on Tsoungiza and at the Sanctuary of Zeus (Table 9.5). They all are probably less than 2 ha, and four are between 0.30 and 0.85 ha (maximally estimated) and, as the investigators observe, the largest are located at the head of the valley at the center of which is Tsoungiza (Cherry *et al.* 2002; Cherry and Davis 2001: 148–50). Assessment of site functions is still underway and there is little that can be said at this point. But the authors have plotted the relationship of the 'Mycenaean sites as well as low-density distributions of artifacts [and they] have been found in virtually every part of the Nemea area that has been in cultivation since the 1940s.' They further observe that the soils in these areas 'are most suitable, or only suitable, for olive cultivation [such that] it seems difficult to avoid the conclusion that this crop was a principal component of the Mycenaean agricultural system' (Cherry *et al.* 2002). It seems likely that the distribution reflects a network extending out from Tsoungiza and consisting of roads and paths to agricultural land, springs, cemeteries, and outlying places of small-scale habitation (field shelters, farmsteads).

In my view this extension of settlement, which corresponds to the second peak in the graph, illustrates the period during which the population of the valley became fully integrated into the Mycenaean economy (Dabney 1997: 470–71). As appears to have been the case in the Akte of the Southern Argolid, early Mycenaean settlement represents a time of reoccupation of the landscape and the establishment of quasi-autonomous communities, probably largely self-sufficient; whereas the later period is one of increasing integration into the primate political economy of the central places in the Argive Plain. Small areas with poor arable land, such as the Berbati-Limnes system, show a pattern that is completely dependent upon the ability and need of the primary centers to exploit them during the acme of their existence. Areas like the Nemea Valley were part of larger, richer networks of habitation and agricultural production and may have enjoyed some independence from the centers.

Analysis

This review of the intensively collected evidence from the Berbati-Limnes and Nemea Valleys illustrates the extent to which they were separate from the coastal area of the Gulf of Corinth and Isthmus and instead more closely tied into the network in the Argolid, even though it could only be reached over passes through the low mountains. Missing from this examination is consideration of the excavated settlement at Zygouries, which Blegen (1928) thought to be a direct satellite of Mycenae. Its position at the head of the Longopotamos River is similar to that of Tsoungiza, but – like the Phliasian Valley to the west – that of the Longopotamos is large and geographically complex, with the shrine site of nearby Ayia Triada (Kilian 1992) and the probability of another major settlement located at Ancient Kleonai. This valley also is connected to Mycenae, but by means of a road system that was not constructed before the LH III period. The Berbati-Limnes survey explored the remains of these roads, constructed by Mycenae to facilitate heavy and regular transport between the citadel and these regions to the north (Steffen 1884; McDonald 1964; Mylonas 1966; Lavery 1990; 1995; Schallin 1996: 172–73; Jansen 2002). Thus control of the passes and control of the inland Corinthian valleys went hand in hand. What is not clear is whether Mycenae's control extended to the coastal plains and the Isthmus (Dickinson 1977; Salmon 1984; Vermeule 1987). Morgan

(1999: 352–53, 362) has cautioned that the evidence does not permit a strong argument for any area beyond the southwest Corinthia.

In light of this problem, it is interesting that the graphs of site distribution, both in the Corinthia (Figures 9.4, 9.5) and in the Nemea Valley (Figure 9.13), exhibit a stage-like progression of sites after MH III, since that pattern is different from the rapid and steady rise of sites found in the core areas of the Argolid (Figure 9.6). I think it justifiable to suggest that these two patterns reflect different trajectories of growth and occupational activities: the Argolid core characteristic of a steady development towards centralization, the Corinthia and Nemea Valley more evocative of a loosely affiliated network of settlements.

The emergence of settlements in these upland valleys during the late Middle Helladic and early Mycenaean periods may be characterized by control of their immediate landscape – that is, the adjacent arable and pastoral lands. As economic and other activities expanded beyond that, a variety of factors that had an influence on continued growth came into play. There is reason to think that the Corinthia – at least, the coastal margins – was strongly influenced by settlement on the island of Aigina; while the Akte likely benefited from wider participation in the developing maritime economy of the Southern Argolid and Saronic Gulf. In her study of the MH period in the northeastern Peloponnesos, Lambropoulou (1991) observes that the distribution of the distinctive Aiginetan wares seems to differ between the coastal Corinthian sites and those of the interior. Among the preserved artifacts from the excavations at Korakou and Gonia she found no imported Cycladic or Minoan pottery of the Middle Bronze Age, nor were there any of the lustrous decorated wares among this material (they are first found only in LH I; see Davis 1979). The only imported wares are of the Aeginetan gold mica fabric, and they appear in the varieties of matt-painted, slipped-and-burnished, and cooking and plain wares. They represent *c.* 9% and 18% of the preserved pottery from Korakou and Gonia, respectively (Lambropoulou 1991: 68, 111, 335). Lambropoulou (1991: 336) stresses that 'this pattern changes drastically as one moves into the interior of the Corinthia', for no imports showed up among the 'admittedly small number of MH pieces from Zygouries', and they are also rare in the MH deposits from Tsoungiza (Rutter 1990). So viewed, the original pattern of settlement may have been stimulated by multiple sources, while the later (LH III) period of growth may be understood as coinciding with Mycenae's consolidation of political and economic power throughout most of the northeastern Peloponnesos.

One thing is certain – namely, that sites along the coast, including Korakou, Gonia, and probably also Aetopetra and Arapiza, were more or less continuously occupied throughout the EH, MH and LH periods, while none of the inland sites, having been abandoned throughout almost all of the Middle Bronze Age.

DISCUSSION

This exercise in plotting the distributions of sites according to the extensive and intensive records provides many insights into issues relating to settlement and landuse throughout the northeastern Peloponnesos. Clearly, the effort of breaking the data down into smaller periods of time is worthwhile, since it demonstrates variability in distributions that significantly advance our understanding of developmental stages, both for large regions and for well-defined localities. The significance is enhanced by the extent to which these variations appear in different areas of study and consistently appear whether the data plotted are from extensive, intensive or analytical categories (*cf.* Figures 9.9, 9.10, 9.11). In addition, analyzing the distributions in terms of the problem of settlement contemporaneity produces plots that are significantly different from those of the raw data. This has been especially apparent in that the simulated counts tend to reduce the high raw numbers of sites, shift distributional highs chronologically downwards, and accentuate variation by showing bimodal distributions. With regard to the problem of the high and low chronologies in the Aegean, it is noteworthy that the low chronology most consistently reduces the number of sites in comparison to the raw numbers and also cuts off the peaks and valleys. Although this is not the place to engage the debate concerning the credibility of these two systems of reckoning (Wiener 1998), it is perhaps of interest that Pollock (1999: 63), in her use of Dewar's algorithm, also noted that it consistently lowered the number of sites in comparison to the raw data. For this reason and for others, I think the results based on the low chronology are probably the most reliable.

This study demonstrates three models of site distribution in the northeastern Peloponnesos that are potentially useful for analyzing settlement and landuse. First is what I venture to call the *Central Place Model*, and it is demonstrated by the graphing of the extensive data from the core area of the Argive Plain (Figure 9.6). It shows a pattern of sites occupied for all periods and a relatively steady increase in numbers up to the acme of the Mycenaean era. Unfortunately, this model is not accompanied by data from intensive survey of the immediate region of any of the major settlements in the plain. Only the intensive survey of the Berbati-Limnes Valley can be used for comparison. In so far as these data demonstrate the extent to which site distributions in this hinterland are directly tied to the rise of the palace-center at Mycenae we can consider the results a confirmation of this model. On the other hand, the Berbati-Limnes data show a very different profile than those from the other intensive surveys (Figures 9.14–15). Thus Berbati-Limnes may represent a second model, the *Dependency Model*, which records in particular the intensive exploitation of the immediate hinterlands of the central places. We need to test other areas around palace sites to see if this model holds up. Third is the *Periphery Model*, and it is represented by the data from

the intensive surveys of the Nemea Valley and the Southern Argolid, and perhaps by the extensive data from the coastal area of the Corinthia and the Isthmus (Figures 9.5, 9.9–11, 9.13). The common element in all these is the variable or stepwise distribution of sites between the Middle and early Late Bronze Ages and the later phases of the Late Bronze Age. The former, I believe, represents relatively independent foundations after the collapse at the end of the Early Bronze Age, while the latter reflects varying degrees of integration into the central political economies of the primary Mycenaean palace centers.

The Periphery Model is one on which those of us working in the Aegean need to concentrate some of our research activities, since it is clearly grossly overstated. There is probably considerable difference among the areas to which I have just suggested it may apply. For example, as argued, the Nemea Valley needs to be considered in terms of its strong neighboring area to the west in the Phliasian Valley, and both valleys need to be evaluated in terms of the extent to which they formed a secondary system or network that enjoyed a degree of autonomy and autarky – even though it seems clear that the settlement of these upland and inland areas was very much stimulated by the rise of the central places (Wright *et al.* 1990; Cherry and Davis 2001). Although the Southern Argolid shares with the Nemea-Phliasian region the characteristic of having variable and multiple landscapes for exploitation, it differs in that it is both much more distant from the core area of the Argive Plain and is able to partake in maritime political economies of the eastern coast of the Peloponnesos and the Saronic Gulf. Proximity to maritime resources clearly makes a difference, for this is also what characterizes the Corinthia-Isthmus coastal region, and, as Morgan (1999: 349–67) has suggested, may have facilitated the emergence of a system of interlinked hamlets and villages or towns, without any one becoming dominant over the other.

The Periphery Model might also apply to the Longopotamos Valley to the east of the Nemea Valley. Here we very much need the benefit of intensive survey, since it is unclear whether or not these valleys and their respective settlements at Zygouries and Tsoungiza are similar in functional and systemic terms. Primarily, the question is whether or not Zygouries is a higher order settlement than Tsoungiza, and the evidence for that may rest on its interpretation – probably not as a pottery production center, but rather as a center of oil and unguent production, if Thomas' assessment is correct (Thomas 1988; Morgan 1999: 358–61). Behind this assessment, however, is the question of whether or not there are secondary centers and regions in the Mycenaean political economy of the northeastern Peloponnesos – that is, settlements to be considered as towns that are also administrative seats, as recorded in the Linear B tablets from Pylos and Knossos (Bennet 1985; 1999a; 1999b; Shelmerdine 1999).

This question of the existence or not of secondary centers in the northeast Peloponnesos during the Mycenaean era is fundamental, and our inability to answer it impedes progress in understanding the degrees of variability in the structure and organization of Mycenaean peer-polities. This study is able to frame the question more squarely as one that could most easily be answered through continued intensive survey. In so doing, I emphasize the lacunae in our knowledge of the nature of settlement and landuse in the immediate environs and hinterlands of the major centers of the Argive Plain. What we do not know very well at all, because of a lack of systematic survey and detailed publication of excavated sites, unfortunately makes for a long list (*cf.* Figure 9.2): the areas behind Acrocorinth, the Longopotamos drainage, the eastern Isthmia and Corinthia (now being intensively surveyed), the hinterlands west of Argos, the area to the southeast of Argos (Kefalari and Kokla), the landscape between Mycenae and the Argive Heraion, that surrounding and behind Dendra-Midea, the region ostensibly controlled by Asine, the entire area east of Aria that includes Kazarma, the Epidauria, and the area around Troizen (to cover only the obvious ones).

Our ignorance of these landscapes should give us pause, since they are numerous and diverse, and, with the exception of the Berbati-Limnes survey as an example of a dependency on a major center, there is in my view little reason to think that the information gleaned from study of the areas already subjected to intensive survey provides us with enough insight to be able to develop reliable models of settlement and land use for extrapolation to this list of unexplored areas. Of course, this is not to say that the data from intensive survey are not useful for building models. Quite the opposite: it is only because of intensive survey that we can raise these questions and begin to construct models for further testing. Indeed the variety of the landscapes listed above invites further intensive analysis to refine any models we develop and to formulate new ones that would take into account unknown variables that we might isolate. That the majority of those on this list comprise the immediate territories of the major centers is a concern, because until we understand in detail the changing nature of landuse and settlement in them, we will be hindered in any attempt to explain the processes by which major centers emerge – how they exploit local resources, the geographic dimensions of their demographic expansion, and the nature of their relations with their neighbors – and how they function during the acme of their development.

This study illustrates that information from the pre- and protohistoric Aegean on the distribution of sites is sufficient to explore major questions about settlement and landuse, despite any problems in the comparability and accuracy of the record. At the same time I have demonstrated that an attention to detail is necessary to assess the variability in patterns of settlement and landuse among different localities, even within relatively similar landscapes. Clearly, we would be incorrect to attempt to build models of the hierarchy and articulation of systems of political economies merely on the basis of extensively gathered data. Equally, the existence of the results of several intensive and systematic surveys does not permit the elaboration of such general systems or their application across broad regions. That the emergence of central political economies is constrained by highly variable local circumstances is nothing new, but seems to be a characteristic of complex societies in the Aegean (Hansen 2000a; 2000b). In order to continue to refine our understanding, however, we need not only to commit to continued systematic intensive survey, but also to take advantage of every opportunity to document the extensive record, for the areas that are most threatened by continuing development are the environs of the central places.

ACKNOWLEDGEMENTS

I wish to thank Susan Alcock and John Cherry for inviting me to participate in this conference. I am grateful to Mary Dabney, Malcolm Wiener, Curtis Runnels, Daniel Pullen, Jeremy Rutter, Christopher Mee, Jack Davis, Berit Wells, and Robert Schon who read and commented on this paper, given me references and pointed out errors and inconsistencies. I am particularly indebted to Deepak Kumar of Bryn Mawr College who put Dewar's algorithm on the web, so that I could use it for my calculations (http://mojo.brynmawr.edu/~dkumar/SettlementDynamics/). I remain responsible for any errors or omissions.

REFERENCES

Adams, R. McC. (1981) *Heartland of Cities: Surveys of Ancient Settlement and Landuse on the Central Floodplain of the Euphrates.* Chicago, University of Chicago Press.

Åkerström, Å. (1940) Das mykenische Töpferviertel in Berbati in der Argolis. In *Bericht über den VI. Internationaler Kongress für Archäologie, Berlin 21.–26. August 1939*: 296–98. Berlin, W. de Gruyter.

Åkerström, Å. (1968) A Mycenaean potter's factory at Berbati near Mycenae. In *Atti e memorie del 1° congresso internazionale di micenologia, Roma 27 settembre–3 ottobre 1967. Incunabula Graeca* 25.1: 48–53. Rome, Ateneo.

Alcock, S. E. (1991) Urban survey and the *polis* of Phlius. *Hesperia* 60: 421–63.

Barber, R. (1992) The origins of the Mycenaean palace. In J. M. Sanders (ed.) *ΦΙΛΟΛΑΚΩΝ: Lakonian Studies in Honour of Hector Catling*: 11–23. London, The British School at Athens.

Bennet, J. (1985) The structure of the Linear B administration at Knossos. *American Journal of Archaeology* 89: 231–49.

Bennet, J. (1999a) Pylos: the expansion of a Mycenaean center. In M. L. Galaty and W. A. Parkinson (eds.) *Rethinking Mycenaean Palaces: New Interpretations of an Old Idea*: 9–18. Los Angeles, The Cotsen Institute of Archaeology.

Bennet, J. (1999b) The Mycenaean conceptualization of space, or Pylian geography (…yet again!). In S. Deger-Jalkotzy, S. Hiller and O. Panagl (eds.) *Floreant Studia Mycenaea: Akten des X. Internationalen Mykenologischen Colloquiums in Salzburg vom 1.–5. Mai 1995*: 131–56. Vienna: Verlag der Österreichischen Akademie der Wissenschaften.

Bennet, J. and Galaty, M. L. (1997) Ancient Greece: recent developments in Aegean archaeology and regional studies. *Journal of Archaeological Research* 5: 75–120.

Bintliff, J. L. (1977) *Natural Environment and Human Settlement in Prehistoric Greece: Based on Original Fieldwork.* BAR Supplementary Series 28. Oxford, British Archaelolgical Reports.

Bintliff, J. (1997) Regional survey, demography, and the rise of complex societies in the ancient Aegean: core-periphery, neo-Malthusian, and other interpretive models. *Journal of Field Archaeology* 24: 1–38.

Bintliff, J. and Snodgrass, A. (1985) The Cambridge/Bradford Boeotian Expedition: the first four years. *Journal of Field Archaeology* 12: 123–61.

Bintliff, J., Howard, P. and Snodgrass, A. (1999) The hidden landscape of prehistoric Greece. *Journal of Mediterranean Archaeology* 12: 139–68.

Blanton, R. E. (2001) Mediterranean myopia (Review of G. Barker and D. Mattingly (series eds.) *The Archaeology of Mediterranean Landscapes*, Oxford, Oxbow Books 1999–2000). *Antiquity* 75 (289): 627–29.

Blanton, R. E., Kowalewski, S., Feinman, G. and Appel, J. (1981) *Ancient Mesoamerica: A Comparison of Change in Three Regions.* New York, Cambridge University Press.

Blegen, C. W. (1928) *Zygouries: A Prehistoric Settlement in the Valley of Cleonae.* Cambridge, Mass., Harvard University Press.

Broodbank, C. (2000) *An Island Archaeology of the Early Cyclades.* Cambridge, Cambridge University Press.

Caskey, J. (1960) The Early Helladic period in the Argolid. *Hesperia* 29: 285–303.

Cavanagh, W. (1995) Development of the Mycenaean state in Laconia: evidence from the Laconia Survey. In R. Laffineur and W.-D. Niemeier (eds.) *Politeia: Society and State in the Aegean Bronze Age. Proceedings of the 5th International Aegean Conference University of Heidelberg, Archäologisches Institut, 10–13 April. Aegaeum* 12: 81–88. Liège, Université de Liège, Histoire de l'art et archéologie de la Grèce antique.

Cavanagh, W. and Mee, C. (1998) *A Private Place: Death in Prehistoric Greece. Studies in Mediterranean Archaeology* 125. Jonsered, Paul Åströms Förlag.

Cherry, J. F. and Davis, J. L. (2001) 'Under the sceptre of Agamemnon': the view from the hinterlands of Mycenae. In K. Branigan (ed.) *Urbanism in the Aegean Bronze Age*: 141–59. Sheffield, Sheffield Academic Press.

Cherry, J. F., Davis, J. L. and Mantzourani, E. (2002) Mycenaean Nemea: the results of the Nemea Valley Archaeological Project, Archaeological Survey. http://river.blg.uc.edu/nvap/MycNVAP.html

Dabney, M. (1997) Craft product consumption as an economic indicator of site status in regional studies. In R. Laffineur and P. P. Betancourt (eds.) *TEXNH: Craftsmen, Craftswomen and Craftsmanship in the Aegean Bronze Age. Proceedings of the 6th International Aegean Conference, Philadelphia, Temple University, 18–21 April 1996. Aegaeum* 16: 467–71. Liège, Université de Liège, Histoire de l'art et archéologie de la Grèce antique.

Dabney, M. K. and Wright, J. C. (1990) Mortuary customs, palatial society and state formation in the Aegean area: a comparative study. In R. Hägg and G. C. Nordquist (eds.) *Celebrations of Death and Divinity in the Bronze Age Argolid: Proceedings of the Sixth International Symposium at the Swedish Institute at Athens, 11–13 June, 1988.* Skrifter utgivna av Svenska institutet i Athen, 4°, 40: 45–53. Stockholm, Paul Åströms Förlag.

Davis, J. L. (1979) Late Helladic I pottery from Korakou. *Hesperia* 48: 234–63.

Davis, J. L. (1988) If there's a room at the top what's at the bottom? Settlement and hierarchy in Early Mycenaean Greece. *Bulletin*

of the Institute of Classical Studies, University of London 35: 164–65 [abstract].

Davis, J. L., Alcock, S. E., Bennet, J., Lolos, Y. and Shelmerdine, C. (1997) The Pylos Regional Archaeological Project. Part I: overview and the archaeological survey. *Hesperia* 66: 391–494.

Davis, J. L., Alcock, S. E., Bennet, J., Lolos, Y., Shelmerdine, C. and Zangger, E. (2002) The Pylos Regional Archaeological Project Internet Edition. http://river.blg.uc.edu/prap/PRAP.html.

Demakopoulou, K. (ed.) (1996) *The Aidonia Treasure: Seals and Jewellery of the Aegean Late Bronze Age.* Athens, Ministry of Culture.

Dewar, R. (1991) Incorporating variation in occupation span into settlement-pattern analysis. *American Antiquity* 56: 604–620.

Dewar, R. (1994) Contending with contemporaneity: a reply to Kintigh. *American Antiquity* 59: 149–52.

Dickinson, O. T. P. K. (1977) *The Origins of Mycenaean Civilisation.* Studies in Mediterranean Archaeology 49. Göteborg, Paul Åströms Förlag.

Dickinson, O. T. P. K. (1982) Parallels and contrasts in the Bronze Age of the Peloponnese. *Oxford Journal of Archaeology* 2: 125–38.

Dickinson, O. T. P. K. (1999) Invasion, migration and the Shaft Graves. *Bulletin of the Institute of Classical Studies, University of London* 43: 97–107.

Dietz, S. (1991) *The Argolid at the Transition to the Mycenaean Age.* Copenhagen, National Museum of Denmark.

Dunnell, R. C. (1980) Evolutionary theory and archaeology. *Advances in Archaeological Method and Theory* 3: 35–99.

Forbes, H. (2000) The agrarian economy of the Erminonidha around 1700: an ethnohistorical investigation. In S. B. Sutton (ed.) *Contingent Countryside: Settlement, Economy, and Landuse in the Southern Argolid since 1700:* 41–70. Stanford, Stanford University Press.

Forsén, J. (1992) *The Twilight of the Early Helladics. A Study of the Disturbances in East-Central and Southern Greece Towards the End of the Early Bronze Age.* Studies in Mediterranean Archaeology, Pocket Book Series 116. Jonsered, Paul Åströms Förlag.

Freytag, B. von (1973) *Geologie des Isthmus von Korinth.* Erlanger Geologischen Abhandlungen 95. Erlangen, Erlanger Geologischen Abhandlungen.

Haley, J. and Blegen, C. (1928) The coming of the Greeks. *American Journal of Archaeology* 32: 141–54.

Hansen, M. H. (2000a) Introduction: the concepts of city-state and city-state culture. In M. H. Hansen (ed.) *A Comparative Study of Thirty City-State Cultures. An Investigation Conducted by the Copenhagen Polis Center:* 11–33. Copenhagen, The Royal Danish Academy of Sciences and Letters.

Hansen, M. H. (2000b) The Hellenic *Polis.* In M. H. Hansen (ed.) *A Comparative Study of Thirty City-State Cultures. An Investigation Conducted by the Copenhagen Polis Center:* 141–87. Copenhagen, The Royal Danish Academy of Sciences and Letters.

Higgins, M. D. and Higgins, R. (1996) *A Geological Companion to Greece.* Cornell, Cornell University Press.

Hodder, I. and Orton, C. (1976) *Spatial Analysis in Archaeology.* Cambridge, Cambridge University Press.

Hope Simpson, R. (1965) *A Gazetteer and Atlas of Mycenaean Sites.* Bulletin of the Institute of Classical Studies, Supplement 161. London, University of London.

Hope Simpson, R. and Dickinson, O. (1979) *A Gazetteer of Aegean Civilisation in the Bronze Age.* Studies in Mediterranean Archaeology 52. Göteborg, Paul Åströms Förlag.

Jameson, M., Runnels, C., and van Andel, T. (1994) *A Greek Countryside: The Southern Argolid from Prehistory to the Present Day.* Stanford, Stanford University Press.

Jansen, A. G. (2002) *A Study of the Remains of Mycenaean Roads and Stations of Bronze-Age Greece.* Lewiston, N.Y., Edwin Mellen Press.

Kalogerou, A. (n.d.) Unpublished manuscript on the Early Helladic artifacts from the archaeological survey of the Nemea Valley Archaeological Project.

Kilian, K. (1987) L'architecture des residences mycéniennes: origine et extension d'une structure du pouvoir politique pendant l'âge du bronze récent. In E. Lèvy (ed.) *Le système palatial en Orient, en Grèc, et à Rome: Actes du colloque de Strasbourg, 19–22 juin 1985*: 203–217. Strasbourg, Université des sciences humaines de Strasbourg.

Kilian, K. (1988a) The emergence of the wanax ideology in the Mycenaean palaces. *Oxford Journal of Archaeology* 7: 291–302.

Kilian, K. (1988b) Mycenaeans up to date: trends and changes in recent research. In E. B. French and K. A. Wardle (eds.) *Problems in Greek Prehistory: Papers Presented at the Centenary Conference of the British School of Archaeology at Athens, Manchester, April 1986*: 115–52. Bristol, Bristol Classical Press.

Kilian, K. (1992) Mykenischer Heiligtümer der Peloponnes. In H. Froning, T. Hölscher and H. Mielsch (eds.) *Kotinos: Festschrift für Erika Simon*: 10–25. Mainz, von Zabern.

Kilian, K. (1994) Il mondo miceneo 'aggiornato': tendenze e cambiamenti nell'ambito delle più recenti ricerche. In M. Marazzi (ed.) *La Società Micenea*: 357–419. Rome, Bagatto.

Kintigh, K. (1994) Contending with contemporaneity in settlement-pattern studies. *American Antiquity* 59: 143–48.

Lambropoulou, A. (1991) *The Middle Helladic Period in the Corinthia and the Argolid: An Archaeological Survey.* (Doctoral Dissertation, Bryn Mawr College.) Ann Arbor, University Microfilms.

Lavery, J. (1990) Some aspects of Mycenaean topography. *Bulletin of the Institute of Classical Studies* 37: 165–71.

Lavery, J. (1995) Some 'new' Mycenaean roads at Mycenae. *Bulletin of the Institute of Classical Studies* 40: 264–67.

Lehmann, H. (1937) *Argolis.* Athens, German Archaeological Institute.

Lukerman, F. E. (1972) Settlement and circulation: patterns and systems. In W. A. McDonald and G. Rapp, Jr. (eds.) *The Minnesota Messenia Expedition: Reconstructing a Bronze Age Regional Environment*: 148–70. Minneapolis, University of Minnesota.

Manning, S. (1995) *The Absolute Chronology of the Aegean Early Bronze Age: Archaeology, Radiocarbon and History.* Monographs in Mediterranean Archaeology 3. Sheffield, Sheffield Academic Press.

Maran, J. (1998) *Kulturwandel auf dem griechischen Festland und den Kykladen im späten 3. Jahrtausend v. Chr. Studien zu den kulturellen Verhältnissen in Südosteuropa und dem zentralen sowie östlichen Mittelmeerraum in der späten Kupfer- und frühen Bronzezeit.* Bonn, Habelt.

McDonald, W. A. (1964) Overland communications in Greece during LH III, with special reference to Southwest Peloponnese. In E. L. Bennett, Jr. (ed.) *Mycenaean Studies: Proceedings of the Third International Colloquium for Mycenaean Studies Held at 'Wingspread,' 4–8 September 1961*: 217–40. Madison, University of Wisconsin Press.

McDonald, W. A. and Hope Simpson, R. (1972) Archaeological exploration and Register. In W. A. McDonald and G. Rapp, Jr. (eds.) *The Minnesota Messenia Expedition*: 117–147, 264–309. Minneapolis, The University of Minnesota Press.

Mee, C. and Forbes, H. (eds.) (1997) *A Rough and Rocky Place: The Landscape and Settlement History of the Methana Peninsula, Greece. Results of the Methana Survey Project.* Liverpool, Liverpool University Press.

Morgan, C. (1999) *Isthmia* VIII: *The Late Bronze Age Settlement and Early Iron Age Sanctuary.* Princeton, American School of Classical Studies.

Mountjoy, P.-A. (1995) The pottery of the Late Helladic period. In C. Runnels, D. Pullen and S. Langdon (eds.) *Artifact and Assemblage: The Finds from a Regional Survey of the Southern Argolid, Greece, Volume I. The Prehistoric and Early Iron Age Pottery and the Lithic Artifacts*: 52–56. Stanford, Stanford University Press.

Mylonas, G. (1966) *Mycenae and the Mycenaean Age.* Princeton, Princeton University Press.

Nordquist, G. C. (1987) *A Middle Helladic Village: Asine in the Argolid.* Uppsala Studies in Ancient Mediterranean and Near Eastern Civilizations 16. Uppsala, University of Uppsala.

Nordquist, G. C. (1995) The pottery of the Early Helladic III and Middle Helladic periods. In C. Runnels, D. Pullen and S. Langdon (eds.) *Artifact and Assemblage: The Finds from a Regional Survey of the Southern Argolid, Greece, Volume I. The Prehistoric and Early Iron Age Pottery and the Lithic Artifacts*: 43–51. Stanford, Stanford University Press.

Petronoti, M. (2000) Social and economic formations in Kranidhi (1821–1981): a preliminary investigation. In S. B. Sutton (ed.) *Contingent Countryside: Settlement, Economy, and Landuse in the Southern Argolid since 1700*: 71–83. Stanford, Stanford University Press.

Plog, F. (1973) Diachronic anthropology. In C. Redman (ed.) *Research and Theory in Current Anthropology*: 181–98. New York, Wiley.

Plog, F. Plog, S. and Wait, W. (1978) Decision-making in modern surveys. *Advances in Archaeological Method and Theory* 1: 383–421. Academic Press, New York.

Pollock, S. (1999) *Ancient Mesopotamia: The Eden that Never Was.* Cambridge, Cambridge University Press.

Renfrew, C. (1972) *The Emergence of Civilisation.* London, Methuen.

Runnels, C. and van Andel, T. (1987) The evolution of settlement in the Southern Argolid, Greece. *Hesperia* 56: 303–334.

Runnels, C., Pullen, D. and Langdon, S. (eds.) (1995) *Artifact and Assemblage: The Finds from a Regional Survey of the Southern Argolid, Greece, Volume 1. The Prehistoric and Early Iron Age Pottery and Lithic Artifacts.* Stanford, Stanford University Press.

Rutter, J. (1983) Some thoughts on the analysis of ceramic data generated by site surveys. In D. R. Keller and D. W. Rupp (eds.) *Archaeological Survey in the Mediterranean Area.* BAR International Series 155: 137–42. Oxford, British Archaeological Reports.

Rutter, J. (1990) Pottery groups from Tsoungiza of the end of the Middle Bronze Age. *Hesperia* 59: 375–458.

Rutter, J. (1993a) A group of Late Helladic IIA pottery from Tsoungiza. *Hesperia* 62: 53–95.

Rutter, J. (1993b) Review of Aegean Prehistory II: the prepalatial Bronze Age of the southern and central Greek Mainland. *American Journal of Archaeology* 97: 745–97.

Rutter, J. B. (2002) The Prehistoric Archaeology of the Aegean. http://devlab.dartmouth.edu/history/bronze_age/chrono.html.

Salmon, J. (1984) *Wealthy Corinth.* Oxford, Oxford University Press.

Sanders, W., Parsons, J. and Santley, R. (1979) *The Basin of Mexico: Ecological Processes in the Evolution of a Civilization.* New York, Academic Press.

Schacht, R. (1984) The contemporaneity problem. *American Antiquity* 49: 678–95.

Schallin, A.-L. (1996) The Late Helladic period. In B. Wells (ed.) *The Berbati-Limnes Archaeological Survey 1988–1990*: 123–75. Stockholm, Paul Åströms Förlag.

Shelmerdine, C. W. (1997) The palatial Bronze Age of the southern and central Greek Mainland. *American Journal of Archaeology* 101: 537–85.

Shelmerdine, C. W. (1999) A comparative look at Mycenaean administration(s). In S. Deger-Jalkotzy, S. Hiller and O. Panagl (eds.) *Floreant Studia Mycenaea. Akten des X. Internationalen Mykenologischen Colloquiums in Salzburg vom 1.–5. Mai 1995. Band I*: 555–76. Vienna, Verlag der Österreichischen Akademie der Wissenschaften.

Steffen, J. (ed.) 1884 *Karten von Mykenai*. Berlin, D. Reimer.

Steward, J. (1950) *Area Research, Theory and Practice*. New York, Social Science Research Council.

Sutton, S. B. (1988) What is a village in a nation of migrants? *Journal of Modern Greek Studies* 6: 187–215.

Sutton, S. B. (1994) Settlement patterns, settlement perceptions: rethinking the Greek village. In P. N. Kardulias (ed.) *Beyond the Site: Regional Studies in the Aegean Area*: 313–35. Lanham, MD, University Press of America.

Sutton, S. B. (1999) Fleeting villages, moving households: Greek housing strategies in historical perspective. In D. Birdwell-Pheasant and D. Lawrence-Zúñiga (eds.) *House Life: Space, Place, and Family in Europe*: 73–104. New York, Berg.

Sutton, S. B. (2000a) Introduction: past and present in rural Greece. In S. B. Sutton (ed.) *Contingent Countryside: Settlement, Economy, and Landuse in the Southern Argolid since 1700*: 1–24. Stanford, Stanford University Press.

Sutton, S. B. (2000b) Liquid landscapes: demographic transitions in the Ermionidha. In S. B. Sutton (ed.) *Contingent Countryside: Settlement, Economy, and Landuse in the Southern Argolid since 1700*: 84–106. Stanford, Stanford University Press.

Thomas, P. (1988) A Mycenaean perfumed oil workshop at Zygouries. *American Journal of Archaeology* 92: 254 [abstract].

Topping, P. (2000) The Southern Argolid from Byzantine to Ottoman times. In S. B. Sutton (ed.) *Contingent Countryside: Settlement, Economy, and Landuse in the Southern Argolid since 1700*: 25–40. Stanford, Stanford University Press.

Van Andel, T. and Runnels, C. (1987) *Beyond the Acropolis: A Rural Greek Past*. Stanford, Stanford University Press.

Vermeule, E. (1987) Baby Aigisthos and the Bronze Age. *Proceedings of the Cambridge Philological Society* 33: 122–52.

Warren, P. and Hankey, V. (1989) *Aegean Bronze Age Chronology*. Bristol, Bristol Classical Press.

Wells, B. (1996) The Middle Bronze Age. In B. Wells (ed.) *The Berbati-Limnes Archaeological Survey 1988–1990*: 121. Stockholm, Paul Åströms Förlag.

Wells, B., Runnels, C. and Zangger, E. (1990) The Berbati-Limnes Archaeological Survey: the 1988 season. *Opuscula Atheniensis* 18: 207–238.

Wells, B., Runnels, C. and Zangger, E. (1993) In the shadow of Mycenae. *Archaeology* 46: 54–58, 63.

Wiener M. H. (1998) The absolute chronology of Late Helladic IIIA2. In M. S. Balmuth and R. H. Tykot (eds.) *Sardinian and Aegean Chronology: Towards the Resolution of Relative and Absolute Dating in the Mediterranean. Proceedings of the International Colloquium 'Sardinian Stratigraphy and Mediterranean Chronology', Tufts Universtity, Medford, Mass., March 17–19, 1995. Studies in Sardinian Archaeology* 5: 309–319. Oxford, Oxbow Books.

Wright, J. C. (1990) An Early Mycenaean hamlet on Tsoungiza at ancient Nemea. In P. Darcque and R. Treuil (eds.) *L'habitat égéen préhistorique. Actes de la table ronde internationale, Athènes, 23–25 juin 1987. Bulletin de correspondance hellénique, Supplément* 19: 347–57. Paris, École française d'Athènes.

Wright, J. C. (1995) From chief to king in Mycenaean society. In P. Rehak (ed.) *The Role of the Ruler in the Prehistoric Aegean. Aegaeum* 11: 63–80. Liège, Histoire de l'art et archéologie de la Grèce antique, Université de Liège; Austin, Program in Aegean Scripts and Prehistory, University of Texas at Austin.

Wright, J. C., Cherry, J. F., Davis, J. L., Mantzourani, E., and Sutton, S. B. (1990) The Nemea Valley Archaeological Project: a preliminary report. *Hesperia* 59: 579–659.

Zangger, E. (1993) *The Geoarchaeology of the Argolid. Argolis 2*. Berlin, Mann.

Zerner, C. (1978) *The Beginning of the Middle Helladic Period at Lerna*. Ann Arbor, University Microfilms (7904772).

Zerner, C. (1986) Middle and Late Helladic I pottery from Lerna. *Hydra* 2: 58–74.

Zerner, C. (1988) Middle and Late Helladic I pottery from Lerna. Part II, Shapes. *Hydra* 4: 1–10 and unnumbered ills.

Zerner, C. (1993) New perspectives on trade in the Middle and Early Late Helladic periods on the Mainland. In C. Zerner, P. Zerner and J. Winder (eds.) *Pottery as Evidence for Trade in the Aegean Bronze Age, 1939–1989*: 39–56. Amsterdam, Gieben.

10. Problems and Possibilities in Comparative Survey: A North African Perspective

David L. Stone

In the last 25 years, Tunisia has witnessed a boom in field survey archaeology. The success of regional survey projects in the northern Mediterranean, together with a government-sponsored program to inventory all archaeological sites in Tunisia, has encouraged archaeologists to begin 19 programs of surface survey in this country. With the explosion of this research, survey investigations now form one of the main bodies of evidence for Tunisia's rural landscapes, and significant patterns of landscape exploitation are emerging from these studies.

The benefit of such an extended focus of attention on the countryside is a vast databank of information on rural sites; the challenge for archaeologists comes in discerning how to evaluate that information. It is easy to be pessimistic about the data. The emphasis of recent survey work in this part of the Mediterranean has fallen heavily on recording previously identified sites and monuments, rather than on finding new sites or undertaking rigorous, systematic investigations of the countryside. Such a methodological orientation has not yet enabled archaeological research in Tunisia to play a role in understanding issues of social organization, nor has it led many of the projects conducted there to interest a wide audience of archaeologists. Comparative quantitative analysis of the collected data is feasible on a limited basis, when ideally it would be desirable to use much more frequently. Nonetheless, the basic quantitative data from field surveys are available in sufficient depth that they can be used to construct a 'landscape history'. Even if that history is legible in general rather than specific terms at the present time, a good argument can still be made for the usefulness of a comparative study of the survey data in their current state. Based on the results compiled to date from those 19 field survey projects undertaken in the last 25 years within Tunisia, this study will demonstrate that comparative analysis of survey data clearly indicates long-term changes in the countryside, while recognizing the problems as well as the possibilities inherent in this endeavor.

HISTORY OF SURVEY RESEARCH IN TUNISIA

Landscape archaeology has a long and distinguished history in North Africa. Surveys of the countryside were among the earliest investigations undertaken in the 19th century. The *Atlas archéologique de la Tunisie*, compiled using reports made by French archaeologists, soldiers, and surveying teams working in the late 19th and early 20th centuries, was a formidable achievement of archaeological site recording (Babelon *et al.* 1892–1913; Cagnat *et al.* 1914–32). Each sheet plotted sites in a 20- by 30-km region at the scale of 1:50,000 and located all the known archaeological sites, but described only a selection of the major ones in an attached explanatory text. For its time, this was an in-depth assessment of the rural landscape, even though many of these sites were no more than 'dots on maps,' smaller sites were inevitably overlooked, and the quality of record-keeping for the 60 individual sheets varied tremendously. An archaeological atlas with a similar structure was compiled at the same time in Algeria (Gsell 1911).

Despite this impressive early research, very little survey work was carried out between 1910 and the late 1970s. The only landscape studies to take place in this period occurred around Sufetula, on Cap Bon, and along the southern frontier of Roman expansion. These three projects primarily involved recording known sites. Near Sufetula, the Brathay Survey studied Roman-period farms within a 10-km radius of the town to understand regional economic development (Addyman 1962; Addyman and Simpson 1966). On Cap Bon, researchers investigated the spatial organization of Punic settlements and cemeteries, most of which were located near the coast (Acquaro *et al.* 1973; Barreca and Fantar 1983). On the southern border of the Roman empire, the *Limes Tripolitanus* Survey examined the purpose of the forts, barriers, and outposts erected there (Trousset 1974).

Modern archaeological field survey research is a development of the last quarter-century, when interest in landscape studies re-emerged vigorously. Beginning in the late 1970s and early 1980s, 19 survey projects, many

Survey	Publications
Carte archéologique	Ben Baaziz 1992
Bir Mcherga	Maurin and Peyras 1991
El Meknassi	Ben Baaziz 1991a
Gafsa	Annabi 1991b; Ben Baaziz 1991b
Mididi	Ben Baaziz 1986
Oued Cherita	Annabi 1991a
Oued Sejnane	Ghalia 1992
Rohia	Ben Baaziz 1986
Sidi El Hani	Ben Baaziz 1988
Sousse	Annabi 1988
Sraa Ouertane	Ben Baaziz 1986
Carthage Survey	Greene 1983a; 1983b; 1984; 1986; 1992; forthcoming; Greene and Kehoe 1995
Coastlines Survey	Ben Lazreg *et al.* 1995; Bonifay *et al.* 1992; Chelbi *et al.* 1995; Paskoff *et al.* 1991; Paskoff and Trousset 1991; Trousset 1992
Dougga Survey	De Vos 2000
Jerba Survey	Fentress 2000; 2001
Kasserine Archaeological Survey	Hitchner 1988; 1989; 1990; 1995; Neuru 1987
Leptiminus Archaeological Survey	Mattingly 1992; Mattingly *et al.* 2000; Stone *et al.* 1998
Segermes (Project Africa Proconsularis)	Dietz *et al.* 1995; Ørsted *et al.* 2000
Sahel Pottery Survey	Peacock *et al.* 1989; 1990; Peacock and Tomber 1989
Sufetula-Masclianae Survey	Barbery and Delhoume 1982

Table 10.1 Bibliography of the principal publications of recent field survey projects in Tunisia. (Most projects are listed under the name by which they refer to themselves. The Segermes Survey is also known as Project Africa Proconsularis. The 'Coastlines Survey' is a shortened version of the Programme tuniso-français d'étude du littoral de la Tunisie. *In the case of the Sufetula-Masclianae Survey and the Sahel Pottery Survey, the name has been assigned. The* Carte archéologique *includes multiple regional investigations, listed individually in this table, which are largely comparable to the other survey projects.)*

of which are still ongoing, have generated a large and growing database of information on rural settlement patterns. In this respect, Tunisia has lagged behind some of its Mediterranean counterparts, such as Italy and Greece, where survey work between the 1960s and 1980s led to the testing of new theories and methodologies (McDonald and Rapp 1972; Renfrew and Wagstaff 1982; Cherry 1983); indeed, the impetus provided by successful endeavors in the northern Mediterranean is partially responsible for the application of survey techniques in Tunisia. As another catalyst, one might point also to the inauguration of the *Carte nationale des sites archéologiques et des monuments historiques (*hereafter, *Carte archéologique),* a large-scale initiative to inventory all archaeological remains in the country (Ben Baaziz 1992). The Tunisian government has sponsored the *Carte archéologique* in order to create an inventory of sites, as well as to protect against their destruction in the face of rapid modern development, and to encourage greater public awareness of local heritage. Table 10.1 lists the 19 recent projects, with references to their principal publications; 10 of them were conducted in the context of the *Carte archéologique.*

THE SURVEY DATABASE

At present, Tunisia must be acknowledged as having one of the most comprehensive regional archaeological databases in the Mediterranean. The accelerated pace at which field surveys have started here is remarkable, although the rapid growth of survey as a research methodology in a number of regions of the Mediterranean emerges clearly from other papers in this volume.

The 19 recent survey projects fall within most of the main geographic areas of the country. They have occurred on the north coast, in the upper and lower Tell, the Sahel, the high and low Steppes, and on the island of Jerba in the south (Figure 10.1). Such broad geographic coverage makes it possible to explore variation in the archaeology of several regions of the country. The wide distribution of surveys throughout the country, therefore, supplies an additional motivation for a comparative analysis of their results.

Only the Dougga and Segermes Surveys have published final book-length reports (De Vos 2000; Dietz *et al.* 1995; Ørsted *et al.* 2000). It is thus important to stress that any conclusions drawn from a comparison of surveys here are preliminary. On the other hand, most projects have completed their fieldwork and are currently compiling and

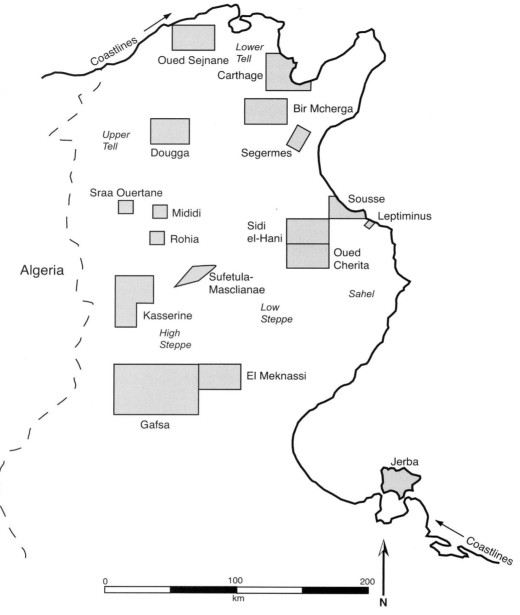

Figure 10.1 Recent field survey projects in Tunisia. (The Sahel Pottery Project [not shown] covers a large area between the Leptiminus and Sufetula-Masclianae Surveys.)

analyzing their data for publication. Preliminary reports in journals or conference proceedings have varied from detailed examinations of individual sites (*e.g.* Kasserine Survey), to overviews of regional trends (*e.g.* the Coastlines, Jerba, and Sufetula-Masclianae Surveys), and to inventories of types of sites discovered (*e.g.* the Sidi el Hani and Sousse Surveys). Some of these reports have considered the importance of the survey data for theorizing about cultural change or spatial patterns in the landscape (*e.g.* the Kasserine and Segermes Surveys). Other surveys, especially those of the *Carte archéologique*, have neither presented their findings in depth, nor come to grips with the data in any synthetic fashion (*e.g.* the Gafsa, Mididi,

Oued Cherita, Rohia, and Sraa Ouertane Surveys). Adequate maps of individual sites are also lacking, again particularly (although not exclusively) among the reports of the *Carte archéologique* surveys. Despite significant differences in extent and quality of publication, all 19 projects have been included here in order to create as large a database as possible for interregional comparison. The volume of the data already collected and presented by these surveys is more than sufficient to justify comparative analysis.

Survey Project	Area (sq. km)	Team Size	Transport	Artifacts	Interdisc.	Off-site data
Carte archéologique Projects						
Bir Mcherga	320	2–3	car			
El Meknassi	640	2–3	car			
Gafsa	2560	2–3	car			
Mididi	c. 100	2–3	car			
Oued Cherita	640	2–3	car			
Oued Sejnane	610	2–3	car			
Rohia	c. 100	2–3	car			
Sidi El Hani	640	2–3	car			
Sousse	420	2–3	car			
Sraa Ouertane	c. 100	2–3	car			
Other Projects						
Carthage Survey	825	1	car	√		
Coastlines Survey	>1300	4+	car		√	
Dougga Survey	150	4+	fw	√	√	
Jerba Survey	580	4+	fw	√	√	√
Kasserine Archaeological Survey	75	4+	fw	√		√
Leptiminus Archaeological Survey	10	4+	fw	√	√	√
Segermes Survey	c. 150	4+	fw	√	√	√
Sahel Pottery Survey	20000>	4+	car	√		
Sufetula-Masclianae Survey	c. 400	2–3	car			

Table 10.2 Methodological comparison of recent surveys in Tunisia. (Key: fw = fieldwalking; interdisc. = interdisciplinary.)

METHODOLOGY

At first observation, the recent survey projects present severe problems of comparability. They have been conducted by both indigenous and foreign scholars, working in several geographic zones, with variably-sized teams and budgets. But perhaps the most critical point to emphasize is that their directors have brought different methodologies to bear upon the landscapes they have studied. Table 10.2 displays the methods used by these surveys. The purpose of the summary in this section is not to debate the relative merits of different techniques (such a debate might be indeed be worthwhile for Tunisian archaeologists to hold elsewhere, since there are real differences of opinion), but to provide an overview of their methods without which any comparative assessment would be impossible. This overview is intended to summarize methodological differences without presenting an exhaustive treatment of every single one.

Survey 'Intensity'

Two groups of 'intensive' and 'extensive' survey projects stand out in Table 10.2. Surface survey by fieldwalkers at a high level of intensity (*i.e.*, at an interval of 25 m or less) has been performed by only five projects in Tunisia (Dougga, Jerba, Kasserine, Leptiminus, and Segermes Surveys). On these surveys, several people (at least three, and usually five to seven) formed the fieldwalking teams. The research design of the other surveys mainly involved re-documenting sites previously found by the 19th-century surveys (see Ben Baaziz 1992 for the *Carte archéologique*; bibliography in Table 10.1 for the other surveys). In most cases, archaeologists on these survey projects explored the landscape by car and worked in teams of one, two, or three

people. They investigated new sites where they discovered them in the course of examining known ones, or where local informants pointed them out. The differences in methodology employed by these two groups of Tunisian survey projects conform to the well-known case of 'earlier' and 'recent' Greek surveys examined by John Cherry. His study demonstrated the impact of methodological differences on site recovery (Cherry 1983: fig. 1; see also Wilkinson *et al.,* Ch. 14, this volume, Figure 14.1), providing empirical evidence that 'intensive', closely-spaced fieldwalking procedures tended to find 70–100 times the density of sites than more 'extensive' archaeological reconnaissance investigations. In addition, it showed that the more intensive surveys found a greater proportion of small-sized sites, and thus revealed a more complete settlement hierarchy.

Table 10.3, a compilation of the basic results from the surveys, reveals a similar, though less pronounced, pattern in the Tunisian evidence. The survey projects which have employed rigorous, systematic methods in collecting their data have found many more sites than the others. Each of the more intensive projects has recorded among the highest totals of sites per sq. km, as shown in Figure 10.2. In all situations the more intensive the survey methodology applied, the more sites were found. Where it was possible to make a comparison to earlier surveys, the *Atlas Archéologique* of the 1880s and 1890s in all cases found fewer sites than the surveys of the 1980s and 1990s (Figure 10.3).

Site Definition and Function

What individual survey projects call a 'site' – a notorious definitional problem in regional archaeology – often

Survey Project	Area (sq.km)	Total sites	Prehist.	Pre-Roman	Roman	Islamic	Modern	Atlas
Carte archéologique								
Bir Mcherga	320	158	0*	4*	143	NR	–	210
El Meknassi	640	85	5*	2*	50	NR	NR	NC
Gafsa	2560	291	30 max.	30 max.	200	85 max.	85 max.	48
Mididi	c. 100	75	–	5	72	–	–	NR
Oued Cherita	640	176	2	2	NR	NR	NR	NC
Oued Sejnane	610	165	2*	37	80	NR	85	25
Rohia	c. 100	22	–	3	19	–	–	NR
Sidi El Hani	640	125	NR	NR	104	NR	NR	81
Sousse	420	186	2*	4*	128	39	4	99
Sraa Ouertane	c. 100	65	0*	42	26	–	–	NR
Other Projects								
Carthage Survey	825	136	0*	57	121	26	40	104
Coastlines Survey	>1300	209	NR	NR	NR	NR	NR	
Dougga Survey	150	206	NR	63	132	2	6	NR
Jerba Survey	580	446	NR	183	216	276	273	NR
Kasserine Survey	75	164	0	23	149	0	12	NR
Leptiminus Survey	10	30	0	3	17	4	6	6
Segermes Survey	c. 150	c. 250	4	8	c. 220	NR	NR	80
Sahel Pottery Survey	20000>	29	–	–	29 kilns	–	–	
Suf.-Masc. Survey	c. 400	125	–	–	125	–	–	NR

*Table 10.3 Basic quantitative results of the recent surveys in Tunisia, based on numbers compiled from the publications listed in Table 10.1. (Key: * = data from the Atlas préhistorique de la Tunisie; – = survey did not investigate this period; NR = not reported in publication; NA = not available; NC = not covered by Atlas archéologique.)*

involves complex issues of interpretation and analysis (Cherry *et al.* 1991: 37–54; Gallant 1986). In general, the more recent Tunisian surveys do not disagree over what they consider a site, but they have many more differences in the use of intensive fieldwalking procedures, collection methods, and interdisciplinary approaches. By contrast, the surveys display a remarkable similarity in their use of the term 'site', employing it to describe a distinct concentration of artifacts related to recurrent patterns of human activity in the past.'

Such a definition distinguishes a site from, for example, lithic artifacts or potsherds not found in association with other artifacts but likely to derive from 'off-site' activities. Investigation of off-site data, which can reveal specific agricultural activities, refuse disposal, and intensity of landuse (see Alcock *et al.* 1994; Foley 1981; Wilkinson 1982; 1989), is a feature of four Tunisian survey projects (the Dougga, Jerba, Leptiminus and Segermes Surveys).

Although there is basic agreement among the Tunisian surveys regarding the definition of site and off-site materials, there is little uniformity in the assignment of a site hierarchy. The Kasserine Survey, for example, has designated a five-tiered typology of Roman rural sites ranging

from *agroville* to villa, *opus africanum* farm, courtyard farm, and small structure (Hitchner 1988). The Carthage Survey identified three levels of Roman rural sites: villages, villas, and small-scale farmsteads (Greene forthcoming). The rest of the surveys have additional categories of site and more or less elaborate site hierarchies. Some of these differences may be due to real variations in the make-up of settlements in the survey region, but they indicate one of the basic ways in which data from individual projects are not directly compatible with those from others.

Artifact Collection and Sampling Methods

Collection of materials from individual sites provides a quantitative basis for the analysis of their dates of occupation, their functions, and their relationships to other sites. Most practitioners of Mediterranean survey would agree that a multi-stage design of increasingly rigorous collection procedures will produce the most reliable results. In the recent Tunisian surveys, only the Carthage, Coastlines, Dougga, Jerba, Kasserine, Leptiminus, Sahel Pottery, and Segermes Surveys have so far collected artifacts from sites (Table 10.2). These projects also

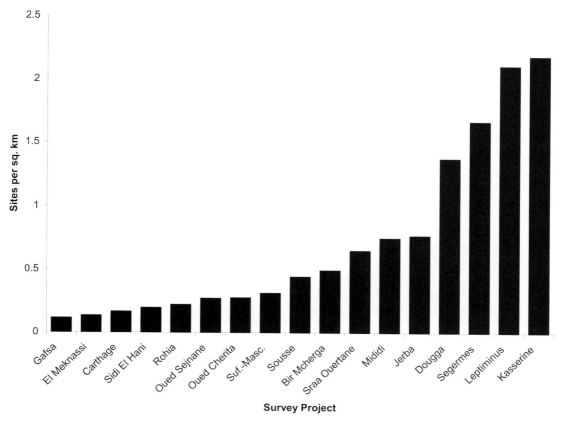

Figure 10.2 Site densities in recent Tunisian surveys (all periods).

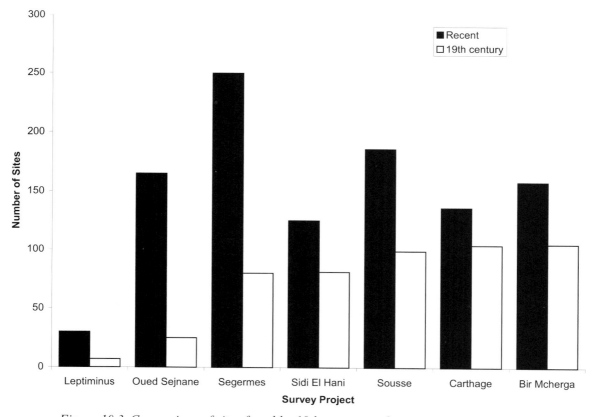

Figure 10.3 Comparison of sites found by 19th-century and recent surveys in Tunisia.

incorporated a multi-stage component into their research design in which sites were revisited, and artifact collection took place with more thorough sampling strategies on subsequent visits. The other projects (the Sufetula-Masclianae and all of the *Carte archéologique* surveys) did not gather artifacts at any stage. Sadok Ben Baaziz, the director of the *Carte archéologique*, has argued (1992: 13) that this approach is not relevant for the broad and rapid coverage of the country which his project aims to accomplish; therefore, archaeologists working on the *Carte archéologique* simply estimate the date of a site based on the brief observation of surface materials. On small sites, if the density and scatter of artifacts are restricted, a subjective analysis of date and function may be fairly easy to make; but on larger sites, where the surveyor may not have had the ability to investigate all remains closely, the subjectivity of the analysis inevitably increases. For a functional interpretation of each site, the *Carte archéologique* relies upon surviving architectural elements, whereas the collection of artifacts enables other projects to draw on a wider array of material evidence. These differences in collection methods mean that detailed information about sites is available from some surveys, while others have gathered basic data only.

Single-period Emphasis

Virtually all of the recent survey projects have examined sites of all periods from prehistoric to modern, but it is clear that Roman archaeology has been their principal focus. Two have even concentrated exclusively, or almost exclusively, on Roman data (the Sahel Pottery and Sufetula-Masclianae Surveys). Finally, Roman archaeologists comprised the principal staff even on survey projects which evaluated sites from all periods in their regions (the *Carte archéologique*, Dougga, and Leptiminus Surveys). In part, the single-period emphasis is due to the fact that rural settlement was widespread in the Roman period, and therefore the presence of Roman archaeologists in Tunisian regional surveys is essential. But this emphasis also derives in part from the guidelines of some permits issued to foreign archaeologists, which stipulated that in-depth research could be carried out only on the Roman-period sites. The Segermes Survey, which included specialists from a number of different periods (Prehistoric, Punic, Roman) and disciplines (archaeology, ceramics, geology, palaeobotany) on its staff, appears different from the other surveys, although even this project systematically examined material from only the Prehistoric, Punic, and Roman periods. The Jerba Survey, co-directed by Roman and Medieval archaeologists, is the sole project that has a fully diachronic focus, and its results accordingly show a much greater balance of site numbers between periods (Table 10.3).

Site Dating and Artifact Chronologies

One issue affecting use of data from different surveys is the employment of variant chronological schemes or terminologies. Alcock (1989: 11, n. 20; 1993) found the use of multiple chronological schemes to be a difficult, but not irresolvable, problem in her comparative study of Greek surveys. In Tunisia, individual surveys constructed their own chronological systems without regard to whether they conformed with the systems used by other survey projects, presenting problems of data compatibility. For example, the Carthage and Segermes Surveys spent considerable time collecting and dating pottery from their sites and have broken them down by arbitrary 50-year (Segermes) and 100-year (Carthage) periods. Such categories are more precise than those employed by the Coastlines and Dougga Surveys which subdivide pottery from broad periods (such as Roman) into multiple components (such as early, middle, and late Roman). By contrast, the *Carte archéologique* has not made artifact collection a priority: it assessed the date of a site by brief observation of surface remains and therefore did not divide periods into multiple units. Recorded Roman sites date between the first century BC and the seventh century AD, but only occasionally did the author of a *Carte archéologique* publication specify a smaller window within these eight centuries.

Interdisciplinary Studies

Contrary to many current Mediterranean investigations, field survey projects in Tunisia have concentrated narrowly on the archaeological record alone and have avoided interdisciplinary investigations. Two exceptions are the Segermes and Coastlines Surveys. At Segermes, palynological and geological studies have substantially improved knowledge of vegetational history and the formation of the natural landscape (Dietz *et al.* 1995). The union of geomorphological and archaeological techniques on the Coastlines Survey has provided a detailed landscape reconstruction of the lower Medjerda valley over the past 6,000 years (Chelbi *et al.* 1995). Other surveys carrying out interdisciplinary analyses in Tunisia have yet to publish many of their studies, though that picture may change before long.

Summary

It is obvious that the quality of the data available from Tunisian surveys varies significantly. Archaeologists who consider comparative studies of survey databases elsewhere similarly face this critical problem. Are some surveys simply too extensive in approach to provide any worthwhile information? Should one omit the evidence from these surveys and evaluate instead only the more rigorous ones? Beyond this question, of course, lie further problems of comparability among the intensive surveys, such as the use of different collection methods or chronological systems. How big a role do these methodological differences play?

Survey project	Survey area (sq. km)	Roman sites	Oil presses	Presses/sq. km	Presses/site
Kasserine	75	149	40	0.13	0.27
Mididi	100	72	29	0.29	0.40
Segermes	150	220	27	0.18	0.12
Sufetula-Masc.	400	125	44	0.11	0.35
Rohia	100	19	11	0.11	0.58
Sraa Ouertane	100	26	5	0.05	0.19
Oued Sejnane	610	80	22	0.04	0.28
Carthage	825	121	13	0.02	0.11
Sousse	420	128	4	0.01	0.03
Sidi El Hani	640	104	2	0.003	0.02

Table 10.4 Olive oil presses found by recent Tunisian surveys (ranked by presses/sq. km).

COMPARING THE DATA

Given the preliminary nature of many of the survey publications, as well as the methodological discrepancies, there are limits to the questions that can be asked. It seems best to begin with an evaluation of site numbers and site types for both the pre-Roman and Roman periods. In the following section, a synthetic analysis of the 19 most recent projects presents the long-term trends in patterns of settlement and landuse which the surveys have documented.

Pre-Roman Period

From approximately the 7th to 2nd centuries BC, the emerging Numidian kingdom and the Carthaginian state controlled different parts of Tunisia. To simplify the terminology, this period will be defined as pre-Roman, rather than Protohistoric, Punic or Numidian; each of the latter, though commonly used, refers to part but not all of Tunisia during this time period. Survey data from the pre-Roman period indicate several activities taking place in the countryside and significant regional variation in the types of sites found. A small number of towns and tombs have been identified in the areas of the Dougga, Jerba, and Leptiminus Surveys. The Sraa Ouertane and Kasserine Surveys, respectively, found 42 and 23 megalithic tombs, but no settlements. Cemeteries containing rock-cut tombs known as *haouanet* are present in other survey regions such as the Oued Sejnane (37) and Segermes (2).

In only two survey areas is there much evidence for widespread rural activity beyond the construction of tombs. The Carthage Survey data show minor occupation of the city's hinterland during the 7th to 5th centuries BC (7 sites) and the 4th century BC (9 sites), but a very significant rise in settlement density marked the 3rd to 2nd centuries BC (50 sites). Three factors suggest that the expansion of rural activity may well have been linked to the presence of new agricultural installations. First, the hill-country in the hinterland of Carthage, where the new 3rd- and 2nd-century BC sites are located, consists of easily exploitable soils. Second, the overall site distribution pattern in the Roman period, when these sites contain numerous agricultural features (presses, millstones, irrigation), is quite similar. Finally, the presence of Punic fine wares and amphoras also suggests occupation (Greene, forthcoming).

The Jerba Survey has likewise documented the presence of rural sites in the 3rd and 2nd centuries BC. On Jerba, rural villas and smaller farms make up a landscape that seems geared toward surplus production of wine and olive oil, based on the evidence of pottery from nearby kilns. These products were likely exchanged for cereals, as subsistence crops fare poorly on the island (Fentress 2001: 262–64). The survey has also documented the presence of isolated tombs and cemeteries in the rural landscape.

Thus, the evidence from recent surveys argues for significant developments in Tunisian landuse in the 3rd and 2nd centuries BC, although rural exploitation varied by region. At Carthage and on Jerba, isolated rural settlements as well as moderately-sized villages first filled the countryside at this time; such organization, in which communities relied on small-holders and peasants who commuted between town and country, is typical of more developed societies in the eastern Mediterranean in the contemporary Hellenistic period. Elsewhere in Tunisia, where surveys made an effort to study the pre-Roman period, high concentrations of funerary monuments were present in the rural landscape. These areas contained *haouanet*, or megalithic tombs, which seem to have developed in the 4th, 3rd, and 2nd centuries BC in response to the increasing expropriation of territory by the Numidian kings and Carthage. The overall picture – of a landscape with rural farms emerging in two coastal zones, but dominated in all other areas by small towns and cemeteries – is clear.

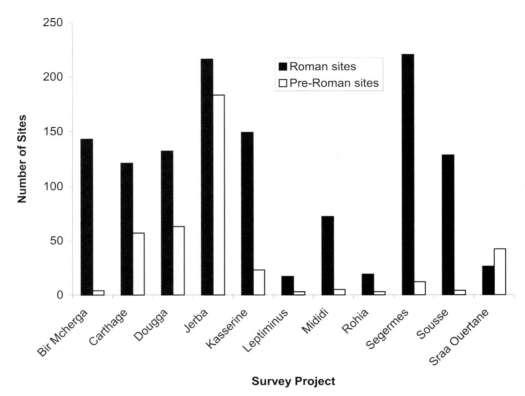

Figure 10.4 Pre-Roman and Roman site numbers compared in several survey areas.

Roman Period

During the Roman period the number of rural sites increased significantly in almost every region of Tunisia. Table 10.3 presents the total number of sites for all periods studied by the recent Tunisian surveys; Roman sites surpassed pre-Roman sites in all but one case, often by several times. The high density of rural sites occupied in the Roman period appears clearly in Figure 10.4. The character of the new sites, moreover, signifies an important change in the nature of landuse in the Roman period. All of the surveys found evidence for rural farms, a form of settlement which became the new ordering mechanism of the landscape at this time, in contrast to the presence of farms in just two of the survey areas from the pre-Roman period. Roman-period farms have courtyards with attached buildings, cisterns, and a range of ceramic wares, arguing for year-round occupation, rather than seasonal use at the large majority of the sites (*e.g.* the Dougga, Kasserine, and Segermes Surveys). The substantial number of sites with agricultural features, such as olive-presses, millstones, and water-related facilities, points to the surplus production and export of grain, and olive oil, a link especially well attested by the Coastlines, Dougga, Kasserine, Leptiminus, Mididi, Sahel Pottery, and Sufetula-Masclianae Surveys. Estimates of total production capacities of olive oil for the Kasserine Survey area in years with average or high rainfall reach well beyond regional subsistence requirements (Mattingly 1988; 1994). As the density of olive-presses in other survey areas indicates, some regions

may have equalled or nearly attained the levels produced around Kasserine (Table 10.4). The Roman-period landscape in Tunisia contains additional features such as roads, bridges, cemeteries, boundary stones, and kilns, although farms significantly outnumber other site types (see the Dougga and Segermes Surveys). The chronology of rural development is not well documented, though the 'boom' visible in the survey data appears to start earlier and finish later in coastal regions.

Beyond this general picture, individual survey areas exhibited some difference in settlement patterns during the Roman period. Figure 10.5 displays the number of Roman sites per sq. km found by all of the surveys. These numbers relate to actual densities of settlement in antiquity, but are also shaped by other factors such as survey intensity, the durability of local building materials, and post-abandonment conditions. Nonetheless, the numbers demonstrate regional variation, with many sites appearing in surveys in the high steppe and Sahel and comparatively fewer sites per km in the low steppe, upper Tell, and lower Tell. Within Tunisia, there were 'discrepant experiences' under Roman rule, as the decline in site numbers in the Sraa Ouertane in particular suggests (Mattingly 1997; Said 1993: 31–43). Some regions responded more rapidly or favorably to the imposition of empire, although the general trend points toward a significant expansion of rural settlement everywhere.

Based on the evidence collected by the surveys, it is currently impossible to carry this analysis further into the

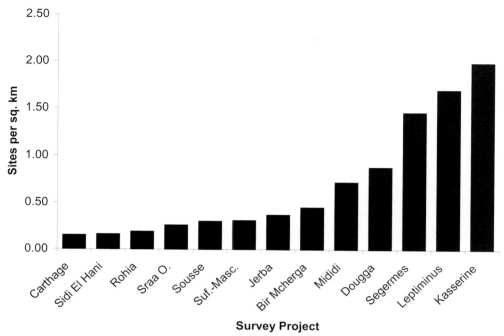

Figure 10.5 Site densities for the Roman period.

Arab, Ottoman, or French colonial periods. With the exception of the Jerba Survey, recent Tunisian projects have placed very little emphasis on recording material from these periods; it is true that excavations have neglected to undertake detailed relevant site and ceramic studies as well. An inability to recognize ceramic evidence from these periods may contribute to their present low site totals.

CONCLUSION

Although recent surveys in Tunisia ranged from extensive projects conceived for the purpose of recording the presence of sites and monuments, to intensive projects aimed at producing detailed multi-period reconstructions of landscapes, such methodological variance has not precluded comparative study. From the pre-Roman to the Roman period, as the Tunisian countryside came to participate in a wider sphere of economic and cultural relations, the survey data from many regions lead to a similar conclusion. There appeared a transformed landscape, characterized by frequent rural farming settlements and agricultural facilities, rather than scattered towns and cemeteries. Without evidence from field surveys, this transformation would hardly be so visible. Prior to the recent survey projects, scarce references in ancient texts, limited surface reconnaissance, and inadequate – mostly unscientific – excavations offered only a very imprecise picture of the changes between the pre-Roman and Roman periods. There is no doubt that on its own the survey evidence provides a more accurate historical reconstruc-

tion, since this evidence can be assessed in quantitative terms.

Even though many projects have not yet completed their analysis and publication, this comparative study has been useful in taking stock of the present situation. It has illustrated the methodological shortcomings of current work and enumerated areas to be explored in future investigations. Nor should archaeologists be hesitant to undertake such an analysis before final publication of results occurs; a reluctance to undertake a comparative analysis of survey data at an early stage will only prolong the time before survey data become useful and will only delay the development of a suitable agenda for future research.

The results summarized here should offer encouragement that survey work in Tunisia has a key role to play in the future. At the moment, several concerns must be raised. Field surveys in Tunisia must strive to include a wider variety of specialties as regular foci of investigation. Too few surveys have considered geomorphological, palaeoenvironmental, and other questions pertaining to landscape evolution, in addition to acquiring archaeological data. Reconstructing the history of fertile and marginal zones will greatly improve the comprehension of landuse and settlement patterns. Detailed ceramic analysis must also become a more prominent feature of survey reports since it is impossible to document the extent of occupation or the range of functional activities on a site without knowledge of its ceramic assemblage. Two potential issues to be studied through ceramic analysis include the chronology of the appearance of rural farms in the country and the arrival in quantity of imported consumer goods (signified, for example, by the presence of Dressel 2/4 amphoras). A diachronic approach to regional history must also be adopted. The distribution of Neolithic sites in coastal areas is poorly understood, the placement of saint's tombs in the landscape may signal religious changes in the country-side during the Arab period, and the construction of wells for irrigation in the Ottoman era may point to the arrival of a new phase of olive oil exportation. These three issues (and many others) could be illuminated by greater attention to all material evidence in the countryside. The suitability of field survey as a technique for the study of the Tunisian landscape no longer needs justification, but – in order to make new contributions – individual survey projects must begin to address some of these methodological concerns in a serious fashion.

ACKNOWLEDGEMENTS

I would like to thank Sue Alcock, John Cherry, Bruce Hitchner, and David Mattingly for their excellent advice and suggestions while I worked on the topic discussed in this paper, first as part of my Ph.D. dissertation for the University of Michigan, and second in the course of this conference. Elizabeth Fentress kindly offered data in advance of the Jerba Survey publication. Several other members of the conference offered comments on my paper for which I am also grateful.

REFERENCES

Acquaro, E., Bartoloni, P., Ciasca, A. and Fantar, M. (1973) *Prospezione archeologica al Capo Bon* I. Collezione di studi fenici 2. Rome, Consiglio nazionale delle richerche.

Addyman, P. (1962) The archaeology of the Sbeitla area: interim report. *Brathay Exploration Group Annual Report*: 60–77.

Addyman, P., and Simpson, W. G. (1966) Archaeology of the Sbeitla area: second interim report. *Brathay Exploration Group Annual Report*: 153–70.

Alcock, S. E. (1989) Roman imperialism in the Greek landscape. *Journal of Roman Archaeology* 2: 5–34.

Alcock, S. E. (1993) *Graecia capta: The Landscapes of Roman Greece*. Cambridge, Cambridge University Press.

Alcock, S. E., Cherry, J. F., and Davis, J. L. (1994) Intensive survey, agricultural practice, and the Classical landscape of Greece. In I. Morris (ed.) *Classical Greece: Ancient Histories and Modern Archaeologies*: 137–70. Cambridge, Cambridge University Press.

Annabi, M. K. (1988) Prospection archéologique dans la région de Sousse. *Bulletin de l'Institut National de l'art et l'archéologie* Comptes Rendus (Fascicule 2): 17–31.

Annabi, M. K. (1991a) Archéologie de paysage à oued Cherita. *Bulletin de l'Institut National de l'art et l'archéologie* Comptes Rendus (Fascicule 4): 7–28.

Annabi, M. K. (1991b) Prospections archéologiques en Tunisie: le site de Henchir Bir Ennadhour. In *Colloque sur l'Histoire et l'Archéologie de l'Afrique du Nord* 4: 549–54. Paris, Editions du CTHS.

Babelon, E., Cagnat, R. and Reinach, S. (1892–1913) *Atlas archéologique de la Tunisie*. Paris, E. Leroux.

Barbery, J., and Delhoume, J.-P. (1982) La voie romaine de piedmont Sufetula-Masclianae (Djebel Mrhila, Tunisie centrale). *Antiquités Africaines* 18: 27–43.

Barreca, F., and Fantar, M. (1983) *Prospezione archeologica al Capo Bon* II. Collezione di studi fenici 14. Rome, Consiglio nazionale delle richerche.

Ben Baaziz, S. (1986) L'occupation humaine dans la plaine de Rohia et le Sraa Ouertane dans l'antiquité. In *Colloque sur l'Histoire et l'Archéologie de l'Afrique du Nord* 3: 289–300. Paris, CTHS.

Ben Baaziz, S. (1988) Les sites antiques de la région de Sidi El Hani. *Bulletin de l'Institut National de l'art et l'archéologie* Comptes Rendus (Fascicule 2): 7–15.

Ben Baaziz, S. (1991a) Prospection archéologique de la région d'el Meknassi (premier bilan). *Bulletin de l'Institut National de l'art et l'archéologie* Comptes Rendus (Fascicule 4): 29–39.

Ben Baaziz, S. (1991b) Les sites archéologiques de la région de Gafsa. In *Colloque sur l'Histoire et l'Archéologie de l'Afrique du Nord* 4: 535–48. Paris, Editions du CTHS.

Ben Baaziz, S. (1992) La carte nationale des sites archéologiques et des monuments historiques. *Bulletin de l'Institut National du Patrimoine*: 1–15.

Ben Lazreg, N., Bonifay, M., Drine, A. and Trousset, P. (1995) Production et commercialisation des *salsamenta* de l'Afrique ancienne. In P. Trousset (ed.) *Productions et exportations Africaines: actualités archéologiques en Afrique du nord antique et medievale*. Colloque sur l'Histoire et l'Archéologie de l'Afrique du Nord 6.1: 103–42. Paris, Cahiers des Travaux Historiques et Scientifiques.

Bonifay, M., Oueslati, A., Paskoff, R., Slim, H. and Trousset, P. (1992) Programme tuniso-français d'étude du littoral de la Tunisie: bilan des travaux 1987–1990. *Bulletin de l'Institut National du Patrimoine* Comptes Rendus (Fascicule 5, Janvier-Juin 1990): 95–116.

Cagnat, R., Babelon, E., Reinach, S. and Merlin, A. (1914–32) *Atlas archéologique de la Tunisie*. 2nd edition. Paris, E. Leroux.

Chelbi, F., Paskoff, R. and Trousset, P. (1995) La baie d'Utique et son évolution depuis l'antiquité: une réévaluation géoarchéo-logique. *Antiquités Africaines* 31: 7–51.

Cherry, J. F. (1983) Frogs round the pond: perspectives on current archaeological survey projects in the Mediterranean region. In D. Keller and D. Rupp (eds.) *Archaeological Survey in the Mediterranean Area*: 375–416. BAR International Series 155. Oxford, British Archaeological Reports.

Cherry, J. F., Davis, J. L. and Mantzourani, E. (1991) *Landscape Archaeology as Long-Term History: Northern Keos in the Cycladic Islands*. Monumenta Archaeologica 16. Los Angeles, UCLA Institute of Archaeology.

De Vos, M. (2000) *Rus Africum. Terra, acqua, olio nell'Africa settetrionale. Scavo e ricognizione nei dintorni di Dougga (alto tell tunisino)*. Trento, Università degli studi di Trento.

Dietz, S., Ladjimi Sebai, L. and Ben Hassen, H. (eds.) (1995) *Africa Proconsularis: Regional Studies in the Segermes Valley of Northern Tunesia*. 2 vols. Aarhus, Aarhus University Press.

Fentress, E. (2000) The Jerba Survey: settlement in the Punic and Roman periods. *L'Africa romana* 13(1): 73–85.

Fentress, E. (2001) Villas, wine and kilns: the landscape of Jerba in the late Hellenistic period. *Journal of Roman Archaeology* 14: 249–68.

Foley, R. A. (1981) Off-site archaeology: an alternative approach for the short-sited. In I. Hodder, G. Isaac and N. Hammond (eds.) *Pattern of the Past: Essays in Honour of David Clarke*: 157–183. Cambridge, Cambridge University Press.

Gallant, T. W. (1986) Background noise and site definition: a contribution to survey methodology. *Journal of Field Archaeology* 13: 403–418.

Ghalia, T. (1992) Approches du paysage antique de la vallée de l'Oued Sejnane (Feuille n. 5 au 1/50,000). *Bulletin de l'Institut National du Patrimoine* Comptes Rendus (Fascicule 5. Janvier-Juin 1990): 33–57.

Greene, J. A. (1983a) 'Atlas archéologique de la Tunisie' and recent archaeological reconnaissance near Carthage. In D. Keller and D. Rupp (eds.) *Archaeological Survey in the Mediterranean Area*: 133–36. BAR International Series 155. Oxford, British Archaeological Reports.

Greene, J. A. (1983b) Carthage survey. In D. R. Keller and D. W. Rupp (eds.) *Archaeological Survey in the Mediterranean Area*: 197–99. BAR International Series 155. Oxford, British Archaeological Reports.

Greene, J. A. (1984) Canadian Carthage survey 1983: preliminary report. *Échos du monde classique/Classical views*: 214–18.

Greene, J. A. (1986) The Carthaginian Countryside: Archaeological Reconnaisance in the Hinterland of Ancient Carthage. Ph.D. Thesis, University of Chicago.

Greene, J. A. (1992) Une reconnaissance archéologique dans l'arrière-pays de la Carthage antique. In A. Ennabli (ed.) *Pour sauver Carthage: Exploration et conservation de la cité punique, romaine, et byzantine*: 195–97. Paris, UNESCO.

Greene, J. A. (forthcoming) *Ager and 'Arosot: Rural Settlement and Agrarian History in the Carthaginian Countryside.*

Greene, J. A. and Kehoe, D. P. (1995) Mago the Carthaginian on agriculture: archaeology and the ancient sources. In M. Fantar (ed.) *Actes du IIIᵉ congrès international des études phéniciennes et puniques* II: 110–17. Tunis, Institut National du Patrimoine.

Gsell, S. (1911) *Atlas archéologique de l'Algérie.* Algiers, A. Jourdan.

Hitchner, R. B. (1988) The Kasserine Archaeological Survey, 1982–86. *Antiquités Africaines* 24: 7–41.

Hitchner, R. B. (1989) The organisation of rural settlement in the Cillium-Thelepte region (Kasserine, Central Tunisia). *L'Africa romana* 6: 387–402.

Hitchner, R. B. (1990) The Kasserine Archaeological Survey, 1987. *Antiquités Africaines* 26: 231–60.

Hitchner, R. B. (1995) Irrigation, terraces, dams and aqueducts in the region of Cillium (mod. Kasserine). In P. Trousset (ed.) *Productions et Exportations Africaines: Actualités Archéologiques en Afrique du nord antique et medievale.* Colloque sur l'Histoire et l'Archéologie de l'Afrique du Nord 6.1: 143–58. Paris, Cahiers des Travaux Historiques et Scientifiques.

McDonald, W. A. and Rapp, G. R. (eds.) (1972) *The Minnesota Messenia Expedition: Reconstructing a Bronze Age Regional Environment.* Minneapolis, University of Minnesota Press.

Mattingly, D. J. (1988) Oil for export? A comparative study of olive-oil production in Libya, Spain, and Tunisia. *Journal of Roman Archaeology* 1: 33–56.

Mattingly, D. J. (1992) The field survey: strategy, methodology, and preliminary results. In N. Ben Lazreg and D. J. Mattingly (eds.) *Leptiminus (Lamta): A Roman Port Town in Tunisia. Report no. 1.*: 89–120. *Journal of Roman Archaeology* Supplementary Series 4. Ann Arbor, Journal of Roman Archaeology.

Mattingly, D. J. (1994) Regional variation in Roman oleoculture: some problems of comparability. In J. Carlsen, P. Ørsted and J.-E. Skydsgaard (eds.) *Landuse in the Roman Empire.* Analecta Romana Supplement 22: 91–106. Rome, Danish Institute at Rome.

Mattingly, D. J. (1997) Imperialism and territory: Africa, a landscape of opportunity? In D. J. Mattingly (ed.) *Dialogues in Roman Imperialism: Power, Discourse, and Discrepant Experience in the Roman Empire*: 117–39. *Journal of Roman Archaeology* Supplementary Series 23. Portsmouth, RI, Journal of Roman Archaeology.

Mattingly, D. J., Stone, D. L., Stirling, L. M. and Ben Lazreg, N. (2000) Leptiminus (Tunisia): a producer city? In D. Mattingly and J. Salmon (eds.) *Economies beyond Agriculture in the Ancient World*: 66–89. London, Routledge.

Maurin, L. and Peyras, J. (1991) Romanisation et traditions africaines dans la région de Bir Mcherga. *Cahiers de Tunisie* 154–55: 105–148.

Neuru, L. (1987) Red-slipped wares of southwestern central Tunisia: new evidence. *Rei Cretariae Romanae Fautorum Acta* 25–26: 175–88.

Ørsted, P., Carlsen, J., Sebai, L. L. and Ben Hassen, H. (eds.) (2000) *Africa Proconsularis: Regional Studies in the Segermes Valley of Northern Tunisia. Vol. III: Historical Conclusions.* Aarhus, Aarhus University Press.

Paskoff, R., Slim, H. and Trousset, P. (1991) Le littoral de la Tunisie dans l'antiquité: cinq ans de recherches géoarchéologiques. *Comptes Rendus à l'Academie des Inscriptions et Belles-Lettres*: 515–46.

Paskoff, R. and Trousset, P. (1991) Les sites submergés de Tunisie. In M. Lazarov (ed.) *Thracia Pontica IV, actes du symposium international de Sozopol (octobre 1988)*: 367–84. Sofia. Centre d'archéologie subaquatique.

Peacock, D. P. S., Bejaoui, F. and Ben Lazreg, N. (1989) Roman amphora production in the Sahel region of Tunisia. In *Amphores romaines et histoire économique: dix ans de recherches*: 179–222. Collection de l'Ecole Française de Rome 114. Rome, Ecole Française de Rome.

Peacock, D. P. S., Bejaoui, F. and Ben Lazreg, N. (1990) Roman pottery production in central Tunisia. *Journal of Roman Archaeology* 3: 59–84.

Peacock, D. P. S. and Tomber, R. (1989) Roman amphora kilns in the Sahel of Tunisia: petrographic investigation of kiln material from a sedimentary environment. In I. Freestone and A. Middleton (eds.) *Recent Developments in Ceramic Petrology.* British Museum Occasional Paper 81: 289–304. London, British Museum.

Renfrew, C. and Wagstaff, M. (eds.) (1982) *An Island Polity: The Archaeology of Exploitation in Melos.* Cambridge, Cambridge University Press.

Said, E. W. (1993) *Culture and Imperialism.* New York, Knopf.

Stone, D. L., Stirling, L. M., and Ben Lazreg, N. (1998) Suburban land-use and ceramic production around Leptiminus (Tunisia): interim report. *Journal of Roman Archaeology* 11: 304–317.

Trousset, P. (1974) *Recherches sur le limes Tripolitanus: du chott el-Djerid à la frontière tuniso-libyenne.* Paris, Centre National de la Recherche Scientifique.

Trousset, P. (1992) La vie littorale et les ports dans la Petite Syrte à l'époque romaine. In *Afrique du Nord antique et médiévale: spectacles, vie portuaire, religions.* Colloque sur l'Histoire et l'Archéologie de l'Afrique du Nord 5: 317–32. Paris. Editions du CTHS

Wilkinson, T. (1982) The definition of ancient manuring zones by means of extensive sherd sampling techniques. *Journal of Field Archaeology* 9: 323–33.

Wilkinson, T. (1989) Extensive sherd scatters and land-use intensity: some recent results. *Journal of Field Archaeology* 16: 31–46.

ISSUES AND IMPLICATIONS

11. Accounting for ARS:
Fineware and Sites in Sicily and Africa

Elizabeth Fentress, Sergio Fontana, R. Bruce Hitchner and Philip Perkins

In a brief paper written 15 years ago two of us attempted to pull together the evidence for the importation of African Red Slip (ARS) deriving from field surveys in the Western Mediterranean (Fentress and Perkins 1988; see also Cambi and Fentress 1989). On that occasion we published composite diagrams of the import curves from a series of projects, comparing them to the curve derived from the average of all the finds. The principle, then as now, was that deviations from the average curve would reflect specific aspects of the history of the area surveyed, while the full curve would reflect the rhythms of production and distribution in the centers of production.

In the past 15 years much new material has come out, as well as studies of various production centers (Peacock *et al.* 1990; Mackensen 1993; 1998a; 1998b; Mackensen and Schneider 2002 [which appeared too late to be taken into account here]; Tortorella 1983; 1995; 1998; Lund 1995; Hayes 1998). Our database now includes 18,840 sherds from 16 projects, classified according to form, while the 1988 article was based on 7,960 sherds from seven projects. It is notable that at the time that work was done none of the Tunisian field surveys had received full publication, so that our only 'African' project was Cherchell (Leveau 1984), more distant from the centers of production than Rome itself. This new study seeks to fill that gap, using the rich material from the African projects of the last 20 years: the Unesco Libyan Valleys Survey (ULVS), (Barker *et al.* 1996*)*, the Kasserine Survey (Hitchner 1988; 1990), the Jerba Survey (Fentress 2001; Drine *et al.* forthcoming), the Segermes Survey (Dietz *et al.* 1995), and the Leptiminus survey (Ben Lazreg and Mattingly 1992, Stone *et al.* 1998). To these we have added three Sicilian projects, the Morgantina Survey, the Contrada Mirabile (Marsala) Survey (Fentress *et al.* 1986) and the Monreale Survey. Although two of these projects have received full publication, the others are known only from preliminary reports, and this article is thus based on unpublished information shared, with extraordinary generosity, by the projects themselves. Our particular gratitude is due to John Dore for the ULVS databases, to John Dore and Karen Carr for the Leptiminus databases, to Lucinda Neuru for

the Kasserine databases and to Stephen Thompson and Sebastian Heath for the Morgantina databases. Our overall database may be consulted by anyone interested in adding to it, in comparing their curves to our averages, or in analyzing the material in other ways.

We have three main objectives in writing this essay. First, we want to compare the results of the pottery analysis with those of 15 years ago, and examine the various issues that have since arisen. How valid is the curve as a whole, and what factors may be affecting its shape? Second, we want to deal with an aspect of the distribution of ARS which could not have been examined then – the distribution of the products of the various production centers in Africa Proconsularis, and the role of regional production centers in the supply of African sites. These include the well-known Tripolitanian Red Slip Wares (TRS), and the 'E' wares of Byzacena. Their distribution in the wider Mediterranean market is fairly limited, but in Africa itself they played an important role in import substitution, a common indicator of economic growth (Reynolds 1986: 56–57; Hitchner 1993: 504). Finally, the settlement histories in the individual survey areas will be examined in the light both of their pottery imports and of their total numbers of sites throughout the Roman period.

THE PRODUCTION CURVE OF ARS OVER THE PERIOD CONSIDERED

The methodology used in this study is essentially the same as that used in 1987. This was decided both because we wanted to be able to compare the data, and because we find the more sophisticated approach of Millett (1991) places rather too much confidence in the bell curve. The principal aim of this project is to study the chronological and spatial distribution of fine wares, particularly African Red Slip ware, as an economic phenomenon, and to relate that to settlement histories. Each African Red Slip ware form has its own particular date range; some had a very short date range, others remained current for many years. This means that a count of the frequencies of individual forms does not have a direct relation to chronological time. Therefore a method was devised to map the date range of forms onto calendar years. It was assumed that each form had an equal probability that it was made in each year of its date range. Thus a pot with a date range of 100 years was considered to have a probability of 1/100 that it was made in each year of its date range. This probability was then multiplied by the total number of sherds of that form so that, for example, 200 sherds would result in a probable distribution of two pots per year. This method was repeated for each form in turn to produce cumulative totals of African Red Slip ware distribution through time for each of the assemblages. The cumulative totals for each assemblage were combined to produce a mean representing a global total of African Red Slip ware production: this is the 'mean' that appears on all figures. The totals were calculated at five-year intervals, whereas in 1987 a 10-year interval was used. This is a result of the increase in computing capacity rather than any perceived shift in the precision of African Red Slip ware dating. The sherd counts from the various data sets were used to generate a relative frequency of African Red Slip ware production over some 700 years: we should note that this data set includes all the projects treated in 1988, those treated here, and some further collections of pottery, from Sardinia (Dyson and Rowland 1992) and the upper Adriatic (Pröttel 1996).

The causes of variability in the histograms

There are three causes for the variability in the results obtained. The first, obviously, is time, the second the sherd counts, and the third the date ranges assigned to each form. Each individual data set suffers from a variety of post-depositional processes that will have altered the composition of the assemblage in the transition from a new piece of tableware to a published (or soon to be published) sherd. It is not possible to compensate system-atically and reliably for any biases that this may have caused in the assemblages. We can only hope that the large sample size, the geographical spread and the variety of the types of collection combine to minimize bias caused by any individual sample.

The date range assigned to each form clearly has an impact on the results of the method. This can be explored by using simulated data sets. The first approach is to generate a random data set and process it (Fig.11.1). In the parts of the histogram where the mean and the random curves are similar to one another, the implication is that the curve derives from the structure of the date range applied to each form rather than the frequency of individual forms. This phenomenon may be further illustrated by considering a second simulated data set where an even distribution of forms is generated, *i.e.* one sherd of each form (Figure 11.2). The resultant curve is similar to the random data set: this is not surprising, since the even distribution is effectively a summation of an infinite number of random data sets and because each sherd has

Random % ARS / year

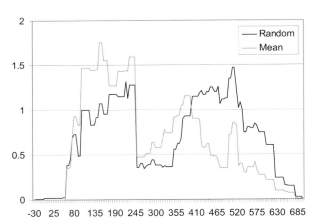

Figure 11.1 A graph of a data set created from random frequencies for each ARS form compared to the mean derived from the dates of each form used in this paper (the 2002 mean).

Even % ARS / year

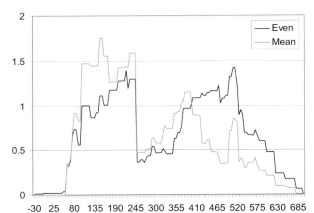

Figure 11.2 A graph of a data set created from even frequencies for each ARS form compared to the mean derived from the dates of each form used in this paper (the 2002 mean).

an equal probability of being represented in the data set, *i.e.* a probability of one.

The simulated data suggest that the following features of the mean curve are artifacts of the precise dating ranges used:

1) The rapid rise up to AD 100: 63 new forms first appear between AD 50 and 100.
2) The sharp drop between AD 245 and 250; this is the result of 45 forms having a latest date of 250, including some of the most common forms (*e.g.* Hayes 8b, 9b, 27, 31).
3) The AD 500–520 peak. 25 forms are first dated to 500–510 and 22 have a latest date of 500. Clearly, if

the 22 with a latest date of 500 had in fact ceased to be produced in 490 then the change would be somewhat less abrupt.

4) The slow rise between AD 245 and 300.

These traits shared by the two simulated data sets and the mean combine to form traits which we might expect to observe in the individual African Red Slip ware assemblages, and so where they diverge from this pattern there is a clear indication of a local archaeological phenomenon to be interpreted. Furthermore, these observations reinforce the notion that the curves should not be taken at face value, and that – for example – the precipitous drop in AD 245–250 is not a clear illustration of the sudden onslaught of the '3rd century crisis', although the generally low level of production of the second half of the 3rd century cannot be denied: indeed, it is more marked now than it was in 1988. However, as the principal factor affecting the simulated data sets is the number of forms produced in any given period, the changes in them cannot simply be written off as a random artifact of the data, as we might expect that the production of multiple forms in a given period, and the innovation implied by the production of new forms, would be at least an indicator of economic vitality.

Testing the 1988 data

Although the methodology is little changed since 1987, the data set has expanded considerably, so a first question is to what extent the new data have altered our calculation of total relative African Red Slip ware production. A comparison of the mean of ARS supply calculated in 1987 and in 2002 indicates that there is little significant change (Figure 11.3). Much of that change is a result of using a revised and up-to-date set of dates for the various African Red Slip ware forms. This can be seen in comparing the two curves for the 1987 data set, presented using both the date ranges employed in 1987 and 2002. The largest differences between the means calculated 15 years after the first attempt are that the peak of A wares and cooking wares between AD 100 and 195 has reduced by about 0.5%, the trough between 250 and 350 has deepened and the small peak between 500 and 520 has increased by almost 0.5%. The mean in the 4th century AD and in the 6th and 7th centuries has also increased. The 500–520 peak derives principally from the Mirabile, Segermes, Upper Adriatic and Jerba data sets, where forms 87b and 88 are common and have a narrow date range: in Segermes there are 260 sherds of form 88, while in the Upper Adriatic there are 90 sherds of Hayes 87b. The peak is also present in the randomised and even-distribution simulated data sets, indicating that it is partially derived from the overlapping date ranges of the common forms 99 and 103 coinciding at the beginning of the 6th century with the 87b and 88 dates. The heavy dependence of this peak in 500–520 on the dating assigned to the individual forms in this period makes it slightly difficult to relate it,

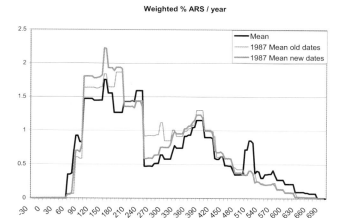

Weighted % ARS / year

Figure 11.3 A comparison of the mean of ARS supply calculated in 1987, the mean of ARS supply calculated in 1987 recalibrated with the current datings for each form, and the mean calculated with the 2002 data set and current datings.

as Zanini has done, to the revival of the Byzantine grain shipments to Italy (Zanini 1996). However, the new figures make the increase even clearer, which does seem to suggest some change in the pattern of trade and production.

It was argued in our 1988 paper that the production and distribution curves had an economic basis. A challenge to this view has been made by Hawthorne, who suggests that the cause of variability is to be found in the changing vessel capacity over time (Hawthorne 1996; 2000). He attempts to explain the overall fall in the number of African Red Slip ware sherds in the 3rd century by observing that, as sherd counts fall, the capacity of the individual vessels increases. Thus overall the capacity does not fall in the 3rd century, even if there are fewer sherds. Hawthorne explains the reduction in the quantity of African Red Slip ware in the 3rd century as a change in eating habits and questions the economic explanations of African Red Slip ware variability that we prefer (Hawthorne 2000: 23). Hawthorne further argues that the shift to communal platters should be seen as related to the growth of Christianity in the Western Mediterranean: this is possible, but there is no way at present to confirm this on archaeological grounds.

There are a number of additional problems with this argument. First, although it is true that the platters of the 3rd and 4th centuries have much larger capacities, it is equally true that they have much larger diameters, which means that they will produce, on average, more sherds. Thus a cup of the common form Hayes 8 has a circumference of around 50 cm, while a platter of form 50 has a circumference of around 106 cm. It would thus take two bowls of Hayes 8 to produce as many rim sherds as a Hayes 50, assuming that they were broken into equal-sized sherds. Further, while it is undeniable that there is a change in African Red Slip ware to large forms, presumably indicating that table ware vessels may no longer constitute a personal service in the style of Augustan-period *terra sigillata italica* 'services' (Hayes 1997: 44–45), a change in the capacities of the vessels is not the only alteration which occurred in African Red Slip ware in this period. A major change, with major economic consequences – and almost certainly causes – was the decline in the manufacture of African Red Slip ware A wares in northern Tunisia and the growth of African Red Slip ware C wares in central Tunisia. Hawthorne assumes that he is studying a single production of African Red Slip ware, whereas the reality is that the change in vessels is paralleled by a change in fabrics and production centers. It is only the modern archaeologist who can view African Red Slip ware production as a single ceramic 'production' lasting for over 600 years: this characterisation of ceramic as a single category of artifact is unlikely to have been shared by the ancients. We would reiterate the point made in 1988 (Fentress and Perkins 1988: 208) that the mean histogram with its 3rd-century trough is really a combination of the curves for the larger African Red Slip ware A and D productions which form the peaks to either side of the lesser C production.

A final argument for an economic interpretation of the data is that all of the data sets from around the western and central Mediterranean used in this study are a direct result of trade. The vessels, whatever their size, were items of trade of one sort or another. That is how they got from Africa to the remainder of the Mediterranean basin. Certainly, abstract economic explanations and interpretations can have no monopoly on understanding ceramic assemblages; questions of culture and identity are also relevant, but economic factors mediate the other roles that ceramics performed in the ancient world (Perkins 2000: 200–205). But as we shall see, the growth of C wares mirrors the corresponding growth in settlement in the area in which they were produced. That third-century Byzacena could not only create import substitution, but also compete with Northern Tunisia on the international market, is a clear illustration of the relationship between pottery production and economic development.

The production curve and African history

Where the overall mean diverges from the even and random patterns there is clearly some feature of the overall African Red Slip ware production to be interpreted. The peak and fall between AD 100 and 175 is an example of this and clearly relates to the commonness of the main African Red Slip ware A ware series of bowls Hayes 3, 6, 8 and 9, all of which disappear around 175. The peak falls between AD 150 and 155. This could be related to one of the few firm historical dates associated with exports from Africa: the establishment of the imperial *annona* fleet, the *classis Africana,* in AD 150 by Commodus (*Scriptores Historiae Augustae, Commodus* 17.7; Rickman 1981: 129–30). We might expect that this new infrastructure would have enhanced the possibility of marketing fine-

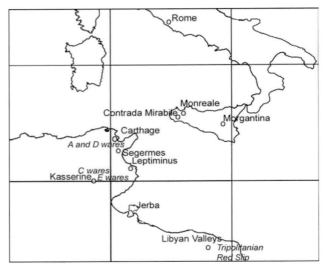

Figure 11.4 The area studied.

wares, although it may be that the *navicularii* were not permitted to carry additional non-*annona* cargos, and so that, rather than gaining a distributional advantage in subsidized transport, African Red Slip ware lost one. Another possible cause for the decline after AD 160 might be the Antonine plague between roughly AD 165 and 182, which Galen refers to as exceptionally long-lasting, and which may have affected the production and distribution of the pottery (Duncan-Jones 1996). The various economic indicators (building inscriptions, army diplomas, etc.) charted by Duncan-Jones for the period show very similar low points in this period to our own material.

A second period where the mean diverges from the even distribution is throughout the 5th century where the percentage of African Red Slip ware continually falls from a peak between AD 380 and 395, whereas the even distribution continues to rise. In 1987 we suggested that the peak might be related to the ending of the revolt of Firmus or increased circulation of gold in the province (Fentress and Perkins 1988: 209); however, neither of these explains why the production should fall. Paradoxically, the major catastrophe of the 5th century – the Vandal capture of Carthage in AD 439 – is marked only by a slight halt in the fall in African Red Slip ware production. Whatever the impact of the Vandals on Africa they cannot be held to account for causing any particular disruption in African Red Slip ware production and supply.

Finally, the AD 500–525 peak should be associated with the renewal of trade with the eastern Mediterranean, signaled in Meninx by a massive importation of eastern amphorae. In this context, it is worth remembering Procopius' statement that it was merchants who convinced Justinian to undertake the reconquest of Africa. Hilderic (AD 523–30) had developed closer ties with the Byzantine state and had ended persecutions of Catholic Africa. He had also raised expectations among merchants of closer relations between Africa and the East. It was his deposition by Gelimer that led to the Byzantine invasion (Procopius,

Segermes % ARS / year

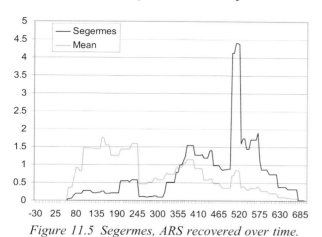

Figure 11.5 Segermes, ARS recovered over time.

Segermes (66 sites)

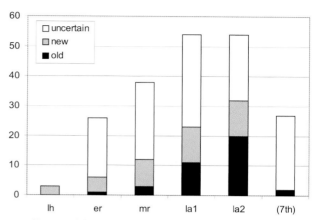

Figure 11.6 Segermes, site numbers over time.

Bellum Vandalicum 2.5.8; also 1.10.20). Thus the upswing in trade would have started in the period before the 530s (*cf.* Zanini 1996).

The African and Sicilian surveys

It is now necessary to introduce the surveys that form the basis for this paper (Figure 11.4). The first five give us samples from Africa Proconsularis, later the provinces of Zeugitania, Byzacena and Tripolitania, while the last three derive from Sicily. We regret not being able to include the Dougga survey (De Vos 2001) for lack of a detailed table of the ceramic finds.

The inclusion of the Sicilian surveys allows us to compare the two regions, both of which were major producers of crops for the Roman market. For each survey we will give the ARS curve and a histogram showing site numbers divided into old, new and uncertain. The information on the periods comes in most cases from the site databases, although for Segermes we have used the more refined published breakdown (Dietz *et al.* 1995) with 'possible' referring to periods covered only by sherds which can be dated to two periods: *e.g.* form 50, which runs between AD 230 and 400. The periods given are not uniform, because of being dependent to a certain extent on the chronology of the dominant class of sherds, particularly (for Early Roman) Italian sigillata. They are: Late Hellenistic (200–30 BC), Early Roman (30 BC–AD 100), Middle Roman (AD 100–300), Late Antique I (AD 300–500) and Late Antique II (AD 500–700). The last figure gives certain 7th century sites, in practice those with forms 99c, 104c, 109, etc.

ZEUGITANIA

Segermes (Figures 11.5 and 11.6)

The Africa Proconsularis survey (1987–89), directed by

Soren Dietz, Peter Ørsted, Laila Ladjimi Sebaï and Habib Ben Hassen for the University of Copenhagen and the Institut National du Patrimoine, involved both survey and excavation at the Roman town of Segermes and its territory (Dietz *et al.* 1995). Within an area of 600 sq. km, intensive fieldwalking was carried out over a total 26 sq. km split into 11 sample sectors. All pottery observed by the survey was counted (114,000 sherds) and its density across the landscape mapped, though only diagnostics were collected (*c.*10,000 sherds). A total of 193 sites was recorded, of which 66 could be dated in the Roman period. 1,939 sherds of ARS were recovered.

BYZACENA

Kasserine Survey (Figures 11.7 and 11.8)

The Kasserine Survey (1982–89), directed by R. Bruce Hitchner, was designed to investigate changes in rural settlement and economy in the Tunisian high steppe in the Roman period (Hitchner 1988; 1990). The survey focused initially on the investigation of previously recorded rural settlements around ancient Cillium. This was followed by more intensive survey over an area of some 175 sq. km subdivided into five sectors, in which some 200 sites were recorded, planned, and sherded: 64 of these were dated settlements. Approximately 25,000 sherds were collected and processed, of which 502 were ARS.

Leptiminus (Figures 11.9 and 11.10)

This survey (1990–99) concentrated on the harbour town of Leptiminus and its immediate surroundings, and included the excavation of several sites within the city (Ben Lazreg and Mattingly 1992; Stone *et al.* 1998). One of these was a pottery kiln producing Hayes cooking ware forms 181 and 182: this is one of the reasons for the

Kasserine % ARS / year

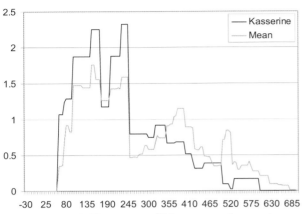

Figure 11.7 Kasserine, ARS recovered over time.

Kasserine (64 sites)

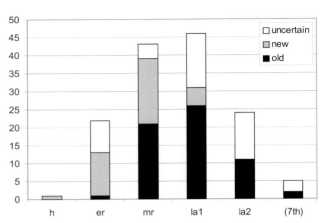

Figure 11.8 Kasserine, site numbers over time.

Leptiminus (R) % ARS / year

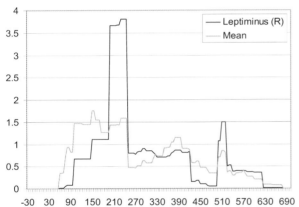

Figure 11.9 Leptiminus rural survey, ARS recovered over time.

Leptiminus (U) % ARS / year

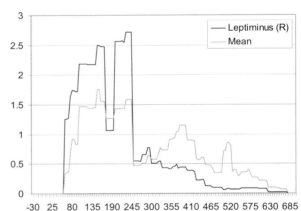

Figure 11.10 Leptiminus urban survey, ARS recovered over time.

spectacularly high curve in the period AD 100–250. The curves given here represent the rural survey, conducted outside the walls by David Stone, and the urban survey, including the excavation, conducted by David Mattingly, Najib Ben Lazreg and Leah Stirling. 464 sherds of ARS were recovered from the rural survey, 2,142 sherds from the urban survey.

TRIPOLITANIA

Jerba (Figures 11.11 and 11.12)

The Jerba Survey was a joint undertaking of the Tunisian Institut National du Patrimoine, the American Academy of Rome, and the University of Pennsylvania, directed by Ali Drine, Elizabeth Fentress and Renata Holod (Fentress 2001; Drine *et al.* forthcoming). Its purpose was to record the settlement history of the Tunisian island of Jerba in all

periods through a combination of extensive and intensive survey, geophysical survey, and excavation. 490 sites were found, of which 203 were dated settlements of the Roman period. 681 ARS sherds were recovered from the survey.

UNESCO Libyan Valleys Survey (ULVS) (Figures 11.13 and 11.14)

The UNESCO Libyan Valleys Survey (1979–89), directed for the Libyan Society by Graham Barker, Barri Jones, David Mattingly and David Gilbertson, investigated the long-term relationship between settlement, land-use and environment in the desert-margins with particular emphasis on the period of classical antiquity (Barker *et al.* 1996). Work was concentrated in the wadi systems of the Sofeggin and Zem-Zem basins *c.*100 km south of Tripoli. More than 2,500 sites were recorded, of which 425 could be dated to the Roman period, and over 55,000 sherds collected and processed, of which 1,154 were ARS.

Jerba % ARS / year

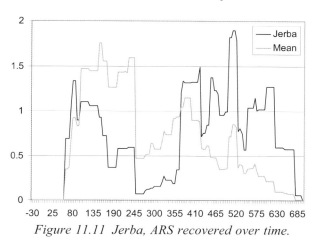

Figure 11.11 Jerba, ARS recovered over time.

Jerba (203 sites)

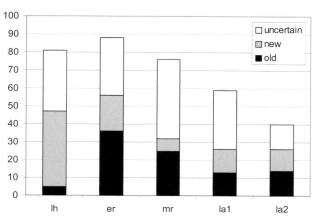

Figure 11.12 Jerba, site numbers over time.

Libyan Valleys % ARS / year

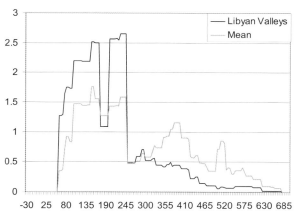

Figure 11.13 UNESCO Libyan Valleys survey, ARS recovered over time.

ULVS (425 sites)

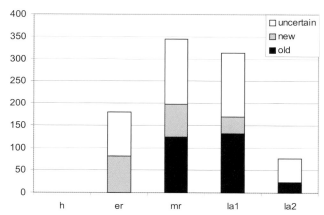

Figure 11.14 UNESCO Libyan Valleys survey, site numbers over time.

SICILY

The Monreale Survey (Figures 11.15 and 11.16)

Directed by Jeremy Johns with Philip Perkins between 1982–1987, the Monreale Survey intensively investigated 40 sq. km between San Giuseppe Iato and Corleone, to the south of Palermo, and neighbouring areas less intensively. Although the primary focus of the survey was the land owned by the medieval Abbey of Monreale, all periods of occupation were covered. 1,172 sherds of ARS were found.

Contrada Mirabile (Figs.11.17 and 11.18)

A small survey was carried out in 1988 by Elizabeth Fentress and Derek Kennet in conjunction with the excavation of a substantial villa of the early 2nd century BC in the hinterland of Marsala, ancient Lilybaeum (Fentress *et al.* 1986). 24 sites were recorded in an area of 12 sq. km,

with other sites recorded during earlier intensive survey. 766 ARS sherds were recovered.

Morgantina (Figures 11.19 and 11.20)

The survey of the territory of Morgantina was directed by Stephen Thompson between 1993 and 1996. It aimed at recovering the settlement history of the territory, with particular attention to the effects of the Romanization of this part of central Sicily. 59 sites were recovered datable to the period dealt with here, and 659 ARS sherds found.

THE SITES AND THEIR SHERDS: ARS CONSUMPTION AND IMPORT REPLACEMENT

The first point that emerges from the comparison of the site numbers and the sherds recovered is their utter lack of correlation. Of course, for the late Hellenistic and Early

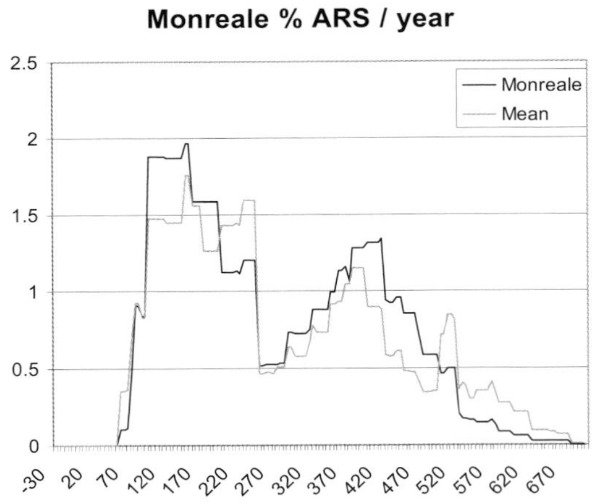

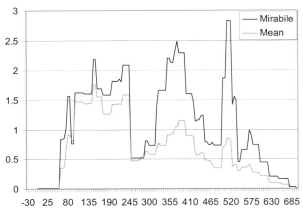

Figure 11.15 Monreale survey, site numbers over time.

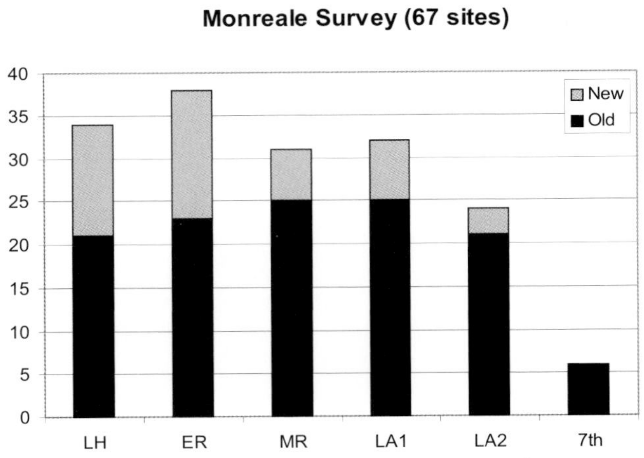

Figure 11.16 Monreale survey, ARS recovered over time.

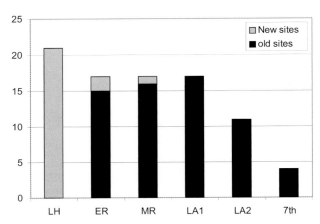

Figure 11.17 Contrada Mirabile survey, ARS recovered over time.

Figure 11.18 Contrada Mirabile survey, site numbers over time.

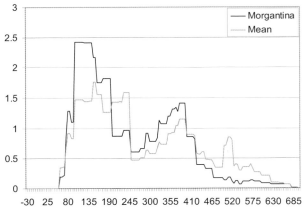

Figure 11.19 Morgantina Survey, ARS recovered over time.

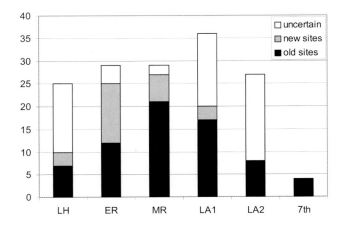

Figure 11.20 Morgantina Survey, site numbers over time.

Roman periods the dating comes from very different materials, black glaze and Italian and Gallic sigillata. However, even if we only consider the mid-Roman and Late Antique periods, the lack of fit is striking. The '3rd century crisis' so clear in the fall in pottery production in the second half of the 3rd century is never reflected in the occupation of sites, while the massive imbalance towards the 1st and 2nd centuries seen at ULVS and Jerba seems to be a far greater reflection of their imports at this time than it is of their real settlement history. The only point at which the occupation history of the sites and the imports of ARS agree is at the end of the sequence, when both sites and sherds disappear around the beginning of the 7th century. Even here the correlation is not evident, for Segermes' one surviving site has so much 7th-century pottery that its pottery curve clocks in at substantially above the mean.

It is, however, appropriate to change from this rather negative picture to the more interesting results to be obtained from a comparison of the assemblages within the sites. The first is the rather surprising conclusion that the African sites receive overall far less ARS than the Sicilian sites. If we remove the pottery from the city of Meninx, which constitutes a large element in the Jerban assemblage, it emerges that Kasserine, Jerba and the ULVS sites tend to have less than eight sherds per site (counting only identifiable sherds) (Figure 11.21). Segermes, close to the production centers at Carthage, stands out for its wealth of material. Far less easy to understand are the rich assemblages of the Sicilian sites. In general, however, we might observe that most of these sites, from the Early Roman period onwards, were very large villas, with a heavy consumption of finewares. Yet this is only a partial answer, as many of the African sites are equally large, but it is unusual to find as many as 30 ARS sherds on any of them. Further, none of the Sicilian surveys covered coastal areas, although Contrada Mirabile lay around 10 km from the coast. They thus cannot be seen to have any particular advantages *vis-à-vis* their access to the pottery. This explains the far higher level of uncertainty in dating the African sites, for there are many periods with only one or two sherds to date them. The relative dearth of ARS on African sites is a phenomenon requiring explanation, for it raises some interesting questions about the extent to which ARS was embedded in Africa. An argument might be made that ARS was primarily intended for export and that its appearance on African sites was really a by-product of the export production. Areas closer to export centers, such as Segermes, have more ARS, while those further away have less. However, more data would be necessary to confirm this: on a small survey in the Belezma mountains it was noted that local red slip could form up to 50% of the finds, while it was extremely common in central Numidia (Fentress *et al.* 1991).

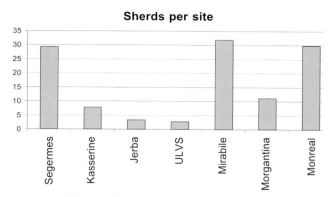

Figure 11.21 Sherds of ARS per site.

THE TUNISIAN PRODUCTIONS AND THEIR DISTRIBUTION BETWEEN THE 3RD AND THE 5TH CENTURIES

The picture of the various productions of ARS suggested by Hayes and the *Atlante* (1981) has in recent years been expanded by the identification of numerous production centers. In particular, the research of Michael Mackensen (on the sites of El Mahrine and Sidi Marzouk Tounsi) and that of David Peacock, Fathi Bejaoui and Najib Ben Lazreg (on the production centers of central Tunisia) have been fundamental for enlarging our knowledge of these sites, although the general outlines of Hayes' scheme (1972) remain the same.

The importance of this sort of quantitative approach to the assemblages containing ARS has often been underlined, because simple presence/absence data give no real sense of the distribution for objects this common. Only through an evaluation of the resemblances between the various contexts in the same periods can we form some idea of the different importance of the products distributed by long-distance, regional and local trade, whether this involves commerce by sea or by land (Fontana 1991a; 1991b).

Various difficulties were encountered in the very different assemblages, particularly in the identification of the smaller local productions. In order to overcome this, we have concentrated on those forms identified by Hayes, defining the ones that are most characteristic of the individual assemblages. Those which appear particularly significant are the wares characterized as A/D, for the period between AD 180–270, and the C wares of Byzacena (C1–3 for the period between AD 230 and 350, C3–4 between 300 and 450, and C5 between 430 and 530). Another distinctive production is that of the D1 forms, produced in the kilns of El Mahrine between AD 300 and 450. Finally, the E productions of southern Tunisia and the Tripolitanian Red Slip wares were considered for the period between AD 370 and 450.

Evaluating the percentage for each survey context, Figures 11.22–24 give the percentage of the most characteristic forms of each production in relation to the all

A/D

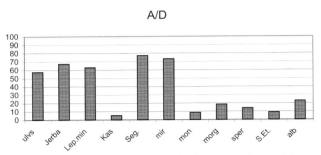

Figure 11.22 The percentage of A/D wares (forms 18, 28, 29, 32 and 33) in the third-century (in comparison to other sources, A2 and A/C).

C 1-3

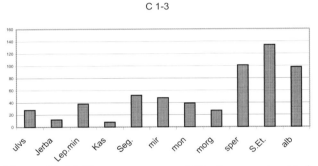

Figure 11.23 The percentage of C1–3 wares in third-fourth-century AD assemblages (forms Hayes 37, 39, 40, 41, 42, 44, 46, 47, 48, 49, 50, 57).

D1

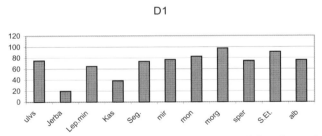

Figure 11.24 D1 wares as a percentage of fourth- and early fifth-century AD ARS productions.

the contemporary material found on the same project. To the African and Sicilian sites studied we have added, for comparison, three surveys from central Italy: the Albegna Valley Survey (Carandini *et al.* 2002), the South Etruria Survey, and the huge pottery deposits from the imperial villa at Sperlonga (Saguì 1980). The material from these three surveys was analyzed in 1988: however, that from South Etruria has undergone a major re-analysis by Sergio Fontana in the context of the Tiber Valley Project, directed by Helen Patterson for the British School at Rome.

Figure 11.22 shows that the relative frequency of A/D wares on the various sites. The production centers for these forms are unknown, although it is presumed that

they are to be found in Northern or Central Tunisia. In all of the African surveys (except Kasserine) these wares form over 50% of the whole assemblage, with a peak at Segermes of 78%, clearly dependent on its nearness to the production site. In contrast, on Italian and Sicilian sites the incidence of this ware sinks to between 10 and 25%, with a far higher proportion of the products of other Tunisian industries, the A2 and C1–2 fabrics. The exception is Contrada Mirabile, where – again – the ware reaches 70% of the assemblage, similar to the African sites. As we will see for other periods, Contrada Mirabile presents marked similarities to the context at Segermes. However, there is little doubt that this product tended to be distributed with a far greater frequency in Africa than in Italy.

Figure 11.23 shows that the C wares were produced in central Tunisia, particularly at the important site of Sidi Marzouk Tounsi. It is clear that for the first phase this ware was particularly common in central Italy, rising to as much as 30% of the identified forms of the same period. In Africa only Segermes shows any substantial percentages of the ware, while in Sicily the attestations vary between 13% at Monreale and 27% at Contrada Mirabile. It thus seems to have been produced especially for long-distance trade. Even on the Tunisian sites closest to its production centers, particularly Kasserine, it is an extremely rare find. To underline this fact, we note that the form Hayes 50, which is very common indeed on Italian sites, is an oddity in the African contexts. Later phases of this ware are everywhere less common. This decline is less obvious in the southern sites, where the pottery continued to enjoy some regional circulation, but clear at the Sicilian and Italian sites, where the productions of the Byzacena kilns were outsold by the D wares of Zeugitania.

Figure 11.24 shows the frequency of the D1 wares, whose principal production center is found at El Mahrine, in northern Tunisia, between the 4th and the first half of the 5th centuries. It is by far the most common fineware (Hayes forms 58, 59, 61a, 67, 76, 80a). On Italian and Sicilian sites the percentage of these wares in the assemblages ranges from 78% to as much as 97% at Morgantina and 91% in the South Etruria survey. At Segermes, close to the production centers, they were almost equally common, but this is true, as well, in the Libyan Valleys. Only at Jerba and at Kasserine do the percentages fall below 50%.

Overseas and local productions: distribution and the question of import substitution

The 4th century saw a boom in new regional productions, particularly in Africa. E wares and other local fabrics (Hayes forms 66, 68, 70, 92) were produced in the 4th and 5th centuries in central and southern Tunisia. They seem to have had an almost exclusively regional distribution, and are rare in northern Tunisia, Sicily and central Italy. Only at Jerba and, to a lesser degree, Kasserine do they

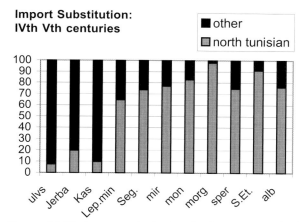

**Import Substitution:
IVth Vth centuries**

■ other
▨ north tunisian

Figure 11.25 Import substitution in the areas studied.

occupy a significant market share. In Tripolitania the production of TRS began around the same period; a production site for the ware has recently been identified at the Wadi Taraglat, inland from Misurata (Felici and Pentiricci 2002).

The phenomenon was not limited to Byzacena and Tripolitania, but extended in particular to Numidia. Local productions have been examined at Sétif, where there is an excellent case to be made for import substitution (Fentress 1991: 193): imported ARS constituted 18% of the ensemble in the 3rd century, and only 2% by the 5th. However, locally produced Red Slip had more than substituted for the imported wares, constituting 19% of the whole ensemble.

Figure 11.25 shows the relative proportions of the north Tunisian D1 wares and regional productions. These are represented in Libya by Tripolitanian Red Slip, and in Jerba and at Kasserine by local Red Slip and the E wares. It is clear that the regional productions are heavily represented on the sites of Tripolitania and Byzacena. They are rarer in northern Tunisia and at Leptiminus, and extremely rare in Sicily and central Italy. It seems to have been advantageous for the areas of Numidia, Tripolitania and Byzacena to replace the imported D wares with their own products, sold at local markets but, in general, rarely exported.

The very similar assemblages of the Sicilian and Italian sites, which comprise almost exclusively mainstream ARS productions, reflect the similarities of their curves to the western Mediterranean average (particularly in the case of Monreale). This suggests the important conclusion that their supply functioned by other mechanisms. Already in the 3rd and early 4th centuries the Monreale Survey and Morgantina strongly resembled central Italy, although the assemblage at Contrada Mirabile more closely resembled that of Segermes in the large quantities of A/D wares. This seems to imply a direct trading relationship with Carthage, along the old Punic route between Carthage and Lilybaeum, only 20 km away from Contrada Mirabile. We must imagine that traders there were supplying them-

selves on the local Carthaginian markets. Outside of the area of Lilybaeum there is little representation of regional African productions, and only the generally traded pottery finds its way into the distribution system, leading to very homogenous assemblages.

Two mechanisms, which are not necessarily exclusive, will be explored here to explain these differences. The first is the potential role of *cabotage* as a distribution mechanism for ARS, given the proximity of Sicily to Africa; and the second is the potential role of Rome as an entrepôt between Africa and the western Mediterranean in the redistribution of ARS, given the pivotal role played by Rome in the economy of the Mediterranean. *Cabotage*, or the small-scale but intensive exchange by coastal trading, could theoretically result in a homogenous assortment of ARS being available in Sicilian markets, the result of what Horden and Purcell have recently termed the 'Brownian motion' of *caboteurs* (Horden and Purcell 2000: 137–43). This mechanism could be invoked to explain the longevity of the patterning in the assemblages, and would seem to be extremely resilient; for example, contrary to the suggestion of Wilson (1990: 255), the particular curves do not reflect the heavy Vandal raids on Sicily between 440 and 475, since the 5th century is generally a period of diminishing ARS supply. These small-scale merchants would have been linked in some way to both the producers and the consumers. In Africa and Sicily we may assume the functioning of local markets, redistributing the wares imported by *caboteurs*, but what about the other end of the chain of supply: where and how did the *caboteurs* obtain their supplies of ARS? The volume, widespread distribution and ubiquity of ARS surely indicates that it was produced for a pan-Mediterranean market, and we must consider that the connection between producers and distributors was highly organised, and question whether distribution could have been left to intensive, but essentially haphazard *cabotage*. The evidence from the C wares, which appear preponderantly on the international rather than the local market would have to be explained here.

Both Africa and Sicily were areas closely linked to Rome by economic ties, Africa by oil and grain, including the *annona* supply, Sicily by grain. However these shipments functioned in detail – Domenico Vera suggests that both African and Sicilian grain were furnished as tax (1996) – on a practical level the grain ships left Carthage and Palermo or Syracuse destined for Rome, and would not have returned empty, but with whatever cargo they could pick up there. It is possible that ships from Carthage carried ARS as a part of their cargo and the ceramics – and indeed other African produce such as oil, could then have been traded on from Rome, either by *caboteurs* to other parts of the western Mediterranean or back to Sicily on the way to Africa. In such a mechanism we can conclude that individual merchants would have obtained ARS in a single market – the ports of Rome. This could mean that the merchandise tended to travel to the ports of Rome, at Ostia and at Portus, where it was then resold to the *cabotage* traders, or even as return cargo on Sicilian grain ships. Thus in addition to direct trade between the African coast and the Sicily we must add the possibility that some of their supply came directly from Rome.

This model, in which Rome acted to some degree as an entrepôt between Africa and Sicily, probably constituted the continuation of a pattern of trade interwoven with taxation by *annona* which would have developed between Campania and Sicily during the Republican period. Here we should bear in mind the massive importation of Campanian wine in Dressel 1 and 2–4 amphorae for which there is evidence on numerous Sicilian sites. This must be seen as a return cargo on the *annona* ships from Sicily. Africa itself may also have received produce from Rome in these currents of trade. However, in areas away from the Proconsularis-Rome axis of the *annona*, local fineware productions developed with less competition.

SETTLEMENT HISTORIES

The great strength of the African surveys has always been the extraordinary preservation of the sites. Thus Kasserine, ULVS and Segermes have given us detailed pictures of every building in a particular landscape, showing not only the major farms but also their dependent structures – Jerba is alone in resembling the Italian sites, where stone robbing and continuous cultivation have left nothing but sherds. The picture presented here is naturally much less rich. The histograms provided for each project give a very bare notion of their settlement histories, and the level of uncertainty in the African curves leaves even these slightly in doubt. But it seems worthwhile briefly to compare those bare outlines, if only to underline the lack of similarities between them.

The only area to have a settlement history stretching back to the classical period is Jerba, where the towns of Bourgou and Meninx, as well as two small ports, were occupied at least from the 4th century BC (Fentress 2001). By the 2nd century BC a complex settlement hierarchy was fully developed: in addition to the towns, large villas and villages farmed the territory, with numerous small farms scattered between them. Wine and oil, as well as murex, were exported from their ports. We seem to see here a precocious development fully integrated into the Mediterranean economy and closely linked to the Sicilian settlement of the same period (Fentress 2001). Leptis Magna, too, was closely tied into this economy, producing and selling large amounts of oil (*Bellum Africum* 97.3; Mattingly 1985: 32; 1988: 37). Leptis Magna also probably served as a terminus for the sub-Saharan slave trade of the Garamantes. This may have been the case at Jerba as well; it was certainly so in the middle ages (Savage 1997). Coastal villas show signs of early construction, as many of them yield finds of black glaze. By the time of Augustus this settled agricultural production was clearly beginning to penetrate into the distant hinterland rep-

resented by the ULVS surveys, which have a significantly higher amount of Arretine and Gaullish sigillata (338 examples from 122 sites) than any other of the projects except Jerba (with 675 sherds). The earliest settlements were probably promontory villages, but this quickly developed into a complex settlement hierarchy, with some large farms built in the 'urban' *opus africanum* technique. However, there are no cities in the area and we must assume that trade was channeled through the towns of the coast, particularly Leptis Magna. The other areas considered were settled much more slowly, surprisingly so in the case of Segermes, which lies relatively close to the Carthaginian heartland. Here earlier settlement is testified to by several tombs of Hellenistic type, which Ferchiou suggests signal the properties of elite owners in the area (Ferchiou 1994), and by two large sites marked by Punic rock-cut tombs (Dietz *et al.* 1995: 790). On both these sites black glaze pottery and Punic coins were recovered. However, only 23 sites were settled in the 1st century, and of these most are dated to the last decades of the century by early ARS (the high level of uncertainty is explained by the fact that most of these forms run on into the 2nd century). Italian sigillata is conspicuously absent, being recovered from only four sites. Most of these sites are classified as 'agglomerations rurales', suggesting that the earliest settlement was heavily nucleated. Only four villas and one small farm are known from the 1st century. Kasserine, too, gets off to a much slower start. We may imagine that its pastoral base was slowly transformed into an agricultural economy. ARS of the 1st-century is recovered largely in sector 1, the area of the Musuni Regiani tribe, around Cillium. In the mountainous Djebel Selloum area, 1st-century ARS is found at only two complex sites, farm 27 and a fortified site 82 in the mountains. Finally, ARS and one piece of Gallic Sigillata were recovered at the major agro-town, Ksar el Guellal, between Cillium and Sufetula.

The 2nd century brought little change to Jerba, except for a contraction in the number of small farms, and what appears to have been a concentration of settlement on the villas and villages. However, towards the end of the century the old agro-town of Bourgou began to lose its inhabitants in favour of the contemporary expansion of Meninx, the great murex-producing center on the coast. In contrast to this minimal change in an already well-developed settlement pattern, the period between AD 100 and 300 was one of maximum growth for the sites of the interior, with a great diversification in the type and complexity of settlement. At Segermes, the eponymous *municipium* was apparently founded in the second half of the 2nd century: confusingly, it gained municipal status under Marcus Aurelius in AD 180, but the first datable pottery appears to be of 200 (Dietz *et al.* 1995: 791). This should suggest that the earliest levels are buried beneath later occupation. Around AD 200 there was a burst of new settlements, ranging from large agglomerations to villas where the presence of bath houses and mosaics testifies to a certain amount of luxury. Only small farms remain rare. The picture appears to be one in which production was concentrated on large estates and villages, fairly evenly distributed throughout the territory.

At Kasserine a very substantial growth in settlement started in the 2nd century. Growth was heaviest in sector 5, a low piedmont area dominated by small farms to the west of Cillium, and to a lesser degree in sector 1 where some smaller farms emerge against the backdrop of the larger production centers first established in the 1st century. Finally, settlement numbers in the Libyan valleys almost doubled during the Middle Roman period, with a continuous investment in new structures and 'filling-in' of the previously occupied areas. This conclusion is paralleled by the research of Longerstay (1999: 64), whose work in similar valleys of the Syrtis shows a peak of settlement between the 1st and the 3rd centuries AD.

The 4th century brought some pronounced settlement changes to the Libyan Valleys, including the shift from the open *opus africanum* olive farms to the fortified *ksour*, whose construction had begun in the last years of the 3rd century. This presumably reflects a concern for defense, as well as the growing importance of dominant families in the settlement hierarchy. These concerns are also reflected on Jerba, where most of the small farms were abandoned by the 4th century. New settlements tended to be villages, and – although Meninx evidently continued to flourish – we can see a growing nucleation of the habitat. At Kasserine a few sites dropped out of use by the 5th century, but there was no significant decline in settlement, and new sites suggest continuous investment. The continuity of sites in Kasserine in the 5th century may be related to the fact that many private and imperial estates in Byzacena were appropriated as part of the royal domains set up by the Vandals, which were exempt from taxation (Victor Vitensis 1. 13; Procopius, *Bellum Vandalicum* 1.5.12). The exception to this general pattern of slight contraction is Segermes, where growth continued unabated in all levels of the settlement hierarchy. The 6th century brought no arrest to this expansion. Much of this growth reflects the continuous establishment of large villas in the area, which continued until the beginning of the 5th century. This signifies a continuity of elite investment, although it may not be related to intensive farming, insofar as olive production was found on only two of the sites. In any case, the reduction in sites in all of the other areas suggests that we may be witnessing a demographic shift towards the north and the region of Carthage. In this context it is interesting to note the position of the Byzantine *limes* in this period: the line of mainland fortifications runs around the rim of the low steppe (Pringle 1981).

Elsewhere the 6th century produced a marked drop-off in settlement. In the Libyan valleys there were no new sites founded after AD 500, and the number of occupied sites shrank by almost 70%, from 294 to 76. This must reflect the great insecurity of the area in this period. Not surprisingly, the fortified *ksour* remained in occupation

the longest. At Kasserine the decline was slightly less drastic, from 46 to 24 sites. Again, the principal victims were the small farms, and we can see a marked tendency towards the nucleation of settlement on easily defended sites. At Jerba the decline was even lower, from 40 to 28, and some activity is evident in the construction of new villages. We may imagine that the island was relatively protected from the growing insecurity in the interior. However, occupation at Meninx thinned out drastically by the middle of the 6th century. It may be that the ever-more restricted trade left this city vulnerable to famine, as its hinterland was hardly able to support it without the continuous import of grain from elsewhere. The port town may also have been particularly receptive to the Justinianic plague. The new villages seem to suggest a de-urbanization of the population, which returned to the agricultural pursuits that at least guaranteed subsistence.

By the 7th century occupation was extinguished in almost all the areas surveyed. No sites in the Libyan Valleys were apparently occupied (although the cessation of imports may have rendered such occupation invisible), while at Kasserine the period witnesses wholesale disappearance of settlement in all sectors. Only large villa sites show evidence of continuity into the 7th century. Meninx and Leptiminus were apparently deserted, although sites in the countryside seem to have resisted the general collapse: again, the island's role as a refuge was probably important here. At Segermes only one site was certainly occupied, although doubt remains on a number of others. Again, we might suggest that we are witnessing a demographic contraction towards the north of the country. This would have become ever more pronounced with the Arab raids, between the battle of Sufetula in AD 647 and the fall of Carthage in 698. However, the twin processes of settlement contraction and the cessation of regional trade were clearly well underway by the time that these raids started.

This brief summary has necessarily left out many of the nuances of the settlement history of the surveyed areas. Our discussion of the Sicilian surveys will be even briefer, in that there is far less to relate. To generalize, settlement in Sicily was significantly different from the African surveys, being overwhelmingly concentrated in large villas. Although settlement in the late Hellenistic period was reasonably well diversified, with small farms alongside larger villas, by the 2nd century AD if not earlier almost all of the settlement was concentrated on the larger sites. Further, towns in these areas are all but absent. Lilybaeum continued to flourish, but Morgantina was abandoned by the end of the 1st century BC (Strabo 6.2.4) and in the area of the Monreale survey the city of Iatas was also abandoned, in the early 1st century AD. In Sicily as a whole cities in the interior were rare, and the Hellenistic pattern of urban centers with diversified rural settlement of villas and smaller sites changed in the imperial period to a non-urban pattern. However, the absence of cities was partially compensated for by a number of large villages, which became increasingly common in the late antique period (Wilson 1990: 223–31). Although there is a substantial continuity of settlement in all three areas up until AD 500 (at Morgantina) and through the 6th century (at Monreale and Contrada Mirabile), we see little in the way of new building; once settled, sites remained occupied. The four villa sites at Contrada Mirabile for which there is evidence in the 7th century were still occupied in the 12th century, but no new sites were built in the intervening period. This picture of extreme stagnation and settlement concentration on the properties of landowning families must be related to the vocation of the island in the Roman period, as one of the principal sources of grain for the empire.

What remains to be explained are the vast differences between Sicily and Africa during the period we are examining. Sicily remained a vital production center of grain for the Roman market through the 7th century. Its advantages in terms of 'piggy-back' trade, with 'free' shipping provided by the charges of grain for Rome, were no less obvious than those of Africa Proconsularis. Yet Sicily produced no fine pottery after the cessation of black glaze production in the 1st century AD until the 6th century (Wilson 1990: 451–54). When such a production did emerge, at Naxos, it was crude and poorly distributed. We have no evidence for other productions in Sicily, with the exception of some early imperial lamps (Wilson 1990: 260), a small quantity of wine amphorae (also from Naxos; Wilson 1990: 254) and a small, regional, production of brick and tile. Indeed, Sicily imported tiles from elsewhere (Wilson 1990: 270). It is not enough to say that the African productions dominated Sicilian consumption – 'sweeping all before it and banishing serious competition for fine wares' (Wilson 1990: 254). As we have seen, this is precisely what did not take place in Africa, where regional production centers spread throughout the provinces. Even oil was largely imported from an early date – African amphorae are an extremely common site find in the Monreale Survey area – as if Sicily was incapable of supplying its own regional market. Wine from Naxos was the only product we know of with a distribution outside the island itself (Wilson 1990: 264). In this way the Sicilian evidence throws light on the African evidence: what was the difference between the two?

Although the answer for the moment remains somewhat simplistic, the clearest difference between Sicily and Africa lies in the settlement patterns themselves. The considerable settlement differentiation in Africa is a reflection of many factors. The landscape of northern and coastal Tunisia was already dominated by agricultural towns and estates at the time of the Roman conquest, whereas the southern part of the province, although less heavily populated, was the home of numerous tribes practicing both agriculture and pastoralism. In the 1st and 2nd centuries AD, Roman colonization in both areas introduced new structures of settlement and land use (colonies, *municipia*, centuriation, etc.) on top of the indigenous system. The establishment of private and imperial estates introduced a further level of complexity to the pattern of agricultural organization. This was probably in part through the creation of leasing contracts (*locatio-conductio*) between owners and manager/tenants – a development which accounts perhaps for the many industrial villas and associated small farms in the Kasserine region (Vera 1986; 1988; Garnsey 2000; Whittaker 2000). In spite of a tendency to agglomerate, the African countryside remained marked by a highly differentiated settlement pattern, with villages, small farms and towns surviving beside the villas of the urban elite. In these lived an equally motley assortment of people, from *coloni* on the estates to artisans in the villages: the existence of these rather modest producers in Africa is typified by Alfius Caecilianus, duumvir of the little town of Abthugni, who was a weaver with a small workshop at the beginning of the 4th century (Lepelley 2001).

In Sicily a similar hierarchy is apparently absent. The large villas built between the 2nd century BC and the 1st century AD lived on, perhaps as villages, and were not replaced. The villa at Contrada Mirabile is a case in point: it burned down in the 2nd century and was replaced by a ragged group of houses which lived on through the 6th century (Fentress *et al.* 1986). The small farms did not survive, and most of the towns that flourished in the Hellenistic period were gone by the 1st century AD. The Late Roman villas at Piazza Armerina, Tindaris and Patti Marina are well-known exceptions to the view that there was little new investment in the countryside, but these were huge and luxurious establishments that seem to have been devoted as much to the recreation of their senatorial owners as to production. Indeed, as Vera has remarked, Roman senators, whether indigenous or foreign, are conspicuous by their absence throughout Sicilian history (Vera 1996: 51). In general, we must see the Sicilian countryside as relatively stagnant, with none of the investment so visible in each of the African areas. The great late villas were centers of consumption as well as production. The turn-around begins to come in the 6th century, marked by new coastal villages such as Caucana and the Naxos kilns. There may even have been some demographic increase at the time, as Wilson argues. We might imagine that immigrants from an increasingly unstable Africa could have contributed to some of this. But the complex structures of property, and the substantial artisan class which we know from Africa, seem to have found no place among the landscape of the Sicilian *latifundia*.

This study is based on what is still a woefully small set of data, and we have no doubt of the precarious nature of its conclusions. However, it reveals the potential value of comparative regional studies for our understanding of economic growth (or the lack thereof) in the Roman provinces. As one of us has argued elsewhere, within any model of economic activity in the Roman Empire we must allow for considerable diversity in the structure, scale and performance of regional economies (Hitchner, forthcoming). In the case of Roman Africa, while there is nothing in the evidence from the four surveys that would counter the view that the province, broadly speaking, experienced economic growth between roughly the 1st and 4th centuries, it does appear that the regional economy of Jerba was substantially less affected across time than the Libyan Valleys, Segermes and Kasserine by their incorporation into the Roman economic system. The latter experienced remarkable change in patterns of settlement and the organization of production under the empire, reflecting their transformation from pre-desert, chiefly pastoral societies to areas of intensive surplus-producing olive farms and stock-raising. The inter- and intra-regional exchange of artisan productions, particularly ARS, went hand in hand with the production of grain and oil for export in an economy that seems not to have lost its vitality until the 6th century AD. The distribution of ARS is a key illustration of the connected and integrated nature of the Roman economy.

REFERENCES

Atlante delle forme ceramiche I. (1981) *Ceramica fine romana nel bacino mediterraneo (medio e tardo impero)*, Enciclopedia dell'arte antica, classica e orientale 1. Roma, Istituto della Enciclopedia italiana.

Barker, G. W. W., Gilbertson, D. D., Jones, G. D. B. and Mattingly, D. J. (eds.) (1996) *Farming the Desert: The UNESCO Libyan Valleys Archaeological Survey*. 2 vols. Paris and London, UNESCO Publishing.

Ben Lazreg, N. and Mattingly, D. J. (1992) *Leptiminus (Lamta): A Roman Port City in Tunisia. Report no. 1 (JRA* Supplementary Series 4). Ann Arbor, Journal of Roman Archaeology.

Cambi, F. and Fentress, E. (1989) Villas to castles: first millennium AD demography in the Albegna Valley. In K. Randsborg (ed.) *The Birth of Europe: Archaeology and Social Development in the First Millennium AD* (Analecta Romana Instituti Danici, Supplementum XVI): 74–86. Rome, "L'Erma" di Bretschneider.

Carandini, A., Cambi, F., Celuzza, M. and Fentress E. (2002) *Paesaggi d'Etruria*. Rome, Edizioni di Storia e Letteratura.

De Vos, M. (ed.) (2001) *Rus Africum: Terra, acqua, olio nell'Africa settentrionale. Scavo e ricognizione nei dintorni di Dougga (Alto Tell Tunisino)*. Trento, Università degli studi di Trento.

Dietz, S., Ladjimi Sebaï, L. and Ben Hassen, H. (eds.) (1995) *Africa Proconsularis: Regional Studies in the Segermes Valley of Northern Tunesia*. 2 Vols. Copenhagen, Publications of the National Museum of Denmark.

Drine, A., Fentress, E., and Holod, R., (forthcoming) *The Jerba Project* (*JRA* Supplementary Series).

Duncan-Jones, R. P. (1996) The impact of the Antonine plague. *Journal of Roman Archaeology* 9: 108–136.

Dyson, S. L. and Rowland, R., Jr. (1992) Survey and settlement reconstruction in west-central Sardinia. *American Journal of Archaeology* 96: 203–220.

Felici, F. and Pentirici, M. (2002) Per una definizione delle dinamiche economiche e commerciali del territorio di Leptis Magna. *L'Africa Romana* 14: 245–263.

Fentress, E. (2001) Villas, wine and kilns: the landscape of Jerba in the late Hellenistic period. *Journal of Roman Archaeology* 14: 249–269.

Fentress, E. (ed.) (1991) *Fouilles de Sétif 1977–1984* (*Supplément au Bulletin d'archéologie algérienne* 5). Algeria: Agence nationale d'archéologie et de prospection des sites et monuments historiques.

Fentress, E., Aït Kaci, A. and Bounssair, N. (1991) Prospections dans le Belezma: Rapport préliminaire. *Actes du Colloque International sur l'Histoire de Sétif* (*Supplément au Bulletin d'archéologie algérienne* 7): 107–13. Algeria: Agence nationale d'archéologie et de prospection des sites et monuments historiques.

Fentress, E., Kennet, D. and Valenti, I. (1986) A Sicilian villa and its landscape (Contrada Mirabile, Mazara del Vallo). *Opus* 5: 75–90.

Fentress, E. and Perkins, P. (1988). Counting African red slip ware. *L'Africa Romana* 5: 205–214.

Ferchiou, N. (1994) Le paysage protohistorique et pré-Impérial à l'est et au sud de Zaghouan. *Antiquités Africaines* 30: 7–56.

Fontana, S. (1991a) Analisi comparata delle attestazioni della ceramica africana nel V sec.d.C.: un' indagine preliminare. *Archeologia e Calcolatori* 2: 109–122.

Fontana, S. (1991b) Note sulla distribuzione della sigillata africana in Italia. In E. Herring, R. Whitehouse and J. Wilkins (eds.) *Papers of the Fourth Conference of Italian Archaeology, The Archaeology of Power*: 135–45. London, Accordia Research Centre.

Garnsey, P. (2000) The land. In A. Bowman, P. Garnsey and D. Rathbone (eds.) *The Cambridge Ancient History XI: The High Empire, AD 70–192* (2nd edn.): 679–709. Cambridge, University Press.

Hawthorne, J. (1996) Commensalism and common sense: a new approach to archaeological ceramics. *Assemblage* 1: 3–6.

Hawthorne, J. (2000) Vessel volume as a factor in ceramic quantification: the case of African Red Slip ware. In K. Lockyear, T. J. T. Sly and V. Mihailescu-Bîrliba (eds.) *CAA 96: Computer Applications and Quantitative Methods in Archaeology* (British Archaeological Reports International Series 845): 19–24. Oxford, Archaeopress.

Hayes, J. W. (1972) *Late Roman Pottery*. London, British School at Rome.

Hayes, J. W. (1997) *Handbook of Mediterranean Roman Pottery*. London, British Museum Press.

Hayes, J. W. (1998) Introduction. The study of Roman pottery in the Mediterranean 23 years after *Late Roman Pottery*. In L. Saguì (ed.) *Ceramica in Italia: VI–VII secolo. Atti del Convegno in onore di John W. Hayes. Roma, 11–13 maggio 1995* (*Biblioteca di Archeologia Medievale* 14): 9–21. Florence, All'insegna del giglio.

Hitchner, R. B. (1988) The Kasserine Archaeological Survey, 1982–86. *Antiquités Africaines* 24: 7–41.

Hitchner, R. B. (1990) The Kasserine Archaeological Survey, 1987. *Antiquités Africaines* 26: 231–260.

Hitchner, R. B. (1993) Olive oil production and the Roman economy: the case for intensive growth. In M.-C. Amouretti and J.-P. Brun (eds.) *La production du vin et de l'huile en Mediterrannée*: 499–508. Athens, École Française d'Athènes.

Hitchner, R. B. (forthcoming) 'The fairest part of the earth': stagnation or growth in the Roman empire. In J. Manning and I. Morris (eds.) *The Ancient Economy: Evidence and Models*: 32–45. Stanford, Stanford University Press.

Horden, P. and Purcell, N. (2000) *The Corrupting Sea: A Study of Mediterranean History*. Oxford, Blackwell Books.

Lepelley, C. (2001) Chrétiens et païens au temps de la persecution de Dioclétien: le cas d'Abthugni. In C. Lepelley, *Aspects de l'Afrique Romaine. Les cités, la vie rurale, le christianisme*: 323–28. Bari, Edipuglia.

Leveau, P. (1984) *Caesarea de Maurétanie: une ville romaine et ses campagnes* (Collection de l'École Française de Rome 70). Rome, École française de Rome.

Longerstay, M. (1999) Prospection archéologique dans cinq vallées de la region syrtique (Libye) et fouille d'un batiment antique de la vallée du Wadi Herawah: rapport préliminaire. *Bulletin archéologique du Comité des travaux historiques, Afrique du Nord* 25 (1996–1998): 53–68.

Lund, J. (1995) Hellenistic, Roman and Late Roman Fine Ware from the Segermes Valley – forms and chronology. In S. Dietz, L. Ladjimi Sebaï and H. Ben Hassen (eds) *Africa Proconsularis: Regional Studies in the Segermes Valley of Northern Tunisia*: 447–629. Copenhagen, Publications of the National Museum of Denmark.

Mackensen, M. (1993) *Die spätantiken Sigillata- und Lampentöpfereien von El Mahrine (Nordtunesien): Studien zur nordafrikanischen Feinkeramik des 4. bis 7. Jahrhunderts* (Münchner Beiträge zur Vor- und Frühgeschichte 50). Munich, C. H. Beck.

Mackensen M. (1998a) Centres of African red slip ware production in Tunisia from the late 5th to the 7th century. In L. Saguì (ed.) *Ceramica in Italia: VI–VII secolo. Atti del Convegno in onore di John W. Hayes. Roma, 11–13 maggio 1995 (Biblioteca di Archeologia Medievale* 14): 23–39. Florence, All'insegna del giglio.

Mackensen, M. (1998b) Central Tunisian red slip ware with stamped decoration. *Journal of Roman Archaeology* 11: 355–70.

Mackensen, M. and Schneider, G. (2002) Production centres of African red slip ware (3rd–7th c.) in northern and central Tunisia: archaeological provenance and reference groups passed on chemical analysis. *Journal of Roman Archaeology* 15: 159–72.

Mattingly, D. J. (1985) Olive oil production in Roman Tripolitania. In D. J. Buck and D. J. Mattingly (eds.) *Town and Country in Roman Tripolitania: Studies in Honour of Olwen Brogan* (British Archaeological Reports International Series 274): 27–46. Oxford, British Archaeological Reports.

Mattingly, D. J. (1988) The olive boom: oil surpluses, wealth and power in Roman Tripolitania. *Libyan Studies* 19: 21–41.

Millett, M. (1991) Pottery: population or supply patterns? The *Ager Tarraconensis* approach. In G. W. W. Barker and J. Lloyd (eds.) *Roman Landscapes: Archaeological Survey in the Mediterranean Region* (Archaeological Monographs of the British School at Rome 2): 18–26. London, British School at Rome.

Peacock, D. P. S., Bejaoui, F. and Ben Lazreg, N. (1990) Roman pottery production in Central Tunisia. *Journal of Roman Archaeology* 3: 59–84.

Perkins, P. (2000) Power, culture and identity in the Roman economy. In J. Huskinson (ed.) *Experiencing Rome*: 183–212. London, Routledge.

Pringle, D. (1981) *The Defence of Byzantine Africa from Justinian to the Arab Conquest* (British Archaeological Reports International Series 99). Oxford, British Archaeological Reports.

Pröttel, P. M. (1996) *Mediterrane Feinkeramikimporte des 2. bis 7. Jahrhunderts n. Chr. Im oberen Adriaraum und in Slowenien*

(Kölner Studien zur Archäologie der römischen Provinzen 0945-2893, 2). Espelkamp, M. Leidorf.

Reynolds, L. G. (1986) *Economic Growth in the Third World: An Introduction.* New Haven, Yale University Press.

Rickman. G. (1981) *The Corn Supply of Ancient Rome.* Oxford, Clarendon Press.

Saguì, L. (1980) Ceramica africana dalla 'villa di Tiberio' a Sperlonga. *Mélanges de l'Ecole Française de Rome, Antiquité* 92: 471–490.

Saguì, L. (ed.) (1998) *Ceramica in Italia: VI–VII secolo. Atti del Convegno in onore di John W. Hayes. Roma, 11–13 maggio 1995 (Biblioteca di Archeologia Medievale* 14): 9–21. Florence, All'insegna del giglio.

Savage, E. (1997) *A Gateway to Hell, A Gateway to Paradise: The North African Response to the Arab Conquest.* Princeton, Princeton University Press.

Stone, D., Stirling, L. and Ben Lazreg, N. (1998) Suburban landuse and ceramic production around Leptiminus: interim report, 1. *Journal of Roman Archaeology* 11: 304–318.

Tortorella, S. (1983) Produzione e circolazione della ceramica africana di Cartagine (V–VII sec.). *Opus* 2: 15–30.

Tortorella, S. (1995) La ceramica africana: un bilancio dell'ultimo decennio di ricerche. In P. Trousset (ed.) *Productions et exportations africaines* (Colloque international sur l'histoire et l'archéologie de l'Afrique du Nord 6): 79–102. Paris: Editions du CTHS.

Tortorella, S. (1998) La sigillata africana in Italia nel VI e nel VII secolo d.C.: problemi di cronologia e distribuzione. In L. Saguì (ed.) *Ceramica in Italia: VI–VII secolo. Atti del Convegno in onore di John W. Hayes. Roma, 11–13 maggio 1995 (Biblioteca di Archeologia Medievale* 14): 41–69. Florence, All'insegna del giglio.

Vera, D. (1986) Enfiteusi, colonato e trasformazioni agrarie nell'Africa Proconsolare del tardo impero. *L'Africa Romana* 4: 287–93.

Vera, D. (1988) Terra e lavoro nell' Africa romana. *Studi Storici* 29: 967–92.

Vera, D. (1996) Augusto, Plinio il Vecchio e la Sicilia in età imperiale. A proposito di ricenti scoperte epigraphiche e archeologiche ad Agrigento. *Kokalos* 42: 31–59.

Whittaker, C. R. (2000) Africa in the High Empire, A.D. 70–192. In A. Bowman, P. Garnsey and D. Rathbone (eds.) *The Cambridge Ancient History XI: The High Empire, AD 70–192* (2nd edn.): 514–46. Cambridge, University Press.

Wilson, R. J. A. (1990) S*icily under the Roman Empire.* Warminster, Aris and Phillips.

Zanini, E. (1996) Ricontando la terra sigillata africana. *Archeologia Medievale* 22: 677–88.

12. Demography and Survey

Robin Osborne

It is an open question whether we can understand any society unless we know how large it is. Population levels relate directly both to levels of consumption and levels of production: if we know how many mouths there are, we have a shrewd idea of minimum food needs; and if we know how many hands there are, and the level of technological sophistication, we have a good idea of possible production maxima. Population densities impact directly on levels of human interaction: that is dramatically reflected in susceptibility to epidemic diseases, but it has equally direct, if less securely appreciated, effects on possible social and political organisation. Levels of population are also crucial to any attempt to compare one society with another: questions of degrees of urbanisation are only one of the many comparative questions that cannot begin to be broached without an impression of population size.

In this paper I look at the demographic data available to historians of ancient Greece and at the questions that have preoccupied them, before discussing how survey archaeology contributes to the formulation both of the questions and of the possible answers. I limit myself to work on the Greek mainland and islands and to the first millennium BC, both because my own expertise is limited to that area and because, although many of the general issues raised here are of general relevance, issues of the historical interpretation of settlement patterns are not automatically generalisable across different societies.

My discussion of Greek survey archaeology falls into two parts. First, I review major survey publications, their own explicit statements, the form in which they give their site data and the extent to which this enables scholars to generate alternative hypotheses on the basis of different interpretations of the material found. Second, I explore the consequences of approaching the material with assumptions different from those brought by the scholars who made the initial analysis. In the latter activity, as in various particular observations, I follow in the footsteps of Whitelaw (2000). Although my concerns overlap with those discussed by Sbonias (1999a; 1999b), I focus much more narrowly on the interpretation of data collected,

leaving aside – not because it is unimportant, but because my current concern is different – the question of the factors that may have distorted data collection in the first place.

TEXTS AND DEMOGRAPHY: THE HISTORIAN'S AGENDA

Ancient literary sources offer us very little basis for demographic studies in the Greek world in the Archaic, Classical and Hellenistic periods (the situation is not much different for the Roman world). We have an array of army numbers, of varying precision, a few claims about slave numbers at Athens that are more or less (in)credible, and a number of generalisations about city populations. On the basis of the best of the military figures (Thucydides 2.13 is crucial), we can be reasonably confident about the number of adult male citizens in fifth-century BC Athens. On the basis of similar sources we can also more or less agree about the number of Athenian citizens in the fourth century. We get 50,000 as the fifth-century figure, 25,000 as the fourth-century figure, and reasonable confidence that we are not likely to be more than 20% out (*cf.* Gomme 1933; Hansen 1985; 1988).

Doing any more with demography in the Greek world depends upon comparison with societies that are better known. That is true even for the number of women. There is considerable debate, moreover, as to whether or not female infanticide had a lasting demographic impact (Sallares 1991: 151–57). It would certainly have done so if the comic fragment of Poseidippos (frg. 12, Kassel-Austin), which has a character announce that even the rich expose a baby if it is a girl, was telling the truth.

Much of the discussion of ancient demography – and this is true of Rome, as much as of Greece – has been concerned with absolute population figures. We take what figures we have for adult males, or particular sub-sections of the adult male population, guess at the life-expectancy at birth (sometimes helped by the possibility of comparison between different age cohorts) – usually guessing at 25 or

30 – guess at the population being stable and experiencing minimal growth, and then imagine that ancient populations fitted one of the Princeton model life-tables for pre-industrial populations (*cf.* Hansen 1985: 9–11). Out of that we get a total native free-born population.

At this point a certain irony kicks in. Comparative information gives us strong reason to believe that population growth, if not population change, is likely to have been at a very slow rate, even at best. Walter Scheidel (2003) has recently argued that if we take the most probable estimates of population for Mycenaean and for Classical Greece, then in between we can only reckon a population growth rate of 0.2 or 0.3% per annum. There are two basic ingredients to this claim: one is about the extreme difficulty of a population sustaining a higher rate of growth in circumstances of high mortality, while the other is the extreme effects of a higher rate of population growth when sustained over a long period – the compound interest effect. But against this, as Scheidel acknowledges and discusses, both literary and archaeological evidence has been seen to urge, at least for certain periods, strikingly sudden patterns of change.

Take Classical Athens. What I have already said indicates that I think it reasonable to believe that the citizen population of Athens halved itself between its fifth-century peak and its general fourth-century level. And this change takes place over the course of just 30 years – the 30 years of the Peloponnesian War. War, and plague such as that which occurred in Athens during and partly as a result of the war, kill large numbers and may have major demographic effects, and so this dramatic population decrease seems understandable in the light of comparative evidence. But most ancient historians find it hard to credit an Athenian citizen population in 500 BC above the level of fourth-century Athens; that is, they tend to believe, even if they do not articulate their belief, that the population of Athens doubled between 500 and 430 BC. Ancient sources themselves suggest, in the context of explaining Perikles' Citizenship Law of 451/50, which restricted citizenship in future to those whose mothers and fathers could both show that they were of Athenian citizen descent, that the population of Athens increased rapidly in the 30 years after the Persian Wars (see Patterson 1981). But how? We can invent stories – mass Athenian marriage to foreign women, completely lax policing of existing citizenship rules, and so on – but if we do so, we are thereby privileging issues thrown up by the single piece of evidence we have, and without considering what is suggested for other times and places in explanation of not dissimilarly dramatic events.

Those other events are mainly events for the archaeologist. Most familiar is the dramatic evidence from Athenian burials in the eighth century BC and Snodgrass's (1977; 1980) claims of 4% per annum growth in the Athenian population then (see further Morris 1987: 72; Osborne 1996a: 70–81; Scheidel 2003). Even if we want to argue that the Athenian burial evidence does not give direct evidence of population growth in the Geometric period, we have to admit that the rate of appearance of new settlements itself, though less dramatic than the increase in the numbers of burials, points to a substantial increase in population numbers. And once we start thinking about settlement numbers increasing, we will each find ourselves thinking about survey evidence, and in particular the sharp increases in site numbers in, for example, the late Classical and late Roman periods.

It is precisely because the long-run of demographic history has to be a story of overall slow growth, though decline could be more rapid, whereas the short-term of both the historical and the archaeological record indicates periods of rapid growth, that demography has to be on the agenda for all archaeologists and historians. Demographers are happy to allow that populations do indeed fluctuate in their growth rates over the shorter-term, but such fluctuations do not happen without a cause. Part of the problem with interpreting the change of numbers of archaeologically visible burials in eighth-century Attica or Argos as change in population numbers is the inability of any of its advocates adequately to explain why it should or how it could have happened. Neither Snodgrass's putative change from pastoral to arable agriculture (1980: 35–36) nor Sallares's putative decay of age classes (Sallares 1991: 160–92) has been able to muster more than the most exiguous and debatable evidence on its side and as a result neither has carried conviction.

Had it been possible to show that the burial explosion in the eighth century in Attica was also a population explosion, then that demographic revolution would itself have been sufficient to generate explanations for many further changes that are visible in the archaeological record (settlements abroad, hoplite armies) or hinted in the literary evidence (changes from monarchy to tyranny, perhaps). Demographic change is a very powerful motor. It is for that reason that the demographic implications of the changing site numbers and site distribution now well attested by survey have to be one of the priorities in the interpretation of those data. But as I will attempt to show in some detail below, changing site numbers cannot be read as a direct map of changing population in the way that many have in the past suggested (Sallares 1991: 60–65). Both absolute population numbers and the way that population is distributed are vital ingredients of an understanding of the Greek city; of that there is no better illustration than the debate over whether or not it is appropriate to refer to the Greek city as a 'face-to-face' society, or the discussion of participation levels in political institutions.

SURVEYING SURVEYS: THE DEMOGRAPHIC RECORD

What *can* we do with survey and demography? Consciousness of the importance of demography is clear from the first reports on the new wave of survey until the present, as the following review indicates.

Melos

An Island Polity: The Archaeology of Exploitation in Melos (Renfrew and Wagstaff 1982) devotes a whole chapter to 'Settlement and population change' (Wagstaff and Cherry 1982a) and discusses the topic repeatedly elsewhere (*cf.* the section 'Population and settlement pattern' in the chapter on 'Animal husbandry, population and urbanisation' [Gamble 1982: 165–66]; all the discussions are easily traced in the excellent index). For the Early Bronze Age, Wagstaff and Cherry (1982a: 136–39) argue that settlements and cemeteries should be seen as closely paired in this period, and that since cemeteries on average yield only the number of dead that a single family would yield over a century, the sites should be taken to represent only single families. That is, from survey all that is taken over is the *presence* of a site; the deductions about site size are indirect, generalising, and make no use of any particular features of the sites surveyed. For the period from *c.* 2000 BC onwards (pp. 139–40), when settlement evidence from Melos is largely limited to Phylakopi, population estimates depend upon the area of Phylakopi and a density figure that is adopted from cross-culturally derived formulae.

Subsequent to the Bronze Age, the basis for calculation changes. Geometric population change is tentatively inferred from changes in the numbers of published Melian pots. Changing numbers of rural sites are noted, along with their small size, but the only suggestion made about population is that the decline in rural site numbers in the Classical and Hellenistic periods should be taken as indicative of nucleation rather than of population change. The authors (pp. 144–45) decline to attempt to derive a population figure for Melos from the size (15 ha) of Melos town and choose instead a figure of 2,000–3,000 on the basis of Thucydides' notice that the Athenians sent 500 settlers (add their wives and children). For Hellenistic demographic history, a story is told on the basis of literary and epigraphic texts and the archaeology is noted simply to be 'not at variance' with that literary picture (p. 145), but for the Roman period the increasing number of sites *is* taken as a basis for supposing it reasonable 'that the island population grew larger in Roman times than in any earlier period'. There is discussion of the wider range of types of site visible in the Roman period, but nothing is fed back from that discussion into demography, no doubt in part because of the continuing dominance of Melos town. Of later periods of history I note only the calculation later in the book, that the figures offered by Olivier for 1798 and Leake for 1806 imply a population growth of 37.5% per annum: 'Immigration is likely, but not on the required scale. We are forced to conclude that the gross changes in population were not as great as presented...' (Wagstaff and Cherry 1982b: 255).

The site catalogue in *An Island Polity* (Cherry 1982) gives an estimate not only of the size of the site but of the percentage of arable land within a 1 km radius. It gives no indication of density of sherd material.

Boiotia

Demographic discussion is central to the preliminary report of the Boiotia survey published in the *Journal of Field Archaeology* (Bintliff and Snodgrass 1985). Indeed, no fewer than five pages are devoted to 'An excursus on population density' (pp. 140–45). This concerns the Archaic to early Hellenistic periods, and turns on literary evidence. On the basis of the overall number of troops mustered in fifth-century Boiotia, the authors offer a guess at an overall population of 165,500. Among other things, this guess assumes (surely falsely) that (a) Boiotian rowers were drawn from those who did not also fight on land; and (b) that Boiotian ships were manned by free citizens of Boiotia, rather than at least in part by paid rowers originating outside Boiotia. Having arrived at their guess for the total population, Bintliff and Snodgrass then deduct the number of people living in towns or villages in order to calculate the number living in farms in the countryside. To do this, they first construct a figure for towns, assuming a population of 5,000 for Thespiai city and then multiply that by 11, on the grounds that Thespiai supplied one of the 11 Boiotarchs. We might ask (though they do not) whether that was not 'Thespiai' as a *polis*, not Thespiai as a town. What we are in fact told at *Hellenika Oxyrhynchia* 16.3 is that Thespiai plus Thisbe and Eutresis supplied two of the 11 Boiotarchs. Bintliff and Snodgrass construct a figure for villages by taking Askra to have 1,000 inhabitants and supposing there might be 12 Askra-sized communities in Boiotia. The density of occupation of the countryside is then calculated both as an overall figure (98,500 inhabitants spread over 2,580 sq. km = 38 per sq. km) and as a figure based on the assumption that they all will have lived in the 40% of Boiotia that was cultivated (95 inhabitants per cultivated sq. km). They then compare the population they regard as indicated by survey finds (on the basis of 11 'large-medium' sites, totalling 1,250 people – the basis for assuming 113.64 people per large-medium site is not revealed – and 57 farms, ranging in area from 0.007 ha to 0.5 ha, at 5 people per farm, totaling 285 people) with the predicted population on the grounds that they have surveyed 21 sq. km of good arable land: 21 at 95 per sq. km = 1,796. They suggest that the difference between the 1,535 'found' in survey and the 1,796 predicted is due to the loss of poor farms – no fewer than 52 of them. That is, survey picks up only just over 50% of farms.

The reader has a strong sense of being in the hands of skilled jugglers here. The idea that only just over half the farms of antiquity were recovered in survey seems so striking that the reader is inclined to assume that changing the assumptions slightly would not make much difference (up to two-thirds, perhaps, or three-quarters, or down to one-third?). In fact, certain of the assumptions are absolutely crucial. I draw attention to just some. First, the calculations are done on a Boiotia-wide basis: that is, the assumption is made that the distribution of population between town and countryside was consistent all over

Boiotia. Even if 1/11 of the Boiotian population did live in towns, that does not mean that 1/11 of the population of Thespiai did so. Second, the round figures for city and satellite-town population are never justified, and nor is the number for, or of, 'satellite towns'. The satellite-town figure is particularly tricky, since identity as a 'satellite town' whose population does not count for the 5,000 urban residents per Boiotarch, seems to depend entirely on not being mentioned in *Hellenika Oxyrhynchia*. Third, the assumption is made that all rural sites which show signs of Classical occupation at all were occupied simultaneously. Not all of these considerations point in the same direction, but it becomes clear that relatively small variations in assumptions will allow one to believe either that recovery of rural settlements is practically complete or that it is very much more incomplete than Bintliff and Snodgrass suggest.

Bintliff himself has recently (1997) returned to the question and redone the calculations, basing himself much more upon the built-up area of Boiotian cities rather than on assumptions culled from *Hellenika Oxyrhynchia*, and thus addressing my second complaint. He has indeed found it possible to account for all the rural population, but the problems of assuming uniform density of occupation across Boeotia, and, as it happens, also assuming simultaneous and continuous occupation of sites, remain. Bintliff also sticks to the original calculation for total Boiotian population. I note only that if their naval provision is cut in half (and there are strong grounds for reducing it still further), the consequent total population is reduced to 140,500. If one then maintain all the other assumptions made by Bintliff and Snodgrass in 1985, the rural population is reduced to 73,500, the population density per cultivated sq. km to 71, and the number of rural inhabitants in the area surveyed is predicted as 1,491, compared with the 1,535 'actually found'. On these calculations, survey found 44 more people (= 9 more farms) that were occupied, a recovery rate for farms of 119%. Such a recovery rate is, of course, given discontinuity of occupation, perfectly plausible.

All we currently have from the Boiotia survey remains the preliminary report and papers on more specialised aspects of the survey and its findings. In consequence, no detailed data have yet been presented; but I note that, for the purposes of the calculation, it appears that Bintliff and Snodgrass operated in 1985 with 5 grades of site: the 'city' (Thespiai), the 'satellite town' (Askra), the 'large' and 'medium' rural site (village/hamlet) and the farm. All farms are taken as the same size in population terms, with no attempt to differentiate by area or by intensity of occupation. Bintliff (1997) equivocated as to whether population should be ascribed to 'large sites' (= hamlets) simply by ascribing to them the residue rural population not accounted for by the farms (which results in 32 people per 'large site'), or rather by assigning them 12.1 × 5 (= 61 persons) as their population, since on average they were 12.1 times larger than the smallest sites. By comparison, Bintliff had calculated the population of all villages and towns (of >10 ha) by assuming 56% to be

domestic and the density of population in domestic occupation to be 225 persons per ha. If we apply those sorts of calculations to sites that average 2.5 ha, they would have *c*. 250 inhabitants, not 61, let alone 32.

Northern Keos

Landscape Archaeology as Long-Term History (Cherry *et al.* 1991) discusses population both in relation to the *polis* of Koressos, where epigraphic evidence had been used by earlier scholars to posit a total population, and in relation to rural settlement. On the epigraphic front, Cherry *et al.* rightly point out the problems of moving from epigraphic lists and data on sacrificial victims to population totals, but note that, whatever one's reservations, that evidence is hard to square with a population of much below 1,000 and is compatible with a population of *c*. 1,300 (pp. 236–37). On rural sites (pp. 337–46), they offer both a maximum population (essentially = the number of rural sites with any evidence from the period x 5) and a more conservative figure (= the number of rural sites with more than three datable artefacts from a period × 5). The latter figure is characteristically one third or less of the former figure. For the Classical period the difference is between 75 and 200, when the population at the *polis* centre of Koressos may be *c*.1,000. Problems of whether sites were permanently occupied and whether they were all occupied at the same time are explicitly flagged up, as are the fact that town and country populations seem to be directly, and not inversely, correlated. The overall demographic history is of growth and decline – the extremes of the estimates for town and country offered amount to 575–745 in the Archaic period, 975–1,400 for the Classical period, and <490 to <605 for the Hellenistic period. Given the length of the periods involved there is nothing here that could not be accommodated on the basis that neither growth nor decline exceeded 0.5% per annum.

The only information about rural sites used in the population estimate is their existence and the strength of the evidence for use in any particular period. On site size it is simply remarked that none seem large enough to allow residence by more than a single family. In revisiting all of this, Whitelaw (1998; 2000) has employed (along with slightly different data) a more differentiated model of rural residence, taking variation in area of scatter to correspond to the presence of more than one residential unit, and together with the inclusion of sites not counted by Cherry *et al*. This has the effect of increasing the rural population to 82 families – on the normal assumption some 410 individuals. In *Landscape Archaeology* the Gazetteer of Archaeological Sites (pp. 69–156) supplies an estimate of site area, an indication of the periods represented and the number of diagnostic pieces by which they are represented. The density of the pottery scatter is indicated only in the prose description – 'abundant pottery...', 'a low-density scatter...', 'high-density scatter', etc. Individual sherds are described.

The Southern Argolid

A Greek Countryside (Jameson *et al.* 1994) includes a whole long appendix (pp. 539–67), ill-signalled in its index, on 'The population of the southern Argolid'. Populations are there calculated on the basis that villages have a population density of 125 persons per ha, towns of 250 persons per ha, and that smaller sites come in multiples of a household unit of 5 persons. For the Geometric period there is one town (Hermion), 3 villages of 2 ha or more, 3 sites of *c.* 0.5 ha and 11 one-family sites, giving a total of *c.* 1,100 persons. For the Archaic period they calculate that, given simultaneous occupation, some 2,550 people lived in five villages of larger than 1 ha, five hamlets of 0.2–1 ha, and 27 farms, compared to 3,330 people living in Hermion and Halieis. For the Classical period the urban total rises to 4,845, the rural falls to 2,035, since although the number of farms increases from 27 to 44, there are only three hamlets of less than 1 ha and the total area of the 5 village sites larger than 1 ha falls. In the late Classical and Hellenistic periods the town population again rises, to 8,000, and the rural population increases to 2,885, with a slight increase in the number and size of hamlets and villages and a further marked increase in the number of small sites (to 98). The succeeding late Hellenistic and early Roman period sees major settlement dislocation, with the abandonment not just of Halieis but of several villages and hamlets and the number of small sites falling to 17. Nevertheless, although the total population falls from 10,855 to 4,570, the rural population falls only from 2,885 to 1,735.

The basic ingredients to the non-urban population figures here are site numbers and site size. 0.2 ha is taken as the threshold for a site that represents more than a single family, a signal for the density operator of 125 persons per ha to be brought into play. All sites from 0.2 ha upwards use that multiplier unless they are towns, in which case the figure is differently computed. All sites below 0.2 ha are taken to be single-family occupation.

The 'Register of Sites' (pp. 415–538) records area, height above sea level, percentage of site sampled, and periods of material, and it gives a prose description which may describe the material in some detail and always records the number of sherds and tile fragments collected. The overall density of sherd material is nevertheless not always easy to deduce, even in broad terms, since although 'small but dense concentration of artifacts' is pretty clear, 'a well-defined concentration of artifacts' is not.

Methana

A Rough and Rocky Place (Mee and Forbes 1997) has no index entry for population or demography. This does indeed correspond to a rather passing concern for population in the book itself, which lacks any synthetic account of changing settlement on the peninsula, contenting itself with chapters devoted to specific periods. These chapters give an account of what sites were found in what periods, and how their distribution and typology change over time, but they rarely relate this to demography. The chapter on Early Iron Age and Archaic Methana observes of population only that 'Despite the fact that the number of major sites on the Methana peninsula contracts at the start of the Archaic period, the size of the remaining centres seems to have increased. This would suggest a more nucleated society as well as a larger population' (p. 60). For the Classical period we are told 'These data [*sc.* absence of processing equipment] suggest that only a small proportion of the population worked the land from permanent bases outside the major centres of population'. For the Hellenistic period there is no clear discussion of rural sites at all and population is mentioned only in connection with denying that the Hellenistic period was one of recession on Methana.

What *A Rough and Rocky Place* does provide is graphic representation of the distribution of site sizes in each period along with tables of data which give not only area and components, but also density of material. All this information is given again, in slightly different form, in the 'Catalogue of Sites' (pp. 118–210), which also gives height above sea level.

Laconia

The shyness about making any estimation of, or even comment on, population seems to have become widespread in recent discussions. Neither the preliminary report of the Nemea Valley Archaeological Project (Wright *et al.* 1990) nor that of the Pylos Regional Archaeological Project (Davis *et al.* 1997) make any attempt to discuss population levels or population change. As on Methana, so in the Nemea Valley there is allusion to the problems of assuming uninterrupted settlement on a site just because there is material from different periods: 'Our evidence suggests instead a much more dynamic and discontinuous pattern of ebb and flow in settlement, at the level both of individual site and of the region as a whole' (Wright *et al.* 1990: 617).

The first volume of the Laconia survey (Cavanagh *et al.* 2002) however, as I know from a preview which Richard Catling was kind enough to afford me, is bolder. Catling (2002), in his section on the Early Iron Age to Classical periods (1050–323 BC), devotes a section to a tentative discussion of population estimates. On the basis of their area, he suggests classifying his rural sites as farmsteads (= 5 people), villas (= 15 people), hamlets (at 5 people per 0.1 ha) and villages (at 5 people per 0.05 ha). This produces an Archaic-early Classical population for the survey area of 1,025, with 300 in the one village, 155 in hamlets, 255 in villas and 315 in farmsteads. In the Classical period the population reduces to 855, with 300 in the village, 270 in hamlets, 150 in villas and 135 in farmsteads. Catling also reveals that in AD 1700 the same area seems to have had a total population of 779, of whom 523 resided in one village, Chrysapha. Interestingly, those

Survey Project	Urban density (persons per ha.)	Upper area limit for farmsteads (= 5 people)
Melos	1,037–1,666 in area of dwelling houses (taken to be 75% of site, for Phylakopi)	Sites of *mean* area of 1.2 ha taken to be farmsteads; range 0.2–7 ha.
Boiotia (Bintliff 1997)	225 for domestic occupation (taken to be 56% of site) (=126 for total site area)	1 ha
Keos	150	2 ha
S. Argolid	250 in walled towns 125 outside walled towns	0.2 ha
Laconia	100 for villages (3.0 ha up) 50 for hamlets (0.4 ha up)	0.14 ha (0.15–0.39 ha = villa = 15 people)

Table 12.1 The variety of assumptions about town and farm in selected Greek surveys.

779 came from 217 families, giving a family size of 3.6 (to compare with the figure of five more or less universally assumed for antiquity). In a subsequent section, Catling examines site function, adding in data for the types of pottery found (tablewares, food preparation types, storage vessels, loomweights). Some seven small sites lack both storage vessels and food preparation vessels, even more (27) have food preparation vessels but lack storage vessels, while 11 have storage vessels but lack food preparation types; all have tablewares and in greater quantities than either food preparation wares or storage vessels. The demographic calculation assumes five people for each of these sites, regardless of this evidence for functional differentiation: Catling observes that storage is vital for survival at subsistence level, but may have been accomplished by vessels which do not survive to be identified in the archaeological record.

Volume 2 of the Laconia survey, which includes the Survey site catalogue (pp. 315–438), gives height above sea level, slope, area, sherd density (including a measure of continuity, which is explained in Volume 1).

ANALYSING SURVEYS: ASSUMPTIONS AND THEIR EFFECTS

Setting the data from these Greek surveys side-by-side reveals certain common assumptions and certain common items of information (Table 12.1). All the published surveys give at least some indication of site area, and the vast majority believe that small sites translate into family residences for which an average of five inhabitants should be supposed. Several surveys have played with calculating the population of larger sites from formulae for density that may be explicitly cross-culturally derived or calculated on the basis of local evidence. But against this general pattern of uniformity of approach there is, in fact, very wide variety in detail. How much difference does this make?

Even if we ignore the density per ha employed for Bronze Age Phylakopi (and the figure there is far from impossible – compare the figure of 1,205 persons per ha estimated by Postgate [1994; *cf.* Wilkinson 1999: 46] as the upper end of the range at Abu Salabikh in Iraq), the range of practice here is considerable. The more or less universal employment of densities from 100 to 250 persons per ha for villages and towns masks considerable variation

as to the lower size limit for towns and villages. Correspondingly, the repeated assumption that farms count as five persons masks variation by a factor of 15 in the upper size limit for such farms – again even ignoring Melos (where I may have read the account unsympathetically).

In illustration, if I re-run the Laconia calculations on the original Keos assumptions, and allow 150 persons per ha for the one Classical village site larger than 2 ha, then I generate a village population of 450 (against Catling's 300), but I reduce the rest of the rural population from his 925 to 220. Settlements below the level of the village now account for approximately one-third of the population, compared with two-thirds in Catling's calculation. What is more, the total population of the countryside is virtually halved. Similarly, if I re-run the data from Classical Keos (as reworked and augmented by Whitelaw 2000) on Catling's assumptions, then there are 18 certain or probable sites of 0.4 ha or above and less than 3 ha (amounting to 510 persons); 24 certain or probable sites of 0.15 to 0.39 ha (amounting to 360 people); and 15 sites of 0.15 ha or less, yielding 75 people. Total population of the Classical countryside leaps from *Landscape Archaeology*'s 200 to 945. If we keep to the total population estimates for the *polis* derived from texts, the effect of this is more or less to depopulate the town of Koressos – down to perhaps 300 people. Alternatively, if we keep even the *village* population density that Catling suggests and apply it even to the 6–8 ha of Koressos which Cherry *et al.* (1991: 278) suggest was densely occupied, then we have an urban population of 600–800 and a total population of between 1,545 and 1,745 (with consequences for our confidence in deductions from texts).

There are various points to be made here. The first is the degree of uncertainty among survey archaeologists as to what the sorts of small scatter that they most commonly find amount to. The Keos Survey was content to imagine that a single family residence might create a scatter as large as 1 ha, a figure used also in Boiotia, and they even contemplate it perhaps creating one as large as 2 ha (*cf.* Cherry *et al.* 1991: 336). From the Melos survey publication, it is apparently thought possible that even larger scatters might be from a single family. By contrast, a site 1 ha in area is translated by the Argolid survey into 125 people, and by the Laconia survey into 50 people. If the sceptical historian asked to credit the archaeological evidence is alerted to the fact that archaeologists cannot

Survey	Period	>10 ha	5–10 ha	2–4.9 ha	1–1.9 ha	0.5–0.9 ha	0.2–0.4 ha	<0.2 ha
Keos	A		?	0	0	8	23	11
	C	1	0	0	0	10	29	18
	HL	1	0	0	1	3	19	11
S. Argolid	A	0	4	2	1	2	3	27
	C	1	1	2	3	1	2	44
	C/HL	2	1	1	5	3	0	98
Methana	A	0	2	0	1	1	1	5
	C/HL	–	2	1	2	3	5	9
Laconia	A/Early C	–	1	1	1	3	13	68
	C	–	1	1	2	3	10	29

Table 12.2 Distribution of site sizes for selected Greek surveys (A = Archaic; C = Classical; HL = Hellenistic; data for Keos from Whitelaw 1998 and 2000).

agree as to whether a scatter of sherds equates to 5 residents or 125 residents, it is hard to believe that she or he will ever open a survey publication again.

The second point to be made is that early survey publications, by their tendency to work on the basis that anything that was not a village was a single farm, have encouraged the belief that it is the number/density of spots on the map that is the most important key to understanding rural settlement and exploitation. But from the point of view of possible demographic consequences, site size is vital. Discussions of the distribution of site size across various surveys has generally taken place in discussions of survey technique, with a more or less self-congratulatory emphasis by the proponents of very intensive survey on their ability to find a high proportion of tiny sites (*cf.* Cherry *et al.* 1991: 18–20, fig. 2.3). The differential distribution of site sizes across more or less equally intensive surveys has rarely been signalled as of any historical interest. But the more confident we become – and Todd Whitelaw's reassessment of the Keian data, together with Richard Catling's recently published work, suggests that people are becoming more confident – that size of scatter equates reasonably closely to number of possible residents, then the size of the sites represented by dots on the map becomes a crucial variable.

Table 12.2 presents the Classical (and, for the southern Argolid, late Classical) site-size distribution for those cases where evidence is readily to hand. If we are not seeing here simply the different ways in which different surveys determined site boundaries, and that is certainly a real issue, then we have some distinctly different patterns. The Classical/Hellenistic Argolid emerges as a place where what is volatile over time is (only) the very small site, and where the number of very small sites in the Classical period differs from the number of larger sites by a very great factor. By contrast on Methana, although small sites are more numerous than any other single size-category, this is only by a factor of less than two, and the increase in site numbers with decreasing site size is in the Classical period relatively smooth and gentle. Although Lakonia is the survey whose pattern most closely approaches that of the Argolid, its site-size distribution is not in fact very similar,

since it has a substantial number of not-quite-so-small sites. Keos offers a different pattern again, with the smallest sites significantly outnumbered by the not-so-small sites.

Historical geographers have thought a lot about the significance of the size distribution of towns, in particular with regard to the rank-size rule. Jan de Vries' classic and eye-opening *European Urbanisation 1500–1800* (de Vries 1984) shows just how much can be done. For antiquity, there are all sorts of problems about doing a parallel exercise for towns: not only do we not have population figures for individual towns, but there is nothing that can act as a proxy for population (walled area, the most promising candidate, being notoriously loosely connected to population). There is in fact much more reason to think that our proxy data are good at the bottom end of the size range, and yet no-one has taken much interest in the distribution of numbers and sizes of small sites. For progress to be made in the historical interpretation of survey data, however, it is to these small sites that attention must be devoted. What is the social significance of these rather different patterns? How can we explain why, if that is what we are indeed seeing, in some areas of Greece individual families set up on their own, whereas in others they more normally operate in clusters? The sorts of crude manipulation involving decisions to reside in town or in country, in which some of us indulged in the first flush of enthusiasm for survey's results (*cf.* Osborne 1987), need to become very much more subtle: not all decisions to reside in the countryside meant the same thing.

It is not hard to see from these data why it is in the Argolid and Laconia that the survey archaeologists have been keen to see anything larger than 0.15 or 0.2 ha as constituting something more substantial than the 'family farm'. Equally, it is apparent why assumptions about the relationship between site size and numbers of inhabitants for the size range 0.2–0.9 ha are of trivial impact for the southern Argolid, but have drastic effects on the interpretation of the Keian data. The point which I made in reviewing *A Greek Countryside* (Osborne 1996b) – that the demographic impact of the sites recorded in the countryside was, on the surveyors' own assumptions, minimal – is absolutely dependent on the tiny size of the vast majority of the sites in question, with so little between the village and the putative 'family farm'. The story for Keos is, as we have already seen, quite different – or at least might be, depending on the assumptions about the relationship between area of scatter and numbers of ancient residents that we care to apply. I note that although the Pylos project (Davis *et al.* 1997), for example, has directed some attention to sites as small as 0.23 ha, that attention has not been able to determine whether or not the site in question was a permanent residence (and perhaps could hardly be expected to do so). Some of us will continue to wonder whether what the southern Argolid survey found in such profusion were not farms but seasonal shelters, a mark not of changes of residence but of intensity of land-exploitation (*cf.* also Acheson 1997).

It is not inevitable, of course, that size of scatter relates to numbers of residents in the same way in every area. It is more than conceivable that local practices for the location of yards in relation to buildings, or for how middens relate to residences, may result in the same number of residents producing smaller or larger scatters of artefacts. It may therefore be entirely appropriate that different surveys employ different assumptions both as to the threshold for the 'family farm' and as to the numbers of people per ha to assume for larger sites. But if different assumptions are to be made in different areas, the differences clearly need to be argued for: if we cannot currently distinguish yard and midden material from domestic assemblages, then clearly we urgently need to do more work on those questions.

BACK TO THE HISTORIAN'S QUESTIONS

I return in conclusion to the considerations with which I began. What sort of absolute population levels and what sort of a pattern of population change does survey give us good reason to believe in?

This paper should only have made clearer what is familiar enough, but still admitted only with reluctance: that survey itself offers no way in to absolute population levels. Survey data yield figures for numbers of inhabitants only when we apply a series of assumptions derived from non-survey, and frequently from non-archaeological, evidence. Survey itself cannot even show that the assumption that 'family farms' were on average the residences of five people is justified. The density figures for larger settlements are at best derived from local excavation evidence (via further hypotheses which are not themselves testable on the basis of archaeological material); more normally, they come from cross-cultural data whose comparability is not explored.

What I have tried to make more visible than others have previously done is that even in the case of the demographic relationship between different settlements in the same survey area, or more crudely between 'town' and 'country',

the story that we tell hangs to a very large extent upon the assumptions that are imported in order to turn areas of unusually dense sherd material into a number of residents. Figures are adopted with little argument and on the basis of assumptions (*e.g.* that hamlets were less densely packed than villages, and villages less so than towns) for which no archaeological support is enlisted (or locally available). Changing the assumptions about the density of occupation of any class of site, or about the size thresholds for the class, can transform our picture both of the absolute number of people involved and of the relationship between town and country, village and farm. All this is quite apart from the purely archaeological problems of interpreting what one has got (or missed) in the first place, which others have well discussed (*cf.* Sbonias 1999a: 2–8).

When we turn to patterns of population change, some of the same difficulties continue to arise. In as far as different periods see different classes of site more or less prominent in the survey record, interpretation of change over time is going to be crucially affected by the assumptions made about site size and population density. But two positive points should be clear.

First, short of contentions that ancient towns were garden cities with very low population densities indeed, or conversely that sites in the countryside were extremely densely packed with human residents, no survey in the Greek world that has included or considered town as well as countryside has been able to suggest that changes in the countryside have anything but the most trivial demographic implications by comparison to changes in the town. The idea that the number of sites in the countryside is a good proxy for population, and that what survey is counting when it counts dots on maps is the population at one remove, is simply untenable: changes in the occupation of towns are what will have much more significant demographic impact.

Second, nothing that survey has uncovered offers any serious threat to the contention that population grew only very slowly. Wherever we look, if we are prepared to smooth out the sharp changes produce by grouping material crudely into periods that are rarely shorter than 200 years, then we can accommodate practically all change within a population growth figure of 0.5% per annum. Such greater fluctuations as there were, and it is rather unlikely that there were none, do not currently emerge from the quality of data that we have. In demographic terms, the findings of intensive survey are almost uniformly undramatic. The more than doubling of the number of small sites in the southern Argolid survey area between the Classical and the late Classical periods is a dramatic event, and it remains dramatic even if those small sites are non-residential; but neither the causes nor the consequences are likely to be demographic. As a general proxy for degree of agricultural intensity, there is still good reason to think that the number of small sites is important and useful; but although agricultural intensity and demographic pressure are unlikely to be unrelated, greater agricultural intensity certainly does not necessarily imply demographic change (it might, for instance, mark external food resources becoming unavailable).

As John Chapman (1999: 66) has observed, population is central to what remain survey's basic questions of site numbers, relations and functions. Unless survey gives up any pretensions to tell us something about historical societies, it is hard to see that that will change. But looking at the major intensive surveys of Classical Greece side-by-side, it is striking how limited the archaeological work has been that has been concerned with providing evidence for the basic demographic reconstructions without which the collections of sherds remain collections of sherds. The questions of permanent or temporary residence at small sites, which have been prominent on the agenda (though often generating heat rather than light), are actually demographically trivial. Survey archaeologists need to focus upon site hierarchy and the density of human occupation which it is reasonable to ascribe to the not-quite-so-small sites. And historians need to contemplate, as they have not yet done, what they are to make of the very different site hierarchies that are emerging in different areas.

REFERENCES

Acheson, P. (1997) Does the economic explanation work? Settlement, agriculture and erosion in the territory of Halieis in the late Classical–early Hellenistic period. *Journal of Mediterranean Archaeology* 10: 165–90.

Bintliff, J. L. (1997) Further considerations on the population of ancient Boeotia. In J. L. Bintliff (ed.) *Recent Developments in the History and Archaeology of Central Greece. Proceedings of the 6th International Boeotian Conference* (*BAR International Series* 666): 231–52. Oxford, British Archaeological Reports..

Bintliff, J. L. and Snodgrass, A. M. (1985) The Cambridge/Bradford Boeotia Expedition: the first four years. *Journal of Field Archaeology* 12: 123–61.

Bintliff, J. L. and Sbonias, K. (eds.) (1999) *Reconstructing Past Population Trends in Mediterranean Europe (3000 BC – AD 1800)* (*The Archaeology of Mediterranean Landscapes* 1). Oxford, Oxbow Books.

Bintliff, J. L. and Sbonias, K. (2000) Demographic and ceramic analysis in regional survey. In R. Francovich, H. Patterson and G. Barker (eds.) *Extracting Meaning from Ploughsoil Assemblages* (*The Archaeology of Mediterranean Landscapes* 5): 244–58. Oxford, Oxbow Books.

Catling, R. W. V. (2002) The survey area from the Early Iron Age to the Classical period (*c.* 1050 – *c.* 300 B.C.). In W. G. Cavanagh, J. Crouwel, R. W. V. Catling and G. Shipley, *Continuity and Change in a Greek Rural Landscape: The Laconia Survey* Vol. 1. London, British School at Athens.

Cavanagh, W. G., Crouwel, J., Catling, R. and Shipley, G. (1996) *Continuity and Change in a Greek Rural Landscape: The Laconia Survey* Vol. 2. London, British School at Athens.

Cavanagh, W. G., Crouwel, J., Catling, R. and Shipley, G. (2002) *Continuity and Change in a Greek Rural Landscape: The Laconia Survey* Vol. 1. London, British School at Athens.

Chapman, J. (1999) Archaeological proxy-data for demographic recnstructions: facts, factoids or fiction? In J. L. Bintliff and K. Sbonias (eds.) *Reconstructing Past Population Trends in Mediterranean Europe (3000 BC – AD 1800)* (*The Archaeology of Mediterranean Landscapes* 1): 65–76. Oxford, Oxbow Books.

Cherry, J.F. (1982) Appendix A: Register of archaeological sites on Melos. In C. Renfrew and M. Wagstaff (eds.) *An Island Polity: The Archaeology of Exploitation in Melos*: 291–309. Cambridge: Cambridge University Press.

Cherry, J., Davis, J., and Mantzourani, E. (1991) *Landscape Archaeology as Long-term History: Northern Keos in the Cycladic Islands.* Los Angeles, UCLA Institute of Archaeology.

Davis, J. L., Alcock, S. E., Bennet, J., Lolos, Y. G. and Shelmerdine, C.W. (1997) The Pylos Regional Archaeological Project. Part I: Overview and the archaeological survey. *Hesperia* 66: 391–494.

de Vries, J. (1984) *European Urbanisation 1500–1800*. Cambridge, Mass., Harvard University Press.

Francovich, R., Patterson, H. and Barker, G. (eds.) (2000) *Extracting Meaning from Ploughsoil Assemblages* (*The Archaeology of Mediterranean Landscapes* 5). Oxford, Oxbow Books.

Gamble, C. (1982) Animal husbandry, population and urbanisation. In C. Renfrew and M. Wagstaff (eds.) *An Island Polity: The Archaeology of Exploitation in Melos*: 161–71. Cambridge, Cambridge University Press.

Gomme, A. W. (1933) *The Population of Attica in the Fifth and Fourth Centuries BC.* Oxford, Clarendon Press.

Hansen, M. H. (1985) *Demography and Democracy: The Number of Athenian Citizens in the Fourth Century BC.* Herning, Systime.

Hansen, M. H. (1988) Athenian population losses 431–403 BC and the number of Athenian citizens in 431 BC. In M. H. Hansen, *Three Studies in Athenian Demography* (*Historisk-filosofiske meddelelser* 56). Copenhagen, Royal Danish Academy of Sciences and Letters.

Jameson, M., Runnels, C. and van Andel, Tj. (1994) *A Greek Countryside: The Southern Argolid from Prehistory to the Present Day.* Stanford, Stanford University Press.

Mee, C. and Forbes, H. (eds.) (1997) *A Rough and Rocky Place: The Landscape and Settlement History of the Methana Peninsula, Greece.* Liverpool, Liverpool University Press.

Morris, I. M. (1987) *Burial and Ancient Society: The Rise of the Greek City-state.* Cambridge, Cambridge University Press.

Osborne, R. (1987) *Classical Landscape with Figures: The Ancient Greek City and its Countryside.* London, George Philip.

Osborne, R. (1996a) *Greece in the Making, 1200–479 BC.* London, Routledge.

Osborne, R. (1996b) Survey and Greek society. *American Journal of Archaeology* 100: 165–69.

Patterson, C. (1981) *Pericles' Citizenship Law of 451–50 BC.* New York, Arno.

Postgate, N. (1994) How many Sumerians per hectare? Probing the anatomy of an early city. *Cambridge Archaeological Journal* 4: 47–65.

Renfrew, C. and Wagstaff, M. (eds.) (1982) *An Island Polity: The Archaeology of Exploitation in Melos.* Cambridge, Cambridge University Press.

Sallares, J. R. (1991) *The Ecology of the Ancient Greek World.* London, Duckworth.

Sbonias, K. (1999a) Introduction to issues of demography and survey. In J. L. Bintliff and K. Sbonias (eds.) *Reconstructing Past Population Trends in Mediterranean Europe (3000 BC – AD 1800)* (*The Archaeology of Mediterranean Landscapes* 1): 1–20. Oxford, Oxbow Books.

Sbonias, K. (1999b) Investigating the interface between regional survey, historical demography and paleodemography. In J. L. Bintliff and K. Sbonias (eds.) *Reconstructing Past Population Trends in Mediterranean Europe (3000 BC – AD 1800)* (*The Archaeology of Mediterranean Landscapes* 1): 219–34. Oxford, Oxbow Books.

Scheidel, W. (2003) The demographic background of the Greek expansion. *Journal of Hellenic Studies* 123 (forthcoming).

Snodgrass, A. M. (1977) *Archaeology and the Rise of the Greek State*. Cambridge, Cambridge University Press.

Snodgrass, A. M. (1980) *Archaic Greece: The Age of Experiment*. London, Dent.

Wagstaff, M. and Cherry, J. F. (1982a) Settlement and population change. In C. Renfrew and M. Wagstaff (eds*.) An Island Polity: The Archaeology of Exploitation in Melos*: 136–55. Cambridge, Cambridge University Press.

Wagstaff, M. and Cherry, J. F. (1982b) Settlement and resources. In C. Renfrew and M. Wagstaff (eds*.) An Island Polity: The Archaeology of Exploitation in Melos*: 246–63. Cambridge, Cambridge University Press.

Whitelaw, T. (1998) Colonisation and competition in the polis of Koressos: the development of settlement in north-west Keos from the Archaic to the Late Roman periods. In L.G. Mendoni and A. Mazarakis Ainian (eds.) *Kea-Kythnos: History and Archaeology*: 227–58. Athens: Research Centre for Greek and Roman Antiquity, National Hellenic Research Foundation.

Whitelaw, T. (2000) Reconstructing a classical landscape with figures: some interpretive explorations in North-West Keos. In R. Francovich and H. Patterson (eds.) *Extracting Meaning from Ploughsoil Assemblages* (*The Archaeology of Mediterranean Landscapes* 5): 227–43. Oxford, Oxbow Books.

Wilkinson T. (1999) Demographic trends from archaeological survey: case studies from the Levant and Near East. In J. L. Bintliff and K. Sbonias (eds.) *Reconstructing Past Population Trends in Mediterranean Europe (3000 BC – AD 1800)* (*The Archaeology of Mediterranean Landscapes* 1): 45–64. Oxford, Oxbow Books.

Wright, J. C., Cherry, J. F., Davis, J. L., Mantzourani, E., Sutton, S. B. and Sutton, R.F., Jr (1990) The Nemea Valley Archaeological Project: a preliminary report. *Hesperia* 59: 579–659.

13. Mapping the Roman World:
The Contribution of Field Survey Data

David Mattingly and Rob Witcher

INTRODUCTION

There has been much debate about the appropriate territorial unit of analysis in archaeological field survey (Francovich *et al.* 2000). Favoured solutions have included: an urban territory (*e.g.* Barker *et al.* 1993; Carreté *et al.* 1995); a bounded topographical feature, such as a river valley (*e.g.* Attolini *et al.* 1991; Barker 1995) or an island (*e.g.* Cherry *et al.* 1991; Renfrew and Wagstaff 1972); or a modern political or cartographic unit (*e.g.* Croft and Mynard 1993; Muzzioli 1980; RCHM 1980). The intensification of survey method since the great pioneer surveys of the 1950s and 1960s (MacDonald and Rapp 1972) has meant that the territorial focus of most surveyors today is a micro-region of tens or hundreds of sq. km (Barker 1991a; Bernardi 1992; Cherry 1983; Schofield 1990).

However, although the results achieved by such intensification are to be applauded, recent field survey is also open to the accusation that it has become obsessed with minutiae of the relation of people and landscape, sometimes failing to address the bigger picture of the regional settlement pattern (see the pertinent comments of Fentress 2000a). Part of the problem here is a lack of ambition in certain quarters, since the archaeological data now available in many regions should allow the sort of regional synthesis attempted by Alcock for Greece (Alcock 1993; 1997; *cf.* Mattingly 1997b; 1998; 1999; Stone 1997, for Africa). Indeed, the amount and quality of archaeological data on regional settlement patterns is widely acknowledged as having a major impact on the overall view of the ancient world (Horden and Purcell 2000, 176–77; Shaw 2001, 426–34).

The focus of this paper is a review of how data on rural settlement patterns are used in the cartographic representation of the ancient world. The current state of mapping of the ancient world will be assessed, starting with the *Barrington Atlas* (Talbert 2000a). We shall review the extent to which field survey (and air-photographic) data have fed into regional mapping projects of the Roman world. However, the main focus of the paper is the potential for even coarse-grained survey data now held (especially through the use of digital formats) to contribute to a radically different cartographic vision of the ancient world.

THE STATE OF THE ART?

The *Barrington Atlas* is a long-awaited and a much-needed tool in Classical Studies (Talbert 1992; 2000b). It has been rightly praised as 'comprehensive and comprehensible' within the parameters set by its editorial team (Alcock *et al.* 2001: 457). There is no doubting the exceptional quality of the map production or the rigour of the map research. This will be an enduring work of reference on the geography of the ancient world and its 'look' will shape our collective view of the Greco-Roman world for years to come. A particular feature of the way the maps treat the Roman provincial landscapes is the delineation of centuriated areas (visually stunning in the context of Provence or the Po Valley). The two-volume Map-by-Map Directory that accompanies the Atlas is an impressive gazetteer of ancient toponyms, modern equivalents, site phasing and relevant bibliography on every site. All its positive qualities make it a difficult work to criticise.

It is also immediately apparent, however, in turning the pages of the Atlas that the traditional image of Classical antiquity as a 'world of cities' has not been superseded here and that knowledge of rural settlement has been drastically under-represented. For example, there is little evidence of the settlement hierarchy of either the centuriated or the non-centuriated landscapes in the *Barrington Atlas*. As such, the resulting maps do not represent as great a leap forward in knowledge from the last great age of atlas-making in the late 19th century as one might expect. In particular, the results of regional surveys have been largely ignored (Alcock *et al.* 2001: 458–59). All of us involved in landscape archaeology cannot but be disappointed at the outcome, when the results of our labours have been so blatantly and publicly ignored. Considering the growing importance of survey in Classical archaeology through the late 20th century and the balance of fieldwork now existing between excavation and survey archaeology, the non-representation of the results of the latter area of research should actually be a cause of concern. How could this result have been avoided and how best could the barren landscapes of the *Barrington Atlas* have been populated? These are germane questions for landscape archaeologists to consider. In part, at least, the responsibility rests with survey archaeologists like ourselves who have not always been good at considering the bigger picture, into which their catalogue of, for example, 1 small town, 10 villas, 26 farmsteads, 10 possible habitations, 4 cemeteries, etc. needs to be fitted.

As a compiler of maps for the *Barrington Atlas* (Mattingly 2000a–e), the first-named author of this paper has an insider's view of the debate that went on during the early stages of the map commissioning and of the compromises that were thrashed out in the later stages to even out somewhat the differences of approach taken by individual compilers. In defence of the team of editors and compilers involved in the project, there are fundamental differences between the various regions of the ancient world, in the history of their archaeological investigation and in the specialist expertise and interests of the various compilers. It is clear that these differences rendered complete homogeneity of approach impossible.

One of the great lessons of this sort of map-making is to discover the extent of our ignorance of the ancient world. Yet many of the blank areas on the *Barrington Atlas* maps could have been populated, and the suspicion must remain that an opportunity has been missed for gaining a genuinely new vision of the ancient world. For certain categories of evidence (such as ancient toponyms and their archaeological correlates), the pool of evidence is now growing very slowly. Archaeological data on settlement patterns, however, are expanding exponentially through air-photography, field survey and professional archaeological activity in many countries. A key obstacle to dealing with the rural sites in the *Barrington Atlas* was the editorial stipulation that all sites mapped should normally have a name on the map and a gazetteer entry. There were also those involved in the project who argued vehemently for a policy of only mapping sites whose ancient name was known – a policy that would have limited the work almost entirely to towns, small towns, sanctuaries and road stations. These issues focused attention on the individual significance of every site, rather than the broader implications of the distribution of a particular class of site. Most compilers understandably shied away from sites for which the data available were slight or ambiguous. Yet even where we lack modern data, there are important indications to be had from earlier investigations. There are areas of North Africa, for instance, where the existence of sites of some size and complexity is known, but where there has been virtually no investigation beyond that carried out by French map-makers in the late 19th century (see Fentress 2000b: 483, on the

earlier detailed mapping work of Stephane Gsell). This raised the question of whether it was worse to have large blank areas on our maps (when we knew there were sites there) or to include sites about which the data were very incomplete. To avoid the issue and neglect rural settlement completely (as some contributors appear to have done) places the *Barrington Atlas* map for certain areas behind the corresponding sheet of the *Tabula Imperii Romani*, where that existed – something that seemed at odds with the overall aims of the new Atlas (compare Talbert 2000a: maps 69–70 showing Palestine, with the Israel sheet of the *Tabula Imperii Romani* [1993]). In the end, contributors negotiated their individual position with the editor and, although there were in theory standard rules governing the map-making process, the inconsistencies of approach are plainly visible when one compares a group of neighbouring maps.

As an example of this point, let us review some of the map sheets from North Africa. The territory of Caesarea (modern Algeria) was the subject of a pioneering survey by Phillipe Leveau (1984) that was important not least for the demonstration of the difference in settlement type between the core urban territory and the wider hinterland. The corresponding map in the *Barrington Atlas* contains very few rural sites – only the very largest villas and villages (sites of > 1 ha size), plus some enigmatic and apparently isolated tumuli (Potter 2000). The distinction between Caesarea and its hinterland, so clear in Leveau's publication, is completely lost. Other compilers have been more inclusive of rural sites, incorporating data from recent surveys as well as from French colonial surveys, though Fentress (2000b; 2000c) has focused on villages or nucleated settlements of > 1 ha area, whilst Hitchner (2000a; 2000b) has also included 'villas'. Hitchner's maps represent one of the fullest attempts to map rural settlement anywhere in the Atlas (but are still an oversimplification of the best of the data; *cf.* Dietz *et al.* 1996; Hitchner *et al.* 1990). In the sequence of maps extending from southern Tunisia to the western Egyptian desert, Mattingly attempted to depict wherever possible something of the overall pattern of sites by including a cross-section of rural settlement, including some sites of < 1 ha area, especially where they have been featured in the archaeological literature (Mattingly 2000a–e). Where more detailed studies exist, as in the Libyan predesert region, the compromises made for the *Barrington Atlas* map are clear from comparison with the more detailed maps (Barker *et al.* 1996a; 1996b). An important feature of this group of *Barrington Atlas* maps is the depiction of oasis sites and native sites beyond the Roman frontiers; in the past, many maps of the ancient world have resorted to large capital letters when dealing with the territory of non-Roman peoples and ignored the character of their settlement sites. On the other hand, it should be self-evident that the locations of communication networks and population centres beyond the frontiers of the empire have a real importance when considered alongside, for example, Roman military dispositions.

PROBLEMS WITH MAPPING RURAL
SETTLEMENT AT SMALL SCALES

There are obvious problems with representing rural settlements on small-scale maps. Provincial mapping tends to be at scales of between 1:500,000 and 1:1,000,000 and these do not allow inclusion of every minor rural site (consider the look of a modern road atlas). So selection of detail for inclusion is a natural consequence – though layered data in a modern GIS will in future allow digital maps at small scales to handle much larger quantities of data. For an example of what is possible, we could consider the mapping of settlement data for medieval England, where *c.* 11,000 sites from small hamlets to towns have been included on a map at a scale of 1:2,000,000, but with the same large dataset also explored at a variety of larger scales (Roberts and Wrathmell 2000: maps 3, 5, 13). There are, of course, problems of spatial discontinuities of the data on rural settlement. Contiguous areas of the landscape may appear to contain radically different densities and types of sites simply because one area has been subjected to intensive modern survey and the other has not. It can be argued that the patchiness of survey data is at best distracting and at worst seriously misleading. In this context, it is notable that in the most-cited example of comparative survey, Alcock's (1993) *Graecia Capta*, there are no maps of rural settlement density at a scale beyond that of the individual surveys (a similar cartographic tendency is present in Leveau *et al.* 1993). But a further problem concerns the extent to which selection is representative of the total settlement hierarchy or exclusive of settlements below a certain level. For the Roman world, provincial mapping is mostly pre-defined in terms of the most 'Romanised' sites and landscape features. An academic agenda that prioritises certain categories of site and ignores others will perpetuate such an approach for desk-based scholars, but will produce maps that do not match the perceptions of field archaeologists.

Dating is a further concern. All maps tend to be chronological fictions, conflating data from different phases of activity and creating an artificial image of the province that is 'true' for no one moment in time. However, the dating evidence of many rural sites tends to be weaker than for urban or military sites and, as a result, most rural settlement is likely to be weeded out by any test based on chronological diagnostics. These problems raise the issue of whether survey data are thus suitable for inclusion in province-wide maps of the ancient world? The answer to this question may be different depending on whether one looks back at traditional paper maps or thinks forward to future digital resources, linked to large databases with GIS functionality. But even with the traditional folded or atlas map, it is arguable that we have not exploited the full explanatory power of the available evidence of rural settlement.

To illustrate this point, let us consider Roman Britain, one of the most thoroughly mapped provincial areas of the empire. The Barrington maps (Esmonde Cleary 2000a–

b) are supplemented by the *Tabula Imperii Romani* sheets (1983/1987) and the Ordnance Survey (OS) map, now in its fifth edition (Ordnance Survey 1924; 1927; 1956; 1978; 1994; 2001). There is also an entire Atlas dedicated to Britain and a series of detailed studies of rural settlement (Jones and Mattingly 1990; *cf.* Dark and Dark 1997; Hingley 1989). Yet close scrutiny of the available map coverage highlights the problems of integrating data from fieldwalking and air-photographic survey within a framework that is explicitly selective and subjective. Esmonde Cleary (2001) comments on the 5th revision of the OS map:

> All the main categories of Romanised site are depicted. Strict site selection criteria have been used: accurate location and a high degree of certainty over interpretation of the site were required... The small rural settlements of the native British population that never achieved a high degree of Romanisation, but which underpinned the economy of the whole province are not shown... Although as complete as possible, the features depicted on this map are not exhaustive and are shown subject to the limitations imposed by the scale of the mapping [1:625,000].

This seems reasonable at first sight (and one must have sympathy for the editorial committee responsible for the selection from a very large and rich British database); but the academic priorities have produced a map of Roman Britain, rather than Britain in the Roman empire (and these two things are not the same at all). The desire to avoid clutter on the map is understandable, but in the case of the 5th edition OS map of Roman Britain the omission of some Roman-period data was in itself necessitated by the decision to superimpose the selected features onto a topographic base, showing thousands of largely irrelevant modern roads, towns and villages across the length and breadth of the country.

The main categories of site mapped on the OS map have remained fairly consistent since the early editions (though nomenclature has changed slightly, the underlying criteria for selection have remained Romano-centric): major towns, defended small towns ('settlement, defended'), a selection of other nucleated settlements (essentially those along the major roads of the province), spa towns, villas, other substantial rural buildings, temples, legionary fortresses, forts, fortlets, signal stations, temporary camps, frontier works, roads, milestones, lighthouses, aqueducts, artificial watercourses, mineral extraction sites, salt-making sites, pottery/tile production sites, barrows or mausolea (but not other cemeteries), major hoards. It is worth considering what is not mapped: a large number of substantial villages/hamlets (especially those away from the main road network), distinctive regional settlement types – such as fortified major settlements in the north and west of Britain (for instance, the rounds of Cornwall, nucleated defended sites in Wales, brochs and duns in Scotland). Even the largest native sites are excluded as settlement sites, however: to take one notable example, the hillfort of Traprain Law in Scotland is marked, but not named, as the location of a major hoard. There is thus a clear 'Roman' bias in the selection of what to map – what we see are primarily the features of government and domination, and that part of elite society that was most closely aligned with the imperial power. The policy is both elitist and 'racist' in that we map one branch of society down to milestones and isolated hoards, while ignoring even the major settlements of another significant branch. An alternative vision of Britain in the Roman period would be one that brought out more detail of the regional variability in settlement morphology and gave greater consideration to the less Romanised sections of the landscape than is conventionally done.

Just as the selection of typological categories is a subjective choice on the part of the compiler, the sub-sampling within categories to determine which sites to include on the map is also a source of potential bias. For example, 'villa' is a very broad category, covering a wide range of sites from palatial country retreats (Woodchester, Fishborne) to small cottage-like farms of 'Romanised' appearance (Dark and Dark 1997: 43–75). The division of known sites between the 'villa' and 'other substantial building' categories will inevitably be easier for areas where more extensive excavation has been carried out. The small town/undefended settlement category is another type where much responsibility for inclusion or exclusion rests with the compiler. Not since the OS 2nd edition has the category 'village' been used, though the potential importance of widespread small nucleated centres in Britain is once more becoming increasingly recognised (Dark and Dark 1997; Hingley 1989; 1997). This issue clearly intersects with the question of whether or not to map native settlements in the less Romanised parts of the province.

'Stray finds' have traditionally appeared on the OS map of Roman Britain, though one suspects that the data behind the distribution were increasingly outmoded. In the most recent edition (Ordnance Survey 2001), they have been removed from southern Britain and only retained for Scotland. The decision is a curious one, since many of these finds in fact designate sites occupied in the Roman period, but of non-Roman type. The reasons for privileging such information from Scotland over, say, Wales or Cornwall are unclear. And what of parts of the lowland landscape where there are no villas, such as the Fenland? (This is left blank on Ordnance Survey 2001, though a small map incorporated in the text of the border does show a detail of the dynamic settlement evidence from here; for a new study of the Fenland landscapes, see Fincham 2001.)

Air-photography has had a far more dramatic impact in British archaeology (*e.g.* Wilson 1982), than is the case for the Mediterranean countries, but its value is all the greater when combined with field survey results (for instance, Bewley [1994] shows the combined impact of air-photography and field survey on the landscapes of the

northern frontier region). A major study of rural settlement of Iron Age and Roman date in England has recently been undertaken by Jeremy Taylor on behalf of English Heritage, combining the results of local/regional Sites and Monuments Records, archaeological surveys and air-photographic records into a huge GIS database (currently with over 70,000 sites in it). The quality of the data may be variable, but the sheer quantity of information and its geographical coverage creates dramatic new possibilities for analysing settlement at the provincial level. It is on this foundation that future studies of the rural geography of Roman Britain will be built.

OTHER APPROACHES TO MAPPING THE ROMAN WORLD

A key cartographic issue is scale. Conventional paper mapping demands that a decision be made about a single scale of presentation. This will always be a compromise between detail and the physical size of the map. This decision automatically excludes a certain amount of data – such as the small and densely distributed rural sites of antiquity. In contrast, one of the most significant aspects of new digital map technology is that a single data set can be analysed at a variety of different scales; it also permits much greater flexibility to mix and match data of different scales. In other words, zooming-in may allow us to see data and spatial relationships more clearly, but can also allow us to view a different range of larger-scale data. For example, a site may be represented as a dot at 1:25,000, an area at 1:10,000 and a scatter of individual artefacts at 1:2,000. In general, archaeologists have endeavoured to increase the accuracy and precision with which evidence is mapped, aided by such developments as GPS (Global Positioning Systems). In particular, this has attempted to move away from the use of points to represent sites and instead to record them as areas. In trying to map macro-regional patterns, therefore, we need to think of similarly innovative ways to present data at smaller scales. For example, we need to look at alternatives to maps of sites each represented by an individual dot or symbol (see below for an example). Zooming-in, we could then switch to more detailed and appropriate mapping of individual sites. This regional approach may, in fact, be well suited to the types of data with which we are dealing. Surface data are notoriously ephemeral ('coming on and off like traffic lights') and at a small scale of mapping it can be argued that individual sites are less significant than the overall impression of settlement density or forms. Comparative geography provides good examples of what can be achieved in terms of mapping at small scales. Rather than try to represent every known site on a map, one solution is to convert what we know of settlement density into conventional shadings. Bekker-Nielsen (1989) produced an interesting series of maps of northwestern Europe based on the density of urban centres of Roman date (see also

Jongman 1988: fig. 2, for urbanism in Italy), and the same approach perhaps merits extension to other classes of rural site. On the other hand, maps can bear an amazing amount of detail (a common experience of many contributors to the *Barrington Atlas* was surprise at seeing how their densely-packed overlay sheets translated into printed maps with ample space between sites, captions, etc.). As mentioned above, Roberts and Wrathmell (2000) have shown what is possible with rural settlement data for medieval England and the results are compelling evidence that maps can be produced that contain many thousands of settlement sites (though, of course, it is easier to read the detail when these are reproduced at larger scales). Another of the key characteristics of cartography is that it presents (or creates) definitive versions of geographical phenomena (see Wood 1993). Further, the reader of a map makes implicit assumptions about the evenness of spatial and thematic coverage. In contrast, however, much rural survey data is unstable and derives from erratic spatial coverage. Indeed, without care, GIS and database architecture may gloss over much of this ambiguity and uncertainty (Miller and Richards 1995). However, this need not be the case, and it will be argued here that GIS provides the type of flexible environment in which to emphasise and understand this inherent fuzziness.

Problems of data compatibility can be divided into spatial, chronological and interpretative issues. At a macro-regional scale, the spatial distribution of survey data is extremely uneven: some areas are much better studied than others (*e.g.* in Italy, areas close to Rome and along the coastal plains have been surveyed much more intensively). The chronological distribution of sites is also highly variable – in part, this relates to differences in dates of conquest by Rome. More significant (though not unrelated) is considerable variation in ceramic typologies and chronological diagnosticity. Finally, the criteria for the definition and interpretation of sites (*e.g.* farm or villa) may vary significantly. Arguably, we have hardly begun to use the potential of (digital) cartography to express these kinds of uncertainty, doubt, bias and unevenness.

One approach to is to develop a series of 'filters' or weights designed to correct for these problems. These can – but do not have to – be quantitative; they could simply use GIS to help us identify and visualise biases and errors. GIS may also provide a flexible means of inferring the evidence of small well-studied or re-surveyed areas across wider regions (see papers in Gillings *et al.* 1999; Lock and Stančič 1995; for examples of both visual and quantitative approaches, see below). Here, it is worth stating that we can never create a bias-free picture of past settlement; but GIS techniques can allow us to recognise where such discrepancies might be, and to comprehend their significance.

The potential of integrated, multi-scale GIS is not easily demonstrated in the format of a paper or electronic document. Apart from issues of scale, the use of colour and so on, this relates to the 'fixed' nature of these maps.

The surveyor decides what is included and excluded and in what format, restricting the reader's understanding of the data to a particular perspective. User-defined maps that allow individuals to construct 'maps-to-order' have much to recommend them – permitting others to question existing theories and present alternatives (for a growing archive of online/down-loadable data, see Archaeology Data Service 1996–2003). However, it is worth commenting that this is not an argument for simply putting all survey data on the Internet and letting the user get on with it. It is still vital for surveyors to take responsibility for the explanation and interpretation of their results – no amount of metadata can be a substitute for first-hand experience of a survey (for fully integrated digital publications and archives, see *Internet Archaeology*, *e.g.* Perkins 1998). Regional mapping might also make use of other techniques for visualising data. For example, the shifting location and density of settlement might be well served through phase-by-phase animation (for a different example of animation in the visualisation of archaeological data, see Exon *et al.* 2000).

A CASE STUDY FROM ROMAN ITALY

There is a long tradition of topographical and landscape studies in Italy (see Cambi and Terrenato 1994). Over time, the focus of this research has shifted and the techniques improved; in Etruria, for example, attention was long directed towards rock-cut tombs and in the *suburbium* of Rome towards aqueducts, roads and monumental villas. The South Etruria survey of the 1950s and 1960s helped to shift attention towards artefact scatters identifying an unimagined wealth of small, densely distributed farms (Potter 1979). Over the last 25 years in particular there has been a vast amount of field survey by both Italian and foreign scholars (see papers in Barker and Lloyd 1991). One of the key themes to develop from this work is the diversity of Italian regional landscapes (Terrenato 2001: 2–3). The potential of these data for a comparative study was noted 20 years ago (Celluzza and Regoli 1982; Cherry 1983: 383–89) and has been an implicit theme in much subsequent work (*e.g.* Patterson 1987: 134–38; Sbonias 1999: 15–16). However, despite the wealth of evidence and the awareness of its potential to illustrate significant patterning, attempts at comparing and mapping at a macro-regional scale have been limited.

The *Barrington Atlas* divides Italy into 8 sheets (plus Sicily and Sardinia), with a strong emphasis on towns, roads and centuriation. Such features clearly comprise an important part of the landscape of Roman Italy. In many ways, however, they imitate an official, Romano-centric perspective. Still more problematical is that the enormous density – and diversity – of rural settlement brought to light over the last 50 years is nowhere apparent. For example, field survey has demonstrated the *suburbium* of Rome to have been one of the most densely occupied

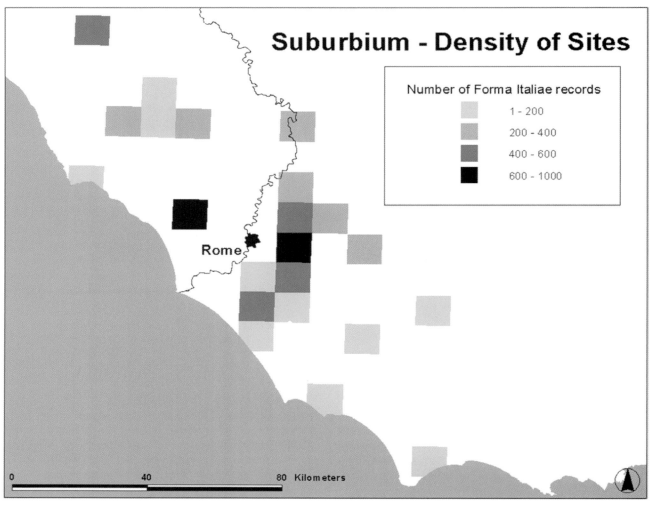

Figure 13.1 Forma Italiae: *density of settlement in the Roman* suburbium.

areas of Italy (and the Mediterranean), producing a sub-stantial part of the metropolis' near insatiable demand for food and other supplies (Morley 1996); yet, even in the 1:150,000 detailed coverage (Talbert 2000a: Map 43, *cf.* also Map 44), its countryside is almost as sparsely occu-pied as the rest of the peninsula.

As discussed above, this situation is partly an issue of scale; the density of settlement is such that it would require an impossibly large scale to show each individual site. GIS clearly has a role to play in this context. However, there is a range of methodological considerations, which are more difficult to resolve. These include variation in the intensity of coverage and significant differences in the archaeological definition of site types (Lloyd 1991). Other problems are more 'structural': for example, differing levels of archaeological knowledge of ceramic typologies and unsuitable survey conditions across wide areas such as alluvial river valleys (*e.g.* the Po valley) and wooded and/or mountainous regions.

Some of the problems of comparative survey can be addressed through the re-study of material collected by earlier surveys and through the use of targeted re-survey.

For example, the British School at Rome's Tiber Valley Project is currently re-studying *c.*100,000 artefacts col-lected during the South Etruria Survey; for the first time, this will provide a sound basis for identifying similarities and differences within the middle Tiber valley (*c.* 2000 sq. km, Patterson and Millett 1998; Patterson *et al.* 2000). The project is also using targeted re-survey to clarify the results of earlier projects (*e.g.* Di Giuseppe *et al.* 2002), as is the 'Pathways to Complexity Project' of the Uni-versities of Amsterdam and Groningen which is comparing the Pontino, Sibaritide and Salento regions (Attema and van Leusen, Ch. 7, this volume; Attema *et al.* 1998; http:/ /odin.let.rug.nl/RPC/).

This section presents some preliminary attempts to map the results of Italian survey at a macro-regional scale emphasising the similarities and differences in regional settlement. An important starting point for any landscape and settlement study of Italy is the *Forma Italiae* series. This comprises a series of surveys usually covering a single *Istituto Geografico Militare* mapsheet (*c.* 10 x 10 km); there is a particular concentration in the Roman *suburbium*. Figure 13.1 shows the total number of archaeological

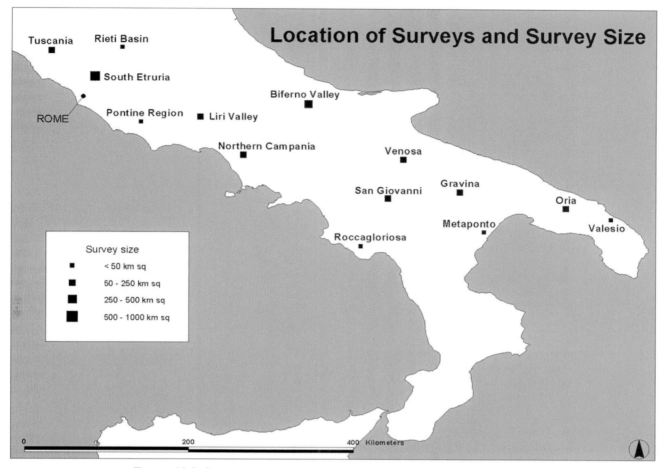

Figure 13.2 Surveys in Central and Southern Italy mentioned in the text.

findspots identified by the *Forma Italiae* volumes in the immediate vicinity of Rome. The shading represents the number of records, though as most of these surveys cover roughly the same area (*c.* 100 sq. km), the map can be read in terms of density.

This map quickly reveals some significant differences in the density of archaeological findspots around Rome. The highest densities are closest to Rome with some fall-off with distance; however, in the area immediately south of the city, there is a rather mixed picture. One important consideration in using these particular surveys is the date at which they were completed. Not least, a notable increase in the number of surface scatters identified in the most recent volumes suggests that techniques have become more intensive; without changes in agricultural practice, the easily eroded tufa landscape of much of this area might lead us to expect a long-term reduction, not increase, in the number of such sites. One approach to this variation of survey intensity could be to map ratios of standing structures to surface scatters or of large to small scatters. However, all of these measures must be treated with caution – ultimately, they are not independent of the genuine patterns of variation in the data that we seek.

It is clear that there is some diversity in settlement

patterns within the *suburbium*; but this is still a comparatively small region. Is it possible to map this diversity at a still smaller scale? Figure 13.2 shows the location of 14 surveys from Central and Southern Italy. The surveys used here are, from north to south: Tuscania (Barker *et al.* 1993; Rasmussen 1991); Rieti Basin (Coccia and Mattingly 1992; 1995); South Etruria (Patterson *et al.* 2000; Potter 1979); Pontine region (Attema 1993; Attema *et al.* 1998); Liri Valley (Hayes and Martini 1994); Biferno Valley (Barker 1991b; Barker 1995); Northern Campania (Arthur 1991); Venosa (Marchi and Sabbatini 1996); San Giovanni (Roberto and Small 1994, 19–23); Gravina (Basilicata and Apulia, Small 1991); Roccagloriosa (western Lucania, Gualtieri and de Polignac 1991); Metaponto (Carter 1990); Oria (Yntema 1993); Valesio (Boersma *et al.* 1991).

Figure 13.3 shows the distribution of Early Imperial settlement identified by these 14 surveys. At this scale, it is neither possible to show every site, nor is the precise location of each individual site of significance – it is the overall impression that is of importance. The map therefore simulates the surveys' results: each dot represents three actual sites and the distribution of dots within each area is random.

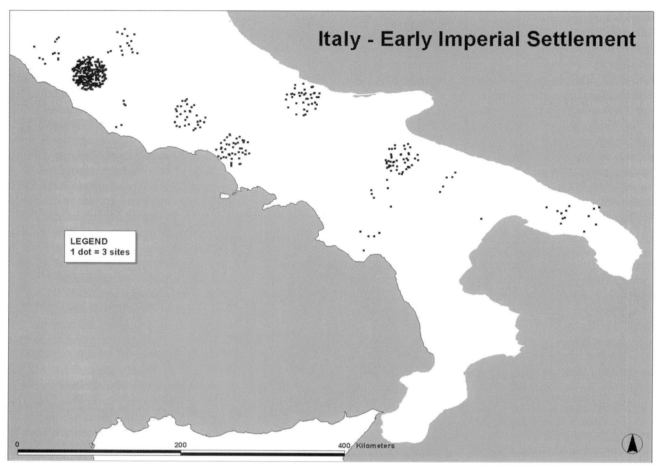

Figure 13.3 Numbers of Early Imperial period settlements in Central and Southern Italy.

The dense distribution of sites identified by the South Etruria survey contrasts sharply with other areas; the thin settlement of southern Italy is also notable (Figure 13.3). As with the map of *Forma Italiae* surveys, however, it is important to add some context to this distribution, in order to tease genuine variation in the archaeological record from methodological considerations. These figures relate to the actual number of Early Imperial sites located; but there are significant differences in the areas covered by these surveys (from 22 to *c*. 1000 sq. km). It is therefore necessary to map the densities instead of the numbers of Early Imperial settlement in order to facilitate comparison. As we have already seen, this can be done with shading. However, we can also continue to use dots and therefore make use of a familiar cartographic convention. In this case, each dot is the equivalent of 0.1 site per sq. km; the total number of dots for each survey represents the overall density of settlement. Hence, two dots indicate a density of 0.2 sites per sq. km; ten dots is the equivalent of 1 site per sq. km (Figure 13.4).

Settlement density in South Etruria now no longer stands out as anomalous, being equalled by the Rieti, Venosa, Valesio and Northern Campania surveys. The Biferno valley, on the other hand, now appears much more

like Southern Italy than previously. Broadly, there is a greater density of Early Imperial settlement closer to Rome. However, as with the *Forma Italiae* surveys, there is further variation in survey methodology which needs to be taken into consideration. Perhaps the most important of these is survey intensity, since it has been repeatedly demonstrated that the greater the intensity of survey techniques, the more sites it is possible to identify (Cherry 1983: fig. 1; Schiffer 1987). This can be measured in various ways, for example, the number of person-days per sq. km or the spacing of walkers. Few surveys, however, have published a full range of methodological details with which to attempt widespread systematic mapping of these measures (see Mattingly 2000f; Witcher 1999). As an alternative approach, these surveys have been classified into three classes of intensity: medium, high and very high (some of the earlier *Forma Italiae* would be classified as low) (Figure 13.5). This is a simplistic measure based upon assessment of a range of methodological information such as survey objectives, person-days, techniques for dealing with visibility, and so on. This information can be displayed alongside settlement densities in order to help visualise and assess patterning in the data.

Combining the settlement density plots with a visual

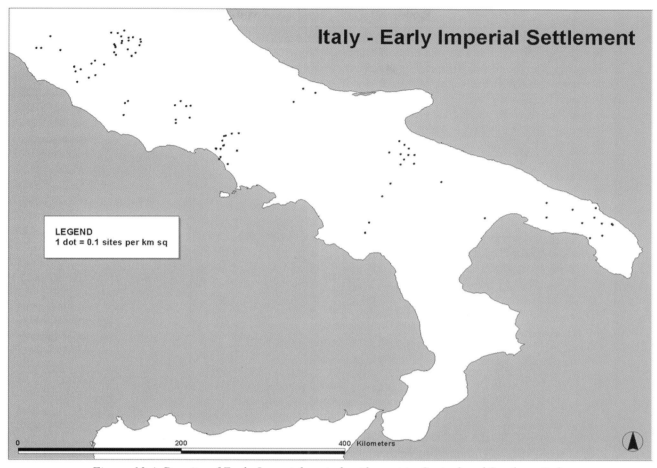

Figure 13.4 Density of Early Imperial period settlement in Central and Southern Italy.

representation of survey intensity provides useful contextual information with which to identify possible biases and assess patterning in the data. It now becomes clear that the high density of settlement at Rieti and Valesio, for example, coincides with particularly intensive surveys. The low densities recorded by surveys in southern Italy is also notable: where survey techniques in this area have been intensified (Venosa, Oria and especially Valesio), settlement numbers are notably higher, though never quite as high as the levels identified in Central West Italy. However, not all the patterns can be explained by survey intensity. For example, despite the high intensity of survey coverage at Tuscania, Early Imperial site density is still comparatively low, indicating a genuine contrast with the neighbouring South Etruria survey area. The density of settlement in Northern Campania is also extremely high despite the relatively low intensity of coverage, again indicating a genuine density of sites.

It should by now be clear that at a macro-regional scale, methodological issues are as likely to exercise influence on patterning as genuine variation in the distribution of Roman settlement. Valid comparisons, therefore, clearly requires some estimation of bias so that we can compensate for such differences.

As a preliminary experiment in weighting survey results for varying survey intensity, the densities from the medium category were doubled and those from the high category increased by 50% to make them comparable with the very high category (Figure 13.6). Clearly these multipliers are arbitrary: firstly, they are likely to vary region by region, depending on the nature of past settlement and the archaeological record; and secondly, they are likely to affect different periods to varying degrees, again depending on the nature of settlement (*e.g.* dispersed, nucleated, etc.). Nonetheless, GIS provides a flexible space in which to quickly and easily explore such multiple alternative scenarios. In fact, these particular multipliers may be quite conservative – there is good evidence that higher survey intensity can significantly increase site numbers (*e.g.* a resurvey of the *Forma Italiae* of the Cures Sabini region near Rome identified three times the number of mid-Republican sites: Di Giuseppe *et al*. 2002; Muzzioli 1980).

The resulting map shows calculated Early Imperial settlement density, evening out some of the gross biases caused by survey methodology. Patterns to note include a general rise in settlement density in Southern Italy, though it is still lower than that found in Central West Italy. In contrast to Figure 13.3, Northern Campania now stands

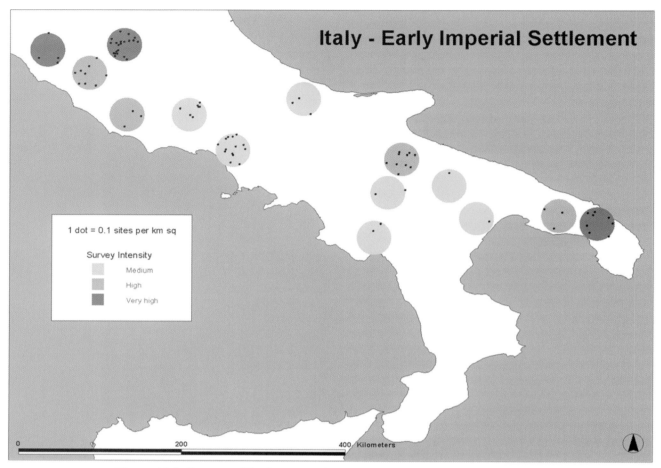

Figure 13.5 Density of Early Imperial period settlement, with survey intensity.

out as an area of particularly dense settlement, as does another area of colonisation, around Venosa. Tuscania and the Pontine Region demonstrate comparatively low settlement density in comparison to nearby areas in the vicinity of Rome such as South Etruria and Rieti. The density of settlement in the latter area is still noticeably (though not implausibly) high.

This distribution of rural settlement is supplemented through an indication of urban density, these data being derived from a simple count of contemporary urban centres mapped in the *Barrington Atlas*, taking into account all significant population centres, including road stations. (It is worth pointing out that collecting the basic data for this simple measure would have been a major task without the Atlas!) The results are displayed through shading, which illustrates marked contrasts in the distribution and density of urban and nucleated settlement in Early Imperial Italy. Read together with the rural settlement evidence, we can begin to identify general patterns and associations. Broadly, though not exclusively, areas of high urbanisation also demonstrate dense rural settlement (Campania, Etruria, Lazio); in contrast, areas of limited urbanisation have much lower densities of dispersed rural settlement (*e.g.* Basilicata, Northern Puglia). At a basic level, this is what we

might expect – urban centres require a certain surplus from their hinterlands in order to fund urban munificence and support non-producing populations, and so on. At a wider scale, the correspondence of these high urban and rural densities with Rome's immediate hinterland also points to the strong influence of the City's economic demand, as well as the means of marketing this surplus (*cf.* Morley 1996). Dynamic versions of such mapping could help to clarify many aspects of the development and transformation of settlement and economy. Other patterns which might merit more attention include the rather mixed picture from the Salento peninsula (Southern Puglia). More generally, the key to the settlement patterns of Southern Italy might lie in between our arbitrary distinction of urban and rural – the *vicus* is a category of settlement which is comparatively rare in the historical sources (and the *Barrington Atlas*), although widely identified by surveys in the area as sites of a few hectares (*e.g.* Small 1991). Although not fully urban in the generally-accepted sense, they undoubtedly served as not only population, but also economic, centres and continued a long history of nucleated settlement in this area. Such observations demonstrate the importance of integrating some form of settlement hierarchy into our new small-scale maps.

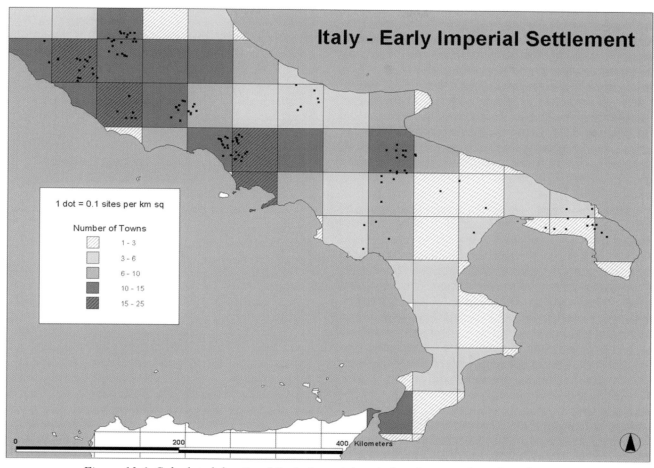

Figure 13.6 Calculated density of Early Imperial period settlement, plus urban densities.

Clearly, this is a very coarse approach that needs to be refined. Nonetheless, it demonstrates a series of potential approaches to visualising and assessing macro-regional settlement patterns. Improvement of survey character-isation could include recent agricultural histories and proximity to modern towns. Such reconstruction of the history of research in a region can provide valuable insights into the structure of archaeological datasets: for example, Rajala *et al.* (1999) identified changing relationships between survey objectives and intensity and the distri-bution of sites of all periods in relation to Roman roads. The discontinuous nature of survey coverage is also evident; again, GIS may be able to address this issue through the interpolation of settlement evidence to cover less well-studied areas (see Kuna 2000).

Beyond methodological considerations, the attention of comparative survey must also shift towards the inter-pretative significance of settlement distributions. As already mentioned, the definition of villas is perhaps one of the most discussed issues with regards (Italian) survey; unsurprisingly, therefore, no-one has yet produced a detailed map of Roman villas across Central and Southern Italy. Yet such a map would be invaluable in the debate about their spatial distribution, origins and social and

economic functions. Again, we need not restrict ourselves to plotting specific site types. We should also think about producing maps which show ratios of different settlement types (*e.g.* the ratio of villas to other rural settlements) which may help to visualise variation in settlement hier-archy at a macro-regional scale, or maps of average length of site occupation to assess settlement continuity or instability.

To summarise, the potential of a comparative study of Italian surveys remains largely undeveloped since first being raised 20 years ago. Perhaps this is partly due to an initial over-optimism towards the data previously available; however, over the last 20 years, the quantity and quality of data has grown rapidly. Just as importantly, the widespread adoption of GIS has provided a vital tool with which to help facilitate such comparison. As well as developing techniques to understand how datasets can be integrated (such as re-survey, re-study of material, and setting out basic standards for methodology and publication), it is also important to develop innovative ways of mapping these data to exploit their potential for understanding macro-scale patterning across the Italian peninsula and beyond.

CONCLUSIONS

It is critical that archaeologists highlight more clearly than has been achieved to date the differences between sub-regions of the Roman world. Most current mapping tends to exaggerate the degree of similarity between and within provinces, because of the academic agendas that lie behind the inclusion or exclusion of data. The emphasis on similarity is partly a result of academic interest in certain key features (towns, military installations, villas, etc.), and partly to do with the small scale of mapping. These features are often well-known both archaeologically and historically. The omission of perceived non-Roman settlement types and the mapping of Roman material culture in 'native' areas (as 'stray finds', whilst excluding 'native' material culture) perpetuates an implicit idea of Romans and Others which no longer enjoys wider theoretical currency. Once we shift our attention to rural settlement, issues of data compatibility become more significant. The sites and scatters that we wish to map are known through quite different circumstances: they must be actively sought on the ground, not through the written sources. In contrast to the basically similar patterns of features presented by the *Barrington Atlas*, mapping of rural settlement will often demonstrate quite dramatic diversity relating both to methodological considerations and historical differences. Such bias is often not quantifiable; it cannot, however, be ignored and GIS presents one medium through which such unevenness might be tackled.

One of the effective requirements of mapping at a macro-regional scale is that we may need to adjust the way we present our data. It may be less important to plot each individual settlement and to focus instead on the wider picture through a range of simplified and indicative shading and symbols. At no stage does this preclude high-resolution mapping of survey – but rather should complement it, as a means of visualising these extraordinary quantities of data. The type of mapping work described above is dependent upon a degree of consistency in the collection and publication of survey data that has not yet materialised. Survey archaeologists therefore need to plan ahead for how to integrate their data into the bigger picture of the ancient world – to move from the local to the macro-scale inter-regional picture. Without prescribing specific methodological practices, it should still be possible to improve the compatibility of our data. Publication of methods ('metadata') as well as results is one key desideratum. Once we begin to comprehend the significance of these metadata for understanding individual surveys we can move on to compare between surveys. There are currently no accepted techniques for either visualising or attempting to correct survey data at the scales discussed here. However, as techniques to represent these biases develop and data are collected with which to address them, new cartographic models will undoubtedly emerge and facilitate more inclusive approaches to mapping the Roman world.

REFERENCES

Special abbreviation: *Barrington Atlas* = R. J. A. Talbert (ed.) (2000a) *Barrington Atlas of the Greek and Roman World*. Princeton, Princeton University Press.

Alcock, S. E. (1993) *Graecia Capta: The Landscapes of Roman Greece*. Cambridge, Cambridge University Press.
Alcock, S. E. (1997) Greece: a landscape of resistance? In D. J. Mattingly (ed.) *Dialogues in Roman Imperialism: Power, Discourse and Discrepant Experience in the Roman Empire*. Journal of Roman Archaeology, Supplementary Vol. 23: 103–115. Portsmouth, RI, Journal of Roman Archaeology.
Alcock, S. E., Dey, H. and Parker, G. (2001) Sitting down with the Barrington Atlas. *Journal of Roman Archaeology* 14: 454–61.
Archaeology Data Service (1996–2003) http://www.ads.ahds.ac.uk.
Arthur, P. A. J. (1991) *The Romans in Northern Campania: Settlement and Land Use around the Massico and the Garigliano Basin*. Archaeological Monograph of the British School at Rome 1. London, British School at Rome.
Attema, P. A. J. (1993) *An Archaeological Survey in the Pontine Region 1: Text*. Groningen, University of Groningen.
Attema, P. A. J., Burgers, G.-J., Kleibrink, M. and Yntema, D. G. (1998) Case studies in indigenous developments in early Italian centralization and urbanization, a Dutch perspective. *European Journal of Archaeology* 1(3): 326–81.
Attolini, I., Cambi, F., Castagna, M., Celuzza, M., Fentress, E. W. B. and Perkins, P. (1991) Political geography and productive geography between the valleys of the Albegna and the Fiora in northern Etruria. In G. W. Barker and J. Lloyd (eds.) *Roman Landscapes: Archaeological Survey in the Mediterranean Region*. BSR Archaeological Monograph 2: 142–52. London, British School at Rome.
Barker, G. W. (1991a) Approaches to archaeological survey. In G. W. Barker and J. Lloyd (eds.) *Roman Landscapes: Archaeological Survey in the Mediterranean Region*. BSR Archaeological Monograph 2: 1–9. London, British School at Rome.
Barker, G. W. (1991b) Two Italy's, one valley: an *Annaliste* perspective. In J. L. Bintliff (ed.) *The Annales School and Archaeology*: 34–56. London, Leicester University Press.
Barker, G. W. (ed.) (1995) *A Mediterranean Valley: Landscape, Archaeology and* Annales *History in the Biferno Valley*. 2 vols. London, Leicester University Press.
Barker, G. W. and Lloyd, J. (eds). (1991) *Roman Landscapes. Archaeological Survey in the Mediterranean Region*. BSR Archaeological Monograph 2. London, British School at Rome.
Barker, G. W., Grant, A. and Rasmussen, T. (1993) Approaches to the Etruscan landscape: the development of the Tuscania survey. In P. Bogucki (ed.) *Case Studies in European Prehistory*: 229–57. Boca Raton, CRC Press.
Barker, G. W., Gilbertson, D. D., Jones, G. D. B. and Mattingly, D. J. (1996a) *Farming the Desert: The UNESCO Libyan Valleys Archaeological Survey. Vol. 1, Synthesis*. Paris and London, UNESCO and Society for Libyan Studies.
Barker, G. W., Gilbertson, D. D., Jones, G. D. B. and Mattingly, D. J. (1996b) *Farming the Desert: The UNESCO Libyan Valleys Archaeological Survey. Vol. 2, Gazetteer and Pottery*. Paris and London, UNESCO and Society for Libyan Studies.
Bekker-Nielsen, T. (1989) *The Geography of Power: Studies in the Urbanisation of Roman North-West Europe*. British Archaeological Reports S 477. Oxford, British Archaeological Reports.
Bernardi, M. (1992) *Archeologia del Paesaggio*. Florence, All'Insegna di Giglio.
Bewley, R. (1994) *Prehistoric and Romano-British Settlement in the Solway Plain, Cumbria*. Oxford, Oxbow Books.
Boersma, J. S., Burgers, G.-J. and Yntema, D. G. (1991) The Valesio

Project: final interim report (campaign of 1990). *Bulletin Antieke Beschaving* 66: 115–32.

Cambi, F. and Terrenato, N. (1994) *Introduzione all'archeologia dei paesaggi.* Rome, La Nuova Italia Scientifica.

Carreté, J.-M., Keay, S. and Millett, M. (1995) *A Roman Provincial Capital and its Hinterland: The Survey of the Territory of Tarragona, Spain, 1985-90. Journal of Roman Archaeology*, Supplementary Vol. 15. Portsmouth, RI, Journal of Roman Archaeology.

Carter, J. C. (1990) Metapontum – land, wealth and population. In J.-P. Descoeudres (ed.) *Greek Colonists and Native Populations. Proceedings of the First Classical Australian Congress of Classical Archaeology, Held in Honour of A. D. Trendall*: 405–441. Canberra and Oxford, Humanities Research Board and Clarendon Press.

Celluza, M. G. and Regoli, E. (1982) La Valle d'Oro del territorio di Cosa. Ager Cosanus e ager Veientanus a confronto. *Dialoghi di Archeologia* 4: 31–62.

Cherry, J. F. (1983) Frogs around the pond: perspectives on current archaeological survey in the Mediterranean region. In D. R. Keller and D. W. Rupp (eds.) *Archaeological Survey in the Mediterranean Area.* BAR International Series 155: 375–416. Oxford, British Archaeological Reports.

Cherry, J. F., Davis, J. L. and Mantzourani, E. (1991) *Landscape Archaeology as Long-term History: Northern Keos in the Cycladic Islands.* Los Angeles, UCLA Institute of Archaeology.

Coccia, S. and Mattingly, D. J. (1992) Settlement history, environment and human exploitation of an intermontane basin in the Central Apennines: the Rieti Survey, 1988–1991. Part 1. *Papers of the British School at Rome* 60: 213–89.

Coccia, S. and Mattingly, D. J. (1995) Settlement history, environment and human exploitation of an intermontane basin in the Central Apennines: the Rieti Survey, 1988–1991. Part 2. Land-use patterns and gazetteer. *Papers of the British School at Rome* 63: 105–158.

Croft, R. A. and Mynard, D. C. (1993) *The Changing Landscape of Milton Keynes.* Aylesbury, Buckinghamshire Archaeological Society.

Dark, K. and Dark, P. (1997) *The Landscape of Roman Britain.* Gloucester, Sutton.

Di Giuseppe, H., Sansoni, M., Williams, J. and Witcher, R. (2002) The *Sabinensis Ager* revisited: a field survey in the Sabina Tiberina. *Papers of the British School at Rome* 70: 99–150.

Dietz, S., Ladjimi Sebaï, L. and Habib, B. (1996) *Africa Pro-consularis: Regional Studies in the Segermes Valley in Northern Tunesia.* 2 vols. Copenhagen, Carlsberg Foundation.

Esmonde Cleary, S. (2000a) Britannia Superior. In *Barrington Atlas*: map 8 and Map-by-Map Directory p. 111–26.

Esmonde Cleary, S. (2000b) Britannia Inferior. In *Barrington Atlas*: map 9 and Map-by-Map Directory p. 127–35.

Esmonde Cleary, S. (2001) Text accompanying Ordnance Survey, *Map of Roman Britain.* Fifth edition. Southampton, Ordnance Survey.

Exon, S., Gaffney, V., Woodward, A. and Yorston, R. (2000) *Stonehenge Landscapes. Journeys Through Real and Imagined Worlds.* (CD ROM). Oxford, Archaeopress.

Fentress, E. W. B. (2000a) What are we counting for? In R. Francovich, H. Patterson and G. Barker (eds.) (2000) *Extracting Meaning from Ploughsoil Assemblages.* Archaeology of Mediterranean Landscapes 5: 44–52. Oxford, Oxbow Books.

Fentress, E. W. B. (2000b) Cirta. In *Barrington Atlas*: map 31 and Map-by-Map Directory p. 483–92.

Fentress, E. W. B. (2000c) Numidia. In *Barrington Atlas*: map 34 and Map-by-Map Directory p. 520–28.

Fincham, G. (2001) *Landscapes of Imperialism: Roman and Native Interaction in the East Anglian Fenlands.* Unpublished Ph.D. thesis, University of Leicester.

Francovich, R. and Patterson, H. (eds.) (2000) *Extracting Meaning from Ploughsoil Assemblages.* Archaeology of Mediterranean Landscapes 5. Oxford, Oxbow Books.

Gillings, M., Mattingly, D. J. and van Dalen, J. (eds.) (1999) *Geographical Information Systems and Landscape Archaeology.* Archaeology of Mediterranean Landscapes 3. Oxford, Oxbow Books.

Gualtieri, M. and de Polignac, F. (1991) A rural landscape in Western Lucania. In G. W. Barker and J. Lloyd (eds.) *Roman Landscapes: Archaeological Survey in the Mediterranean Region.* BSR Archaeological Monograph 2: 194–203. London, British School at Rome.

Hayes, J. W. and Martini, I. P. (eds.) (1994) *Archaeological Survey in the Lower Liri Valley, Central Italy.* BAR International Series 595. Oxford, British Archaeological Reports/Tempus Reparatum.

Hingley, R. (1989) *Rural Settlement in Roman Britain.* London, Seaby.

Hingley, R. (1997) Resistance and domination: social change in Roman Britain. In D. J. Mattingly (ed.) *Dialogues in Roman Imperialism: Power, Discourse and Discrepant Experience in the Roman Empire. Journal of Roman Archaeology*, Supplementary Vol. 23: 81–100. Portsmouth, RI, Journal of Roman Archaeology.

Hitchner, R. B. (2000a) Carthago. In *Barrington Atlas*: map 32 and Map-by-Map Directory p. 493–509.

Hitchner, R. B. (2000b) Theveste-Hadrumetum. In *Barrington Atlas*: map 33 and Map-by-Map Directory p. 510–19.

Hitchner, R. B. (1990) The Kasserine archaeological survey 1987. *Antiquités africaines* 26: 231–60.

Horden, P. and Purcell, N. (2000) *The Corrupting Sea: A Study of Mediterranean History.* Oxford, Blackwell.

Internet Archaeology. http://intarch.ac.uk.

Jameson, M. H., Runnels, C. and van Andel, T. (1994) *The Southern Argolid: A Greek Countryside from Prehistory to the Present.* Stanford, Stanford University Press.

Jones, B. and Mattingly, D. J. (1990) *An Atlas of Roman Britain.* Oxford and New York, Blackwell (reprinted 2002, Oxford, Oxbow Books).

Jongman, W. (1988) *The Economy and Society of Pompeii.* Amsterdam, Gieben.

Kuna, M. (2000) Session 3 discussion: Comments on archaeological prediction. In G. Lock (ed.) *Beyond the Map. Archaeology and Spatial Technologies*: 180–86. Amsterdam, IOS Press.

Leveau, P. (1984) *Caesarea de Mauretanie. Une ville romaine et ses campagnes.* Rome, Ecole Française.

Leveau, P., Sillières, P. and Vallat, J.-P. (1993) *Campagnes de la Méditerranée romaine.* Paris, Hachette.

Lloyd, J. (1991) Forms of rural settlement in the early Roman Empire. In G. W. Barker and J. Lloyd (eds.) *Roman Landscapes: Archaeological Survey in the Mediterranean Region.* BSR Archaeological Monograph 2: 233–40. London, British School at Rome.

Lock, G. and Stančič, Z. (eds). (1995) *Archaeology and Geographic Information Systems: A European Perspective.* London, Taylor and Francis.

MacDonald, W. and Rapp, G. R. (1972) *The Minnesota Messenia Expedition: Reconstructing a Bronze Age Regional Environment.* Minneapolis, University of Minnesota Press.

Marchi, M. L. and Sabbatini, G. (1996) *Venusia. Forma Italiae* 37. Florence, La Sapienza, Università di Roma and Olschki.

Mattingly, D. J. (ed.) (1997a) *Dialogues in Roman Imperialism: Power, Discourse and Discrepant Experience in the Roman Empire. Journal of Roman Archaeology*, Supplementary Vol. 23. Portsmouth, RI, Journal of Roman Archaeology.

Mattingly, D. J. (1997b) Imperialism and territory: Africa, a landscape of opportunity? In D. J. Mattingly (ed.) *Dialogues in*

Roman Imperialism: Power, Discourse and Discrepant Experience in the Roman Empire. Journal of Roman Archaeology, Supplementary Vol. 23: 115–38. Portsmouth, RI, Journal of Roman Archaeology.

Mattingly, D. J. (1998) Landscapes of imperialism in Roman Tripolitania. *L'Africa romana* 12: 163–79.

Mattingly, D. J. (1999) Mapping the ancient world: Libyan problems and perspectives. In B. Amendolea (ed.), *Carta archeologica e pianificazione territoriale: un problema politico e metodologico*: 258–63. Rome, Fratelli Palombi Editori.

Mattingly, D. J. (2000a) Tripolitana. In *Barrington Atlas*: map 35 and Map-by-Map Directory p. 529–44.

Mattingly, D. J. (2000b) Garama. In *Barrington Atlas*: map 36 and Map-by-Map Directory p. 545–51.

Mattingly, D. J. (2000c) Syrtica. In *Barrington Atlas*: map 37 and Map-by-Map Directory p. 552–57.

Mattingly, D. J. (2000d) Cyrene. In *Barrington Atlas*: map 38 and Map-by-Map Directory p. 558–69.

Mattingly, D. J. (2000e) Ammon. In *Barrington Atlas*: map 73 and Map-by-Map Directory p. 1108–16.

Mattingly, D. J. (2000f) Methods of collection, recording and quantification. In R. Francovich, H. Patterson and G. Barker (eds.) *Extracting Meaning from Ploughsoil Assemblages*. Archaeology of Mediterranean Landscapes 5: 5–15. Oxford, Oxbow Books.

Miller, P. and Richards, J. (1995) The good, the bad, and the downright misleading: archaeological adoption of computer visualisation. In J. Huggett and N. Ryan (eds.) *Computer Applications and Quantitative Methods in Archaeology – CAA 94*: 19–22. Oxford, British Archaeological Reports.

Morley, N. (1996) *Metropolis and Hinterland: The City of Rome and the Italian Economy 200 BC – AD 200*. Cambridge, Cambridge University Press.

Muzzioli, M. P. (1980) *Cures Sabini. Forma Italiae, Regio 4,* Vol. 2. Florence, Olschki.

Ordnance Survey (1924) *Map of Roman Britain*. 1st edition. Southampton, Ordnance Survey.

Ordnance Survey (1928) *Map of Roman Britain*. 2nd edition. Southampton, Ordnance Survey.

Ordnance Survey (1956) *Map of Roman Britain*. 3rd edition. Southampton, Ordnance Survey.

Ordnance Survey (1978) *Map of Roman Britain*. 4th edition. Southampton, Ordnance Survey.

Ordnance Survey (1994) *Map of Roman Britain*. Revised 4th edition. Southampton, Ordnance Survey.

Ordnance Survey (2001) *Map of Roman Britain*. 5th edition. Southampton, Ordnance Survey

Patterson, H. and Millett, M. (1998) The Tiber Valley Project. *Papers of the British School at Rome* 66: 1–20.

Patterson, H., Di Gennaro, F., Di Giuseppe, H., Fontana, S., Gaffney, V., Harrison, A., Keay, S. J., Millett, M., Rendeli, M., Roberts, P., Stoddart, S. and Witcher, R. (2000) The Tiber Valley Project: the Tiber and Rome through two millennia. *Antiquity* 74 (284): 395–403.

Patterson, J. R. (1987) Crisis: what crisis? Rural change and urban development in Imperial Appennine Italy. *Papers of the British School at Rome* 55: 115–46.

Perkins, P. (1998) Etruscan Pottery from the Albegna Valley/Ager Cosanus Survey. *Internet Archaeology* 4 [http://intarch.ac.uk/journal/issue4/perkins_index.html].

Potter, T. W. (1979) *The Changing Landscape of South Etruria*. London, Elek.

Potter, T. W. (2000) Iol Caesarea. In *Barrington Atlas*: map 30 and Map-by-Map Directory p. 475–82.

Rajala, U., Harrison, A. and Stoddart, S. K. F. (eds.) (1999) *The Enhancement of the South Etruria Survey: GIS in the Study of the Research History of the Southern Faliscan Area*. BAR International Series 750. Oxford, British Archaeological Reports.

Rasmussen, T. (1991) Tuscania and its territory. In G. W. Barker and J. Lloyd (eds.) *Roman Landscapes: Archaeological Survey in the Mediterranean Region*. BSR Archaeological Monograph 2: 106–114. London, British School at Rome.

RCHM (1980) *Northamptonshire: An Archaeological Atlas*. London, HMSO.

Renfrew, C. and Wagstaff, M. (eds.) (1982) *An Island Polity. The Archaeology of Exploitation in Melos*. Cambridge, Cambridge University Press.

Roberto, C. and Small, A. M. (1994) The field survey. In A. Small, and R. J. Buck (eds.) *The Excavations of San Giovanni di Ruoti 1. The Villas and their Environment*: 19–23. Toronto, University of Toronto Press.

Roberts, B. K. and Wrathmell, S. (2000) *An Atlas of Rural Settlement in England*. London, English Heritage.

Sbonias, K. (1999) Introduction of issues in demography and survey. In J. Bintliff and K. Sbonias (eds.) *Reconstructing Past Population Trends in Mediterranean Europe (3000 BC–AD 1800)*. Archaeology of Mediterranean Landscapes 1: 1–20. Oxford, Oxbow Books.

Schiffer, M. B. (1987) *Formation Processes of the Archaeological Record*. Albuquerque, University of New Mexico Press.

Schofield, J. (1990) *Interpreting Artefact Scatters*. Oxford, Oxbow Books.

Shaw, B. D. (2001) Challenging Braudel: a new vision of the Mediterranean. *Journal of Roman Archaeology* 14: 419–53.

Small, A. M. (1991) Late Roman rural settlement in Basilicata and Western Apulia. In G. W. Barker and J. Lloyd (eds.) *Roman Landscapes: Archaeological Survey in the Mediterranean Region*. BSR Archaeological Monograph 2: 204–222. London, British School at Rome.

Stone, D. L. (1997) *The Development of an Imperial Territory: Romans, Africans and the Transformation of the Rural Landscape of Tunisia*. Unpublished Ph.D. thesis, University of Michigan.

Tabula Imperii Romani (1983) *Condate-Glevum-Londinium-Lutetia*. London, British Academy.

Tabula Imperii Romani (1987) *Britannia Septentrionalis*. London, British Academy.

Tabula Imperii Romani (1993) *Iudaea-Palestinae*. Jerusalem, Israel Academy of Sciences.

Talbert, R. J. A. (1992) Mapping the classical world: major atlases and map series 1872–1990. *Journal of Roman Archaeology* 5: 5–38.

Talbert, R. J. A. (ed.) (2000a) *Barrington Atlas of the Greek and Roman World*. Princeton, Princeton University Press.

Talbert, R. J. A. (2000b) Introduction and Guidelines for Reference. In *Barrington Atlas*: xix–xxviii.

Terrenato, N. (2001) Introduction. In S. Keay and N. Terrenato (eds.) *Italy and the West: Comparative Issues in Romanization*: 1–6. Oxford, Oxbow Books.

Wilson, D. R. (1982) *Air Photographic Interpretation for Archaeologists*. London, Batsford.

Witcher, R. (1999) *Modelling Roman Imperialism: Landscape and Settlement in Italy*. Unpublished Ph.D. thesis, University of Leicester.

Wood, D. (1993) *The Power of Maps*. London, Routledge.

Yntema, D. G. (1993) *In Search of an Ancient Countryside: The Amsterdam Free University Field Survey at Oria, Province of Brindisi, South Italy (1981–1983)*. Amsterdam, Thesis Publishers.

WIDER PERSPECTIVES

14. From Nucleation to Dispersal: Trends in Settlement Pattern in the Northern Fertile Crescent

T. J. Wilkinson, Jason Ur and Jesse Casana

INTRODUCTION

When compared with Mediterranean surveys, most surveys conducted in the Near East seem extensive, inaccurate and idiosyncratic. Interestingly, however, some of the problems raised by these apparently coarse-grained surveys raise issues of wider relevance, especially to the development of early states and empires. Here we discuss how some recent surveys conducted in Upper Mesopotamia and the Levant contribute to an understanding of a major structural transformation of settlement that occurred in the Near East between the Early Bronze Age and the Roman period. This transition in settlement represents a shift from nucleated tell-based settlement in the Early Bronze Age to a more dispersed pattern of frequently small settlements in the Iron Age and Roman-Byzantine periods. Sometimes this shift took place progressively over the entire second millennium BC, while in some cases this phase of dispersal and settlement extension had not manifested itself fully until the Roman period.

At face value, this shift in settlement structure appears to represent a change from one very basic form of political organization – the 'city-state' or chiefdom (itself a contentious issue!) – toward a settlement pattern that developed in association with large territorial empires. If such a relationship can be demonstrated, it has significant implications for the understanding of historical trends in the Near East, as well as processes that took place further to the west in the Mediterranean region. In order to tackle this problem, it is necessary to compare evidence from archaeological surveys conducted over a large geographical area, as well as to make certain that there is some degree of comparability of evidence. These factors are essential because over the last few years it has become clear that the rather coarse techniques of traditional surveys in the Near East are, in fact, quite successful at recording the settlement of certain periods. Nevertheless they prove to be hopelessly inadequate for other periods.

First we compare Near Eastern surveys with those conducted in the Mediterranean basin; second, changes in settlement structure and density are described for several surveys conducted from northwest Iraq to the Medi-terranean; and third, changes in settlement structure are related to changes in the social structure, potential land-holding strategies and the political economy of the regions in question.

COMPARISONS WITH MEDITERRANEAN SURVEYS

In order to draw a comparison with surveys conducted in the Mediterranean, it is most appropriate to employ the 'Cherry Chart' (Cherry 1983), with modifications. Interestingly, this shows that surveys in, for example, the plains of upper Mesopotamia (including more recent surveys with off-site control) have a stubborn tendency to remain in a fairly 'extensive' category compared with Mediterranean surveys. When the number of sites is plotted according to the size of the survey area, Near Eastern surveys recover between 1 site per 10 sq. km and 1 site per sq. km (Figure 14.1). In other words, they show a higher rate of recovery than 'earlier Greek surveys' (*i.e.* those before the 1970s), but are well below those conducted between, say, 1970 and the early 1980s, and certainly much less than the surveys of the 1990s. Even when occupation periods (*i.e.* on multi-period sites) are plotted per survey area, the number of occupations per sq. km still does not attain that of most intensive Mediterranean surveys (Figure 14.1: 4a, 5a and 8a). This suggests immediately that Near Eastern surveys continue to be somewhat antiquated in terms of techniques of site recognition and recovery.

Alternatively, however, these statistics may represent a *real* difference between the pattern of settlement in the Near East and the Mediterranean, and surveys in the Upper Mesopotamian plains could imply that site densities were, in fact, significantly lower than in the Mediterranean. That this is the case is suggested by some surveys conducted in arid areas along the desert margins. These yield higher 'site' densities than occur in sub-humid regions. This unexpected disparity can be explained in the following ways:

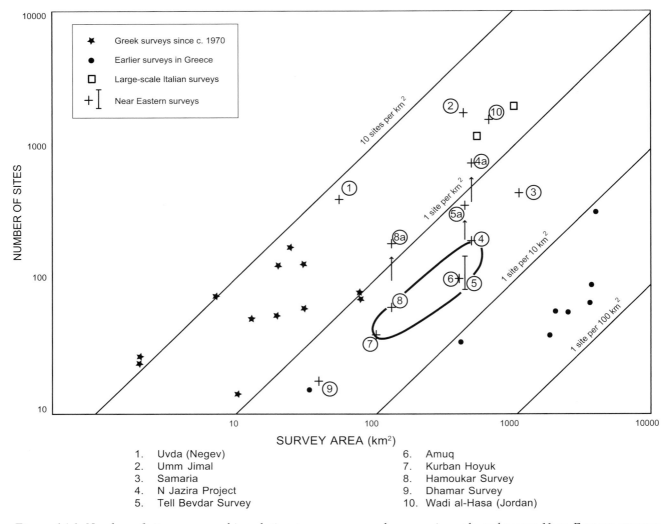

Figure 14.1 Number of sites recovered in relation to area surveyed, comparing selected recent Near Eastern surveys with those conducted in Greece and Italy before and since the 1970s (after Cherry 1983: fig. 1). Note that 4a, 5a and 8a refer to occupation periods per survey area, not sites (see text).

- We are not comparing like with like, because very different settlement traces are being compared.
- Landscape 'taphonomy' results in very different levels of site preservation in sub-humid versus arid areas (as discussed below).
- Markedly different processes of site formation are in operation (*e.g.* agro-pastoral communities; temporary nomadic settlements; cultic features in the desert margins versus long-term sedentary settlement in the sub-humid to semi-arid plains).

THE SIGNIFICANCE OF LANDSCAPE TRANSFORMATIONS

Statistics on site density demonstrate that the total number of sites in an area will vary according to how an archaeological site is defined. A fundamental issue here is that in the desert fringes the concept of 'site' becomes less useful

and the often subtle traces of individual structures or activity areas can hardly be accorded the same weight (in terms of population or archaeological significance) as the much larger and frequently multi-period sites found in more humid areas of the Near East.

In addition, processes of landscape transformation, both physical and cultural, are crucial to interpreting site recovery statistics (Schiffer 1987). Even during the earlier stages of landscape archaeology there was an awareness that the cultural landscape had suffered progressive attrition of features through time, and Bradford (1957) showed how, for example, systems of Roman centuriation experienced the progressive attrition of field boundaries through time. In 1972 Christopher Taylor provided a significant stepping-stone in the debate, and his conceptual framework of 'landscapes of destruction' and 'landscape of survival' enabled British archaeologists to take account of the likelihood of feature survival when assessing the landscape record (Taylor 1972). This simple concept

Class	Sub-humid zone. Bronze Age	Sub-humid zone. Post-Bronze Age	Semi-arid zone. Bronze Age	Semi-arid zone. Post-Bronze Age	Arid margin zone. Bronze Age	Arid margin zone. Post-Bronze Age	Arid zone. Bronze Age	Arid zone. Post-Bronze Age
Nucleated 1a	▓		▓					
Nucleated 1b			▓					
Dispersed 2a		▓		▓		▓		
Dispersed 2b		▓		▓	▓			
3 Disp. Agro-pastoral					▓	▓		
4 Min.-mobile							▓	▓

Notes:
Major settlement /landscape classes:
1a.   Nucleation in mounded sites without field scatter
1b.   Nucleation in mounded sites with field scatter
2a.   Dispersal of small, low sites without field scatter
2b.   Dispersal of small, low sites with field scatter
3.   Dispersal with traces of temporary agro-pastoral settlement
4.   Min-mobile: mobile groups with relatively brief residence time.
Additional classes of settlement landscape not considered here include: elongate sprawling sites in irrigated areas (especially post-Bronze Age settlements); hilltop locations in rocky uplands, dispersed rural settlement in many uplands. Note that settlement locational stability (i.e. continuity) is greater in the moister areas, less in drier arid margins, minimal in the desert. In addition taphonomic disturbance should be higher in the moister areas, least in the desert.

Table 14.1 Class of settlement plotted according to environmental zone. Shading implies significant presence of the stated settlement landscape within the zone in question. Blanks do not indicate absence of these landscapes, but rather that there is a less significant presence.

received less attention than it deserved, but for the British Isles it has now been revised by Tom Williamson, who refers to a complex kaleidoscope of patterned creation and destruction (Williamson 1998: 6 and fig. 3).

The Taylor-Williamson model clearly puts landscape transformations at center stage in the interpretation of landscape and settlement data. Although these processes have been recognized by landscape archaeologists in the Mediterranean for a number of years they have not been applied formally. Suitably amended, the Taylor model can now be effectively applied to the ancient Near Eastern landscape as follows. Landscapes with the greatest probability of feature survival occur in deserts and high mountains, whereas progressive loss of features is at its maximum in areas of long-term cultivation and is rather less so in marginal zones of settlement. Finally, the coastal zone experiences a patterned loss and survival depending upon coastal sedimentation and currents.

CONTRASTS BETWEEN DESERT FRINGE AND SUB-HUMID AREAS OF THE NEAR EAST

Viewed at a very schematic level, if we chart the number of 'sites' per sq. km according to environmental zone from arid to sub-humid, there appears to be a rough trend from a low density of archaeological sites per sq. km in the true desert, high densities in some desert margins, and rather lower densities in the semi-arid to sub-humid zones where nucleated tell-based settlements predominated during certain periods. Table 14.1 summarizes some of

these trends by sketching some temporal and geographical trends in settlement type in the Fertile Crescent.

Overall, we suggest that in the extensive sub-humid or semi-arid plains of the Fertile Crescent settlement nucleation operates during certain periods and that, in such cases, sites are also re-occupied more frequently. As a result, there is apparently increased locational 'stability' during these periods. In contrast, after the Bronze Age as well as within the desert margins and some upland areas, dispersed settlement can be more common.

TEMPORAL PATTERNS OF NUCLEATION AND DISPERSAL

In addition to the above-mentioned geographical patterning of settlement types, there is a temporal component in the form of cycles of nucleation and dispersal. For example, in the semi-arid plains of Upper Mesopotamia, settlement nucleation into tells is more characteristic of the Bronze Age, whereas dispersal of settlement occurred in the post-Bronze Age (*i.e.* the first millennium BC and later; Wilkinson 2000a). In Upper Mesopotamia, Bronze Age nucleation takes the form of prominent mounds that range from less than 1 ha in area to somewhat over 100 ha in area (Weiss 1986), whereas post-Bronze Age dispersed settlement appears as low, often straggling, mounds of farmsteads and villages. Towns and cities of course occur in the post-Bronze Age periods, but these are usually extensive mounds that are more widely distributed. These include, for example, regional Neo-Assyrian centers such as Til Barsip (57 ha) and Dur Katlimmu (105 ha), or major imperial capitals on the scale of Nineveh, Nimrud and Khorsabad, at 750, 360–430 and 300 ha, respectively.

In the sub-humid plains of western Syria and southern Turkey, although the same pattern is evident, it is less clear and instead there is a tendency for Iron Age settlements to exhibit a mixed tell-based (nucleated) and dispersed pattern of settlement. In this region, the dispersed pattern of rural settlement only becomes clearly evident well into Seleucid or Roman times. The following examples from recent surveys conducted along an east-to-west line from north-western Iraq to southern Turkey illustrates these broad temporal trends in settlement (Figure 14.2).

Northern (Upper) Mesopotamia

The dramatic shift from nucleated tell-based settlement to a dispersed pattern of small villages has been recently documented by several intensive full-coverage surveys in semi-arid regions of Northern Mesopotamia (Wilkinson 2000a). These include the North Jazira Survey of northern Iraq (NJS: Wilkinson and Tucker 1995), the Tell Beydar Survey in the eastern Upper Khabur Basin (TBS: Wilkinson 2001), and the Tell Hamoukar Survey in the western Upper Khabur basin (THS: Ur 2002a; 2002b) (Figure 14.3). These surveys covered lowlands which have supported dry-farming settlements since the late Neolithic (i.e. since at least 6,000 BC). Because of their fertility, these plains have attracted near-continuous habitation since their initial settlement. The effects of such long-term settlement and cultivation have impacted the patterns recoverable by archaeological survey; thus these areas of Northern Mesopotamia can be classed as 'landscapes of destruction.'

All three surveys used a similar methodology. A full-coverage approach was employed, with each unit of the survey universe being examined with an equal intensity. Sites were initially identified via remote sensing: aerial photography, and detailed topographic maps (NJS), SPOT imagery (TBS), and CORONA satellite photography (THS; see Ur 2003); these sites were then visited by vehicle and collected by dividing up the surface into topographically discrete units from which a large sample of diagnostic sherds was collected. The North Jazira and Hamoukar surveys both included a program of off-site survey, which entailed walking systematic transects between sites or according to a grid-pattern of sample points. By collecting field-scatters and pinpointing (remarkably rare) minor artifact-scatters, this program allowed us roughly to compare these north Mesopotamian surveys with the more intensive surveys conducted around the Mediterranean.

The definition of a 'site' is of particular relevance to this comparison. In the three surveys discussed here, a site was regarded as a locus of concentrated human activity, assumed to entail residence for all or part of a year. This definition distinguishes traditional 'sites' from field-scatters, which also represent human activity but at a much

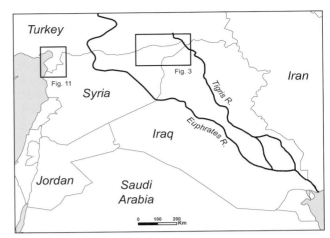

Figure 14.2 Locational map of surveys showing the eastern Jazira (cf. Figure 14.3) and the Amuq (cf. Figure 14.11).

lower intensity. A combination of three criteria was used to identify and delimit sites archaeologically: sherd density, topography, and soils. On-site sherd density tended to be at least 150–200 sherds per 100 sq. m under most site surface conditions; field scatter density averaged between 10–60 sherds per 100 sq. m on fallow fields, although proximity to third-millennium sites and local field conditions affected these averages. Field-scatters are nearly invisible in plowed fields, and are frequently in the range of 70–100 sherds per 100 sq. m within 1500 m of urban third-millennium sites. On the Upper Mesopotamian plains, mudbrick was the primary building material, and thus ancient sites tend to be mounded. On the one hand, concentrated on-site human activity inhibited soil formation, whereas the contribution of human and animal waste-products and middens resulted in a lighter and finer-grained anthropogenic soil, which stands out from the darker and red-hued calcareous soils (calcic xerosols) of the plains.

All three surveys revealed a highly nucleated Early Bronze Age (EBA) pattern. In the NJS (Figure 14.4), 20 late EBA sites (referred to as 'later third millennium') were recovered; the 66 ha settlement of Tell al-Hawa stood at the apex of a three-level hierarchy of towns and villages, all located on multi-period tell sites. The TBS produced a linear pattern of 17 large villages, evenly spread out along what are today seasonal watercourses, centered on the 23-ha town of Tell Beydar (Figure 14.6). The THS was focused on the immediate hinterland of the 105-ha EBA city of Hamoukar; although eight other contemporary sites were identified, Hamoukar represented 92% of the settled area within the survey territory at the time (Figure 14.8).

Associated with these nucleated tell sites were two types of off-site landscape phenomena which highlight the degree of population concentration and the intensity of agricultural and pastoral land use in the EBA. Traces of ancient road systems are preserved in the form of hollow-ways – that is, broad linear depressions which radiate out from EBA sites, connecting them with their satellites, as

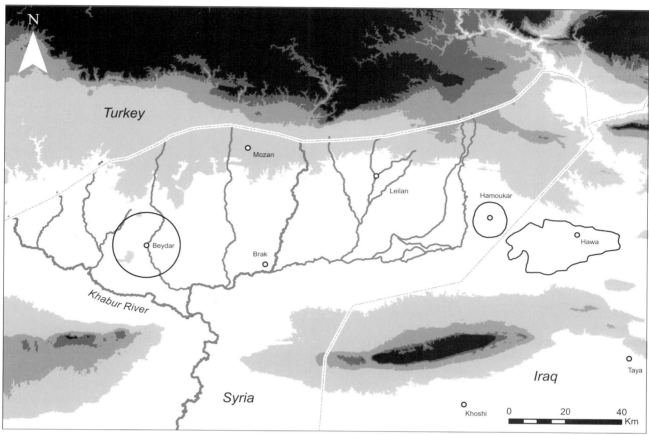

Figure 14.3 Khabur basin in northeastern Syria and part of northwestern Iraq: the location of the North Jazira Survey (around Tell al-Hawa), the Hamoukar and Beydar Surveys.

Survey	Area (sq. km)	Total Sites	Sites/sq. km	Periods/sq. km	EBA*	IA*
North Jazira Survey (NJS)	475	184	0.39	1.51	20 sites	78 sites
					146 ha	123 ha
Tell Beydar Survey (TBS)	450	82	0.18	0.77	17 sites	35 sites
					98 ha	97 ha
Tell Hamoukar Survey (THS)	125	67	0.54	1.36	9 sites	20 sites
					114 ha	64 ha

Table 14.2 Comparison of intensive Northern Mesopotamian surveys and their results for the EBA and Iron Age periods (* = number of sites and aggregate area).

well as their associated agricultural land and pasture land beyond (Van Liere and Lauffray 1954–55; Wilkinson 1993; Ur 2003). Early Bronze Age sites are also surrounded by a low-density carpet of abraded artifacts (field-scatters). These are interpreted as the result of agricultural intensification in which settlement-derived debris was spread on fields around the settlement as manure in an attempt to increase crop yield; the non-organic component survived and can be archaeologically detected (Wilkinson 1982; Ur 2002b).

This nucleated pattern broke down during the second millennium BC. The western Upper Khabur basin experienced settlement abandonments in the early second millennium BC: 16 of the 17 EBA sites in the TBS area were abandoned. In all three survey areas, the Late Bronze

Age (LBA) pattern was one of towns or villages clinging to the sides of the abandoned EBA tells or occasional minor outlying settlements. The transformation was completed by the Iron Age or Neo-Assyrian period (early first millennium BC). The NJS area supported 78 Iron Age villages in the range of 1–5 ha, which were evenly spaced across the plain (Figure 14.5). In the Tell Beydar area, following the early second-millennium abandonment and LBA resettlement, a scatter of some 35 sites of Iron Age date was established in valley floors, on low upland watersheds and even on the otherwise unoccupied basalt plateau (updated from Wilkinson and Barbanes 2000: 413–14) (Figure 14.7). Of these, most were single-period 'new foundations', although some also yielded pottery of the LBA and even Mittanian periods. In the THS area, four of

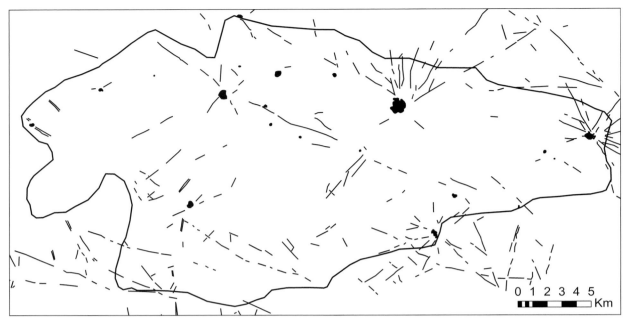

Figure 14.4 The North Jazira Survey: the pattern of nucleated EBA settlement and ancient 'hollow-way' roads.

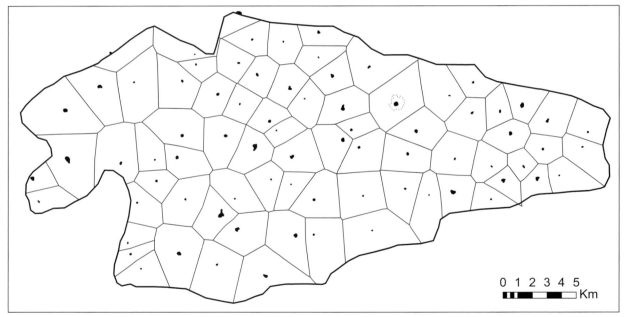

Figure 14.5 The North Jazira Survey: the pattern of dispersed Iron Age settlement, with Thiessen polygons as an indication of notional settlement territories.

the five largest EBA tells had Iron Age 'lower town' settlements; the other 16 Iron Age sites were either new foundations on the plain or were reoccupations of low mounds which had been abandoned since the fourth millennium or earlier (Figure 14.9).

The landscape features associated with the nucleated EBA pattern appear to be absent or much less commonly seen with the dispersed Iron Age settlements. In the THS area, only where Iron Age settlements are found on the

slopes of EBA tells are they associated with denser field-scatters (Figure 14.9), and in those situations the field scatters appear to contain predominantly EBA ceramic types. In areas adjacent to single-period Iron Age settlements or those on small prehistoric mounds, field-scatters are normally in the background range of 10–25 sherds per 100 sq. m. In the NJS area, Iron Age ceramics were found in field-scatters, but only half as frequently as EBA types (Wilkinson and Tucker 1995: 62). Very rarely are Iron

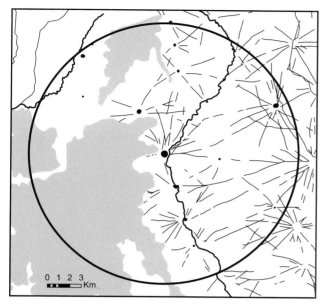

Figure 14.6 The Tell Beydar Survey: nucleated EBA settlement with ancient 'hollow-way' roads.

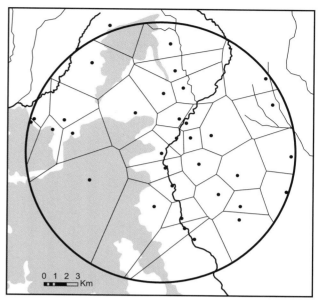

Figure 14.7 The Tell Beydar Survey: the pattern of dispersed Iron Age settlement with Thiessen polygons showing notional territories.

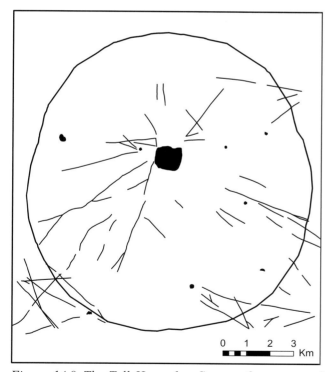

Figure 14.8 The Tell Hamoukar Survey: the pattern of nucleated settlement of the EBA with ancient 'hollow-way' roads.

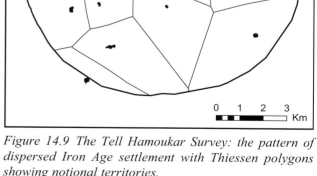

Figure 14.9 The Tell Hamoukar Survey: the pattern of dispersed Iron Age settlement with Thiessen polygons showing notional territories.

Age sites associated with hollow-ways; only those Iron Age settlements on older EBA sites have associated hollow-ways, but in many cases these can be directly associated with features of the EBA site such as walls and gates, rather than with any features dating to the Iron Age.

SURVEY RATES OF RECOVERY AND INTER-REGIONAL COMPARABILITY

Even in the THS, where the small survey area allowed for the greatest survey intensity, settlement density is still substantially lower than in the more recent Mediterranean surveys. Are these surveys overlooking smaller sites? Most Middle Eastern surveys cannot be compared with Mediterranean surveys for methodological reasons: they tend to rely heavily on non-systematic vehicular reconnaissance supplemented by remote-sensing sources, as opposed to the systematic field-walking transect methods favored in the Mediterranean.

While non-systematic field-walking (*i.e.* following wadi courses) has been included as a part of several recent intensive Middle Eastern surveys, few have included a program of systematic 'off-site' transect-walking at set intervals. However, the NJS and the THS included systematic 'off-site' landscape observation as part of the study of field-scatters. In the NJS, radial transects were walked around and between the major EBA sites and many kilometers of sections of a 500 m irrigation canal grid were systematically investigated for traces of buried sites (Wilkinson and Tucker 1995: 17). In the THS, a three-person team made 100 sq. m field-scatter unit collections in a 200 m UTM-based grid; this involved walking transects at 200 m intervals (Figure 14.10). Admittedly, this resolution is coarse when compared to Mediterranean surveys, but the Jaziran sample methods do serve as a rough check on the remote-sensing sources. In the fall of 2000, when the THS transects were made, most fields were fallow or harvested and grazed. Visibility was very high; we estimate that each field-walker could cover a range of 3–4 m on either side, and possibly further under certain light conditions. In the NJS area, only a few buried sites were found where modern canals cut through the alluvial belt of minor wadis. This evidence, together with records of soil sections along the canals, led to the observation that alluviation was not obscuring sites. After walking over some 56,000 m of transects and collecting almost 500 units, the THS found no sites that had not already been recognized on CORONA photographs (for other archaeological applications of CORONA satellite photographs, see Kennedy 1998; Philip *et al.* 2002).

To what extent, then, are the low-relief plains of Northern Mesopotamia a landscape of destruction? Within the Taylor-Williamson model, these are areas where progressive loss of features should be at its maximum, and where we should expect to find 'ghosts' of sites remaining. Yet when field-walking has been included in the survey methods (NJS and THS), very few additional sites have been recovered. We would argue that the choice of mudbrick as the primary building materials and the floodplain geomorphology in these regions have acted to make sites much more visible than in the Mediterranean area. Scarcity of timber resources in these and other areas of the Middle East has meant that mudbrick has been the most common building material almost since the beginnings of sedentary settlement. Since it is more efficient to make new mudbricks than to reuse old ones, there has been little, if any, deconstruction or robbing of abandoned settlements for building materials. Mudbrick sites pose few difficulties for agriculture: whereas a stone settlement leaves material which will impede a plow and must be cleared out of fields, a mudbrick site can be plowed over directly. This process results in the slight dispersal of archaeological materials across the landscape, but even on late Neolithic sites, mounding is still preserved after millennia of subsequent agriculture and a half-century of mechanized plowing. In other words, although long-term taphonomic processes have resulted in the attrition of many (but not all) landscape features, a large number of the original settlements appear to remain.

We conclude that in the Jazira of upper Mesopotamia, if high-resolution remote-sensing sources are combined with intensive field-survey, a reasonable approximation of full recovery is theoretically possible. Moreover, a degree of site recovery comparable to that of the intensive Mediterranean surveys is possible using much less intensive methods. This statement applies only to the plains of northern Syria and northern Iraq; few highland areas of Northern Mesopotamia have been subjected to intensive survey. These near-ideal survey conditions may not pertain for much longer, however; within the last several decades, mechanized plowing, bulldozing of sites, the extension of irrigated cotton agriculture, the expansion of towns and villages, and state-sponsored dam and irrigation projects have begun to take a serious toll on site preservation. Moreover, probably the greatest cause of loss of archaeological sites is where they are obscured below modern villages. Even where pottery can be recognized between the modern houses the individual sherds are frequently abraded down to small sizes so that they are difficult to place typologically.

If Near Eastern intensive field-survey methods are not capable of finding additional small sites, how can the discrepancy in site density between the Near East and the Mediterranean be explained? It is possible that real differences in long-term cultural practices existed between these regions, particularly a 'settlement inertia' on the plains of North Mesopotamia, whereby a positive feedback-loop caused people both to remain within their communities and to return to previously settled places (see below).

The Amuq Plain of Southern Turkey

The northern Levant is an ideal region for comparing trends in archaeological settlement between northern Mesopotamia on the one hand, and Greece and the Aegean on the other. The region is not only roughly equidistant between these areas, but it also has a long historical and cultural pedigree as a part of both the Syro-Mesopotamian and Greco-Roman worlds. Surveys in the northern Levant have often reflected the academic divide between Classical and Near Eastern archaeological traditions – not only in terms of the sites they have recorded, but also in the regions they have chosen to survey. For instance, in northwest Syria surveys by Near Eastern archaeologists have tended to focus on lowland plains, such as the Orontes River Valley, and were primarily interested in recording large

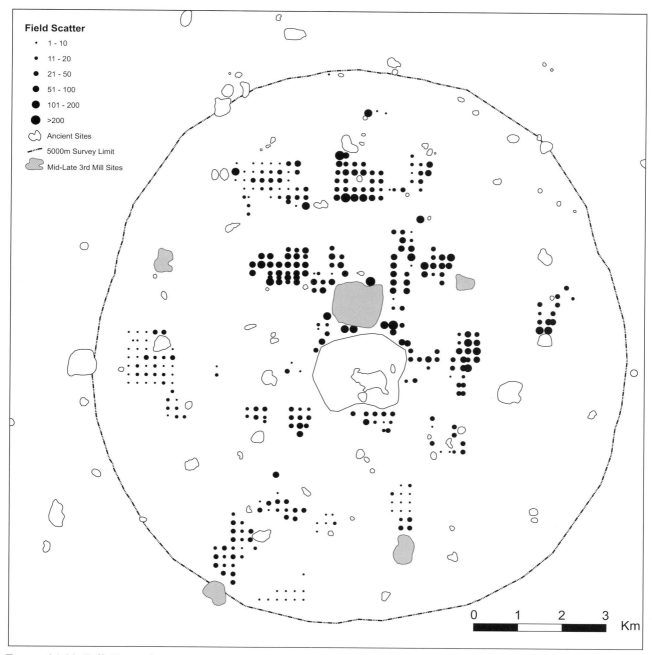

Figure 14.10 Tell Hamoukar Survey field-scatter collection units and off-site sherd-scatter densities per 100 sq. m collection unit.

Bronze and Iron Age tell sites (*e.g.* Courtois 1973). Classical archaeologists, on the other hand, have predominantly worked in upland areas, such as the *massif calcaire* or Hauran of Syria, and have recorded Roman and Late Antique remains almost exclusively (Tchalenko 1953–58; Tate 1992). The disjuncture is perhaps understandable, given that early tell sites are relatively common in lowland plains, while few contemporary settlements are known in the uplands. Meanwhile, the limestone hills of northwest Syria (the *massif calcaire*) form a textbook 'landscape of preservation', and are home to hundreds of

spectacularly preserved Late Antique villages, the so-called 'Dead Cities'. However, the gulf in the academic interests of such survey projects and their focus on entirely different types of landscape has resulted in records of settlement that are difficult to compare both spatially and temporally. Moreover, the geographical and chronological separation in the interests of most surveys in the northern Levant has drawn attention away from the major transformation in settlement that occurs across this academic watershed.

As in northern Mesopotamia, in the first millennium

BC the northern Levant witnessed a pronounced dispersal of settlement away from nucleated tell sites, and towards much smaller sites that are spread across the plains and into surrounding highlands. However, this transformation has not been explicitly investigated nor well documented until recently. The original archaeological survey of the Amuq Plain by Robert Braidwood (1937) mapped the basic framework of tell-based settlement in the region, recording some 178 sites. The survey was remarkably innovative for the 1930s, and succeeded in discovering many small sites in addition to larger tells, including those of Roman to Late Roman date. Nevertheless, without the advantage of more recently developed intensive survey methodologies, most of the small, flat sites that typify the Hellenistic to Late Roman periods were not recovered by the project, the result being that those phases of settlement were severely under-represented. Additionally, the project did not seek to investigate the uplands where later settlement has been found to be particularly dense.

Recent archaeological survey by the Oriental Institute's Amuq Valley Regional Project (AVRP) has begun to reveal the profundity of the structural transformation in settlement that occurred in the late first millennium BC (Figure 14.11). The vast majority of Chalcolithic through Late Bronze Age (6000–1150 BC) occupation was concentrated at a relatively small number of tell sites, almost all of which were located in the lowland plain. For example, in the mid-third millennium BC, 42 sites have been found to have evidence of occupation, most of which are at large tells. Only one of these sites is located in the uplands, and is not a typical occupational site, but rather a stone building-complex, possibly of ritual or military function (Verstraete and Wilkinson 2000: AS 208). By way of contrast, more than 150 sites have been recorded in the plain that have some evidence of Roman-Late Roman occupation. Many of these sites are very small, often less than 1 ha, and frequently have little or no topographic relief.

Surveys employed a vehicle to undertake a broad full-coverage survey for the entire area of some 1200 sq. km, while pedestrian transects run at 100 m intervals were used for local checking of areas between sites. Although this only provided a sample of off-site areas, it gave a good idea concerning the location and appearance of minor occupations. As in northern Mesopotamia, CORONA satellite imagery has proven to be a tremendously valuable tool for the Amuq Valley survey, because many previously undocumented sites appear with great clarity. For instance, in the area around Tell Tayinat and Tell Atchana located in the southern plain, the original survey, as well as the more recent AVRP surveys, failed to locate a large number of very small, flat sites that are visible in the vicinity (Figure 14.12). The image clearly illustrates the dispersal of settlement, because while virtually all Early Bronze through Iron Age occupation in the area was concentrated at the two large tells, Hellenistic through Early Islamic settlement is located at the many small sites that surround them.

Overall, CORONA imagery has revealed the location of nearly 100 additional small possible sites throughout the plain. While only a sample of these sites has been visited, nearly all that have been recorded are Hellenistic to Early Islamic in date, suggesting that these periods may still be significantly under-represented in the survey data. Similarly, the off-site transects conducted by Jan Verstraete mainly recovered the remains of flat artifact-scatters of Roman and Byzantine date. Additionally, there is evidence to suggest that many of the tell sites in the Amuq had minor Roman-Byzantine occupation on them. Excavations at Chatal Höyük found that the large Iron Age city at the site was replaced by a minor Late Antique village, and work at Tell Judaidah shows a similar pattern (Haines 1971). Many other tell sites in the valley are predominantly Bronze and Iron Age, but a small amount of Roman-Byzantine material is frequently found on them, suggesting a situation similar to that at Chatal Höyük and Tell Judaidah, in which small villages or farmsteads were located on top of older mounds. These later occupations at tell sites are sometimes nearly invisible to archaeological survey because they are lost against an overwhelming percentage of earlier materials. For instance, at Tell Atchana a systematic surface collection of over 3,000 diagnostic sherds recovered only 12 Late Antique sherds and 4 roof-tile fragments. The presence of the tiles, as well as a Late Antique field-scatter to the north of the mound, suggests that there was probably some Roman-Byzantine occupation at the site, not merely stray sherds (Casana, forthcoming).

Unlike northern Mesopotamia, where large areas of the plains appear relatively stable geomorphologically, resulting in very good preservation of many landscape features such as hollow-ways, the plains of the northern Levant have experienced significant aggradation over the past several millennia. In addition, this area has probably experienced the degradation of earlier landscape features and minor sites as a result of long-term agricultural practices. Because alluvial and colluvial activity can bury much of the ancient landscape, archaeological surveys in the region must be closely tied to geomorphological investigations in order to interpret settlement data critically. Such work in the Amuq Valley has demonstrated that while the plain is deceptively flat, it is actually a complex patchwork of high and low sedimentation zones (Wilkinson 2000b). Archaeological survey on the western side of the plain, where alluvial fans have built up some 3 m of gravel fill since the Hellenistic/Roman period, has recorded few early sites. Similarly, examination of sections through sediments on the Orontes River floodplain in the southern Amuq Valley has shown that the area witnessed extreme flooding and aggradation of several meters of sediment since the Late Antique period. The rapid aggradation of the plain buried the earliest layers of Tell Atchana/Alalakh as well as much of the Roman city of Antioch, and may have obscured many archaeological sites as well. Conversely, some areas in the central Amuq Plain have experienced little or no sedimentation since the early

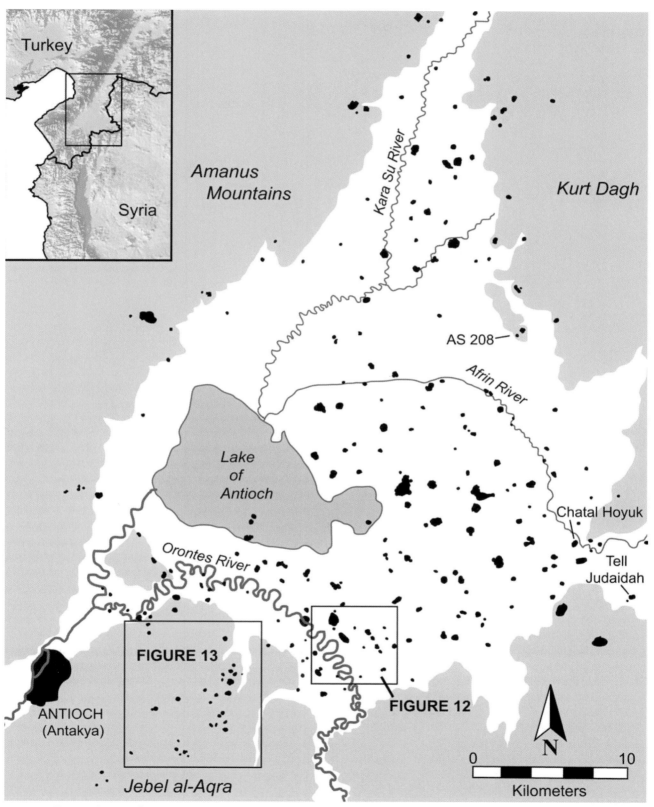

Figure 14.11 The Amuq plain and neighboring uplands, showing sites and subsidiary survey areas.

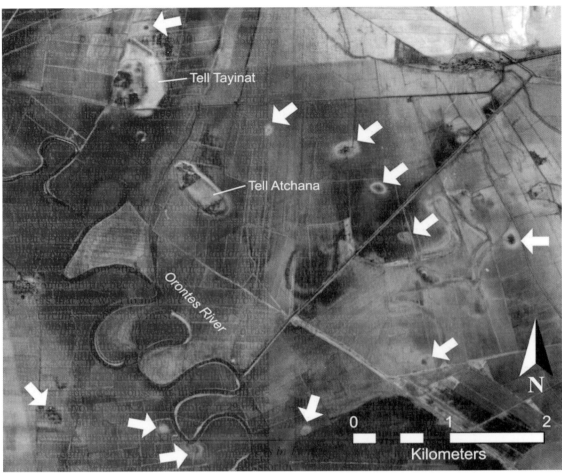

Figure 14.12 CORONA image showing the nucleated pattern of settlement around Tells Tayinat (early third and first millennium BC) and Atchana (mainly second millennium BC), together with outlying small sites, mainly of post Iron Age date (arrowed). (Photograph courtesy of the U.S. Geological Survey).

Holocene. These areas provide us with 'sedimentary windows' in which there has been little loss of sites and other features to alluvial processes, and which therefore can be used to suggest the extent to which the archaeological landscape has been obscured on other parts of the plain. For instance, in one sedimentary window around the large site of Chakal Tepe, archaeological survey documented an unusually large number of early Neolithic and Chalcolithic sites, and off-site transects found a relatively dense artifactual field-scatter. Examination of CORONA satellite imagery of the area suggests that there are many other still unrecorded archaeological sites in the area. The high density of settlement and the unusual concentration of early sites in the sedimentary window may imply that similar landscapes have been obscured on other parts of the plain.

Records of settlement from lowland plains and river valleys are notoriously difficult to compare with highland areas, owing to problems of site visibility and preservation, as well as the constraints on sampling techniques imposed by steep and unforgiving terrain (Banning 1996). In the Amuq Valley, the Amanus Mountains to the west, the Jebel al-Aqra to the south and the Kurt Dagh to the east

provide a different challenge for archaeological survey than does the plain. While CORONA imagery has proven an indispensable tool for locating archaeological sites in the plain, virtually no sites are evident on the imagery in upland areas. Furthermore, from the ground, sites are often far less obvious than on the plain because mounding is rare, and when present is often difficult to differentiate against the natural topography. However, recent semi-intensive survey employing walking transects at roughly 100-m intervals in a valley in the Jebel al-Aqra has documented a rich archaeological landscape in which settlement is widely dispersed throughout all topographical zones. All evidence of Chalcolithic through Iron Age settlement is concentrated at two tell sites, both located on the narrow valley floor. However, beginning in the Hellenistic period small sites are found on hillsides throughout the valley, and by the Late Roman period, small settlements are found on many hill-slopes and summits visited by the survey (Figure 14.13). The dramatic increase in upland settlement in the Hellenistic to Late Roman periods contributed to a local increase in soil erosion, well illustrated near the mouth of the valley where

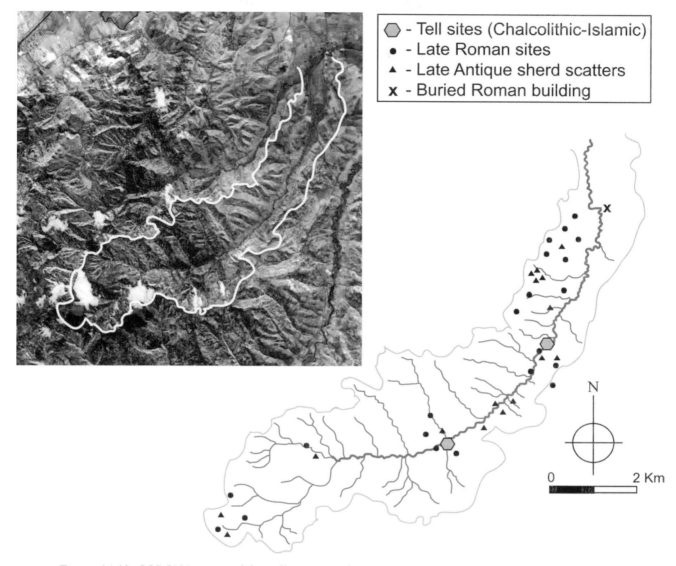

Figure 14.13 CORONA image of the valley surveyed in 2001, and the tells and later sites recorded.

a Roman building has been buried by over 4 m of sediment. Surveys to the west of the Amuq Plain in the Amanus foothills suggest that there was a similar extension of upland settlement there and a parallel increase in erosion that deposited large alluvial fans on the valley floor.

The fact that highland areas in the northern Levant seem to have been sparsely occupied in early periods suggests that survey projects which do not investigate lowlands may fail to record the early component of settlement (*e.g.* Blanton 2000). Furthermore, in areas that are susceptible to erosion, dense occupation of uplands may contribute to significant increases in erosion from slopes and the consequent burial of earlier sites on valley floors.

The combined and critical use of imagery-based and more traditional intensive survey methodologies has enabled us to document a widespread and fundamental transformation in the history of human occupation in the Amuq Valley. Unlike northern Mesopotamia where the dispersal of settlement away from tell sites appears to begin in the Late Bronze Age, or even slightly earlier, the structurally parallel change in the Amuq Valley does not begin until the Hellenistic period, and reaches a peak in the Late Roman period (Casana, forthcoming). The enormous chronological range between these two cases, and indeed among the many geographically disparate cases throughout the Near East, suggests that the causes of the transformation are probably not any single, local, historical event. More likely, the dispersal of settlement in the Amuq Valley, northern Mesopotamia and elsewhere in the Near East is related to very basic and sweeping changes in the structure of the ancient economy, in systems of land-tenure and agricultural production, and in the integration of the regions into territorial empires.

DISCUSSION

Overall, in northern Iraq, northern Syria and southern Turkey traditional surveys appear to have been reasonably effective at recognizing the basic pattern of Bronze Age settlement, but they have proved to be woefully inadequate for accurately recovering the pattern of settlement of the Iron Age, Hellenistic and later periods. In many areas, settlement dispersal commenced during the second half of the second millennium BC, and by the Iron Age there had been a pronounced extension of settlement into the steppe or uplands. This dispersal has been recorded in much of the Jazira (Morandi 2000; Wilkinson and Barbanes 2000), the Jabbul plain (Schwartz *et al.* 2000), and the Levant (Finkelstein 1998). Furthermore, during the Hellenistic, Roman and Late Antique periods the development of a rural landscape dominated by a dispersed pattern of rural settlement became even more pronounced in the southern Levant, as well as the Euphrates region of southern Turkey and parts of northern Syria (Wilkinson 1990; Algaze *et al.* 1994). The recent surveys support and locally amplify Alcock's statement (1994: 181) that for the Hellenistic period:

> Assembling all available hints from Syrian surveys, however, it can tentatively be stated that an increase in settlement numbers and population, with more territory placed under cultivation than before, did indeed occur.

Recent surveys undertaken at a greater level of intensity and with more regard for smaller sites, support the above statement, but in the Jazira of Northern Syria and Iraq, this statement is more appropriate for the Iron Age, as well as for the later periods in some parts of the region. For much of the Levant, northwestern Syria, and southern Turkey recent surveys describe a particularly densely settled countryside during the late first millennium BC and early first millennium AD. In many areas this resembles the 'busy countryside' described for Italy by Lloyd (1991; see also Barker 1996). Although such a growth of rural settlement and rural agricultural production may, in some areas, have been associated with the implantation of new Seleucid cities (Grainger 1990: 110–19; also Alcock 1994: 181), in other places this pattern of dispersed settlement appears to have been built upon foundations that were laid during the Iron Age (*e.g.* northern Iraq: Wilkinson and Tucker 1995). Overall, the massive expansion of rural settlement over the Levantine uplands and into parts of Anatolia must be partly a result of increased commercialization of agricultural production, particularly of olive-oil and wine (Ward-Perkins 2000), in association also with the massive growth in demand provided by cities such as Antioch and Apamea.

The striking change in settlement structure that took place between the mid-third and the first millennium BC appears to represent a major shift from complex 'city-state'-type settlement systems during the Bronze Age toward the territorial empires of the first millennium BC

and later. Such a transformation, which was probably associated with the collapse of the Late Bronze Age political economy, may be linked to wide-ranging changes in land-tenure, as well as to shifts in the exercising of power and population redistributions. However, before such links between settlement structure and the political economy can be established it is crucial for settlement surveys to be conducted, in both lowlands and nearby uplands, to a rigorous and standardized methodology. Moreover, it is also important to take into account differences in landscape taphonomy (both physical and cultural transformations), as well as local mechanisms of site development that reinforce earlier patterns of settlement.

In the context of tell formation, an abandoned mound is a good place for settlement because its elevation provides improved drainage and a favorable micro-climate. By settling on mounds, incoming inhabitants would not reduce the available agricultural land surrounding the site. Furthermore, sites with mudbrick buildings usually have associated borrow-pits, from which building materials were extracted; these depressions continue to collect moisture and thus remain an attractive water supply, as well as a resource for building materials for subsequent settlers. The troughs of hollow-ways also capture moisture; in the THS it can be demonstrated in several places that subsequent (post-EBA) settlements took advantage of the borrow-pit potential of disused hollow-way troughs (Ur 2002b).

From a social and ideational perspective, tells and mounds probably retained a deeper significance that cannot be recovered archaeologically. Fundamental to the process of settlement nucleation is that, for the communities in question, there may have been more of an incentive to live as an aggregated community, rather than dispersing out to their fields. Thus Roberts (1996: 35–37) defines three basic conditions of 'communality' that may contribute to settlement nucleation:

- Communality of assent is the tendency for family ties to hold groups together in the same settlement.
- Communality to economize operates because community action can be more productive than action by small groups, especially for the mobilization of group labor.
- Communality of enforcement is evident in the case of settlements growing up around fortified places or centers of power or religion.

Additional social factors contribute to nucleation. If deceased family members were interred beneath the floors of their houses, settlements or abandoned sites would probably be closely associated with ancestors, real or imagined; even in the last millennium, when sedentary settlement was at a nadir in the Upper Khabur basin, mobile pastoral groups used tells as the preferred place for burials. Moreover, continuity of religion, well exemplified by superimposed temples at Middle and Late Bronze Age Atchana (Alalakh) in the Amuq, must also contribute to settlements remaining in one place and communities clustering together.

The nature of land-holding may also have militated against settlement dispersal. In a large part of the semi-arid Fertile Crescent, cultivated land has traditionally been held according to the *musha 'a* system, under which the agricultural land is held not by individuals but by the community (Granott 1952: 213–48). As a result, fields are redistributed periodically among the members of the community according to a generally accepted scheme, often simply by drawing lots. A by-product of this system is that because no individual holds exclusive right to any field parcel, it is difficult for any person to move out of the village (*e.g.* for reasons of a dispute with another member of the community) and establish a new dwelling within the cultivated territory of the village. In such cases, the only recourse would be to establish a new residence in another community (itself presumably a nucleated settlement with a *musha 'a* land-holding system), or as a satellite community on waste ground beyond the village fields. In a similar manner, if a family should own parcels of land that are dispersed throughout the agricultural territory, this again makes a location within a central settlement the most obvious choice of residence. Such corporate land-holding systems, although not practiced over the entire Fertile Crescent, were widespread until recent land reforms and they appear to be remarkably ancient, being traceable back to the Late Bronze Age and almost certainly earlier (Renger 1995).

Interestingly, maps of traditional Levantine villages with their fields show a distinct pattern of nucleated villages, within a matrix of surrounding strip-like fields, which are accessed by means of radial tracks, forked at appropriate points in order to optimize access to the outermost fields (Weulersse 1946: fig. 37). Such a pattern resembles that observed around Early Bronze Age tells in the Jazira, and it can be speculated that such Bronze Age settlements also employed a similar land-holding system. The corporate nature of these village communities therefore contributed to their long-term stability in the landscape, as well as to the overall continuity of settlement nucleation in the extensive plains of the Fertile Crescent.

Because the *musha 'a* system was a predominant form of land holding in the Ottoman period, one cannot simply equate corporate settlements and a communal land-holding system uniquely with the Bronze Age, and then some other form of land-holding in the post-Bronze Age. Rather, there appears to have been a complex alternation between nucleated corporate communities and dispersed settlement systems through time. Nevertheless, it is significant that the dispersal of settlement that took place after the Bronze Age was into areas that extended beyond the long-term settlement on the plains. The new lands which experienced such settlement may therefore have been either deliberate re-settlement schemes of land not previously cultivated (as in the case of Neo-Assyrian re-settlement), spontaneous settlement by nomadic groups (such as the Aramaeans),

or perhaps piecemeal settlement of uplands by individuals who acquired or purchased land outside the traditional land-holding system. Overall, it can be argued that the various factors of communality discussed above must have contributed to the nucleation into the tell-based systems recognized in the Bronze Age, whereas the break-down of this system (which started in the second millennium and continued in the first) may have contributed to the well-attested dispersal recorded in the surveys discussed above.

The tendency toward settlement nucleation and continuity manifests itself archaeologically in the form of multi-period sites. For example, in the NJS only 13% of sites were occupied in a single period; in the TBS and NJS, over 50% of sites had four or more periods of occupation. In an attempt to compare with the Mediterranean settlement data, we have calculated periods per sq. km – that is, counting the total number of periods for each site and dividing this figure by the total survey area (Table 14.2). When this figure is plotted in the 'Cherry Chart' (Figure 14.1), although our rate of site recovery is improved, it still fails to match the record of 'Greek surveys since the 1970s'. This implies that even when allowance is made for successive occupations occurring in the same place, the plains of Upper Mesopotamia still favor a markedly nucleated pattern of settlement.

Overall, the record of landscape and settlement in the Near East is now starting to suggest a more coherent narrative than hitherto. The marked regional zonation of environmental zones shows a number of signature landscape-types (although the degree of regional variation is considerable). Processes of landscape transformation are clearly important, because in the more verdant and long-settled areas a significant (albeit unknown) part of the landscape record is missing. This is well illustrated from the Amuq survey where off-site transects recorded flat artifact-scatters remaining as 'ghosts', and CORONA images record sites that appear to have minimal topographic expression and appear to have been degraded by long-term taphonomic processes. On the other hand, it does seem that the relatively low density of settlement remaining in the landscapes of the Jazira to the east may be real, and reflect a process of positive feedback that maintains sites in one general location. What is important in terms of survey is that when mound accumulation takes place, the resultant sites are easy to find, but the component occupations become progressively obscured; on the other hand, when settlements are dispersed and form single-period flat sites, their recognition is difficult, but each occupational phase can be more securely dated because of the lack of overlying deposits. There is therefore a trade-off between high visibility, multi-period mounds with progressively obscured earlier occupations, and low-visibility, flat sites in which the component occupations remain visible.

Although certain settlement landscapes may tentatively be related to the prevailing political economy, the tantalizing relationship between settlement pattern and large-scale administrative structures, such as states or empires, will need considerably more research to determine whether it can be upheld. More important, we believe, are factors that lead to changes in settlement structure and morphology. In areas near the Mediterranean where there is clear evidence for Hellenistic-Byzantine settlement dispersal, surveys are in danger of identifying the dispersed phase of settlement in the uplands, but missing the long-term record of lowland settlement. This is because lowland settlement may have been obscured by deposition, especially by sediments eroded from the surrounding hills during the post-Hellenistic phase of settlement dispersal. The final result of such a survey – very little occupation on the plains and post-Hellenistic settlement on the hills – could therefore show little resemblance to the true picture of long-lived settlement (*i.e.* prehistoric to Iron Age) on the plain and post-Hellenistic settlement on the uplands. Overall, rather than becoming obsessed with the details of site recovery, it is necessary for surveyors to also become more sensitive to settlement structure, landscape taphonomy, processes of settlement formation, as well as interactions between settlement and geomorphology. Attention to these factors, together with site recovery and comparability of data-collections, should considerably improve our ability to compare neighboring survey records.

ACKNOWLEDGEMENTS

Many thanks go to the following for providing help and advice to the following surveys. The North Jazira Project (Iraq): Manhal Jabr, Dr. Mu' ayyad Sa'id Damerji, and Moslem Mohammed (Directorate General of Antiquities in Iraq), as well as to Warwick Ball and David Tucker; Hamoukar Project (Syria): Prof. Dr. Abd al-Razzak Moaz, Dr. Michel Maqdisi, Prof. Dr. Sultan Muhesen, Mr Abdul Massieh Bagdo, Dr. Amr al-Azm and Dr. McGuire Gibson; Tell Beydar (Syria): Dr. Marc Lebeau, Dr. Anton Suleiman and Dr. Karel Vanlerberghe; the Amuq (Turkey): Dr. K. Aslihan Yener and Dr. Hatice Pamir, as well as the Turkish Ministry of Culture, Directorate General of Monuments and Museums. Funding was provided by the National Geographic Society and British School of Archaeology in Iraq for the North Jazira Project; the Oriental Institute, and various private donors, for the Hamoukar and Beydar surveys; in addition, Jason Ur received funding from the Ryerson fund and the ASOR Mesopotamian Fellowship for work at Hamoukar; the National Geographic Society and a grant from the Ryerson Fund to Jesse Casana provided funding for the Amuq Survey. Thanks also go to Peggy Sanders for drafting Figure 14.1.

REFERENCES

Alcock S. E. (1994) Breaking up the Hellenistic world: survey and society. In I. Morris (ed.) *Classical Greece: Ancient Histories and Modern Archaeologies*: 171–90. Cambridge, Cambridge University Press.

Algaze, G., Breuninger, R. and Knutstad, J. (1994) The Tigris-Euphrates Archaeological Reconnaissance Project: final report of the Birecik and Carchemish Dam survey areas. *Anatolica* 20: 1–96.

Banning, E. B. (1996) Highlands and lowlands: problems and survey frameworks for rural archaeology in the Near East. *Bulletin of the American Schools of Oriental Research* 301: 25–45.

Barker, G. W. W. (1996) Regional archaeological projects: trends and traditions in Mediterranean archaeology. *Archaeological Dialogues* 2: 160–75.

Blanton, R. E. (2000) *Hellenistic, Roman and Byzantine Settlement Patterns of the Coast Lands of Western Rough Cilicia.* BAR International Series 879. Oxford, Archaeopress.

Bradford, J. (1957) *Ancient Landscapes: Studies in Field Archaeology.* London, Bell (reprinted Westport, CT, Greenwood Press, 1980).

Braidwood, R. J. (1937) *Mounds in the Plain of Antioch: An Archaeological Survey.* Oriental Institute Publication 48. Chicago, Oriental Institute.

Casana, J. (forthcoming) The archaeological landscape of Late Roman Antioch. In J. A. R. Huskinson and B. Sandwell (eds.) *Culture and Society in Late Roman Antioch.* London and New York, David Brown Book Company.

Cherry, J. F. (1983) Frogs round the pond: perspectives on current archaeological survey projects in the Mediterranean area. In D. R. Keller and D. W. Rupp (eds.) *Archaeological Survey in the Mediterranean Area*: 375–416. BAR International Series 155. Oxford, British Archaeological Reports.

Courtois, J.-C. (1973) Prospection archéologique dans la moyenne vallée de l'Oronte. *Syria* 50: 53–99.

Finkelstein, I. (1998) The great transformation: the 'conquest' of the highlands frontiers and the rise of the territorial states. In T. E. Levy (ed.) *The Archaeology of Society in the Holy Land*: 349–65. Leicester, Leicester University Press.

Grainger, J. (1990) *The Cities of Seleucid Syria.* Oxford, Clarendon Press.

Granott, A. (1952) *The Land System in Palestine: History and Structure.* London, Eyre and Spottsiwoode.

Haines, R. C. (1971) *Excavations in the Plain of Antioch*, Vol. 2. *The Structural Remains of the Later Phases: Chatal Hoyuk, Tell al-Judaidah, and Tell Ta'yinat.* Oriental Institute Publication 95. Chicago, Oriental Institute.

Kennedy, D. (1998) Declassified satellite photographs and archaeology in the Middle East: case studies from Turkey. *Antiquity* 72: 553–61.

Lloyd, J. (1991) Conclusion: archaeological survey and the Roman landscape. In G. Barker and J. Lloyd (eds.) *Roman Landscapes: Archaeological Survey in the Mediterranean Region*: 233–40. British School at Rome, Archaeological Monograph 2. Rome, British School at Rome.

Morandi, D. B. (2000) The Syrian Jazireh in the Late Assyrian period: a view from the countryside. In G. Bunnens (ed.) *Essays on Syria in the Iron Age*: 349–96. Ancient Near Eastern Studies 7 (supplement). Louvain, Peeters Press.

Philip, G., Donoghue, D., Beck, A. and Galiatsatos, N. (2002) CORONA satellite photography: an archaeological application from the Middle East. *Antiquity* 76: 109–18.

Renger, J. M. (1995) Institutional, communal, and individual ownership or possession of arable land in Ancient Mesopotamia from the end of the fourth to the end of the first millennium B.C. *Chicago-Kent Law Review* 71(1): 269–319.

Roberts, B. K. (1996) *Landscapes of Settlement: Prehistory to the Present.* London, Routledge.

Schiffer, M. B. (1987) *Formation Processes of the Archaeological Record.* Albuquerque, University of New Mexico Press.

Schwartz, G. M., Curvers, H. H., Gerritsen, F. A., MacCormack, J. A., Miller, N. F. and Weber, J. A. (2000) Excavation and survey in the Jabbul Plain, Western Syria: the Umm al-Marra Project 1996–1997. *American Journal of Archaeology* 104: 419–62.

Tate, G. (1992) *Les campagnes de la Syrie du Nord du IIe au VIIe siècle, 1*. Bibliothèque archéologique et historique Vol. 133, Institut français d'archéologie du Proche-Orient. Paris, Librarie orientaliste Paul Geuthner.

Taylor, C. C. (1972) The study of settlement pattern in pre-Saxon Britain. In P. J. Ucko, R. Tringham and G. W. Dimbleby (eds.) *Man, Settlement and Urbanism*: 109–114. London, Duckworth.

Tchalenko, G. (1953–58) *Villages antiques de la Syrie du nord, I–III*. Paris, Librairie orientaliste Paul Geuthner.

Ur, J. (2002a) Surface collection and off-site studies at Tell Hamoukar, 1999. *Iraq* 64: 15–44.

Ur, J. (2002b) Settlement and landscape in Northern Mesopotamia: the Tell Hamoukar Survey 2000–2001. *Akkadica* 123: 57–88.

Ur, J. (2003) CORONA satellite photography and ancient road networks: a Northern Mesopotamian case study. *Antiquity* 77: 102–115.

Van Liere, W. J. and Lauffray, J. (1954–55) Nouvelle prospection archéologique dans la Haute Jezireh Syrienne. *Les Annales archéologiques de Syrie* 4–5: 129–48.

Verstraete, J. and Wilkinson, T.J. (2000) The Amuq Regional Archaeological Survey. In K. A. Yener, C. Edens, T. P. Harrison, J. Verstraete, and T. J. Wilkinson, The Amuq Valley Regional Project, 1995–1998. *American Journal of Archaeology* 104: 163–220.

Ward-Perkins, B. (2000) Specialized production and exchange. In A. Cameron, B. Ward-Perkins and M. Whitby (eds.) *The Cambridge Ancient History, Vol. XIV. Late Antiquity: Empire and Successors A.D. 425–600*: 346–91. Cambridge, Cambridge University Press.

Weiss, H. (1986) The origins of Tell Leilan. In H. Weiss (ed.) *The Origins of Cities in Dry-Farming Syria and Mesopotamia in the Third Millennium BC*: 71–108. Guilford, Four Quarters.

Weulersse, J. (1946) *Paysans de Syrie et du Proche-Orient*. Paris, Gallimard.

Wilkinson, T. J. (1982) The definition of ancient manured zones by means of extensive sherd-sampling techniques. *Journal of Field Archaeology* 9: 323–33.

Wilkinson, T. J. (1990) *Town and Country in SE Anatolia, Vol.1. Settlement and Land Use at Kurban Hoyuk and Other Sites in the Lower Karababa Basin*. Oriental Institute Publications 109. Chicago, Oriental Institute.

Wilkinson, T. J. (1993) Linear hollows in the Jazira, Upper Mesopotamia. *Antiquity* 67: 548–62.

Wilkinson, T. J. (2000a) Regional approaches to Mesopotamian archaeology: the contribution of archaeological surveys. *Journal of Archaeological Research* 8: 219–67.

Wilkinson, T. J. (2000b) Geoarchaeology of the Amuq Plain. In K. A. Yener, C. Edens, T. P. Harrison, J. Verstraete, and T. J. Wilkinson, The Amuq Valley Regional Project, 1995–1998, *American Journal of Archaeology* 104: 168–79.

Wilkinson, T. J. (2001) Archaeological survey of the Tell Beydar region, Syria, 1997: a preliminary report. In K. Van Lerberghe and G. Voet (eds.) *Tell Beydar: Environmental and Technical Studies*: 1–37. Subartu VI. Turnhout, Brepols.

Wilkinson, T. J. and Barbanes, E. (2000) Settlement patterns in the Syrian Jazira during the Iron Age. In G. Bunnens (ed.) *Essays on Syria in the Iron Age*: 397–424. Ancient Near Eastern Studies 7 (supplement). Louvain, Peeters Press.

Wilkinson, T. J. and Tucker, D. (1995) *Settlement Development in the North Jazira, Iraq*. Warminster, Aris & Phillips.

Williamson, T. (1998) Questions of preservation and destruction. In P. Everson and T. Williamson (eds.) *The Archaeology of Landscape: Studies Presented to Christopher Taylor*: 1–24. Manchester, Manchester University Press.

15. Settlement Pattern and Population Change in Mesoamerican and Mediterranean Civilizations: A Comparative Perspective

Richard E. Blanton

Increasingly, in both Mesoamerica and the Mediterranean, archaeologists and historians are using the results of settlement pattern surveys to understand the past (*e.g.*, Alcock 1993; Blanton *et al.* 1993; Cherry 1983; 1994; Davis 1994; Kardulias 1994; Lloyd 1991; Snodgrass 1990; Wallace-Hadrill 1991), but the research potential of comparative analysis of settlement pattern data has not often been realized (though see now Smith 2002). In this chapter, I analyze settlement pattern survey data coded from published sources to compare these two civilizations, emphasizing similar and contrastive patterns of long-term sociocultural evolutionary change. By undertaking this ambitious task, I hope to illustrate the potential value of comparison of settlement pattern data for theory development, following the lead of Wright (1986), who first hinted at the usefulness of such an approach. Comparison based on survey data can be an important analytical strategy that will allow us to build on the findings of earlier comparativists whose work was influential, but largely qualitative and difficult to evaluate empirically (*e.g.* Adams 1966; Service 1975).

I suggest that now is the time for survey-oriented archaeologists to devote more effort to comparison. A vast amount of survey data has accumulated over the past 30 years from various world areas, much of it based on field methods that grew out of research in Mesopotamia (*e.g.* Adams 1981) and the Valley of Mexio (Millon 1973; Sanders *et al.* 1979). Survey methods vary somewhat, reflecting (among other factors) a combination of the archaeologist's preferences, environmental conditions, and the type of permit with which the archaeologist is working; but most contemporary survey archaeologists in the Mediterranean and Mesoamerica are working within the framework of that larger methodological tradition and its associated problem orientation. This shared knowledge provides a foundation for within- and cross-regional comparative analysis.

Most of the comparative literature based on settlement pattern data emphasizes regional and temporal differences within larger civilizational traditions (Alcock 1993; Bintliff 1997; Blanton *et al.* 1993). Is it reasonable to compare across two civilizations? I first pondered this while engaged in my own survey in Rough Cilicia, on the south coast of Turkey. After having devoted many field seasons to survey in highland Mesoamerica, I was surprised at the similarities I encountered in the scale and complexity of the Turkish sites, their surface visibility, and ceramic densities. To this Mesoamericanist, however, differences were also apparent. Most notable was the fact that my colleagues and I were able to do this project even though no one had ever studied the locally-produced pottery. Pottery reflecting what I will refer to below as 'metropolitan styles' – in our case, Hellenistic and Roman (or local imitations thereof) – was present in sufficient density, even on small rural sites, to provide for basic site periodization. This is very much unlike Mesoamerica, where we encounter a greater degree of ceramic provincialism. It was not until late in the prehispanic sequence that several perhaps analogous metropolitan pottery types were in use over a wide area and across social segments, including Chalco-Cholula polychrome (Smith and Heath-Smith 1982). I was also surprised to find such an attenuated occupational sequence in the Rough Cilician survey area, and it was this singular fact that prompted me to attempt a comparative study of Mediterranean regions based on archaeological survey data (Blanton 2000), to find out just how common it was for a region to be missing whole archaeological periods.

While coding data for this small comparative project, it seemed to me that in prehispanic Mesoamerica long-term demographic change, viewed broadly, was unlike what I was finding in the Mediterranean survey data. My suspicion could only be confirmed by developing a coding system for data from two civilizations, but this presented methodological difficulties. In some important respects, survey projects in the two regions are often not highly comparable, even though they draw from a common pool of methodological exemplars. Mediterranean lithic and ceramic sequences are far more complex than those found in Mesoamerica, limiting the degree to which surface areas of components of multi-period sites can be accurately measured by visual inspection of surface artifacts, as we routinely do in the course of Mesoamerican survey.

Furthermore, Mediterranean surveys are generally smaller than their Mesoamerican counterparts, in part owing to the fact that permits for large-scale surveys are not often obtainable, especially in Greece. In the surveys analyzed for this paper, the mean area of the Mediterranean surveys is 350 sq. km (ranging from 18 to 3,250), while the Mesoamerican surveys average 838 sq. km (ranging from 200 to 2,150). Small surveys are problematic in a number of respects. We know from our Mesoamerican experience that local-scale demographic change does not always reflect more general patterns being played out at a regional scale (Kowalewski n.d.); so some of the variation over time in population densities seen in the Mediterranean surveys could be an artifact, in part, of the smaller scale of survey projects there. Additionally, while all the Mesoamerican surveys based their methodology on the exemplars mentioned previously, some of the larger Mediterranean surveys included in my coding were done before systematic settlement pattern methodology was fully developed (especially the South Etruria surveys conducted by John Ward-Perkins and others, and the Lower Guadalquivir survey by M. Ponsich). As a result, some categories of data could not be reliably derived from these cases.

DATA SOURCES

Some Mediterranean data analyzed here were carried over from my previous comparative study (Blanton 2000: Appendix 3), although I dropped some surveys from that list and included others, given that I added variables for this project, including nearest-neighbor measures for rank one and rank two centers (described below). My goal was to include surveys in which: a) survey maps, as well as site-by-site descriptions, are available in accessible publications; b) the archaeologist(s) made use of systematic field-by-field survey (or a method I judged similar to contemporary standards) over an area I judged to be at least reasonably representative of larger regional-scale processes; c) a full-coverage approach was employed (*e.g.* Fish and Kowalewski 1990), as opposed to a sampling method; and d) all periods were studied (in the Mediterranean, Neolithic through Late Roman; in Mesoamerica, Early Formative through Late Postclassic) (Table 15.1). In my original sample, I had emphasized the European Mediterranean, and this same bias has been carried forward to the present study, although below I tabulate selected nearest-neighbor data from Africa, as well as other cases not included in the coded sample. Two of the requirements, full-coverage and all periods, were sometimes not met in the cases I coded, and this resulted in 'no data' entries for some variables or missing periods. All-period archaeological survey in the Mediterranean is notoriously difficult, owing to the complexity of the lithic and ceramic sequences, and some archaeologists have tended to focus on

just one, or a few, periods. I included such surveys if useful data could be coded for the period(s) represented.

One of the variables added to this study, but not in my original study, is a nearest-neighbor measure for distance between centers. While a number of studies have made use of inter-center distances for comparative analysis (*e.g.* Bekker-Nielsen 1989), I coded only cases where distance between centers can be ascertained from systematic archaeological survey maps. Although the completeness of survey coverage is quite variable for the Mediterranean, I selected cases done sufficiently intensively so that it was likely that all central places of significant size were located. An additional factor figuring into my case selection was the requirement that site size and/or site population estimate be included, so that I could calculate total population density in persons per sq. km by period (as well as other density measures described below). Some surveys were included primarily for their potential for nearest-neighbor and other measures, but could not serve as reliable sources for population estimates.

The data are included in two appendices. Appendix 1 codes each survey area by period, and emphasizes site and population density measures of several types for each area and period as a whole (totaling 172 cases). Appendix 2 codes for centers by period, and emphasizes center size and nearest-neighbor measures for each center (343 cases).

Using these selection criteria, and with the resources available, I identified 13 Mediterranean and 8 Meso-american surveys. The coded surveys, with main sources and area surveyed, are the following:

Mediterranean

1. Lower Guadalquivir (Ponsich 1974) (3,250 sq. km)
2. Saint-Blaise, Provence (Trément 1999) (100 sq. km)
3. Albegna Valley and Ager Cosanus (Perkins 1999) (260 sq. km)
4. S. Etruria, combining Kahane *et al.* (1968) (Ager Veientanus); Duncan (1958) (Sutri); Jones (1962; 1963) (Ager Capenas); Frederiksen and Ward-Perkins (1957) (Ager Faliscus); and the summary in Potter (1979) (694 sq. km)
5. S. Euboea (Keller 1985) (41 sq. km)
6. N. Keos (Cherry *et al.* 1991) (18 sq. km)
7. S. Argolid (Jameson *et al.* 1994) (225 sq. km)
8. Melos (Renfrew and Wagstaff 1982) (34 sq. km)
9. Lasithi (Watrous 1974; 1982) (66 sq. km)
10. Pylos (Davis *et al.* 1997) (40 sq. km)
11. Kavousi (Haggis 1996) (21 sq. km)
12. Palaipaphos (Cyprus) (Rupp *et al.* 1984) (73 sq. km)
13. Rough Cilicia (Blanton 2000) (80 sq. km)

Mesoamerica

1. Amatzinac, Morelos (Hirth 1980) (454 sq. km)
(2–6.) Valley of Mexico. Given the Valley's tendency over most of its prehispanic periods to have been politically

Years Ago	Mesoamerican Period	Valley of Mexico Phase	Valley of Oaxaca Phase	Mediterranean Period
500				
	Late Postclassic	Late Aztec	Monte Albán V	
		Early Aztec		
1000	Early Postclassic	Mazapan	Monte Albán IV	
		Coyotlatelco		
	Late Classic	Metepec	Monte Albán IIIB	
1500		Xolalpan		Late Roman
	Early Classic	Tlamimilolpa	Monte Albán IIIA	
		Miccaotli		Early Roman
2000	Late Formative	Tzacualli	Monte Albán II	
		Patlachique	Monte Albán Late I	Hellenistic
		Ticoman	Monte Albán Early I	
2500	Middle Formative			Classical
		Zacatenco	Rosario	Archaic
			Guadalupe	Geometric
3000			San José	
	Early Formative	Ixtapaluca		
			Tierras Largas	Late Bronze
3500				
4000				Middle Bronze
4500				
				Early Bronze
5000				
5500				
6000				
6500				Late/Final Neolithic
7000				
7500				
				Middle Neolithic
8000				
8500				Early Neolithic
9000				

Table 15.1 Chronology chart for Mesoamerica and the Mediterranean. The Mesoamerican dates, and Mediterranean dates before the beginning of the Geometric Period, are based in part on calibrated radiocarbon dates.

fragmented (the Middle Horizon and the Late Aztec being the major exceptions to this), the Valley of Mexico surveys have been coded separately:

2. Chalco-Xochimilco (Parsons *et al.* 1982) (650 sq. km)
3. Ixtapalapa (Blanton 1972) (200 sq. km)
4. Texcoco (Parsons 1971) (600 sq. km)
5. Teotihuacan Valley (Cowgill 1997; Evans *et al.* 2000; Millon 1973; Nichols 1994; Parsons and Sanders 2000; Sanders *et al.* 1975; Sanders 1986–87; 1996;

Sanders and Evans 2000) (550 sq. km)
6. Zumpango (Parsons *et al.* 1983; the latter and Sanders *et al.* 1979 were also consulted for the Valley of Mexico region as a whole) (600 sq. km)
7. The Valley of Oaxaca was coded as one region, given its tendency to have been politically and economically integrated during and after Period I (Blanton 1978; Blanton *et al.* 1982; Kowalewski *et al.* 1989) (2,150 sq. km)
8. Mixteca Alta (Balkansky *et al.* 2000; Stiver 2001) (1,496 sq. km)

This sample totals 11,602 sq. km of systematically surveyed area (4,902 sq. km Mediterranean and 6,700 sq. km Mesoamerican), within which 12,657 sites (components) were located and described (2,827 Mediterranean and 9,830 Mesoamerican). I am not sure to what extent these impressive numbers go to the issue of validity of the conclusions of this paper. Even though the total area is large, the hard-won product of many thousands of foot-bruising days of survey, we need more data. For example, the number of Bronze Age centers in the sample is quite small, and the major Bronze Age polities have not been completely surveyed. In spite of these shortcomings, the extant data are rich; what is attempted here represents only a fraction of what could be learned from them. It is my hope that others will be intrigued by these findings and pursue other research problems based on comparison.

A COMPARATIVE METHOD FOR THE SETTLEMENT PATTERN ANALYSIS OF CENTERS

Much of the analysis that follows reflects the approach used by Kowalewski (1990), in which he characterized change in social complexity in the prehispanic Valley of Oaxaca based on the region-wide systematic archaeological survey that provided data on all classes of settlements – ranging from central places to villages and isolated residences, as well as special-purpose sites such as boundary fortifications (Kowalewski *et al.* 1989). While Kowalewski's paper is a useful model for addressing complexity issues with settlement pattern data, in trying to replicate his approach beyond Oaxaca, I found that in most instances the requisite information is not available from published settlement pattern surveys. In the Mediterranean, especially, surveys often covered quite small areas, so that the settlements found are not reflective of the overall complexity of a social formation at a particular time period. Additionally, supraregional or other high-ranking centers are rarely found within the surveys that have been done (in some survey areas, no centers at all are found, at least in some periods). In order to pursue a comparative study of settlement patterns, given these data limitations, I modified Kowalewski's approach. Several of his variables could be coded from certain surveys, including estimates of center population and total population by period. For comparative purposes, I converted the latter values to population density (persons per sq. km) by period. I also borrowed his measure of urbanization, which is the percentage of the population residing in communities of more than 1,000 persons. This value did prove useful for cross-regional comparison, since in many cases the scale of cities and towns is highly comparable for the regions and periods considered. Although this figure of 1,000 should not be regarded as necessarily having intrinsic sociocultural or demographic significance, it is of interest to note that, for both civilizations, it is close to, or somewhat higher than, an estimated upper limit of population size for a largely agrarian

community with an agricultural catchment of 2 km, as I discuss below.

The most difficult problem facing the comparative researcher surrounds the question of central place hierarchy. All the surveys did distinguish between centers (cities and towns), villages, and isolated residences (in addition to special-function sites, such as industrial sites, or culturally-specific sites, such as Mediterranean villas), although the classifying criteria vary somewhat according to region, time period, and the archaeologist's preferences. In some study regions, a considerable hierarchical depth is evident for centers, ranging up to five identified levels for some periods in Oaxaca, for example, while in other surveys little center hierarchical differentiation was evident.

In order to maximize the amount of information that could be coded from sometimes small regional surveys, I developed a comparative method that focuses analytical attention on local cities or towns (I call these 'rank 1 and 2 centers') (cf. Engels 1990: 175). Ranks 1 and 2 refer to rank in relation to the local system of central places, not the social system as a whole, which usually cannot be studied with the territorially limited settlement pattern data. In cases where a supraregional center was located within a survey area (*e.g.* Teotihuacan and Monte Albán), it was regarded as a rank-1 center, since such centers would have provided central-place services to a local hinterland population in addition to serving as the capital of a multi-regional state, while not including their values in calculations of average center size or related calculations tied to their population sizes.

The center category did not include all large sites; those that had specialized functions – for example, industrial production – were not included with the rank 1 and 2 centers. I assume that, when an archaeologist identifies a site as a city, town, or center, he or she is referring to a community that served as a locus of central-place transactions, especially market and administrative transactions. These centers often had additional functions (*e.g.* break-of-bulk, shrines, or defense), but the remains of recognized forms of public architecture and public spaces suggest that they served as central places. In the sample, centers of ranks 1 and 2 as defined here served adjacent populations within hinterlands 3 to 15 km in radius, with hinterland areas ranging from roughly 20 sq. km or less up to roughly 500 sq. km (*e.g.* Blanton 2000: Appendix 3). By comparison, a Late Imperial Chinese local system focused on an intermediate market town that occupied an average of 350 sq. km (Skinner 1964: 18, 33). Some survey areas I coded included multiple centers of this scale with interlocked hinterlands, along the interstices of which developed secondary centers (rank 2) in positions suggesting the playing out of Christaller's K=3 or K=4 spatial configurations (*e.g.* in the Postclassic Valley of Mexico in Blanton [1996: figs. 3–8, 3–9]; *cf.* Skinner's [1964] 'standard market towns' in relation to intermediate market towns). In other cases, secondary centers appear to have developed as nearby outliers of particular centers, rather than in interstitial positions between multiple centers, perhaps linking subsets of a center's hinterland into its territorial system, as in the case of the Christallerian K=7 or administrative pattern – for example, the Texcoco domain of the Late Postclassic Valley of Mexico (Blanton 1996: 72–73).

I included only these rank 1 and rank 2 centers in my center coding, an analytical approach that has some consequences for comparative study:

1) I ignore what are sometimes called 'lower-limb' centers with ranks below one and two. In the survey reports coded here, such sites were often difficult to interpret in regional functional terms (*cf.* Bennet 1990: 197, 201), or they had specialized or limited functions. In the coded regions, I came across local community administrative sites, industrial sites, road stations along major highways in South Etruria, and shrine and tomb complexes in some other areas, none of which fit my definition of a rank 1 or 2 center. I included such localities in my 'village' category if they were thought to have had a resident population (as used here, 'village' is applied to sites that were neither rank 1 or 2 centers, nor isolated residences).

2) By focusing on local cities and towns, this method cannot address whole-system complexity, especially in cases of large states or empires. On the other hand, analysis at a middle scale, centered around the spacing and sizes of local centers, not only permits cross-regional comparison with limited data, but it also opens a window onto domains of social action that are likely to have been significant in the everyday lives of the great majority of persons. Here I refer to the importance of local centers in the ordinary routines of households whose domestic economies must account for the time and energy costs of frequent trips for market exchanges, administrative transactions, temple services, entertainment, and similar frequently occurring social transactions. The spatial patterning of local centers is highly relevant to many aspects of domestic life, for example, in relation to market choices, degree of commercialization, time and labor costs of transport to centers, and degree of access to public goods and political participation (*e.g.* Smith 1976). Viewed from the perspective of governing officials, these same settlement pattern variables are relevant to the cost and effectiveness of social control and of the mobilization of surpluses, among other functions of a polity or its local administrative organs (as I discuss in more detail below).

Data Organization

Data from the survey reports have been coded in two overlapping but distinct formats (Appendices 1 and 2). In the first data set, the unit of analysis is the survey area, for which each archaeological period was coded separately,

and placed chronologically at the mid-point of the period. For each survey area, I coded for total estimated population density by period (in persons per sq. km) and percent urban (percent in settlements of 1,000 or more), also recording whether the population size represented growth of 30% or more from the prior period (coded as '1'), about the same population size (coded as '0'), or decline of 30% or more from the prior period (coded as '-1'), in order to detect population transitions of large magnitude, without having to assume that population estimates are necessarily highly accurate. I coded for the number (per 100 sq. km) of centers of ranks 1 and 2 (combined), villages, isolated residences, and villas, as well as the contribution each settlement type made to total population density.

In cases where the settlement pattern report did not provide a ranking of centers, I looked at a combination of population size and scale of public architecture to identify centers of the top two ranks (in some cases, only one center category could be identified). In some of the larger surveys, where numerous central places were identified, I found myself at times making arbitrary decisions regarding which centers to include or exclude. This was a particular problem in the Lower Guadalquivir survey (a real monster by Mediterranean standards, covering more than 3,000 sq. km), where only minimal data are provided for cities and towns, and where it is likely that centers of ranks 1 through 3 or possibly 4 can be distinguished. In the Mediterranean, isolated residences were usually described as farms in the survey reports, but I included all sites with surface areas of less than about 0.2 ha in this category (most were less than 0.1 ha in area). Villages included sites greater than 0.2 ha. For the Mesoamerican surveys, isolated residences had estimated populations of less than 15 (or were described as isolated residences), while villages included all residential sites above an estimated 15 persons that were not identified as rank 1 or 2 centers.

In the second data set, the units of analysis are the rank 1 and 2 centers, with a separate coded entry for each center by time period. For each center, I coded survey area, region, time period (as the mid-point of the period), population size estimate, rank, and distance to nearest neighbor in km (recorded simply as straight-line distance, although I measured around major topographic obstacles to movement). In cases where distance to the edge of the survey is less than distance to the nearest other center within the survey area, no value was recorded, unless it was clear that no closer center existed outside the survey area.

FARMING IN TWO CIVILIZATIONS

Comparing two such highly distinct and historically disconnected civilizations is clearly not a methodologically trivial exercise. Here I support my proposition that comparison is possible, by pointing to similarities in several factors that

	Mediterranean (wheat)	*Mesoamerica (maize, net production)*
Average productivity of the major grain(kgs/ha /year)	600 (gross) (estimates range from 240 to 1000 (Bintliff and Snodgrass 1985: 318; Davis 1991; Gallant 1991: Table 4.7; Halstead 1981: 318; Jameson 1977/78: 131; Jameson et al. 1994: 283, 550) 500 (net for hoe cultivation) (subtracts 17% for seed reserves, from Stirling 1965: 85) 400 (net for plow cultivation) (subtracts 17% for stall feeding of draft animals, from Stirling 1965: 85)	(Late Formative) Type I Irrigable 581 Type II Irrigable 375 Type III Dry Farmed 250 (Classic/Postclassic) Type I Irrigable 1000 Type II Irrigable 664 Type III Dry Farmed 415 (values for both periods are based on figures for the Valley of Oaxaca in Kowalewski 1982: Table 9-3, and Kirkby 1973: Ch. 5; *cf.* Charlton 1970: Table 3; Hirth 2000, Vol. 1: Table 8.3; Sanders 1976: Table 9 for comparable values for the Central Highlands; the net value subtracts 17% for seed reserves)
Average grain consumption (kgs/person/ year)	200 (Foxhall and Forbes 1982: 69; Jameson 1977/78: 131)	200 (for both periods, based on Kowalewski 1982: 158; cf. Parsons 1976)
Fallow	Each year, 50% of outer fields (grain) are bare fallowed (Halstead 1987: 82)	Type I land is continuously cultivated, while Types II and III use a 50% fallow (Sanders 1976: Table 9; Hirth 2000, Vol. I: Table 8.3)
A household of 5 persons can cultivate (maximum) in ha/year	2.5 (hoe cultivation) (assumes that hoeing requires 50% or more labor per ha than plowing, cf. Gallant 1991: 51; Manning 1994: 236; White 1970: 336) 5 (plow cultivation) (Kehoe 1988: 16; White 1970: 181)	5 Using the *coa* and related hand tools (Rojas Rabiela 1984), and assuming one person can cultivate 2 ha, and that 50% of an average 5-person household works in the fields (Kirkby 1973: 73; Kowalewski 1982: 156)

Table 15.2 Key agronomic variables for the comparison of two civilizations.

are relevant to understanding variation in the coded settlement pattern data. We can start with the agricultural variables set out in Table 15.2. For both the Mediterranean and Mesoamerica, I use the main grain crop (wheat and maize) as a proxy for agricultural productivity, since the basic grain constituted the foundation of the typical diet in both cases. More importantly for regional analysis, the major grains took up the largest cultivated areas (*e.g.* Nowicki 1999: 163), and thus were crucial in determining the sizes of community agricultural catchments. Subsidiary crops in both cases were often grown intensively as smaller infield garden crops, or were intercropped with the major grain (*e.g.* olives in the Mediterranean; beans and squash in Mesoamerica). Wheat (or barley) is different from maize in two important respects that are evaluated in Table 15.2. Mediterranean grain productivity appears to have been more inelastic in response to intensification than maize. Increased agricultural production was achieved primarily

through manure fertilizing (Alcock *et al.* 1994) and through the labor-intensive intercropping of grain with pulses, reducing the usual 50% fallow period (Davis 1991: 138; Halstead 1987: 82). Maize intensification could involve fertilizing and reduced fallow too; but while dry farming prevailed in the European Mediterranean (*e.g.* White 1984: 168), the key to increased maize productivity was irrigation. Hence, I have followed Kirkby (1973) and Kowalewski (1982) in calculating maize productivity according to degree of irrigation (in Table 15.2, Type I land is canal or well-irrigated, Type II is flood-water irrigated, and Type III is dry-farmed).

Maize, unlike wheat (or barley), was also different in that it was a continually evolving biotechnology over the periods in question (Kirkby 1973: fig. 48), while wheat productivity estimates do not vary over time. In fact, some estimates indicate higher productivity for Neolithic wheat than later periods, because it would have been grown only

A 2 km radius catchment is 1256 ha, of which I assume 60% is used for grain cultivation (754 ha). I assume a 50% fallow for wheat fields, giving 377 ha cultivated in one year.

I. Hoe cultivation, @ 500 kgs/ha net   Total Annual Production 188,400 kg

  At 200 kgs/person/year, this production supports a population of 942

  Households needed to cultivate 377 ha: 151

  This implies that 151 farm households can support 37 other households (0.6 to 1) (actual figures for households supported will be lower, because not all households will cultivate the maximum possible 2.5 ha).

II. Plow cultivation, @ 400 kgs/ha net   Total Annual Production 150,800 kg

  At 200 kgs/person/year, this production supports a population of 754

  Households needed to cultivate 377 ha: 75

  This implies that 75 farm households can support 76 other households (1 to 1) (actual figures for households supported will be lower, because not all households will cultivate the maximum possible 5 ha).

Table 15.3 Key agronomic variables for a Mediterranean community with an agricultural catchment of two km radius. (Calculations based on Table 15.2.)

on selected high-productivity soils (Halstead 1981: 318). Therefore, Table 15.1 contrasts Late Formative (*c.* 200 BC) maize productivity values as a proxy for the Formative Period as a whole, with estimates for approximately AD 500 as a proxy for Classic and Postclassic Periods (which, generally, are grouped together in the following discussion).

Per capita consumption and grain reserving have similar values for maize and wheat, but while all maize cultivation was based on the *coa* (digging stick and related implements: Rojas Rabiela 1984), wheat production displays a significant difference based on whether cultivation was by hoe or plow (Manning 1994: 236). Plowing increases production because it allows for the annual cultivation of roughly twice the area per farm family (and allows the cultivation of more marginal land), but some grain must be devoted to stall feeding of draft animals, reducing the productivity per ha.

The values in Table 15.2 can be made relevant to the variables I coded by investigating some demographic implications of various agronomic regimes. This is attempted in Tables 15.3, 15.4, and 15.5, where I calculate the population parameters of several hypothetical communities. For each, I assume a community with an agricultural catchment radius of 2 km. This does not imply that all agrarian communities would be limited to a 2 km catchment radius, only that beyond this distance preindustrial farmers begin to experience diminishing returns to their efforts, owing to excess travel times to most distant fields (*e.g.* Halstead and Jones 1989; Vita-Finzi and Higgs 1970). Given that communities in both areas may have catchments

truncated by steep terrain, coastal location, etc., it has also been assumed that an average of 60% of each catchment is usable; a much more detailed analysis than is possible here would estimate each site's actual catchment (*e.g.* Blanton 2000: 14–15). While travel-to-field (or travel-to-market) costs in time and energy could have been somewhat mitigated using domesticated animals in the Mediterranean, it is also the case that animal-based transport is not only energetically costly, but may not significantly reduce travel time. Oxen travel at a leisurely pace that is roughly one-half human speed, and they can work only five hours per day (Engels 1978: 15). Mules and horses travel further per day than oxen, carrying three times what humans can carry, but may consume nearly proportionately that much more food energy (Engels 1978: 17; *cf.* Hassig 1985: 218, who points out that the pre-Hispanic mode of transport using human carriers continued well into the Colonial Period). Engels (1978: 17) concludes: 'It should be remembered that because of the inefficient throat and girth harness, manpower was as effective as horsepower in antiquity.' My own conclusion is that the presence or absence of domesticated animals is not a fundamental factor differentiating the farm economies of the two civilizations (*e.g.* Clark and Haswell 1970: 204), at least not in terms of the variables addressed here.

From Table 15.3, the more 'primitive' hoe cultivation system supports a higher potential community population (942) than the plow-based system (754 people), but requires more households to cultivate the estimated 754 ha catchment. The corresponding Mesoamerican estimates in Tables 15.4 and 15.5 bracket the Mediterranean values;

A 2 km radius catchment is 1256 ha, of which I assume 60% is used for grain cultivation (754 ha). Based on the average area for land types from Kowalewski 1982: 153), this would imply:

Type I (irrigable, continously cultivated) 10% @581 kg/ha 43,800 kg
Type II (irrigable, 50% fallow) 10% @ 375 kg/ha 14,138 kg
Type III (dry-farmed, 50% fallow) 80% @250 kg/ha 75,425 kg

Total Annual Production 133,400 kg

Average maize productivity 321 kg/ha

At 200 kgs/person/year consumed, this production supports a population of 667

Households needed to cultivate 415 ha: 83

This implies that 83 farm families can support 51 other families (.6 to 1)
(actual figures for families supported will be lower, because not all
farmers will cultivate the maximum possible 2 ha).

Table 15.4 Key agronomic variables for a Mesoamerican Late Formative community with an agricultural catchment of two km radius. (Calculations based on Table 15.2; Kirkby 1973: Ch. 5; Kowalewski 1982: 153, Table 9.3. Estimated maize productivity values for the Valley of Oaxaca, Monte Albán Late I have been used.)

A 2 km radius catchment is 1256 ha, of which I assume 60% is used for grain cultivation (754 ha). Based on the average area for land types from Kowalewski 1982: 153), this would imply:

Type I (irrigable, continously cultivated) 10% @1,000 kg/ha 75,400 kg
Type II (irrigable, 50% fallow) 10% @ 664 kg/ha 25,000 kg
Type III (dry-farmed, 50% fallow) 80% @415 kg/ha 125,000 kg

Total Annual Production 225,600 kg

Average maize productivity 545 kg/ha

At 200 kgs/person/year, this production supports a population of 1,128

Households needed to cultivate 415 ha: 83

This implies that 83 farm families can support 143 other families (1.7 to 1)
(actual figures for families supported will be lower, because not all
farmers will cultivate the maximum possible 2 ha).

Table 15.5 Key agronomic variables for a Mesoamerican Classic/Postclassic community with an agricultural catchment of two km radius. (Calculations based on Table 15.2; Kirkby 1973: Ch. 5; Kowalewski 1982: 153, Table 9–3. Estimated maize productivity values for the Valley of Oaxaca, Monte Albán IIIB have been used.)

while Formative Period production would support only an estimated 670, by the Classic/Postclassic the estimate is 1,128. Given that any Mediterranean community could potentially have a mixture of hoe- and plow-cultivated fields, it is not clear which of the two figures should be used for comparison. Animal-drawn ard or plow cultivation has been practiced since the late fourth millennium BC, but even in the Roman period poorer farm households could not afford draft animals (White 1970: 273). But if we assume that agronomic variables contributed importantly to the variation in population size of communities, as well as variation in regional population density, then the largely overlapping values seen in Tables 15.3–5 should predict broadly overlapping population-density values and community sizes in the two civilizations. Theoretically, and looking only at agronomic variables, Classic and Postclassic Mesoamerica should display higher population densities and larger community sizes overall. What I found, however, is both no and yes – no, Mesoamerican population density was not always higher in the later periods (although the mean values for both civilizations, as described below, are very similar); but, yes, Mesoamerican centers were, on average, larger than their Mediterranean counterparts. However, as I discuss below, it is unlikely that the difference can be attributed to agronomic factors.

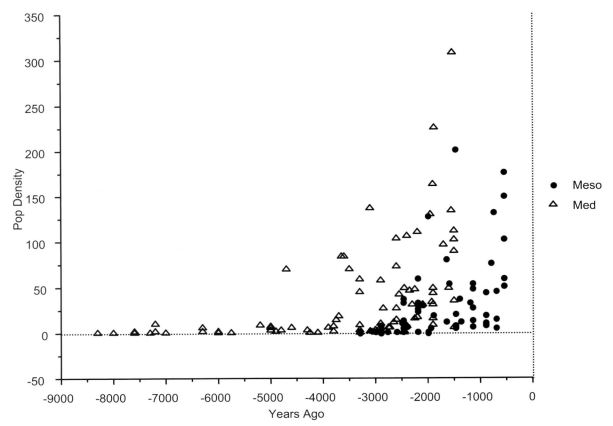

Figure 15.1   Estimated population densities (in persons per sq. km) of the coded surveys, plotted by years ago and split by Mesoamerica and the Mediterranean.

POPULATION GROWTH IN TWO CIVILIZATIONS

Site population estimates in my data sets follow the archaeologists' estimates where these are provided, but otherwise population size has been estimated from site area using standard conversion values widely used in the two regions (*e.g.* Jameson *et al.* 1994: 542–50; Sanders *et al.* 1979: 34–40). Figure 15.1 plots the population density values by years ago, split by Mesoamerica and the Mediterranean. Obviously, the Mediterranean has a longer history of settled village life and ceramic technology. Based on these data, however, it exhibits little or no net gain in population density during the Neolithic (although some denser 'patches' of Neolithic population are known in areas apart from the surveys included here [Perlès 2001: 113]), and significant population growth was delayed until after about 4,000 years ago. Mesoamerican agricultural village life started later, but growth was comparatively rapid following initial sedentism. After about 2,500 years ago there is a considerable degree of overlap of population density values for the two civilizations. In both, the highest values are late in the respective archaeological sequences evaluated here. Had even later periods been coded, both would also show major declines, in the Mediterranean following the Late Roman Period, and in Mesoamerica following the Spanish conquest.

I use a linear regression and correlation approach to illustrate the main growth trends (Figures 15.2 and 15.3). (In these figures and in the following discussion, Bronze Age pertains to 5,200 to 3,000 years ago; Classical Antiquity, 3,000 to 1,500 years ago; Formative Period, 2,600 to 1,800 years ago; and Classic/Postclassic, 1,800 to 500 years ago.) While the position and slope of the Neolithic regression line is unlike other periods evaluated here (in Figure 15.3), the slope and position of the regression line for the Formative Period is roughly similar to the Mediterranean Bronze Age (although the latter tends toward higher population densities). Likewise, the Mediterranean Historical Period (hereafter referred to as 'Classical Antiquity') and the Classic/Postclassic Periods display similar positions and slopes of their respective regression lines (again, with the Mediterranean tending toward higher population densities). These central tendencies in patterns of population growth mask important differences that are evident with more detailed analysis of the population estimates.

Population Growth and Collapse

While their population-density values are broadly over-lapping, in other measures Mesoamerican and Medi-

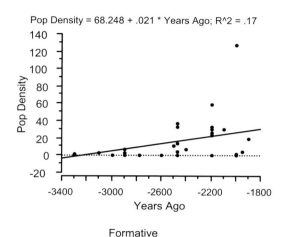

Formative

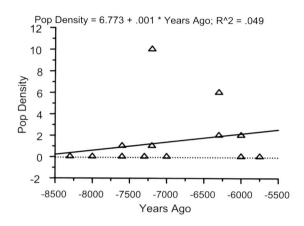

Neolithic

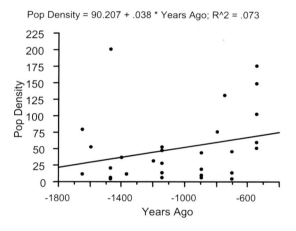

Classic and Postclassic

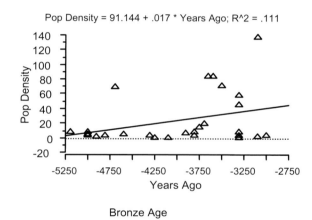

Bronze Age

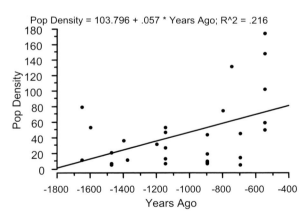

Classic and Postclassic, Excluding Classic Period Teotihuacan

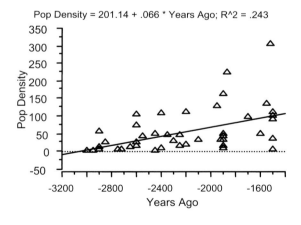

Classical Antiquity

Figure 15.2 A regression and correlation method for summarizing broad population growth trends for the Mesoamerican Formative and the Classic/Postclassic. (Population density is in persons per sq. km, based on estimates from the coded surveys; the regression lines summarize overall growth trends.)

Figure 15.3 A regression and correlation method for summarizing broad population growth trends for three segments of the Mediterranean sequence considered here. (Population density is in persons per sq. km, based on estimates from the coded surveys; the regression lines summarize overall growth trends.)

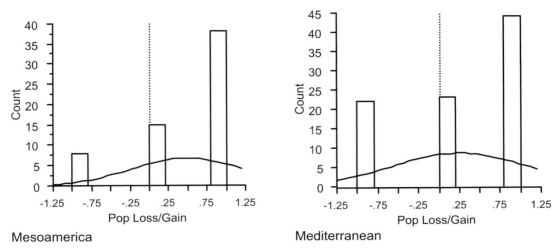

Figure 15.4 Frequency distributions of population loss and gain, based on population estimates from the coded surveys. (-1 signifies loss of 30% or more from the prior period, 0 signifies less than 30% change from the prior period, and +1 signifies 30% or more gain from the prior period; the lines show the expected frequency curves for a normal distribution with the same mean and standard deviation as the variable.)

terranean civilizations displayed contrasting population dynamics over the periods in question. Figure 15.4 plots the frequency of substantial population loss and gain for each survey area (as already noted, 30% or more loss from the prior period is coded as '-1', population about the same as '0', and growth of 30% or more from the prior period as '1'). While the linear regression lines in Figures 15.2 and 15.3 summarize overall growth trends, local population histories were more complex, especially in the Mediterranean, where episodes of 30% or more loss from the prior period occurred roughly three times as often as in the Mesoamerican survey areas. In Mesoamerica, by contrast, most episodes of significant demographic transition between periods involved rapid growth, and most of the extreme decline episodes can be tied to a single event, namely the consolidation of Terminal Formative (Tzacualli phase) population at Teotihuacan and the corresponding emptying-out of adjacent areas including the Texcoco, Ixtapalapa, and Chalco-Xochimilco regions (Sanders *et al.* 1979: 105–108). Tables 15.6–8 document this aspect of contrastive population histories by summarizing growth and decline episodes and instances of extremely low or non-existent population in the two areas, and they demonstrate that decline episodes and low population densities were both comparatively frequent in the Mediterranean and occurred across a variety of time periods and places. While Horden and Purcell (2000: 266) perhaps overstep the data when they claim that there was no sustained population growth in the pre-modern Mediterranean (there was overall growth, at least from the Bronze Age through Classical Antiquity), they nonetheless correctly identify a significant local demographic pattern in which episodic population growth and agricultural intensification in many cases were undone by decline and disintensification (*e.g.* Horden and Purcell 2000: 279). According to them, this

dynamic reflects, in part, a tendency toward 'substantial horizontal movements of population' (2000: 267; *cf.* Driessen 2001: 53 and *passim*). I return to this point below.

Urbanism and Population Sizes of Centers

Another difference in the demographic patterns of the two civilizations pertains to the population sizes of centers and the relative proportion of persons living in centers and villages. Mesoamerican rank 1 and 2 centers were as large or larger than their Mediterranean counterparts. Table 15.9 summarizes population means for these centers during the Bronze Age, Classical Antiquity, the Formative period, and the Classic/Postclassic period. Some Bronze Age centers reached population sizes considerably above the period mean of 850 indicated in this table. For example, the Palace of Nestor in the Pylos region is estimated as at least 12 ha during the Late Helladic IIIB period (Davis *et al.* 1997: 430), probably indicating well over 2,500 persons if one employs the standard multiplier of 210 persons per ha; Knossos peaked at an estimated 75 ha in Middle Minoan III–Late Minoan IA (Manning 1999), indicating a population of around 15,000 (*cf.* Branigan 2001: 39). But the average estimated center population of 850 is in the middle of the values in Table 15.3 calculated from agronomic variables for a largely agrarian community cultivating a catchment with the cost-effective 2 km radius.

Like the Bronze Age, the Formative period mean center size of 1,059 is superceded by a few larger centers of the period. For example, Late I Monte Albán is estimated at over 15,000 (Blanton 1978: 44), the same as the estimate for Knossos. But the mean value for the period is only marginally higher than the corresponding agronomic estimate given in Table 15.4 (670), suggesting that, to some degree, in both the Bronze Age and the Formative,

Albegna Valley and the Ager Cosanus	7th century BC (2800) to 6th century BC (10,500) 4th century BC (12,000) to 3rd century BC (3800)	X 3.8 -72%
S Etruria	L Bronze (500) to Villanovan (3200) Villanovan (3200) to E Etruscan (10,000) E Etruscan (10,000) to Republican (20,500) E Roman (21,500) to L Roman (3500)	X 6.4 X 3 X 2 -84%
N Keos	E Cyc. I (0) to E. Cyc. II (1200) E Cyc. II (1200) to M Cyc. I-II (100?) M Cyc. I-II (100?) to M Cyc. III/L Cyc. II (1500) M Cyc. III/L Cyc. II (1500) to L Helladic IIIC (50?) Geometric (100?) to Archaic (1300) Classical/E Hellenistic (1900) to L Hellenistic (550) E Roman (800?) to L Roman (2000)	 -92% X 15 -97% X 13 -71% X 2.6
S Argolid	Final Neolithic (450?) to E Helladic I-II (1900) E Helladic I-II (1900) to E Helladic III (0?) M Helladic (450?) to L Helladic (1800) L Helladic (1800) to Protogeometric and E Geometric (0) Protogeometric and E Geometric (0) to L Geometric (1100) L Geometric (1100) to Archaic (5900) Late Classical/Hellenistic (10,900) to E Roman (3400) E Roman (3400) to L Roman (8,100)	X 4 -100% X 4. -100% X 5.3 -69% X 2.4
Melos	Final Neolithic (0) to E Bronze (700?) M Bronze (250) to L Bronze (1800) L Bronze (1800) to E Geometric (0) E Geometric (0) to Classical (3600) E Roman (5600, estimated for whole island) to L Roman (15,000, estimated for whole island)	 X 7.3 -100% X 2.7
Lasithi	E Minoan II (200?) to M Minoan III (2900) E Roman (550?) to L Roman (6700)	X14.5 X 12
Pylos	E Helladic (120?) to L Helladic II (3300)	X 20
Kavousi	M Minoan II (400) to L Minoan I (1500) L Minoan I (1500) to Postpalatial (70?) E Iron (1200?) to Classical (0) Classical (0) to E Roman (1000?)	X 3.9 -95% -100%
Palaipaphos	E Cypriote (0) to M Cypriote (950?) M Cypriote (950?) to L Cypriote (4000?) L Cypriote (4000?) to Cypro-Geometric (700?) Cypro-Geometric (700?) to Cypro-Archaic (7500?) Cypro-Archaic (7500?) to Cypro-Classical (50?) Cypro-Classical (50?) to Hellenistic (8000?)	 X 4.2 -82% X 10.7 -99% X 160
Rough Cilicia	Classical (negligible) to Hellenistic (1350) Hellenistic (1350) to E Roman (18,000)	 X 13.3

Table 15.6 Examples of substantial demographic transitions between archaeological periods, based on the coded Mediterranean surveys. (Approximate population totals for periods are indicated in parentheses; the right column indicates the scales of approximate growth or decline as a multiple or percent population loss.)

center population size was limited by local agronomic factors. Bronze Age centers served as nodes in the management of agricultural production and storage for small polities (Bennet 1990: 94; Chadwick 1976; Halstead 1981; Renfrew 1972: 296–97; Schoep 2001). From Table 15.9, it is evident that such agronomic limits were less restrictive during later periods in both areas. For the Mediterranean, the transition to larger center size from the Bronze Age to later periods is consistent with information from textual and other sources that point to the central-place functions of centers in relation to market and administrative hinterlands (Engels 1990), reflecting the development of elab-

Amatzinac	Terminal Formative (2400) to E Classic (5200)	X 2.2
Chalco-Xochimilco	E Form (500) to M Form (5000)	X 10
	M Form (5000) to L Form (21,800)	X 4.4
	T Form (Patlachique) (18,000) to Tzacualli (0)	-100%
	Classic (4400) to Coyotlatelco (9000)	X 2
	Mazapan (7200) to E Aztec (30,000)	X 4
	E Aztec (30,000) to L Aztec (67,000)	X 2.2
Ixtapalapa	Patlachique (6700) to Tzacualli (40)	-94%
	Tzacualli (40) to E Classic (4150)	X 104
	E Aztec (2900) to L Aztec (12,000)	X 4.1
Texcoco	M Form (1900) to L Form (8100)	X 4.3
	L Form (8100) to Patlachique (18,000)	X 2.2
	Patlachique (18,000) to Tzacualli (700)	-96%
	Classic (3600) to Coyotlatelco (28,700)	X 8
	Coyotlatelco (28,700) to Mazapan (6000)	-79%
	E Aztec (20,000 min.) to L Aztec (105,400)	X 4?
Teotihuacan	M Form (500) to L Form (3000)	X 6
	L Form (3000) to Patlachique (33,000)	X 11
	Patlachique (33,000) to Tzacualli (70,300)	X 2.1
	Classic (111,000) to Coyotlatelco (29,500)	-73%
Zumpango	Coyotlatelco (4000) to Mazapan (12,000)	X 3
	Mazapan (12,000) to E Aztec (3750)	-69%
	E Aztec (3750) to L Aztec (31,000)	X 8.3
Valley of Oaxaca	Tierras Largas (300) to San José (2000)	X 6.2
	Rosario (1800) to Early I (14,500)	X 8
	Early I (14,500) to Late I (51,000)	X 3.5
	Period II (41,300) to Period IIIA (115,200)	X 2.8
	Period IV (70,000) to Period V (162,500)	X 2.3

Table 15.7 Examples of substantial demographic transitions between archaeological periods, based on the coded Mesoamerican surveys. (Approximate population totals for periods are indicated in parentheses; the right column indicates the scales of approximate growth or decline as a multiple or percent population loss. Demographic transitions attributable to the consolidation of population at Teotihuacan are underlined.)

S Etruria	All Neolithic, E and M Bronze Age
S Euboea	All Neolithic
N Keos	All Neolithic, E Cycladic I, M Cycladic I-II, L Helladic IIIC, Geometric
S Argolid	E, M, and L Neolithic, E Helladic II, Protogeometric, E Geometric
Melos	All Neolithic, E Geometric
Lasithi	All Neolithic through E Minoan II
Kavousi	E through L Neolithic
Palaipaphos	All Neolithic, Chalcolithic, E Cypriote, Cypro-Classical
Rough Cilicia	Neolithic through Classical
Chalco-Xochimilco	Tzacualli
Ixtapalapa	Tzacualli
Texcoco	E Form, Tzacualli
Teotihuacan	E Form, M Form
Zumpango	E Form, M Form, L Form
Valley of Oaxaca	Tierras Largas

Table 15.8 Periods with no or negligible population. (Periods where low population is attributed to migration to Teotihuacan are underlined.)

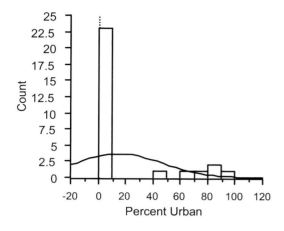

Bronze Age

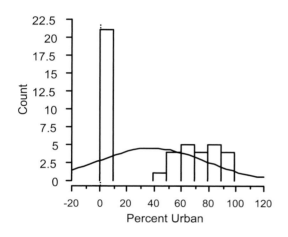

Classical Antiquity

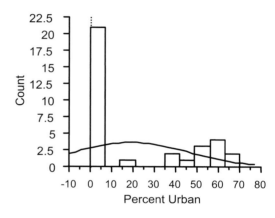

Formative Period

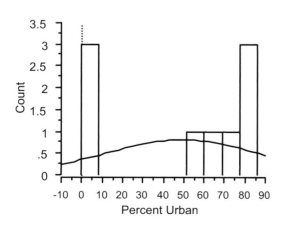

Early Roman

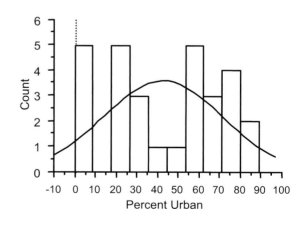

Classic and Postclassic Periods

Figure 15.5 Mediterranean frequency distributions of percent urban (percent of total population living in communities of 1,000 or more), based on site population estimates from the coded surveys. (The lines show the expected frequency curves for a normal distribution with the same mean and standard deviation as the variable.)

Figure 15.6 Mesoamerican frequency distributions of percent urban (percent of total population living in communities of 1,000 or more), based on site population estimates from the coded surveys. (The lines show the expected frequency curves for a normal distribution with the same mean and standard deviation as the variable.)

Bronze Age
Mean Center Population 850
SD=856, N=18
Classical Antiquity
Mean Center Population 2375
SD=1,946, N= 50
Mesoamerican Formative Period
Mean Center Population 1059
SD=1040, N=83
(excludes Teotihuacan and Monte Albán)
Classic/Postclassic Period
Mean Center Population 4416
SD=5,213, N=129
(excludes Teotihuacan and Monte Albán)

Table 15.9 Mean center population size.

Bronze Age	Mean Population Density 25 Population Density, Centers 18 Population Density, Villages 5 Population Density, Isolated Residences (IR) 2
Classical Antiquity	Mean Population Density 53 Centers 43 Villages 18 IR .5
Formative	Mean Population Density 14 Centers 9 Villages 5 IR .1
Classic and Postclassic	Mean Population Density 50 (Excluding Teotihuacan 44) Centers 27 (all sites) (Excluding Teotihuacan 21) Villages 23 IR .6

Table 15.10 Mean population densities, in persons per sq. km, for four periods, and the contribution to overall mean population density made by centers, villages, and isolated residences. Owing to missing data for some categories of sites, center, village, and isolated residence population densities do not always equal the values for overall population density.

orate commercial systems (Chaniotis 1999; Hopkins 1983; Sherratt and Sherratt 1993). Grain supplies and other commodities would have derived from market hinterlands of much larger size than a community's immediate agricultural catchment, among various possible sources of food supplies and other commodities. The growth in center size in the Mesoamerican transition from the Formative to the Classic/Postclassic suggests a parallel development from a situation where local agronomic factors strongly influenced center size earlier, while to a greater degree commercial and other central place functions probably would have to be considered in explaining center sizes in later periods.

Why Mesoamerican centers, on average, should be nearly double the size of the Mediterranean centers (Table 15.9) is not clear, although Table 15.5 does show that some agronomic limits to center growth were more relaxed by the Classic/Postclassic periods. Perhaps more importantly, as I discuss below, in Mesoamerica centers were more widely spaced – at least in general, if not in specific cases – suggesting that more central-place services were concentrated in fewer centers, each servicing a comparatively larger market and administrative hinterland.

During the coding, I was surprised to find another broad similarity between two civilizations – namely, that the percentage of the population in communities of 1,000 or more ('percent urban') was often quite high. Figure 15.5 illustrates this for the Mediterranean, with histograms for the Bronze Age, Classical Antiquity, and the Early Roman period, where it is evident that the number of survey areas with periods that are above c. 50% or more urban tended to increase over time. The Formative period histogram also displays periods of population concentration in a number of survey areas, as does the Classic/Postclassic; in the latter period, however, there is a greater range of variation in percent urban (Figure 15.6).

The frequent occurrence of population in larger communities is also indicated in Table 15.10, where total mean population density is considered to be made up of three components: (1) mean population density in all survey areas of persons living in centers of ranks 1 and 2; (2)

mean population density of persons living in communities larger than isolated residences, but not in centers of ranks 1 and 2 (here labeled 'villages'); and (3) mean population density represented by isolated residences. Overall, Mediterranean mean population density is higher than in Mesoamerica, but the figures for Classical Antiquity and the Classic/Postclassic are surprisingly similar, at about 50 per sq. km. In all four time periods, isolated residences contributed very little to total population density (Figure 15.7, top), although the Mediterranean values tend to be a little higher (especially in eastern regions), and a few Mediterranean surveys found quite high values, primarily dating from Classical through Early Roman periods (S. Etruria, S. Euboea, N. Keos, S. Argolid, and Lasithi [Late Roman]), and two surveys found high densities dating to the Bronze Age (Pylos [Early Helladic], and Kavousi [Middle Minoan II and Late Minoan I]).

Although Mesoamerican centers tended to be larger in population size in both periods than their Mediterranean counterparts (Table 15.9), center population contributed less to the total mean population density in the New World cases (Table 15.10), because in Mesoamerica the number of centers per sq. km was often lower (as discussed below). In Mesoamerica, villages accounted for more of the total mean population density (36% in the Formative period, over half in the Classic/Postclassic), while in the Mediterranean, the corresponding figures are 20% for the Bronze Age and 34% for Classical Antiquity. During the Late Postclassic, in particular, a pronounced process of ruralization is evident (see Figure 15.7); but, in both civilizations, a relative increase in rural population density

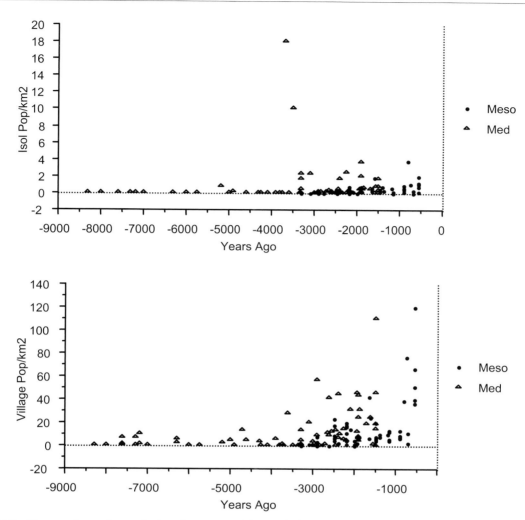

Figure 15.7   Top: estimated population densities of the coded surveys (in persons per sq km), calculated from the number of isolated residences, by years ago and split by Mesoamerica and the Mediterranean. Bottom: estimated population densities of the coded surveys (in persons per sq km), calculated from population estimates of all sites that were larger than isolated residences but not classified as centers of ranks 1 or 2 ('villages'), by years ago and split by Mesoamerica and the Mediterranean.

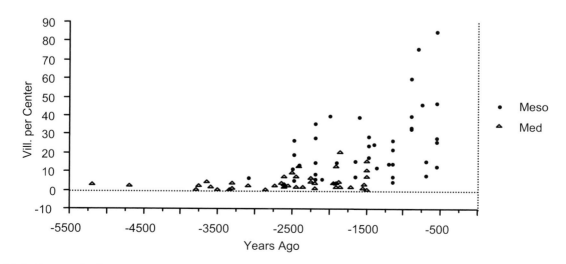

Figure 15.8   Ratio of villages per center (number of villages divided by number of centers of ranks 1 and 2), for the coded surveys, plotted by time and split by Mesoamerica and the Mediterranean.

Bronze Age	1.6
Classical Antiquity	4.5 600-400 BC Only=9 Early Roman Only =6.4
Formative	15.5
Classic/Postclassic	28.6

Table 15.11 Mean number of villages per center.

was a concomitant of long-term sociocultural evolutionary change.

A useful measure indicating the relative importance of center and non-center population in a region is the ratio of villages to centers (villages per center), first used by G. W. Skinner. For Late Imperial China, he found an average ratio of 18 villages per market town (Skinner 1964: 18). Figure 15.8 plots the village-to-center ratio over time for all coded survey areas, distinguishing between Meso-american and Mediterranean cases. While generally these values increased over time, and again illustrate the tendency toward ruralization in the later periods in both civilizations, the Mesoamerican values show more ruralization than the Mediterranean, and, toward the end of the pre-Hispanic sequence, they were well above the values for Late Imperial China (Table 15.11).

CENTER SPACING AND THE EVOLUTION OF COMMERCIALIZED LANDSCAPES

Center density (estimated as the number of centers per 100 sq. km) is a key measure providing us with a window onto differing modes of regional organization in Medi-terranean and Mesoamerican civilizations. While Meso-american centers (of ranks 1 and 2 as coded here) tended to be larger in population size (Table 15.9), especially in the later periods, there were fewer of them in most of the landscapes studied (Table 15.12) – a result that is not easily explained. One might expect an opposite outcome, if we assume that, in the Mediterranean, the costliness of trips from rural settlement to town, using pack animals and carts, would have been comparatively less. Hence, market and other central-place hinterlands could have been larger than Mesoamerican hinterlands, on average; but, instead, we see a Mediterranean that was more parceled out into comparatively small center hinterlands, with a higher density of centers. In Mesoamerica, generally, center population size was larger, while, at the same time, a greater proportion of the total population resided in communities smaller than centers of ranks 1 and 2. In part, the observed difference may be an artifact of my method, which emphasizes centers of the top two ranks. A greater proportion of the Mesoamerican population resided in settlements not coded as centers (Table 15.10), but some of the smaller sites not included in the center coding

Bronze Age	1.5 (SD=2.5)
Classical Antiquity	2.0 (SD=2.1)
Formative	0.3 (SD=.34)
Classic/Postclassic	0.5 (SD=.3)

Table 15.12 Mean values of centers of ranks 1 and 2 (combined) per 100 sq. km.

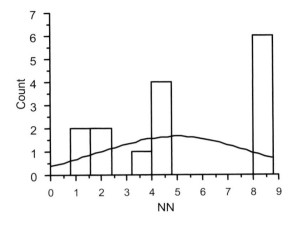

Bronze Age Mean=4.9 kms (SD=2.9, N=15)

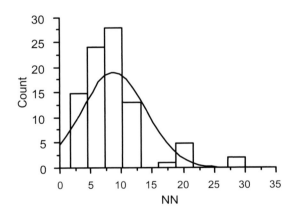

Classical Antiquity Mean=8.8 kms (SD=5.2, N=88)

Figure 15.9 Frequency distributions and summary stat-istics for nearest-neighbor distances (in km) of centers of ranks 1 and 2, for two Mediterranean time-periods. (The lines show the expected frequency curves for a normal distribution with the same mean and standard deviation as the variable.)

probably were 'lower limb' central places of ranks 3–5, so that some part of the observed difference may be attributable to the fact that Mesoamerican central-place systems tended toward a greater degree of vertical hier-archical complexity. This is an issue that will require further investigation using a method distinct from that developed here. Another hypothesis to consider is that Mesoamerican market services were offered in fewer places, but more frequently, compared with the Medi-

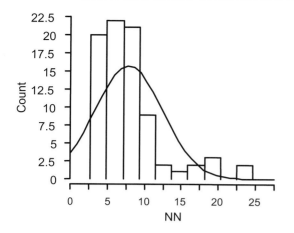

Formative Period   Mean=7.9 km (SD=4.6, N=81)

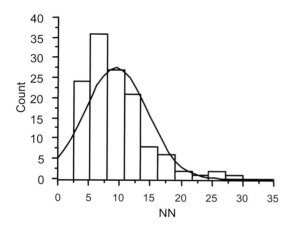

Classic and Postclassic   Mean=9.4 km (SD=5.1, N=128)

Figure 15.10 Frequency distributions and summary statistics for nearest-neighbor distances (in km) of centers of ranks 1 and 2, for two Mesoamerican time periods. (The lines show the expected frequency curves for a normal distribution with the same mean and standard deviation as the variable.)

terranean. By the end of the pre-Hispanic period, the standard market periodicity in Central Mexico was a five-day cycle (Hassig 1985: 80), while the Roman period market cycle in Italy was eight days (de Ligt 1993: 26).

Differences in the spacing of centers also show up in the center nearest-neighbor measures (Figures 15.9 and 15.10). Interestingly, in spite of the overall differences in center spacing (comparing Bronze Age with Formative, and Classical Antiquity with Classic/Postclassic – the Mediterranean tending toward smaller values), in both civilizations center spacing tended to increase over time. While the largest number of nearest-neighbor values for all four periods is around 8 km, for the Bronze Age a number of smaller distances were found and no larger values (although the sample is rather small). Classical Antiquity and Classic/Postclassic, by contrast, include some values larger than 8

km (these latter two periods show not only similar mean values for nearest neighbor, but nearly identical standard deviations). Given that the number of Bronze Age centers included in the sample is small, I looked for additional center spacing information from regions not included in the coded data (Table 15.13). This search produced a few additional cases, and these support the validity of the values derived from the coded sample. All the Bronze Age values are less than 5 or 6 km, while all the values for Classical antiquity are above 10 km.

I return to a previously-suggested hypothesis that proposed a larger role for agronomic factors in determining center size in the Bronze Age (and Formative), while later centers, in both civilizations, had more commercial and other central-place functions. These same factors are relevant to understanding change over time in center spacing. In a managed agricultural economy such as those of the Bronze Age polities, the economics of center spacing would be strongly constrained by the energy and time costs of moving goods and information to and from rank 1 centers and secondary administrative and storage locations (*cf.* Van Andel and Runnels 1988: 241). This is similar to a locational model first proposed by Steponaitis (1978), in which he argued that the most efficient location for secondary centers in a highly administered regional system is not one in which they are central to their local hinterlands, but rather one where they are 'pulled in' toward the rank 1 center, to minimize center-to-center movement costs. The only locational constraint for inter-center distance in a situation such as this, where center populations are largely agrarian, is that center agricultural catchments not overlap. Assuming 2- to 3-km catchments for Bronze Age centers of about 850 persons (my period average), this would imply that a spacing of 4 to 6 km between rank 1 and 2 centers is likely (*cf.* Bennet 1990: 197).

By contrast with these heavily administered situations, the locational economics of more commercialized landscapes reflect, in part, competition between centers for market hinterlands (*e.g.* Hodder and Orton 1976: 63). For preindustrial societies, maximum travel distance from house to market is often noted to be 10 km or less (*e.g.* Blanton 1996: 57–59), implying at most a 20 km round-trip, or one full day of travel (rarer trips to more distant markets are of course undertaken, but require overnight stays). These limits imply market hinterlands with a radius of about 10 km, at most, and inter-center spacing of 20 km, although greater inter-center distances are found in situations of low population density or low levels of household market participation (*e.g.* the northern Valley of Mexico Late Postclassic in Blanton 1996: 71). In the model proposed by Skinner (1964: 16; 1965: 195–211), population growth and/or increased demand for market services (commercialization) can be met through a doubling of market days in existing markets, or the addition of new markets in locations along the edges of existing market hinterlands, in locations where new market-places can service households most distant from existing markets,

Region	Bronze Age (mean values)	Classical Antiquity (mean values)
Upper Guadalquivir (Ruiz Rodríguez *et al.* 1991: Figure 4) Early Roman		11.7 km
Khania Region, Crete (Moody 1987)	E Minoan 5.2 km MM II-Old Palace 5.2 km MM III-LM I 2.7 km LM III 6 km	
Roman-British Walled Towns (not based on systematic survey) (Hodder and Orton 1976: 63)		34.6 km
Mycenean Late Bronze Age (Bintliff 1977: Table 3) (not based on systematic survey)	Argos region 3.9 km Sparta region 3.1 km Helos region 2.5 km	
Roman Tripolitania (not entirely based on systematic survey) (Mattingly 1994: Figure 0: 2)		34.1 km
Roman Corinth (not based on systematic survey) (Engels 1990: Map 5)		10.7 km

Table 15.13 Nearest neighbor distances (in km) for rank 1 and 2 centers, from archaeological surveys not included in the coded data.

close to the 10 km movement limit. All other things being equal, regional evolution would imply the foundation of new central places in interstitial positions, resulting in market hinterlands 5 km or less in radius and inter-center spacing of about 10 km. The latter value is similar to mean nearest-neighbor values for Classical Antiquity and Classic/Postclassic periods (Figures 15.9 and 15.10).

I can evaluate the hypothesis that the nearest-neighbor data allow me to distinguish more administered from more commercial locational patterns of centers by looking at one of its test implications. In all periods, central places no doubt provided a mix of commercial, administrative, temple, and other services, so this is not a comparison of central-place types as much as it is an evaluation of tendencies toward one or another locational pattern. In regional systems where market factors are important determinants of center spacing, increased population density (and commercialization, although I lack a commercialization measure) will result in smaller values of inter-center spacing, giving a negatively-sloping regression of population density by center nearest-neighbor values. By contrast, in a more centrally administered regional economy, agricultural catchment radius is a limiting factor, so growth occurs through the addition of secondary centers at a consistent small distance interval. In this case, nearest-neighbor measures should not be negatively related to population density. The hypothesis that regional settlement-pattern changes reflect an evolution from more administered to more commercialized in both civilizations is supported by a regression analysis of the coded data, with nearest-neighbor values as the dependent variable and population density as the independent variable. The results are as follows:

Bronze Age
nearest neighbor = 4.09 + 0.016 × pop. density (R-squared = 0.067)

Classical Antiquity
nearest neighbor = 9.24 - 0.022 × pop. density (R-squared = 0.217)
Late and Terminal Formative
nearest neighbor = 7.6 + 0.003 × pop. density (R-squared = 0)
Classic and Postclassic (excluding Teotihuacan)
nearest neighbor = 10.9 - 0.02 × pop. density (R-squared = 0.04)

While the R-squared values are not statistically significant, the hypothesis is supported, since both Classical Antiquity and the Classic/Postclassic have the predicted negatively sloping regression lines, while the Bronze Age and Formative slopes are flat (Mesoamerica) or have a mildly positive slope (Bronze Age).

Increased center spacing over time and the regression analysis suggest the evolution of market systems in the later periods of both civilizations. This finding supports the 'service city' theories of later Mediterranean urbanism (*e.g.* Engels 1990; Hopkins 1978), as opposed to the 'consumer city' theory of substantivists such as Finley (1973; *cf.* Whittaker 1990). However, it would be a mistake to pose a simple evolutionary scenario, in which managed economies are always early and market economies are always later. It is not yet clear to what degree commercial transactions occurred in Bronze Age economies (*cf.* Lamberg-Karlovsky 1996). Market systems are thought to have originated in the Mesoamerican Late Formative (Blanton 1983), although they were probably more institutionally complex and pervasive by the Postclassic. However, in Mesoamerica, some subregional systems exhibited partially managed economies that departed from the expectations of market location theory, even in the later Postclassic periods (*e.g.* Blanton 1996: 65–66, 72–74). I doubt if it will be possible to classify regional systems in any simple typological scheme, but parallel long-term social change

	S. Argolid *E. Helladic I-II*	*V. of Oaxaca* *Period Late I*	*S. Etruria* *Early Roman*	*V. of Oaxaca* *Early Classic*	*V. of Mexico* *Late Aztec*	*V. of Oaxaca* *Period V*
NN Mean (km)	5.6 N=3	7.6 N=13	12 N=5	12.5 N=12	7 N=21	13.2 N=12
Mean Center Population	408	810 (exc. Monte Albán)	3500	3960	6063	5890
Villages /100 sq. km	4.4	17	.6	22	29	43
Isolated Residences /100 km sq.	8.9	10	51	25	15	54
Population Density	8	17 (exc.Monte Albán)	31	54	115	76
Villas/100 sq. km	0	0	33	0	0	0
Percent Urban	0	14	73	64	46	57
Villages per Center	2.7	29	.8	39	35	76

Table 15.14 Statistical summary of selected variables from selected regions chosen from the coded settlement pattern data.

in the direction of greater commercialization can be discerned in two civilizations.

A COMPARISON OF SELECTED REGIONS

Several aspects of difference and similarity I have addressed are evident when selected variables are summarized from a sample of the survey regions and time periods (Table 15.14). The Bronze Age survey selected for inclusion here (the Southern Argolid), as expected, has the smallest mean value in the table for distance to nearest neighbor for rank 1 and 2 centers, while the later periods in both civilizations have larger mean inter-center distances. However, the Late Aztec (Late Postclassic) Valley of Mexico also has a comparatively small mean nearest-neighbor value – the result of the addition of new market centers, in the context of rapid population growth to the highest density levels anywhere in Mesoamerica at that or any other period. In the Valley of Oaxaca Early Classic (Monte Albán IIIA), a drastic reformulation of regional organization took place, characterized by a more dispersed central-place settlement pattern (compare with Late I), but dispersion of central places was not a simple directional change in the Valley of Oaxaca. By the Late Classic Monte Albán IIIB, the region had cycled back to a regional organization featuring closely-spaced centers (mean nearest-neighbor distance = 7.7 km). Interestingly, the most dense packing of IIIB centers occurred in the same Etla and Central Valley subregions where this pattern had originally developed during the Formative Period (Kowalewski *et al.* 1989: fig. 9.3). By Period V, the regional system had cycled back to a more dispersed center pattern, in some respects similar to that of Period IIIA.

Center-size data summarized in Table 15.14 also reflect the variation found in the coded sample as a whole. While mean center size for the Early Roman Period in South Etruria is close to the mean value for the Valley of Oaxaca in the Classic Period, the Postclassic Mesoamerican centers were more populous than their Mediterranean

counterparts. In South Etruria, the combination of a high density of villas with a high density of isolated residences constitutes a mode of rural organization not found in Mesoamerica. Rather than commercial farms and isolated residences, Table 15.14 portrays a picture of rural social organization of Mesoamerican regions built around the village. While South Etruria's extremely low density of villages is somewhat anomalous, even by Mediterranean standards, the values for Mesoamerican village density (and villages per center) still serve to reaffirm the presence of a persistent institutional arrangement that had its roots in the Formative Period, and that has continued to the present (Chambers and Young 1979).

Bronze Age Similar to the Mesoamerican Formative Period?

Interpreting Late Formative Mesoamerica in comparative terms presents some challenges. In Table 15.14, mean inter-center distance for the Valley of Oaxaca Late I is less than the Classic/Postclassic for all except the high-density Valley of Mexico Late Aztec Period. But Late I is more like the Southern Argolid in Early Helladic I–II, in having a comparatively small mean center population and a population density far below those of later periods in the sample of regions. This suggests agronomic limits to center growth and center spacing constrained by high inter-center administrative costs. Could these statistics be interpreted to mean that the Late Formative Valley of Oaxaca (and other Late Formative periods considered here) was in some ways analogous to the heavily administered Bronze Age social formations? Comparison is problematic, because none of the major Bronze Age polities has been completely surveyed archaeologically, but several measures based on textual and survey sources for the Pylian state summarized in Bennet (1995; *cf.* Davis *et al.* 1997) can be used to carry a Bronze Age/Mesoamerican Formative comparison further. Davis and his co-authors (1997: 422) and Bennet estimate that the Pylian state occupied an area of 2,000 sq. km (an estimate not based entirely on survey), larger than the mean estimated territory sizes for Bronze Age polities of about 1,000 sq. km (Bennet 1990: table 1). Of 150 Pylian sites mentioned in texts, two were major centers, including the Palace of Nestor at Pylos, and there were 17 smaller administrative centers or towns, for a total of 19 administrative centers of ranks 1 and 2, as I think I would have interpreted them from survey data. This represents a density of approximately 0.95 centers per 100 sq. km. The Late I state probably controlled the entire Valley of Oaxaca, an area of slightly more than 2,000 sq. km (and the statistics in Table 15.14 are based on the valley as a whole), but the settlement pattern data suggest a more-integrated territory of roughly 1,000 sq. km and a less-integrated outer zone, also of about 1,000 sq. km (Kowalewski *et al.* 1989: 151). Within the inner zone there were 12 centers of ranks 1 and 2, giving a center density of 1.2 per 100 sq. km (and a mean nearest-neighbor value of 6.3 km), very close to the Pylian value.

Taken together, the similarities across several regional measures allow me to hypothesize that in some respects Bronze Age and Late Formative social formations were similar in scale, complexity, and modes of integration. More particularly, the dense packing of centers suggests strongly administered polities, at least by comparison with the later, more commercialized regional systems. How the Mesoamerican polities may have been administered, however, is not clear. From what we know about Late I, nothing seems analogous to the Bronze Age administrative texts, seals, and pottery-markings, or the capacious public storage facilities (Blanton *et al.* 1999: 118–20).

The Evolution of Two Core Regions

Two of the regions characterized in Table 15.14 deserve comment for what they can tell us about similarities and differences in one aspect of regional evolution. The South Etruria and Valley of Mexico surveys studied areas adjacent to imperial capitals, during and just prior to the Early Roman Period (centered on Rome) and during the Late Aztec period (centered on Tenochtitlan-Tlatelolco). In both, demographic transitions and changes in regional organization reflect political strategies and economic demand emanating from their respective capitals (*e.g.* Potter 1979: 93–137; Blanton 1996; Hodge 1996; Sanders *et al.* 1979: 153–81) – hence, the evolution of two social and agroecological landscapes tells us something about contrastive modes of political economy in two civilizations. The emerging settlement pattern of South Etruria featured a proliferation of large commercial farms (villas) and numerous isolated residences. In the Valley of Mexico, the number of villages increased, and their residents' production, for sale and tribute, was channeled through a complex system of market and administrative central places (Blanton 1996; Hicks 1987).

Both regions were strongly politically integrated into their respective imperial systems, their residents benefiting from intense urban demand for goods, but differences are evident in how political capitals restructured their respective rural hinterlands. Rome's thalassocracy supported its population with provisions arriving from Africa, Gaul, and elsewhere, in addition to local production in adjacent areas such as South Etruria. By contrast, Tenochtitlan-Tlatelolco was provisioned from a much smaller catchment, restricted in scale by the energy limits of transport using human carriers (Drennan 1984; Hassig 1985: 40). This limit was mitigated somewhat by canoe transport in the Valley of Mexico (Hassig 1985: 61–66), but, nonetheless, rapid population growth in the Late Horizon Mesoamerican capital coincided with local agricultural intensification, population growth, and market-system evolution in the Valley of Mexico as a whole that far surpassed comparable changes in the analogous Republican and Early Roman Periods in South Etruria. This is indicated most clearly by population density in the two regions. At 115 per sq. km (average for all survey areas), the Valley of Mexico was nearly four times as densely populated as Early Roman South Etruria (31 per sq. km). The latter estimate might have been somewhat higher had the South Etruria surveys been methodologically more like the Valley of Mexico surveys; but they were sufficiently intensive and systematic that they could not have missed anything like the astonishing density of villages and populous cities that the Valley of Mexico survey crews encountered. Similarly, a human-engineered landscape analogous to the intensely cultivated *chinampa* farm-land that marked the densely populated rural core of the Aztec empire could not have been missed in South Etruria. The *chinampas* covered hundreds of sq. km and required massive water-management facilities (Armillas 1971). They were capable of an average production of 3,000 kg of maize per ha annually (Sanders 1976: table 9). The South Etruria landscape was transformed, gradually, after the fifth century BC, reflecting the growing economic influence of Rome, but agroecological change primarily entailed forest clearance and swamp drainage aimed at increasing the amount of arable land. In Potter's description of this process (1979: 52–137), there is no mention of agrohydraulic projects of the scale seen in the Late Aztec Valley of Mexico (Sanders *et al.* 1979: 277–81).

CONCLUSIONS, I: PATHWAYS TO WORLD-SYSTEM DEVELOPMENT IN TWO CIVILIZATIONS

The settlement pattern data suggest both broad similarities in the evolution of two civilizations – for example, increasing commercialization – but also point to differences that suggest distinct pathways to social complexity. World-system development and structure is one aspect of difference. In their social architecture, large-scale Mesoamerican polities and economies embodied elements of core-periphery systems, as they are conceived of in the recent world-system literature (*e.g.* Chase-Dunn and Hall 1991). Cores were the foundational elements of sociocultural evolutionary change, where political consolidation occurred alongside intensive commercial development, sustained population growth, and agricultural intensification. (Mesoamerican examples of cores included in the coded survey regions include the Teotihuacan Valley [Terminal Formative and Classic Periods], the Valley of Oaxaca [Late and Terminal Formative through Monte Albán IIIA], and the Valley of Mexico [Late Aztec Period].) Neoevolutionist theory, influenced by the Weberian perspective that sees the state as an institution controlling a discrete territory (*e.g.* Mann 1986: 37), has generally identified this kind of core development as the central process in the evolution of early complex societies (Harris 2001: 103–105; Service 1975: 273–75). Political and economic expansion outward from the core incorporated distant indigenous populations into core-centered world economies or empires through a process much like the periphery incorporation of world-system theorists (Hall 1986; Woolf 1990: 47; *cf.* on the Aztec empire, Berdan 1996; Smith 1996).

In the Mediterranean, periphery incorporation of formerly independent populations did occur (*e.g.* Egypt in the Roman empire). But, given the highly volatile and patchy nature of Mediterranean demography, world-system growth did not always involve periphery incorporation as it is usually conceived of in world-system theory. Instead, in some cases it involved the colonization of unoccupied or sparsely populated localities – for example, as Davis (1992: 706) describes Minoan expansion into the Southern Aegean, through the establishment of new communities 'de novo on virgin soil.' Rather than periphery incorporation of indigenous populations, that typically results in some combination of diffusion and indigenous social and cultural change (Hall 1986), in the Mediterranean this process involved an active social construction of peripheries making use of social and cultural forms contrived by metropolitan social actors, and in many cases it even involved the populating of the periphery with colonists where little indigenous population was found. This alternative form of world-system process had distinct outcomes that are evident in the settlement pattern data:

1. In the Mediterranean, extreme between-period changes in population density and settlement pattern are often thought to reflect changing ties to distant metropolitan social formations, rather than reflecting the influence of local environmental factors or indigenous social forces (*e.g.* Jameson *et al.* 1994: 366–67). Metropolitan systems were able to stimulate immigration and perhaps other sources of population growth, even in locations far from their key cities; but the rise and decline of particular metropolitan systems and shifts over time in Mediterranean-wide world-system geography frequently brought periphery decline and emigration, evidently because in many cases local systems were not viable without metropolitan involvement (*cf.* Horden and Purcell 2001: 279). By contrast,

in Mesoamerica, local populations experienced various episodes of periphery incorporation, but often remained demographically comparatively stable, while at the same time retaining aspects of their traditional cultures, languages, and technologies, as well as strong symbolic associations with place. For example, it is difficult to find any physical trace of the Aztec empire outside its core region (Umberger 1996). By comparison with Mesoamerica, in the Mediterranean people were more likely to migrate long distances and to adopt metropolitan ways of living, including the consumption of metropolitan-style goods; local demography was comparatively volatile. But differences have to be viewed in relative terms, not as absolutes. Teotihuacan's emergence was associated with a marked demographic transition involving migration and a wide dissemination of something approximating a metropolitan culture (Millon 1992), and substantial periphery to core migration is documented in the growth history of Tenochtitlan-Tlatelolco (Bray 1978).

2. In the Mediterranean, modes of regional organization, including rural-urban relations, commercial systems, and modes of appropriation of surpluses varied through time and space, in part dependent on policies of distant and often culturally distinct political and economic actors who, in various times and places, made use of different strategies for regional and world-system organization. Scanning across periods and survey areas from the coded data, one sees sometimes a predominance of villages, sometimes a preponderance of isolated residences, urban nucleation in yet other cases, not to mention a high density of villas in others besides. Beyond the coded surveys, other modes of periphery construction have been identified, including rural collectives such as the Roman Libyan *gasr* (Burns and Mattingly 1980–81), and state-sponsored *coloni* (Kehoe 1988), as yet other possibilities; but none of these forms necessarily left very much of a lasting institutional or cultural imprint in any particular area, once metropolitan involvement ceased. Mesoamerican complexity was more often built from the middle – in the social space, so to speak, between household and polity – rather than from top down, based on a foundation of local village-based organizational complexity and demographic stability, so that if one were to measure social complexity of the system as a whole, it could be said to have been more evenly apportioned from top to bottom. This need not imply that any particular village would necessarily have had a multi-period occupational history, but that, over time, villages tended to be socially reproduced as key building-blocks of social complexity.

CONCLUSIONS, II: RETHINKING NEOEVOLUTIONIST THEORY FROM A MEDITERRANEAN PERSPECTIVE

For neoevolutionist theory to mature, its practitioners should do more to absorb the lessons that can be learned from the Mediterranean experience. Obviously, some of this civilization's uniqueness is attributable to a primacy of maritime social interaction not duplicated elsewhere, but social and demographic processes encountered in the ancient Mediterranean can be productively incorporated into an expanded theory of social evolution. The contrasting modes of rural core evolution in South Etruria and the Valley of Mexico, discussed above, can serve as a segue to a broader discussion of the evolution of social complexity hinted at in the coded settlement pattern data. From this vantage-point, it is evident that the Mesoamerican experience better illustrates the expectations of world-system theory than does the Mediterranean; but it also better illustrates the causal model proposed by neoevolutionist theory for the primary evolution of complex society, in which the origins of complexity are found in the agrohydraulic development of core regions. While some degree of core-zone agricultural intensification could be found in places like South Etruria, Mediterranean social complexity was based primarily on thalassocratic expansion, rather than core agricultural intensification and population growth (*cf.* Horden and Purcell 2001: 396 and *passim*). Neoevolutionist theory has comparatively little to say about the Mediterranean mode of social evolution. Marvin Harris (2001: 104–105) recognizes a form of complex society he calls 'rainfall states,' that lack the agrohydraulic intensification found in his 'hydraulic empires,' but he describes these as 'secondary formations brought into existence to take advantage of the opportunity for trade and plunder created by the expansion of hydraulic empires' (2001: 105).

Although we still do not fully understand how social complexity in the Mediterranean developed in relation to Egypt and Greater Mesopotamia, some researchers have suggested a more complex model for the Mediterranean and similar situations (*e.g.* Knapp and Cherry 1994: 123–55). I suggest that what can be termed a 'non-nuclear' theory, such as that proposed for state formation in Southeast Asia by Winzeler (196) and Bently (1986: 276), requires further elaboration, so that we can incorporate situations such as the thalassocratic societies of the Mediterranean more effectively than Harris's simplistic scheme can do. To develop such a perspective would require that we expand beyond our usual analytical focus on variables related to intensification and appropriation of agricultural surpluses in core zones (the 'tributary mode of production'), to investigate causal variables pertaining to the long-distance movement of people and goods (*cf.* Cherry 1987: 166; Knapp and Cherry 1994: 123–55). Migration, obviously central to understanding Mediterranean social change, is rarely evaluated by neoevolutionists, who tend to assume a constant growth of highly bounded population units (*e.g.* Logan and Sanders 1976). Political scientists have often noted the significance of migration in the evolution of political systems (Hirschman 1970), and the pattern of Mediterranean social evolution suggests we should be following their lead. In Barfield's 'maritime trade empires' (2001: 35–36), rather than reflecting the domination of territory and production, political evolution was based on the control of valuable goods and their transport over vast distances (*e.g.* Subramanyam 2001). An expanded neoevolutionist theory better able to account for migration, exchange, and consumption will not only allow us to incorporate the Mediterranean experience more directly into theory-building, but will also give us a fresh view of civilizations such as Mesoamerica.

ACKNOWLEDGEMENTS

I thank Sue Alcock and John Cherry for inviting me to participate in their 'Side-by-Side Survey' conference. Stephen Kowalewski read an early draft of my chapter and provided many useful comments.

REFERENCES

Adams, R. McC. (1966) *The Evolution of Urban Society: Early Mesopotamia and Prehispanic Mexico*. Chicago, Aldine-Atherton.

Adams, R. McC. (1981) *Heartland of Cities: Surveys of Ancient Settlement and Land Use on the Central Floodplain of the Euphrates*. Chicago, University of Chicago Press.

Alcock, S. E. (1993) *Graecia Capta: The Landscapes of Roman Greece*. Cambridge, Cambridge University Press.

Alcock, S. E., Cherry, J. F. and Davis, J. L. (1994) Intensive survey, agricultural practice and the classical landscape of Greece. In I. Morris (ed.) *Classical Greece: Ancient Histories and Modern Archaeologies*: 137–70. Cambridge, Cambridge University Press.

Armillas, P. (1971) Gardens on swamps. *Science* 174: 653–61.

Balkansky, A. K., Kowalewski, S. A., Stiver, L. R., Pluckhahn, T. J., Beliaev, D., Chamblee, J. F., Heredia, V. Y., Rodríguez, V. P. , Pérez, R. S. and Smith, C. A. (2000) Archaeological survey in the Mixteca Alta of Oaxaca, Mexico. *Journal of Field Archaeology* 27: 365–89.

Barfield, T. J. (2001) The shadow empires: imperial state formation along the Chinese-nomad frontier. In S. E. Alcock, T. N. D'Altroy, K. D. Morrison, and C. M. Sinopoli (eds.) *Empires: Perspectives from Archaeology and History*: 10–41. Cambridge, Cambridge University Press.

Bekker-Nielsen, T. (1989) *The Geography of Power: Studies in the Urbanization of Roman North-West Europe*. BAR International Series 477. Oxford, British Archaeological Reports.

Bennet, J. (1990) Knossos in context: comparative perspectives on the Linear B administration of LM II–III Crete. *American Journal of Archaeology* 94: 193–211.

Bennet, J. (1995) Space through time: diachronic perspectives on the spatial organization of the Pylian state. In W.-D. Niemeier, and R. Laffineur (eds.) *Politeia: Society and State in the Aegean Bronze Age*. Aegaeum 13: 587–602. Liège, The University of Liège.

Bently, G. C. (1986) Indigenous states of Southeast Asia. *Annual Review of Anthropology* 15: 275–305.

Berdan, F. F. (1996) The tributary provinces. In F. F. Berdan, R. E. Blanton, E. H. Boone, M. G. Hodge, M. E. Smith and E. Umberger (eds.) *Aztec Imperial Strategies*: 115–36. Washington, D. C., Dumbarton Oaks Research Library and Collection.

Bintliff, J. L. (1977) *Natural Environment and Human Settlement in Prehistoric Greece*. BAR Supplementary Series 28. Oxford, British Archaeological Reports.

Bintliff, J. L. (1997) Regional survey, demography, and the rise of complex societies in the ancient Aegean: core-periphery, neo-Malthusian, and other interpretive models. *Journal of Field Archaeology* 24: 1–38.

Bintliff, J. L. and Snodgrass, A. M. (1985) The Cambridge/Bradford Boeotian expedition: the first four years. *Journal of Field Archaeology* 12: 123–61.

Blanton, R. E. (1972) *Prehispanic Settlement Patterns of the Ixtapalapa Peninsula Region, Mexico*. Occasional Papers in Anthropology, Department of Anthropology, The Pennsylvania State University 6. University Park, Pennsylvania, The Pennsylvania State University.

Blanton, R. E. (1978) *Monte Albán: Settlements Patterns at the Ancient Zapotec Capital*. New York, Academic Press.

Blanton, R. E. (1983) Factors underlying the origin and evolution of market systems. In S. Ortiz (ed.) *Economic Anthropology: Topics and Theories*. Society for Economic Anthropology, Monographs in Economic Anthropology 1: 51–66. Lanham, University Press of America.

Blanton, R. E. (1996) The Basin of Mexico market system and the growth of empire. In F. F. Berdan, R. E. Blanton, E. H. Boone, M. G. Hodge, M. E. Smith, and E. Umberger (eds.) *Aztec Imperial Strategies*: 47–84. Washington, D. C., Dumbarton Oaks Research Library and Collection.

Blanton, R. E. (2000) *Hellenistic, Roman, and Byzantine Settlement Patterns of the Coast Lands of Western Rough Cilicia*. BAR International Series 879. Oxford, Archaeopress.

Blanton, R. E., Feinman, G. M., Kowalewski, S. A. and Nicholas, L. M. (1999) *Ancient Oaxaca: The Monte Albán State*. Cambridge, Cambridge University Press.

Blanton, R. E., Kowalewski, S. A., Feinman, G. M. and Appel, J. (1982) *Monte Albán's Hinterland, Part I: The Prehispanic Settlement Patterns of the Central and Southern Parts of the Valley of Oaxaca, Mexico*. Memoirs of the Museum of Anthropology, University of Michigan 15. Ann Arbor, Museum of Anthropology, The University of Michigan.

Blanton, R. E., Kowalewski, S. A., Feinman, G. M. and Finsten, L. M. (1993) *Ancient Mesoamerica: A Comparison of Change in Three Regions*. Cambridge, Cambridge University Press.

Branigan, K. (2001) Aspects of Minoan urbanism. In K. Branigan (ed.) *Urbanism in the Aegean Bronze Age*: 38–50. London, Sheffield Academic Press.

Bray, W. (1978) Civilizing the Aztecs. In J. Friedman and M. Rowlands (eds.) *The Evolution of Social Systems*: 373–98. Pittsburgh, The University of Pittsburgh Press.

Burns, R. and Mattingly, D. J. (1980–1981) The Wadi N'F'D survey. In G. W. W. Barker and G. D. B. Jones (eds.) *Farming the Desert: The UNESCO Libyan Valleys Archaeological Survey*: 24–42. London, Society for Libyan Studies.

Chadwick, J. (1976) *The Mycenean World*. Cambridge, Cambridge University Press.

Chambers, E. J. and Young, P. D. (1979) Mesoamerican community studies: the past decade. *Annual Review of Anthropology* 8: 45–69.

Chaniotis, A. (ed.) (1999) *From Minoan Farmers to Roman Traders: Sidelights on the Economy of Ancient Crete*. Stuttgart, Franz Steiner.

Charlton, T. (1970) Contemporary agriculture in the Teotihuacan Valley. In W. T. Sanders, A. Kovar, T. Charlton, and R. A. Diehl (eds.) *The Teotihuacan Valley Project Final Report, Volume 1: The Natural Environment, Contemporary Occupation, and 16th Century Population of the Valley*: 251–361. Occasional Papers in Anthropology, Department of Anthropology, The Pennsylvania State University 3. University Park, Pennsylvania, The Pennsylvania State University.

Chase-Dunn, C. and Hall, T. D. (1991) Conceptualizing core/periphery hierarchies for comparative study. In C. Chase-Dunn and T. D. Hall (eds.) *Core/Periphery Relations in Precapitalist Worlds*: 5–44. Boulder, Westview Press.

Cherry, J. F. (1983) Frogs round the pond: perspectives on current archaeological survey projects in the Mediterranean region. In D. R. Keller and D. W. Rupp (eds.) *Archaeological Survey in the Mediterranean Area*: 375–416. BAR International Series 155. Oxford, British Archaeological Reports.

Cherry, J. F. (1987) Power in space: archaeological and geographical studies of the state. In J. M. Wagstaff (ed.) *Landscape and Culture*: 146–72. Oxford, Basil Blackwell.

Cherry, J. F. (1994) Regional survey in the Aegean: the new wave (and after). In P. N. Kardulias (ed.) *Beyond the Site: Regional Studies in the Aegean Area*: 91–112. Lanham, University Press of America.

Cherry, J. F., Davis, J. L. and Mantzourani, E. (eds.) (1991) *Landscape Archaeology as Long-Term History: Northern Keos in the Cycladic Islands from Earliest Settlement Until Modern Times*. Monumenta Archaeologica 16. Los Angeles, UCLA Institute of Archaeology.

Clark, C. and Haswell, M. (1970) *The Economics of Subsistence Agriculture*. London, MacMillan.

Cowgill, G. L. (1997) State and society at Teotihuacan, Mexico. *Annual Review of Anthropology* 26: 129–61.

Davis, J. L. (1991) Contributions to a Mediterranean rural archaeology: historical case studies from the Ottoman Cyclades. *Journal of Mediterranean Archaeology* 4: 131–215.

Davis, J. L. (1992) Review of Aegean Prehistory I: the islands of the Aegean. *American Journal of Archaeology* 96: 699–756.

Davis, J. L. (1994) Regional studies in Greece: a vade mecum? In P. N. Kardulias (ed.) *Beyond the Site: Regional Studies in the Aegean Area*: 373–88. Lanham, University Press of America.

Davis, J. L., Alcock, S. E., Bennet, J., Lolos, Y. G., and Shelmerdine, C. W. (1997) The Pylos Regional Archaeological Project, Part I: overview and the archaeological survey. *Hesperia* 66: 391–494.

de Ligt, L. (1993) *Fairs and Markets in the Roman Empire: Economic and Social Aspects of Periodic Trade in a Pre-industrial Society*. Amsterdam, J. C. Gieben.

Drennan, R. D. (1984) Long-distance transport costs in pre-Hispanic Mesoamerica. *American Anthropologist* 86: 105–12.

Driessen, J. (2001) History and hierarchy: preliminary observations on the settlement pattern in Minoan Crete. In K. Branigan (ed.) *Urbanism in the Aegean Bronze Age*: 51–71. London, Sheffield Academic Press.

Duncan, G. C. (1958) Sutri: notes on southern Etruria, 3. *Papers of the British School at Rome* 26: 63–134.

Engels, D. (1978) *Alexander the Great and the Logistics of the Macedonian Army*. Berkeley, University of California Press.

Engels, D. (1990) *Roman Corinth: An Alternative Model for the Classical City*. Chicago, University of Chicago Press.

Evans, S. T., Sanders, W. T. and Parsons, J. R. (2000) The Teotihuacan Valley project: Aztec period site descriptions. In S. T. Evans and W. T. Sanders (eds.) *The Teotihuacan Valley Project Final Report, Volume 5: The Aztec Period Occupation of the Valley, Part I*: 85–499. Occasional Papers in Anthropology, Department of Anthropology, The Pennsylvania State University 25. University Park, Pennsylvania, The Pennsylvania State University.

Finley, M. I. (1973) *The Ancient Economy*. Berkeley, University of California Press.

Fish, S. K. and Kowalewski, S. A. (eds.) (1990) *The Archaeology of Regions: A Case for Full-Coverage Survey*. Washington, D. C., Smithsonian Institution Press.

Foxhall, L. and Forbes, H. A. (1982) *Sitometreia*: the role of grains as a staple food in classical antiquity. *Chiron* 12: 41–90.

Frederiksen, M. W. and Ward-Perkins, J. B. (1957) The ancient road systems of the central and northern Ager Faliscus. *Papers of the British School at Rome* 25: 67–208.

Gallant, T. W. (1991) *Risk and Survival in Ancient Greece: Reconstructing the Rural Domestic Economy*. Stanford, Stanford University Press.

Haggis, D. C. (1996) Archaeological survey at Kavousi, east Crete: preliminary report. *Hesperia* 65: 373–432.

Hall, T. D. (1986) Incorporation in the world-system: toward a critique. *American Sociological Review* 51: 390–402.

Halstead, P. (1981) Counting sheep in Neolithic and Bronze Age Greece. In I. Hodder, G. Isaac, and N. Hammond (eds.) *Pattern of the Past*: 307–40. Cambridge, Cambridge University Press.

Halstead, P. (1987) Traditional and ancient rural economy in Mediterranean Europe: plus ça change? *Journal of Hellenic Studies* 107: 77–87.

Halstead, P. and Jones, G. (1989) Agrarian ecology in the Greek islands: time stress, scale and risk. *Journal of Hellenic Studies* 109: 41–55.

Harris, M. (2001) *Cultural Materialism* (updated edn.). Walnut Creek, AltaMira Press.

Hassig, R. (1985) *Trade, Tribute, and Transportation: The Sixteenth-Century Political Economy of the Valley of Mexico*. Norman, University of Oklahoma Press.

Hicks, F. (1987) First steps toward a market-integrated economy in Aztec Mexico. In H. J. M. Claessen and P. van de Velde (eds.) *Early State Dynamics*: 91–107. Leiden, E. J. Brill.

Hirschman, A. O. (1970) *Exit, Voice, and Loyalty: Responses to Decline in Firms, Organizations, and States*. Cambridge, Harvard University Press.

Hirth, K. (1980) *Eastern Morelos and Teotihuacan: A Settlement Survey*. Vanderbilt University Publications in Anthropology 25. Nashville, Vanderbilt University.

Hirth, K. (2000) *Ancient Urbanism at Xochicalco: The Evolution and Organization of a Pre-Hispanic Society, Volume 1*. Salt Lake City, University of Utah Press.

Hodder, I. and Orton, C. (1976) *Spatial Analysis in Archaeology*. Cambridge, Cambridge University Press.

Hodge, M. G. (1996) Political organization of the central provinces. In F. F. Berdan, R. E. Blanton, E. H. Boone, M. G. Hodge, M. E. Smith, and E. Umberger (eds.) *Aztec Imperial Strategies*: 17–46. Washington, D. C., Dumbarton Oaks Research Library and Collection.

Hopkins, K. (1978) Economic growth and towns in classical antiquity. In P. Abrams and E. A. Wrigley (eds.) *Towns in Societies*: 35–79. Cambridge, Cambridge University Press.

Hopkins, K. (1983) Introduction. In P. Garnsey, K. Hopkins, and C. R. Whittaker (eds.) *Trade in the Ancient Economy*: ix–xxv. Berkeley, University of California Press.

Horden, P. and Purcell, N. (2000) *The Corrupting Sea*. Oxford, Blackwell.

Jameson, M. H. (1977/78) Agriculture and slavery in classical Athens. *The Classical Journal* 73: 122–45.

Jameson, M. H., Runnels, C. N. and van Andel, Tj. H. (1994) *A Greek Countryside: The Southern Argolid from Prehistory to the Present Day*. Stanford, Stanford University Press.

Jones, G. D. B. (1962) Capena and the Ager Capenas, Part I. *Papers of the British School at Rome* 30: 116–207.

Jones, G. D. B. (1963) Capena and the Ager Capenas, Part II. *Papers of the British School at Rome* 31: 100–158.

Kahane, A., Threipland, L. M. and Ward-Perkins, J. (1968) The Ager Veientanus, north and east of Rome. *Papers of the British School at Rome* 36: 1–218.

Kardulias, P. N. (1994) Paradigms of the past in Greek archaeology. In P. N. Kardulias (ed.) *Beyond the Site: Regional Studies in the Aegean Area*: 1–24. Lanham, University Press of America.

Kehoe, D. P. (1988) *The Economics of Agriculture on Roman Imperial Estates in North Africa*. Göttingen, Vandenhoeck and Ruprecht.

Keller, D. R. (1985) Archaeological survey in Southern Euboea, Greece: a reconstruction of human activity from Neolithic times through the Byzantine period. PhD dissertation, Indiana University.

Kirkby, A. V. T. (1973) *The Use of Land and Water Resources in the Past and Present Valley of Oaxaca, Mexico*. Memoirs of the Museum of Anthropology, University of Michigan 5. Ann Arbor, Museum of Anthropology, The University of Michigan.

Knapp, A. B. and Cherry, J. F. (1994) *Provenience Studies and Bronze Age Cyprus: Production, Exchange, and Politico-Economic Change*. Monographs in World Archaeology 21. Madison, Prehistory Press.

Kowalewski, S. A. (n.d.) Scale and demographic change: a 3500-year population curve for the Valley of Oaxaca. Unpublished paper.

Kowalewski, S. A. (1982) Population and agricultural potential: Early I through V. In R. E. Blanton, S. A. Kowalewski, G. M. Feinman, and J. Appel, *Monte Albán's Hinterland, Part I: The Prehispanic Settlement Patterns of the Central and Southern Parts of the Valley of Oaxaca, Mexico*: 149–80. Memoirs of the Museum of Anthropology, University of Michigan 15. Ann Arbor, Museum of Anthropology, The University of Michigan.

Kowalewski, S. A. (1990) The evolution of complexity in the Valley of Oaxaca. *Annual Review of Anthropology* 19: 39–58.

Kowalewski, S. A., Feinman, G. M., Finsten, L., Blanton, R. E. and Nicholas, L. M. (1989) *Monte Albán's Hinterland, Part II: Prehispanic Settlement Patterns in Tlacolula, Etla, and Ocotlán, the Valley of Oaxaca, Mexico*. Memoirs of the Museum of Anthropology, University of Michigan 23. Ann Arbor, Museum of Anthropology, The University of Michigan.

Lamberg-Karlovsky, C. C. (1996) The archaeological evidence for international commerce: public and/or private enterprise in Mesopotamia. In M. Hudson and B. A. Levine (eds.) *Privatization in the Ancient Near East and Classical World*. Peabody Museum Bulletin 5: 73–108. Cambridge, Mass., Peabody Museum of Archaeology and Ethnology.

Lloyd, J. (1991) Conclusion: archaeological survey and the Roman landscape. In G. Barker and J. Lloyd (eds.) *Roman Landscapes*. Archaeological Monographs of the British School at Rome 2: 233–40. London, British School at Rome.

Logan, M. H., and Sanders, W. T. (1976) The model. In E. R. Wolf (ed.) *The Valley of Mexico: Studies in Pre-Hispanic Ecology and Society*: 31–58. Albuquerque, University of New Mexico Press.

Mann, M. (1986) *The Sources of Social Power, Volume 1: A History of Power from the Beginning to A. D. 1760*. Cambridge, Cambridge University Press.

Manning, S. (1994) The emergence of divergence: development and decline on Bronze Age Crete and the Cyclades. In C. Mathers and S. Stoddart (eds.) *Development and Decline in the Mediterranean Bronze Age*. Sheffield Archaeological Monographs 8: 221–70. Sheffield, J. R. Collis.

Manning, S. (1999) Knossos and the limits to settlement growth. In P. Betancourt, V. Karageorghis, R. Laffineur, and W.-D. Niemeier (eds.) *Meletemata: Studies in Aegean Archaeology Presented to Malcolm H. Wiener As He Enters his 65th Year*. Aegaeum 20: 469–80. Liège: University of Liège.

Mattingly, D. J. (1994) *Tripolitania*. Ann Arbor, University of Michigan Press.

Millon, R. (ed.) (1973) *Urbanization at Teotihuacán, Mexico.* Austin, University of Texas Press.

Millon, R. (1992) Teotihuacan studies from 1950 to 1990 and beyond. In J. Berlo (ed.) *Art, Ideology, and the City of Teotihuacan*: 339–429. Washington, D. C., Dumbarton Oaks Research Library and Collection.

Moody, J. (1987) The environmental and cultural prehistory of the Khania region of W. Crete: Neolithic through Late Minoan III. PhD dissertation, University of Minnesota.

Nichols, D. (1994) The organization of provincial craft production and the Aztec city-state of Otumba. In M. Hodge and M. E. Smith (eds.) *Economies and Polities in the Aztec Realm*. Studies on Culture and Society 6: 175–93. Albany, Institute for Mesoamerican Studies, State University of New York at Albany.

Nowicki, K. (1999) Economy of refugees: life in the Cretan mountains at the turn of the Bronze and Iron Ages. In A. Chaniotis (ed.) *From Minoan Farmers to Roman Traders: Sidelights on the Economy of Ancient Crete*: 145–71. Stuttgart, Franz Steiner.

Parsons, J. R. (1971) *Prehistoric Settlement Patterns in the Texcoco Region, Mexico*. Memoirs of the Museum of Anthropology, University of Michigan 3. Ann Arbor, Museum of Anthropology, The University of Michigan.

Parsons, J. R. (1976) The role of *chinampa* agriculture in the food supply of Aztec Tenochtitlan. In C. Cleland (ed.) *Cultural Change and Continuity*: 233–58. New York, Academic Press.

Parsons, J. R., Brumfiel, E., Parsons, M. H. and Wilson, D. J. (1982) *Prehispanic Settlement Patterns in the Southern Valley of Mexico: The Chalco-Xochimilco Region*. Memoirs of the Museum of Anthropology, University of Michigan 14. Ann Arbor, Museum of Anthropology, The University of Michigan.

Parsons, J. R., Kintigh, K. W. and Gregg, S. A. (1983) *Archaeological Settlement Pattern Data from the Chalco, Xochimilco, Ixtapalapa, Texcoco, and Zumpango Regions, Mexico*. Technical Reports of the Museum of Anthropology, The University of Michigan 14. Ann Arbor, Museum of Anthropology, The University of Michigan.

Parsons, J. R. and Sanders, W. T. (2000) The 1966 survey of Zones 10 and 17 of the Teotihuacan Valley. In W. T. Sanders and S. T. Evans (eds.) *The Teotihuacan Valley Project Final Report, Volume 5: The Aztec Period Occupation of the Valley, Part 2*: 501–564. Occasional Papers in Anthropology, Department of Anthropology, The Pennsylvania State University 26. University Park, Pennsylvania, The Pennsylvania State University.

Perlès, C. (2001) *The Early Neolithic in Greece*. Cambridge, Cambridge University Press.

Perkins, P. (1999) Reconstructing the population history of the Albegna Valley and Ager Cosanus, Tuscany, Italy, in the Etruscan Period. In M. Gillings, D. J. Mattingly, and J. van Dalen (eds.) *The Archaeology of Mediterranean Landscapes, Volume 3: Geographical Information Systems and Landscape Archaeology*: 103–15. Oxford, Oxbow Books.

Ponsich, M. (1974) *Implantation rurale antique sur le Bas-Guadalquivir*. Paris, E. de Boccard.

Potter, T. W. (1979) *The Changing Landscape of South Etruria*. New York, St. Martin's Press.

Renfrew, C. (1972) *The Emergence of Civilization: The Cyclades and the Aegean in the Third Millennium BC*. London, Methuen.

Renfrew, C. and Wagstaff, M. (eds.) (1982) *An Island Polity: The Archaeology of Exploitation in Melos*. Cambridge, Cambridge University Press.

Rojas Rabiela, T. (1984) Agricultural implements in Mesoamerica. In H. R. Harvey and H. J. Prem (eds.) *Explorations in Ethnohistory: Indians of Central Mexico in the Sixteenth Century*: 175–204. Albuquerque, University of New Mexico Press.

Ruiz Rodríguez, A., Molinos, M. and López, M. C. (1991) Settlement and continuity in the territory of the Guadalquivir valley (6th century BC – 1st century AD). In G. Barker and J. Lloyd (eds.) *Roman Landscapes*. Archaeological Monographs of the British School at Rome 2: 29–36. London, British School at Rome.

Rupp, D. W., Sorensen, L. W., King, R. H. and Fox, W. (1984) Canadian Palaipaphos (Cyprus) survey project: second preliminary report, 1980–82. *Journal of Field Archaeology* 11: 133–54.

Sanders, W. T. (1976) The agricultural history of the Basin of Mexico. In E. R. Wolf (ed.) *The Valley of Mexico: Studies in Pre-Hispanic Ecology and Society*: 101–60. Albuquerque, University of New Mexico Press.

Sanders, W. T. (1986–87) *The Teotihuacan Valley Project Final Report, Volume 4: The Toltec Period Occupation of the Valley, Parts 1 and 2*. Occasional Papers in Anthropology, Department of Anthropology, The Pennsylvania State University 13–14. University Park, Pennsylvania, The Pennsylvania State University.

Sanders, W. T. (1996) *The Teotihuacan Valley Project Final Report, Volume 3: The Teotihuacan Period Occupation of the Valley, Part 3*. Occasional Papers in Anthropology, Department of Anthropology, The Pennsylvania State University 21. University Park, Pennsylvania, The Pennsylvania State University.

Sanders, W. T. and Evans, S. T. (2000) *The Teotihuacan Valley Project Final Report, Volume 5: The Aztec Period Occupation of the Valley, Part 2*. Occasional Papers in Anthropology, Department of Anthropology, The Pennsylvania State University, no. 26. University Park, Pennsylvania, The Pennsylvania State University.

Sanders, W. T., Parsons, J. R. and Santley, R. S. (1979) *The Basin of Mexico: Ecological Processes in the Evolution of a Civilization*. New York, Academic Press.

Sanders, W. T., West, M., Fletcher, C. and Marino, J. (1975) *The Teotihuacan Valley Project Final Report, Volume 2: The Formative Period Occupation of the Valley, Part I*. Occasional Papers in Anthropology, Department of Anthropology, The Pennsylvania State University 10. University Park, Pennsylvania, The Pennsylvania State University.

Schoep, I. (2001) Managing the hinterland: the rural concerns of urban administration. In K. Branigan (ed.) *Urbanism in the Aegean Bronze Age*: 87–102. London, Sheffield Academic Press.

Service, E. R. (1975) *Origins of the State and Civilization*. New York, W. W. Norton.

Sherratt, S. and Sherratt, A. (1993) The growth of the Mediterranean economy in the early first millennium BC. *World Archaeology* 24: 361–78.

Skinner, G. W. (1964) Marketing and social structure in rural China, part I. *Journal of Asian Studies* 24: 3–43.

Skinner, G. W. (1965) Marketing and social structure in rural China, part II. *Journal of Asian Studies* 24: 195–228.

Smith, C. A. (1976) Regional economic systems: linking geographical models and socioeconomic problems. In C. Smith (ed.) *Regional Analysis: Volume I, Economic Systems*: 3–63. New York, Academic Press.

Smith, C. A. (2002) *Concordant Change and Core-Periphery Dynamics: A synthesis of highland Mesoamerican Archaeological Survey Data*. Ph.D. Dissertation, University of Georgia, Athens GA.

Smith, M. E. (1996) The strategic provinces. In F. F. Berdan, R. E. Blanton, E. H. Boone, M. G. Hodge, M. E. Smith and E. Umberger (eds.) *Aztec Imperial Strategies*: 151–80. Washington, D. C., Dumbarton Oaks Research Library and Collection.

Smith, M. E. and Heath-Smith, C. M. (1982) Waves of influence in Postclassic Mesoamerica? A critique of the Mixteca-Puebla concept. *Anthropology* 4: 15–50.

Snodgrass, A. M. (1990) Survey archaeology and the rural landscape of the Greek city. In O. Murray and S. Price (eds.) *The Greek*

City: From Homer to Alexander: 113–36. Oxford, Clarendon Press.

Steponaitis, V. P. (1978) Location theory and complex chiefdoms: a Mississippian example. In B. D. Smith (ed.) *Mississippian Settlement Patterns*: 417–53. New York, Academic Press.

Stirling, P. (1965) *Turkish Village*. London, Weidenfeld and Nicolson.

Stiver, L. (2001) Prehispanic Mixtec settlement and state in the Teposcolula Valley of Oaxaca, Mexico. PhD dissertation, Vanderbilt University.

Subrahmanyam, S. (2001) Written on water: designs and dynamics in the Portuguese Estado da India. In S. E. Alcock, T. N. D'Altroy, K. D. Morrison and C. M. Sinopoli (eds.) *Empires: Perspectives from Archaeology and History:* 42–69. Cambridge, Cambridge University Press.

Trément, F. (1999) Prospection archéologique et démographie en Provence: approche paléodémographique de la rive occidental de L'Etang de Berre sur la longue durée. In J. Bintliff and K. Sbonias (eds.) *The Archaeology of Mediterranean Landscapes, Volume 1: Reconstructing Past Population Trends in Mediterranean Europe:* 93–113. Oxford, Oxbow Books.

Umberger, E. (1996) Aztec presence and material remains in the outer provinces. In F. F. Berdan, R. E. Blanton, E. H. Boone, M. G. Hodge, M. E. Smith and E. Umberger (eds.) *Aztec Imperial Strategies*: 151–80. Washington, D. C., Dumbarton Oaks Research Library and Collection.

van Andel, Tj. H. and Runnels, C. N. (1988) An essay on the emergence of civilization in the Aegean world. *Antiquity* 62: 234–47.

Vita Finzi, C. and Higgs, E. S. (1970) Prehistoric economy in the Mount Carmel area of Palestine: site catchment analysis. *Proceedings of the Prehistoric Society* 36: 1–37.

Wallace-Hadrill, A. (1991) Introduction. In J. Rich and A. Wallace-Hadrill (eds.) *City and Country in the Ancient World*: ix–xviii. London, Routledge.

Watrous, L. V. (1974) An archaeological survey of the Lasithi Plain in Crete from the Neolithic to the Late Roman period. PhD dissertation, University of Pennsylvania.

Watrous, L. V. (1982) *Lasithi: A History of Settlement on a Highland Plain in Crete*. Hesperia Supplement 18. Princeton, American School of Classical Studies at Athens.

Winzeler, R. L. (1976) Ecology, culture, social organization, and state formation in Southeast Asia. *Current Anthropology* 17: 623–40.

White, K. D. (1970) *Roman Farming*. Ithaca, Cornell University Press.

White, K. D. (1975) *Farm Equipment of the Roman World*. Cambridge, Cambridge University Press.

White, K. D. (1984) *Greek and Roman Technology*. Ithaca, Cornell University Press.

Whittaker, C. R. (1990) The consumer city revisited: the *vicus* and the city. *Journal of Roman Archaeology* 3: 110–18.

Woolf, G. (1990) World-systems analysis and the Roman empire. *Journal of Roman Archaeology* 3: 44–58.

Wright, H. T. (1986) The evolution of civilizations. In D. J. Meltzer, D. D. Fowler and J. A. Sabloff (eds.) *American Archaeology: Past and Future*: 323–68. Washington, D. C., Smithsonian Institution Press.

Appendix 1

Survey	Years Ago	KmArea	PopDen	L/G	%Urban	CP/100km	V/100km	IR/100km	Villas/100km	CP/Vill	IRPop	CPPop	Vpop	Comments
L Guadal	-1850	3250	.	.	.	0.4	0.6	9.2	3	1.4	0.65	.	.	
St Blaise	-2450	100	.	.	.	4	21	.	0	7	.	.	.	
St Blaise	-1850	.	.	.	.	2	40	.	5	20	.	.	.	
St Blaise	-1650	.	.	.	.	2	12	.	1	15	.	.	.	
St Blaise	-1500	.	.	.	.	4	60	.	1	3	.	.	.	
Ager Cosanus	-2650	260	11	.	0	0.8	2.3	.	0	.	.	.	.	
Ager Cosanus	-2550	.	41	1	60	1.5	2.3	.	0	1.5	0	28.9	12.2	
Ager Cosanus	-2450	.	49	0	58	2	2.7	.	0	1.4	0	36	13.4	
Ager Cosanus	-2350	.	46	0	63	2	2.3	.	0	1.2	0	36	10.1	
Ager Cosanus	-2250	.	15	-1	0	2	0	.	0.4	.	0	.	.	
S Etruria	-5750	694	0	.	0	0	0	0	0	.	0	0	0	
S Etruria	-3100	.	1	1	0	0.1	.	.	.	.	.	.	.	
S Etruria	-2750	.	5	1	0	0.7	.	.	.	.	.	.	.	
S Etruria	-2600	.	14	1	50	1	.	43	0	.	.	.	.	
S Etruria	-2300	.	30	1	75	0.7	.	73	0	.	.	.	.	
S Etruria	-1900	.	31	0	73	0.7	0.58	51	33	0.8	3.6	21.6	.	
S Etruria	-1500	.	5	-1	86	0.4	0	5.2	3.9	0	0.36	4.3	0	
S Euboea	-8000	41	0	.	0	0	0	0	0	.	.	.	.	
S Euboea	-7600	.	0	0	0	0	0	0	0	.	0	0	7	
S Euboea	-7300	.	0	0	0	0	0	0	0	.	0	0	7	
S Euboea	-6000	.	2	1	0	0	.	.	.	.	.	.	.	
S Euboea	-5000	.	7	1	0	0	4.9	0	0	.	.	.	.	
S Euboea	-3800	.	7	0	0	0	2.4	0	0	.	.	.	.	
S Euboea	-3300	.	0	-1	0	0	0	0	0	.	.	.	.	
S Euboea	-2600	.	.	1	.	2.4	0	0	0	.	.	.	.	
S Euboea	-2400	.	7	1	0	0	2.4	71	0	.	.	.	.	
S Euboea	-2200	.	.	1	94	2.4	4.9	41	0	.	.	.	.	
S Euboea	-1900	.	163	0	80	7.3	22	27	5	3	1.9	154	6.15	
S Euboea	-1550	.	133	0	98	5	2.4	10	5	0.5	0.68	131	1.2	
N Keos	-8300	18	0	.	0	0	0	0	0	.	0	0	0	
N Keos	-7600	.	0	0	0	0	0	0	0	.	0	0	0	
N Keos	-7200	.	10	1	0	0	11	0	0	.	0	0	10	
N Keos	-6300	.	6	-1	0	0	5.6	0	0	.	0	0	6	
N Keos	-4700	.	69	1	80	5.6	11	0	0	2	0	55.6	13.4	
N Keos	-3900	.	6	-1	0	0	5.6	0	0	.	0	0	6	

Survey	Years Ago	KmArea	PopDen	L/G	%Urban	CP/100km	V/100km	IR/100km	Villas/100km	CP/Vill	IRPop	CPPop	Vpop	Comments
N Keos	-3650	.	83	1	67	5.6	22	.	0	4	.	.	.	
N Keos	-3000	.	3	-1	0	0	5.6	0	0	.	.	.	3	
N Keos	-2900	.	6	-1	0	0	5.6	0	0	.	.	.	.	
N Keos	-2600	.	72	1	0	5.6	39	11	0	7	0	31	41	
N Keos	-2400	.	106	1	58	5.6	67	22	0	12	1.6	61	44	
N Keos	-2100	.	31	-1	0	0	44.4	0	0	.	0	0	31	
N Keos	-1900	.	43	0	0	0	44.4	0	0	.	0	0	43	
N Keos	-1500	.	111	1	0	0	111	11	0	.	0.8	0	110	
S Argolid	-7600	225	1	0	0	0	0.4	0	0	.	0	0	1	
S Argolid	-7200	.	1	0	0	0	0.4	0	0	.	0	0	1	
S Argolid	-6300	.	2	1	0	0	0.8	0	0	.	0	0	2	
S Argolid	-5200	.	8	1	0	1.3	4.4	8.9	0	2.7	0.7	5.4	2.3	
S Argolid	-4250	.	0	-1	0	0	0	0	0	.	.	.	0	
S Argolid	-3800	.	2	1	0	0	1.3	0.9	0	.	0	0	.	
S Argolid	-3300	.	8	1	0	1.3	3.1	5	0	3	0.44	3.3	4.2	
S Argolid	-3000	.	0	-1	0	0	0	0	0	.	0	0	0	
S Argolid	-2725	.	5	1	0	1.3	3	2	0	2	0.16	3.9	0.84	
S Argolid	-2600	.	26	1	55	1.3	3.6	2.7	0	2.7	0.19	17.4	8.4	
S Argolid	-2250	.	47	1	73	1.8	6.7	34	0	3.8	2.4	40.6	5.5	
S Argolid	-1900	.	15	-1	82	0.44	5.3	1.8	0	12	0.12	10.7	4.3	
S Argolid	-1500	.	35	1	47	0.9	6.2	12	0.9	7	0.8	19.7	15	
Melos	-8000	34	0	.	0	0	0	0	0	.	0	0	0	
Melos	-7600	.	0	0	0	0	0	0	0	.	0	0	0	
Melos	-7300	.	0	0	0	0	0	0	0	.	0	0	0	
Melos	-6000	.	0	0	0	0	0	0	0	.	0	0	0	
Melos	-4800	.	.	1	0	0	20.5	0	0	.	0	.	0	
Melos	-3800	.	.	-1	0	0.6	0	0	0	0	0	.	0	
Melos	-3350	.	.	1	100	0.6	0	0	0	0	0	0	0	
Melos	-2950	.	0	-1	0	0	0	0	0	.	0	0	0	
Melos	-2500	.	.	1	70	0.6	23.5	2.9	0	9	0	.	.	
Melos	-2250	.	.	0	80	0.6	17.6	0	0	6	0	20.2	14	
Melos	-1925	.	33	1	56	1.2	14.7	0	2.9	.	0	20.2	12.6	Est. for Whole Island
Melos	-1500	.	89	1	63	1.8	41	0	2.9	.	0	42	46	Est. for Whole Island
Lasithi	-5000	66	3	.	0	0	4.5	7.5	0	.	.	0	.	
Lasithi	-4300	.	3	0	0	4.5	4.5	4.5	0	.	0	0	3	
Lasithi	-3300	.	44	1	0	4.5	14	0.24	0	3	1.7	28.8	13.5	
Lasithi	-2850	.	26	-1	99	1.5	0	3	0	0	0.2	26	0	
Lasithi	-2650	.	11	-1	0	0	9	4.5	0	.	0.3	0	10.7	
Lasithi	-2400	.	7	-1	0	0	4.5	1.5	0	.	0.1	0	6.7	
Lasithi	-2300	.	.	0	0	0	3	0	0	.	.	.	.	

Survey	Years Ago	KmArea	PopDen	L/G	%Urban	CP/100km	V/100km	IR/100km	Villas/100km	CP/Vill	IRPop	CPPop	Vpop	Comments
Lasithi	-1900	.	8	0	0	0	1.5	1.5	0	.	0.1	0	8	
Lasithi	-1500	.	102	1	79	1.5	15	23	0	10	1.6	80.3	19	
Pylos	-4800	40	3	.	0	0	0	30	0	.	0	.	.	
Pylos	-3600	.	83	1	45	5	5	0	0	1	0	55	28	
Pylos	-3100	.	136	1	70	5	7.5	0	0	1.5	2.3	113.4	20.5	
Kavousi	-5000	21	5	1	0	0	9.5	0	0	.	0	0	5	
Kavousi	-4600	.	5	0	0	0	9.5	0	0	.	0	0	5	
Kavousi	-3700	.	18	1	0	0	0	250	0	.	18	0	0	
Kavousi	-3500	.	70	1	0	9.5	0	143	0	0	10	60	0	
Kavousi	-3300	.	3	-1	0	0	0	33	0	.	2.3	0	0	
Kavousi	-2900	.	57	1	0	0	48	0	0	.	0	0	57	
Kavousi	-2450	.	0	-1	0	0	0	0	0	.	0	0	0	
Kavousi	-1900	.	48	1	0	.	90	0	0	.	0	23.8	24.2	Rough Est. of Pop
Kavousi	-1600	.	48	0	0	.	90	0	0	.	0	23.8	24.2	Rough Est. of Pop
Palaipaphos	-7000	73	0	.	0	0	0	0	0	.	0	0	0	
Palaipaphos	-4900	.	1	.	0	0	0	1.4	0	.	0.14	0	0	
Palaipaphos	-4100	.	0	-1	0	0	0	0	0	.	0	0	0	
Palaipaphos	-3750	.	14	1	0	1.4	2.7	0	0	2	0	13	1	
Palaipaphos	-3300	.	58	1	84	2.7	1.4	0	0	0.5	0	57	1	
Palaipaphos	-2900	.	10	-1	0	0	8.2	2.7	0	.	0.19	0	9.4	
Palaipaphos	-2600	.	103	1	65	5.5	5.5	2.7	0	1	0.19	94	8.8	
Palaipaphos	-2450	.	1	-1	0	0	0	5.5	0	.	0.38	0	0	
Palaipaphos	-2200	.	110	1	83	5.5	2.7	4.1	0	0.5	0.3	105	4.7	
Palaipaphos	-1950	.	129	0	65	5.5	17.8	5	0	3.3	0.4	83	46	
Palaipaphos	-1700	.	96	-1	65	4	1.3	6.8	0	1.3	0.5	77	18.5	
R Cilicia	-2200	80	17	1	0	1.3	3.8	0	0	3	0	12	5	
R Cilicia	-1875	.	225	1	86	5	20	6.3	0	4	0.44	194	30.6	
R Cilicia	-1525	.	307	0	92	6.3	15	7.5	0	2.4	0.5	282	24.5	
Amatzinac	-1950	454	5	0	0	0.9	2.6	8.6	0	4	0.6	2.3	2.4	
Amatzinac	-1650	.	12	1	20	0.9	6.6	7.5	0	7.5	0.54	4	7	
Amatzinac	-1375	.	13	0	32	0.44	5.3	4.8	0	12	0.34	5.2	7.7	
Chalco-Xoch	-3300	650	1	.	0	0	0.6	0.15	0	.	0.01	0	0.74	
Chalco-Xoch	-2900	.	8	1	57	0	2	0.6	0	.	0.04	0	7.6	
Chalco-Xoch	-2475	.	34	1	63	0.3	5.8	2.8	0	19	0.19	9.9	23.5	
Chalco-Xoch	-2200	.	27	0	57	0.46	6.9	2.9	0	15	0.2	10.6	16.2	
Chalco-Xoch	-2000	.	0	-1	0	0	0	0	0	.	0	0	0	
Chalco-Xoch	-1475	.	7	1	0	0	6.6	2.8	0	.	0.19	0	6.5	
Chalco-Xoch	-1150	.	14	1	67	0.6	4.5	1.5	0	7.5	0.11	8.7	4.8	
Chalco-Xoch	-900	.	11	0	21	0.2	9.1	6	0	60	0.42	2.3	8.4	
Chalco-Xoch	-700	.	46	1	76	0.8	11.8	5.2	0	15.4	0.33	35	10.8	

Survey	Years Ago	KmArea	PopDen	L/G	%Urban	CP/100km	V/100km	IR/100km	Villas/100km	CP/Vill	IRPop	CPPop	Vpop	Comments
Chalco-Xoch	-550	.	103	1	49	0.9	26	29	0	28.2	2	50.7	50.7	
Ixtapalapa	-3300	200	2	.	0	0	1.5	0.5	0	.	0.01	0	0.74	
Ixtapalapa	-2900	.	3	1	0	0	2	0	0	.	0	0	3	
Ixtapalapa	-2475	.	37	1	52	1	5.5	0	0	5.5	0	19.1	18	
Ixtapalapa	-2200	.	33	0	57	1	6	0.5	0	6	0.4	13	19.9	
Ixtapalapa	-2000	.	1	-1	0	0	1	0	0	.	0	0	0.2	
Ixtapalapa	-1475	.	21	1	0	0	13	5	0	.	0.35	0	20.4	
Ixtapalapa	-1150	.	28	1	57	0.5	7	3	0	14	0.21	16	12.1	
Ixtapalapa	-900	.	8	-1	0	0	16	8.5	0	8	0.6	0	7.5	
Ixtapalapa	-700	.	15	1	83	0.5	4	3.5	0	.	0	12.2	2.4	
Ixtapalapa	-550	.	60	1	55	1	26	15	0	26	1.05	22.7	36.25	
Texcoco	-3300	600	0	.	0	0	0	0	0	.	0	0	0	
Texcoco	-2900	.	3	1	0	0	3.2	0	0	.	0	0	3	
Texcoco	-2475	.	14	1	49	0.2	4.5	0	0	27	0	4.4	9.1	
Texcoco	-2200	.	30	1	39	0.7	6	0.17	0	9	0	11.9	18.3	
Texcoco	-2000	.	1	-1	0	0	1.7	0	0	.	0	0	1	
Texcoco	-1475	.	6	1	0	0.2	4	1.5	0	24	0.1	1	5	
Texcoco	-1150	.	48	1	75	0.5	2.3	0.5	0	4.7	0.04	34	13.8	
Texcoco	-900	.	10	-1	19	0.2	5.7	3	0	34	0.2	2.5	7.2	
Texcoco	-700	.	.	1	.	0.33	.	.	0	.	.	.	.	
Texcoco	-550	.	176	1	65	1	13	1.5	0	13	0.1	109	66.6	
Teotihuacan	-3300	550	0	1	0	0	0	0	0	.	0	0	0	
Teotihuacan	-2900	.	1	1	0	0	0.8	0	0	.	0	0	1	
Teotihuacan	-2475	.	5	1	0	0	4	0	0	.	0	0	5	
Teotihuacan	-2200	.	60	1	94	0.2	6.5	0	0	36	0	55	4.5	
Teotihuacan	-2000	.	128	1	97	0.2	7.3	0	0	40	0	124	4	
Teotihuacan	-1475	.	202	1	93	0.73	13	5.5	0	18	0.4	193	8.2	
Teotihuacan	-1150	.	54	-1	89	0.2	4	0	0	22	0	47.7	5.9	
Teotihuacan	-900	.	45	0	30	0.55	22	.	0	40	.	.	.	
Teotihuacan	-700	.	.	.	.	0.2	.	.	0	.	.	.	.	
Teotihuacan	-550	.	150	1	36	0.55	47	0.1	0	85	0.73	29.8	119.5	
Zumpango	-3300	600	0	.	0	0	0	0	0	.	0	0	0	
Zumpango	-2900	.	0	0	0	0	0	0	0	.	0	0	0	
Zumpango	-2475	.	1	0	0	0	0.17	0	0	.	0	0	.	
Zumpango	-2200	.	1	1	0	0	2.2	2.3	0	.	0.16	0	0.98	
Zumpango	-2000	.	2	0	0	0	3.5	0	0	.	.	.	.	
Zumpango	-1475	.	8	1	0	0.33	9.7	4.2	0	29	0.3	2.3	5.4	
Zumpango	-1150	.	7	0	27	0.2	4.5	0.3	0	27	0.02	1.9	5	
Zumpango	-900	.	20	1	19	0.7	22	12.5	0	33	0.88	6.1	13	
Zumpango	-700	.	6	-1	.	0.2	.	.	0	.	.	4.3	.	

Survey	Years Ago	KmArea	PopDen	L/G	%Urban	CP/100km	V/100km	IR/100km	Villas/100km	CP/Vill	IRPop	CPPop	Vpop	Comments
Zumpango	-550	.	51	1	23	0.7	31	17.2	0	47	1.2	10.6	39.5	
V of Oaxaca	-3300	2150	1	.	0	0	0.7	0.5	0	.	0.04	0	0.11	
V of Oaxaca	-3000	.	1	1	70	0	0.8	1	0	.	0.07	0	0.83	
V of Oaxaca	-2775	.	1	0	0	0	1	1	0	.	0.06	0	0.77	
V of Oaxaca	-2600	.	1	0	0	0.4	1	2.2	0	2.3	0.15	0.5	0.2	
V of Oaxaca	-2400	.	7	1	43	0.5	6.3	5.2	0	13.6	0.36	4	2.5	
V of Oaxaca	-2200	.	24	1	40	0.6	17.3	10	0	28.5	0.72	11.6	11.36	
V of Oaxaca	-1900	.	19	0	50	0.7	10.7	11.3	0	15.3	0.8	12.2	6.2	
V of Oaxaca	-1600	.	54	1	64	0.6	22	25	0	39.4	1.8	27.9	23.9	
V of Oaxaca	-1400	.	37	-1	76	0.6	14.7	10.8	0	24.4	0.76	25.7	10.2	
V of Oaxaca	-1200	.	33	0	78	0.5	7.3	9.4	0	14.2	0.66	21.6	10.3	
V of Oaxaca	-800	.	76	1	57	0.6	42.6	54	0	76.3	3.8	32.9	38.9	
Mixteca Alta	-3100	1496	3	.	0	0.27	1.74	0.8	.	7	0.06	1.3	1.3	
Mixteca Alta	-2500	.	11	1	18	0.6	7.1	3.1	.	11.8	0.25	3.7	7	
Mixteca Alta	-2100	.	31	1	62	0.8	4.7	1.6	.	5.8	0.13	16.7	14.3	
Mixteca Alta	-1650	.	80	1	60	1	16	0.25	.	16	0.25	37	42	
Mixteca Alta	-750	.	132	0	58	0.8	37	13	.	46	1	53.5	77.1	

Appendix 2

Region	Site	NN (km)	Years Ago	Center Pop
L Guadal	Carmona	11	-1850	
L Guadal	L del Rio	9	-1850	
L Guadal	Castillejo	6	-1850	
L Guadal	Cantillana	9	-1850	
L Guadal	Alcala del Rio	10	-1850	
L Guadal	Italica	8	-1850	
L Guadal	Sevilla	8	-1850	
L Guadal	Cerro	11	-1850	
L Guadal	C d Toruno	6	-1850	
L Guadal	Mairena d Acor	6	-1850	
L Guadal	Canania	7	-1850	
L Guadal	Tocina	7	-1850	
L Guadal	Gelves	8	-1850	
L Guadal	A d Aljarefe	12	-1850	
St Blaise	Castellan	6.2	-2450	
St Blaise	St.-Blaise	6.2	-2450	
St Blaise	Martigues	8.5	-2450	
St Blaise	Fos	10	-1850	
St Blaise	Martigues	10	-1850	
St Blaise	Fos	10	-1650	
St Blaise	Martigues	10	-1650	
St Blaise	St. Michel	8	-1500	
St Blaise	St-Blaise	5	-1500	
St Blaise	Fos	5	-1500	
St Blaise	Martigues	8	-1500	
SC Etruria	Cosa	7	-2250	
SC Etruria		13	-2250	
SC Etruria	Saturnia	30	-2250	
SC Etruria	Cosa	7	-2180	
SC Etruria		13	-2180	
SC Etruria	Saturnia	30	-2180	
SC Etruria	Cosa	7	-2120	
SC Etruria		13	-2120	
SC Etruria	Heba	13	-2120	
SC Etruria	Saturnia	19	-2120	
S Etruria	Veii	13	-2750	
S Etruria	MS Angelo	11	-2750	
S Etruria	Narce	6	-2750	
S Etruria	Nepi	6	-2750	
S Etruria	Falerii	7	-2750	
S Etruria	Veii	11	-2600	5000
S Etruria	MS Angelo	11	-2600	
S Etruria	Sutri	7	-2600	200
S Etruria	Nepi	7	-2600	450
S Etruria	Falerii	8	-2600	650
S Etruria	Narce	7	-2600	325
S Etruria	Capena	10	-2600	125
S Etruria	Sutri	10	-2300	2500
S Etruria	Nepi	6.5	-2300	2500
S Etruria	F Novi	6.5	-2300	5000
S Etruria	L Feroniae	19	-2300	2500
S Etruria	Veii	19	-2300	1000
S Etruria	Nepi	6.5	-1900	4000
S Etruria	F Novi	6.5	-1900	5000
S Etruria	Sutri	9	-1900	2500
S Etruria	Veii	19	-1900	2500
S Etruria	L Feroniae	19	-1900	
S Etruria	Nepi	9	-1500	
S Etruria	Nazanno	18	-1500	
S Etruria	Sutri	9	-1500	
S Argolid	Fournoi	4	-5200	600
S Argolid	Mases	4	-5200	250
S Argolid	A6/9	8.8	-5200	375
S Argolid	Mases	4	-3300	250
S Argolid	Fournoi	4	-3300	275
S Argolid	Ermioni	8	-3300	225
S Argolid	F32/16	4	-2725	375
S Argolid	Mases	4	-2725	250
S Argolid	A-9	9	-2725	250
S Argolid	Mases	11	-2600	250
S Argolid	Halieis	11	-2600	1200
S Argolid	Hermion	6	-2600	2000
S Argolid	Halieis	9.5	-2250	3800
S Argolid	Hermion	9	-2250	4200
S Argolid	Eileoi	9	-2250	500
S Argolid	Mases	9	-2250	625
S Argolid	Hermion		-1900	2800
S Argolid	Hermion	9.5	-1500	3800
S Argolid	Mases	9.5	-1500	625
N Keos	Ayia Irini		-4700	1000
N Keos	Ayia Irini		-3650	1000
N Keos	Koressos	4	-2600	550
N Keos	Koressos	4	-2400	1100
Melos	Phylakopi		-3800	250
Melos	Phylakopi		-3350	1825
Melos	Melos		-2500	2500
Melos	Melos		-2250	2500
Melos	Melos	3.3	-1925	2500
Melos	Site 17	3.3	-1925	945
Melos	Melos	2.2	-1500	3150
Melos	Emborio	3.9	-1500	2100
Melos	Site 63	1.8	-1500	1900
Lasithi	Site 18	2	-3300	650
Lasithi	Site 12	2	-3300	
Lasithi	Kastellon	3.6	-3300	650
Lasithi	Papoura		-2850	1700
Lasithi	Kardamoutsa		-1500	5300
Pylos	Palace of Nestor	8	-3600	1500
Pylos	Koryfasio	8	-3600	700
Pylos	Palace of Nestor	8	-3300	3800
Pylos	Koryfasio	8	-3300	700
Kavousi	Tholos Bay	0.8	-3500	750
Kavousi	Ayios Antonios	0.8	-3500	500
Kavousi	Tholos Bay		-1900	500
R Cilicia	Iotape		-2200	945
R Cilicia	Iotape	7.7	-1875	2200
R Cilicia	Selinus	2.3	-1875	2300
R Cilicia	Cestrus	2.3	-1875	3360
R Cilicia	Antiochia	5	-1875	7665
R Cilicia	Iotape	7.7	-1525	2184
R Cilicia	Selinus	2.3	-1525	4900
R Cilicia	Cestrus	2.3	-1525	3360
R Cilicia	Nephelion	1.8	-1525	3150
R Cilicia	Antiochia	1.8	-1525	9000
Amatzinac	Site 20	6.8	-1950	263
Amatzinac	Site 50		-1950	95
Amatzinac	Site 78		-1950	613
Amatzinac	Site 84	8	-1950	72

Region	Site	NN (km)	Years Ago	Center Pop	Region	Site	NN (km)	Years Ago	Center Pop
Amatzinac	Site 14	11.3	-1650	289	Ixtapalapa	Culhuacan	3.2	-540	2438
Amatzinac	Site 78	7.5	-1650	1073	Texcoco	Tepetlaoxtoc	9.8	-540	10125
Amatzinac	Site 84	8.8	-1650	110	Texcoco	Texcoco	4.8	-540	18750
Amatzinac	Site 172	7.5	-1650	345	Texcoco	Huexotla	2.7	-540	17250
Amatzinac	Site 78		-1375	1929	Texcoco	Coatlinchan	2.7	-540	8250
Amatzinac	Site 14	15	-1375	416	Texcoco	Coatepec	6.3	-540	1875
Chalco-Xoch	CH-LF-5	3	-2475	3900	Texcoco	Chimalhuacan	9.4	-540	9000
Chalco-Xoch	CH-LF-6	3	-2475	2550	Teotihuacan	Teotihuacan	7.8	-540	
Ixtapalapa	IX-LF-6	10	-2475	2440	Teotihuacan	Otumba	9.6	-540	
Ixtapalapa	IX-LF-2	10	-2475	1400	Teotihuacan	Acolman	7.8	-540	
Texcoco	TX-LF-12	10	-2475	2625	Zumpango	ZU-AZ-130	7	-540	1650
Teotihuacan	Teotihuacan	11	-2200	30246	Zumpango	ZU-AZ-172	7	-540	1800
Chalco-Xoch	CH-TF-9	4.1	-2200	2250	Zumpango	ZU-AZ-255	8.8	-540	300
Chalco-Xoch	CH-TF-14	2.9	-2200	3000	Zumpango	ZU-AZ-276	8.8	-540	2625
Chalco-Xoch	CH-TF-16	2.9	-2200	1650	V of Oaxaca	SJ Mogote	6.4	-2600	564
Ixtapalapa	IX-TF-4	7.5	-2200	1388	V of Oaxaca	Yeguih	2.7	-2600	132
Ixtapalapa	IX-TF-5	7.5	-2200	1200	V of Oaxaca	Tlapacoyan	24.7	-2600	70
Texcoco	TX-TF-1	9.1	-2200	1900	V of Oaxaca	Tilcajete	4.9	-2600	34
Texcoco	TX-TF-17	6.8	-2200	2625	V of Oaxaca	Mazaltepec	9.3	-2600	25
Texcoco	TX-TF-30	6.8	-2200	1500	V of Oaxaca	Cacaotepec	4	-2600	28
Texcoco	TX-TF-50	14	-2200	1125	V of Oaxaca	Tierras Largas	5.9	-2600	53
Teotihuacan	Teotihuacan		-2000	68234	V of Oaxaca	SB Coyotepec	4.9	-2600	48
Teotihuacan	Teotihuacan	11.3	-1475	103233	V of Oaxaca	Hac Alferez	2.7	-2600	81
Teotihuacan	TC-83	9.1	-1475	1373	V of Oaxaca	Monte Alban	6	-2400	5250
Teotihuacan	TC-73	6.9	-1475	945	V of Oaxaca	Yeguih	4.4	-2400	578
Teotihuacan	TC-40	6.9	-1475	428	V of Oaxaca	SJ Mogote	6.4	-2400	1112
Texcoco	TX-EC-32	30	-1475	600	V of Oaxaca	SD Tlaltinango	8.7	-2400	272
Zumpango	ZU-EC-56	18	-1475	750	V of Oaxaca	Cacaotepec	6.4	-2400	210
Zumpango	ZU-EC-84	8.8	-1475	600	V of Oaxaca	Pueblo Nuevo	6	-2400	210
Teotihuacan	Teotihuacan	11.5	-1150	32500	V of Oaxaca	SA dl Juntas	8.7	-2400	179
Chalco-Xoch	CH-ET-24	4.9	-1150	1800	V of Oaxaca	04/03/2023	7.1	-2400	256
Chalco-Xoch	CH-ET-31	7.5	-1150	600	V of Oaxaca	Tilcajete	7.1	-2400	225
Chalco-Xoch	CH-ET-28	4.9	-1150	2625	V of Oaxaca	SJ Guelavia	4.4	-2400	289
Chalco-Xoch	CH-ET-7	9.8	-1150	900	V of Oaxaca	Monte Alban	7.3	-2200	15300
Ixtapalapa	IX-ET-13	17.5	-1150	3200	V of Oaxaca	Suchilquitongo	7.3	-2200	1392
Texcoco	TX-ET-4	3.4	-1150	5400	V of Oaxaca	Mag Apasco	4.7	-2200	1475
Texcoco	TX-ET-7	3.4	-1150	6000	V of Oaxaca	SJ Mogote	3.3	-2200	1946
Texcoco	TX-ET-18	12.5	-1150	9000	V of Oaxaca	Reyes Etla	3.3	-2200	336
Zumpango	ZU-ET-12	25	-1150	1125	V of Oaxaca	SA dl Juntas	8	-2200	658
Chalco-Xoch	CH-LT-13	12.1	-1000	1500	V of Oaxaca	Tilcajete	5.3	-2200	879
Texcoco	TX-LT-53	12.1	-1000	1500	V of Oaxaca	Yeguih	23.6	-2200	648
Teotihuacan	Otumba	9.6	-1000		V of Oaxaca	SB Coyotepec	6.7	-2200	263
Teotihuacan	Acolman	7.8	-1000		V of Oaxaca	La Cienega	6.9	-2200	606
Teotihuacan	Teotihuacan	7.8	-1000	7500	V of Oaxaca	La Soledad	5.3	-2200	616
Zumpango	ZU-LT-75	6.3	-1000	300	V of Oaxaca	Cuilapan	7.3	-2200	289
Zumpango	ZU-LT-87	6.3	-1000	225	V of Oaxaca	SL Beltran	9.9	-2200	607
Zumpango	ZU-LT-135	6.3	-1000	900	V of Oaxaca	Monte Alban	7.3	-1900	14475
Zumpango	ZU-LT-211	21.3	-1000	2250	V of Oaxaca	Suchiquitongo	4.4	-1900	1947
Chalco-Xoch	Chalco	9.1	-700	9375	V of Oaxaca	SF Tejalapan	8.3	-1900	1240
Chalco-Xoch	Amecameca	18.4	-700	3750	V of Oaxaca	SD Tlaltinango	3.7	-1900	727
Chalco-Xoch	Xico	2.5	-700	1200	V of Oaxaca	M Apasco	3.7	-1900	1771
Chalco-Xoch	Cuitlahuac	9.1	-700	2813	V of Oaxaca	Reyes Etla	3.3	-1900	387
Chalco-Xoch	Xochimilco	7.5	-700	5625	V of Oaxaca	SJ Mogote	3.3	-1900	1100
Ixtapalapa	Culhuacan	7.5	-700	2438	V of Oaxaca	Cacaotepec East	4.7	-1900	560
Texcoco	Huexotla	2.7	-700	11250	V of Oaxaca	Cuilapan	7.3	-1900	423
Texcoco	Coatlinchan	2.7	-700	8250	V of Oaxaca	SB Coyotepec	5.3	-1900	249
Zumpango	Xaltocan	15.6	-700	2550	V of Oaxaca	06/03/1940	5.3	-1900	979
Chalco-Xoch	Cuitlahuac	6.3	-540	3375	V of Oaxaca	06/03/1956	8.5	-1900	343
Chalco-Xoch	Chalco	9	-540	9375	V of Oaxaca	Tlalixtac	11.1	-1900	671
Chalco-Xoch	Amecameca	9.5	-540	7500	V of Oaxaca	Dainzu	8.3	-1900	993
Chalco-Xoch	Mixquic	5.9	-540	1688	V of Oaxaca	Yeguih	8.3	-1900	455
Chalco-Xoch	Xochimilco	7.5	-540	8025	V of Oaxaca	Monte Alban	6.4	-1600	16507
Chalco-Xoch	Tlalmanalco	9.5	-540	3000	V of Oaxaca	Suchiquitongo	26.3	-1600	1789
Ixtapalapa	Ixtapalapa	3.2	-540	2100	V of Oaxaca	Xoxocotlan	6.4	-1600	2014

Region	Site	NN (km)	Years Ago	Center Pop
V of Oaxaca	Cuilapan	6.7	-1600	803
V of Oaxaca	Trinidad Zaachila	8.7	-1600	1266
V of Oaxaca	Jalieza	12	-1600	12835
V of Oaxaca	SC Mixtepec	14.7	-1600	3219
V of Oaxaca	T d Morelos	13.3	-1600	1937
V of Oaxaca	El Choco	13.3	-1600	1320
V of Oaxaca	4-8-133,160,163	12.7	-1600	12300
V of Oaxaca	Quialana	12.7	-1600	1575
V of Oaxaca	El Palmillo	16.7	-1600	4517
V of Oaxaca	Monte Alban	6	-1400	24189
V of Oaxaca	Suchiquitongo	4	-1400	3959
V of Oaxaca	SF Tejalapan	4	-1400	1493
V of Oaxaca	Tlaltinango	4	-1400	1106
V of Oaxaca	M Apasco	4	-1400	2416
V of Oaxaca	Reyes Etla	5.3	-1400	2560
V of Oaxaca	S G Etla	5.3	-1400	2904
V of Oaxaca	L de Trapiche	6.4	-1400	4516
V of Oaxaca	El Mirador	4	-1400	1677
V of Oaxaca	SP Ixtlahuaca	5.7	-1400	1656
V of Oaxaca	Zaachila	11.3	-1400	2135
V of Oaxaca	T de Morelos	22	-1400	1215
V of Oaxaca	Tlacachahuaya	18.7	-1400	5352
V of Oaxaca	Monte Alban	8.7	-1200	4062
V of Oaxaca	Loma dl Montura	5.3	-1200	1929
V of Oaxaca	A Trujano	5.3	-1200	1121
V of Oaxaca	Jalieza	18	-1200	16117
V of Oaxaca	El Choco	13.3	-1200	4047
V of Oaxaca	SC Mixtepec	13.3	-1200	1501
V of Oaxaca	Macuilxochitl	8	-1200	6222
V of Oaxaca	SA d Valle	4.1	-1200	3590
V of Oaxaca	Yagul/Tanivet	5.3	-1200	2784
V of Oaxaca	Mitla	9.3	-1200	2354
V of Oaxaca	Lambityeco	4.1	-1200	2702
V of Oaxaca	Sa'a Yucu	13.7	-800	13573
V of Oaxaca	SD Barrio Alto	15.3	-800	1563
V of Oaxaca	SL Beltran	15.3	-800	2506
V of Oaxaca	Coyotepec	12	-800	1968
V of Oaxaca	Jalieza	12	-800	6649
V of Oaxaca	El Choco	21.3	-800	1627
V of Oaxaca	Tlalixtoc	6.7	-800	6609
V of Oaxaca	SJ Teitipac	12	-800	2051
V of Oaxaca	Macuilxochitl	12	-800	13831
V of Oaxaca	Yagul	12	-800	6324
V of Oaxaca	Mitla	12	-800	10551
V of Oaxaca	S P Martir	14	-800	3430
Mix Alta	SJD 7	20	-3100	867
Mix Alta	XAC 4	8.5	-3100	761
Mix Alta	TEC 4ii	13.5	-3100	193
Mix Alta	YBA 2		-3100	131
Mix Alta	TIL 7	20	-2500	1602
Mix Alta	YOS 1	7	-2500	1287
Mix Alta	SAT 42	7	-2500	801
Mix Alta	SPP 29	18.2	-2500	74
Mix Alta	YBA 1		-2500	369
Mix Alta	CAT 8	16	-2500	464
Mix Alta	MOR 4		-2500	444
Mix Alta	YOL 6	12.8	-2500	141
Mix Alta	YUC 21		-2500	400
Mix Alta	TIL 1		-2100	3889
Mix Alta	TIP 1	10	-2100	5974
Mix Alta	SJT 20	8.6	-2100	1534
Mix Alta	YUC 16	8.6	-2100	1988
Mix Alta	SPP 55	5.1	-2100	2297
Mix Alta	SDH 2	17.6	-2100	2081

Region	Site	NN (km)	Years Ago	Center Pop
Mix Alta	SPT 3	9.6	-2100	1504
Mix Alta	YPD 6		-2100	1891
Mix Alta	ODA 10		-2100	1192
Mix Alta	YOL 37	6.4	-2100	1181
Mix Alta	SPP 3	5.1	-2100	1512
Mix Alta	TOP 1	4.8	-2100	780
Mix Alta	TIP 1	4.8	-1500	17180
Mix Alta	SMO 1		-1500	6619
Mix Alta	TLA 42	5.8	-1500	4623
Mix Alta	TOP 1	4.8	-1500	4000
Mix Alta	SVN 3	7	-1500	3485
Mix Alta	TLA 1	5.8	-1500	3129
Mix Alta	SPP 55	5.1	-1500	3568
Mix Alta	SJT 20		-1500	1643
Mix Alta	TLA 36		-1500	943
Mix Alta	SPP 2	10.2	-1500	1497
Mix Alta	YOL 27	14.7	-1500	2095
Mix Alta	SBY 3	10.2	-1500	1710
Mix Alta	TIL 24		-1500	1944
Mix Alta	YPD 6	5.1	-1500	1895
Mix Alta	YUC 20	8	-1500	975
Mix Alta	TIP 1	8.5	-750	32000
Mix Alta	SPP 1	11.2	-750	7214
Mix Alta	SIP 5		-750	6000
Mix Alta	SBY 3	9.6	-750	6000
Mix Alta	TIL 7		-750	5180
Mix Alta	TLA 42		-750	4883
Mix Alta	SMA 4	9.6	-750	1077
Mix Alta	SAT 9	4.5	-750	4159
Mix Alta	SJT 21	8	-750	4739
Mix Alta	SCA 2	6.4	-750	4183
Mix Alta	TGO 2	8	-750	2550
Mix Alta	YOL 4	9.9	-750	2145

APPENDIX

16. Appendix. Internet Resources for Mediterranean Regional Survey Projects: A Preliminary Listing

Jennifer E. Gates, Susan E. Alcock and John F. Cherry

As noted in the Introduction (Ch. 1), the basic premise of this volume – that there is a growing interest in attempting intra- and inter-regional studies encompassing multiple sets of Mediterranean survey data – immediately raises the question of access to those data, in sufficient detail to allow meaningful comparison and "source criticism". Relying on final publication in the traditional formats of the printed article or monograph can often mean a long wait, and in any case precludes the use of digital data. So the Internet seems an obvious solution to the problems of data-sharing. Attempts to establish centralized archives or databanks serving digital data via the World Wide Web have so far foundered from an insufficiency of funding or of archaeologists willing to contribute information. But to what extent have individual regional projects "published" detailed data on the web, and how suitable are such data for comparative purposes?

Although familiar with a number of websites dealing with survey projects in the Mediterranean, we had no clear impression of how common such sites might be, nor of the general level of data presentation to be found within them. Consequently, it seemed a useful exercise, as part of our preparation for the Workshop in 2002, to compile a systematic (if not comprehensive) database of survey projects available via the Internet. What appears in this Appendix, then, is a version of the information compiled for that database, updated in early 2003.

The websites listed below were in most cases located as the result of a series of fairly diligent and systematic Google searches on the Internet, using search terms such as "archaeological survey", "archaeology survey", "regional analysis", or "regional analysis survey" (and repeating these with the names of various countries attached: *e.g.* "archaeological survey Egypt"). Not surprisingly, visits to the sites thrown up by these searches in many cases revealed links to other possibly relevant sites, which were also checked. Once these sources seemed to have been exhausted, we turned to examine the listings of fieldwork projects to be found on the websites of the Archaeological Institute of America (AIA), the Society for American Archaeology (SAA), and other such professional organizations; we also looked at the annual fieldwork opportunity bulletins maintained by the AIA, the Council for British Archaeology, and others. Finally, we have consulted colleagues (among them, naturally, many of the contributors to the present volume), asking them to look over our lists of websites for particular regions, and to report omissions or suggest further avenues we might pursue, especially in cases where our searches had produced meager results.

The number of websites, Mediterranean-wide, is apparently quite modest – certainly fewer than we had supposed might exist – and, despite much casual talk about "web publishing", very few of them in fact present data at the level of detail that would be standard in a printed final publication. Partly in reaction to this fact, we have been catholic in our decisions about what to list here (including, for instance, a few non-Mediterranean countries, such as Sudan and Hungary, and parts of the Near East, if the websites seemed of interest). On the other hand, websites that proved, on inspection, to contain relatively little useful information and those seemingly created only as publicity vehicles (*e.g.* for field schools) have not been listed at all.

We have opened, and tried to navigate systematically within, each of the websites whose URLs are given below, and the very fact of their inclusion indicates that, at least at the time of our visit to the website, they were functioning satisfactorily (a number of others were eliminated on these grounds). But by the time you, the reader, see these words and perhaps try to visit these same websites, it is inevitable that some of them will have turned into dead links, or migrated to new URLs, or been transformed into non-active (archived) websites, or simply become hopelessly out-of-date, as a result of lack of attention from a webmaster. All this is to be expected in a volatile medium that is expanding so fast; the very notion of an "exhaustive listing" is meaningless, where websites are concerned. But this does not necessarily render the present Appendix useless as soon as it appears in print. We hope that parts of it will indeed be of some practical value to readers, at least for a little while. But in the longer run its interest will be as a record of where things stood, in 2002–2003, in terms of the use of the Internet to promulgate information about archaeological surveys and regional analysis in the Mediterranean area.

ABU DHABI

http://www.adias-uae.com/ (2002)
Abu Dhabi Islands Archaeological Survey (ADIAS)
•   Directed by Dr. Geoffrey King under auspices of the Govt. of UAE.
•   Clear explanations of methodology and goals. Still under development. No maps or images of finds. Primarily a compilation of references to available publications and popular articles on the archaeology of the UAE.

ALBANIA

http://www.lamp.ac.uk/archaeology/amarkp/ALBANIA/ALBANIA.HTM (1996)
Butrint
•   University of Wales, Lampeter; Butrint Foundation.
•   Links to survey reports and introductory description included. Website now rather out-of-date (and soon to be replaced).

http://www.butrintfound.dial.pipex.com/ (2002)
The Butrint Foundation
•   The Butrint Foundation.
•   Primarily an overview of the Foundation's organization and funding, but also includes an annual report which details excavation and survey work of recent years.

http://river.blg.uc.edu/mrap/MRAP.html (2001)
The Mallakastra Regional Archaeological Project (MRAP)
•   University of Cincinnati; Institute of Archaeology, Tirana, Albania; Millsaps College.
•   Site includes a series of yearly interim reports that present all aspects of the survey fieldwork and excavation results, supplemented by figures and maps. Specialists' reports are also included.

CROATIA

http://www.zrc-sazu.si/pic/pub/gaffney/gaffney.htm (2003)
Island Crossings: The Role of the Central Dalmatian Islands in Prehistory and Antiquity
•   University of Birmingham.
•   Site briefly describes methodology and aims of the project, while presenting detailed results by period. Related publications also listed.

CYPRUS

http://www.taesp.arts.gla.ac.uk/ (2002)
Troodos Archaeological and Environmental Survey Project
•   University of Glasgow; University of Cyprus; Oregon State University.
•   Extensive resources and clear explanations of objectives, methodology provided. Links to seasonal reports, some GIS data, including DEM and maps.

http://www.scsp.arts.gla.ac.uk/ (1999)
Sydney Cyprus Survey Project: An Interdisciplinary Regional Survey Project in the Northern Troodos Foothills, Central Cyprus
•   University of Glasgow.
•   Succinct introduction to the project with useful links to published reports and bibliography. Maps and distributions provided. Site to be updated mid-2003, to coincide with publication of final monograph on this project.

http://www.arcl.ed.ac.uk/arch/lemba/homepage.html (1999)
Lemba Archaeological Project
•   University of Edinburgh.
•   Survey reports located in the "projects" section. Includes annual survey reviews and preliminary analyses.

http://www.davidson.edu/academic/classics/AAP/aap.htm (2000)
Athienou Archaeological Project
- Davidson College.
- Brief description of site and project supplemented by photos of selected finds and photographs. Published reports also linked to site.

http://www.latrobe.edu.au/archaeology/research/marki/marki.html (2002)
Marki-Alonia Archaeological Project
- La Trobe University, Melbourne.
- User-friendly site with descriptions of methodology, photographs of wide range of finds. Selective publication of certain buildings and site discoveries.

EGYPT

http://rome.classics.lsa.umich.edu/projects/coptos/desert. html (1993)
Archaeological Survey in the Eastern Desert of Egypt
- University of Michigan; University of Asiut.
- Publication of the report submitted to the Egyptian Antiquities Organization on survey around Coptos. Detailed publication of survey includes rough digitized maps and catalogs of sites by period.

http://millennium.arts.kuleuven.ac.be/visitklass/hawara/ (2000)
Hawara 2000 Archaeological Survey
- Katholieke Universiteit, Leuven.
- Informative, if largely descriptive, account of survey by area. Includes some photographs of landscape and finds, as well as general results.

http://www-oi.uchicago.edu/OI/PROJ/DES/Desert_Road. html (2000)
The Luxor-Farshut Desert Road Project/The Theban Desert Road Survey
- Oriental Institute, University of Chicago.
- Links to series of annual reports with images of finds.

FRANCE

http://www.informatics.org/france/france.html (2001)
GIS and Remote Sensing for Archaeology: Burgundy
- University of North Carolina, Chapel Hill; Informatics International, Inc.
- Long-term regional project with considerable breadth of research techniques applied to its geophysical data. Extensive description of technological aspects, with emphasis on these above data. Excellent links section.

GREECE AND THE AEGEAN

http://eleftheria.stcloudstate.edu/eks/ (2001)
Eastern Korinthia Archaeological Survey
- St. Cloud State University, Minnesota.
- Includes project overview, yearly field reports, methodology and research goals. Detailed maps of survey area, downloads of GIS and geophysical survey data for project. Bibliography and funding proposals also included.

http://rome.classics.lsa.umich.edu/NVAP.html (2000)
Nemea Valley Archaeological Project Archaeological Survey Internet Edition
- Bryn Mawr College; University of Michigan; University of Cincinnati.
- Straightforward, well organized site with basic publication data.

http://classics.lsa.umich.edu/PRAP.html (1996)
Pylos Regional Archaeological Project Internet Edition
- University of Michigan; University of Cincinnati; University of Wisconsin, Madison; University of Ioannina.
- Clear and well-organized. Extensive data presented for specialized audience.

http://sphakia.classics.ox.ac.uk/ (2002)
Sphakia Survey: the Internet Edition
- Queens University; University of Minnesota; University of Cambridge.
- Excellent site with easily navigable sections covering all aspects of the excavation. All results are not included, but useful case studies are profiled.

http:www.nottingham.ac.uk/archaeology/research/balkans /greece/gcount.html (2000)
Field Survey at Louloudies: a new Late Roman Fortification in Pieria
- University of Nottingham.
- Small site geared to a general audience. Includes descriptions of methodology and general results with images.

http://www1.ims.forth.gr/ArchGeolab/ArchLasithi/html-end/html-map-page1.htm (2001)
Digital Archaeological Map of Lasithi, Crete
- Institute for Mediterranean Studies; Foundation for Research and Technology, Hellas.
- Site focuses on the technical presentation of GIS map and associated database. One of few sites to emphasize the technological aspects over the information itself. Thorough and easy to use.

http://halai.fac.cornell.edu/chelp/home.htm (2002)
Cornell Halai and East Lokris Project
- (Cornell University).
- Excavation and survey briefly summarized, with links to online reports and images.

http://www.archaeology.usyd.edu.au/research/kythera/index.html (1998)
The Australian Paliochora-Kythera Archaeological Survey
- University of Sydney.
- Description of project goals and methods. Information for interested students and description of possible results.

http://www.ucl.ac.uk/kip (2003)
Kythera Island Project
- University College London.
- Site initially presents an overview of project methods and results, with excellent GIS graphics. Additional datasets to be added as their study is completed.

http://www.uni-heidelberg.de/institute/fak8/ufg/forschung /maran3/phliasia.htm (2001)
Phlious Archaeological Project
- Ruprecht-Karls University, Heidelberg.
- Excellent graphics, short description of project objectives and preliminary results. (In German).

HUNGARY

http://people.bu.edu/mcg/ (1999)
Valeria Archaeological Survey Project
- Boston University.
- Well-organized, engaging site with reports, catalogs of maps, artifact drawings and site photographs.

IRAN

http://www-oi.uchicago.edu/OI/PROJ/FAR/Fars.html (2001)
Archaeological Survey in Northwestern Fars, Iran
- Oriental Institute, University of Chicago.
- Ethnoarchaeological survey with excavation component. Links to annual reports which include description of proceedings and finds. Some basic maps and photos included.

IRAQ

http://www.dur.ac.uk/~drk0dk/samarra.htm (1999)
Sammara' Archaeological Survey
- University of Durham, Université de Paris.
- Single page of descriptive text narrating the history of the site, the remains and the results of excavations. Single aerial photograph of site provided.

ISRAEL

http://www.tau.ac.il/~archpubs/megiddo/index.html (2002)
Megiddo Excavation and Survey
•   Tel Aviv University; Pennsylvania State University; other consortium partners.
•   Information on survey included under the "projects" segment of the site. Brief description, some bar graphs with site frequency percentages included, as well as GIS information.

ITALY

http://www.lamp.ac.uk/archaeology/amarkp/SICILIA/SURV1996.HTM (1996)
Torcicoda Valley (Sicilia) Archaeological Project
•   University of Wales.
•   Straightforward report, with no images or maps, of the first season of work.

http://www.bufau.bham.ac.uk/research/forum_novum/Default.htm (2002)
Forum Novum-Vescovio
•   University of Birmingham.
•   Preliminary results only of large survey. Methodologies described in detail and history of site provided.

http://www.sardinia.arts.gla.ac.uk/riumannu.htm (2001)
The Riu Mannu Regional Archaeological Project
•   Leiden University; University of Glasgow.
•   Site presents only basic information at this time, including study aims and methodologies. Results forthcoming.

http://www.bsr.ac.uk/tvproject.html (2001)
The Tiber Valley Project
•   British School at Rome.
•   Useful descriptions of background, methodology and preliminary results. Some images.

http://www.arch.cam.ac.uk/TROINA/ (2001)
The Troina Project (Sicily)
•   University of Cambridge.
•   Brief but thorough descriptions of current work, past publications, team members and methodology. Some images.

http://www.arch.cam.ac.uk/~jer39/BMAP/ (2001)
Bova Marina Archaeological Project
•   University of Southampton.
•   Site provides thorough introduction to project aims and methodologies, as well as general overview of results. A separate GIS section provides some spatial data and project objectives.

http://www.utexas.edu/research/ica/metaponto/index.html (2001)
Metapontum Project
•   University of Texas.
•   Thorough presentation of survey methods and results by period.

http://odin.let.rug.nl/RPC/ (2000)
Regional Pathways to Complexity
•   University of Groningen; Free University, Amsterdam.
•   Unique regional-comparative approach presents detailed information on several large projects. Each segment is explained in detail. (*cf.* also Ch. 7, this volume)

http://dig.anthro.niu.edu/fldschl/ (2003)
Monte Polizzo Excavations and Survey
•   American Academy in Rome; Stanford University; Northern Illinois University; Lund University.
•   Site introduced and fieldwork objectives explained for a general audience, including this project's field school. Some survey results presented in yearly summaries.

http://www.arch.cam.ac.uk/projects/etruria/ (1999)
South Etruria Enhancement Project
- University of Cambridge; University of Bristol; SUNY, Buffalo; Soprintendenza Archeologica per l'Etruria Meridionale.
- Brief summary of research aims, results and bibliography. Part of the Middle Tiber project of the British School at Rome; the aim is to bring the results of the British School surveys in the area north of Rome up to date.

http://www.arch.soton.ac.uk/Research/Falerii/ (2000)
Falerii Novi Geophysical Survey
- University of Southampton.
- Interactive map, published as part of Tiber Valley Project.

JORDAN

http://www.stfx.ca/people/bmacdona/tbasweb/welcome. htm (2001)
Tafial-Busayra Archaeological Survey, Jordan
- St. Francis Xavier University.
- Links to reports and project bibliography with drawings and photographs.

http://www.wam.umd.edu/~amsii/welcome.htm (2002)
Wadi-Araba Archaeological Research Project, East-Central Araba Archaeological Survey
- Wadi Araba Archaeological Project, independent group.
- Online field publications. Includes links to several other affiliated survey projects at Bir Madhkur, East-Central Araba survey and survey components of the Roman Aqaba project.

http://weber.ucsd.edu/Depts/Anthro/classes/tlevy/Fidan/Fidan01.html (2002)
Archaeology in the Levant: Jabal Hamrat Fidan Project, Nahal Tillah, Shiqmim and Gilat
- University of California, San Diego.
- A useful site with links to several projects with survey components. Information on the use of GIS in archaeology.

http://www.archaeology.usyd.edu.au/research/rukeis/jordan.html (1998)
University of Sydney Expedition to the Hauran
- University of Sydney.
- Short description of site and research objectives. Maps and photo.

http://www.wwc.edu/academics/departments/theology/mpp/ (2002)
Madaba Plains Project including Tall al'Umayri, Tall Hisban, Tall Jalul and the Hinterland Survey
- Andrews University; Walla Walla College; La Sierra University; Canadian University College; Pacific Union College.
- Attractive photography and easy to use.

http://archaeology.asu.edu/Jordan/mars2000.html (2000)
The Moab Archaeological Resource Survey
- Jordanian Department of Antiquities.
- The field report for the 2000 season has been transferred to the web, with the addition of photos and graphics, where available.

http://www.chass.utoronto.ca/~banning/Ziqlab/ (2001)
Wadi Ziqlab Project Home Page
- University of Toronto.
- Good range of information for introductory purposes and publication. Artifact illustrations, maps and up-to-date results from very recent excavations and surveys.

http://www.ucl.ac.uk/archaeology/research/profiles/kwright/wadires.htm (1999)
Wadi Feinan in the Fourth and Third Millennium BC/Wadi Feinan Regional Project
- British Institute at Amman for Archaeology and History (BIAAH); Institute of Archaeology, UCL; Department of Antiquities, Hashemite Kingdom of Jordan.
- Short description of survey project.

LIBYA

http://www.cru.uea.ac.uk/~e118/Fezzan/fezzan_home. html (2001)
The Fezzan Project: Geoarchaeology of the Sahara
- University of Leicester; University of Newcastle; University of Reading; King's College London.
- Topical summations of various project components and a very useful links section. Images nicely integrated and high quality.

http://museums.ncl.ac.uk/garamantes/feztop.htm (2000)
The Garamantes of the Fezzan: the archaeology of Saharan Oasis Dwellers
- University of Leicester; University of Newcastle.
- Excellent, with succinct overviews of methodology and regional information, some ceramic profiles included.

SUDAN

http://www.spicey.demon.co.uk/Nubianpage/mahas.htm (2002)
The Mahas Survey Project
- University of Khartoum.
- Site presents description of project goals and preliminary results. Some images of finds and landscape photos on site-by-site basis, as well as numerous topical links.

PORTUGAL

http://www.arch.soton.ac.uk/Research/AveValley/ (1998)
The Ave Valley, northern Portugal: an archaeological survey of Iron Age and Roman Settlement
- University of Southampton; Universidade Fernando Pessao.
- Fairly detailed illustrated summary, with links to separate databases (not accessible except by subscription to e-journal) that present field and find reports. GIS analysis.

SPAIN

http://www.monza.demon.co.uk/fede/ (1995)
The application of GIS to the study of the development of the Roman settlement pattern in Spain
- University of Southampton.
- Project combines non-systematic survey data with GIS analysis. Brief description of methodology and bibliography. No results available.

http://www.arch.soton.ac.uk/Research/Ciudades/ (2002)
Ciudades Romanas Project
- University of Southampton.
- Excellent site with introductory texts for project goals and results, along with searchable databases of selected finds and results by site.

TUNISIA

http://www.arthistory.upenn.edu/jerba (2000)
Jerba, Le Projet Tuniso-Américain
- University of Pennsylvania; American Academy in Rome.
- Thorough overview of fieldwork and results, some photographs and maps.

http://rome.classics.lsa.umich.edu/projects/lepti/lepti.html (1994)
Report on the site of Leptiminus and fieldwork from 1990–1993
- University of Michigan; Institut National du Patrimoine.
- Short fieldwork summary and some images, but no quite out-of-date.

TURKEY

http://catal.arch.cam.ac.uk/catal/Newsletter2/regional. html (1996)
Regional Site Survey, part of Çatalhöyük newsletter publication
- Çatal Trust.
- Brief description of methodology and results from survey. Single map.

http://www-oi.uchicago.edu/OI/PROJ/AMU/Amuq.html (2002)
The Amuq Valley Regional Projects
- Oriental Institute, University of Chicago.
- Sophisticated site that presents survey results from multiple sites. Reproduces OI Annual reports in some cases but supplements these with images and maps.

http://www.metu.edu.tr/home/wwwkerk/ (2002)
The Kerkenes Project Homepage
- Middle East Technical University; Yozgat Museum; University of California, Berkeley; British Institute of Archaeology at Ankara.
- Attractive and sophisticated site with excellent publication of GIS and traditional data. Reports and bibliography provided as well as didactic presentations of GIS material. Very user-friendly.

http://pandora.nla.gov.au/nph-arch/O1998-Feb-24/http://adhocalypse.arts.unimelb.edu.au/Dept/Arch/NETurkey/home. html (1997)
The University of Melbourne Northeastern Turkey Archaeological Project
- University of Melbourne.
- Archived (non-active) site includes survey coverage and some results. Very brief.

http://www.choma.org/~mgarriso/Drafts/HMSurvey.html (2001)
The Hacımusular Project
- Ministry of Culture; Bilkent University; Associated Colleges of the South; DePauw University; the College of the Holy Cross.
- Excellent introduction to survey methodology and technology, user-friendly graphics and explanations.

http://pasture.ecn.purdue.edu/~rauhn/ (2002)
The Rough Cilicia Archaeological Survey Project
- Purdue University; University of Nebraska at Lincoln; Clark University, Loyola Marymount University.
- Extensive site with detailed GIS and DEM data, ceramic distributions, etc. Also useful sections with discussions of survey methods and problems for the general public.

YEMEN

http://www.aiys.org/webdate/zim.html (2000)
Middle Hadramawt Archaeological Survey
- University of Pennsylvania.
- Preliminary Results, October 1999 season. Brief description of general methods and results of survey. Includes two maps and some landscape photos.

YEMEN/SYRIA/IRAQ/TURKEY

http://www-oi.uchicago.edu/OI/PROJ/CAMEL/Main.html (2001)
Center for the Archaeology of the Middle East Landscape (CAMEL)
- Oriental Institute, University of Chicago.
- Site provides links to series of regional project reports which present detailed results supplemented by images.

REFERENCE AND OTHER MISCELLANEOUS RESOURCES

http://rome.classics.lsa.umich.edu/welcome.html (2000)
Classics and Mediterranean Archaeology
- University of Michigan, webmaster Sebastian Heath.
- The earliest, and still one of most comprehensive, websites collecting links to Internet resources of interest to classicists and Mediterranean archaeologists. The section on "Field Projects and Site- or Region-Specific Resources" is most relevant. Excellent search tools built into the site.

http://ourworld.compuserve.com/homepages/mjff/homepage.htm (2000)
The Satellite Remote Sensing and Archaeology Homepage
- Martin J.F. Fowler, webmaster, no institutional affiliation given.
- Survey bibliography organized by region. Impressive satellite imagery for archaeological sites world-wide.

http://www.ees.ac.uk/ (2000)
Egypt Exploration Society
- EES.
- Contains lists by region of very brief descriptions of projects, including some surveys, underway in Egypt. No links to further web publications provided, but this could be a useful reference source for surveys in Egypt.

http://www.petranationaltrust.com/archaeological.html (1998)
Archaeological Survey for the Wadi Mousa Water Supply and Wastewater Project
- Petra National Trust.
- Limited description of survey of water line conducted within Petra preserve. Several photos.

http://antichita.let.uniroma1.it/ricerca/r_italia.htm
Carta Archeologica d'Italia – Forma Italiae
- Consiglio Nazionale delle Ricerche.
- The traditional 'topographic explorations' aimed at producing a comprehensive archaeological map have been updated and the old institute responsible for the maps of the *Forma Italiae* (*cf.* also Ch. 13, this volume) has been reinvented in a remarkable way.
  See also, as examples
  Around Segesta (Sicily):
  http://www.archeo.unisi.it/Segestaweb2/prima.htm
  The provinces of Siena and Grosseto:
  http://192.167.112.135/NewPages/CARTOGRAFIA/home.html

http://www.antony-aubert.org/ (2003)
Le Portail de l'archéologie
- Antony Aubert.
- Comprehensive list of topical pages and project links by region is well-organized and a useful research tool. Provides links to wide range of bibliographic databases and archaeological organizations with emphasis on European materials.

http://www.staff.ncl.ac.uk/kevin.greene/wintro/ (2002)
Archaeology: An Introduction – the Online Companion
- Kevin Greene, University of Newcastle.
- An online supplement to a widely-used introductory textbook, this site presents web links accompanying each chapter and topic. The explanation of survey and illustrative links are particularly useful.

http://www.depauw.edu/acad/geology/website/cgma/about .html (2001)
Collaboratory for GIS and Mediterranean Archaeology
- Rebecca K. Schindler and Pedar W. Foss, De Pauw University, Greencastle, IN.
- CGMA aims to begin construction on the first Mediterranean-wide GIS system for archaeology, providing a functional framework for broad studies of the interactions of humans and their environment in antiquity. (But no data are yet available through this website.)